THE URBAN WORLD AND THE FIRST CHRISTIANS

The Urban World
and the First Christians

Edited by

Steve Walton
Paul R. Trebilco
and
David W. J. Gill

WILLIAM B. EERDMANS PUBLISHING COMPANY
GRAND RAPIDS, MICHIGAN

Wm. B. Eerdmans Publishing Co.
2140 Oak Industrial Drive N.E., Grand Rapids, Michigan 49505
www.eerdmans.com

23 22 21 20 19 18 17   1 2 3 4 5 6 7

ISBN 978-0-8028-7451-1

Library of Congress Cataloging-in-Publication Data

Names: Walton, Steve, 1955- editor.
Title: The urban world and the first Christians / edited by Steve Walton,
    Paul R. Trebilco, and David W. J. Gill.
Description: Grand Rapids : Eerdmans Publishing Co., 2017. | Includes
    bibliographical references and index.
Identifiers: LCCN 2017012591 | ISBN 9780802874511 (pbk.)
Subjects: LCSH: Church history—Primitive and early church, ca. 30-600. |
    Cities and towns—Religious aspects—Christianity.
Classification: LCC BR166 .U73 2017 | DDC 270.1—dc23
    LC record available at https://lccn.loc.gov/2017012591

Contents

Contributors

Piotr Ashwin-Siejkowski is Visiting Research Fellow, King's College London, UK, and Assistant Priest, St Mary's Church, Twickenham.

Cédric Brélaz is Professor of Ancient History, Université de Fribourg, Switzerland.

Paul Cloke is Professor of Human Geography, University of Exeter, UK.

David W. J. Gill is Professor of Archaeological Heritage and Director of Heritage Futures, University Campus Suffolk and University of East Anglia, UK.

David G. Horrell is Professor of New Testament Studies and Director of the Center for Biblical Studies, University of Exeter, UK.

Chris Keith is Professor of New Testament and Early Christianity and Director of the Centre for the Social-Scientific Study of the Bible, St Mary's University, Twickenham, UK.

Anthony Le Donne is Assistant Professor of New Testament, United Theological Seminary, Dayton, Ohio, USA.

Jutta Leonhardt-Balzer is Senior Lecturer in New Testament, University of Aberdeen, UK.

Helen Morris is Lecturer in Applied Theology, Moorlands College, Sopley, Dorset, UK.

Ian Paul is Honorary Assistant Professor in New Testament, University of Nottingham, UK.

Volker Rabens is *Wissenschaftlicher Mitarbeiter* in New Testament Studies at Friedrich Schiller University Jena, Germany, and Extraordinary Associate Professor at the Faculty of Theology at North-West University, South Africa.

Anders Runesson is Professor of New Testament, University of Oslo, Norway.

Matthew Sleeman is Lecturer in New Testament, Oak Hill College, London, UK.

Joan E. Taylor is Professor of Christian Origins and Second Temple Judaism, Kings College, London, UK.

Paul R. Trebilco is Professor of New Testament Studies, University of Otago, Dunedin, New Zealand.

Steve Walton is Professor in New Testament, St Mary's University, Twickenham, UK.

Wei Hsien Wan recently completed his PhD in Theology and Religion (New Testament) at University of Exeter, UK, and is engaged in postdoctoral research.

Abbreviations

Other than those listed below, abbreviations used are those found in Billie Jean Collins, Bob Buller, and John F. Kutsko, eds., *The SBL Handbook of Style: For Biblical Studies and Related Disciplines,* 2nd ed. (Atlanta: SBL Press, 2014).

ABib	Academia Biblica
ABSA	Annual of the British School at Athens
AJEC	Ancient Judaism and Early Christianity
Am. Anthropol.	*American Anthropologist*
ArtB	*Art Bulletin*
AYBRL	Anchor Yale Bible Reference Library
BAR.I	British Archaeological Reports, International Series
BEHE.H	Bibliothèque de l'école des hautes études. Sciences historiques et philologiques
BHGNT	Baylor Handbook on the Greek New Testament
BICS	*Bulletin of the Institute of Classical Studies*
BICSSup	*Bulletin of the Institute of Classical Studies* Supplement Series
BSASup	British School at Athens Supplement Series
BST	The Bible Speaks Today
CbNT	Commentaire biblique: Nouveau Testament
CCEL	Christian Classics Ethereal Library
CMRDM	E. N. Lane, *Corpus monumentorum religionis dei Menis.* 4 vols. Études préliminaires aux religions orientales dans l'Empire romain 19. Leiden: Brill, 1971–1978.

COQG	Christian Origins and the Question of God
CR	*Classical Review*
Cult. Geogr.	*Cultural Geography*
EaChrCon	Early Christianity in Context
EC	Epworth Commentaries
ENT	Erläuterungen zum Neuen Testament
Env. Plan. A	*Environment and Planning A*
Env. Plan. D	*Environment and Planning D*
Geogr. Ann. B	*Geografiska Annaler Series B*
Geogr. Compass	*Geography Compass*
Hist. Theory	*History and Theory*
HTA	Historisch-theologische Auslegung
IGSK	Inschriften griechischer Städte aus Kleinasien
Int. J. Urb. Reg. Res.	*International Journal of Urban and Regional Research*
IvEph	Hermann Wankel et al., *Die Inschriften von Ephesos.* IGSK 11.1–17.4. Bonn: Rudolf Habelt, 1979–1984.
JAJ	*Journal of Ancient Judaism*
JRASup	*Journal of Roman Archaeology* Supplementary Series
JSHJ	*Journal for the Study of the Historical Jesus*
LHJS	Library of Historical Jesus Studies
MAPS	Memoirs of the American Philosophical Society
MEFRA	*Mélanges de l'école française de Rome: Antiquité*
NHMS	Nag Hammadi and Manichaean Studies
NIVAC	New International Version Application Commentary
NVBS	New Voices in Biblical Studies
PAPS	*Proceedings of the American Philosophical Society*
PBM	Paternoster Biblical Monographs
Prog. Hum. Geogr.	*Progress in Human Geography*
SCJ	*Stone-Campbell Journal*
Soc. Cult. Geogr.	*Social and Cultural Geography*
Sociol. Relig.	*Sociology of Religion*
Trans. Inst. Br. Geog.	*Transactions of the Institute of British Geographers*
Urban Geogr.	*Urban Geography*
Urban Stud.	*Urban Studies*
VCSup	Supplements to *Vigiliae Christianae*
ZECNT	Zondervan Exegetical Commentary on the New Testament

Cities as More Than "Scenery"

THE EDITORS

1. Introduction

Cities were key places in the establishment, growth, and development of earliest Christianity, and they have continued to be so throughout history. This book seeks to explore the relationship between the earliest Christian believers and the city environment by focusing on two areas. First, we look at how the urban environments of the ancient Mediterranean basin affected the ways in which early Christianity progressed; secondly, we reflect on how the earliest Christians thought and theologized in their engagement with cities and urban environments, which could be challenging and difficult as well as open and receptive.

To approach these areas fruitfully requires the tools and expertise of more than one discipline, and to this end we here bring together studies by human geographers, who have rigorous ways of studying urban settings, and classicists, who know the ancient world and its cities, as well as New Testament scholars of various interests and approaches, whose texts speak of the early Christian stories and reflections. The essays in this book were originally presented at a multidisciplinary conference hosted by the Centre for the Social-Scientific Study of the Bible at St Mary's University, Twickenham (London), UK, in May 2015, and the cross-fertilization between different perspectives within the conference has contributed helpfully to the revised essays that you see here. Thus, readers will find in these pages a rich variety of expertise and scholarship, all focused on our key questions about cities and earliest Christianity.

2. Early Christianity in Its Ancient Urban Setting(s)

Part I focuses on our first area, the impact of cities on earliest Christianity. Some scholars argue that the Greek word *Ioudaios,* traditionally translated "Jew," would better be translated "Judean," partly to guard against the danger of "reading back" modern Judaism into our ancient sources. *Anthony Le Donne* enters this debate and considers how ethnic groups were identified in the first century. He argues that first-century people were identified by their connection with a mother city, and thus that the identity of *Ioudaioi* came from their connection with Jerusalem, rather than their "ethnicity" in today's terms. *Matthew Sleeman* keeps the spotlight on Jerusalem by considering Paul's final visit to the city in Acts 21. Sleeman brings expertise as both a human geographer and a NT scholar to this enterprise, and uses ideas from legal geography to consider how Paul seeks to remake spaces he enters as places where the heavenly Christ is known to dwell and reign. *Joan Taylor*'s essay keeps us with Paul in Acts by considering Caesarea Maritima, a city mentioned many times in Acts, and a place where Paul was held under arrest for two years. Taylor shows how our archaeological and other evidence portrays Caesarea as a city that "performed" Rome, and how these data illuminate the narrative of Acts.

David Gill casts the net wider, using his classical learning to inform our reading of the developments of earliest Christianity in key Roman colonies in the Greek East of the empire: Corinth, Philippi, and Pisidian Antioch. He shows how knowledge from the ancient world meshes with texts from Acts, Galatians, and 1 Corinthians, illustrating the tensions and issues that arose as believing communities were established in these Roman cities. *Jutta Leonhardt-Balzer* extends our thinking on Paul and cities by comparing and contrasting Paul's attitudes to Jerusalem and Rome with those of a contemporary Hellenistic Jew, Philo of Alexandria. In both men she detects an ambivalence, to varying degrees and with varying emphases, between valuing Jerusalem as "mother city" and being independent of that city, and between seeing Rome as strategically and politically important and adopting a cautious approach to Rome's power and claims. *Volker Rabens* considers how Paul approached his mission, to make Christ known, in the urban settings of the first-century Roman Empire, discussing how Paul chose the cities he visited and how he acted once he arrived in a city. Rabens argues that Paul was no mere pragmatist, but that his highly flexible practice and missiological principles were closely interlocked.

A series of studies then consider Christian engagement with particu-

lar cities. *Cédric Brélaz* uses data from recent French archaeological work
in Philippi to recontextualize Paul's mission in this city, which Acts desig-
nates—unusually—as a Roman colony (16:12). *Helen Morris* examines Paul's
use of "body" imagery in 1 Cor 12:12–31 for the believing communities, and
she compares and contrasts it with the use of the "body" in the context of
cities to encourage social harmony. Morris argues that Paul regards the city
of Corinth as neither "friend" (uncritically accepted) nor "foe" (unbendingly
opposed), but as a foil to his argument—the eschatological tension within
which the church lives produces elements of both conformity and subversion
in Christian engagement with the city-state. *Paul Trebilco* compares and contrasts two different early Christian approaches to the city of Ephesus, those
found among the Pauline communities (attested by 1 and 2 Timothy) and
among the Johannine communities (attested by 1, 2, and 3 John). Trebilco
identifies a significant contrast between engagement and withdrawal (respectively) as the default mode of relating to the city and society of Ephesus
and elucidates the rationale and practice of these two Christian approaches.
Chris Keith takes us to Rome in the second century, through the eyes of
Justin Martyr and Hermas, to consider how widespread literacy and literate
education were in that city, against the backdrop of the common scholarly
claim that there was much greater literacy in urban settings. He argues that
the evidence runs against a straightforward correlation, and he uses the discussion to critique some reconstructions of early Christian transmission of
their traditions through written notes. *Piotr Ashwin-Siejkowski* stays in the
later centuries with a focus on the growth of Christianity in Alexandria in
Egypt. He identifies features of the city's life that made it fertile soil for the
planting and growth of believing communities: its intellectual legacy, its
urban institutions (such as libraries), and its geographical location.

3. Early Christian Thinking about Cities

Part II turns to consider how the earliest Christians regarded cities in general, and some specific cities in particular. *Anders Runesson* considers Matthew's portrait of Jerusalem, which has alternatively been argued to be either
"city of God" or home of traitors and killers. He walks carefully through the
evidence to offer a fresh perspective that recognizes that the "first urban
Christians" were located outside Jerusalem and Judea. *Steve Walton* considers the use of "heavenly citizenship" language in Philippians in relation to
Paul's use of his Roman citizenship in Philippi, and he argues that this lan-

guage indicates Paul as appropriating "city" language that was well-known to the inhabitants of Philippi and its environs but applying it to the believing communities as outposts of the heavenly city. *Paul Cloke* applies models of "spiritual landscapes" from modern human geography to reading the letter to the Colossians, noticing ways in which the Roman Empire maintained its colonial control over the city, the presence of invisible "spiritual" powers in the city for which Paul offers "alternative imaginaries," and the faithful improvisation of life into which the believing community was being called by God-in-Christ. *David Horrell,* in conversation with the human geographers Edward Soja and David Harvey, reflects on the setting of 1 Peter by considering how the letter constructs space. This approach allows him to elucidate the letter's view of the believers' situation living under the Roman Empire, a view elucidated by an alternative way of seeing reality, an alternative geography. *Wei Hsien Wan* explores 1 Peter further by considering how imperial cults configured physical and ideological space under Roman domination. Wan contrasts the Roman construction of space with the "spiritual house" to which believers belong, which allows them to resist the romanization of space and relocates them in a new spatial reality as a dwelling place for the Spirit. *Ian Paul* considers the seven cities of Revelation 2–3 in the wider context of the two cities of Babylon and the new Jerusalem. Paul presents the seven cities as the arena of discipleship, whereas the two cities make mutually incompatible claims on people's loyalty.

4. Conclusion

We would like to thank our publisher, Eerdmans, and especially our editor Michael Thomson, for their collaboration in producing this book. We are also very grateful to all of the contributors who have patiently answered the many questions we have had. Dave Smith, then a PhD student at St Mary's University, Twickenham, did sterling work in compiling the consolidated bibliography, and we thank him for his labors. The Centre for the Social-Scientific Study of the Bible, to which Steve Walton belongs, under the fine leadership of its director, Professor Chris Keith, proved to be a very congenial location for this project, and we acknowledge with thanks the support of the Centre and the university's vice-chancellor, Francis Campbell.

PART I

Early Christianity in Its Ancient Urban Setting(s)

Complicating the Category of *Ethnos* toward Poliscentrism

A Possible Way Forward within Second Temple Ethnography

Anthony Le Donne

Modern historians have long described Second Temple Jews as members of a religion called Judaism. Religious specialists have traditionally acknowledged that the people we label "ancient Jews" were delineated by ethnicity too. But most of our collective efforts have been dedicated to the religious elements of the Second Temple period. While this is still common practice, some have challenged the category of "religion" as applied to this people and period. Perhaps, it is argued, religion was not a category emic to ancient worldviews.[1] Indeed, the fact that the term *Ioudaismos* is not well attested in the Second Temple period invites us to rethink our (perhaps anachronistic) categories. Furthermore, if we are on shaky ground with religious categorization, perhaps we will find more solid footing with ethnic categorization.

Can we avoid the modern conceptual baggage associated with the term "Jew" when translating *Ioudaios*? Maybe the term "Judean" would better represent the conceptual mapping of this period. But such a move assumes that ethnic categorization is less problematic. In this chapter I will argue that it is not. Because our efforts have been dedicated to the religious elements of Second Temple Jews/Judeans, much less effort has been invested in defining the emic category of *ethnos*. In this chapter I will suggest a few avenues that might lead to a better understanding of ethnicity as it was understood by Second Temple Jews/Judeans. Chief among these avenues is the way that

---

1. E.g., Steve Mason, *Josephus, Judea, and Christian Origins: Methods and Categories* (Peabody, MA: Hendrickson, 2009), ch. 5.

ethnos was defined in relationship to the concept of *polis*. Orientation toward the governance, customs, worship, etc. of a particular city was primary in determining *ethnos* in the Second Temple period.

This chapter will: (1) discuss how physical traits associated with "race" by modern minds were seen differently in Hellenistic antiquity; (2) discuss how Hellenistic thinkers conceptualized *ethnos* as an extension of poliscentrism; (3) suggest that Second Temple *Ioudaioi* were poliscentric with varying ways of expressing their orientation toward Jerusalem.

1. Phenotypes and Physiognomic Stereotypes

Hellenic and Hellenistic antiquity did not suffer from the baggage created by nineteenth-century scientific racism. Stereotypes based on physicality influenced both thought-worlds, but in much different ways.

Modern, Western minds tend to relate certain characteristics of physicality to ethnic delineation. The "popularly used physical features to define races" tend to be the most easily recognizable features like "skin pigmentation, hair type, lip size," etc.[2] From the 1800s onward such associations gave way to the analysis of genetic and phrenological consistency within races. Enlightenment thinkers such as Arthur de Gobineau (1816–1882) emphasized physically internal factors with the hope that certain moral and cultural tendencies would be demonstrated biologically. The simplistic associations between race and physical traits were problematized as early as the work of Franz Boas (1858–1942).[3] Ethnologists now give almost no credence to anthropometric methodologies of earlier generations except to explain the emergence of scientific racism. It is now commonplace in ethnic studies to describe race as a social construct that reinforces political, economic, and other cultural hierarchies.[4] It would be safe to say that contemporary ethnic studies do not study race as their primary object, but rather racism. Consider these words of Benjamin Isaac, "race does not exist,

2. Martin N. Marger, *Race and Ethnic Relations: American and Global Perspectives* (Belmont, CA: Wadsworth, 2012), 408.

3. Franz Boas, "Changes in Bodily Form of Descendants of Immigrants," *Am. Anthropol.* 14 (1912): 530–63. For a more recent treatment, see Clarence C. Gravlee, H. Russell Bernard, and William R. Leonard, "Heredity, Environment, and Cranial Form: A Reanalaysis of Boas's Immigrant Data," *Am. Anthropol.* 105 (2003): 125–38.

4. Cf. the influential work of Michael Omi and Howard Winant, *Racial Formation in the United States: From the 1960s to the 1980s* (New York: Routledge, 1986).

racism does."[5] Isaac does not represent every ethnologist in this statement, but such statements are commonplace in the field. He explains:

> Since the concept of race as such is merely theoretical, since it is a quasi-biological construct invented to establish a hierarchy of human groups and to delineate differences between them, and since it does not work in practice, attempts have been made from the beginning [of racial theory] to incorporate other features which are not physiological. The designation "race" in the sense of subspecies cannot be applied by definition to language groups (the Aryan race), national groups (the English race), religious groups (the Christian or Jewish race), groups with one or more physical features in common, such as skin color, or the entire species of humans (the human race): such usages are biologically and scientifically meaningless.[6]

Even if Isaac is viewed as extreme, he points to a common principle in ethnic studies: implicit in racial theory is the notion of superior and inferior races. Race is as much a matter of perception as it is anything else. At the same time, these perceptions have created realities in the modern world that cannot be ignored.[7]

> Physical anthropologists distinguish major categories of human traits as either phenotypes—visible anatomical features such as skin color, hair texture, and body and facial shape—or genotypes—genetic specifications inherited from one's parents. Races have traditionally been classified chiefly on the basis of the most easily observable anatomical traits, like skin color, internal and blood traits have been de-emphasized or disregarded.[8]

While the genotypes of race are de-emphasized or disregarded, the problem of racism persists and thus the anthropological significance of phenotypes continues to be of interest. The object of study here is the social reality created by the popular and entrenched racial interpretations of "skin pigmen-

---

5. Benjamin Isaac, *The Invention of Racism in Classical Antiquity* (Princeton: Princeton University Press, 2004), 33.

6. Isaac, *Invention*, 33.

7. Along these lines we might point to the instrumental functions of ethnicity toward political and economic ends. See Jonathan Hall, *Ethnic Identity in Greek Antiquity* (New York: Cambridge University Press, 1997).

8. Marger, *Race and Ethnic Relations*, 408.

tation, hair type, lip size," etc. And, moreover, these interpretations vary from culture to culture.

As we turn to the question of perceptions of *ethnos* in the Second Temple period we must acknowledge that ancient interpretations of phenotypes differ from our modern, racially-invested interpretations. One possible avenue to discover such differences is by way of classical physiognomic discussions.

Hellenistic physiognomic ideology supposed that it was possible to recognize personality traits by observing a person's physical features. Analogues to "known" animal characteristics were often employed or presupposed. Cross-species comparison was fundamental to this school of thought (e.g., large cow-like eyes bespoke cowardice because cows lack courage). Also fundamental was a set of ideals that bespoke nobility of character. Perceptions of moderate characteristics were more ideal than extremes (e.g., being of middle-range height was better than being too tall or too short). I do not put forth this short section on physiognomy as an explanation of ancient ethnic categorization. Nor do I have the space to offer a robust history of the idea. Rather, I include only a few examples to demonstrate how some ancient minds perceived and categorized the social world based on what we have called phenotypes.

According to Ps.-Aristotle, the "soul and body react on each other; when the character of the soul changes, it changes also the form of the body, and conversely, when the form of the body changes, it changes the character of the soul."[9] In this introduction to a physiognomic perspective, one's external characteristics reflected something of one's personality and vice versa.

Consider then this description of Caligula by Suetonius:

> He was very tall, and extremely pale, with a huge body, but very thick neck and legs. His eyes and temples were hollow, his forehead broad and grim, his hair thin and entirely gone on the top of his head, though his body was hairy. While his face was naturally forbidding and ugly, he purposely made it even more savage, practicing all kinds of terrible and fearsome expressions before a mirror. (*Cal.* 50)[10]

Caligula is a helpful example because he represents a figure who was almost universally despised in retrospect and who departs in so many ways from

---

9. Ps.-Aristotle, *Physiognomics* 808b 11–13 (W. S. Hett; LCL).

10. As quoted from Elizabeth Evans, *Physiognomics in the Ancient World*, TAPS 59 (Philadelphia: American Philosophical Society, 1969), 55. My thanks to my student Gregg Hemminger, who alerted me to several ancient physiognomic descriptions.

Suetonius's physiognomic ideal. Suetonius emphasizes Caligula's goat-like appearance and disposition: "The goat was of this appearance. Creatures with hairy legs are sensual. . . . He has a pale skin and is covered with black, straight hair, which is a sign of cowardice, which indicates stupidity and foolishness." Notice, for the purpose of this chapter, that Caligula is described as pale-skinned twice and that his black, straight hair is emphasized. According to this physiognomy, such features indicate cowardice. There is no indication that a pale-skinned, straight-haired man might be considered "white" in Hellenistic antiquity in the way that he might in a modern mind. Moreover, in this context it was superior to be darker-skinned and have curly hair. Consider Homer's description of Eurybates:

> Furthermore, a herald attended [Odysseus], a little older than he, and I will tell you of him, too, what manner of man he was. He was round-shouldered, dark of skin, and curly-haired, and his name was Eurybates; and Odysseus honored him above his other comrades, because he was like-minded with himself. (*Od.* 19.245 [Goold, LCL])

Modern readers might associate the description of a man "dark of skin and curly-haired" to be a statement of racial heritage. But in this ancient context, these phenotypes bespoke the camaraderie and honor of the individual man. Finally, Suetonius's description of Augustus suggests that physiognomic ideals differed in many ways from modern, phenotypical aesthetics.

> He was unusually handsome and exceedingly graceful at all periods of his life, though he cared nothing for personal adornment. His expression, whether in conversation or when he was silent, was so calm and mild. He had clear, bright eyes, in which he liked to have it thought that there was a kind of divine power, and it greatly pleased him, whenever he looked keenly at anyone, if he let his face fall as if before the radiance of the sun; but in his old age he could not see very well with his left eye. His teeth were wide apart, small, and ill-kept; his hair was slightly curly and inclined to golden; his eyebrows met. His ears were of moderate size, and his nose projected a little at the top and then bent slightly forward. His complexion was between dark and fair. He was short of stature (although Julius Marathus, his freedman and keeper of his records, says that he was five feet and nine inches in height), but this was concealed by the fine proportion and symmetry of his figure, and was noticeable only by comparison with some taller person standing beside him. (*Aug.* 79 [J. C. Rolfe, LCL])

Notice in this case that one could be seen as handsome with ill-kept teeth, an irregular nose, and a unibrow. As with much of the physiognomic literature, the most important features of a man are his eyes. But even with the failing of his left eye, Augustus was considered "unusually handsome and exceedingly graceful at all periods of his life."[11] His height is questionably ideal, according to Suetonius, but this does not detract from Augustus's otherwise stellar countenance. Within this context, notice that his hair is slightly curly and his complexion was "between dark and fair." In other words, he did not suffer from pale skin and straight hair as did Caligula. Generally speaking, the physiognomic writers had no conception of "black" vs. "white" as racial categories. The important categories were moderate vs. extreme. The former bespeaks virtue; the latter bespeaks vice.[12]

Many more examples are available and provide windows into a bygone culture wherein phenotypes bespoke personal character traits. For the purposes of this chapter it will suffice to point out that phenotypes were not associated first and foremost with *ethnos*. Indeed, the classical voices most interested in phenotypes are more interested in cross-species comparison (e.g., between humans and goats) than they are in the way that phenotypes remain consistent within any particular *genos* or *ethnos*.

This is not to give the impression that phenotypes were not associated with geographical populations. Some ancient writers assumed that climates and landscapes conditioned skin color, hair, etc. (cf. Plato, *Laws* 5.747d). But what authors like Plato found most interesting were the general customs and driving motivations of people groups; very limited space was devoted to phenotypes when the topic turned to *ethnoi*. By comparison, the physiognomic literature places a great deal of weight on phenotypes. I would suggest that future analyses of Hellenistic ethnographies take care to distinguish between phenotypical stereotypes and ethnographic stereotypes. These conceptual worlds overlapped at times but not to the extent that they do in many modern cultures. As we move forward, therefore, I

11. The popularly disseminated image of Augustus was so influential that it was mimicked in personal portraiture. "The much-admired portrait style of the imperial house apparently inspired the most conscientious imitators to suppress even their own individual features in favor of depersonalized formulas expressing dignity and moral worth." Paul Zanker, *The Power of Images in the Age of Augustus*, trans. Alan Shapiro, Thomas Spencer Jerome Lectures (Ann Arbor: University of Michigan Press, 1990), 295.

12. For a survey of the political aspects of Hellenistic and Roman portraiture, see Roland R. R. Smith, *Hellenistic Royal Portraits*, Oxford Monographs on Classical Archaeology (Oxford: Clarendon, 1988), esp. 109–43.

will sideline the significance of phenotypes to focus on a key factor in the conceptualization of *ethnos*.

2. *Ethnos* as Poliscentric

Modern ethnologists now deemphasize or reject the popular notions of race that emerged from nineteenth-century pseudoscience. An ethnic community is now defined by one introduction as a people with varying combinations of (1) a common proper name; (2) a myth of common ancestry; (3) shared commemoration; (4) one or more elements of common culture, e.g., religion, customs, language; (5) a link with a (physical or symbolic) homeland; (6) a feeling of solidarity among (at least portions of) the population of the ethnic community.[13]

Applying the conclusions of ethnic studies to the Second Temple period is helpful inasmuch as it problematizes our standard projections. But we do better to remember that the modern concept of ethnicity was reinvented in response to scientific racism. As such, our preconceived notions of race remain in play even as we attempt to define ethnicity in counter-distinction to a discredited science. Such conceptual baggage might mislead us when applied to antiquity. If an *ethnos* was not primarily associated with phenotypes or genotypes in the classical world, *what did Hellenistic people think about when they thought ethnographically?*

Perhaps the first step toward an emic solution relates to the importance of urban cultures. Amselle writes, "For the Greeks, the notion of *ethnos* was a political category. It constituted one pole in the hierarchization that evolved between the two principal forms of societies: *polis* and *ethnos*."[14] *Polis* is a Greek word that we translate as "city" and from which we borrow in the words politics, cosmopolitan, metropolis ("mother city"), etc. But *polis* means more in antiquity than is conveyed in the word "city." The concept of the *polis*—a carryover from the conceptual map of the Greek city-state— was a constellation of relationships between urban center, geography, law (or customs), worship, citizenship, wider community, and—of key importance—self-sufficiency. Those within the cultural orbit of an urban center

13. John Hutchinson and Anthony D. Smith, "Introduction," in *Ethnicity*, ed. John Hutchinson and Anthony D. Smith (Oxford: Oxford University Press, 1996), 3–16, here 6–7.
14. Jean-Loup Amselle, *Mestizo Logics: Anthropology of Identity in Africa and Elsewhere*, trans. Claudia Royal (Stanford: Stanford University Press, 1998), 6.

would be identified as members of that center. I call this a "poliscentric" worldview.[15]

In order to understand poliscentrism it might be helpful to begin with the more common reality of clan-centrism. In clan-centrism families coalesced (most often) around a father figure. The good of the clan was found within the gravitational force of family honor and longevity of continuous progeny. This worldview bleeds into Greek and Roman thought as evinced by the concept of *paterfamilias* (father of the family). The ideal father figure would serve as the public face of the wider clan, control wealth, property, marriage, and most major decisions.[16] Importantly, he would provide for those under his care. Aristotle's description is apt: "The rule of a father over his children is royal, for he rules by virtue both of love and of the respect due to age, exercising a kind of royal power" (*Pol.* 1259b 9–13).[17] But by the Second Temple period the *paterfamilias* was just one dynamic in play in a world of larger networks. Aristotle discusses this shift in terms of commerce:

> For the members of the family originally had all things in common; later, when the family divided into parts, the parts shared in many things, and different parts in different things, which they had to give in exchange for what they wanted, a kind of barter which is still practiced among barbarous nations who exchange with one another the necessaries of life and nothing more; giving and receiving wine, for example, in exchange for coin, and the like. (*Pol.* 1257a 15–20)

Key factors for Aristotle are the motives of necessity and self-sufficiency (both are key themes throughout *Politics*). Social institutions often emerge from postures of security. As families grew and divided, more innovative

15. In previous decades studies of this period would have emphasized the distinction between *astu* (life nearer to the urban center) and *chōra* (life in the countryside). More recently scholarship has blurred this distinction. See, e.g., Neville Morley, "Cities in Context: Urban Systems in Roman Italy" in *Roman Urbanism: Beyond the Consumer City*, ed. Helen M. Parkins (London: Routledge, 1997), 42–58, here 44–45.

16. I discuss this more fully in my *The Wife of Jesus: Ancient Texts and Modern Scandals* (London: Oneworld, 2014).

17. All quotations of *Politics* are taken from the Benjamin Jowett translation unless otherwise noted; http://classics.mit.edu/Aristotle/politics.html (accessed 8 October 2015) provides an accessible resource. It is also worth noting that the most up-to-date treatments of ethnographic study in Hellenism treat Aristotle's *Politics* as primary and central to the discussion. Cf. Kostas Vlassopoulos, *Unthinking the Greek Polis: Ancient Greek History beyond Eurocentrism* (Cambridge: Cambridge University Press, 2007).

ways to provide for them emerged including exchange within and between clans. This explains, in part, the evolution from household to village.

Another important element for this Greek mapping of the world is the process of contradistinction. Hellenistic minds tended to map the world in binary opposites. It was not their tendency to study a phenomenon in isolation, but by way of contrast. As part of this tendency, they looked for antithetical relationships mirrored by a complementary opposite. The concepts of household (*oikos* or *oikia*) and village (*kōmē*) were juxtaposed, just as the concepts of village and city were juxtaposed.[18] Thus we enter into a discussion of the *polis*. I would suggest that a poliscentric worldview stands in contrasting relationship to previous clan-centric views. Moreover, from Aristotle's perspective, we witness a cultural advance.

Size was an important point of distinction for Aristotle's ideal: a *polis* must be larger than a village but small enough so that all members of the community know one another. Beyond this critical mass of intimacy, the participation of each individual in decision-making was nearly impossible (*Pol.* 1326b 12–17). So, for Aristotle the size of the *polis* was critical for its definition as such because it related to self-sufficiency.[19] In addition, the *polis* differed from the village because the *polis* was (relatively) self-governed and had an urban center. In sum, a process of expansion and contradistinction explains the evolution from household to village to *polis* in this worldview. And here we find the necessary link between *polis* and *ethnos*.

In the antithetical world of the Greeks, *polis* and *ethnos* stood in a contrasting but often necessary relationship. If a grouping of people was too large, they would cease to be a *polis*. Generally speaking, any large people group that could not be classified as a *polis* was called an *ethnos* (*Pol.* 1326b 3–5).[20] Edward Cohen points out that in much of classical Greek literature the term *ethnos* is often accompanied by its counterpart *polis*. In Aristotle's

---

18. Edward E. Cohen, *The Athenian Nation* (Princeton: Princeton University Press, 2000), 23. He writes, "In the fourth century [BCE], numerous nouns were available to denote a farrago of differentiable sites smaller than a polis—*kōmion, khōrian, topos, epineion, amphodon, limēn, hieron, tonos, manteion, polikhnē*, and many others—but all were encompassed within the general term 'village,' itself a contrast to 'household' (*oikos* or *oikia*)."

19. It was possible for an *ethnos* to become self-sufficient by way of several collaborating villages and thus have no urban center. This network of villages would not have been considered a *polis* by Aristotelian standards.

20. Cohen, *Athenian*, 28, argues that urban groupings like Athens and Babylon would have been too large to be considered *poleis*. Indeed, some urban groupings would have been larger than many nations and would have therefore been *ethnē*. Cohen concedes, however, that Herodotus calls Babylon a *polis* in *Hist.* 1.90–91.

Politics, the author never uses the term *ethnos* without a mention of *polis*. In many places in Greek literature, if the writer wanted to speak of the entire population of the world, he would refer to "all cities (*poleis*) and nations (*ethnē*)." Cohen writes, "*polis* and *ethnos* together encompassed all units larger than a *kōmē*."[21]

It is therefore commonplace in ethnographic treatments of Hellenistic thought to point to the contrasting relationship between *polis* and *ethnos* in a binary way. After all, classical writers such as Herodotus and Aristotle describe the logical process as such. But more recent studies demonstrate that the classical descriptions of Greek thought do not always represent the complexity of the relevant associations from which these categories derive. "The *ethnos* is now envisaged not as an alternative to the *polis*, but as a complex organisational linking of political forms and communities both above and below the *polis*."[22] But whether we are dealing in binary contrasts or with a more sophisticated network of relationships, the consensus is clear: in Hellenistic thought, the concept of *ethnos* was defined in relationship to *polis*.

Christopher P. Jones explains that Herodotus used both *genos* and *ethnos*, but not interchangeably. For Herodotus, *genos* refers to descendance; *ethnos* refers to a people unified as a geographical unit.[23] So, in simple terms, ethnicity was related to geography. But "geography" is too imprecise to be of much help.[24] The mapping of the Hellenistic world included gravitational centers of culture. Amselle hits the mark succinctly when he explains that the *polis* "was a precisely defined and valorized category, one in which the Greeks found their plentitude of being." This is what I have called poliscentrism. Jones explains that *ethnos* is therefore defined in contradistinction:

21. Cohen, *Athenian,* 24.

22. Vlassopoulos, *Unthinking,* 194

23. Christopher P. Jones, "ἔθνος and γένος in Herodotus," *ClQ* 46 (1996): 315–20. He writes: "Herodotus uses *ethnos* in a very restricted way, and practically every case can be translated 'people' or 'nation'" (316); cf. also the more recent nuances of Vlassopoulos, who argues that "the supposed tribal affinities of the *ethnos* are fictive; the Greeks of the *ethnē* were capable of inventing and forging ties of political, social and religious kinship, as the Greeks of *poleis* were" (*Unthinking the Greek Polis,* 194). If Vlassopoulos is correct, a more sustainable emic definition of *ethnos* rests on the myth of a shared tribe rather than any genotypical connection to the past.

24. Cf. Catherine Morgan, "Ethnic Expression on the Early Iron Age and Early Archaic Greek Mainland: Where Should We Be Looking?" in *Ethnic Constructs in Antiquity: The Role of Power and Tradition,* ed. Ton Derks and Nico Roymans, Amsterdam Archaeological Studies[0] 13 (Amsterdam: Amsterdam University Press, 2009), 11–36; this essay serves as an excellent starting point for assessing the relationship(s) between *ethnos* and *polis*.

"the category of *ethnos*, in contrast [to *polis*], was vague and deprecatory."[25] We should nuance this a bit, however, and point out that in some cases *ethnē* orbited a *polis* center and was rendered distinct by this cultural force of gravity.[26] Athens, according to Cohen, provides the prime example of this relationship. In sum, while many *ethnē* were not oriented toward a *polis*, some very important *ethnē* were. Most importantly, the Greeks used the concept of *polis* to define the concept of *ethnos*. *Ethnos* is first and foremost a poliscentric category.

3. Jews/Judeans as Poliscentric People

At this point, the definitive tone of my essay must soften. We can be confident that *ethnos* is a poliscentric category within Hellenistic thought. We can also be confident that Hellenism seeped into the pores of Jewish life in innumerable ways and to varying degrees. But defining the fluid phenomenon of Jewish identity is problematic and the literature treating this topic is oceanic. As John Barclay writes, "'Jewish identity' is, of course, a multifaceted phenomenon. Jews had (and have) a triple identity: how they viewed themselves, how they were viewed by other Jews and how they were viewed by outsiders."[27] Shaye Cohen complicates the nature of the problem even further:

> There were few mechanisms in antiquity that would have provided empirical or "objective" criteria by which to determine who was "really" a Jew and who was not. Jewishness was a subjective identity, constructed by the individual him/herself, other Jews, other gentiles, and the state. . . . The boundary was fluid and not well marked; we must allow for a variety of competing definitions and for the influence of the perspective of the observer.[28]

We may add to these complexities the concerns of Adele Reinhartz who reminds us that redefining the identities of historical Jews has political and

---

25. Amselle, *Mestizo Logics*, 6.
26. Thucydides describes Khios and Lesbos as *ethnē*-encompassing *poleis* (2.9.4).
27. John M. G. Barclay, *Jews in the Mediterranean Diaspora: From Alexander to Trajan (323 BCE–117 CE)* (Berkeley: University of California Press, 1996), 400.
28. Shaye J. D. Cohen, *The Beginnings of Jewishness: Boundaries, Varieties, Uncertainties* (Berkeley: University of California Press, 1999), 3, 4.

moral implications for the present.[29] But the way forward is not hopeless, as the work of Barclay demonstrates. In the space remaining, I will argue that poliscentrism is an apt category for Second Temple Jewish life.

Many Iron Age rural sites have been revealed in and around the modern city of Jerusalem. Most of these were abandoned during the neo-Babylonian period and resettled around the Second Temple period.[30] That Jerusalem in the Second Temple period was a *polis* with an orbiting *ethnos* is not a matter of dispute. It is the nature and extent of the orbit that introduces significant complexity.

Within Judea a diversity of ideologies and power positions would have factored into various kinds and levels of investment in Jerusalem. *Ioudaioi* of Galilee, Idumea, among the Yahad, and in diaspora *poleis* all over the Roman Empire had various ways of orienting themselves toward the *polis*. Diaspora communities would have been variously influenced by their environs. And, as Barclay writes, "there were no 'typical' diaspora conditions. Understanding the social milieu of diaspora Jews requires attention to each individual site and period as well as the peculiar circumstances of Jewish individuals and communities in each environment."[31]

Strabo provides one Greek perspective on Jewish political identity. He credits Moses for gathering and unifying *Ioudaioi* (themselves having an Egyptian heritage) and for leading them to Jerusalem. Strabo derides several of what he regards as the customs, superstitions, and corruptions of the Jerusalem leadership but praises their relationship with the Acropolis (and presumably the Temple Mount).

> Respect, however, was paid to the Acropolis; it was not abhorred as the seat of tyranny, but honored and venerated as a temple. This is according to nature, and common both to Greeks and barbarians. For, as members of a civil community, they live according to a common law; otherwise it would be impossible for the mass to execute any one thing in concert (in which consists a civil state), or to live in a social state at all. (*Geography* 16.2.37–38 [H. L. Jones, LCL])

29. "The Vanishing Jews of Antiquity"; http://www.marginalia.lareviewofbooks.org/vanishing-jews-antiquity-adele-reinhartz/.

30. Avraham Faust, *Judah in the Neo-Babylonian Period: The Archaeology of Desolation* (Atlanta: SBL, 2012), 39. Faust argues compellingly that some sites in Judea were not vacated during this period but maintained continuous use.

31. Barclay, *Diaspora*, 399.

For Strabo, the topics of importance—the factors first and foremost in explaining the identity of *Ioudaioi*—relate to the story of Moses's leadership, the establishment and customs of Jerusalem, and Jerusalem's relationship with the Acropolis. Thus, to be Jewish, according to Strabo, was to be oriented toward and invested in Jerusalem. But this poliscentrism did not preclude respect and veneration of other Greek *poleis*. Consider again the language used by Strabo:

> For, as members of a civil community (πολιτικοί), they live according to a common law; otherwise it would be impossible for the mass to execute any one thing in concert (in which consists a civil state), or to live in a social state (πολιτεύεσθαι). (H. L. Jones, LCL)

This description emphasizes the *polis*-connectedness of Jewish life and represents, from Strabo's perspective, the civility of *Ioudaioi*.

Philo's now famous veneration of Jerusalem as the mother-*polis* of diaspora *Ioudaioi* is important for my thesis in two ways: (1) we hear an echo of Aristotle's definition of an *ethnos* as it relates to a *polis;* (2) we learn that *Ioudaioi* outside of Judea are defined as "Jews" by way of their orientation toward Jerusalem.

> ... no single country can contain the Jews because of their multitude, and for this reason they inhabit the most extensive and wealthiest districts in Europe and Asia both on islands and on mainlands, and while they regard the Holy City as their mother-city, in which is founded and consecrated the temple of the most high God, yet they severally hold that land as their fatherland which they have obtained by inheritance from fathers and grandfathers and great-grandfathers and still more remote ancestors for their portion to dwell in, in which they were born and reared. (*Flacc.* 46)

Philo, writing from Alexandria, calls Jerusalem both *hieropolis* ("holy city") and *metropolis* ("mother city"). In keeping with Aristotle's definition of an *ethnos*, Philo emphasizes the large population of *Ioudaioi*. As seen above, the size of the population was an important factor in distinguishing a *polis* from an *ethnos*. In the case of Philo's description, we have an example of an *ethnos* orbiting a *polis* even when the orbit extends to Alexandria. So the Jewish *ethnos* is not contrasted with the *polis* in this case; rather the *ethnos* is defined in relation to Jerusalem positively. Jewish relationships with Jerusalem are primary, thus confirming that Philo viewed diaspora *Ioudaioi* as a poliscentric people.

Philo's description is relevant to my argument in an additional way as he also emphasizes ancestral inheritance in relation to Jewish identity. Maren Niehoff argues that Philo invents a myth of progeny from Jerusalem so that diaspora *Ioudaioi* will see themselves as colonists, much as Greeks would owe allegiance first and foremost to the *polis* of their ancestors. She argues that Philo viewed Jerusalem as a mother city in mirror image to the Roman metaphor of Rome as mother. According to this view, Romans who used this metaphor of Rome and Philo who used a similar metaphor did so to demonstrate ultimate allegiance to their true *polis* in distinction from any allegiances they felt toward their colonies of residence.[32] Sarah Pearce has taken Niehoff to task for drawing too close a parallel between Rome and Jerusalem. The concept of the Holy City as "mother" is better understood as rooted in the longstanding Hebrew metaphors.[33] Whatever his motive, and however legendary, Philo is interested in connecting Jewish *ethnos* to Jerusalem in terms of ancestry. So, while *ethnos* and *genos* are distinct categories in Herodotus, the conceptual spheres of poliscentrism and genotypical links overlap in the minds of at least some Second Temple Jews. Consider Barclay's observation of one example from the diaspora. In the *Letter of Aristeas*, *Ioudaioi* are a *genos* but presented as *politai* (citizens[34]):

> In the case of *The Letter of Aristeas*, though the Jews are introduced as a *genos* (6), the narrator, the high-priest and the king all refer to Eleazar's fellow-Jews as "citizens" (*politai*, 3, 36, 44, 126), and the metaphor may be carefully chosen to throw emphasis on the political and cultural, rather than the genealogical, aspects of Judaism.[35]

This letter also refers to the Jews as a *politeuma*—perhaps in a technical sense—denoting the diaspora community as "an organisation of aliens re-

---

32. Maren Niehoff, *Philo on Jewish Identity and Culture*, TSAJ 86 (Tübingen: Mohr Siebeck, 2001), 29–30.

33. Sarah Pearce, "Jerusalem as 'Mother-City' in the Writings of Philo of Alexandra," in *Negotiating Diaspora: Jewish Strategies in the Roman Empire*, ed. John M. G. Barclay, LSTS 45 (London: T&T Clark, 2004), 19–36, here 27–30.

34. "The Greek word *politeia* means in the first instance 'citizenship,' the quality of being a citizen (a *politēs*). By extension the word also refers to the institutions and conventions within which a citizen exercises his citizenship" (Cohen, *Beginnings*, 125). I will note additionally that the term is a poliscentric category as is evident both in etymology and in usage.

35. Barclay, *Diaspora*, 406.

siding in a foreign city."[36] This definition of diaspora Jewish folk may well be supported by two examples of epigraphy from Berenice in Cyrenaica. "They consist of decrees which had been promulgated by a Jewish organisation called 'The Politeuma of the Jews in Berenice'."[37] This group might have comprised the sum total of all Jews living in a foreign *polis* or it might have been limited to the political leaders of the group.[38] In either case, the fact that some diaspora Jews self-identified with such a term bespeaks a sense of political identity (i.e., relating to their orientation to the Judean *polis*) in terms of self-governance.[39] The use of this term in *The Letter of Aristeas* (§310) supports Barclay's suggestion that the diaspora Jews referred to in the letter are presented as citizens.

One of Pearce's arguments is that Romans thought of their relationship to their mother-*polis* primarily in terms of citizenship. If Barclay's suggestion is correct, *Ioudaioi* were capable of using similar categories when presenting Jewish life to outsiders. "Both Josephus and Philo were aware of this complexity."[40] Eric Barreto succinctly explains, "Like ethnicities, ethnic terminologies are flexible and subject to change in different narrative contexts."[41]

I will round out this section by discussing two very problematic references to "Judaism" or "Judaizing" in 2 Maccabees. I reiterate that this chapter intends to suggest possible avenues for conceptualizing *Ioudaios* as a poliscentric category. By providing these examples, I merely point in a direction; I do not claim that a solution can be had in this limited space.

The following two passages suggest an ideological abstraction by certain Second Temple *Ioudaioi*. These are cases that Steve Mason might call "Judaizing"—that is, attempts to adopt the customs of Judea with great fervor.

---

36. Gert Lüderitz, "What Is the *Politeuma*?" in *Studies in Early Jewish Epigraphy*, ed. Jan Willem van Henten and Pieter Willem van der Horst, AGJU 21 (Leiden: Brill, 1994), 183–225, here 183. Lüderitz writes that *politeuma*, if used in a technical sense, "can either represent a political body which is part of the administrative organisation of a Greek *polis*, or it can stand for other organised groups of people. Formally a Jewish *politeuma*—as an alien body in a Greek city—should of course be included within the second category, but . . . in some respects the Jewish *politeuma* could have borne a closer resemblance to the *politeumata* of the first category" (185).

37. Lüderitz, "*Politeuma*," 183.

38. Lüderitz, "*Politeuma*," 214.

39. A more comprehensive study would, no doubt, be supported by greater attention to the epigraphy of Jews inside and outside Judea.

40. Barclay, *Diaspora*, 404; see further Cohen, *Beginnings*, 125–29.

41. Eric Barreto, *Ethnic Negotiations: The Function of Race and Ethnicity in Acts 16*, WUNT/2 294 (Tübingen: Mohr Siebeck, 2010), 24.

Mason has argued in multiple publications that projecting religious denotation into this semantic range is anachronistic. Fitting hand-in-glove with this thesis, Mason prefers "Judean" rather than "Jew" when rendering *Ioudaios* in English. In the Second Temple period, so goes the logic, a Judean is someone who lives in Judea and practices the customs of Judea. By contrast, Daniel Schwartz argues that while many occurrences of *Ioudaios* connote geographical affiliation (cf. *Apion* 1.177; *Ant.* 18.196), others are clearly religious.[42] Or, following the thesis of another (Seth) Schwartz, we might say that we witness the seeds of Judaism already germinating in the Second Temple period. 2 Macc 2:20–22 and 8:1–3 illustrate the problem. Schwartz, contra Mason, reads these passages as religious representations of Second Temple Jews.[43]

> . . . and further the wars against Antiochus Epiphanes and his son Eupator, and the appearances that came from heaven to those who fought bravely for Judaism ['Ιουδαϊσμοῦ], so that though few in number they seized the whole land and pursued the barbarian hordes, and regained possession of the temple famous throughout the world, and liberated the city [τὴν οἰκουμένην ἱερὸν ἀνακομίσασθαι καὶ τὴν πόλιν ἐλευθερῶσαι] and reestablished the laws that were about to be abolished, while the Lord with great kindness became gracious to them. (2 Macc 2:20–22 NRSV)

Daniel Schwartz downplays the geographical affiliation of this passage. He writes that "it is clear that *Ioudaios* must define a person not by reference to his place, Judea, but, rather, by relation to religion—what this book indeed terms '*Ioudaismos*.'"[44] While I am sympathetic to his overall thesis, this passage is clearly geographically oriented. The designation *Ioudaismos* does not speak to the region of residence necessarily, but it may well indicate the *polis* of orientation. Mason's alternative reading does not quite hit the mark either. To label these zealous "Judaizing Jews" as people with geographical ties is much too vague. Given our brief survey of poliscentrism above, I would suggest that these *Ioudaioi* are orienting themselves toward the *polis* and temple with renewed zeal. If so, perhaps poliscentrism is a better way to think of the identity showcased in this passage. Consider also:

42. Daniel R. Schwartz, "'Judean' or 'Jew'? How Should We Translate *Ioudaios* in Josephus?" in *Jewish Identity in the Greco-Roman World*, ed. Jörg Frey, Daniel R. Schwartz, and Stephanie Gripentrog, AGJU 71 (Leiden: Brill, 2007), 3–27.
43. Seth Schwartz, "How Many Judaisms Were There? A Critique of Neusner and Smith on Definition and Mason and Boyarin on Categorization," *JAJ* 2.2 (2011): 208–38, here 225.
44. Schwartz, "'Judean' or 'Jew'?" 13.

Meanwhile Judas, who was also called Maccabeus, and his companions secretly entered the villages and summoned their kindred and enlisted those who had continued in the Jewish faith [τοὺς μεμενηκότας ἐν τῷ Ἰουδαϊσμῷ], and so they gathered about six thousand. They implored the Lord to look upon the people who were oppressed by all; and to have pity on the temple that had been profaned by the godless; to have mercy on the city [πόλιν] that was being destroyed and about to be leveled to the ground; to hearken to the blood that cried out to him. (2 Macc 8:1–3 NRSV)

This passage is especially problematic for Mason's argument (cf. 4 Macc 4:26). There is no reference to "Judaizing" in the sense of adopting new regional customs. The *Ioudaioi* here are continuing to practice something called *Ioudaismos*. But Schwartz's claim that this is a religious rather than geographical category misses the mark too. These *Ioudaioi* are explicitly oriented toward and invested in Jerusalem and the Jerusalem temple. I would suggest that the category of poliscentrism might provide a better reading of this passage.

4. Concluding Remarks

I hope that this chapter has problematized the retreat from religious categorization to ethnic categorization. As demonstrated here, the problem of ethnicity in the Second Temple period is just as complex as the problem of emerging religious identities. We cannot assume that our own ethnic categories translate simply to other cultures, much less the cultures of Hellenistic antiquity.

In the Hellenistic world *ethnos* was a poliscentric category. If, then, *Ioudaios* is such a category, it is less helpful to think of *Ioudaioi* of this period in terms of "race" as we conceptualize racial categories in the modern Western world. I have suggested that Second Temple *Ioudaioi* were poliscentric as they lived within the orbit of the Jerusalem temple. They were an *ethnos* too numerous and widespread to function collectively as a *polis* by Aristotle's definition. But their *polis* was central to their identity as an *ethnos*. Variations in orientation toward Jerusalem had the power to create different ways of expressing Jewishness.

Paul, Pentecost, and the Nomosphere

The Final Return to Jerusalem in the Acts of the Apostles

MATTHEW SLEEMAN

Acts engages with many cities, but none as much as Jerusalem. After dominating the narrative's opening chapters, and having been an occasional setting up until the Acts 15 council, Jerusalem hosts one final visit by Paul (following a brief visit alluded to in 18:22) during the second Pentecost festival recounted in Acts.

In this chapter I reappraise this final return to Jerusalem using a broad range of spatial lenses such as I have elsewhere argued are required for a Critical Spatial Theory 2.0.[1] One premise of my argument is that readings of Scripture can be enhanced by using spatial theories; also, although less often demonstrated, spatial theories can benefit from historical case studies drawn from antiquity,[2] including biblical texts, and can require realignment in order to apprehend the theological *Tendenz* of Scripture. To this end, I use two spatial lenses here. First, drawing from the social theorist and activist Henri Lefebvre (1901–1991), I shall unpack the ways in which Paul asserts a "right to the city." Also, taking up recent work from critical legal geography, I shall explore how Paul navigates within Jerusalem what David Delaney calls the nomosphere. Then, having gleaned some of the insights for reading Acts 21 that these two theoretical lenses bring us, I appraise

---

1. Matthew Sleeman, "Critical Spatial Theory 2.0," in *Constructions of Space V: Place, Space and Identity in the Ancient Mediterranean World*, ed. Gert T. M. Prinsloo and Christl M. Maier, LHBOTS 576 (London: Bloomsbury/T&T Clark, 2013), 49–66.

2. E.g., Eleonora Redaelli, "Becoming a Creative City: Perspectives from Augustus' Rome," *Urban Geogr.* 36 (2015): 608–23, esp. 609–10.

their usefulness for illuminating how Acts presents and reworks Jerusalem as both peopled place and placed people (noting these dual uses of πόλις in Acts 21:29, 30).

1. Reading the City

Both Lefebvre and Delaney challenge static, singular, and positivistic notions of the city and resist reducing space to either a background container for life or history, or to a merely discursive, disembodied symbol. Instead, they both reflect the predominant understanding within urban studies that cities are performed artifacts, always an *assemblage*, constructed and struggled over, made up of multiple scales and settings, unstable in their forms, and open to challenge, even to change. They would concur with writers such as Engin Isin that the city is both "the battleground through which groups define their identities, stake their claims, wage their battles, and articulate citizenship rights and obligations" *and* "an object of thought and experience [which] emerges out of these practices."[3]

First, then, what does Lefebvre offer to a reading of Acts 21? Although widely cited within spatial readings of Scripture, Lefebvre might well need some introduction here. Over the last two decades there has been a "spatial turn" within the wider humanities, a new concern with space and place as explanatory factors for life, a concern which increasingly includes biblical studies. Lefebvre has been seminal in this new interest in space and place, both through one particular writing and through an influential popularizer of it.[4] Lefebvre's basic thesis concerning space is that it cannot—and should not—be reduced either simply to inert physical spaces or only to mentalities conceiving space in an abstracted, disembodied sense. Space, and diverse realizations of spatiality, are too lively for such reductions. Rather, space is also always "lived": that is, far from being simply a physical container

---

3. Engin F. Isin, *Being Political: Genealogies of Citizenship* (Minneapolis: University of Minnesota Press, 2002), 50. See 1–51 "City as a Difference Machine," esp. 42–50 "Space Is the Machine."

4. Henri Lefebvre, *The Production of Space,* trans. Donald Nicholson (Oxford: Blackwell, 1991); trans. of *La Production de l'espace* (Paris: Anthropos, 1974). Lefebvre's work was popularized by Edward Soja, originally in Edward W. Soja, *Postmodern Geographies: The Reassertion of Space in Critical Social Theory* (London: Verso, 1989). Soja was subsequently pivotal for the later "spatial turn": Barney Warf and Santa Arias, eds., *The Spatial Turn: Interdisciplinary Perspectives* (London: Routledge, 2009).

or staging for life, or merely dots or lines on a map, spaces and places are struggled over, inhabited. Their meanings are contested, and constantly so.

Here, I am assuming this dynamic understanding of space but drawing on another related aspect of Lefebvre's many writings, one that previously has not been evident within biblical studies. Lefebvre's "right to the city"[5] means a right not only to inhabit the city, but also for inhabitants to be able "to produce urban life on new terms . . . [and] to remain unalienated from urban life."[6] For Lefebvre, "the city is an *oeuvre*, closer to a work of art than to a simple material product."[7] It is intensely human, produced by the daily labor and activities of its inhabitants. Lefebvre thus espouses a right to make and remake ourselves by changing the city via its everyday activities and practices at varying scales, ranging from the intensely personal to the broader structural parameters of society. As well as opening new vistas for reading New Testament cities as lived experience, this also helps address potential criticisms of too narrow an appropriation of Lefebvre's work within biblical studies.[8]

Lefebvre's "right to the city" needs contextualizing and transposing if it is to function as a lens for reading Acts. Contextually, Lefebvre espoused this renewed right for the citizens to shape the city, their city, as part of a revolutionary critique of everyday life issued in response to the alienations engendered by capitalist solutions to the French post-war housing crisis. His grounded, relational approach seeking a concrete and not merely cognitive utopianism influenced the politics of urban space espoused by the Situationists, a group seeking anti-authoritarian alternatives to capitalist urban life in 1960s France,[9] and informed the urban riots in France during 1968. More recently, it has spurred the Occupy movement and theorizing

5. Henri Lefebvre, *Writings on Cities*, trans. Eleonore Kofman and Elizabeth Lebas (Oxford: Blackwell, 1996), 158: "the *right to the city* is like a cry and a demand. . . [for] a transformed and renewed *right to urban life*" within daily life (emphasis original).

6. Kafui A. Attoh, "What *Kind* of Right Is the Right to the City?," *Prog. Hum. Geogr.* 35 (2011): 669–85, here 674.

7. Lefebvre, *Writings on Cities*, 101.

8. Stuart Elden, "Politics, Philosophy, Geography: Henri Lefebvre in Recent Anglo-American Scholarship," *Antipode* 10 (2001): 809–25. Elden criticizes Soja (through whom many biblical scholars encounter Lefebvre) for presenting too narrow a reading of Lefebvre, focused excessively on the first chapter of *The Production of Space*.

9. David Pinder, "'Old Paris Is No More': Geographies of Spectacle and Anti-Spectacle," *Antipode* 32 (2000): 357–86; David Pinder, "Reconstituting the Possible: Lefebvre, Utopia and the Urban Question," *Int. J. Urb. Reg. Res.* 39 (2015): 28–45. Cf. also A. E. Souzis, "Momentary Ambiances: Psychogeography in Action," *Cult. Geogr.* 22 (2015): 193–201.

of urban exploration and trespass as alternative ways of "being" within the city.[10] Yet Lefebvre developed the notion only sporadically and, while a radical openness or strategic fuzziness can foster an initial solidarity between differing causes and interests, the progressive potential of a right to the city still remains to be worked out and realized in the practical trade-offs inherent within real politics.[11]

Looking toward exegesis, Lefebvre's concrete utopianism raises interesting questions for reading Acts, but also needs careful transposition if it is to be exegetically useful. Just as when drawing Lefebvre's twentieth-century politics into urban struggles today,[12] caution is required when using Lefebvre's work to read ancient texts. But Acts does invite such comparisons. Via its wider and orienting ascension geography,[13] Acts resists a locality "trap,"[14] that is, a prioritizing of the local scale above all others. Also, its ascension geography does not isolate or over-privilege the urban: Acts also lays claim to a right to the village (8:25; cf. 1:8). Nevertheless, the urban is clearly in view, and Jerusalem is not the only focus within Luke's urban interests.[15] In various ways (e.g., 20:20, and in numerous cities he visited), Paul's "ministry" has already asserted a right to the city across the wider region in which he has worked. Importantly for employing Lefebvrian categories for exegesis, Acts, when narrating and theologizing "Jerusalem," does not relate with a stable, external, thing-in-itself (nor does it so regard any other place, for that matter). Instead, as shall be seen, it engages with existing first-century Jewish construals of Jerusalem, as it shapes its own performative portrait. It is therefore legitimate to look in Acts for a particular theologically and christologically charged "right to the city," which forms an integral but relatively unexplored part of the certainty, an inherently spatialized "certainty" that is being communicated to Theophilus and to other ancient readers/ auditors (Luke 1:1–4).

10. Bradley L. Garrett, *Explore Everything: Place-Hacking the City* (London: Verso, 2013).

11. Attoh, "What *Kind* of Right."

12. Justus Uitermark, Walter Nicholls, and Maarten Loopmans, "Cities and Social Movements: Theorizing beyond the Right to the City," *Env. Plan. A* 44 (2012): 2546–54.

13. Matthew Sleeman, *Geography and the Ascension Narrative in Acts*, SNTSMS 146 (Cambridge: Cambridge University Press, 2009).

14. Mark Purcell, "Urban Democracy and the Local Trap," *Urban Stud.* 43 (2006): 1921–41.

15. Elden, "Politics," 816 criticizes Soja for a localized particularism, for an overfocusing on Los Angeles.

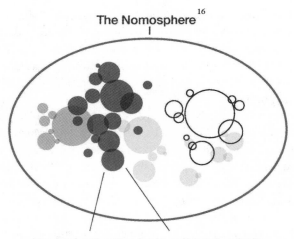

The Nomosphere [16]

Interrelated nomic settings forming multiple and overlapping,
fluid and dynamic nomoscapes within the nomosphere.

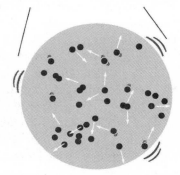

Each nomic setting home to (and formed by) active and interactive
nomic traces joined together in particular performances of nomicity.

A similar foregrounding of the performativities that constitute the city is evident in David Delaney's 2010 book, subtitled *Nomospheric Investigations*.[17] As with Lefebvre, it is necessary to show how this can offer a useful lens for exegesis, particularly regarding Acts 21.

16. I am grateful to Matt Peckham for producing the diagrammatic representation used here.

17. David Delaney, *The Spatial, the Legal, and the Pragmatics of World-Making: Nomospheric Investigations* (Abingdon: Routledge, 2010).

Unapologetic about coining the neologism "nomosphere," Delaney likens it to the biosphere—itself once an innovative term—as a useful means for examining at different analytical scales certain relations within life-ordering and space that we might otherwise dismiss or not be able to articulate. When uncovered, here lies its benefit for exegesis.

Delaney uses *nomos* to appraise law and things legal, but his use extends beyond conventional New Testament glosses for the Greek word νόμος to include more informal ways of ordering life: it incorporates conventions, customs, and even what we might call cultures. In short, for Delaney, nomicity projects wide-reaching understandings of what is "normal" within human lived experience. Crucially, such normative deliberations are not abstract things-in-themselves: they are always embodied, performed, played out in actual places—they are, as Delaney characteristically terms it, "worlded." As such, Delaney's understanding of *nomos* allows a wider and more integrated aperture for reading Paul's engagement with Jerusalem in Acts 21. A brief survey of how Delaney builds an analytical framework from *nomos* to the nomosphere will establish this claim.

Viewed from the ground up, the nomosphere is built from infinite nomic traces, which agents performatively construct into nomic settings, each with ambiguous and contested boundaries. Nomic settings occur on every scale and are layered and flexible, nesting between the global and the intensely local; they—and we—are soaked with rules, customs and directives for moral conduct and for wider life. Individuals and groups inhabit multiple nomic settings that, for them, then cohere together to form nomoscapes, where particular performances of normality are both pursued and challenged. Again, their boundaries are ambiguous, open for challenge, and multiple nomoscapes—upheld by different individuals and groups—rub up one against another in various ways and in the same locations. Together, these nomoscapes constitute the nomosphere that, like our planet's physical atmosphere, is ubiquitous, inescapable in and for life; it is always around us, we are always located within it. It makes us and we make it but, typically, this is routine, unnoticed and unconscious, except in times and places where the nomosphere undergoes a disturbance. Such nomic disturbances can be momentary, or enduring; terrifying, or liberating; routine, or memorable. In them, worlds are made, unmade, and remade.

With these things in mind, we turn to Acts 21, where Jerusalem, in many ways *the* archetypal nomic city, is rich with such disturbances that inform the text's narrative-theology and the message it seeks to proclaim.

2. Reading Paul's Arrival in Jerusalem

Why does Paul go to Jerusalem for a final time in Acts? On an immediate level, the clearest answer is that Paul is under a compulsion in his spirit/the Spirit, which gradually becomes clearer over the span of Acts 19–21 (19:21, 21:4, 21:11–14; cf. 23:11). Such an impetus to visit a place is not unusual in Acts,[18] but this is the only time when it is overlaid with an explicit time constraint—Paul wants to be in Jerusalem in time for "the day of Pentecost" (20:16).[19] Given that elsewhere in Acts times and seasons are judged to be outside of mortal control (1:6, 17:26), this urgency on Paul's part could indicate a heavenly-directed appointment with Jerusalem as a particular time and place. At very least, Paul is eager to reach Jerusalem. Viewed broadly, the localized lived experience provided by festival time-space[20] offers rich missionary and networking potential for Paul. More specifically here, "the day of Pentecost" recalls Acts 2, with its festival crowds hearing and seeing the witness to Jesus. For Lefebvre, festivals offer particular potential for emancipatory or revolutionary change:[21] Luke would concur regarding festal Jerusalem, while appreciating that this festal potential cuts both ways, toward both life and death (Luke 22:7–23; Acts 12:3).

While Acts does not explicitly state that Paul arrived in time for Pen-

---

18. See, e.g., Acts 1:8; 8:26, 29, 40; 9:1–2, 11; 10:5–6, 20; 16:9–10; 18:21; 19:21.

19. The polite refusal to stay in Ephesus in Acts 18:21 does not make explicit any such time constraint although, significantly, Paul is on his way to Jerusalem (cf. 18:22). The only other time constraint in Acts, albeit in very different circumstances, concerns the overwintering of a ship (27:12; cf. vv. 9–10, 21).

20. Regarding the temple and its ritual life, including the lived experience of pilgrim festivals, see E. P. Sanders, *Judaism: Practice and Belief 63 BCE–66 CE* (London: SCM, 1992), 47–145. Also, variously, Josephus, *Ant.* 4.203–4; Deut 16:16; Josephus, *J.W.* 6.420–27; Craig S. Keener, *Acts: An Exegetical Commentary*, 4 vols. (Grand Rapids: Baker Academic, 2012–15), 1:797–98; and Stephen C. Barton, "Why Do Things Move People? The Jerusalem Temple as Emotional Repository," *JSNT* 37 (2015): 351–80, here 363–64. Spencer misses the spatial-temporal pragmatic politics of festival when noting (correctly) that the references to festivals in Acts 20 are "generally reminding us of Paul's loyalty to Jewish traditions as a means of undercutting the Jewish opposition against him" and "evoke particular memories from the larger Lukan narrative" (F. Scott Spencer, *Journeying through Acts: A Literary-Cultural Reading* (Peabody, MA: Hendrickson, 2004), 200).

21. For a pointed example of Lefebvre's concern for festival time and the seasonal rhythms of nature as offering moments of emancipatory potential, see his polemic against a rural Roman Catholic church, "Notes Written One Sunday," 221–47, esp. 231–32, in Henri Lefebvre, *Critique of Everyday Life: The One-Volume Edition*, trans. John Moore (London: Verso, 2014).

tecost, the text's lack of any stated frustration for his plan, combined with Paul's acceptance of more lengthy hospitality progressively closer to Jerusalem, suggests that he did arrive in time for the festival. Hearers/readers of Acts thus envision Paul in the midst of the crowded temple-city, with the festival heightening its sense of Jewishness.

And, in another crucial sense, Paul is not alone in the city. Although 21:29 denies the accuracy of the charge rendered by the Jews from Asia, it reveals a telling point about Paul's presence in Jerusalem which I think informs his Lukan purpose for being there. The mention of Trophimus the Ephesian seems initially slight, but is an important nomic trace. As a particular, partially locatable, and even messy "small story," 21:29 provides an entry point into a localized performance of knowledge, a microhistorical clue illuminating a bigger circumstance.[22] It evokes the earlier mention of Paul's companions listed in 20:4, who in turn folded into the "we" passage beginning in 20:5 and leading into Jerusalem itself, even into the encounter with James and the elders in 21:18–25. Commentators generally agree that those listed in 20:4 reflect the geographical distribution of much of Paul's previous ministry;[23] Paul thus arrives back in Jerusalem surrounded by the

22. Hayden Lorimer, "Telling Small Stories: Spaces of Knowledge and the Practice of Geography," *Trans. Inst. Br. Geog.* 28 (2003): 197–217; Matti Peltonen, "Clues, Margins, and Monads: The Micro-Macro Link in Historical Research," *Hist. Theory* 40 (2002): 347–59.

23. With differing estimations of the historical veracity of the list, compare Richard I. Pervo, *Acts*, Hermeneia (Minneapolis: Fortress, 2008), 507–9 with Ben Witherington III, *The Acts of the Apostles: A Socio-Rhetorical Commentary* (Grand Rapids: Eerdmans, 1998), 603. Cf. Luke Timothy Johnson, *The Acts of the Apostles*, SP 5 (Collegeville, MN: Liturgical, 1992), 355: "the passage testifies to the complexity of the Pauline mission. . . ." Mikeal C. Parsons, *Acts*, Paideia (Grand Rapids, Baker, 2008), 286 goes as far as to comment: "The coworkers total seven, and the number indicates both the Gentile mission and a certain completeness of the same (cf. the Seven appointed to represent the concerns of the Hellenists in Acts 6)." This is a maximal reading, but at least one, Trophimus, appears to be a gentile. John R. W. Stott, *The Message of Acts*, BST (Leicester: Inter-Varsity Press, 1990), 318 sees them as bearing witness to "the growth, unity, and even . . . 'catholicity' of the church," as well as "the fruitfulness of Paul's missionary expeditions" who "give evidence of the missionary-mindedness of the young Christian communities, which already gave up some of their best local leadership to the wider work and witness of Christ's church." As such, they function to keep alive within a particular lived experience the vision of local churches sustaining fellowship across distances which is inherent in Acts 15:19–35. Robert C. Tannehill, *The Narrative Unity of Luke-Acts: A Literary Interpretation.* Volume Two: *The Acts of the Apostles* (Minneapolis: Augsburg Fortress, 1990), 246: they are "the fruit of Paul's labors in the various areas of his work," who "resemble the companions of Jesus, who journeyed with him to Jerusalem." The difference, however, is that one of them, Trophimus, will

embodied evidence of his ministries among the diaspora and the nations. As earlier in Philippi (16:17), and previously in Jerusalem (4:23, 29; cf. 2:18), the group and not simply an individual is in view. Thus, Paul's report in 21:19 of "the things that God had done among the gentiles through his ministry" is both discursive *and* embodied: it is heard and it is seen (cf. 1:1; 2:32–33).[24] This duality feeds into the likelihood that Jewish believers "will certainly hear" that Paul has come to Jerusalem (21:22).

As with twenty-first-century urban trespass, reentering the conventional city is a politically-charged event that raises tensions and highlights cracks and fault lines within that city's presentation of itself. Reemergence carries an implicit "you could do this," and reveals the cracks in the facade of the urban spectacle. Like trespass, its transgressive qualities trigger "connections . . . which would never have been obvious from the view of 'everyday space'," provoking a recoding of the urban spectacle.[25] Just as the Lukan version of the parable of the great supper (Luke 14:15–24) launched and anticipated transgressive entries disrupting the conventional urban form,[26] so too Paul's reemergence posits to other inhabitants who witness it alternative ways of being within the city. It unsettles the status quo, provoking the keepers of the city to police, persecute, and even punish deviant performances of the city.

Paul's reentry into Jerusalem after some years away in the diaspora, an arrival together with at least one uncircumcised gentile believer and timed to coincide with the festival, seems to maximize intentionally its impact within and upon the city. It emphasizes both Paul's Jewishness and the transgressive nature of that Jewishness, in its distinctively "Christian" embodiment within the "we" group (here using "Christian" in the Acts 11:26 sense of Jews and gentiles together, in close proximity, *as* Jews and *as* gentiles). Also, Paul's arrival enhances existing, perhaps chronic rumors about the impact of his

---

provide the tinder for the explosion that erupts in Jerusalem in 21:28–30. Regarding textual variants in 20:4, see, e.g., C. K. Barrett, *The Acts of the Apostles*, ICC, 2 vols. (Edinburgh: T&T Clark, 1994, 1998), 2:947–49. Commentators variously discuss, and seek to account for, the apparent absences of representatives from, e.g., Philippi and Corinth; such absences need not affect us here. More generally, regarding Paul's companions and coworkers, see Eckhard J. Schnabel, *Early Christian Mission*, 2 vols. (Downers Grove, IL: InterVarsity Press, 2004), 2:1425–45.

24. For the content of this report in 21:19, the reader/auditor fills the gap with evidence drawn from Acts 13–20, maybe particularly from the summative address in 20:18–35, or assumes a parallel to 15:12.

25. Garrett, *Explore Everything*, 127, 128.

26. Richard L. Rohrbaugh, *The New Testament in Cross-Cultural Perspective* (Eugene, OR: Cascade, 2014), 160–74.

ministry on religious observance among Jewish believers within the diaspora (21:21). In short, akin to Lefebvre's theory of "moments" imbued with everyday revolutionary potential,[27] it creates and feeds a nomic situation.

Verse 21 "they have been told" (cf. v. 24) also fits with Pieter Botha's recent work on rumor.[28] Botha posits rumors as often having their own demonstrable logic, being improvised news that, in the face of important, ambiguous events, assembles a reality from available traces.[29] While Acts 15 dealt with gentile circumcision, it made no comment on the requirement for continuing *Jewish* circumcision. Here is the ambiguity. It is clear from 11:3 and 15:1, 5 that circumcision is an important nomic trace for Jews in Acts.[30] Failure to perform it—if indeed that is the case—requires an explanation. Paul—from a Jerusalem-based perspective, and in light of the earlier narrative (cf. 15:12; 21:19)—provides a known, plausible and contentious agency on whom can be tied circumcision's possible non-performance by diaspora Jewish believers. His synagogue teaching regarding the limits of Torah (e.g., 13:38–39) might well feed rumors in Jerusalem far more than isolated acts such as Timothy's circumcision (16:3) would count against it. In Botha's calculation, "Rumour = importance x ambiguity,"[31] but—beyond the maths—rumor is also *placed*:[32] it is part of the production of the city as

27. Lefebvre, *Critique of Everyday Life*, 634–52. Paul, here, is more directional than the Situationist practice of *derive*, "a type of free-form but critical drift through urban terrain," David Pinder, "Subverting Cartography: The Situationists and Maps of the City," *Env. Plan. A* 28 (1996): 405–28, here 416. Elsewhere, *derive* might be more indicative of Paul's urban engagement, e.g., Acts 17:16.

28. Pieter J. J. Botha, *Orality and Literacy in Early Christianity*, Biblical Performance Criticism 5 (Eugene, OR: Cascade, 2012).

29. Botha, *Orality*, 141–43.

30. Nomic traces can assume different signification within varying particular Jewish nomoscapes. Regarding the diversity of Jewish views of circumcision within the diaspora, see Eric D. Barreto, *Ethnic Negotiations: The Function of Race and Ethnicity in Acts 16*, WUNT/2 294 (Tübingen: Mohr Siebeck, 2011), 98–110. Such diversity has its own geographies: in broad terms, however, Acts 11, 15 and 21 cast Jerusalem as a likely epicenter for heightened nomic signification being attached to circumcision.

31. Botha, *Orality*, 143 n. 31.

32. Different kinds of speech occur within, and help construct and define, different kinds of space. Interweaving and distinguishing "gossip" and "rumor," Marianne Bjelland Kartzow, *Gossip and Gender: Othering of Speech in the Pastoral Epistles*, BZNW 164 (Berlin: de Gruyter, 2009) presents gossip as a placed, often gendered, activity "which makes public what was supposed to be private... talk about the private by means of the public" (33). It is not easily differentiated from rumor in practice (73). Destructive rumors were a commonplace danger in an ancient city (53), crossing gendered and placed divides.

oeuvre. Also, it probably accelerates with Paul's arrival in Jerusalem, which enhances its importance, being compounded by festivals functioning as hubs for rumors.[33] The rumor does necessarily communicate the truth, but it disturbs the nomoscape and presents a live issue for James and Paul regarding Paul's return to Jerusalem.

Contrary to some scholars, but following David Rudolph's recent reading of Acts 21 within his study on 1 Corinthians 9,[34] I do not see a tension, far less a conflict, between Paul and James at this juncture. Paul has shown himself to be an enthusiastic and observant Jew, albeit within some contentious nomic practices that are unwanted or unwelcomed by some Jews (e.g., Acts 16:1–3; 18:18; 20:16; and, also, his repeated and prioritized synagogue ministries). Also, James has already functioned as a visionary joint architect with Paul in brokering what nomicity Jews expect from gentile believers in 15:15–21. That was the second of three stages in this realization of Jew-gentile space, the first having articulated and accepted in 11:1–18 that Jews can enter and eat within gentile space (v. 3), and can treat uncircumcised gentile believers as fellow recipients of the Holy Spirit.

Now, in Acts 21 at this third stage in the Jerusalem believers' discernment of Jew-gentile placemaking, James's retrospective words in v. 25 link back to the previous decision in Acts 15, just as Peter's words in 15:7–11 recalled, and connected with, 10–11:18. Whereas Acts 15 dealt with a gentile question ("But as for the gentiles"), James's proposal in Acts 21 deals with an intra-Jewish question, namely whether or not Paul is teaching diaspora Jews to forsake their Mosaic heritage (v. 21). Far from being disagreeable or disingenuous for Paul, or sinister on the part of James, the plan in vv. 23–24 is intended to quash rumors and further enhance the believers' lived experience in this city, what we might term their pursuit of variegated but proximate and unified catholicity.[35]

Also, James's proposal coheres with, and asserts, Paul's right to be in the city during festival time, as a diaspora missionary to *both* Jew and gentile. Significantly, the proposal assumes remaining together in one fellowship in

33. Botha, *Orality*, 146. Acts also reports other rumors, e.g., 6:1, 12–14; 9:26; 11:1–2, and recounts various concerns regarding Paul expressed in particular places, differentially cohering into charges, accusations, and attack. If anything, the *absence* of rumor regarding Paul in Rome in 28:21 forms a noteworthy exception.

34. David J. Rudolph, *A Jew to the Jews: Jewish Contours of Pauline Flexibility in 1 Corinthians 9:19–23*, WUNT/2 304 (Tübingen: Mohr Siebeck, 2011), 53–73. Cf., e.g., Stanley E. Porter, *The Paul of Acts*, WUNT 115 (Tübingen: Mohr Siebeck, 1999), 172–86.

35. Stott, *Acts*, 318, quoted earlier.

the same place: even—particularly—within Jerusalem. Nothing is said by James regarding restrictions on the gentiles with Paul, beyond his low-key reassertion of what was decided, communicated and accepted in Acts 15. Thus Paul continues to engage with the city as both a faithful Jew and one who is intimately involved with uncircumcised gentile believers *with him in Jerusalem*. As such, Acts emphasizes that he inhabits and theologizes the space between,[36] a third space shared differentially between Jew and gentile, in the name of Jesus. In so doing his "world-making" stretches, and reworks, the city's ideological values and physical fabric, and the other nomoscapes performed there by other Jews, even at the festival.

How, then, does a nomospheric reading appraise the place of Torah embedded in Acts 21? While agreeing with much of Rudolph's analysis, I think he risks too simple a dichotomy as to whether Paul is observant or non-observant of Torah. Instead, Torah, understood nomically, is *always* "worlded" in a particular performance, in a particular place, its nomic traces selectively and strategically assembled in ways that other Jews might accept or might condemn. Thus, Paul's negotiation of Torah observance is complex, layering embodiment, subversion, compliance and—implicitly—Christocentric fulfillment, even replacement. Likely, however, lived experience cannot be neatly parsed out into discrete models. Rather, nomicity bridges and requires dynamic, hybrid strategies.[37] To quash rumor, Paul needs to perform Torah in the present (both the temporal and spatial present). He must embody it. Words and debate and clarification might well come later, as part of forming a "case" for his orthodoxy, but James rightly recognizes and Paul readily concurs that localized embodiment in Jerusalem is needed first. Rumor forms a soft underbelly for rhetorical management and control, and more than speech is needed. Later, perhaps, more distant discursive traces such as Timothy's circumcision (16:3) might then be brought into play. First, however, Paul must be seen to perform Torah; he must negotiate the inhabited physicality of Jerusalem as a nomic center and arbiter of public reputation.

36. Cf. Kathy Ehrensperger, *Paul at the Crossroads of Cultures: Theologizing in the Space Between*, LNTS 456 (London: Bloomsbury T&T Clark, 2013), who addresses the epistolary Paul but not the Paul of Acts. Ehrensperger demonstrates how first-century bilingualism and biculturalism did not necessarily lead to fusing or confusing of particularity and difference, nor to a diminished sense of belonging. Her insights deserve mapping into Acts, regarding both Paul and the wider Jesus movement narrated there.

37. Cf. Daniel Marguerat, *Paul in Acts and Paul in His Letters*, WUNT 310 (Tübingen: Mohr Siebeck, 2013), 48–65, regarding the dialectical construction of "continuity and rupture within Israel" (64) "based on the Lukan use of the term ἔθος" (62).

In short, James's proposal requires that Paul enters Jerusalem's public space, something not required for the earlier resolutions of Jew-gentile placemaking in Acts 11 and 15. Indeed, the narrative has not entered this arena since Acts 12, where public space was risky, life-threatening, and required Peter's departure to "another [unnamed] place" (v.17). Now, though, Paul reenters public space within Jerusalem to negotiate and advertise his own performance of Jewish nomicity. In this, *being seen* is important and intended. Both the setting—the temple—and his fellow actors—Nazirites—emphasize this (21:26, 27).[38] But, as has been evident previously in Lystra (14:8–19) and Philippi (16:16–24), the nomic significances accruing from being seen in urban public space are hard to control. Nomic traces can be bundled together differently, to form alternative, opposing nomoscapes, which can erupt quickly, violently, and unexpectedly.

Being in the temple, the epicenter of Jewish nomicity, is thus fraught with risk. Delaney emphasizes law as always "worlded";[39] in the case of the Jerusalem temple, this worlding is multidimensional and vast in its effects. It leads, directs and instructs an understanding of both urban and wider life as it constructs space, time, desires and personhood and thus shapes "an emotional regime."[40] In this passionate and energized setting, Paul's nomospheric project, intended to assert his own variegated lived experience among Jews and gentiles together in particular places, is intended to assist and influence nomospheric change among the Jerusalem believers. And the plan almost works—"the seven days were almost (ἔμελλον) completed" (21:27) before it encounters sharp opposition. Verse 27 hints at tragic irony for the Jerusalem church and indeed Jerusalem itself, in light of the hopes expressed by James in v. 24b.[41] Neither Paul's nomospheric project nor that of the Jerusalem believers can stand alone and detached: each necessarily interacts with other projects and agendas, forming a nomoscape ambiguously

38. Whether they are long-haired or shaven at this point, Nazirites exhibited heightened visibility.

39. Delaney, *Nomospheric,* 27.

40. Barton, "Emotional Repository," 370. Barton, however, does not pursue this reading across Acts. Briefly addressing Acts 1–2 (364) and Acts 6–7 (358), he omits Acts 21–22 and reiterates Barrett's determination of a Lukan uncertainty regarding the Jerusalem temple in Acts (C. K. Barrett, "Attitudes to the Temple in the Acts of the Apostles," in *Templum Amicitiae: Essays on the Second Temple Presented to Ernst Bammel,* ed. William Horbury, JSNTSup 48 [Sheffield: Sheffield Academic, 1991], 345–67).

41. This is irony within limits, however: Jerusalem's rejection of his message might surprise Paul, but it does not surprise Jesus (Acts 22:17–21).

overlaid with others within the "worlding" of both law and temple within the city, and within Judaism itself.

If the Jerusalem believers exhibited chronic nomic anxiety regarding Paul's mission, which James and Paul seek to resolve via the temple's everyday practices, then "the [unbelieving] Jews from Asia" in v. 27 quickly transform the tacit performance of the temple's routine practices into a more acute nomospheric disturbance. Nomospheric situations are, as Delaney asserts, layered, flexible, and ultimately uncontrollable by any one individual. As Acts has demonstrated elsewhere, how believers inhabit lived space is ultimately beyond their mortal manipulation (e.g., 14:11; 17:6–9). Here, like anyone navigating the nomosphere, Paul-in-the-temple (21:27) carries with him multiple nomic traces—whether formal or informal, general or highly specific, tacit or explicit—traces from other places, other spaces. For these Asian Jews, these traces include their recent sighting of Paul-in-the-city. So they see both Paul-in-the-temple *and* Paul-in-the-city, having earlier seen him in the public company of Trophimus, possibly their fellow—but certainly an uncircumcised—Ephesian. Once again, public company within the city locates someone's position within it (cf. 5:13; cf. 9:19b–21, 28).

These dual traces, then, together with traces of Paul-in-Ephesus, and of Trophimus-in-Ephesus, trigger for these Asian Jews a crisis in their own right to the city, provoking them to define and exclude. Like the Lystrans in 14:11–12, they incorporate Paul and his message into their existing frame of reference. As in Ephesus, the lived experience and outworkings of the Jesus message engender apparently unsought temple anxiety among those committed to the local cult.[42] Here, regardless of their view of gentiles elsewhere within Jerusalem,[43] their suppositional connection of Paul-in-the-city with

---

42. Regarding parallels between Acts 21:27–23:22 and 19:23–40, see Jeffrey M. Tripp, "A Tale of Two Riots: The *Synkrisis* of the Temples of Ephesus and Jerusalem in Acts 19–23," *JSNT* 37 (2014): 86–111. Tripp is correct to identify *synkrisis* between the temple riots in Ephesus (Acts 19) and Jerusalem (Acts 21–23), but his reading of temple worship as being replaced by house-church worship (98, 105–7) is misplaced on three grounds. First, Jerusalem's Temple is, for Luke, of a different salvation-historical order than any other temple. Second, the temple is not to be isolated from its surrounding cityscape in Acts, nor set in tension with it. Third, there is no house-church in Acts 21–22: instead, the comprehensive inclusion in 24:12 recalls earlier symbiotic paralleling of home and temple in 5:42. Further, the house in 28:23, 30 presents a particular constraint, not a normative model.

43. Luke and Acts populate Jerusalem with varied non-Jews, e.g., Pilate (Luke 23:1–15, 52; Acts 4:27–28) and various Roman military forces (Luke 23:47; Acts 21:31–40; 22:24–30; 23:10, 17–31), an Ethiopian eunuch (8:27), even the devil (Luke 4:9–12). It is where Caesar circulates on coins (Luke 20:24), and where attacking armies will come (Luke 21:20) and

Paul-in-the-temple is what triggers charges of defilement (κεκοίνωκεν[44]) regarding "this holy place" (21:28; cf. 6:13). Paul's attempted negotiation of the nomosphere now also confronts rumors against him that closely parallel earlier false charges against Stephen (21:21; cf. 6:14). This and other parallels—such as both protagonists failing to placate their opponents—contribute toward a picture of Jerusalem tragically hardened against the word concerning Jesus and the realignments of space it engenders.

The narrator exonerates Paul from the opponents' supposition (21:29); what they miss are the limits within Paul's nomic practices. Jew-gentile fellowship is real and proximate, but the "we" group's presence in Jerusalem is not absolute, totalizing, and seeking to erase all difference. Trophimus has *not* been brought into areas of the temple closed to Jews.[45] A spatial eschatological reserve remains, befitting 3:20–21. For Paul's opponents, however, their performance of the Jerusalem Temple configures it absolutely, as "a place to be 'zealous' for, to struggle over, to die for, even to kill for."[46] As such, the temple setting itself might well exacerbate or amplify existing threats and tensions.[47]

Only a third act of "seeing," in 21:32 (cf. vv. 27, 29)—their seeing hegemonic and unclean Roman military force arriving to intervene to reassert its own nomoscape within the city—makes Paul's potential murderers draw back. This intervention confounds and parochializes their assertion that a widespread and settled nomicity is being unsettled by Paul (v. 28),[48] even as it creates the rhetorical space on the steps of the barracks exploited by Paul

where gentiles will trample (Luke 21:24). It is the beginning for mission to all the nations (Luke 24:47).

44. The perfect tense suggests "ongoing" profanation, which is "only to be eliminated if its cause is wiped out" (Witherington, *Acts,* 654).

45. Regarding the bounded spatiality inscribed within the temple area, see Keener, *Acts,* 3:3148–49.

46. Barton, "Emotional Repository," 358, not specifying this occasion in Acts.

47. That the plot against Paul in Acts 20:3 is narrated immediately prior to mention of the diverse group in 20:4 might suggest that Paul's visible lifestyle within a mixed Jewish-gentile company fueled that earlier conspiracy. Clearly the murderous intent evident in 21:31a connects closely with the accusation in 21:28. Perhaps in both instances, and later in 23:12–14, this intent arises from Paul's close association, as a Jew, with uncircumcised gentile companions, in practices that threatened existing nomospheric practices such as synagogue solidarity (cf. also 19:9, in Asia; 18:6–8, in Corinth; 21:21, in Jerusalem).

48. The rhetorically neat "everyone everywhere" captures well πάντας πανταχῇ (v. 28); an astute reader/auditor might hear an echo of πάντας πανταχοῦ (17:30; cf. 24:3!), but would note that utterance as focusing on the universal invitation to repentance, not on a Jewish neglect of circumcision.

as Acts continues to unfold (21:37–22:21). More immediately, their charge and plea in v. 28 is sufficient to ignite the city against Paul (21:30–31a).[49] The "many thousands"[50] of believers reported by James (v. 20) need not be implicated in this opposing crowd; nor, though, do their numbers guarantee an easy right to the city. Acts 21 communicates that the city is a more slippery space than that. Indeed, what ensues is a catastrophic slippage and unravelling for James and Paul's strategy within it.

If, as Rudolph cogently claims,[51] neither James nor the Jerusalem believers betray or sabotage Paul, was Paul naïve in his negotiation of the city's nomosphere? Not really: it was impossible at a mortal level to anticipate this dual embodied encounter with the Ephesian Jews, and the narrative casts Paul as well aware of the risks facing him in Jerusalem (20:22–23, 25, 38; 21:4, 11–14). Thus boldness, rather than naïveté appears to predominate. As such, Paul's spatial-rhetorical performance echoes earlier prayers regarding the believers' right to Jerusalem (4:23–31), and fits with the narrative's final note, in Rome, the imperial city, in 28:31.

Understood in this vein, Acts 21 casts Paul as a resilient and innovative place-maker—even, we might say, place-hacker—within Jerusalem. Just as previously the apostles were reluctant to cede Jerusalem even in the face of great persecution (8:1), and nowhere in Acts has the growing word ever retreated from a place, so here, the fraught nomosphere of Jerusalem during the festival does not become a no-go area for Paul short of his arrest. Paul is "making public" (διαγγέλλων [21:26]): his involvement in the temple sacrificial system occurs *while* being seen associating with Trophimus the Ephesian. Acts wants to hold together Paul-in-the-city (publicly associating with the mixed Jew-gentile "we" group) with Paul-in-the-temple (as observant and pious Jew). His identity, and that of his mission, within "the events that have been fulfilled among us" (Luke 1:1) are irrevocably bound up with both these nomic performances by Paul, and in the "and more" resulting from holding them together. This "and more" is more than simply the sum of their

49. Witherington, *Acts*, 655 concedes "a certain amount of rhetorical hyperbole" but, from Josephus's accounts, defends the possibility of a "massive and unified response" from "the large Jewish crowd which was present." Narratively, Luke and Acts characteristically show whole cities being confronted, and affronted, by the Jesus message (cf. Luke 23:13, 18; Acts 13:44; 14:4; 19:10; 25:23).

50. Taken on face value, πόσαι μυριάδες (21:20) suggests tens of thousands of believers, an impressive culmination to the growing numbers of believers outlined earlier in Acts (and the plural form of μυριάς in Luke 12:1). For wider discussion, see Keener, *Acts*, 3119–23.

51. Rudolph, *A Jew to the Jews*, 53–73.

parts: it is the embodied and durative—and, I would say, proximate—"right to difference," to Jews remaining Jewish and gentiles remaining uncircumcised and both doing so in the same place, in fellowship with one another. *Precisely because* the Jews from Asia misconstrue and oppose this duality and its third space, this right to difference in Jerusalem, it must be defended by Paul. The accusation within Acts 21:29 might well threaten Paul's other gentile traveling companions, Luke among them.[52] Thus internally and externally, this right to difference preserves the Lukan word's right to the city from becoming deradicalized and collapsing "into reactionary and exclusivist defence of locality."[53]

3. Appraising Paul's Arrival in Jerusalem

In sum, Paul's arrival in Jerusalem has disturbed the nomosphere by asserting an alternative right to the city. Four final observations locate this reading of Acts 21 within Acts and Luke's theologizing of the city.

First, Paul's right to the city is predicated, theologically, on Christ's right to the city, befitting Jesus as "Lord of all" (10:36). His first encounter with Jesus demonstrated to Paul that Jesus had "matters in place already in Damascus,"[54] and this remains so in other cities across Acts. An active urban Christology has been formative in Jerusalem (e.g., 9:27), Antioch (11:19–30), Corinth (18:9–10) and elsewhere, both for Paul and for the believers more generally.

Acts 22 sustains this christological right to the city, as the activist assertion over the city in Acts 21 leads into Paul's rhetorical response to the nomospheric disturbance. As well as defending his loyalty to Jerusalem and recounting his Damascus road experience (22:1–16), Paul also proclaims an earlier vision of Jesus (22:17–21, an event probably contemporaneous with 9:30). This helps position Paul's actions in Acts 21. Evoking Isaiah 6, the vision both reinforces a high divine Christology by casting Jesus as the one who commissions from within the Jerusalem temple, and reorients the

52. Martin Hengel, *Between Jesus and Paul: Studies in the Earliest History of Christianity*, trans. John Bowden (London: SCM, 1983), 127. This might help explain Paul's appeal to his Roman citizenship in Acts 22:25.

53. Chris Butler, *Henri Lefebvre: Spatial Politics, Everyday Life and the Right to the City* (Abingdon: Routledge, 2012), 134.

54. Keener, *Acts*, 2:1638 regarding 9:6. Keener's comment appraises well vv. 3–25 as a narrative unit.

temple's performative role within the city. Conventionally, the temple is "the place to 'see' God"[55] but, by this christological insertion, Acts alters both temple and city. The temple becomes the place of commission to the gentiles, even at the cost of Jerusalem rejecting and losing another key testifier to Jesus.[56] There, Jesus continues to challenge other rights to Jerusalem and also to other cities among the nations. Simultaneously, Jesus asserts *his* right to determine difference, and he continues to rewrite theological identities at a national and even individual level (Acts 3:22–23).

This christocentric reading of the temple as performed space within the wider city rejects C. K. Barrett's view of Acts as inconsistent regarding the temple.[57] First, Barrett's reading fails to locate the temple within wider Jerusalem, as a located place. Also, Barrett does not consider the theological consistency that drives the temple's presentation in Acts: he misses the christological dimension in 22:17–21, seeing it as "God" who commissions Paul.[58] Also, Barrett lacks sensitivity to the temple's performative dynamics, which Barton expounds well,[59] even while failing to differ from Barrett's conclusions regarding the temple in Acts.

This present reading also qualifies any easy unilinear movement within Acts away from the physical temple.[60] In the narrative's final view of the temple, Jesus is *in* it; and even the final allusion to its ongoing performance in Acts (26:7) binds it with Christ. Not that this is the final location of *Jesus* within the narrative: 23:11 preludes any static view of Jesus occupying the temple. Tellingly, Acts does not replace the temple, but Jesus uses it, subversively fulfilling it, for his purposes.

Second, this performance of a different Jerusalem remains sharply opposed. In 22:22, the city interrupts and rejects both Paul and Jesus.[61] The two

55. Barton, "Emotional Repository," 357, 358, recalling the temple's parallelism with heaven in Ps 11:4.
56. Previously Jerusalem has rejected Jesus himself, Stephen (Acts 6:8–8:1; 22:20), and James, the brother of John (12:2–3a). Not that Jerusalem is left in Acts without a testimony, either earlier (9:30–31) or now (21:20).
57. Barrett, "Attitudes to the Temple."
58. Barrett, "Attitudes to the Temple," 355.
59. Barton, "Emotional Repository," esp. 364–65.
60. Such a trajectory is possible within Steve Walton, "A Tale of Two Perspectives? The Place of the Temple in Acts," in *Heaven on Earth: The Temple in Biblical Theology*, ed. T. Desmond Alexander and Simon Gathercole (Carlisle: Paternoster, 2004), 135–49.
61. Acts 22:22 reprises 8:33 and with 21:36 also echoes Luke 23:18 (Andrew Clark, *Parallel Lives: The Relation of Paul to the Apostles in the Lucan Perspective*, PBM [Carlisle: Paternoster, 2001], 181).

are speaking as one (cf. 26:23): the earlier temple vision exerts a durative hold on the city and its performance asserts Jerusalem's place within his wider geography of difference. The city's verdict in 22:22 can only ironically confirm and lead to the fulfillment of Jesus's word concerning Paul. The ambiguity of γῆ as either "earth" (NRSV) or "land" in 22:22 (αἶρε ἀπὸ τῆς γῆς τὸν τοιοῦτον) bridges Paul and Jesus, generating differing ironies for Jesus's death, resurrection and ascension and for Paul's movement toward Rome.

Third, Paul and Jesus both nevertheless maintain a claim over the whole city. If 22:21 forms Jesus's first heavenly riposte regarding the events triggered in Acts 21, then 23:11 represents his second such riposte. The first, coming from within the temple, reported after its doors are closed in 21:30,[62] confirms a continued temple presence for Jesus even after Stephen's critique of the temple and subsequent death in Acts 7. The second riposte comes within the Roman barracks (23:11), broadening the expression of Jesus's right and rule to the city even into its most colonized and Romanized spaces.[63] This christophany occurs within the seemingly stable spatial frame for Paul's custody within Jerusalem established by the repeated phrase εἰς τὴν παρεμβολήν ("into/to the barracks," 21:34, 37; 22:24; 23:10, 16, 32).

In a differently ordered claim to the whole city, Paul asserts a tripartite scope for his ministry within Jerusalem, covering temple, synagogues and wider residential areas (24:12). The plural "synagogues" recalls Stephen's earlier engagement with Jews from Asia (6:9–10), and Paul's own ministry in Jerusalem (9:29). In both instances those proclaiming Jesus risk death (cf., also, 9:2). "Throughout the city" (κατὰ τὴν πόλιν) evokes other areas of the city, such as πλατεῖαι, the wide streets or squares forming hubs for urban activity (Acts 5:15; cf. Luke 10:10; 13:26; 14:21), as well as other urban settings implicit elsewhere in Acts (e.g., 13:44–48; 17:17; 18:3). This final phrase in Acts 24:12 also evokes "publicly and from house to house" (δημοσίᾳ καὶ κατ᾽ οἴκους), an earlier assertion of a "right to the city" in Asia (20:20; cf. 5:42), itself recalling Paul's move beyond the synagogue in 19:9. Acts 20:23 "in every city" invites such cross-urban comparisons. In sum, the narrative's final description of the cityscape reprises earlier scenes in Acts. These earlier

---

62. An unknown agency closes the temple doors. This closure stands against—but does not overcome—God opening both missional doors among the gentiles (Acts 14:27) and physical doors imprisoning his missionaries (5:19; 12:10; 16:26), and the ability of Jesus to open hearts (Luke 24:45; Acts 16:13).

63. Matthew L. Skinner, *Locating Paul: Places of Custody as Narrative Settings in Acts 21–28*, AcBib 13 (Atlanta: SBL, 2003), 111–19 presents the barracks as a hybrid location, but does not connect it with an overall right to the city.

negotiations of the city's public space underpin and reflect this claim to the whole city in 24:12, a claim for Paul himself and for other believers remaining there. Viewed as a whole, Luke-Acts assumes a Lefebvrian revolutionary capacity within everyday life, claiming space for deeds in keeping with repentance (Luke 3:8; Acts 26:20), deeds that bring believers into distinctive everyday practices and interrelationships (e.g., 2:40–47) that have to happen some*where*.[64]

Fourth, however, this universal claim to the city remains rendered through the heavenly Christ. At the first Pentecost in Acts, Jesus was declared in Jerusalem as the reigning monarch of Ps 110:1 (Acts 2:34–35); in this second Pentecost his rule over the city is sustained even in the midst of his foes (Ps 110:2). The earth is his footstool (Acts 7:49), but enemies remain presently unsubdued and seemingly in control of the city (7:57–58). This eschatological reserve, declared in 2:14–40, continues to hold within Jerusalem for the duration of the Acts narrative. An active-on-earth ascended Christ links both Pentecosts and orders earthly spaces and places through them. If rights claims need to rely on a particular theory of justice, then in the latter part of Acts it is possibly Roman justice, but behind it is the eschatological justice of Christ at the resurrection of the dead, which underpins Paul's claim to the city.

As such, regarding both space and Christ, this eschatological cry and demand differs so fundamentally from Lefebvre's right to the city, that at least a supplementary hermeneutic is required.[65] This supplementation is partly theological-political, and partly generic.

Theologically-politically, Dietrich Bonhoeffer's use of *Lebensraum* is helpful here.[66] Bonhoeffer presents believer-space as taking up physical, public, territorial space on earth that is widespread and universal but, crucially, is created by the living Word and Spirit of God: in the framing of Acts, it is mediated by the heavenly ruling Christ. As such, this is not the conquered space of conventional earthly empires; rather, prior to the eschaton, it is narrow, minimalist, and measured out in suffering. Bonhoeffer's vision anticipates a blending of 14:22 with 22:22: "when the Christian

---

64. See, e.g., Reta Finger, *Of Widows and Meals: Communal Meals in the Book of Acts* (Grand Rapids: Eerdmans, 2007), esp. 241–42.

65. Cf. the commentary on, and critique of, Lefebvre's phobic reaction against Roman Catholicism provided by Roland Boer, *Criticism of Heaven: On Marxism and Theology* (Leiden: Brill, 2005), 161–214.

66. Donald Fergus, "*Lebensraum*—Just What Is This 'Habitat' or 'Living Space' That Dietrich Bonhoeffer Claimed for the Church?," *SJT* 67 (2014): 70–84.

community has been deprived of its last inch of space here on earth, the end will be near."[67] If, for Paul at least, the right to the city is inherently a right to *suffer* (9:16; 20:23–24; 21:13), then conventional rights-based discourses are inverted—or better, given Paul's willingness to appeal to his citizenship, subverted in the name of Christ. A wider conversation between Lefebvre and Bonhoeffer concerning the shape of the claim to the city in Acts would be both conflicting and illuminating.

Lefebvre also needs supplementing on the grounds of genre. Acts is a literary text, not a social movement. How does it seek to revolutionize the real world? Again, a wider conversation needs to follow, but Acts 21 makes a rhetorical play for "implacing" believers—both Jewish and gentile—within a reimagined Jerusalem.[68] As such, Acts is neither anti-introspective,[69] nor setting introspection against action: both cohere dialectically in its narrative.

Also, as narrative literature, Paul's right to *this* city takes particular shape within the salvation-historical/geographical specificities of Jerusalem but, by Acts 21, Jerusalem is now bound within wider mobilities. Again, this is predicated on Jesus's ascension, both as the ultimate act of human mobility and given its accompanying commission to Spirit-empowered mobility in 1:8. This anticipated mobility is not simply centrifugal, nor is it between fixed and isolated places. Rather, anticipating geography's new mobilities paradigm by nearly two thousand years, Acts recursively draws "a complex relationality of places and persons connected through performances" wherein places are networked rather than isolated, complex rather than simple, and dynamic rather than fixed.[70] A mobilities paradigm, potentially a third spatial lens employed here, emphasizes this mobility across Acts. Acts, then, asserts a right to *cities*, not just to one city, reaching "under heaven" to both Jerusalem and Rome, and *beyond* their spheres of influence. Its rich and differing interplays between local identities and cosmopolitan identity, of

67. Dietrich Bonhoeffer, *The Cost of Discipleship*, trans. R. H. Fuller (New York: Touchstone, 1995), 267.

68. For a reading of Isa 60 generating rhetorical "implacement" of Jerusalem for believers in Jerusalem, see Christopher M. Jones, "'The Wealth of Nations Shall Come to You': Light, Tribute, and Implacement in Isaiah 60," *VT* 64 (2014): 611–22. An analogous reading of Jerusalem in Acts helps place a Lukan "right to the city" within a wider biblical-theological frame of reference befitting the framing established by Luke 24:45–47.

69. Michal Beth Dinkler, "'The Thoughts of Many Hearts Shall Be Revealed': Listening in on Lukan Interior Monologues," *JBL* 133 (2015): 373–99. Lukan interior monologues aim at lived spatial production and interpretation, in the city and beyond.

70. Mimi Sheller and John Urry, "The New Mobilities Paradigm," *Env. Plan. A* 38 (2006): 207–26, here 214.

the one and the many, of *e pluribus unum,* will outrun the urban politics of Jerusalem, Rome, or elsewhere.

4. Conclusion

This right to the city and to difference was seen, in embryo, in the differing languages heard declaring God's deeds of power at Pentecost in Acts 2:5–11, itself predicated on Jesus's ascension. It is also evident, in miniature, in the "we" group around Paul at this Pentecost, striving in their utopian occupation of the city of Jerusalem for the seemingly impossible, a realized and lived manifestation of the Spirit's inbreaking times and spaces of refreshing—that is, Jews and gentiles together within Jerusalem.

Here in Acts 21, however, the fruits of Paul's mobility must be brought back, and lived out one last time, in the place of initial moorings in Acts: Jerusalem. The "we" group brings others from elsewhere; but this city is not the destination (23:11), as neither, ultimately, is even Rome itself. Yet Jerusalem still matters. The interplay of mobilities around the Mediterranean rim and moorings in the historic city, within a wider and overarching ascension geography, means Jerusalem is both needed and needled by the Lukan mission to both Jews and gentiles. The city illuminates the tensions within this mission, and demonstrates that not only does the mission have to be embodied in lived experience *somewhere,* it has to be embodied *here,* in the city where Luke's narrative began and from where the mission sprang.

Paul's Caesarea

JOAN E. TAYLOR

In recent years the narrative of the Acts of the Apostles has been increasingly studied by New Testament scholars to fine-tune our awareness of the historical and rhetorical aspects of this text.[1] In such studies, locations are defined and evaluated as narrative settings or spaces important for meaning. As Resseguie states, a "close reading of setting adds to the interpretation of characterization, plot, theme, and point of view."[2] Such settings can also provide subtle messages: for example, in the Gospel of Mark both John the Baptist and Jesus have narrative settings of wilderness and water, to which the character of the amorphous "crowd" is drawn; thus Mark effectively emphasizes to the audience that the two figures are linked together.[3] In terms

---

1. See Mark Allan Powell, *What Is Narrative Criticism?* GBS (Minneapolis: Fortress, 1990); David M. Gunn, "Narrative Criticism" in *To Each Its Own Meaning: An Introduction to Biblical Criticisms and Their Applications*, ed. Stephen R. Hayes and Steven L. McKenzie, rev. ed. (Louisville: Westminster John Knox, 1999), 201–9; James L. Resseguie, *Narrative Criticism of the New Testament: An Introduction* (Grand Rapids: Baker Academic, 2005). We see the employment of narrative criticism finely done in works such as Robert C. Tannehill, *The Narrative Unity of Luke-Acts: A Literary Interpretation*, 2 vols. (Philadelphia: Fortress, 1986, 1990); William S. Kurz, *Reading Luke-Acts: Dynamics of Biblical Narrative* (Louisville: Westminster John Knox, 1993), and David G. Peterson, *The Acts of the Apostles*, PNTC (Grand Rapids: Eerdmans, 2009).

2. Resseguie, *Narrative Criticism,* 94, and discussion (94–120). For the seminal exploration of setting, see Elizabeth Struthers Malbon, *Narrative Space and Mythic Meaning in Mark*, NVBS (San Francisco: Harper & Row, 1986).

3. See Federico Adinolfi and Joan E. Taylor, "John the Baptist and Jesus the Baptist: A Narrative Critical Approach," *JSHJ* 10 (2012): 247–84.

of the cities of the Acts of the Apostles, they may be presented on the basis of well-known features about them,[4] but narrative criticism requires us to consider these as not mere backdrops for the action of a scene, but as literary "actors" themselves, containing elements through which the narrator can emphasize meanings.

The city of Caesarea, center of Roman government in Judea, does not appear at all in the gospels: we meet only the Roman governor, Pontius Pilate, in Jerusalem. However, in Acts, Caesarea is explicitly named in the narrative as a place that needs no introduction, second to Jerusalem as the most mentioned city in the book (fifteen times: 8:40; 9:30; 10:1, 24; 11:11; 12:19; 18:22; 21:8, 16; 23:23, 33; 25:1, 4, 6, 13), and just ahead of (Syrian) Antioch (at thirteen times: 6:5; 11:19, 20, 22, 25, 26, 27; 13:1; 15:22, 23, 30, 35; 18:22).[5]

1. Caesarea as a Narrative Setting in Acts

If we consider how Caesarea functions as a setting in Acts,[6] one should at the outset note that urban spaces (as opposed to the countryside of the gospels) are in general identified as loci of evangelization within the book.[7] One would therefore expect this aspect to be key as a typifying feature. Indeed, the city first appears in regard to Philip, as the final destination of the deacon as he heads north from the Hellenistic coastal city of Azotus: "Philip was found at Azotus and then he was journeying through all the cities telling the good news until his coming into Caesarea" (Φίλιππος δὲ εὑρέθη εἰς Ἄζωτον· καὶ διερχόμενος εὐηγγελίζετο τὰς πόλεις πάσας ἕως τοῦ ἐλθεῖν αὐτὸν εἰς

4. Colin J. Hemer, *The Book of Acts in the Setting of Hellenistic History*, ed. Conrad H. Gempf, WUNT 49 (Tübingen: Mohr Siebeck, 1989), 104, 107.

5. Interestingly, while Ephesus is mentioned nine times and Rome six, Corinth appears only three times (18:1, 8; 19:1) in Acts.

6. While there have been summaries of Christians in Caesarea, a narrative critical study focusing on setting has not hitherto been done. For the summaries, see Glanville Downey, "Caesarea and the Christian Church," in *Studies in the History of Caesarea Maritima*, vol. 1 of *The Joint Expedition to Caesarea Maritima*, ed. Charles T. Fritsch, BASORSup 19 (Missoula, MT: Scholars, 1975), 23–42; Lee I. Levine, *Caesarea under Roman Rule*, SJLA 7 (Leiden: Brill, 1975), 24–26; Edgar Krentz, "Caesarea and Early Christianity," in *Caesarea Papers: Straton's Tower, Herod's Harbour, and Roman and Byzantine Caesarea*, ed. Robert Lindley Vann, JRASup 5 (Ann Arbor, MI: Journal of Roman Archaeology, 1992), 261–67.

7. E. M. de Ste. Croix, *The Class Struggle in the Ancient Greek World* (London: Duckworth, 1981), 9–19.

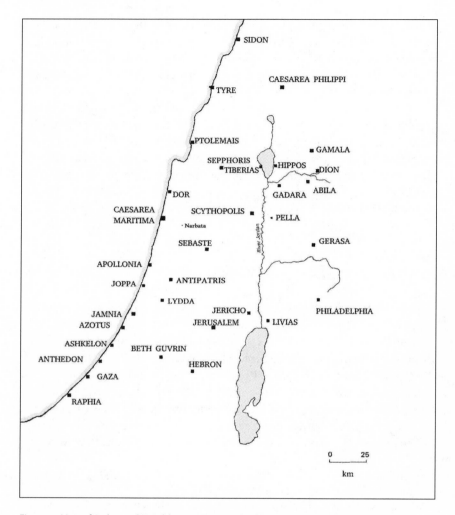

Figure 1. Map of Judea and Neighboring Cities in the First Century CE © Joan E. Taylor

Καισάρειαν [Acts 8:40]).[8] Philip is left entering Caesarea and telling the good news, primed for his reappearance later on.

The name of Caesarea itself is given baldly, without any explanation, as is the name of Azotus, which only appears in the New Testament here in Acts. Intermediate cities between Azotus and Caesarea are alluded to

8. Translations of Greek texts are the author's own throughout.

44

within the designation αἱ πόλεις πᾶσαι "all the cities," and a certain amount of audience knowledge might be assumed here. The cities (including their city territories) lying between Azotus (ancient Ashdod) and Caesarea were Jamnia, Lydda, Joppa, Apollonia and Antipatris (see Figure 1), but they did not all have the same status, in that while Lydda and Joppa headed Judean toparchies, Azotus and Jamnia were imperial estates, administered by an imperial procurator at Jamnia.[9] Apollonia was another autonomous πόλις, not part of Judea but lying directly under the Roman governor of Syria, while Antipatris, founded by Herod the Great, would likely have been administered as part of the king's domains by the prefect/procurator of Judea in Caesarea.[10] At any rate, Caesarea and Azotus are linked together in the narrative as the starting and ending points of Philip's mission and the imperial status of Azotus might be implicit. As for Caesarea, any city named Καισάρεια implies a special association with the Roman emperor, in which one would expect a temple for the imperial cult. It is "Caesar's City," and as such it performs Rome.

At this mention of Caesarea there is a break, concluding the story of the hero character of Philip, and the narrative moves back to Jerusalem with "Saul": "But Saul, still breathing threats and slaughter toward the disciples of the Lord, went to the High Priest" (Ὁ δὲ Σαῦλος, ἔτι ἐμπνέων ἀπειλῆς καὶ φόνου εἰς τοὺς μαθητὰς τοῦ κυρίου, προσελθὼν τῷ ἀρχιερεῖ [9:1]). The focus is now on Paul's conversion on the way to Damascus, and then his fairly unsuccessful visit to Jerusalem, where Barnabas takes Paul under his wing (9:1–29). Hearing then that Hellenic Jews in Jerusalem now want to kill Paul, "the brothers and sisters took him down to Caesarea and despatched him to Tarsus" (οἱ ἀδελφοὶ κατήγαγον αὐτὸν εἰς Καισάρειαν καὶ ἐξαπέστειλαν αὐτὸν εἰς Ταρσόν [9:30]). Thus, Caesarea culminates this story of Saul/Paul as it culminates the story of Philip.

9. Pliny, *Nat.* 5.70; Josephus, *Ant.* 18.158; *J.W.* 3.51; Michael Avi-Yonah, "Historical Geography," in *The Jewish People in the First Century: Historical Geography, Political History, Social, Cultural and Religious Life and Institutions*, ed. S. Safrai and M. Stern, CRINT (Assen: Van Gorcum, 1974), 95–115, here 98.

10. Avi-Yonah, "Historical Geography," 102. It may be that in the narrative of Acts Philip's intention to go to Gaza (8:26), another autonomous city, implies that his brief was to evangelize non-Judean cities along the coast in general (though it is never said that he actually reached Gaza), since it is Peter who actually goes to Lydda and Joppa (9:32–43). Thus "all the cities" in 8:40 would mean "all the cities not in Judea"—Azotus, Apollonia, Antipatris and Caesarea—though this may at first sight seem curious given Caesarea's recognized status as the Roman capital of Judea.

45

With Paul's departure it is indicated that Caesarea was a port, a place with ships large enough to take Paul away from Judea, to his hometown, out of the way of the Way. Caesarea is the "transit city." Paul's ship leaves the harbor in the direction of Tarsus, but the narrative locality remains Caesarea. Note also the language of "going down" to Caesarea, which continues the language in Scripture (Septuagint included) of "going up" to Jerusalem, the holy city in the hills, and "going down" from it.[11]

In terms of the chronological sequence, there is no mention of Philip at this point of Paul's transit, and the parallel story of Philip within the narrative framework might not even be intended to be prior. Paul's story in 9:1 begins with "But Saul" ('Ο δὲ Σαῦλος), with no chronological indicator, and really continues the story of Saul/Paul interrupted at 8:4 with the story of Philip. It seems therefore to be defined as alternate rather than sequential, ending in the same place.

The introduction of the ship in association with Paul is significant. Up until this point in the narrative of Luke-Acts, the movement of the "hero" characters has been entirely overland or on the lake of Gennesaret. It is only when we have mention of Caesarea in Acts 9:30 that we are introduced to the concept of going offshore, away from land. Caesarea is therefore associated with Paul's first sea voyage, as indicated in the narrative: a feature that will become a *leitmotif* for his story in the latter part of the work.

Once Paul is away on the water, we return to a lull, in Acts 9:31, creating a closure to this introductory Paul story: "So the church through all Judea and Galilee and Samaria had peace, and was increased, being built up and journeying with the awe of the Lord and in the comfort of the Holy Spirit" ('Η μὲν οὖν ἐκκλησία καθ' ὅλης τῆς Ἰουδαίας καὶ Γαλιλαίας καὶ Σαμαρείας εἶχεν εἰρήνην, οἰκοδομουμένη καὶ πορευομένη τῷ φόβῳ τοῦ κυρίου, καὶ τῇ παρακλήσει τοῦ ἁγίου πνεύματος ἐπληθύνετο). This comment functions as a break, underlining Paul's departure at Caesarea, before movement begins again with the hero character of Peter.

Peter never goes offshore like Paul in Acts; he only goes as far as Caesarea, like Philip. As with the story of Paul, the narrator avoids the language of chronological sequence, and while we may wish to impose chronology here it is not necessarily the case that the Peter sequence as it stands in Acts 9–11 is intended to indicate that the actions of Peter occurred subsequently to Philip's in terms of the city of Caesarea. Narrative movement in ancient

---

11. E.g., Pss 121–22; Mic 4:2–3, inter alia, as also found in the saying of Jesus in Luke 18:31 (and parr.).

historiography does not necessarily indicate chronological movement, since here the introductory words "It happened that" ('Εγένετο δέ [9:32]) do not indicate subsequent action. What is more interesting is a duplication of movement in regard to both Philip and Peter: Philip is appointed as a deacon in Jerusalem (6:5), and then he goes down (from Jerusalem) to "the/a city of Samaria" (8:5), meaning Sebaste (ancient Samaria) or else Sichem (Balata).[12] Peter is also in Jerusalem, but then he follows Philip to Samaria, tackling the issues of Simon Magus and water-only baptism (8:14–24). Philip and Peter then move in different directions. As noted above, Philip goes south toward the Hellenistic city of Gaza (8:26), baptizes the Ethiopian eunuch (8:26–39), and goes purposefully from Azotus to Caesarea (8:40). Peter appears in Lydda (9:32) and goes to Joppa (9:36–43), and then is forced to Caesarea (10:24). The implication appears to be that Cornelius did not know of Philip, who plays no part in his conversion story. This suggests in itself that sequential reading is to be avoided, since Peter may well have arrived in the city ahead of Philip.[13] In between these two stories, the narrative has the story of Paul, which as we have seen also culminates in Caesarea. In terms of the structure, Caesarea—Caesar's City—becomes the culminating point in the three parallel stories, and this appears more important than chronological sequencing. All roads lead to Caesarea.

As for the start of Peter's story, in Acts 10:1 Caesarea is the city of Cornelius: "A certain man was in Caesarea, named Cornelius, a centurion from the so-called Italian regiment" ('Ανὴρ δέ τις ἐν Καισαρείᾳ ὀνόματι Κορνήλιος, ἑκατοντάρχης ἐκ σπείρης τῆς καλουμένης Ἰταλικῆς). The *Cohors II Italica Civium Romanorum*, a corps of freedman, is indeed known to have been in Syria from 69 CE at the latest.[14] With this information, the

12. In the narrative, the current name of the city of Samaria, Sebaste, is not given, perhaps because it would muddy the waters in regard to Caesarea itself as performing Rome. Sebaste, named in accordance with the Greek version of "Augustus" (Σεβαστός, Acts 25:21, 25; cf. 27:1) was, like Caesarea, also the locus of a great temple to the imperial cult, built by Herod the Great (see Joan E. Taylor, "Pontius Pilate and the Imperial Cult in Roman Judaea," *NTS* 52 (2006): 555–82. However, that Sichem might be indicated is also a possibility. For these localities, see Avi-Yonah, "Historical Geography," 101–2.

13. Krentz, "Caesarea and Early Christianity," 262, notes just how absent Philip is in this story: "In all of this Philip is not mentioned; he does not function as a leader of the church at Caesarea; he does not accept Cornelius into the Christian community; he is not asked to ratify Peter's action; that is done by the Apostles and Christians in Judea and Jerusalem."

14. William M. Ramsay, "Cornelius and the Italic Cohort," *The Expositor*, 5th series 4 (1896): 194–201. See also Irina Levinskaya, "The Italian Cohort in Acts 10:1," in *The New*

city's character as a center of the Roman military is clearly defined. This is the Roman military not constituted by Syrian or other local auxiliaries, but by Italian Roman citizens in this regiment. We are in a locus of *Romanitas*, "Roman-ness."

Caesarea is also a place of some Jews, since Cornelius is said to have given generously in what we may construe as synagogue charity: he was "pious and in awe of God with all his house, making many charitable gifts to the people, and always praying to God" (εὐσεβὴς καὶ φοβούμενος τὸν θεὸν σὺν παντὶ τῷ οἴκῳ αὐτοῦ, ποιῶν ἐλεημοσύνας πολλὰς τῷ λαῷ καὶ δεόμενος τοῦ θεοῦ διὰ παντός [10:2]), and "a righteous man and one in awe of God, and as witnessed by all the nation of the Judeans/Jews" (ἀνὴρ δίκαιος καὶ φοβούμενος τὸν θεὸν μαρτυρούμενός τε ὑπὸ ὅλου τοῦ ἔθνους τῶν Ἰουδαίων [10:22]). We have here the fundamental characterization of a "good" Roman[15] that will set a tone for Caesarea itself: whereas Jerusalem is a place of hostility, governed by the institutions of Judean law, Caesarea is Roman. Caesarea is not a transit city in this story of Peter, but a city performing Rome, and it points forward to the activity of the Holy Spirit continuing to move Paul to Rome at the end of the narrative of Acts as a whole.

In Acts 11:1–18, Caesarea is mentioned again as we get a concluding postscript narrated in Jerusalem of the important story of the conversion of Cornelius and his household, though here his name and identity as a Roman centurion are not provided; he is simply a "gentile." Peter describes how three men came from Caesarea and stopped at the house where he was staying. Peter is called to the city by messengers, clearly not intending to go there without such a plea (unlike Philip, whose mission appears to be directed there). In terms of the structure, this recap by Peter essentially culminates the three stories of Philip, Paul and Peter that have all ended with the hero characters in Caesarea, and it ends with a summation that links Caesarea with one of the main themes of the entire work: "Now God has also granted to the gentiles repentance toward life!" (Ἄρα καὶ τοῖς ἔθνεσιν ὁ θεὸς τὴν μετάνοιαν εἰς ζωὴν ἔδωκεν).

At this point, the narrative takes a different trajectory. The structure returns to the scattering of disciples after the death of Stephen in 8:1–4, at which point the three hero stories of Philip, Paul and Peter began, and we

---

Testament in Its First Century Setting: Essays on Context and Background in Honour of B. W. Winter on His 65th Birthday, ed. Peter J. Williams et al. (Grand Rapids: Eerdmans, 2004), 106–25.

15. For a detailed study of his characterization, see Bonnie Flessen, *An Exemplary Man: Cornelius and Characterization in Acts 10* (Eugene, OR: Wipf & Stock, 2011).

briefly follow the hero character of Barnabas. The narrative progresses to Antioch, where gentiles are coming into the church. Barnabas brings Paul from Tarsus (11:25–26), and there is a prophet from Jerusalem named Agabus who predicts a famine, occurring in the reign of Claudius (11:27–30; though cf. Josephus, *Ant.* 20.49–53, 101), and relief is brought from Antioch to Jerusalem by Barnabas and Paul. Then, abruptly, there is an insertion of the final Peter story. A new client ruler of Judea appears, defined simply as "King Herod" (actually Herod Agrippa I, reigning 41–44 CE), who kills James, the brother of John (12:2), an action that "pleased the Judeans" (12:3), and he arrests Peter (in Jerusalem), though he escapes (12:4–18).

Caesarea is identified again in 12:19 as the Roman locus of "Herod," the Roman client ruler: "After Herod had a thorough search made for him (Peter) and did not find him, he examined the guards and ordered that they be executed; then Herod went down from Judea to Caesarea and stayed there" (Ἡρῴδης δὲ ἐπιζητήσας αὐτὸν καὶ μὴ εὑρὼν ἀνακρίνας τοὺς φύλακας ἐκέλευσεν ἀπαχθῆναι, καὶ κατελθὼν ἀπὸ τῆς Ἰουδαίας εἰς Καισάρειαν διέτριβεν). Here it may be noted that it is not simply a case of going down from Jerusalem to Caesarea, but from "Judea" to Caesarea, indicating that in the narrative space of Acts Caesarea is configured as lying outside Judea. While there are Jews in the city, including Christian Jews, the typifying feature of Caesarea is that it is Roman and gentile, *not* part of Judea—the locus of Judean law. The client king who rules Judea leaves Judea in order to "go down" to Caesarea. However, by this time the narrative has also shown Caesarea as a place of the action of the Holy Spirit. Herod Agrippa is portrayed as a villain: executing James by the sword, arresting Peter, killing his guards. The scene is set for a lesson about what will happen to the persecutors if they do not repent.

In Acts 12:20–23 Caesarea is the location of Herod Agrippa's bizarre death, and the narrative provides an aside containing a flurry of facts: Herod was on bad terms with the Tyrians and Sidonians—people of other port districts to the north—and when a deputation was received with the support of Blastus, the king's chamberlain, a treaty was negotiated. There was a day fixed for this, and Agrippa, wearing fine robes and seated on a dais on a *bēma*, began to make a speech. People said, "It's a god speaking, not a man," but at that moment the angel of the Lord struck him down; he was eaten by worms and died, because he had not given the glory to God (12:23). The city of Caesarea here then functions as a locus of divine actions, via an avenging angel of the Lord, though in fact the story as told does not give as a rationale for Herod Agrippa's death his persecution of apostles but rather his self-aggrandizement and neglect of glorifying God.[16] Caesarea, in Acts, is therefore not a safe place for those who are enemies of the church. While only positive things have happened to Christian missionaries here, the ruler appointed by Rome comes to a sorry end. The entire hero-story of Peter concludes at this point, with Peter free in Jerusalem and "Herod" dead in Caesarea.

The main hero character for the remainder of Acts is of course Paul, and there are a few linking verses in 12:24–25 in which Paul and Barnabas are said to have completed their famine-relief task in Jerusalem: "they turned back bringing John called Mark with them" (ὑπέστρεψαν . . . συμπαραλαβόντες Ἰωάννην τὸν ἐπικληθέντα Μᾶρκον). We understand here that they came back to Antioch, and their journey may well have been via Caesarea, but the words as stated are brief and neither city is explicitly mentioned. The visit of Paul and Barnabas to Jerusalem therefore forms bookends for the story of Peter and Herod Agrippa, ending with the king's death in Caesarea. In terms of the Peter sequence, the centurion Cornelius and the Roman client king Herod act as opposites within the context of the city.

Everything regarding Caesarea that precedes the main part of Paul's story in Acts prepares us for Paul's reentry into Caesarea and provides the essential features of the city in the narrative. In relation to Paul, Caesarea has just been the transit city (9:30), not a place of evangelization. Thus, when Caesarea reappears in Acts 18:22, it is also a transit city: "when he had come down [from the ship] at Caesarea, he went up [to Jerusalem] and greeted the church, and then went down to Antioch" (καὶ κατελθὼν εἰς Καισάρειαν, ἀναβὰς καὶ ἀσπασάμενος τὴν ἐκκλησίαν, κατέβη εἰς Ἀντιόχειαν). He arrives and departs, which underscores what we should expect. However, for Paul, the city of transit becomes a place of restraint, before he is moved to his final location in the hands of the Romans.

Chapters 21 to 28 tell of how Paul is arrested in Jerusalem by the Roman tribune Claudius Lysias and taken into custody, then marched off to Caesarea, where he is tried by the governor Felix according to Roman law as a Roman citizen and then sent off by the new governor Festus to Rome by ship. For Paul, Caesarea—the transit city—continues in performing Rome in Judea, as his trajectory goes in the direction of Rome itself.

The story of Paul in Caesarea in Acts is now told not only in the third

---

16. While a similar story told by Josephus in *Ant.* 19.343–50 places the situation of Herod Agrippa's death in the stadium, we are not told exactly where this occurred in Acts.

person singular but the first person plural[17] and thus in Acts 21:1-7 "we" sailed from Ephesus, to Cos, to Rhodes, to Patara, to Tyre, where disciples told Paul "in the Spirit" not to travel to Jerusalem, and then from Tyre to Ptolemais, and "leaving the next day, we came into Caesarea, and went off to the house of Philip the evangelist, who was one of the Seven [deacons], and we stayed with him" (τῇ δὲ ἐπαύριον ἐξελθόντες ἤλθομεν εἰς Καισάρειαν, καὶ εἰσελθόντες εἰς τὸν οἶκον Φιλίππου τοῦ εὐαγγελιστοῦ ὄντος ἐκ τῶν ἑπτὰ ἐμείναμεν παρ' αὐτῷ). The four virgin daughters of Philip, all prophets, are identified. In Philip's house the Holy Spirit is active through his work and also within the prophecy of the daughters. The narrative had previously parked Philip on reaching Caesarea, but in going back to that point (8:40) we get a sense that Philip has been here for some time, marrying and having four daughters. The prophet called Agabus arrives "from Judea" (ἀπὸ τῆς Ἰουδαίας [21:10]), a comment providing another indication that in the portrayal of Acts' narrative space Caesarea lies beyond Judea, not in it. In Acts 21:16, after Paul has received the warning, the "we," comprised by Paul and an unidentified "Other," go up to Jerusalem, and "some of the disciples from Caesarea also went along with us" (συνῆλθον δὲ καὶ τῶν μαθητῶν ἀπὸ Καισαρείας σὺν ἡμῖν [21:16]).

When Paul takes that road again, it is when he is sent back to Felix, the governor (23:24),[18] at the third hour of the night (9 p.m.), accompanied by "two hundred soldiers, seventy horsemen and two hundred spearmen" (στρατιώτας διακοσίους καὶ ἱππεῖς ἑβδομήκοντα καὶ δεξιολάβους

17. For a recent treatment from a narratological perspective see William S. Campbell, *The "We" Passages in the Acts of the Apostles: The Narrator as Narrative Character*, SBLStBL 14 (Atlanta: SBL, 2007). These passages have been associated with sea voyages: Vernon K. Robbins, "By Land and by Sea: The We-Passages and Ancient Sea Voyages" in *Perspectives on Luke-Acts*, ed. Charles Talbert (Danville, VA: Association of Baptist Professors of Religion, 1978), 215–42, though this is probably not entirely correct. For a critique of Robbins, see Susan M. Praeder, "The Problem of First Person Narration in Acts," *NovT* 29 (1987): 193–218, here 214; Colin J. Hemer, "First Person Narrative in Acts 27–28," *TynBul* 36 (1985): 79–109, here 85; and discussion in Stanley E. Porter, *The Paul of Acts: Essays in Literary Criticism, Rhetoric and Theology*, WUNT 115 (Tübingen: Mohr Siebeck, 1999), 10–46. Traditionally, the "Other" is considered to be Luke, companion of Paul, who tells things from his own perspective at certain points. For a suggestion that the Other is Paul's "sister" companion, see Joan E. Taylor, "Two by Two: The Ark-etypal Language of Mark's Apostolic Pairings," in *The Body in Biblical, Christian and Jewish Texts*, ed. Joan E. Taylor (London: T&T Clark Bloomsbury, 2014), 58–82, here 78–79.

18. Antoninus Felix, procurator of Judea 52–59 CE. In Acts, he is repeatedly called the "governor" (ἡγεμών, 23:24, 26, 33; 24:1, 10).

διακοσίους [Acts 23:23]), as decreed by the tribune Claudius Lysias. Lysias commands his soldiers "to prepare beasts of burden to bear Paul" (κτήνη τε παραστῆσαι ἵνα ἐπιβιβάσαντες τὸν Παῦλον), the plural κτήνη and corresponding verb ἐπιβιβάσαντες indicating then that "Paul" means Paul and the Other, of the "we" category. Paul had outed himself as a Roman citizen in 22:25–29. The tribune Lysias was alarmed that he had put a Roman citizen in chains, and from this point there is the sense of Paul and his companion being given very special treatment. The massive convoy to Caesarea seems to be designed for his protection: it is not because Paul is dangerous, but because Paul is in danger.

When the cavalry arrive in Caesarea, they hand over Paul to the governor (Acts 23:33), who orders him to be held in a place very specifically labeled "Herod's praetorium" (τὸ πραιτώριον τοῦ Ἡρώδου [23:35]). The designation might be local since this structure was indeed built by Herod the Great (see below), but the narrative signals the royal authority of the only Herod mentioned thus far—Herod Agrippa. It therefore creates a strange juxtaposition between the royal residence of the Judean king with a (Greek transliteration of a) very distinctive Roman term, the Latin *praetorium*, which can only mean Felix's own residence now that "Herod" is dead.

Paul and the Roman governor therefore occupy the same location in Herod's praetorium, the palace of the Roman governor. The city of transit is also at the same time a city of detention. Paul is at the heart of Roman civil and military administration in a city named after the emperor. There is no reference at all to Paul being put in prison here, despite his capture. There is even a sense in which things go well in Caesarea, as if the city itself is benevolent in terms of the Christians, and harsh to those—like Herod Agrippa—who oppose them.

Danger still emanates from the Judean authorities, with their center in Jerusalem, supported by Hellenic Jews. In Acts 24:1 it is stated that after five days the High Priest, Ananias, κατέβη, "came down," (from Jerusalem/Judea) to Caesarea with some of the elders and an advocate named Tertullus, who put a case against Paul. In 24:1–23 the city of Caesarea then becomes the locus for Roman law, as opposed to Judean law, with the Roman-named Tertullus acting for the Judean authorities.[19] The defence

19. For further on this trial see Joan E. Taylor, "The *Nazoraeans* as a 'Sect' in 'Sectarian' Judaism? A Reconsideration of the Current View via the Narrative of Acts and the Meaning of *Hairesis*," in *Sects and Sectarianism in Jewish* History, ed. Sacha Stern (Leiden: Brill, 2011), 87–118.

of Paul is provided in detail, and Felix ends up adjourning the case until Lysias should come down from Jerusalem, with orders that Paul should be given some freedom: "having commanded the centurion to keep him, but to have ease and not to forbid those of his own to serve him" (διαταξάμενος τῷ ἑκατοντάρχῃ τηρεῖσθαι αὐτὸν ἔχειν τε ἄνεσιν καὶ μηδένα κωλύειν τῶν ἰδίων αὐτοῦ ὑπηρετεῖν αὐτῷ).

Again, this is not a picture of Paul in chains and in prison in Caesarea, though he is held and restricted as a detainee. Felix is described as arriving with his wife "Drusilla who was a Judean" (a rather cursory way of referring to the daughter of Herod Agrippa), and as sending for Paul and discussing matters with him, though he is unable to make up his mind (24:24–26).

After two years, when Felix is succeeded by Porcius Festus (60–62 CE), Festus, like his predecessor, left Paul "in custody" (δεδεμένον), because he was "wishing to gain favors with the Judeans/Jews"; the words used still do not present Paul as being in prison, as such. While δέω literally means "tie up," Paul is not seen as having been put in chains, as we have learned from 22:25–29; it can also mean "to be hindered" or "constrained."[20]

Three days after his arrival Festus "went up to Jerusalem from Caesarea" (25:1), a comment that depicts Festus as arriving in Caesarea as the main center of Roman command, and then going to Jerusalem. "Caesarea" remains pitted against "Jerusalem," the locus of the authority of the "chief priests and leaders of the Jews/Judeans" (abbreviated to the "Judeans"), and to each location there is attached a competing legal authority.

In 25:1–12 the two areas of authority, Roman and Judean, are clearly defined. Judean authorities want Paul transferred back, to be tried by Judean law; this cannot take place in Caesarea. Festus answers that Paul was in custody in Caesarea, where he would be returning, and the Judean authorities could come there to make their case. This they do: "he went down to Caesarea and the next day he took his seat on the tribune and ordered Paul to be brought in" (καταβὰς εἰς Καισάρειαν, τῇ ἐπαύριον καθίσας ἐπὶ τοῦ βήματος ἐκέλευσεν τὸν Παῦλον ἀχθῆναι [Acts 25:6]). Paul is accused by "the Judeans" who accuse him of transgressions. Festus asks, "Are you willing to go up to Jerusalem and be tried on these charges before me there?" and Paul responds, "I am standing before the tribune of Caesar and this is where I should be tried" (25:10). The name of the city, Caesarea (Καισάρεια), now

---

20. LSJ 383, 3 and 4. Cf. "δέω," BDAG, 221–22, the first definition being "to confine a person or thing by various kinds of restraints." Sense 3 is "to constrain by law and duty": people are "bound by rules."

becomes a cipher for the name Caesar (Καῖσαρ), in this passage, and the
repetition is powerful: "I appeal to Caesar," says Paul, in Caesarea (25:11),
and Festus replies, "You have appealed to Caesar; to Caesar you shall go"
(25:12). The names Καισαρεία and Καῖσαρ are constantly repeated, drum-
ming themselves through this passage (25:1–12), eight times in twelve verses.
We are clearly in the realm of *Romanitas*. *Romanitas* acts protectively, and
hostile Judea is outside it.

We then have another appearance of the Herodian dynasty, client rulers
of Rome, now in the form of Herod Agrippa II, "King Agrippa,"[21] and his
sister Bernice (in fact also the sister of Drusilla), who hear Paul's case in the
auditorium (ἀκροατήριον) of Festus (25:23). They were gathered also "with
the tribunes and the men of high standing in the city" (σύν τε χιλιάρχοις καὶ
ἀνδράσιν τοῖς κατ᾽ ἐξοχὴν τῆς πόλεως). We learn that Judeans/Jews both
in Jerusalem and in Caesarea had petitioned Festus about Paul. It seems
here then that Agrippa and Bernice are brought in as alternative Judeans
regarding a Judean issue, since Agrippa can make an assessment in matters
independently of the Judean religious authorities centered in Jerusalem.[22]
We then have Paul's defence, and Agrippa and Bernice and those with them
agree that Paul did not deserve death, and could have been set free if he had
not appealed to Caesar (Acts 26:32).

At this point, the narrative returns to the "we" voice comprising Paul
and the Other, and Caesarea is very much a transit place. The Other (who is
not imprisoned though a companion) gives us the facts (27:1–2):

> They handed over Paul and some other prisoners to a centurion named
> Julius of the Augustan cohort. We boarded a vessel from Adramyttium
> bound for ports on the Asiatic coast and put to sea; we had Aristarchus
> with us, a Macedonian of Thessalonica.
>
> παρεδίδουν τόν τε Παῦλον καί τινας ἑτέρους δεσμώτας ἑκατοντάρχῃ
> ὀνόματι Ἰουλίῳ σπείρης Σεβαστῆς. ἐπιβάντες δὲ πλοίῳ Ἀδραμυττηνῷ
> μέλλοντι πλεῖν εἰς τοὺς κατὰ τὴν Ἀσίαν τόπους ἀνήχθημεν, ὄντος σὺν
> ἡμῖν Ἀριστάρχου Μακεδόνος Θεσσαλονικέως.

21. It is not clear when Herod Agrippa II was given the title of "King," though perhaps
not until after the end of the Judean War in 70 CE, when he was also given the dignity of a
Roman Praetor; in ca. 58–59 he ruled territories to the north of Judea and in Peraea, and
the cities of Tiberius and Tarichaea.

22. This raises questions about how the execution of law worked in regard to the legal
authority of the Herodian dynasty and the priestly authorities in Jerusalem, though this
cannot be discussed here.

It is goodbye to Caesarea, and—soon—hello to Rome: from Caesarea to Caesar himself. One is left with the impression that just as Caesarea was basically a gentle and fair place for Paul and for other Christians, Rome should be also.[23] Paul's situation in Rome, staying in lodgings, is likewise not a case of Paul being held as a prisoner; he is a detainee, under the *custodia libera* of house arrest (28:16). Given this, one may assume a similar situation for him in the years he spent in the praetorium of Caesarea.[24]

2. Locations

In terms of actual locations and topographical features of Caesarea in the narrative of Acts we have the following places identified or implied:

  a. Caesarea: A cult center of Caesar (cf. 25:1–12)
  b. Roads leading to the south (Azotus, Joppa) and southeast (Jerusalem) (8:40; 9:32–43; 10:24; 11:11, 13; 12:19; 24:1; 25:1)
  c. The harbor (9:30; 18:22; 21:1–8; 27:1–2)
  d. A synagogue (10:2, 22)
  e. The house of Philip (21:8)
  f. The house of Cornelius (10:2; 11:12)
  g. The praetorium (palace of Herod) and (within it) the ἀκροατήριον, the hearing chamber, and Paul's quarters (23:35; 25:6, 23)

As for evidence that can shed light on the narrative of Acts and the way Caesarea is configured as a city space, the first material to be considered is the description of the city by Josephus. The question of whether Acts demonstrates a knowledge of Josephus's writings specifically[25] or local knowledge

23. This then would bring into question the assessment of Flessen, *Exemplary Man*, 155–56, that Caesarea represents "the home of ineffectual Roman men who cannot control themselves or others . . . [and is] controlled by the opponents of Paul" (i.e., Felix and Festus; Acts 24:24–27; 25:9). In fact, the Roman governors stymie the hostile purposes of the Judean authorities in Jerusalem; while the Roman governors are not portrayed entirely positively, they still manage to keep Paul safe.

24. That Caesarea is the likely place of authorship of Philippians, which explicitly refers to the praetorium in Phil. 1:13, remains debated, and is not the subject of the present study. For a Caesarean provenance, see the arguments put forward by Gerald F. Hawthorne, *Philippians*, WBC 43 (Waco, TX: Word, 1983), xxxvi–xliv.

25. See Steve Mason, "Josephus and Luke-Acts," in his *Josephus and the New Testament* (Peabody, MA: Hendrickson, 1992), 185–229.

generally may never be solved, but it is of interest that Josephus describes Caesarea in some detail in *J.W.* 1.408–15 (written ca. 73–75 CE). For Josephus, his concern is to report the building of the city by King Herod sometime after 40 BCE on the site of a deteriorated town called Straton's Tower. On the basis of this account, various localities implied in the narrative of Acts do appear. Here Herod built "a splendid palace" (= the praetorium, g.), a magnificent deep harbor "bigger than Piraeus" (c.) with honorifically-named towers, a "temple of Caesar" (a.) in which was a colossal statue of Caesar as Olympian Zeus, coupled with one of Rome as Hera of Argos. In addition, there were a theater, amphitheater, and market-places. As Josephus describes it, this was a city to do Caesar proud, the gateway to the eastern reaches of his empire (implying good road systems, b.).

Caesarea appears elsewhere in *Jewish War* and *Antiquities* as the residence of Roman governors and the location of a disturbance involving the synagogue, the key incident that sparked the revolt against Rome, under the governorship of Felix (*J.W.* 2.266–70, 284–92; *Ant.* 20.173–78, 182–84). As Josephus tells it, the Jewish population of Caesarea argued with the non-Jews (called Syrians or Hellenes/Greeks) on the question of whether Caesarea should be considered a Judean/Jewish city or a Syro-Palestinian one, which was understood by Jews as a question of equality. The matter involved a deputation to Nero (*J.W.* 2.270), who decided in favor of the Hellenes. In the twelfth year of Nero (66 CE), the synagogue of Caesarea, next to a property owned by a Hellene, had the entranceway squeezed into a narrow passage by new building projects. In response, Jewish youths attacked the builders. Furthermore, a huge sum of eight talents was offered by the Jewish community to the new Roman governor Florus as a bribe if he ordered the building work to stop, but he took the money and went to Sebaste (*J.W.* 2.288). A Hellene sacrificed birds on an upturned pot at the entrance to the passage when Jews were assembling on the Sabbath (289); rioting ensued, and Jews took their Torah scroll and fled to nearby Narbata, a Judean toparchy 60 stadia from the city of Caesarea.[26] However, Josephus states that the Hellenes apparently massacred the (remaining) Jewish population (*J.W.* 2.457), leading then to massive retaliations by Judeans.[27]

26. See also Anders Runesson, Donald D. Binder and Birger Olsson, eds., *The Ancient Synagogue from Its Origins to 200 CE: A Source Book* (Leiden: Brill, 2008), 20–22.
27. For discussion of the Jewish population and the events of the years leading up to the outbreak of revolt in 66 CE, see Lee I. Levine, "The Jewish-Greek Conflict in First-Century Caesarea," *JJS* 25 (1974): 381–97; Lee I. Levine, *Caesarea under Roman Rule* (Leiden: Brill, 1975), 22–23; Lee I. Levine, "The Jewish Community at Caesarea in Late Antiquity," in *Cae-*

The significance of all this for Caesarea in the narrative of Acts concerns not only the presence of Jews and the indication of a synagogue (d.), but the language noted above regarding the essential identity of the city as being non-Judean (Acts 12:19; 21:11), since one leaves Judea to go to Caesarea. This does not reflect the views of the Jews of the city as described by Josephus; it reflects the notions of their Syro-Palestinian opponents, as endorsed by the decision of Nero, that Caesarea is outside Judea (and Judean law). The question of whether this does assume knowledge of Josephus on the part of the narrator may be unsolvable, but, if it assumes local historical knowledge, the perspective adopted is that of Rome itself.

In addition, Caesarea is mentioned elsewhere in Josephus's *Jewish War* and *Antiquities* at various critical junctures. It was the residence of the Roman governors, the cavalry, and other troops (e.g., Cumanus, *J.W.* 2.236), and it was in the stadium that Pilate dealt with the demonstration resulting from objections to the Roman standards he wished to take into Jerusalem (*J.W.* 2.169–74; *Ant.* 18.57).[28]

a. Caesarea: A Cult Center of Caesar

There is much in a name, when it comes to cities. Caesarea was Caesar's city, named in honour of Augustus by Herod the Great, and Josephus defines it as a place with a magnificent temple built for the imperial cult to venerate him as a god (*J.W.* 1.414). The entire harbor was dominated by a great temple of Augustus (Figure 2), and in aerial images the sunken arms of the port appear to stretch out from this structure, embracing all the ships that come to berth there. Excavations from 1989 onward in the combined excavation by Avner Raban, Kenneth Holum and Joseph Patrich have brought to light the substructures of

---

sarea Papers: Straton's Tower, Herod's Harbour, and Roman and Byzantine Caesarea, ed. Robert Lindley Vann, JRASup 5 (Ann Arbor, MI: Journal of Roman Archaeology, 1992), 268–73; Ariyeh Kasher, "The Isopoliteia Question in Caesarea Maritima," *JQR* 68 (1978): 16–27.

28. In terms of the people and events associated with Caesarea, the famine during the reign of Claudius, which brought Paul and Barnabas through the port (Acts 11:27–28), is mentioned—though at a slightly different time—in *Ant.* 20.49–53, 101. The death of King Agrippa I (Acts 12:23) is described—though differently—in *Ant.* 19.343–61. Ananias the High Priest (23:2; 24:1), who came to Jerusalem with Tertullus, is mentioned in *Ant.* 20.103. Felix (Acts 24:24) is mentioned in *Ant.* 20.137–44, where it is also noted how he married Drusilla, sister of Agrippa II and Bernice. Agrippa II (Acts 25:13; 26:27–28), given the former territory of his uncle Philip and more, is mentioned in *J.W.* 2.247, 252; *Ant.* 20.137, 145. Festus (Acts 24:27–25:2) appears in *Ant.* 20:182–86.

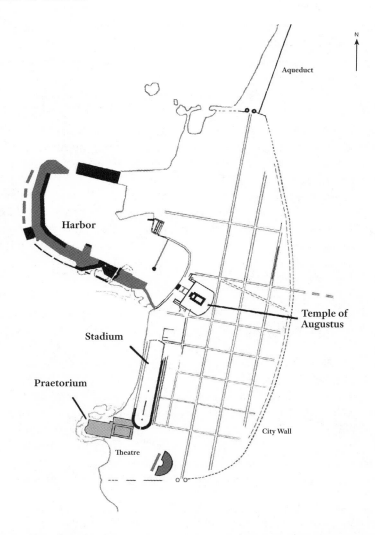

Figure 2. Plan of Caesarea harbor and city, after A. Iamim, Combined Caesarea Expedition.

a temple exceptional in both beauty and size. As noted, Josephus states that there was a colossal statue of Caesar, not inferior to the Zeus at Olympia, which it resembled, and a similarly colossal statue of Roma as Hera at Argos (*J.W.* 1.414; cf. *Ant.* 15:339). This temple was visible from a long way off from those approaching by ship during the day; Josephus said it appeared from a distance like a snow-clad mountain (*J.W.* 5.223). The original assumption of the excavators was that it was made of marble, but it was actually polished limestone. The main staircase was uncovered in 1990s along with a *temenos* platform built on large vaults, the southern one standing 21 m x 7 m x 13 m. Overall the platform was 418 m long and 389 m wide, and surrounded by shops.[29]

There was nothing modest about this structure. Augustus as Olympian Zeus appears to have been used in other imperial cult shrines, and a small version of this statue is now to be seen in the Hermitage Museum, St. Petersburg (A399, found in Cumae). The original statue of Olympian Zeus by Phidias was well known in the ancient world, and to have Augustus as Olympian Zeus in Caesarea clearly provided a locus of propaganda. Rome ruled, and the glory of Augustus was matched by a similar statue of Roma herself. In addition, coins from the time of Nero represent the Tyche of Caesarea, the essential spirit of the city, a cult which may well have been integrated into that of the imperial shrines. One coin shows a laurel wreath of the emperor, with the word ΣΕΒΑΣΤΟΣ ("Augustus" in Greek), with Tyche on the reverse, with a crown of three towers, most likely the towers of the port. A second coin shows laurel-wreathed Nero in profile, with Tyche statue on the reverse, with Λ ΙΔ (L. 14 = 68 CE), and inscriptions (obverse): ΝΕΡΩΝ ΚΑΙΣΑΡ ΣΕΒΑΣΤΟΣ "Nero Caesar Augustus," ΚΑΙΣΑΡΙΑ Η ΠΡΟΣ ΣΕΒΑΣΤΩ ΛΙΜΕΝΙ "Caesarea, which is at the august port," with Tyche standing left holding bust and standard.[30] The second coin (RPC 4862) continues a legend already found on a coin of Herod Agrippa I, dated 43–44 CE, which had the image of Tyche with her hand on a rudder, holding a cor-

---

29. For the temple, see Lisa C. Kahn, "King Herod's Temple of Roma and Augustus at Caesarea Maritima," in *Caesarea Maritima: A Retrospective after Two Millennia*, ed. Avner Raban and Kenneth G. Holum (Leiden: Brill, 1996), 130–45; Kenneth G. Holum, "The Temple Platform: A Progress Report," in *Caesarea Papers 2: Herod's Temple, the Provincial Governor's Praetorium and Granaries, the Later Harbor, a Gold Coin Hoard, and Other Studies*, ed. Kenneth G. Holum, Avner Raban and Joseph Patrich, JRASup 35 (Portsmouth, RI: Journal of Roman Archaeology, 1999), 12–34; Farland H. Stanley, Jr., "The South Flank of the Temple Platform (Area Z2, 1993–95 excavations)," in *Caesarea Papers 2: Herod's Temple, the Provincial Governor's Praetorium and Granaries, the Later Harbor, a Gold Coin Hoard, and Other Studies*, ed. Kenneth G. Holum, Avner Raban, and Joseph Patrich, JRASup 35 (Portsmouth, RI: Journal of Roman Archaeology, 1999), 35–40.

30. Avner Raban suggests this may indicate two harbors with the main harbor itself named separately as "Sebastos" ("Καισαρεια η προς Σεβαστω λιμενι: Two Harbours for Two Entities," in *Caesarea Papers: Straton's Tower, Herod's Harbour, and Roman and Byzantine Caesarea*, ed. Robert Lindley Vann, JRASup 5 [Ann Arbor, MI: Journal of Roman Archaeology, 1992], 68–74). The legend can be pointed as: Καισάρεια ἡ πρὸς σεβαστῷ λιμένι, "Caesarea which is at (the) august/imperial port," since the Greek word σεβαστός is as much an adjective as a noun.

nucopia, and on the back the head of Claudius with the legend ΒΑΣΙΛΕΥΣ ΜΕΓΑΣ ΑΓΡΙΠΠΑΣ ΦΙΛΩΚΑΙΣΑΡ "Great King Agrippa Caesar-loving," which manages to convey both Herod Agrippa's loyalty to Claudius and self-aggrandizement at the same time.[31] The integral relationship between the port, the city, the city-goddess (Tyche), and the imperial cult seems clear from the coinage. The importance of the cult for Roman governors is shown in the evidence of Pontius Pilate, prefect of Judea ca. 26–36, both in his coinage—where Roman cultic items are explicitly shown—and also in the surviving part of an inscription for the Tibereium, dedicated by Pilate.[32]

b. Roads Leading to the South (Azotus, Joppa) and Southeast (Jerusalem)

The roads from Caesarea (see Figure 3), have been defined by Israel Roll, who enumerates five, including a coastal road in which milestones have been found to the north of the city and a road to Antipatris, which seems to have been the route taken to Jerusalem; this became the chief artery for the *cursus publicus*.[33] It was this route probably taken by Philip, as well as Paul; Peter's road would have been the coastal route from Joppa.

c. The Harbor

While in Acts Caesarea is for Paul a place of transit, and his ships sail in and out, there is nothing stated about the harbor itself. For this there is the

---

31. Ya'akov Meshorer, *Jewish Coins of the Second Temple Period* (Tel Aviv: Hassefer and Massada, 1967), 139 no. 90.

32. For the inscription see Clayton M. Lehmann and Kenneth G. Holum, *The Greek and Latin Inscriptions of Caesarea Maritima* (Boston: ASOR, 2000), 67–70, and discussion of this and the coins in Taylor, "Pontius Pilate," 67–69.

33. Israel Roll, "The Roman Road System in Judea," *The Jerusalem Cathedra* 3 (1983): 136–62; Israel Roll, "Roman Roads to Caesarea Maritima," in *Caesarea—A Mercantile City by the Sea*, ed. Ofra Rimon et al. (Haifa: University of Haifa, 1993), 30–33 (map, p. 21); Israel Roll, "Roman Roads to Caesarea Maritima," in *Caesarea Maritima: A Retrospective after Two Millennia*, ed. Avner Raban and Kenneth G. Holum (Leiden: Brill, 1996), 549–58. A plan of the roads with the city territory of Caesarea is found in Kenneth G. Holum et al., *King Herod's Dream: Caesarea on the Sea* (New York & London: Norton, 1988), 76, fig. 42. See also the road system as shown in Joan E. Taylor, ed., *The Onomasticon by Eusebius of Caesarea: Palestine in the Fourth Century*, trans. Greville Freeman-Grenville (Jerusalem: Carta, 2003), maps 4 and 7.

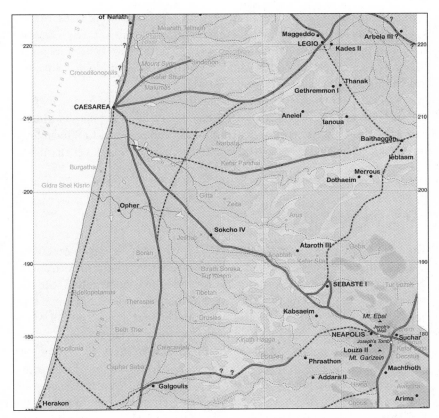

Figure 3. Roads leading to and from Caesarea. © Carta, Jerusalem. Used with permission.

description by Josephus. The full extent of the harbor has been uncovered by underwater archaeology initiated by Avner Raban in 1992, and findings have been presented in numerous volumes.[34] These excavations and aerial

34. Particularly important reports are: Avner Raban et al., eds., *The Site and the Excavations*, vol. 1 of *The Harbours of Caesarea Maritima*, BAR International Series 491 (Oxford: British Archaeological Reports, 1989); Avner Raban, "Sebastos: The Royal Harbour at Caesarea Maritima—A Short-lived Giant," *The International Journal of Nautical Archaeology* 21 (1992): 111–24; John Peter Oleson and Graham Branton, "The Technology of King Herod's Harbour," in *Caesarea Papers: Straton's Tower, Herod's Harbour, and Roman and Byzantine Caesarea*, ed. Robert Lindley Vann, JRASup 5 (Ann Arbor, MI: Journal of Roman Archaeology, 1992), 49–67; Avner Raban et al., "Caesarea and Its Harbours: A Preliminary Report on the 1988 Season," *IEJ* 40 (1990): 241–56; Avner Raban et al., "The Underwater Excavations, 1993–94," in *Caesarea Papers 2: Herod's Temple, the Provincial Governor's Praetorium*

JOAN E. TAYLOR

photography combine to demonstrate that Herod's harbor of Caesarea had
massive artificial arms, on which there were apparently towers to guide ships
to go through the narrow opening. It was one of the largest harbors on the
Mediterranean after Alexandria—built with the latest technological advances
in hydraulic engineering and concrete.

As we can now see it, we may imagine Paul's entries and exits from
Caesarea, to and from Tarsus, or Antioch or elsewhere, as being in a hub of
a massive shipping enterprise, a cosmopolitan and outward-looking market
city designed for trade east to Arabia and west even to Spain. Yet all this was
in the embrace of "Caesar."

d. A Synagogue

The synagogue that was the catalyst for catastrophic events in 66 CE has
not been identified with absolute surety. However, various reports from the
British Mandate period, excavations in 1952 and 1962, and results of the 1982
and 1984 field seasons by the Joint Expedition to Caesarea Maritima have
been collected together in an excellent volume by Marylinda Govaars, Marie
Spiro and L. Michael White.[35] According to John Malalas, *Chron.* 10:261,
lines 13–16, Hadrian erected an Odeon on the site of the/a synagogue, but
in 1930 the finding of an inscribed menorah in a capital integrated into a
Crusader wall led in due course to investigations and discovery of successive
mosaics in what might be a synagogue, located in the northern part of the
city. While excavations in 1956 and 1962 did lead scholars to suggest that the

---

and Granaries, the Later Harbor, a Gold Coin Hoard, and Other Studies, ed. Kenneth G.
Holum, Avner Raban, and Joseph Patrich, JRASup 35 (Portsmouth, RI: Journal of Roman
Archaeology, 1999), 152–68; Avner Raban and Robert Stieglitz, "Caesarea, Ancient Harbor, 1987," *IEJ* 38 (1988): 273–78; Avner Raban and Robert Stieglitz, "Caesarea and Its Harbor—1987–1988," *Excavations and Surveys in Israel* 7–8 (1988–89): 33–41; Avner Raban et al.,
"Land Excavations in the Inner Harbour (1993–94)," in *Caesarea Papers 2: Herod's Temple,
the Provincial Governor's Praetorium and Granaries, the Later Harbor, a Gold Coin Hoard,
and Other Studies,* ed. Kenneth G. Holum, Avner Raban, and Joseph Patrich, JRASup 35
(Portsmouth, RI: Journal of Roman Archaeology, 1999), 198–224; Avner Raban, ed., *Harbour Archaeology: Proceedings of the First International Workshop on Ancient Mediterranean
Harbours, Caesarea Maritima, 24–28.6.83,* BAR International Series 257 (Oxford: British
Archaeological Reports, 1985).

35. Marylinda Govaars, Marie Spiro and L. Michael White, *The Joint Expedition to
Caesarea Maritima Excavation Reports: Field O: The "Synagogue" Site* (Boston: American
Schools of Oriental Research, 2009).

synagogue of Josephus had been found, these conclusions cannot now be verified on the basis of presently available evidence.[36]

e. and f.: *The House of Philip and the House of Cornelius*

There is no clear identification of where these houses were located. In regard to traditional pilgrimage sites, Cornelius's house was pointed out to the Bordeaux Pilgrim in 333 CE (*Itin.* 585.4), as was his "bath," and this house was visited by Paula, friend of Jerome, in the later 4th c. (*Ep.* 108.2), who testified also to "huts of Philip and his four daughters," but these Byzantine sites have not been found.

Wherever the house of Philip was, it was in a densely-packed city with a high population. The theater, with its capacity of four thousand, gives a sense of the size of the town, as does its gigantic hippodrome, which by the time Paul visited had a capacity of about twelve thousand. The population may also be read from the aqueduct, bringing water from the southern side of Mount Carmel, at Shummi, about 10 km to the northeast of the city. The water flowed on a single raised canal, and in one section it is dug into the rock (at Jisr az-Zarka, an Arab village north of Caesarea).

g. *The Praetorium (Palace of Herod), the Hearing Chamber (ἀκροατήριον), and Paul's Quarters*

Of special interest here is the praetorium, the place where Paul was taken under arrest and accommodated, and also the place of the auditorium, ἀκροατήριον, where there was the tribunal in which the governor took his seat. The Praetorium is more popularly known as the Promontory Palace, constructed by Herod the Great between 19 and 10 BCE on a sandstone promontory jutting out into the sea. Until quite recently all that was known of the structure here was a piscina cut into the rocks. However, in surveys done by the Hebrew University (1976) it was realized that there were foundation walls belonging to a large building, and excavations by Ehud Netzer

36. For suggestions of this identification see especially Moses Schwabe, "The Synagogue of Caesarea and Its Inscriptions" [Hebrew] in *Alexander Marx: Jubilee Volume,* ed. Saul Liberman (New York: Jewish Theological Seminary, 1950), 433–50; Michael Avi-Yonah, "Notes and News: Caesarea," *IEJ* 6 (1956): 260–61; Michael Avi-Yonah, "The Synagogue of Caesarea (Preliminary Report)," *Louis Rabinowitz Bulletin for the Study of Ancient Synagogues* 3 (1960): 44–48.

Figure 4. Promontory Palace/Praetorium today looking from northeast corner (area E in Figure 5) to auditorium/*akroaterion*, now covered over. © Joan E. Taylor

and Lee I. Levine brought to light part of a building 110 m by 55 m with a central hall and two small rooms on either side, with pottery dating to the late first century at the earliest. This palace with swimming pool was considered to be the definitive promontory palace until in 1990 a new excavation team came to the site: Ehud Netzer joined forces with Kathryn Gleason and Barbara Burrell from the University of Pennsylvania, and brought to light the upper eastern side of the structure, including the exterior wall. Excavations continued from 1992 with Netzer working with a team on the lower part of the palace and the team from Pennsylvania on the upper level, with a further division of this upper level later on between Gleason and Burrell's team and the Israel Antiquities Authority.

By 1994 the Upper Palace became clearer, with the excavation of rooms around a large peristyle courtyard (45 m x 65 m), with an elevation 3.6 m higher than the lower ground level. The most interesting thing for our purpose is that on the north side a 192 m² hall came to light off the courtyard, identified by the excavators as being the audience hall itself (Figure 5, area E). The palace complex seemed more obviously divided between a lower, private palace and an upper semi-public palace, and indeed the entire palace complex seems to flow on through the hippodrome and to the theater

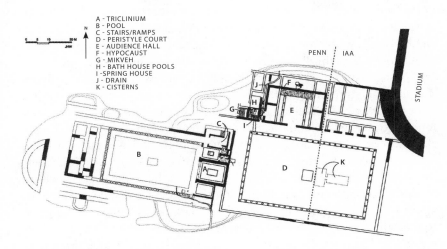

A - TRICLINIUM
B - POOL
C - STAIRS/RAMPS
D - PERISTYLE COURT
E - AUDIENCE HALL
F - HYPOCAUST
G - MIKVEH
H - BATH HOUSE POOLS
I - SPRING HOUSE
J - DRAIN
K - CISTERNS

Figure 5. Promontory Palace/Praetorium Plan. Drawn by J. H. Williams. Reproduced courtesy of the Promontory Palace Excavations.

creating a kind of palace area of the city itself. While this has a resemblance to the palace complex in Alexandria, Gleason has noted that Rome provides an example, with the theater and *domus* of Pompey in the Campus Martius.[37] Thus we have here a physical manifestation of Caesarea performing Rome on the coast of Judea.

If we think particularly of Paul here, first there is something interesting in thinking that a Roman governor, Felix, would insist that Paul, the arrested Roman citizen, should be placed in "Herod's praetorium" (Acts 23:35). Where exactly? Are we to look in fact somewhere in or under the

37. Kathryn Gleason, "Ruler and Spectacle: The Promontary Palace," in *Caesarea Maritima: A Retrospective after Two Millennia*, ed. Avner Raban and Kenneth Holum, DMOA 21 (Leiden: Brill, 1996), 208–27; Kathryn Gleason, with contributions by Barbara Burrell et al., "The Promontory Palace at Caesarea Maritima: Preliminary Evidence for Herod's Praetorium," *JRA* (1998): 23–52. See further Ehud Netzer, "The Promontory Palace," in *Caesarea Maritima, A Retrospective after Two Millennia*, ed. Avner Raban and Kenneth Holum, DMOA 21 (Leiden: Brill, 1996), 193–207; Barbara Burrell, "Palace to Praetorium: The Romanization of Caesarea," in *Caesarea Maritima: A Retrospective after Two Millennia*, ed. Avner Raban and Kenneth Holum, DMOA 21 (Leiden: Brill, 1996), 228–47; Barbara Burrell, Kathryn Gleason and Ehud Netser, "Uncovering Herod's Seaside Palace," *BAR* 19 (1993): 50–57; Barbara Burrell, "Herod's Caesarea on Sebastos: Urban Structures and Influences," in *Herod and Augustus: Papers Presented at the IJS Conference, 21st–23rd June 2005*, ed. David M. Jacobson and Nikos Kokkinos (Leiden: Brill, 2009), 217–33.

praetorium? Joseph Patrich notes that the room that later served as a prison in the late Roman era was indeed *under* the praetorium in a former T-shaped water cistern, where graffiti was found of Christian inscriptions probably dating to the later third and early fourth century.[38] This was not the prison area of the first century. Nevertheless, in the extension toward the hippodrome, Israel Antiquities Authority (IAA) excavations determined the area to be the offices of military personnel, suggested by four Latin inscriptions found in this wing, including a mosaic reading *Spes bona adiutorib(us) officie custodiar(um)*, "Good hope to the assistants of the office of the guards," as well as a club room of the centurions (*schola centurionum*).[39] So this is where the men in charge of Paul spent their time, but where was Paul? Given the model of a *custodia libera* in Rome, in rented apartments, it would not be appropriate to imagine Paul's custody in Caesarea as being in a dungeon. Rather, the statement about the praetorium needs to be taken on its own terms (not "beneath the praetorium" or "adjacent to it"). That there were guards implies perhaps an area that was guarded, close by, yet within the same compound.

Secondly, the auditorium being definitively identified by the University of Pennsylvania team should have caused quite a stir, but, for reasons that have not been explained, the IAA has chosen to cover it all up with concrete and not restore it for eager tourists. In this space, there was a basilical hall with an elevated northern area with underfloor heating on the north side. People coming into the hall would have entered through the main atrium of the praetorium, to the courtyard where a central statue pedestal indicates there was most likely an imposing image of the emperor, which they would have skirted to the right, toward the audience hall of Caesar's representative. As such, this is a very significant find for the life of Paul.

3. Conclusion

That we see Caesarea performing Rome in the narrative of Acts may lead us to consider how the city is described in the writings of Josephus, but this does not need to lead us to an assumption that Josephus was the key

38. Joseph Patrich, "Caesarea in the Time of Eusebius," in *Reconsidering Eusebius: Papers on Literary, Historical, and Theological Issues*, ed. Sabrina Inowlocki and Claudio Zamagni, VCSup 107 (Leiden: Brill, 2011), 1–24, here 15.
39. Hannah M. Cotton and William Eck, "Governors and Their Personnel on Latin Inscriptions from Caesarea Maritima," *PIASH* 7/7 (2001): 215–40.

source, especially given the discrepancies. What one learns from Josephus about Caesarea would have been appreciated instantly by anyone actually visiting the city, and certainly Christians who moved around between Judea and elsewhere were likely to have gone via Caesarea at some stage. Thus, even if the narrator of Acts might not have visited Caesarea, Christians who had visited Judea clearly would have. The narrator could then rely on local knowledge, not just texts.

Moreover, the "we" of the narrative implies an actual visit, and residence in Caesarea at the same time as Paul's detention. To erase the identity of Paul's Other (explained away as a literary device, for example) would mean inventing another narrator with a similar familiarity with the city, and that is certainly not the simplest explanation. It is this personal familiarity that best explains just how Caesarea can function so much as the locus of *Romanitas*, including Roman law. The "we" of the narrative are not on the Jewish side, and are as suspicious of the "Judeans" as the Syrians/Hellenes of Caesarea are in Josephus; "we" simply assume Caesarea is not in Judea. Reasons for any civil dissension do not appear at the very time this dissension was stinging; there is no word of the decision made by Nero. Yet, the effects of knowing what camp you belonged to in Caesarea, in the years 58–60 CE, do appear in the attitude exhibited in this story of Paul. Caesarea is the gentile territory of evangelization and the Holy Spirit, for both Philip and Peter, and it is a transit place of *Romanitas* that—at least temporarily—holds Paul safely in the praetorium itself.

Materially, the image of Caesarea as it is coming to light on the coast of Israel brings us to an awareness of a city performing Rome in its physical structures and spaces. This coheres perfectly with the representation of the city in the narrative of Acts. Archaeology then helps us to map the movements of Paul in a space that is entirely empire, the city of Augustus, the emperor. This is where Paul—the Roman citizen—in appealing to Caesar lost his chance to be set free, despite Rome's friendly face.

Early Christianity in Its Colonial Contexts in the Provinces of the Eastern Empire

DAVID W. J. GILL

1. Introduction

The narrative concerning the spread of Christianity across the eastern prov-inces of the Roman Empire is set against an urban landscape.[1] If we take the sweep of the Acts of the Apostles we start with the city of Jerusalem with its impressive Herodian architecture derived from the Hellenistic kings in the Greek East.[2] Paul's presentation to the Areopagos in Athens is set against the Pericleian architecture of imperial Athens mixed with the monuments to the Attalid dynasty on and around the Athenian acropolis.[3] The riot at Ephesus in the Greek theater merges with the reference to the Artemision, one of the religious wonders of the ancient world. And Luke's narrative ends in one of the megacities of the ancient world, Rome itself, with the symbols of Rome's victories across the then-known world.[4]

1. David W. J. Gill, "The Roman Empire as a Context for the New Testament," in *Handbook to Exegesis of the New Testament*, ed. Stanley E. Porter, NTTS 25 (Leiden: Brill, 1997), 388–406. For the specific background of colonial contexts for the New Testament documents, see Fergus Millar, *The Roman Empire and Its Neighbours*, 2nd ed. (London: Duckworth, 1981), 81.

2. Duane W. Roller, *The Building Program of Herod the Great* (Berkeley: University of California Press, 1998).

3. Jeffrey M. Hurwit, *The Athenian Acropolis: History, Mythology, and Archaeology from the Neolithic Era to the Present* (Cambridge: Cambridge University Press, 1999).

4. Diane G. Favro, *The Urban Image of Augustan Rome* (Cambridge: Cambridge University Press, 1996).

A series of colonies were established in the late Republic and Augustan era to settle the veterans of the major campaigns of the Civil Wars. Augustus himself claimed:

> The Roman citizens who took the soldier's oath of obedience to me numbered about 500,000. I settled rather more than 300,000 of these in colonies (*in colonias*) or sent them back to their home towns (*in municipia*) after their period of service; to all these I assigned lands (*agri*) or gave money as rewards for their military service.[5]

In 29 BCE, following the defeat of Antony, Augustus recorded:

> In my fifth consulship [29 BC] I gave 1,000 sesterces out of booty to every one of the colonists drawn from my soldiers; about 120,000 men in the colonies (*in colonis*) received this largesse at the time of my triumph.[6]

Three of the important Christian communities established during the first century were located in some of the leading Roman colonies in the provinces of the eastern Mediterranean. They were located at Pisidian Antioch in Galatia, Philippi in Macedonia, and Corinth in Achaia.

These colonies were different from other major urban centers in the east as they were constructed along Roman lines: their inhabitants were mainly, though not exclusively, Roman citizens who carried Roman names;[7] their official language was Latin; the architecture reflected Roman, as opposed to Greek, forms; their religious cults were mainly linked to Roman deities.[8] Thus the arrival of Christianity in these centers created an intersection with the Jewish, Hellenic, and Roman groups within a single Roman setting.

The New Testament documents, in particular the Acts of the Apostles and the epistles, contribute in different ways to an understanding of urban and rural life in the provinces of the eastern Mediterranean separate from, but complementary to, their value as biblical documents.[9] The official con-

---

5. *RG* 3.3 (trans. P. A. Brunt and J. M. Moore).

6. *RG* 15.3 (trans. P. A. Brunt and J. M. Moore).

7. For a qualification on this from a New Testament perspective: Peter Oakes, *Philippians: From People to Letter*, SNTSMS 110 (Cambridge: Cambridge University Press, 2001), 13–18.

8. E.g., A. H. M. Jones, *The Greek City from Alexander to Justinian* (Oxford: Clarendon, 1940); E. J. Owens, *The City in the Greek and Roman World* (London: Routledge, 1991).

9. E.g., David W. J. Gill and Conrad H. Gempf, eds., *The Book of Acts in Its Graeco-*

cern about how the riot would be interpreted at Ephesus provides the sort of insight that is rarely obtained from classical texts. So in one sense the New Testament documents provide evidence for urban life in the Greek East alongside rhetorical performances, travelogues, as well as the richness of epigraphy. Indeed, the texts help us to go beyond the muted archaeological evidence of building plans and the stratified debris of occupation.[10]

2. Corinth

The classical city of Corinth was destroyed in 146 BCE and the site deserted. The location was largely deserted for nearly a century until it was founded as a colony by Julius Caesar in 44 BCE.[11] A recent study has been able to identify the limited evidence for occupation in the intervening period.[12] Corinth was one of a limited number of colonies in the province of Achaia.[13] Two others were located in the northern Peloponnese at Dyme and Patrai.[14] A further colony was established at Buthrotum (modern Butrint) in Epirus.[15] Corinth itself was of strategic importance as it commanded the isthmus of Corinth with the two major ports of Cenchreae (on the Saronic Gulf, giving access to the eastern Mediterranean) and Lechaeum (on the Gulf of Corinth, and providing access to Italy).

Considerable research has focused on the Corinthian correspondence and the early church in this colonial setting.[16] This area has drawn on the

Roman Setting, BAFCS 2 (Grand Rapids: Eerdmans, 1994); Daniel Sperber, The City in Roman Palestine (Oxford: Oxford University Press, 1998).

10. For provincial overviews see, e.g., Susan E. Alcock, Graecia Capta: The Landscapes of Roman Greece (Cambridge: Cambridge University Press, 1993); Stephen Mitchell, Anatolia. Land, Men, and Gods in Asia Minor, 2 vols. (Oxford: Clarendon, 1993); Fergus Millar, The Roman Near East 31 BC–AD 337 (Cambridge, MA: Harvard University Press, 1993).

11. Mary E. Hoskins Walbank, "The Foundation and Planning of Early Roman Corinth," JRA 10 (1997): 95–130.

12. Benjamin W. Millis, "'Miserable Huts' in Post-146 BC Corinth," Hesperia 75 (2006): 397–404.

13. For a map of colonies in Achaia and Macedonia, see Alcock, Graecia Capta, 134, fig. 46.

14. For this region: R. Dalongeville, Maria Lakakis, and Athanassios D. Rizakis, eds., Paysages d'Achaie: le bassin du Peiros et la plaine occidentale, Meletēmata 15 (Athens: De Boccard, 1992); Athanassios D. Rizakis, Achaie I. Sources textuelles et histoire regionale, Meletēmata 20 (Athens: De Boccard, 1995).

15. Inge Lyse Hansen, Hellenistic and Roman Butrint (London: Butrint Foundation, 2009).

16. E.g., Andrew D. Clarke, Secular and Christian Leadership in Corinth: A Socio-

literary, epigraphic, historical, and archaeological sources to demonstrate that the appropriate setting for Paul's epistles was not the Hellenistic city, destroyed in the mid–second century BCE, but rather the Roman colony established by Julius Caesar.[17] Excavations by the American School of Classical Studies at Athens have demonstrated that in the first two centuries of the colony Latin was the public language, gradually being eased out from the mid–second century onward.[18] This Roman character of the city was reflected in the coins issued there.[19] The range of Roman cults was also linked to the status of the colony, and the long-established sanctuary of Aphrodite on Acrocorinth became linked to Venus, the mythical ancestor of Julius Caesar.[20] Field survey work has detected the use of centuriation in the laying out of the colony and its territory with a grid system.[21] The

historical and Exegetical Study of 1 Corinthians 1–6, AGJU 18 (Leiden: Brill, 1993); David W. J. Gill, "Corinth: A Roman Colony in Achaea," *BZ* 37 (1993): 259–64; Bruce W. Winter, *After Paul Left Corinth: The Influence of Secular Ethics and Social Change* (Grand Rapids: Eerdmans, 2001). For the Corinthian correspondence against a background of ancient literary, epigraphic, and archaeological evidence: David W. J. Gill, "1 Corinthians," in *Romans to Philemon,* vol. 3 of *Zondervan Illustrated Bible Backgrounds Commentary,* ed. Clint E. Arnold (Grand Rapids: Zondervan, 2002), 100–193; David W. J. Gill and Moyer V. Hubbard, *1 and 2 Corinthians,* Zondervan Illustrated Bible Backgrounds Commentary (Grand Rapids: Zondervan, 2007).

17. Gill, "Corinth: a Roman Colony in Achaea." For a history of the colony: D. Engels, *Roman Corinth: An Alternative Model for the Classical City* (Chicago: University of Chicago, 1990), but see the correcting views in A. J. S. Spawforth, "Roman Corinth and the Ancient Urban Economy," *CR* 42 (1992): 119–20.

18. John Harvey Kent, *The Inscriptions, 1926–1950,* Corinth 8 Part 3 (Princeton: American School of Classical Studies at Athens, 1966); M. Šašel Kos, "A Latin Epitaph of a Roman Legionary from Corinth," *JRS* 68 (1978): 22–25.

19. Mary E. Hoskins Walbank, "Aspects of Corinthian Coins in the Late 1st and Early 2nd Centuries AC," in *Corinth, The Centenary: 1896–1996,* ed. Charles K. Williams II and Nancy Bookidis, Corinth 20 (Princeton: American School of Classical Studies at Athens, 2003), 337–49.

20. Charles K. Williams II, "The Refounding of Corinth: Some Roman Religious Attitudes," in *Roman Architecture in the Greek World,* ed. Sarah Macready and F. H. Thompson, Occasional Papers NS 10 (London: Society of Antiquaries of London, 1987), 26–37.

21. David Gilman Romano, "City Planning, Centuriation, and Land Division in Roman Corinth: Colonia Laus Iulia Corinthiensis and Colonia Iulia Flavia Augusta Corinthiensis," in *Corinth, The Centenary: 1896–1996,* ed. Charles K. Williams II and Nancy Bookidis, Corinth 20 (Princeton: American School of Classical Studies at Athens, 2003), 279–301; David Gilman Romano, "Roman Surveyors in Corinth," *PAPS* 150 (2006): 62–85. For a response to Romano see Mary E. Hoskins Walbank, "What's in a Name? Corinth under the Flavians," *ZPE* 139 (2002): 251–64. See also David Gilman Romano, *Athletics and Mathematics in Archaic Corinth,* MAPS 206 (Philadelphia: American Philosophical Society, 1993).

architectural heart of the forum area reflected the Roman nature of the architecture.[22]

The role of women in the early church at Corinth, identified from the Corinthian correspondence, has been set against epigraphic documents such as the Iunia Theodora dossier celebrating a mid–first century CE Lycian resident of the Roman colony.[23] The series of documents laid out in the inscription are a reminder that a colony such as Corinth, especially with its major harbors, had become a major regional hub with influence beyond its immediate province. New Testament studies have been enhanced, enriched, and strengthened by these new approaches. Classical archaeology, epigraphy, and ancient history no longer need to be deployed merely to confirm the veracity of New Testament documents; for example, the finding of the Erastus piazza inscription outside the theater at Corinth is perhaps linked to the person of the same name who served as the *oikonomos* of the city mentioned in Paul's closing words to the church at Rome.[24] The debate is whether this Greek civic term translates the Latin magistracy of the aedile. Rather, these approaches to the classical world can be deployed to add depth to the background for the interpretation of the New Testament.

The role of the colony as the administrative center for the province is reflected by the attraction of the social elites to the city.[25] Thus the Euryclids, one of the leading families at Sparta who gained citizenship under Augustus, seem to have migrated to Corinth while supporting major projects in Laconia.[26] Among the family members who played an important provincial role

22. Mary E. Hoskins Walbank, "Pausanias, Octavia and Temple E at Corinth," *ASBA* 84 (1989): 361–94.

23. Demetrios I. Pallas, Séraphin Charitonidis, and Jacques Vénencie, "Inscriptions lyciennes trouvées à Solômos près de Corinthe," *BCH* 83 (1959): 496–508; Rosalinde A. Kearsley, "Women in Public Life in the Roman East: Iunia Theodora, Claudia Metrodora and Phoebe, Benefactress of Paul," *TynBul* 50 (1999): 189–211.

24. Rom 16:23. David W. J. Gill, "Erastus the Aedile," *TynBul* 40 (1989): 293–301. See also Andrew D. Clarke, "Another Corinthian Erastus Inscription," *TynBul* 42 (1991): 146–51; L. L. Welborn, *An End to Enmity: Paul and the "Wrongdoer" of Second Corinthians*, BZNW 185 (Berlin: de Gruyter, 2011), 260–83.

25. Antony J. S. Spawforth, "Roman Corinth: The Formation of a Colonial Élite," in *Roman Onomastics in the Greek East: Social and Political Aspects*, ed. Athanassios D. Rizakis, Meletēmata 21 (Athens: De Boccard, 1996), 167–82.

26. Paul Cartledge and Antony Spawforth, *Hellenistic and Roman Sparta: A Tale of Two Cities*, States and Cities of Ancient Greece (London: Routledge, 1989), 103–4. See also Antony J. S. Spawforth, "Balbilla, the Euryclids and Memorials for a Greek Magnate," *ABSA* 73 (1978): 249–60.

was G. Julius Spartiaticus.[27] This pivotal role of Corinth is reflected in the honorific inscription to L. Licinnius Anteros who was granted grazing rights in the polis of Methana in the Peloponnese during the reign of Augustus in return for representing the people in the political heart of the Roman province.[28] These networks suggest a strategy whereby a church established in the provincial center would have an impact in the *poleis* and regions within the province itself. Intensive field surveys in Greece are providing important information about land use in the first century CE, suggesting that the farmers were living in the urban centers and traveling to their land holdings.[29]

3. Philippi

Philippi in Macedonia was one of the key cities on the Via Egnatia that linked the eastern provinces with Rome itself.[30] Excavations by the École française d'Athènes have revealed remains of the colony's forum and administrative buildings, as well as a series of Late Antique basilicas.[31] The city's origins lay with the

27. His role is discussed in detail by Bruce W. Winter, *Divine Honours for the Caesars: The First Christians' Responses* (Grand Rapids: Eerdmans, 2015), 197–209.

28. *IG* 4.853; Lin Foxhall, David W. J. Gill, and Hamish A. Forbes, "The Inscriptions of Methana," in *A Rough and Rocky Place: The Landscape and Settlement History of the Methana Peninsula, Greece. Results of the Methana Survey Project Sponsored by the British School at Athens and the University of Liverpool*, ed. Christopher B. Mee and Hamish A. Forbes (Liverpool: Liverpool University Press, 1997), 273–74, no. 15. The inscription is dated to 1/2 CE, using the new "Actian era" adopted in Achaia.

29. See William Andrew McDonald and George Robert Rapp Jr., eds., *The Minnesota Messenia Expedition: Reconstructing a Bronze Age Regional Environment* (Minneapolis: University of Minnesota Press, 1972); Michael H. Jameson, Curtis N. Runnels, and Tjeerd van Andel, eds., *A Greek Countryside: The Southern Argolid from Prehistory to the Present Day* (Stanford: Stanford University Press, 1994); Rizakis, *Achaie I*; Christopher B. Mee and Hamish A. Forbes, eds., *A Rough and Rocky Place: The Landscape and Settlement History of the Methana Peninsula, Greece. Results of the Methana Survey Project Sponsored by the British School at Athens and the University of Liverpool* (Liverpool: Liverpool University Press, 1997); William Cavanagh, Joost Crouwel, R. W. V. Catling, and Graham Shipley, *The Lakonia Survey: Archaeological Data*, vol. 2 of *Continuity and Change in a Greek Rural Landscape*, BSASup 27 (London: British School at Athens, 1996); *The Lakonia Survey: Methodology and Interpretation*, vol. 1 of *Continuity and Change in a Greek Rural Landscape*, BSASup 26 (London: British School at Athens, 2002).

30. Acts 16:11–40.

31. For a useful overview see Michel Sève, "Philippes: une ville romaine en Grèce" and "Le forum de Philippes," in *L'espace grec. 150 ans de fouilles de l'École française d'Athènes*, ed. Marie-Dominique Nenna (Paris: Fayard, 1996), 89–94, 123–31.

foundation of a settlement by Philip II of Macedon in 365 BCE.[32] The settlement was able to exploit the gold mines found in the vicinity of Mount Pangaion.[33] The Roman colony, *Colonia Augusta Iulia Philippensis*, was established after the battle fought nearby in 42 BCE between Brutus and Cassius, the assassins of Julius Caesar, and Octavian and Mark Antony.[34] The colony was further enhanced by additional settlers following Octavian's victory at Actium in 31 BCE.

Like Corinth, the presence of Latin epigraphy is clear. A prominent example is the funerary monument of C. Vibius Quartus, dating to the first century CE, that lay to the east of the colony.[35] Quartus had served in the V Macedonian legion, and at the end of his career was the military tribune of the II Augustan legion.[36] A long podium at the northeast corner of the forum, adjacent to the temple housing the imperial cult, supported a series of statues of whom four were priestesses of Livia, wife of the emperor Augustus.[37] The base itself, measuring over 7 m in length, may have been erected in the second century CE. In the forum itself there are dedications, some recording benefactions, by L. Tatinius Cnosus, a former soldier in the Praetorian cohort and the XI urban cohort, probably dating to the reign of Domitian.[38] The forum itself was laid out in a Roman plan with Roman architecture adopted for the major public buildings.[39] Some of the earliest work appears to date to the reign of the emperor Claudius.

32. C. Koukouli-Chrysanthaki and Charalambos Bakirtzis, *Philippi* (Athens: Ministry of Culture, 2003); C. Koukouli-Chrysanthaki, "Philippi," in *Brill's Companion to Ancient Macedonia: Studies in Archaeology and the History of Macedonia, 650 BC–300 AD*, ed. Robin J. Lane Fox (Leiden: Brill, 2011), 437–52.

33. Robert Shepherd, *Ancient Mining* (London: Institution of Mining and Metallurgy by Elsevier Applied Science, 1993), 100–102.

34. Appian, *Bell. civ.* 4.105–38.

35. *CIL* 3.647. Athanassios D. Rizakis, "La carrière équestre de C. Vibius Quartus," *Mélanges de l'école française de Rome. Antiquité* 115 (2003): 535–48.

36. For other officers of the II Augustan legion, see Anthony R. Birley, *Officers of the Second Augustan Legion in Britain* (Cardiff: National Museum of Wales, 1990).

37. P. Weber and Michel Sève, "Un monument honorifique au forum de Philippes," *BCH* 112 (1988): 467–79; Michel Sève, "Philippes: une ville romaine en Grèce," in *L'espace grec. 150 ans de fouilles de l'École française d'Athènes*, ed. Marie-Dominique Nenna (Paris: Fayard, 1996), 88–94, 127 (illustration). See also Marie-Dominique Poncin, "Les prêtrises publiques dans la colonie de Philippes," *Cahiers du Centre Gustave Glotz* 12 (2001): 229–52.

38. Paul Collart, "Inscriptions de Philippes," *BCH* 56 (1932): 213–22, nos. 8–9; Paul Collart, "Inscriptions de Philippes," *BCH* 62 (1938): 420–21, no. 7; Weber and Sève, "Un monument honorifique," 472. Cnosus appears to have originated in Philippi.

39. Patrick Weber and Michel Sève, "Le côté Nord du forum de Philippes," *BCH* 110 (1986): 531–81.

And in the city we find Paul interacting with Lydia, a woman who held a position of commercial power within the community.[40] Through Acts it is possible to glimpse the colonial administration at Philippi responding to men who were perceived to be trouble-makers, and then whose status as Roman citizens was revealed to great consternation.[41]

4. Pisidian Antioch

Earlier in Acts Paul had visited the Augustan colony of Pisidian Antioch that lay within the province of Galatia.[42] The site was first identified in the autumn of 1833 by Francis Arundell, followed swiftly by a study conducted by W. J. Hamilton in 1835.[43] In the late nineteenth century there was a growing interest in Anatolia through the work of William Ramsay and the Asia Minor Exploration Fund, and the American topographer J. R. S. Sterrett.[44] Ramsay himself made a more detailed study of the colony in 1905 and he published a full account two years later.[45] More substantial excavations were conducted under the direction of D. M. Robertson during the 1920s.[46] Further survey

40. Acts 16:14.

41. Acts 16:37–39.

42. Acts 13:14–52.

43. Details of early visitors to Pisidian Antioch can be found in Stephen Mitchell and Marc Waelkens, *Pisidian Antioch: The Site and Its Monuments* (London: Duckworth / Classical Press of Wales, 1998), 19–35.

44. For the Asia Minor Exploration Fund: David W. J. Gill, "The British School at Athens and Archaeological Research in the Late Ottoman Empire," in *Archaeology, Anthropology and Heritage in the Balkans and Anatolia: The Life and Times of F.W. Hasluck, 1878–1920,* ed. D. Shankland (Istanbul: Isis, 2004), 1:223–55. For Sterrett: Stephen L. Dyson, *Ancient Marbles to American Shores: Classical Archaeology in the United States* (Philadelphia: University of Pennsylvania Press, 1998).

45. William M. Ramsay, *The Cities of St. Paul: Their Influence on His Life and Thought. The Cities of Eastern Asia Minor,* Dale Memorial Lectures 1907 (London: Hodder and Stoughton, 1907), 246–314; William M. Ramsay, "Colonia Caesarea (Pisidian Antioch) in the Augustan Age," *JRS* 6 (1916): 83–134. For Ramsay's notebooks: Maurice A. Byrne and Guy Labarre, eds., *Nouvelles inscriptions d'Antioche de Pisidie d'après les note-books de W. M. Ramsay,* IGSK 67 (Bonn: Habelt, 2006). For research on Pisidian Antioch in a wider archaeological context: David W. J. Gill, *Sifting the Soil of Greece: The Early Years of the British School at Athens (1886–1919),* BICSSup 111 (London: Institute of Classical Studies, 2011).

46. David M. Robinson, "A Preliminary Report on the Excavations at Pisidian Antioch and at Sizma," *AJA* 28 (1924): 435–44.

work was undertaken by Stephen Mitchell in the early 1980s.[47] Although the New Testament background interest has been in the substantial Jewish community in the colony,[48] a study of the archaeological and epigraphic evidence sheds more light on the background to Acts and, it would suggest, the epistle to the Galatians.

a. Paul's Arrival in Pisidian Antioch

The decision for Paul and his companions to travel through southern Galatia can be highlighted by looking at the immediate Roman background. Barnabas and Paul had left Antioch in Syria for Cyprus, and using the newly constructed Augustan road system, arrived at Paphos, the base for the Roman governor.[49] It was there that Sergius Paulus, the governor (ἀνθύπατος), witnessed the blinding of the magician (μάγος) Elymas and subsequently responded to the Christian message; "then the proconsul believed, when he saw what had occurred, for he was astonished at the teaching of the Lord" (Acts 13:12). Sergius Paulus is known from outside the New Testament documents.[50] He is recorded as one of the water commissioners at Rome during the reign of the emperor Claudius and subsequently becomes suffect consul in 70 CE under Vespasian;[51] as Stephen Mitchell has observed, "he was, as far as we know, the first person of eastern origin to reach that rank."[52]

The family of the Sergii Pauli appears to come from the colony of Pisidian Antioch, and the extent of the family estate is well documented.[53] William M. Calder and William Ramsay were able to establish the extent of the estate in Galatia thanks to the funerary monument of Cn. Cornelius Severinus, the *decurialis viator* of Cn. Pinarius Cornelius Severus; the mon-

47. Mitchell and Waelkens, *Pisidian Antioch*.

48. Paul R. Trebilco, *Jewish Communities in Asia Minor*, SNTSMS 69 (Cambridge: Cambridge University Press, 1991), 21–24. See also Mitchell, *Anatolia*, 2:31–37.

49. Acts 13:4–13. See also David W. J. Gill, "Paul's Travels through Cyprus (Acts 13:4–12)," *TynBul* 46 (1995): 219–28.

50. Gill, "Roman Empire," 389.

51. Alanna Nobbs, "Cyprus," in *The Book of Acts in Its Greco-Roman Setting*, ed. David W. J. Gill and Conrad H. Gempf, BAFCS 2 (Grand Rapids: Eerdmans, 1994), 279–89; Mitchell, *Anatolia*, 1:152; Mitchell, *Anatolia*, 2:6–7; Mitchell and Waelkens, *Pisidian Antioch*, 10. For the inscription from Rome, see *CIL* 6.31545.

52. Mitchell and Waelkens, *Pisidian Antioch*, 10.

53. William M. Ramsay, "Studies in the Roman Province Galatia," *JRS* 16 (1926): 202–6.

ument itself was erected by Severus's wife Sergia L. f. Paullina, a descendant of Sergius Paulus.[54]

It is perhaps significant that it is at this point in the narrative of Acts, as Paul moves from Cyprus to Anatolia, that Saul takes the Roman *cognomen* Paulus.[55] Notice the way that Paul and Barnabas do not appear to stay in Pamphylia:

> Now Paul and his companions set sail from Paphos and came to Perga in Pamphylia. And John left them and returned to Jerusalem, but they went on from Perga and came to Antioch in Pisidia. (Acts 13:13-14)

The change of name to Paul and the subsequent arrival at Pisidian Antioch are perhaps linked. Mitchell has drawn this conclusion: "the proconsul himself had suggested to Paul that he make it his next port of call, no doubt providing him with letters of introduction to aid his passage and his stay."[56] If Mitchell is correct, then Paul would have come to a city with close links to the heart of empire through its association with a senatorial family. Access to the colony would also have been made easy through the construction of new roads, especially the Via Sebaste, into the interior of Anatolia.[57]

b. Chief Men of the City (Acts 13:50)

Paul arrived in a colony that aimed to replicate the city of Rome's architecture of cityscape. Preliminary epigraphic studies by William Ramsay and then by the American and British archaeological teams at the modern Yalvaç have revealed much about the city.[58] Detailed prosopographical work by Barbara Levick has shed light on the detail about the colonial families

54. Mitchell, *Anatolia*, 1:151.

55. Mitchell, *Anatolia*, 2:7 (with earlier references).

56. Mitchell, *Anatolia*, 2:7; Mitchell and Waelkens, *Pisidian Antioch*, 12. Contrast: Wayne A. Meeks, *The First Urban Christians: The Social World of the Apostle Paul* (New Haven: Yale University Press, 1983), 42.

57. David H. French, "The Roman Road-system of Asia Minor," *ANRW* 2.7.2:698-729; David H. French, *Roman Roads and Milestones of Asia Minor,* fasc. 2: *An Interim Catalogue of Milestones,* BAR I 392 (Oxford: British Archaeological Reports, 1988).

58. Barbara Levick, *Roman Colonies in Southern Asia Minor* (Oxford: Oxford University Press, 1967); Mitchell and Waelkens, *Pisidian Antioch*.

especially in the early decades of its foundation.[59] Such studies are key for understanding the reception of Paul and Barnabas. Initially they received a hearing in the synagogue, and later the whole city (πόλις) heard their message;[60] but then there was a change:

> But the Jews incited the devout women of high standing (αἱ σεβόμεναι γυναῖκες αἱ εὐσχήμονες) and the leading men of the city (οἱ πρῶτοι τῆς πόλεως), stirred up persecution against Paul and Barnabas, and drove them out of their district. (Acts 13:50)

Luke seems to be making a distinction here between the Jews and the gentile elite of the colony. His contact has gone beyond the people of Israel and God-fearers first addressed in the synagogue.[61] Mitchell cites an inscription from Acmonia in Phrygia where a gentile woman, Iulia Severa, became the benefactor of the synagogue; he has suggested that there may well have been a strong interest in the synagogue at Pisidian Antioch from the elite colonial families.[62] So what might have happened? Paul presented the gospel in one of the synagogues of the city. Among his hearers were members of the Antioch social elite who had taken an interest in the Jewish community resident in the city.[63] But when members of the gentile social elite responded to the gospel, the Jewish community were worried that their place in the colony might be threatened.

c. "Elementary Principles of the World" (Gal 4)

I am now going to assume that the epistle to the Galatians was addressed to the Christian communities in the southern part of the province of Galatia, communities such as those at Pisidian Antioch, which were established as a result of the preaching of Paul and Barnabas recorded in Acts 13 and 14.[64] It seems less likely that Paul is addressing his letter to communities in cities

---

59. Barbara Levick, "Two Pisidian Colonial Families," *JRS* 48 (1958): 74–78; Barbara Levick, "Two Inscriptions from Pisidian Antioch," *AntSt* 15 (1965): 53–62; Barbara Levick, "Unpublished Inscriptions from Pisidian Antioch," *AntSt* 17 (1967): 101–21.

60. Acts 13:14, 44.

61. Acts 13:16. See also Mitchell, *Anatolia*, 2:8.

62. Mitchell, *Anatolia*, 2:8–9.

63. See also Mitchell and Waelkens, *Pisidian Antioch*, 12.

64. F. F. Bruce, *The Epistle of Paul to the Galatians: A Commentary on the Greek Text*, NIGTC (Exeter: Paternoster, 1982).

such as Ancyra that were located in the northern part of the province. One of the key issues in the first three chapters of Galatians is that Christians from a gentile background need not adopt Jewish customs: "how can you force the gentiles to live like Jews?" (Gal 2:14).

In chapter 4, Paul explores the importance of inheritance. He makes two curious points:

> In the same way we also, when we were children, were enslaved to the elementary principles of the world. (v. 3)
>
> Formerly, when you did not know God, you were enslaved to those that by nature are not gods. But now that you have come to know God, or rather to be known by God, how can you turn back again to the weak and worthless elementary principles of the world, whose slaves you want to be once more? (vv. 8–9 ESV)

Paul uses two phrases: "to the elementary principles of the world" (ὑπὸ τὰ στοιχεῖα τοῦ κόσμου) and "to the weak and worthless elementary principles of the world" (ἐπὶ τὰ ἀσθενῆ καὶ πτωχὰ στοιχεῖα). In the first instance Paul seems to be talking to those from a Jewish background, which included himself: "we also, when we were children . . ." It seems to pick up on the themes of the end of chapter 3: "Now before faith came, we were held captive under the law" (3:23). Is the Mosaic law to be considered by Jews an "elementary principle of the world"?

In the second passage, is Paul addressing those from a gentile background who were enslaved by the "principles" (στοιχεῖα)? Would a gentile understand the term in a different way? The gentile interpretation is supported by the idea that they had formerly been enslaved "to those that by nature are not gods." The idea is similar to that used by Paul in another Roman colony, Corinth, when he discusses food that had been offered to idols:

> . . . we know that an idol has no real existence, and that there is no God but one. For although there may be so-called gods in heaven or on earth—as indeed there are many gods and many lords—yet for us there is one God, the Father, from whom are all things and for whom we exist, and one Lord, Jesus Christ, through whom are all things and through whom we exist. (1 Cor 8:4–6)

Στοιχεῖα can be translated as "elementary principles" or perhaps the "elementary building blocks"; literally "the ABCs of the world." If these were gentiles they would not have been enslaved to the Mosaic law; so what is Paul alluding to here? Philo observes that some define (and indeed deify) αἱ τέσσαρες ἀρχαί—the four elements—as "earth, water, air and fire" (γῆ καὶ ὕδωρ καὶ ἀήρ καὶ πῦρ) or "the sun and moon and the other planets and fixed stars; others again the heaven alone; others the whole world" (δ᾽ ἥλιον καὶ σελήνην καὶ τοὺς ἄλλους πλανήτας καὶ ἀπλανεῖς ἀστέρας, οἱ δὲ μόνον τὸν οὐρανόν, οἱ δὲ τὸν σύμπαντα κόσμον).[65]

New Testament scholars have tended to interpret this against the background of the Olympian or Capitoline deities (e.g., Zeus/Jupiter, Aphrodite/Venus), or sometimes an indigenous Anatolian cult like that of Cybele.[66] However, there is a much stronger candidate at Pisidian Antioch for this Pauline allusion. The main extramural sanctuary of the Roman colony was that of Mên Askaênos, located at Karaküyü in the hills above the colony.[67] This was the key cult for the colony and described as πάτριος θεός,[68] the god of our forefathers (τοῦ πατρίου θεοῦ Μηνός). This classical sanctuary had probably been established in the Seleucid period. Strabo described it as follows:

> [Antioch] is on a hill and has a colony of Romans. The latter [sc. Antioch] was settled by Magnetans who lived near the Maeander river. . . .
> Here there was also a priesthood of Mên Arcaeus, which had a number of temple-slaves and sacred places, but the priesthood was destroyed after the death of Amyntas by those who were sent thither as his inheritors.[69]

The temple was classical in form, Ionic peripteral, and stood in a colonnaded courtyard.[70] Coins of the cult statue standing in the temple suggest that Mên

65. Philo, *Decal.* 53 (F. H. Colson, LCL). Cited in Bruce, *Galatians*, 193.

66. E.g., Susan M. Elliott, "Choose Your Mother, Choose Your Master: Galatians 4:21–5:1 in the Shadow of the Anatolian Mother of the Gods," *JBL* 118 (1999): 661–83.

67. Margaret M. Hardie, "The Shrine of Mên Askaênos at Pisidian Antioch," *JHS* 32 (1912): 111–50; J. G. C. Anderson, "Festivals of Mên Askaênos in the Roman Colony at Antioch of Pisidia," *JRS* 3 (1913): 267–300. See also David W. J. Gill, "Behind the Classical Façade, Local Religions in the Roman Empire," in *One Lord, One God: Christianity in a World of Religious Pluralism*, ed. Andrew D. Clarke and Bruce W. Winter, 2nd ed. (Grand Rapids: Baker, 1992), 85–100; Mitchell, *Anatolia*, 2:9–10.

68. E.g., the victory monuments of Ti. Claudius Marcianus, L. Plotius Marcianus, Cn. Dottius Magnus, and Iulius Cordius Theodoros: Anderson, "Festivals of Mên Askaênos," 286–89, nos. 12–16.

69. Strabo, *Geogr.* 12.8.14 (Jones, LCL).

70. Mitchell and Waelkens, *Pisidian Antioch*, 50–57.

was represented anthropomorphically. However it is also clear that this was not how the worshippers of Mên considered him.[71] Dedications by visitors to the cult center have been found cut onto rocks along the route leading from the colony; others were cut onto the outer blocks of the sanctuary itself; and a number of freestanding stelae have been found. These dedications tell us much about the status of individuals: from freedmen to the elite of the colony.[72] One of the key elements is that Mên was not represented anthropomorphically but instead as a crescent moon. The frequency of crescent moons on a dedication may allude to the number of times that a dedicant had performed specific acts of worship in the sanctuary. Could this moon be one of the "elementary principles" alluded to by Paul in connection with those Christians who had come from a gentile rather than a Jewish background?

It is clear that the people of Pisidian Antioch were also perplexed and puzzled by this deity of Mên. One of the ways that this becomes clear is the way that the elites started to make dedications to Luna, the Roman personification of the moon; but Mên was a male deity. For example, C. Albucius Firmus, who held the rank of both aedile and *duovir* in the colony, helped to establish through his will an athletic event in association with the festival of Luna.[73] This is sometimes obscured in the Latin, rather than Greek dedications, where the dedication itself appears in abbreviated form, LVS, which has been interpreted by Lane as *Luno* (or *Lunae*) *votum solvit*.[74]

It is now clear that the cult of Mên was especially popular in the first century CE. A Greek-style agonistic festival in the god's honor, and apparently held in the mini-stadium at Karaküyü, was established by a member of the civic elite Maximianus and named in his honor, the Maximianeia. The festival seems to have been discontinued, perhaps through lack of sufficient money, and re-established in the 160s during the co-regency of Marcus Aurelius and Lucius Verus and continued into the third century.[75]

---

71. For some of the dedications: Barbara Levick, "Dedications to Mên Askaenos," *AnSt* 20 (1970): 37–50; Eugene N. Lane, *Corpus monumentorum religionis dei Menis (CMRDM)*, 4 vols., EPRO 19 (Leiden: Brill, 1971–1978), vols. 1, 3 and 4.

72. For the elite: C. Ulpius Baebianus and his sister Ulpia Cornelia: Lane, *CMRDM* 4:32, no. 81. See also Mitchell and Waelkens, *Pisidian Antioch*, 13.

73. *CIL* 3.295, 6829. See *CMRDM* 1:113–14, no. 178. See also Mitchell and Waelkens, *Pisidian Antioch*, 13.

74. *CMRDM* 1:100–101, no. 160.

75. The chronology proposed in Anderson, "Festivals of Mên Askaênos," is too late. For caution: Mitchell, *Anatolia*, 2:10 n. 70. A summary of the issues is given by Mitchell and Waelkens, *Pisidian Antioch*, 13.

d. Imperial Cult (Gal 6)

Apart from the cult of Mên, the other main religious focus at Pisidian Antioch was on the imperial cult.[76] The sanctuary for the imperial cult was located in the eastern part of the city and was entered via a monumental propylon that celebrated Augustus's victories.[77] The inside face of the propylon appears to have carried copies of the text of Augustus's *Res Gestae* that were displayed outside the Mausoleum of Augustus in Rome.[78] The gate itself carried a bronze inscription commemorating Augustus that seems to have been dedicated soon after 5 February 2 BCE.[79] The imperial temple, constructed in the Corinthian order, was begun under Tiberius.

The imperial cult may have formed the setting for Galatians 6.[80] Christian converts from a gentile background would be placed in a difficult position; should they continue to be involved in the imperial cult as part of their obligation as Roman citizens, or should they desist along with Jews who were identified as a *religio licita*?[81] Could Christian converts from a Jewish background have suggested circumcision, adherence to the law, and therefore legal protection to their brethren from a gentile background?[82] Pisidian Antioch may well have been one of the first places that the spreading Christian church came into direct contact with the imperial cult in such a developed form. Winter has explored the compulsion for the gentile Christians in Pisidian Antioch to be circumcised and notes Paul's reason for this action: "in order that they may not be persecuted for the cross of Christ" (Gal 6:12).

---

76. Mitchell, *Anatolia*, 1:104; Mitchell and Waelkens, *Pisidian Antioch*, 113–73; Bruce W. Winter, *Divine Honours for the Caesars: The First Christians' Responses* (Grand Rapids: Eerdmans, 2015), 226–49.

77. David M. Robinson, "Roman Sculptures from Colonia Caesarea (Pisidian Antioch)," *ArtB* 9 (1926): 5–69; Mitchell and Waelkens, *Pisidian Antioch*, 146–47.

78. Mitchell and Waelkens, *Pisidian Antioch*, 146.

79. Maurice A. Byrne, "The Date of the City Gate of Antioch," in *Actes du Ier Congrès international sur Antioche du Pisidie*, ed. Thomas Drew-Bear, Mehmet Taşlıalan, and Christine M. Thomas (Lyon: Université Lumière-Lyon, 2002), 193–200; see also Mitchell and Waelkens, *Pisidian Antioch*, 147.

80. Bruce W. Winter, *Seek the Welfare of the City: Christians as Benefactors and Citizens* (Grand Rapids: Eerdmans, 1994), 123–43; Bruce W. Winter, "The Imperial Cult and the Early Christians in Pisidian Antioch (Acts 13 and Galatians 6)," in *First International Conference on Antioch in Pisidia*, ed. Thomas Drew-Bear, Mehmet Taşlıalan, and Christine M. Thomas (Ismit: Kocaeli, 2000), 60–68; Bruce W. Winter, *Divine Honours*, 226–49.

81. Winter, *Seek the Welfare*, 135.

82. Winter, *Seek the Welfare*, 136.

As Winter notes: "Those Gentiles who joined them and observed the Jewish law in daily life would, as Jewish converts, be exempt from the imperial cult."[83] Such an action would give the gentile converts "a good showing," or as Winter has explained it, a good legal status.[84]

A further passage may be linked to the imperial cult. Paul wrote to the Christian community in Galatia, in a section probably addressed to gentile converts: "you observe days and months and seasons and years! I am afraid I may have labored over you in vain" (Gal 4:10–11). Mitchell makes the point that the Roman calendar gave the members of the colony a framework for worshipping the emperor.[85] A Christian from a gentile background would be expected to take part and conform to the pagan norm; and this would be seen as going back to the elementary principles of the world. A Jewish Christian would however be exempt from such requirements; and so it can be understood how there would be an appeal for Christians from a gentile background to adopt Jewish customs.

If Winter is correct, adherence to Jewish customs by gentile converts in a city with a focus on the imperial cult can be understood as giving protection to the Christian community. Paul, however, was alarmed by these developments and the epistle to the Galatians explores the implications for the Galatian Christians in following that route to protect themselves from the worship of the emperor.

e. Hunts and Fighting the Beasts at Ephesus (1 Corinthians 15:32)

One of the allusions in the Corinthian correspondence is to fighting wild animals at Ephesus (1 Cor 15:32). There is a view that such an image would be inappropriate in the eastern provinces where wild-animal hunts were not part of the cultural background for the Greek population. However, a first century CE inscription from Pisidian Antioch relating to a Maximianus shows that wild-animal hunts (*venationes*) and, indeed, gladiatorial shows did take place in Anatolia.[86] This is supported by a second inscription, probably also dating to the first century CE, which records the present of a wooden amphitheater.[87] In the inscription, L. Calpurnius Longus is recorded as the

83. Winter, *Seek the Welfare*, 137.
84. Winter, *Seek the Welfare*, 139.
85. Mitchell, *Anatolia*, 2:10.
86. Anderson, "Festivals of Mên Askaênos."
87. *CIL* 3.6832. William M. Ramsay, "Studies in the Roman Province Galatia," *JRS* 14

first person to promise a *munus* in which gladiators—at least 36 pairs—would fight over an eight-day period. Other amphitheaters in the Greek East are attested by epigraphic and archaeological evidence.[88] Such shows may have been associated with the imperial cult that was certainly active in Antioch at this point.[89]

5. Conclusion

A study of the biblical texts, namely Acts and the epistles to the churches in the colonies of Corinth, Philippi, and Pisidian Antioch, shows how early Christianity developed in Roman urban settings. Converts to Christianity found themselves having to interact with the colonial calendar, civic functions, and religious festivals that were part of the fabric of what were intended as replicas of the city of Rome in the eastern provinces.

The epistle to the Galatians is a good example of how classical scholarship—incorporating epigraphic and archaeological work—can enhance the reading of the biblical text. Likewise, Christian texts provide insights for the social dynamic of life in cities in the eastern Roman Empire. Elite patronage, rivalries, the role of local religious customs as well as the imperial cult all appear to be reflected in Galatians and the corresponding sections in Acts. These issues pose questions. How did the Christian gospel gain a hearing in the cities of the classical world? What were the barriers to faith? How did the first gentile converts try to find a new urban identity when they started to follow Christ? What was the relationship with Judaism? There are hints within the New Testament texts that there were Christians from among the social elite at Pisidian Antioch. Such a strategy for Paul's teaching anticipated the situation in Corinth where members of the colonial elite appear to have been active in the church community.

We can take encouragement from the way that recent research has started to bridge the gap between studies of the diversity of classical urban life in the first century CE and New Testament scholarship. Cousland, writing at the end of the last millennium, has made the key observation: "One of the encouraging features of New Testament scholarship over the last two

---

(1924): 178–79, no. 5; David M. Robinson, "Notes on Inscriptions from Antioch in Pisidia," *JRS* 15 (1925): 253–62; Louis Robert, *Les gladiateurs dans l'Orient grec*, BEHE.H 278 (Paris: Champion, 1940), 140, no. 92; Mitchell and Waelkens, *Pisidian Antioch*, 224–25, no. 7.

88. Mitchell and Waelkens, *Pisidian Antioch*, 225.

89. Mitchell and Waelkens, *Pisidian Antioch*, 225.

decades has been the tendency to interpret the NT within the larger confines of the Classical world."[90]

Other scholars have commented that the research on Acts has attempted to cross the divide between the two disciplines.[91] A study of the colonial settings for first-century churches helps to demonstrate some of the tensions that arose between the faith communities and the wider residents of these Roman urban settings.

90. J. R. C. Cousland, review of *Philo and Paul among the Sophists*, by Bruce W. Winter, *Bryn Mawr Classical Review* (1999), http://bmcr.brynmawr.edu/1999/1999-02-13.html.

91. Thomas A. J. McGinn, "Paul's Women," *CR* 55 (2005): 645–47, reviewing Bruce W. Winter, *Roman Wives, Roman Widows: The Appearance of New Women and the Pauline Communities* (Grand Rapids: Eerdmans, 2003).

Diaspora Jewish Attitudes to *Metropoleis*

Philo and Paul on Balanced Personalities, Split Loyalties, Jerusalem, and Rome

Jutta Leonhardt-Balzer

1. Paul and the Metropolis: The Evidence

Paul was a diaspora Jew, a Jew who lived most of his life outside Jerusalem, but whose awareness circled around that city. According to Acts, he was a Roman citizen (Acts 22:22–29). Even without this evidence, he lived in the Roman Empire, which focused on Rome, its customs, and its laws. Torn between these loyalties he carved out his new existence in Christ, creating a new identity for himself and his communities between these two *metropoleis*. What part do these cities play as parameters in his old and new life? Does the tension between these influences have an effect on his thought and mission? To answer these questions, first I will look at the evidence in Paul, then I will try to answer this question with the help of a contemporary of Paul's, Philo of Alexandria.

In his undisputed letters Paul never uses the term *metropolis*, but of course he mentions Jerusalem and Rome. Rome has an important function in his later mission plans toward the west; Rome is of political and social, but not of theological, relevance.[1] By contrast, right from the beginning Jerusalem is the city that he relates to even after his conversion. Thus, he has to

---

1. Against Robert Vorholt, who claims that Rome is of theological importance for Paul, but fails to give reasons beyond the fact that Paul's mission was organised in the context of the Roman Empire. See Robert Vorholt, "Alle Wege führen nach Rom: Die Hauptstadt im Blickfeld des Paulus," in *Das frühe Christentum und die Stadt*, ed. Reinhard von Bendemann and Markus Tiwald, BWANT 198 (Stuttgart: Kohlhammer, 2012), 208–18, here 215–17.

emphasize that he did not give in to the pull of that city after his conversion, but went to Arabia and then back to Damascus (Gal 1:17).[2] Jerusalem stands here for the main leaders of the budding Christian community, who had chosen this city as their headquarters, although most of these leaders were from Galilee. Paul does not go to Jerusalem until three years later to meet with Cephas and the other leaders (Gal 1:18).[3] After that it took 14 years for him to go back to Jerusalem. Unlike on the previous visits, he did not go alone but took Barnabas, and he emphasizes that he was sent by a revelation in order to guarantee the compatibility of his gospel with that of the Jerusalem leaders (Gal 2:1–2). The reason why he is so hesitant about potential ties to this city at this point is not only that Christ does not require allegiance to Jerusalem, but because for him Jerusalem represents servitude to the Torah, which he believes has been overcome in Christ; consequently, in Gal 4:25–26 he calls the heavenly (not the earthly) Jerusalem (ἄνω Ἰερουσαλήμ) the mother (μήτηρ) of the Christians.[4] Thus, the mother city, the *metropolis* of the Christians, is not the earthly city, but the heavenly one. Paul's account of his early days as a missionary emphasizes that the revelation of Christ did not involve a link to Jerusalem, but called him to go to work where he was.[5] On the other hand, he collects money only for the Jerusalem poor, not for those anywhere else. This indicates that his attitude to the earthly city of Jerusalem is not as straightforward as it seems.

Unlike the dichotomy created in Galatians, in Romans Paul does not feel the need to distance himself from the pull of Jerusalem: in this account, his mission starts with and circles around this city (Rom 15:19).[6] He announces

---

2. There, he rejects the need to go to Jerusalem, and he links the need not with the city itself but with the presence of the other apostles, "those who were apostles before me" (οἱ πρὸ ἐμοῦ ἀπόστολοι).

3. Again, he links the city with the presence of the other apostles: "After three years I went up to Jerusalem to meet Cephas" (Ἔπειτα μετὰ ἔτη τρία ἀνῆλθον εἰς Ἰεροσόλυμα ἱστορῆσαι Κηφᾶν). It does not matter for the present purpose how long the period actually was. It was long enough to indicate independence.

4. The heavenly Jerusalem is Sarah, the free woman, against Hagar, the slave (Gal 4:25–26).

5. For an overview of the texts, not necessarily the dating, see, e.g., Udo Borse, "Paulus in Jerusalem," in *Studien zur Entstehung und Auslegung des Neuen Testaments*, ed. Regina Börschel et al., SBAB 21 (Stuttgart: Katholisches Bibelwerk, 1996), 251–76.

6. According to Rom 15:18–19 the gospel moves in a circle around Jerusalem: "So that I have preached the gospel completely from Jerusalem in a circle as far as Illyricum" (ὥστε με ἀπὸ Ἰερουσαλὴμ καὶ κύκλῳ μέχρι τοῦ Ἰλλυρικοῦ πεπληρωκέναι τὸ εὐαγγέλιον τοῦ Χριστοῦ).

that he is on the road to Jerusalem in order to bring the collection from his communities to the poor in that city (Rom 15:25).[7] He argues that as the gentile Christians in Macedonia and Achaia received their spiritual gifts from Jerusalem, they can be expected to reciprocate with their material property (Rom 15:27). Yet, even here, his attitude to the Christian community in Jerusalem is ambivalent: he continues by asking the Roman Christians to pray for his safe delivery from the Jews in Jerusalem so that his mission is "acceptable" to the Christians there and he can proceed on his mission to Spain (Rom 15:31).[8] The collection is not only mentioned in Romans. In 1 Cor 16:3–4 Paul points out that he will send any people whom the Corinthians trust to Jerusalem with authorising letters and their donation, or even go himself with them.

From these passages it can be seen that there is a contradiction in Paul's attitude regarding Jerusalem like the two sides of a magnet, which push and pull at the same time. Why should his gentile congregations feel the need to send their money there? They already pay taxes to Rome. Why should they pay money to Jerusalem and to the Christians in Jerusalem? It is clear: Jerusalem has a higher status than Rome in Paul's mind. He writes to the Christians in Rome (Rom 1:7), and he wants to visit them, to preach there, exchange views with the existing community, and to convert new people to his gospel (Rom 1:11–13). On the other hand, the fact that he waits to contact them until his preparations for the mission to Spain make contact unavoidable shows that Rome is not his highest priority. They merely have a strategic function, but in this function they are important to him. He wants to preach his gospel there, but only in the sense of being thorough, to preach the gospel to all the nations, the Greeks and barbarians, and in the context of these gentile nations, also to Rome (Rom 1:15–16). Part of his hesitation in contacting the Romans may be due to the fact that the Christian community in Rome already existed before Paul. Among all the preserved Pauline letters, the letter to the Romans is the only one to a community he has not

---

7. Paul mentions that he "travel[s] to Jerusalem in aid of the saints" (Νυνὶ δὲ πορεύομαι εἰς Ἰερουσαλὴμ διακονῶν τοῖς ἁγίοις), for the solidarity of the communities of Macedonia and that Greece has helped "the poor of the saints in Jerusalem" (οἱ πτωχοὶ τῶν ἁγίων τῶν ἐν Ἰερουσαλήμ), Rom 15:25.

8. In Rom 15:31 Paul distinguishes terminologically between the "disobedient people in Judea" (οἱ ἀπειθοῦντες ἐν τῇ Ἰουδαίᾳ) or "obstinate Judeans," from whom he wants to be delivered, and the "saints in Jerusalem" (οἱ ἅγιοι) whose approval he seeks. The context requires the reader to conclude that the term "obstinate Judeans" refers to the Jews in Jerusalem.

founded. In this sense the Roman Christians are special, but Paul does not defer to them (Rom 1:8–15), and, unlike in the case of Jerusalem, he does not even have to argue why he does not do so. They are important, but they do not have an exalted status.

Paul does not give us further background information for his ambivalent attitude to Jerusalem or his views on Rome. There is, however, a contemporary of Paul, another diaspora Jew, who can give some insight into the mentality behind Paul's attitude: Philo of Alexandria.

2. Philo and the *Metropolis*

Philo uses the term *metropolis* in his allegorical commentaries as a metaphor for the relationship between the Logos and other divine powers. The Logos is the μητρόπολις and the powers are the "colonies" (ἀποικίαι [*Fug.* 94–95]). Philo elsewhere associates the Logos with the temple (*Som.* 1.61–67). Thus, by using the term *metropolis* for the Logos metaphorically, without mentioning it explicitly, the term represents Jerusalem in its relationship to the diaspora. The Logos represents the virtuous, spiritual home of the worshipper of the true God. By contrast, Haran is called the "*metropolis* of the senses" in *Som.* 1.41 (μητρόπολίς τις αἰσθήσεων).

Philo also uses the metaphor of the *metropolis* and colony in *Conf.* 77–78 for the relationship between the heavenly home of the soul and the earthly residence, but there is no indication that for him Jerusalem as mother city takes precedence over the colonies.[9] Possibly, the parallel to the Roman citizenship plays a part here as well,[10] but not in the sense that Philo develops a rival model against Rome.[11] The citizenship of the mother city of virtue represents a spiritual interpretation of the *metropolis* as a heavenly city. This concept comes close to Paul's reference to the heavenly Jerusalem as the mother of the Christians in Gal 4:25–26. However, in both allegorical references to the concept of *metropolis* Philo does not mention Jerusalem by name. The concept of the colony and the mother city only applied explicitly

---

9. See Sarah Pearce, "Jerusalem as 'Mother-city' in the Writings of Philo of Alexandria," in *Negotiating Diaspora: Jewish Strategies in the Roman Empire*, ed. John M. G. Barclay, LSTS 45 (London: T&T Clark, 2004), 19–36 here 24–27.

10. See Maren Niehoff, *Philo on Jewish Identity and Culture*, TSAJ 86 (Tübingen: Mohr Siebeck, 2001), 30–36.

11. See Pearce, "Jerusalem as 'Mother-city'," 28–31.

to Jerusalem in the two treatises dealing with the persecution of the Jews[12] and Philo's defence against the charge of double loyalties brought against the Jews.

In the historical treatises, Philo explicitly describes the actual city of Jerusalem as a μητρόπολις. In *Flacc.* 46 the μητρόπολις is paralleled to the "holy city" (ἱερόπολις), where the temple of God is situated.[13] The "holy city" as place for the temple is the technical term for Jerusalem (*Mos.* 2.72; *Legat.* 225, 299), the place of the sanctuary (*Spec.* 3.130), so much so that it can be used even without reference to the temple, as the place where people go to meet the judges (*Spec.* 3.53). The temple is crucially linked to the importance of the city for Jewish life.

The idea of Zion as *metropolis* can already be found in LXX Isa 1:26, but Philo develops it into a concept to explain Jewish life in and outside the city. The Jews do not only live in Jerusalem and its surrounding countryside, because the Jewish nation is too numerous to be contained in one country. Jerusalem is the mother city because it is the "holy city" (ἱερόπολις), where there is "the holy temple of the highest God" (ὁ τοῦ ὑψίστου θεοῦ νεὼς ἅγιος [*Flacc.* 46]), but the local dwelling place of the Jews is their "home country" or "home city" (πατρίς), which he calls a "colony" (ἀποικία). Thus, the Jew is a person living between the mother city, the *metropolis* Jerusalem, and the father, the home country or *patris* (derived from πάτηρ, "father"). The semantic context thus evokes images of family, of permanence, of belonging. It is important that Philo does not use the term "diaspora" in this context. The Jews are not dispersed on account of a failure to obey God. They are so blessed that they multiply. They outgrow a single place, and therefore they settle elsewhere and found colonies, just as the Greek city-states used to, and Rome still did in Philo's time.[14] This use of the term *metropolis* locates Jewish customs in the Greco-Roman culture. It depicts the Jews as a natural part of the Mediterranean world. It also makes the Jewish custom of sending money to the temple, as well as their other religious ties, completely understandable for an ancient reader.[15]

12. See Pearce, "Jerusalem as 'Mother-city'," 31–34.

13. Against the view of David Schwartz, "Temple or City: What Did Hellenistic Jews See in Jerusalem?" in *The Centrality of Jerusalem: Historical Perspectives*, ed. Marcel Poorthuis and Chana Safrai (Kampen: Kok Pharos, 1996), 114–27, who argues that Philo's interest in Jerusalem and the temple is purely spiritual (119–21) and that Hellenistic Jews focused on the city rather than the temple (123–24).

14. See Mireille Hadas-Lebel, *Philo of Alexandria: A Thinker in the Jewish Diaspora*, SphA 7 (Leiden: Brill, 2012), 31.

15. See Pearce, "Jerusalem as 'Mother-city'," 20–23.

The problem that Philo is tackling with this term is that in addition to the local affiliation of the Jews, Jerusalem is the origin and focus of Jewish cultic life. In the *Legatio*, in the mouth of Agrippa, the Jewish king, Jerusalem is called πατρίς and μητρόπολις at the same time, because Agrippa happens to live in Jerusalem. It is the "father city" of its inhabitants, but the "mother city," not only of the Judean land but also of the diaspora Jews "because of the colonies" (διὰ τὰς ἀποικίας) that it establishes all over the inhabited world, not only in the Roman Empire, but also in Babylon and the East (*Legat.* 281–82). For Agrippa, Jerusalem is both mother and father city because he lives there. For the diaspora Jews, it is the mother city, complementing the "father city"[16] where they reside. Philo applies the metaphors deliberately and consistently, indicating that the mother and the father side need to be emphasized equally,[17] and both are needed to shape a balanced personality. Thus, the Jews are not social outcasts or an abnormality within the ancient sociocultural context, but quite the contrary. Philo's language places them in a stable social context through the use of these family metaphors. Judean and diaspora Jews both come from a "stable family background."

Jerusalem and the diaspora together constitute the parentage of the Jewish nation, and thus it is not surprising that family metaphors permeate Philo's account of the pilgrimage in *Spec.* 1.70.[18] Judean and diaspora Jews all observe the Jewish Torah and worship through the temple, but Philo takes great care to communicate that within this worship the loyalty to the emperor is firmly embedded (*Legat.* 279–80), especially in the context of the *Legatio* with its account of Gaius's threat to the temple and the question of

16. It may even here be appropriate to speak of a "fatherland," not just a "father city," because in Philo's conception the term πατρίς comprises also the rural areas of Judea and any other countryside where Jews reside. On the other hand, Philo's worldview is focused on cities. The countryside is a place of retreat, but communal activity mainly takes place in the civic context (probably the Therapeutae were the big exception to this rule, for they withdrew from the temptations of city life to form a community of their own, separated from social and familial ties and wholly dedicated to philosophy, see *Contempl.* 13–20). Thus when speaking of Jewish settlements, he emphasizes that Jewish assemblies were present "in every city" (κατὰ πᾶσαν πόλιν [*Spec.* 1.62]; see *Legat.* 145), a view shared by Josephus (*Ag. Ap.* 2.282); see Jutta Leonhardt, *Jewish Worship in Philo of Alexandria*, TSAJ 84 (Tübingen: Mohr Siebeck, 2002), 83.

17. See Andrea Lieber, "Between Motherland and Fatherland: Diaspora, Pilgrimage and the Spiritualization of Sacrifice in Philo of Alexandria," in *Heavenly Tablets: Interpretation, Identity and Tradition in Ancient Judaism*, ed. Lynn R. LiDonnici and Andrea Lieber, JSJSup 119 (Leiden: Brill, 2007), 193–210.

18. See Lieber, "Between Motherland and Fatherland," 193–98.

Jewish loyalty.[19] Philo himself observed the pilgrimage (*Prov.* 2.107; *Spec.* 1.68) and his account of the pilgrimage in general celebrates the sense of community established by this experience among the Jews from all over the world.[20] The link to Jerusalem is not only maintained through the physical presence of diaspora Jews in the temple during the pilgrimage. Also at home, in their meeting places, which Philo calls προσευχαί,[21] the diaspora Jews collect money to send to the temple, so that everyone who participates in the synagogue worship also participates in what goes on in the sanctuary.[22] There are many προσευχαί in Alexandria, and Philo repeatedly describes their Sabbath meetings as the core means of maintaining Jewish identity, and sending money to the temple is an important part of the synagogues' purpose.[23]

3. Philo and Jerusalem

As can be seen from the previous section, the city of Jerusalem is characterized by its relationship to God. In *Som.* 2:250 Philo calls it first "the . . . city of God" (ἡ . . . θεοῦ πόλις), "called Jerusalem by the Hebrews" (ὑπὸ Ἑβραίων Ἰερουσαλήμ), and then he translates the name as "sight of peace" (ὅρασις . . . εἰρήνης). In the context of the allegorical commentary Philo immediately interprets it symbolically as a metaphor of the soul. This metaphorical use is related to the actual importance of Jerusalem, where the temple provides a visible link to God.

As we have seen in the context of the *metropolis*, the actual city of Jerusalem and the temple can be almost synonymous. Thus, in *Legat.* 157 the people send their sacrifices "to Jerusalem through those who are to offer the sacrifices" (εἰς Ἰεροσόλυμα διὰ τῶν τὰς θυσίας ἀναξόντων). Agrippa emphasizes: "I am born a Jew. Jerusalem is my home, in which the holy

---

19. The splendour of the temple is also described in the account of Agrippa's visit "to the mother city" (εἰς τὴν μητρόπολιν) in *Legat.* 295.

20. See Hadas-Lebel, *Philo of Alexandria*, 35–40.

21. On the προσευχαί, see Leonhardt, *Jewish Worship*, 74–81. The term occurs 19 times in Philo's writings, e.g., *Flacc.* 41, 45, 47–49, 120–23; *Legat.* 134, 346.

22. See Jutta Leonhardt-Balzer, "Priests and Priesthood in Philo," in *Was 70 CE a Watershed in Jewish History? On Jews and Judaism before and after the Destruction of the Second Temple*, ed. D. R. Schwartz, Zeev Weiss, in collaboration with Ruth A. Clements, AJEC 78 (Leiden: Brill, 2011), 121–47.

23. See Leonhardt, *Jewish Worship*, 53–100.

temple of the highest God is erected" (γεγέννημαι μέν . . . Ἰουδαῖος. ἔστι
δέ μοι Ἱεροσόλυμα πατρίς, ἐν ᾗ ὁ τοῦ ὑψίστου θεοῦ νεὼς ἅγιος ἵδρυται,
Legat. 278; see also 312). Because of this link, what happens in Jerusalem
has consequences for all Jews everywhere. When in *Legat.* 288 Agrippa
points out that Gaius's accession to the throne was first announced in
Jerusalem, this emphasizes not only that the people from Jerusalem are
particularly loyal to the emperor, but also that by extension this applies to
all Jews everywhere.

The link between the diaspora and Jerusalem is acknowledged and appreciated by good Roman rulers, such as Augustus. He protects the sending
of first fruits through delegates (*Legat.* 312), the pilgrimage to Jerusalem in
accordance with the ancestral laws (*Legat.* 313), as well as the moneys sent to
Jerusalem, i.e., the temple (*Legat.* 315). These aspects present the relevance
of the actual city of Jerusalem for the Jews exclusively in terms of the cult
and culture. Jerusalem does not represent a rival political power center to
Rome. Thus, in Philo's account there is also the beginning of a distinction
between the political loyalty to Rome and the religious loyalty to Jerusalem.
Philo's argument is that these two do not clash on the part of the Jews (at
least as long as the Roman rulers adhere to their own principles). What is
noteworthily absent is any indication that Jerusalem has a higher power over
the diaspora Jews, even in terms of their religious practices. All the practices
of the Judean and the diaspora Jews are governed by the Torah, not by a
religious authority in Jerusalem, nor even by the High Priest. The reason
behind this avoidance of any Jerusalem influence on the diaspora may be
apologetic, but it is the consistent picture depicted by Philo.

4. Philo and Alexandria

While Jerusalem may be the mother city of all Jews, Alexandria is the ultimate model city for Philo,[24] so much so that he can use its foundation by Alexander the Great as a model metaphor for the creation of the world through
the Logos (*Opif.* 17–18).[25] City life for Philo symbolizes ordered, structured

24. See David T. Runia, "The Idea and the Reality of the City in the Thought of Philo
of Alexandria," *JHI* 61 (2000): 361–79, here 362–64.
25. See David T. Runia, "Polis and Megalopolis: Philo and the Founding of Alexandria,"
in *Exegesis and Philosophy: Studies on Philo of Alexandria,* VCS 332 (Aldershot: Variorum,
1990), 398–412.

community,[26] and he interprets the concept of a city allegorically as a good model, but also sometimes picking up on bad aspects.[27]

This picture of the city in general reflects his own ambivalent experience: on the one hand Alexandria is Philo's home.[28] Philo's family had lived there for generations; they held citizenship and maintained a prominent place not only in the Jewish community, but also in the administration of the city.[29] Philo knows the area and the people around the city, such as the Therapeutae at the Mareotic lake (*Contempl.* 22). He knows the island of Pharos and the difficult waters around it (*Mos.* 2.35). The vast majority of Philo's references to Alexandria, however, occur in the accounts of the pogrom in *Legatio* and *Flaccus*. He mentions the splendid buildings and temples built under Augustus (*Legat.* 150–51). It is the greatest city of the East (*Legat.* 338). He also knows about its history, government, and legal system (*Flacc.* 2, 23, 26–28, 78–80) and particularly Jewish life in it and in Egypt (*Flacc.* 43, 45, 74). Philo displays a fierce loyalty to the Alexandrian Jews and their rights as citizens of Alexandria.[30] On the other hand, he also reflects the experience of very dark aspects of Alexandrian life, and consequently he displays a certain prejudice against the Alexandrian masses, calling "the Alexandrians" a "mixed and promiscuous crowd" (ὁ Ἀλεξανδρέων μιγὰς καὶ πεφορημένος ὄχλος) in the context of the pogroms (*Legat.* 120). They most readily support Gaius in his ambition (*Legat.* 162) to be venerated as a god (*Legat.* 164–65, 170), so that he favors them (*Legat.* 183).

The Alexandrian Jews are numerous (*Legat.* 350). Philo emphasizes that the Jews are Alexandrians and see themselves as such (cf. "we are Alexandrians" [ἐσμὲν Ἀλεξανδρεῖς]). This could imply citizenship or just residence,[31] but there is no need to go into the details of the debate here.[32] Some had

---

26. See Runia, "Idea," 364–66.

27. See Runia, "Idea," 363–72.

28. See David T. Runia, "Philo, Alexandrian and Jew," in *Exegesis and Philosophy: Studies on Philo of Alexandria*, VCS 332 (Aldershot: Variorum, 1990), 1–18.

29. See Hadas-Lebel, *Philo of Alexandria*, 28–31.

30. See Pearce, "Jerusalem as 'Mother-city'," 23–24.

31. See Jonathan Dyck, "Philo, Alexandria and Empire: The Politics of Allegorical Interpretation," in *Jews in the Hellenistic and Roman Cities*, ed. John R. Bartlett (London: Routledge, 2002), 149–74, here 172–73.

32. See already Harry A. Wolfson, "Philo on Jewish Citizenship in Alexandria," *JBL* 63 (1944): 165–68. Against citizenship: e.g., Joseph Mélèze-Modrzejewski, "Esperances et illusions du judaïsme alexandrine," in *Profesorowi Janowi Kodrebskiemu in Memoriam: Mélanges à la mémoire de Jan Kodrębski*, ed. Anna Pikulska-Robaczkiewicz (Łodz: Łodz Publishing House, 2000), 221–35; and the classic Aryeh Kasher, *The Jews in Hellenistic and Roman*

citizenship, such as he and his family, some did not. Philo certainly generalizes and remains deliberately vague in an attempt to create a collective, a common identity that implies citizenship for all. The important point Philo attempts to make is that the Jews in Alexandria are not outsiders, but people who belong there. Yet, in spite of their Alexandrian connections, their loyalty also belongs to Jerusalem. In the threat to the temple in Jerusalem the "whole nation of the Jews" (καθολικωτέρα πολιτεία τῆς Ἰουδαίων) is put in danger (*Legat.* 194). Thus, Jewish life in Alexandria, whether they had citizen status or not, depended on what happened in Jerusalem. This relationship, however, is reciprocal: an attack on the synagogues in Alexandria has effects on the Jews everywhere (*Legat.* 346). Therefore, the relationship between Jerusalem and the diaspora is not that of dominance, but of symbiosis: they are different parts of the body, but each has its function and influences the other. How does Rome fit into this picture?

5. Philo and Rome

Roman culture shaped Philo's time and life in Alexandria in many ways.[33] Yet in Philo's writings, Rome is only mentioned in the *Legatio* and the *Flaccus*. Of course, Philo himself visited Rome for his embassy to the emperor Gaius, and in his account he mentions details of the geography around the city (*Legat.* 185). He claims that the city of Rome together with Italy has amassed more treasures than all the riches of the inhabited world together (*Legat.* 108). His references to "Rome" rarely relate to just the city. The Romans rule the whole world, from the rising to the setting sun (*Legat.* 10). Rome is the empire, not just in the geographical sense, but in an ideal sense. Philo refers to Roman legal customs (*Legat.* 28). He knows that some people "introduced the barbaric custom of *proskynēsis* ('prostrating oneself before a ruler') to Italy" (τὸ βαρβαρικὸν ἔθος εἰς Ἰταλίαν ἤγαγον, τὴν προσκύνησιν), which is alien to the Roman ideas of liberty (*Legat.* 116–17). Philo emphasizes the Jewish interest in maintaining the rights of all nations, especially those of the Romans (*Legat.* 153). Roman citizenship and the Roman constitution are

Egypt: The Struggle for Equal Rights, TSAJ 7 (Tübingen: Mohr Siebeck, 1985), 233–61; for the citizenship of at least sections of the Jewish population, see e.g., Victor A. Tcherikover and Alexander Fuks, *Corpus Papyrorum Judaicarum*, 3 vols. (Cambridge, MA: Harvard University Press / Magness, 1957), 1:55–78; Sylvie Honigman, "Philon, Flavius Josèphe, et la citoyenneté alexandrine: vers une utopie politique," *JJS* 48 (1997): 62–90.

33. This has been studied in detail by Niehoff, *Philo on Jewish Identity and Culture*.

experienced as a privilege (*Legat.* 285), especially when someone is born and bred in Rome (*Flacc.* 158). Roman law and its institutions are guardians against injustice, at least in theory (*Legat.* 287; *Flacc.* 40, 105). Philo does not use the metaphor of the *metropolis* explicitly of Rome; this would be impossible, because for him, Jerusalem is the only *metropolis*, Rome can only be the *patris*, never the *metropolis* of the Jews. Nevertheless, the influence of the mother city on its colonies permeates Philo's depiction of Rome.

The Jews have a dual position in this context. On the one hand, they partake of the good aspects of their *patris*. On the other, as section two on Philo's reading of the *metropolis* (esp. *Flacc.* 46; *Legat.* 281–82) has shown, the loyalty to their own traditions, symbolized by their mother city Jerusalem, complements the influences of the *patris* and balances any negative influences of the place they live in. Thus, far from alienating them from their Roman home, their affiliation to their *metropolis* causes them to stand against imperial abuse of power and for the good principles of the ancient Roman constitution, virtues, and laws, which (almost) match those of Moses. Therefore, according to Philo's picture, the Jews do not let themselves be tempted to bad behavior (unlike the Alexandrians; see *Legat.* 120), and all good Roman rulers appreciate this position. Only the bad rulers doubt the Jewish loyalties. This can be seen in Augustus's disposition toward the Jews versus the threats of Sejanus under Tiberius (*Legat.* 155–60).

Philo's description of Jewish life in Rome is shaped by this argument. The Jews live in a quarter of Rome on the other side of the Tiber (*Legat.* 155). Just as the Alexandrian Jews are called "Alexandrians," he calls the Roman Jews "Romans" (Ῥωμαῖοι), but here he mentions specifically that they received the citizenship as manumitted slaves (*Legat.* 155). Philo feels the need to emphasize that they were not forced to abandon their customs during their slavery. While Philo clearly speaks of actual citizenship here, it is probable that by Philo's time not all Roman Jews were manumitted slaves, and of those who moved there from abroad probably not all held Roman citizenship. Nevertheless, as in the case of Alexandria, Philo develops the concept of a communal Jewish identity that involves full citizenship of their place of residence.

Philo's account continues to specify the conditions in which the Roman Jews express their identity. They "have synagogues" (προσευχὰς ἔχοντας), they meet there, especially on the Sabbath, and they collect the temple dues there to send them to Jerusalem (*Legat.* 156). Augustus never exiled them from Rome; they kept their Roman citizenship in spite of their ties with Jerusalem (*Legat.* 157), and they were allowed to practice their traditions in

Rome as well as collect the money for the temple—Augustus even donated to the temple himself (*Legat.* 157). Even more, the Roman Jews participate in the monthly grain dole, and if that is on a Sabbath, the grain is distributed to them a day later (*Legat.* 158). Philo describes that under the reign of Tiberius, Sejanus threatened these rights of the Roman Jews, but that he did not succeed (*Legat.* 159–60). Even Cicero comments that the half-shekel offering of the diaspora Jews is tied to the rights of the city of Jerusalem (*Flac.* 69), and any threat to the temple affects the Jews in Rome.[34] Thus both Philo and Cicero, the one from an inner-Jewish and the other from an external Roman perspective, saw the temple tax as a sign of Jewish loyalty to Jerusalem.

Philo's depiction presents the Roman Jews of his time as faithful citizens of Rome as well as having strong ties to the temple. They are linked to the *metropolis* of Jerusalem and the *patris* Rome, just as he as an Alexandrian Jew lives between Alexandria and Jerusalem. These ties are above all expressed in the financial contributions to the temple.

6. Paul and the *Metropoleis*: Conclusion

With this in mind, we turn back to Paul. The metaphor of the *metropolis*, which he hints at only once, sheds light on the ambivalence and contradiction within Paul's attitude to Jerusalem: as a diaspora Jew the city of the temple has a strong hold on his perspective on the world. His religious world is focused not so much on the political reality of Rome, but on the spiritual center Jerusalem. Even if he no longer regards the temple worship and observance of the Jewish ritual laws as necessary for gentile Christians, they are still structures that shape his view on Jewish identity as the people of God and therefore they influence his views on how to relate to God: in their assemblies, the Christians mirror the synagogue communities, and these do not exist without a focus on Jerusalem.

Thus Paul's attitude to Jerusalem is nuanced and complex. The gentiles have been given the citizenship of the heavenly (not the earthly) Jerusalem, and the earthly Jerusalem as the holy city has the attraction of the holy place, while at the same time it contains a seduction toward a type of worship that is not required. Therefore, in a context where Jerusalem raises a theological claim to authority, where a threat of Judaizing occurs, Paul is more critical of the place as a focus of Christian orientation. Where this threat is not so

34. See Schwartz, "Temple or City," 125.

prominent, a different attitude can be observed. Thus, the collection for the poor in Jerusalem is not merely an act of charity toward the needy. It is the equivalent of the temple dues that all diaspora Jews send to Jerusalem to demonstrate their unity and their belonging to the one God. What is noteworthy is that Paul himself presents this collection as the result of an agreement with the pillars in Jerusalem.[35] It is not just the spontaneous reaction of diaspora Christians to a famine crisis, or the result of a Pauline "theology of collection" developed from Jewish eschatological expectations.[36] It seems that not just Paul, but also the Christians in Jerusalem regarded the collection as an expression of Christian identity, a claim rooted in Jewish tradition and accepted by Paul. Nevertheless, the acknowledgment of this claim by Paul does not imply his acceptance of any superior spiritual authority of Jerusalem relating to teaching.[37] The self-confidence of the Alexandrian diaspora Jew Philo shows, that in spite of all ritual ties, Jerusalem did not have any theological power or say over what the diaspora thought. The same certainly applies to Paul. For him, the earthly Jerusalem did not have a theological authority, it had a social function. Yet, even this social function is not independent but derives from the heavenly Jerusalem. It is the heavenly Jerusalem that is the mother city and holds together the gentile Christian communities that Paul founded. From the heavenly mother city, however, the claim spills over into Paul's attitude toward the actual Christian community in Jerusalem, so that he is willing to accept the collection on their behalf as an outward sign of Christian unity. The earthly Jerusalem, for Paul as for Philo, is important for the social coherence of the people of God, but it does not have authority over the theological content taught in other places.

35. See Borse, "Paulus in Jerusalem," 47–49, 62–63.

36. Thus Jost Eckert, "Die Kollekte des Paulus für Jerusalem," in *Kontinuität und Einheit: Festschrift für Franz Mußner*, ed. Paul-Gerhard Müller and Werner Stenger (Freiburg im Breisgau: Herder, 1981), 65–80.

37. It is not clear whether this attitude was shared by the Christians in Jerusalem. Probably the Twelve in Jerusalem thought that Paul's agreement did involve acknowledgment of their authority, which is why he has to argue so forcefully in Galatians that it did not.

Paul's Mission Strategy in the Urban Landscape of the First-Century Roman Empire

Volker Rabens

No other figure of the Bible visited more cities than the Apostle Paul. In most of the cities Paul remained for a lengthy stay—weeks, months, and sometimes years. Although his concern was not primarily the study of geography like Strabo's *Geography* or Pausanias's *Description of Greece*, there was a significant overlap between investigations like these and Paul's work: both were interested in people. With regard to Paul, we read in his letters (and in the Acts of the Apostles) that he wanted to pass on to other people what had been a life-transforming event for him—his encounter with the Messiah Jesus. A major concern of Paul's travels was to invite others to join this new relationship and participate in the love and life of God. He wanted to communicate the gospel of Jesus the Messiah, and for him this meant more than a perfunctory evangelistic sermon. Paul did preach, but his preaching was embedded in a more comprehensive service through which he shared his life with others:

> You remember our labor and toil, brothers and sisters; we worked night and day, so that we might not burden any of you while we proclaimed to you the gospel of God. You are witnesses, and God also, how pure, upright, and blameless our conduct was toward you believers. As you know, we dealt with each one of you like a father with his children, urging and encouraging you and pleading that you lead a life worthy of God, who calls you into his own kingdom and glory. (1 Thess 2:9–12 NRSV; cf. 1:5–6)

Paul entered into an intensive relationship with those whom he wanted to reach with the gospel—he even identifies himself as their servant (δοῦλος;

99

VOLKER RABENS

2 Cor 4:5; cf. 12:14–15; Col 1:25). "Mission" is therefore understood in this chapter as the multidimensional engagement of an individual or a faith community, with the goal of attracting others to the message of faith and to the lifestyle related to it. In Paul's case, "multidimensional" meant that his engagement was not limited to verbal proclamation but typically expressed itself in an integrated and reciprocal participation in the lives of others. This participation included working and eating together, theological reflection and discussion, ethical instruction, and the experience of spiritual gifts and miracles (cf. part 1 below).[1]

This chapter investigates Paul's missionary practice among and in the cities of the Roman Empire. My inquiry has two aspects: 1) How did Paul choose the cities that he visited on his missionary journeys? Did he have particular criteria for why he visited Corinth, Ephesus, etc.? 2) What did Paul do once he arrived in a particular city? How did he intend to reach people with the gospel in the context of the social realities of urban life in the Roman Empire?

These two sets of inquiries, which make up the two parts of the present chapter, raise the underlying question whether Paul had a *strategy* in the context of his mission to the cities of the first-century Roman Empire at all. Is there a (conscious?) pattern to his travels and practices among and in the cities? Rodney Stark's *Cities of God* seems to provide an initial positive answer, mainly based on statistics. He formulates three hypotheses regarding Paul's mission:

1) Paul concentrated on the more Hellenized cities.

Paul visited only 8 of the 31 cities, but of these none was among the less Hellenized group. . . . That is, only Hellenic cities were missionized by

---

1. In recent studies on mission in Paul, a number of scholars have aimed at putting forward a comprehensive and integrated concept of "mission," e.g., John P. Dickson, *Mission-Commitment in Ancient Judaism and in the Pauline Communities: The Shape, Extent and Background of Early Christian Mission*, WUNT/2 159 (Tübingen: Mohr Siebeck, 2003), 10; Michael Barram, *Mission and Moral Reflection in Paul*, SBL 75 (New York: Lang, 2006), 175. However, their definitions still tend to focus on describing unilateral missionary activities and overlook the bilateral dynamic of shared lives as we find it in the accounts of Paul's collaborations in the context of founding apostolic communities, e.g., with Aquila and Priscilla in Corinth (Acts 18:2–3). My own approach in this chapter builds on and expands my earlier work, "'Von Jerusalem aus und rings umher . . .' (Röm. 15,19): Die paulinische Missionsstrategie im Dickicht der Städte," in *Das frühe Christentum und die Stadt*, ed. Reinhard von Bendemann and Markus Tiwald, BWANT 198 (Stuttgart: Kohlhammer, 2012), 219–37. I would like to thank Prof. Scott Caulley for providing me with an initial translation of my 2012 article as a starting point for the present chapter.

Paul (Hellenism thereby being a necessary factor), even though many Hellenic cities were not missionized by Paul (Hellenism thereby not being a sufficient factor to have drawn Paul).[2]

2) Paul tended to missionize port cities. Stark admits that this is somewhat obvious because much of Paul's travel was by boat, which was a usual practice in the case of longer-distance travel. Nearly half of the port cities were missionized by Paul, but he visited only 12 percent of the inland cities.[3]

3) Paul tended to missionize cities with substantial Jewish diaspora communities. Stark calculates that two-thirds of the cities with a significant diaspora Jewish community were missionized by Paul, while he visited only two of the cities lacking a diaspora community.[4]

Stark supplies a comprehensive compendium of statistical charts in the appendix of his book in support of his hypotheses, and although his work has been rightly criticized for overdependence on some of these,[5] we can generally agree that Paul followed popular trade routes and tended to visit the larger cities.[6] However, there were also exceptions to these general rules. Stark's statistics agree with that. Therefore, while Stark's statistics-based hypotheses are helpful for tracing Paul's broader movements, we will need to attend to Paul's letters (and, secondarily, to Acts) to fill in more details as we try to find out whether Paul had a cleverly devised strategy to help him a) visit the cities that were significant for his mission, and b) communicate the message of God's reconciliation through Jesus in the most effective way to the people in those cities.

Jörg Frey provides a potential answer to our inquiry: "Paul is the only early Christian missionary for whom we can detect a planned strategic mission, and whose mission is stamped theologically with the marks of his pre-

2. Rodney Stark, *Cities of God: The Real Story of How Christianity Became an Urban Movement and Conquered Rome* (New York: HarperOne, 2007), 132.

3. Stark, *Cities*, 132.

4. Stark, *Cities*, 132.

5. See, e.g., Jan N. Bremmer, *The Rise of Christianity through the Eyes of Gibbon, Harnack, and Rodney Stark*, 2nd ed. (Groningen: Barkhuis, 2010), 64.

6. Thus also another of Stark's hypotheses: "Larger cities had Christian congregations sooner than smaller cities" (Stark, *Cities*, 81). Thomas A. Robinson, *Who Were the First Christians? Dismantling the Urban Thesis* (Oxford: Oxford University Press, 2017), 91–99, rightly insists that Paul may see the countryside included in the orbit of the *polis*, since *polis* and countryside together were a fundamental unit of the economic and political structure of Greco-Roman society. Moreover, as we will see below, when Paul speaks of his mission, he speaks of both regions or provinces as well as individual cities.

Christian upbringing and education, his Scriptural erudition, and his life and occupational experience."[7] Whether one sides with Frey's answer and a series of other authors,[8] or rather agrees with Roland Allen's classic 1912 study that *denied* that Paul had a planned-out mission strategy,[9] depends in large degree upon what one understands by "strategy." One thing should be clear: if by "mission strategy" we mean a consciously worked out program in which strategic points are selected and fit into a timeline, there are hardly any grounds to support this view from Paul's letters and from Acts.

Acts describes Paul's travels from city to city largely in neutral terms (e.g., Acts 17:1; 18:1, 18–19). These reports do not supply any explicit agenda or a formulated mission program that Paul would have followed. Mission is presented as coming from God and is directed by the Spirit (e.g., Acts 16:6–10; 21:4). Paul usually moved on if his hearers rejected the gospel or when conflict arose with opponents (e.g., Acts 14:19–20; 16:39–40; 20:1–3). Paul's letters, however, which have priority for reconstructing a Pauline mission theology, suggest that Paul planned ahead for his travels to various cities (e.g., 1 Thess 2:18; 1 Cor 4:19; 11:34; 16:5–6).[10] The letters also indicate that Paul was frequently forced to change plans because numerous hindrances made particular visits impossible (1 Thess 2:18; 2 Cor 12–13; Rom 1:9–13; 15:22–23), such as antagonisms or conflicts arising from previous visits (e.g., 2 Cor 1:15–24; 12:20–21).

There is at least one passage in the epistles where Paul explicitly reflects on the geographic aspect of his mission endeavor. When he looks back on his former mission travels, Paul says in Romans 15:19–20: "From Jerusalem and

7. Jörg Frey, "Die Ausbreitung des frühen Christentums: Perspektiven für die gegenwärtige Praxis der Kirche," in *Kirche zwischen postmoderner Kultur und Evangelium*, ed. Martin Reppenhagen (Neukirchen-Vluyn: Neukirchener Verlag, 2010), 86–112, here 100; cf. 103.

8. Inter alia, Rainer Riesner, *Die Frühzeit des Apostels Paulus: Studien zur Chronologie, Missionstrategie und Theologie*, WUNT 71 (Tübingen: Mohr Siebeck, 1994), 204–34; Dickson, *Mission-Commitment*, 9–10; Eckhard J. Schnabel, *Paul, the Missionary: Realities, Strategies, and Methods* (Downers Grove, IL: IVP Academic / Nottingham: Apollos, 2008), 22–32; James D. G. Dunn, *Beginning from Jerusalem*, Christianity in the Making 2 (Grand Rapids: Eerdmans, 2009), 555.

9. Roland Allen, *Missionary Methods: St. Paul's or Ours?*, 6th ed. (Grand Rapids: Eerdmans, 1962), 10: "It is quite impossible to maintain that St. Paul deliberately planned his journeys beforehand, selected certain strategic points at which to establish his churches, and then actually carried out his designs." Cf. Robinson, *Christians*, 96–99.

10. On Paul's missionary journeys and their presentation in the Pauline corpus and Acts, see the overview in Eva Ebel, "Paul's Missionary Activity," in *Paul: Life, Setting, Work, Letters*, ed. Oda Wischmeyer (London: T&T Clark, 2012), 111–20, here 112–16.

as far around as Illyricum I have fully proclaimed the good news of Christ. Thus I make it my ambition to proclaim the good news, not where Christ has already been named, so that I do not build on someone else's foundation."[11] This text will be the basis of my discussion of Paul's geographical movement in the first part of this chapter. Apart from providing information on Paul's travels in the urban landscape of the Roman Empire, this passage also points toward an answer to our more general question regarding Paul's mission strategy. Namely, Paul here reveals a fundamental principle of his mission, which is to preach where the gospel had not yet been heard.

Accordingly, if one wishes to speak of Paul's "mission strategy," it seems that this is best understood in terms of *the connection between basic missiological principles and their pragmatic application.* This model of flexible implementation of fundamental tenets also comes to the fore once we turn to Paul's concrete behavior when he arrives in a specific city (part 2). For example, when Paul "entered" a city—he speaks about his "entrance" (εἴσοδος [1 Thess 1:9, 2:1])—he usually did not come just by himself. Rather, his work was embedded in a wide-ranging cooperation with various coworkers (e.g., 1 Cor 3:6; 2 Cor 8:23; Phil 2:25; Rom 16:3, 9, 21). This praxis appears to be based on Paul's theological maxim that the "body of Christ" is made up of many individual members who complement each another. Before we look at this and further cooperations in more detail, we now turn to Paul's reflections on the geography of his missionary journeys.

1. Paul's Travel Procedures among the Cities

Paul was inspired by the universal relevance of the gospel. In 2 Cor 5:19–20 he proclaims that "in Christ God was reconciling the world to himself . . . and entrusting the message of reconciliation to us. So we are ambassadors for Christ, since God is making his appeal through us; we entreat you on behalf of Christ, be reconciled to God." Paul is convinced that the whole world should experience and accept that God has reconciled the world (κόσμος) to himself.[12] God's saving intervention began with Israel, to which God first

11. All biblical quotations in this chapter are from the NRSV.
12. Cf. the investigation of inclusion and exclusion in the context of Paul's mission in Volker Rabens, "Inclusion of and Demarcation from 'Outsiders': Mission and Ethics in Paul's Second Letter to the Corinthians," in *Sensitivity towards Outsiders: Exploring the Dynamic Relationship between Mission and Ethics in the New Testament and Early Christianity,* ed. Jacobus Kok et al., WUNT/2 364 (Tübingen: Mohr Siebeck, 2014), 290–323, here 290–94, 317–19.

devoted himself and made them his people. Therefore the gospel is to the Jews first. However, according to Paul's understanding of the covenant with Abraham (Gen 12:3; 18:18), from the beginning this promise was conceived as a blessing for all people (Gal 3:8).[13] The gospel is "the power of God for salvation to everyone who has faith, to the Jew first and also to the Greek" (Rom 1:16).

Paul understood himself as an apostle called to the gentiles (Gal 2:7-8; Rom 1:5; 11:13; 15:16; etc.). This does not mean that he had given up on Israel. Rather, Paul operates from the premise that through the mission among the gentiles, Israel will also finally be saved (Rom 11:13-14, 25-32). Paul regards his call as a charge that grew out of the call of Israel.[14] He hence bases his fundamental missiological tenets explicitly on the pronouncement found in Isaiah 52:15: "Thus I make it my ambition to proclaim the good news, not where Christ has already been named, so that I do not build on someone else's foundation, but as it is written, 'Those who have never been told of him shall see, and those who have never heard of him shall understand'" (Rom 15:20-21).

Accordingly, Paul set forth to be a pioneer at the frontier of the expanding Christian movement. He committed himself to making known the gospel where no one had yet heard it.[15] The logical consequence for Paul's missionary praxis resulting from this principle was geographical movement in the service of the gospel. Paul himself worked out these practical consequences in the key passage already mentioned above: "Christ has [worked] through me to win obedience from the gentiles, by word and deed, by the power of signs and wonders, by the power of the Spirit of God, *so that from Jerusalem and as far around as Illyricum I have fully proclaimed the good news of Christ*" (Rom 15:18b-19, emphasis added).

The first part of the passage provides one aspect of the answer to our

13. On the implications of the "New Perspective on Paul" for understanding the foundation of Paul's mission, see W. Paul Bowers, "Mission," in *Dictionary of Paul and the Letters*, ed. Gerald F. Hawthorne, Ralph P. Martin, and Daniel G. Reid (Downers Grove, IL: InterVarsity Press, 1993), 608-19, here 613, 618; Dunn, *Beginning*, 533-36.

14. Compare Gal 1:15-16 with Isa 49:1-6 ("I will give you as a light to the nations [εἰς φῶς ἐθνῶν], that my salvation may reach to the end of the earth" [Isa 49:6]) and Jer 1:5 ("a prophet to the nations," προφήτης εἰς ἔθνη). Cf. J. Louis Martyn, *Galatians: A New Translation with Introduction and Commentary*, AB 33A (New York: Doubleday, 1997), 156-57; Roy E. Ciampa, "Paul's Theology of the Gospel," in *Paul as Missionary: Identity, Activity, Theology, and Practice*, ed. Trevor J. Burke and Brian S. Rosner, LNTS 420 (London: T&T Clark, 2011), 180-91, here 183-84.

15. Rome constitutes an exception, as Paul himself makes clear in Rom 15:22-24.

second question regarding Paul's concrete missionary procedure in a given city. Paul describes his entire service as comprised of "word and work" (λόγος καὶ ἔργον). As in other passages, Paul here reports that his missionary service took place "in the power of signs and wonders" (cf. 1 Thess 1:5; 1 Cor 2:4; 2 Cor 12:12). "Work" (ἔργον) in verse 18 should not be limited to this miraculous aspect of Paul's ministry—after all, it was Paul's entire life that gave testimony to the gospel (1 Thess 1:5–6; 2:9–12; 1 Cor 2:16; 3:9–11; etc.).[16] However, the significance of this "charismatic" dimension of Paul's ministry for the reception of the gospel should also not be underestimated (cf. Gal 3:2–5).[17] In the context of Romans 15:14–29, however, the reference to signs and wonders appears primarily to have a different function. Here Paul places himself again in the line of Israelite prophets. Their work too was authenticated through signs and wonders (e.g., Exod 7:3; Deut 7:19; 29:3; 34:11; Ps 135:9). We have already established that Paul understood his missionary enterprise in our passage explicitly against the background of the call of Isaiah (Isa 52:15 is cited in Rom 15:20–21). We find yet another allusion to this tradition in Romans 15:16. There Paul completes his self-portrait as a missionary in the line of Israelite prophets by referencing Isaiah 66:20 as he describes the aim of his "priestly service of the gospel of God" to be "that the offering of the gentiles may be acceptable."[18]

How is the geographic spread of the gospel as it is described in Romans 15:19 to be understood in the context of the urban landscape of the first-century Roman Empire? On the one hand, the reference to Jerusalem as the starting point of the missionary movement can imply the global expansion of salvation ("to the Jew first, and also to the Greek" [Rom 1:16]; cf. Acts 1:8).[19] On the other hand, it could also allude to Paul's own mission

16. Cf. Michael J. Gorman, *Becoming the Gospel: Paul, Participation, and Mission* (Grand Rapids: Eerdmans, 2015), 45.

17. Cf. Wolfgang Reinbold, *Propaganda und Mission im ältesten Christentum: Eine Untersuchung zu den Modalitäten der Ausbreitung der frühen Kirche*, FRLANT 188 (Göttingen: Vandenhoeck & Ruprecht, 2000), 202–204; Volker Rabens, "Power from In Between: The Relational Experience of the Holy Spirit and Spiritual Gifts in Paul's Churches," in *The Spirit and Christ in the New Testament and Christian Theology: Essays in Honor of Max Turner*, ed. I. Howard Marshall, Volker Rabens, and Cornelis Bennema (Grand Rapids: Eerdmans, 2012), 138–55, here 141–43.

18. On this issue, see further Stefan Schreiber, *Paulus als Wundertäter: Redaktionsgeschichtliche Untersuchungen zur Apostelgeschichte und den authentischen Paulusbriefen*, BZNW 79 (Berlin: De Gruyter, 1996), 202; L. J. Lietaert Peerbolte, *Paul the Missionary*, CBET 34 (Leuven: Peeters, 2003), 246–48.

19. Thus various interpreters, as e.g., C. E. B. Cranfield, *A Critical and Exegetical*

activity that, as we have seen above, fits into the idea of global salvation beginning with Israel (thus the flow of Rom 15:18–29; cf. Acts 9:26–29; but see Gal 1:17–18; 2:1–10).[20] This second option, i.e., that Paul is talking here about his own geographical missionary movement, may find support in the wording of the phrase that is central for our question, namely Romans 15:19c: "from Jerusalem *and in an arc/semicircle up to Illyricum*" (ἀπὸ Ἰερουσαλὴμ καὶ κύκλῳ μέχρι τοῦ Ἰλλυρικοῦ).[21] This thesis has been developed in detail by Rainer Riesner. Building on Paul's self-portrait as a missionary in the line of Israelite prophets as outlined above, Riesner argues that Paul here presents his mission activity as a fulfillment of the proclamation of salvation in "Tarshish, Put, and Lud . . . to Tubal and Javan, to the coastlands far away," announced in Isaiah 66:19. These places could have been interpreted by Paul as 1. Tarsus, 2. Cilicia, 3. Lydia, 4. Mysia, 5. Bithynia, 6. Macedonia and 7. the far west. Riesner does not maintain that Paul's mission plans were oriented to Isaiah 66:19 from the beginning, or that this prophecy was the only or the most important among the different reasons for choosing the route Paul traveled. However, the movement from Jerusalem in a northwestern arc to the extreme west described in Isaiah 66:19 corresponds to the idea behind Romans 15:19, and it may be

---

Commentary on the Epistle to the Romans, 2 vols., ICC (Edinburgh: T&T Clark, 1979), 2:760–61.

20. Thus, inter alia, Dieter Zeller, *Juden und Heiden in der Mission des Paulus: Studien zum Römerbrief* (Stuttgart: Verlag Katholisches Bibelwerk, 1973), 227. James D. G. Dunn, *Romans 9–16*, WBC 38B (Waco, TX: Word, 1988), 863–64, holds both options to be convincing. For a nuanced discussion of the locations mentioned in this passage, see further Wayne A. Meeks, *The First Urban Christians: The Social World of the Apostle Paul* (New Haven/London: Yale University Press, 1983), 40.

21. Emphasis added. The translation of κύκλῳ μέχρι as "in a semicircle to" is preferable to the translation "around about," even though the parallel in Ezek 5:5 ("This is Jerusalem; I have set her in the center of the nations, with countries all around her [τὰς κύκλῳ αὐτῆς χώρας]"; cf. James M. Scott, *Paul and the Nations: The Old Testament and Jewish Background of Paul's Mission to the Nations with Special Reference to the Destination of Galatians*, WUNT 84 [Tübingen: Mohr Siebeck, 1995], 67) seems to speak against this. The fact that κύκλῳ can be used to express a circular movement is shown by Philo's use of the expression. In *Leg.* 1.66 Philo describes how the river Pheison (Φεισών) "encompasses the entire land of Evilat" (οὗτος ὁ κυκλῶν πᾶσαν τὴν γῆν Εὐιλάτ): "it encircles in its roundel the land of Evilat" (χορεύει δὲ καὶ κύκλῳ περίεισι τὴν γῆν Εὐιλάτ [Colson, LCL]). The line from Jerusalem to Illyricum runs in a semicircle, as a glimpse at the map quickly makes clear (although Paul did of course not have the maps that we do today). For discussion, see Dunn, *Romans 9–16*, 863–64; Riesner, *Frühzeit*, 214–16; Robert Jewett, *Romans: A Commentary*, Hermeneia (Philadelphia: Fortress, 2006), 910–11.

a key reason why Paul planned to take his mission to Spain, rather than to Gaul or elsewhere.[22]

Along the same lines, James Scott reasons that the apostles had divided the world along the "borders" of the regions inhabited by Noah's offspring as named in the Table of Nations in Genesis 10, such that the region of "Japheth" has fallen to Paul ("from Jerusalem to Illyricum" and Spain).[23] Riesner's and Scott's line of argument has recently been taken up positively by James Dunn. In his monumental trilogy on the expansion of Christianity—and here in the second volume with the fitting title "Beginning from Jerusalem"—Dunn concludes regarding the exposition of Romans 15:19:

> Without subscribing to all details of the theses of Riesner and Scott—given the data, firm conclusions are hardly possible—it is nevertheless likely that Isa. 66.19 provides a shaft of light which illuminates both the rationale of Paul's mission and the compulsion he experienced to reach Spain. If Spain did indeed complete the (half-) circle from Jerusalem, as indicating the limits of Japheth's territory, Paul's compulsion to reach Spain meshes with his hope of winning "the full number of the Gentiles" to faith (Rom. 11.25) and thus of triggering the climax of God's purpose in history and the resurrection of the dead (11.13–15).[24]

However, the suggestions by Riesner and Scott have not always been met with applause.[25] Wright has recently disagreed with Scott in his *Paul and the Faithfulness of God* (he seems to be unaware of Riesner's *Die Frühzeit des Apostels Paulus*, translated into English as *Paul's Early Period*). As a full correspondence between the cities and regions mentioned in Isaiah and those of Paul's missionary journeys cannot be established, Wright concludes "Isaiah 66 . . . hardly matches what we know either of Paul's actual journeys or his future plans."[26] Nevertheless, his own alternative for understanding the reasoning behind Paul's travel procedures among the cities seems even more difficult to prove. According to Wright, Paul's movement was driven

---

22. Riesner, *Frühzeit*, 216–25; cf. Rainer Riesner, *Paul's Early Period: Chronology, Mission Strategy, Theology* (Grand Rapids: Eerdmans, 1998), 241–53.

23. Scott, *Nations*, 135–80; cf. n. 96 in Riesner, *Frühzeit*, 224–25.

24. Dunn, *Beginning*, 544.

25. See inter alia the critical evaluations in Eckhard J. Schnabel, *Urchristliche Mission* (Wuppertal: Brockhaus, 2002), 1239; Lietaert Peerbolte, *Paul*, 249–251.

26. N. T. Wright, *Paul and the Faithfulness of God*, 2 vols., COQG 4 (Minneapolis: Fortress, 2013), 2:1501.

by the agenda to establish messianic communities in those places where Caesar's power was strongest.[27] However, the fact that Paul worked in places that were not Roman provinces (Arabia/Nabatea, cf. Gal 1:17; 2 Cor 11:32) as well as in small towns such as Iconium, Lystra, Derbe, and Beroea, which were not renowned for a particularly strong zeal for the emperor cult, speaks against this thesis. Moreover, while Paul worked in many of the cities for which the imperial cult has been documented, there were many more in which Paul evidently did not preach the gospel.[28] We can hence conclude with Schnabel that Wright's suggestion gives Caesar too much credit for Paul's movements. Paul was less concerned about the emperor than about "all people" and "all gentiles" (1 Cor 9:22; Rom 1:5; 15:11) who needed to hear the gospel, turn away from whatever Greek, Roman, Egyptian, or local deity they worshiped and believe in Jesus and serve the true and living God (cf. 1 Thess 1:1–10).[29]

So, what are we to make of Riesner's proposal? Riesner's approach has received detailed treatment in Ksenija Magda's recent monograph *Paul's Territoriality and Mission Strategy*. Magda criticizes Riesner's model, arguing that Paul's strategy in the context of the cities cannot be connected to a single verse, not least because Paul nowhere explicitly cites this passage (in contrast to other sections of Isaiah).[30] Instead, she is convinced that Paul was influenced and motivated by a Roman geography. Paul repeatedly mentions Roman provinces in his letters. For example, the Thessalonians became an example for all believers in Macedonia and Achaia (1 Thess 1:7–8), and they became imitators of the believers in Judea (2:14). The province of Asia is mentioned several times (1 Cor 16:19; 2 Cor 1:8; Rom 16:5). Furthermore, in Romans 15:19 Paul mentions Illyricum, a province founded in the year 9 BCE. For Magda, the fact that Paul knows Illyricum and refers to it speaks further to the idea that Paul had a Roman understanding of place names and in his missionary travels was exclusively shaped by that understanding.[31]

---

27. Wright, *Paul*, 2:1502.

28. See the details provided in Eckhard J. Schnabel, "Evangelism and the Mission of the Church," in *God and the Faithfulness of Paul: A Critical Examination of the Pauline Theology of N. T. Wright*, ed. Michael F. Bird, Christoph Heilig, and Jay Thomas Hewitt, WUNT/2 413 (Tübingen: Mohr Siebeck, 2016), 688–89.

29. Schnabel, "Evangelism."

30. Ksenija Magda, *Paul's Territoriality and Mission Strategy: Searching for the Geographical Awareness Paradigm behind Romans*, WUNT/2 266 (Tübingen: Mohr Siebeck, 2009), 93.

31. Magda, *Territoriality*, 6–7, 90.

According to Magda, Paul's familiarity with Roman place names is of great significance for our question about his travel customs among the cities, because it is part of the broader concept of *territoriality*. Magda takes over the concept of territoriality from the geographer Robert Sack.[32] A central aspect of territoriality is the interplay of the three components, *nature* (the physical world), *meaning*, and *social relations*. Since these three areas influence each other, we should not underestimate the impact of a specific geographical understanding (which belongs to the area of *nature*) upon the other areas of territoriality, and therefore upon the (missionary) self-understanding of a person. With respect to Paul's territoriality Magda concludes:

> Within his Roman territoriality paradigm, Paul's call by Christ could bring about that serious change in theological understanding which was so difficult for Jerusalem-based apostles. Paul was a Roman citizen with a cosmopolitan feeling for all the nations, far more so than the other disciples of Jesus. In comparison with the territoriality of the other apostles, Paul's is broad enough to include other nations. Indeed, his place is broad enough to give him the freedom to claim that he can be all things to all people (1 Cor 9:22)![33]

Magda thus sees in Paul's Roman "territoriality paradigm" an impetus for his mission to the gentiles. Shaped by this territoriality, it is obvious for Paul that he should view the Roman Empire as made up of targets for the gospel, and he travels through it province by province.

Magda's approach provides a valuable perspective for our discussion. She is correct in her assertion that in his conversion and commissioning experience Paul could hardly have had the geographical information of Isaiah 66:19 in his mind's eye. Rather, he would have been much more likely to interpret his call first against the background of his existing territoriality.[34] We can agree that Paul's missionary journeys were guided by, though

---

32. On the definition of territoriality, see further Robert David Sack, *Human Territoriality: Its Theory and History*, Cambridge Studies in Historical Geography (Cambridge: Cambridge University Press, 1986), 5, 19; Robert David Sack, *Homo Geographicus: A Framework for Action, Awareness, and Moral Concern* (Baltimore: Johns Hopkins University Press, 1997), 1–26. A good illustration of the interplay of the three components is found in Magda, *Territoriality*, 45.

33. Magda, *Territoriality*, 183.

34. When in Gal 1:15–16 Paul describes his mission to the gentiles as a consequence (cf. ἵνα) of his revelatory experience of the risen Christ, the question remains open whether his call as apostle to the gentiles was already a part of that conversion experience (cf. Franz

not totally determined or even limited by, his Roman territoriality. As we have seen above, Paul also worked in places that were not Roman provinces. Moreover, it is worth noting that Riesner does not claim that Paul's mission plans were from the beginning oriented by Isaiah 66:19, or that this prophecy provides the only—or even the most important—reason for the travel routes Paul followed.[35] However, it is clear that in Romans 15:14–24 and in other passages (e.g., Rom 10:14–21; Gal 1:15–16), Paul does interpret his missionary identity against the background of prophetic texts of the Hebrew Bible, especially Isaiah.[36] In this regard, it is striking that Romans 15:16 contains a clear allusion to Isaiah 66:20—i.e., to the verse following directly after 66:19. Even if the concrete geographical information claimed by Riesner only came to the fore in Isaiah 66:19, his interpretation is not just supported by a single verse but by the intertextual echoes of the entire passage of Isaiah 66:18–21 as found in Romans 15:14–24.[37]

It hence suggests itself that—in the context of the announcement in Romans 15:23–24 of his mission to Spain and his visit to Rome—Paul interprets his previous advances in the provinces and cities retrospectively against the background of the prophecies in Isaiah 66:18–21, especially 66:19. Nonetheless, it has to remain open whether this aspect of his territoriality had already guided the *planning phase* of his mission, and to what extent he had integrated this perspective with his Roman understanding of place names. Apart from that, there are other factors shaping Paul's mission activity that integrated well with and were an integral part of Paul's Roman territoriality, namely, the *practical conditions of the Roman Empire*. We will briefly turn to some of these conditions as we conclude the present section.

When one looks at the spectrum of the cities in which Paul worked, one can observe that Paul's mission mainly had to do with large cities.[38]

Mußner, *Der Galaterbrief*, 2nd ed., HTKNT 9 [Freiburg im Breisgau: Herder, 2002], 87–88; Hans Dieter Betz, *Galatians: A Commentary on Paul's Letter to the Churches in Galatia*, Hermeneia [Philadelphia: Fortress, 1979], 71–72). On the interpretation of (spiritual) experiences, cf. the analysis in Rabens, "Power," 138–45.

35. See Riesner, *Frühzeit*, 224–25.

36. On this point, see further William J. Webb, *Returning Home: New Covenant and Second Exodus as the Context for 2 Corinthians 6.14–7.1*, JSNTSup 85 (Sheffield: JSOT, 1993); Florian Wilk, *Die Bedeutung des Jesajabuches für Paulus*, FRLANT 179 (Göttingen: Vandenhoeck & Ruprecht, 1998); Otfried Hofius, "Paulus—Missionar und Theologe," in *Paulusstudien II*, by Otfried Hofius, WUNT 143 (Tübingen: Mohr Siebeck, 2002), 13–16; Dickson, *Mission-Commitment*, 153–77.

37. Cf. Riesner, *Frühzeit*, 218–19.

38. Steven J. Friesen, "Prospects for a Demography of the Pauline Mission: Corinth

For example, Paul remained both in Corinth and Ephesus for a prolonged period during which it was also possible to engage the larger region through coworkers. To expand on Harnack's well-known metaphor,[39] Paul ignited the torch of the gospel in the larger cities along the arc from Jerusalem to Illyricum, so that the light shone into the hinterland. After having made sure that the flame was burning steadily in one place, he moved on to light a new torch—where no flame had yet burned. In the process of spreading the gospel, Paul chose to a great extent centers of concentrated population. Because of the economic dominance, these large cities attracted traders and business people. Because of their advanced infrastructure, such cities offered good conditions for communication and possibilities of contact with other people.[40] Therefore, based on Paul's travel movements among the cities, it is possible to speak of Paul's mission to *urban centers* in their provincial settings.[41]

The external conditions in the Roman Empire during the time of the

---

among the Churches," in *Urban Religion in Roman Corinth: Interdisciplinary Approaches*, ed. Daniel N. Schowalter and Steven J. Friesen, HTS 53 (Cambridge, MA: Havard University Press, 2005), 354, provides a detailed list of the cities where a) Paul founded a church, b) Paul established contact with congregations which he himself had not started, and c) Paul traveled through without founding a church.

39. Adolf von Harnack, *Die Mission in Wort und Tat*, vol. 1 of *Die Mission und Ausbreitung des Christentums in den ersten drei Jahrhunderten*, 4th ed. (Leipzig: Hinrichs, 1924), 80. Cf. Allen, *Methods*, 12; Dunn, *Romans 9–16*, 869; Lietaert Peerbolte, *Paul*, 250; Schnabel, *Paul*, 285–86; Jewett, *Romans*, 914. Reinbold, *Propaganda*, 224–25, however, excludes missions in the surrounding region through coworkers.

40. On the catalytic function of trade in the expansion of religious movements, see more generally Peter Wick and Volker Rabens, eds., *Religions and Trade: Religious Formation, Transformation and Cross-Cultural Exchange between East and West*, Dynamics in the History of Religions 5 (Leiden: Brill, 2014).

41. So, inter alia, Allen, *Methods*, 13–17; Wolf-Henning Ollrog, *Paulus und seine Mitarbeiter: Untersuchungen zu Theorie und Praxis der paulinischen Mission*, WMANT 50 (Neukirchen-Vluyn: Neukirchener Verlag, 1979), 125–26; Reinbold, *Propaganda*, 212; Lietaert Peerbolte, *Paul*, 236, 255. However, Schnabel considers this inference as jumping to conclusions because: 1) We know too little about the first almost fifteen years of Paul's activities in Arabia, Syria, and Cilicia to speak about a *Zentrumsmission* in the time between 32/33 and 45; 2) In his missionary activities during the years 45–57 it appears that Paul did not visit Ankara, the capital of the province of Galatia. Likewise, he probably did not work in other important cities (Side, Termessos, Sagalassos, and Kybistra); 3) According to Acts 13:49, Paul did not limit his missionary activity to cities, but also reached out to those living in the territories around the cities (χώρα), i.e., he also worked among village dwellers (Schnabel, *Mission*, 1242). Cf. Robinson, *Christians*, 65–130, who stresses the dynamic interaction between the cities and the surrounding countryside.

Pauline mission were widely beneficial to the apostle's travels. The rule of Augustus had inaugurated a time of peace and resulted in the flowering of economic and cultural enterprises. Trade could develop, the infrastructure was improved. Methods of travel were relatively safe so that traffic on the Mediterranean Sea and on the main trade roads increased. Travel like Paul's profited from these conditions, a kind of travel that in part might better be referred to as "removal" or "moving household" (cf. Priscilla and Aquila, whom we find first in Rome, then in Corinth, and finally in Ephesus). It hence seems natural to assume that many of Paul's travel procedures were pragmatic decisions based on the concrete shape and practical conditions of the urban landscape of the first-century Roman Empire.

By way of answer to our first question of this chapter, we can conclude that Paul's Roman territoriality and the conditions of the urban landscape of the Roman Empire provided a framework for Paul's travel procedures among the cities. In retrospect, he interpreted his overarching travel directions in the light of the prophecies in Isaiah 66. He wanted to reach the unreached, and it is this focus on people that drove him. He did not just want to win people for the gospel, but he wanted them to "become the gospel," to use the title of Michael Gorman's recent book on Paul, participation, and mission. In order to accomplish this holistic mission, he shared his life with the city dwellers, and a number of times had to return to the cities and regions that he had visited before, so that he could help his assemblies to flourish. In the second part of the chapter we will now look at some of the details of how Paul tried to accomplish this goal once he had arrived in a particular city.

2. Paul's Missionary Procedures upon His Arrival in a City

In the previous section we saw that in his letters Paul does not communicate a detailed mission strategy that would explain the travel plans and program of his ministry in the spreading of the gospel. Paul rather conveys basic principles from which stem practical consequences for his work. These tenets include the precept that Paul wished to work where the gospel was not yet known. Paul's travel routine is based on this foundational truth. Larger cities were particularly well-suited for communicating the gospel. They were pulsing with life and in possession of good infrastructure and access to the surrounding region for which they served as administrative centers.

What awaited Paul in the cities? On the most elementary level, Paul shared the same language (Koine Greek) with the residents of the cities.

Building on this, Paul as a "city dweller" employed rhetoric and verbal images and metaphors from the urban context. In comparison with the Jesus of the gospels, who taught with parables using the rural landscape (seeds, weeds, tenant farmers, etc.), Paul's eloquent Greek more clearly evoked the *gymnasium* and private homes (although he could also use imagery from the world of agriculture, e.g., in 1 Cor 3:6). Apart from that, Paul was also at home in the city because of the practicalities of the urban working environment. In the context of his avocation as a missionary, the cities offered Paul great job opportunities, so that he could support himself and meet other people in a natural way.[42] A further characteristic of the larger cities was that Paul could here find established Jewish communities as well as a great spectrum of non-Jewish inhabitants, including "settlers" (μέτοικοι), who helped open channels of communication with other parts of the non-Jewish world. At the same time, a large city offered a certain amount of anonymity, so that a small, developing group of Christians need not draw unnecessary attention to itself when there were conflicts with people of other faiths.[43]

In the cities Paul met people from a variety of social statuses. Social status is made up of various facets of social identity, such as ethnic origin, nationality, personal freedom, wealth, employment relationships, patron/client relationships, age, gender, marital status, family heritage, public offices, and honors.[44] It is difficult to fathom the precise statistical details of the make-up of the Pauline congregations. Malherbe, Meeks and others are of the opinion that the Pauline assemblies broadly represented an even share of the various statuses which shaped the urban society.[45] Meggitt, Friesen,

---

42. Cf. Meeks, *Urban Christians*, 9. On the physical and social structure of the cities, see esp. Peter Oakes, "Contours of the Urban Environment," in *After the First Urban Christians: The Social-Scientific Study of Pauline Christianity Twenty-Five Years Later*, ed. Todd D. Still and David G. Horrell (London: Continuum, 2009), 21–35; Reinhard von Bendemann and Markus Tiwald, "Das frühe Christentum und die Stadt—Einleitung und Grundlegung," in *Das frühe Christentum und die Stadt*, ed. Reinhard von Bendemann and Markus Tiwald, BWANT 198 (Stuttgart: Kohlhammer, 2012), 9–42; Martin Ebner, *Die Stadt als Lebensraum der ersten Christen*, vol. 1 of *Das Urchristentum in seiner Umwelt*, GNT 1/1 (Göttingen: Vandenhoeck & Ruprecht, 2012). Detailed geographical and archeological maps on Paul's mission in the context of the cities can also be found in Schnabel, *Mission*, 1529–66.

43. Cf. Dunn, *Beginning*, 555–56.

44. Cf. Meeks, *Urban Christians*, 53–55; Friesen, "Demography," 361–62.

45. Abraham J. Malherbe, *Social Aspects of Early Christianity*, Rockwell Lectures, 2nd ed. (Philadelphia: Fortress, 1983), 31, speaks of a developing consensus; Meeks, *Urban Christians*, 72–73, agrees. Cf. Gerd Theißen, *Studien zur Soziologie des Urchristentums*, 3rd ed. (Tübingen: Mohr Siebeck, 1989), 272–89.

and others, however, have strongly emphasized that, just as the majority of the general population was made up of the poorest level of people, so also the majority of church members stemmed from that group.[46] Bruce Longenecker takes a mediating position. He ascribes some significance to the middle class both in society and in the apostolic communities, even if it was minor.[47] No matter which of these analyses one supports, it is clear that a large part of the people in the cities and in the congregations were poor.

The assemblies Paul founded in the cities had something to offer the poorest level of the urban population, including an alternative community with a value system different from the hierarchy of status, honor, and shame. Regarding poverty, Longenecker writes:

> If Paul's communities took initiatives to care for the poor, and if they gathered to share food and drink in corporate dinners and other occasions, it is relatively easy to see what economic attraction such communities would have held for people . . . who fell beyond the structures of a household. Moreover, this dimension might have distinguished groups of Jesus followers from other urban associations, since Greco-Roman associations did not accumulate their membership from among [these] levels.[48]

The apostles were united in giving priority to the care of the poor, and Paul stresses that that "was actually what I was eager to do" (Gal 2:10). This was not just a tactical consideration for "reaching people with the good news," but a theological and ethical reflection that integrated well with Paul's overall mission. The social status and honor of the lower stratum people in the city got enhanced. Equality before God was the new ethos (1 Cor 12:12–26; 2 Cor 8:13–15; Gal 3:28; Rom 10:11–12, etc.).[49] The status change from "slaves" to

46. Justin J. Meggitt, *Paul, Poverty and Survival*, SNTW (Edinburgh: T&T Clark, 1998); Friesen, "Demography," 351–70; cf. Ekkehard W. Stegemann and Wolfgang Stegemann, *Urchristliche Sozialgeschichte: Die Anfänge im Judentum und die Christusgemeinden in der mediterranen Welt* (Stuttgart: Kohlhammer, 1997), 249–71.

47. Bruce W. Longenecker, "Socio-Economic Profiling of the First Urban Christians," in *After the First Urban Christians: The Social-Scientific Study of Pauline Christianity Twenty-Five Years Later*, ed. Todd D. Still and David G. Horrell (London: Continuum, 2009), 36–59. Cf. Bruce W. Longenecker, *Remember the Poor: Paul, Poverty, and the Greco-Roman World* (Grand Rapids: Eerdmans, 2010).

48. Longenecker, "Socio-Economic Profiling," 52.

49. On this point see details in Michael Wolter, *Paulus: Ein Grundriss seiner Theologie* (Neukirchen: Neukirchener Verlag, 2011), 323–327. In addition, Ebel argues that the great intensity of their life together and the renunciation of formal membership requirements

"adopted children of God" (with the attending family imagery of "brothers and sisters") and the experience of the unconditional love of God as "Father" through the Spirit of the Son (Jesus the Messiah) were dimensions of community that had the potential to satisfy the "never-ending hunt for 'honor capture' that marked out Greco-Roman urbanism"[50] (see Rom 5:5, 8; 8:15–17; Gal 4:1–7; etc.).[51]

The factors mentioned above shaped Paul's mission as his gospel and its ethical corollaries engaged the realities of life in the city in the Roman Empire. Next to these formative factors there were some concrete practices and structures of Paul's mission that we will now examine in the remainder of this chapter.

A fundamental characteristic of Paul's missionary work in the urban context was that Paul *traveled with coworkers*. For Paul, mission was a community task for which he could count on an extended network of Jews and non-Jews, women and men, slaves, ex-slaves, and free. In his letters Paul names approximately nineteen "colleagues" ("partners" [κοινωνοί], "fellow slaves" [σύνδουλοι], "fellow prisoners" [συναιχμάλωτοι], and "fellow soldiers" [συστρατιῶται]) who traveled with him. These colleagues worked with him, provided companionship for him, and acted as his representatives (e.g., Timothy in 1 Cor 4:17; 16:10–11; Titus in 2 Cor 2:13; 7:6–15; 8:6, 16–17), or functioned as his host or patron (e.g., Aquila and Prisca in 1 Cor 16:19; Rom 16:3–5).[52] This multifaceted and interactive teamwork in the context of urban mission work touches on the Pauline principle of the church as the body of Christ, in which there are different gifts and tasks (1 Cor 12; Rom 12:4–8; Eph 4:16). Correspondingly, for his missionary work Paul used the fitting picture of building a house, in which he, the wise master builder, has laid the foundation upon which others may build (1 Cor 3:10).

---

made the Christian congregations attractive in the competition with pagan associations in their milieu (Eva Ebel, *Die Attraktivität früher christlicher Gemeinden: Die Gemeinde von Korinth im Spiegel griechisch-römischer Vereine*, WUNT/2 178 [Tübingen: Mohr Siebeck, 2004], 218; cf. Frey, "Ausbreitung," 104–6).

50. Longenecker, "Socio-Economic Profiling," 53.

51. Cf. Jewett, *Romans*, 500; Volker Rabens, *The Holy Spirit and Ethics in Paul: Transformation and Empowering for Religious-Ethical Life*, WUNT/2 283, 2nd ed. (Tübingen: Mohr Siebeck, 2013), 215–41. However, the converse was also true: "The more subversive the early Christian movement appeared, the less attraction it would have held for those enthralled by honor and advancement within Roman urbanism" (Longenecker, "Socio-Economic Profiling," 55).

52. Cf. Ollrog, *Paulus, passim*; Reinbold, *Propaganda*, 213–24. On the meaning of relationships for the life and theology of Paul, see Rabens, *Spirit*, 133–44.

When Paul settled in a city, as a rule *he sought a workplace* (1 Thess 2:9; 1 Cor 4:12; 2 Cor 11:27; 12:14; Acts 20:34). Paul made a living with his hands (according to Acts 18:3 he was a leatherworker or tentmaker). According to Paul's own reports, he spent a great amount of his time in urban business. For example, the apostle reminds the Thessalonians that he and his coworkers labored day and night, taking pains not to become a burden to them (1 Thess 2:9). This practice had at least two consequences for the apostle's life and work. First, it meant that Paul spent the better part of his days in the workshop, probably bent over a workbench next to slaves.[53] In that way Paul's reputation and honor may have suffered—through this practice he was himself probably associated with the status of a slave (cf. Cicero, *Off.* 1.42).[54] On the other side, the apostle's "grounded" existence allowed him to spend a lot of time in daily contact with other people, living and working together. This, in turn, would have produced abundant opportunities for communicating the gospel.[55] Paul thus shared his life with the people of the city—in a thoroughly practical manner.

Also this aspect of Paul's missionary procedure has underlying reasons. The most central motive for earning his own living is stated in 1 Corinthians 9:12-19: the gospel itself is "free of charge" and for that reason he desires to pass it on at no cost.[56] A further cause for Paul financing himself is closely bound up with the first reason: Paul distances himself from wandering preachers who evangelize for the purpose of earning money (1 Cor 9:12; 2 Cor 2:17; 1 Thess 2:3-6). He did not "twist" the gospel (δολοῦν, 2 Cor 4:2) in order to be able to preach more popularly about the crucified Christ (cf. 1 Cor 1:22-23). Furthermore, Dunn suspects that Paul did not want to give up his independence lest he be caught up in new loyalty struggles or power structures, and lest he become a burden to others (1 Thess 2:7, 9; cf. 2 Thess 3:8-9).[57] Even so, Paul could accept

---

53. On the working conditions for leather handwork, see Ronald F. Hock, *The Social Context of Paul's Ministry: Tentmaking and Apostleship* (Philadelphia: Fortress, 1980), 67-68, and the critical discussion in Meggitt, *Poverty*, 65, 76-77.

54. See Steve Walton, "Paul, Patronage and Pay: What Do We Know about the Apostle's Financial Support?," in *Paul as Missionary: Identity, Activity, Theology, and Practice*, ed. Trevor J. Burke and Brian S. Rosner, LNTS 420 (London: T&T Clark, 2011), 220-33, here 222-23.

55. See Hock, *Social Context*, 33, 39-40, 56-57 (mentioning philosophical tutorials in ancient workshops); Dunn, *Beginning*, 565-66.

56. Cf. Gordon D. Fee, *The First Epistle to the Corinthians*, NICNT (Grand Rapids: Eerdmans, 1987), 421: "In offering the 'free' gospel 'free of charge' his own ministry becomes a living paradigm of the gospel itself."

57. Dunn, *Beginning*, 56; cf. Dale B. Martin, *The Corinthian Body* (New Haven/London:

financial gifts in certain circumstances, when these were given not by patrons, but by "partners in the gospel," of their own free will (Phil 1:5). Such gifts did not cover Paul's regular living expenses (Phil 4:10–19; cf. 2 Cor 11:7–8).[58]

Aside from (and presumably during) his daily work, Paul devoted himself to the spreading of the gospel in the city. *Paul preached and discussed in synagogues and houses, and founded apostolic communities.* Acts stereotypically locates the beginning of Paul's preaching activity in the synagogues (e.g., Acts 17:1–2, 10). As we find in Paul no statements of his missionary tactics upon his arrival in a city, and as he says several times that he is an apostle for the gentiles, Wolfgang Reinbold has posed the question whether in this point Acts is historically reliable. In relation to possible preaching activities in the synagogue, Reinbold comes to a negative conclusion. Nonetheless, he grants that Paul may have attended the meetings on the Sabbath and made occasional contacts on this basis.[59] However, while Reinbold is justified in treating Acts' more schematic presentation of Paul's entry into cities with caution, there are good reasons to believe that Paul established significant relationships in the context of his interaction with the synagogues (which may have included teaching). In the synagogues, Paul would have been accepted as a fellow Jewish believer and would find not only a Jewish infrastructure, but also other Jews and Godfearers who were conversant with the essentials of Jewish thinking and in that sense were prepared for the apostle's concerns. Paul thus did not really contradict his principle of gentile mission: in the synagogue both groups would hear the gospel, "the Jew first, and also the Greek" (Rom 1:16). In such a context Paul could also live out one of his related missiological principles:

> To the Jews I became as a Jew, in order to win Jews. To those under the law I became as one under the law (though I myself am not under the law) so that I might win those under the law. To those outside the law I became as one outside the law (though I am not free from God's law but am under Christ's law) so that I might win those outside the law. (1 Cor 9:20–21)

As we have already seen, the salvation of Israel is of great interest for Paul. Since in this passage Paul says that he has directed one part of his missio-

---

Yale University Press, 1995), 79–86; Walton, "Patronage," 232. Walton lists further possible grounds for Paul's practice of financing himself ("Patronage," 224–25).

58. On the potential contradiction, see the detailed discussion in Walton, "Patronage."

59. Reinbold, *Propaganda*, 185–87, 207–10.

logical practice toward "winning Jews," it is only logical that he would seek contact with the synagogue.[60] Judging from his letters, it seems that Paul had a certain amount of success with his mission to his fellow Jews, for he freely presupposes that the members of his assemblies, or at least the teachers, knew the Septuagint as Holy Scripture, acknowledged its authority, and were familiar with Jewish ethics.[61]

To be sure, Paul's interaction with the Jews in the context of his mission did not always meet with success. In his catalog of hardships in 2 Corinthians 11:23–26, Paul writes that he had to suffer five times the punishment of forty lashes minus one.[62] It is most likely that the historical setting of this punishment was his confrontations with the synagogues. Once Paul had to leave a synagogue in a given city, did he then turn to the public squares to preach in the marketplace? This popular image of Paul is based above all on the story of the Areopagus episode in Acts 17 and on the parallels that recount the preaching activity of the Cynic and Sophistic philosophers. However, Stanley Stowers questions these parallels, and argues that the diatribes of the Hellenistic philosophers that have come down to us do not have their *Sitz im Leben* in the marketplace, but in schools.[63] Since Paul's letters provide no

---

60. Against this background Sandnes proposes the hermeneutical principle that the book of Acts deserves attention where it does not contradict Paul's letters. "The dictum of 1 Cor. 9.19–23 becomes almost without reference if Acts is not taken into account" (Karl Olav Sandnes, "A Missionary Strategy in 1 Corinthians 9.19–23?," in *Paul as Missionary: Identity, Activity, Theology, and Practice*, ed. Trevor J. Burke and Brian S. Rosner, LNTS 420 [London: T&T Clark, 2011], 128–41, here 135). Cf. Lietaert Peerbolte, *Paul*, 241; James C. Miller, "The Jewish Context of Paul's Gentile Mission," *TynBul* 58 (2007): 101–15; Reidar Hvalvik, "Paul as a Jewish Believer—According to the Book of Acts," in *Jewish Believers in Jesus: The Early Centuries*, ed. Oskar Skarsaune and Reidar Hvalvik, 2nd ed. (Peabody, MA: Hendrickson, 2007), 121–53. However, one should not go as far as Marius Reiser, "Hat Paulus Heiden bekehrt?," *BZ* 39 (1995): 76–91, who clearly overshoots the target when he denies to Paul any mission outside of the synagogue.

61. Cf. Schnabel, *Mission*, 1242–43; Dunn, *Beginning*, 560.

62. So, among others, Stanley K. Stowers, "Social Status, Public Speaking and Private Teaching: The Circumstances of Paul's Preaching Activity," *NovT* 26 (1984): 59–82, here 64; Margaret E. Thrall, *A Critical and Exegetical Commentary on the Second Epistle to the Corinthians*, ICC (Edinburgh: T&T Clark, 2000), 2:723–58 (with a detailed argument against the thesis that Paul employs the hardship catalog as a parody). Reinbold thinks that the punishment was not carried out because of Paul's preaching, but because of his "un-Jewish" lifestyle (Reinbold, *Propaganda*, 207–210).

63. Stowers, "Status," 59–82, followed by Reinbold, *Propaganda*, 200–202. See the critique in Thomas Schmeller, *Paulus und die 'Diatribe': Eine vergleichende Stilinterpretation*, NTA 19 (Münster: Aschendorff, 1987), 46–52. Stowers sees clear parallels in structure and

information suggesting an extended public preaching ministry in the marketplace, and as Acts gives only a little more (cf. Acts 14:8–18; 20:20; etc.), we can assume with Stowers that preaching in synagogues, schools (cf. Acts 19:9), and private houses was characteristic of Paul. Nevertheless, this certainly does not exclude the possibility that Paul sometimes led philosophical and theological discussions in the public square.[64]

It is indisputable that private houses played a central role in the Pauline mission in the cities. The ancient οἶκος in the sense of "house as living space" and "family household" became the focal point of the early Christian movement. Here arose not only parallels to the teaching activity of the Hellenistic philosophers,[65] but also Jewish converts were familiar with assembling in houses.[66] Furthermore, there is a series of practical reasons that may have led to the significance of houses for the Pauline mission: 1. The houses of new church members were immediately available as meeting places. Remodeling to accommodate the Christian meetings was not necessary. 2. For the central elements of Christian gatherings the private house offered the best conditions: familial community and shared meals at which the Lord's Supper could be celebrated. 3. Private houses made possible relatively in-

---

contents between Hellenistic philosophies (esp. the Stoics) and Paul's theology (Stanley K. Stowers, "Does Pauline Christianity Resemble a Hellenistic Philosophy?," in *Paul beyond the Judaism/Hellenism Divide*, ed. Troels Engberg-Pedersen [Louisville: Westminster John Knox, 2001], 81–102). However, the parallels to Paul's preaching activity should not only be sought among the Hellenistic philosophers (cf. Vítor Hugo Schell, *Die Areopagrede des Paulus und Reden bei Josephus: Eine vergleichende Studie zu Apg 17 und dem historiographischen Werk des Josephus*, WUNT/2 419 [Tübingen: Mohr Siebeck, 2016]), and not all of the supposed parallels between Paul's theology and Stoic philosophy are conclusive (see the critical analysis in, e.g., Volker Rabens, "*Pneuma* and the Beholding of God: Reading Paul in the Context of Philonic Mystical Traditions," in *The Holy Spirit, Inspiration, and the Cultures of Antiquity: Multidisciplinary Perspectives*, ed. Jörg Frey and John R. Levison, Ekstasis 5 [Berlin: de Gruyter, 2014], 293–329, here 306–12). In addition, Philo's teaching (which according to Noack was a missionary activity) offers interesting evidence for the possible circumstances of Paul's preaching. Noack highlights five ideal-typical locations: 1. The synagogue, with the reading and exposition of scripture; 2. The private philosophical school, with a private library and discourse (diatribe); 3. The public lecture hall (Gymnasium, Ephebie); 4. A rich citizen's private villa with philosophical lectures; 5. The marketplace (cf. Philo, *Spec.* 1.319–23) (Christian Noack, *Gottesbewußtsein: Exegetische Studien zur Soteriologie und Mystik bei Philo von Alexandria*, WUNT/2 116 [Tübingen: Mohr Siebeck, 2000], 27–29); cf. Schnabel, *Mission*, 1236.

64. Cf. Reinbold, *Propaganda*, 202.
65. Cf. Stowers, "Status," 81.
66. According to Schnabel, *Mission*, 1244, this applied to Palestine as well as to the diaspora.

conspicuous gatherings—a requirement that became necessary if there were conflicts with non-believers.[67]

In many cities these house communities started to expand in the course of the Pauline mission activity. After the apostle had helped an assembly develop a worship life and had provided guidance for the spiritual and structural growth of the community (cf. 1 Thess 2:10–12, etc.), *Paul moved on*. If, in his estimation, he had "fully proclaimed the gospel of Christ" (πεπληρωκέναι τὸ εὐαγγέλιον τοῦ Χριστοῦ, Rom 15:19), or if he found "no further place" in a city or region (μηκέτι τόπος, 15:23), the apostle would carry on his mission elsewhere—where Christ was not yet known (15:20). Nevertheless, he continued to care for the congregations he founded through visits, letters, and by sending coworkers as emissaries who could build upon the foundation he had laid (1 Cor 3:10).[68]

Did Paul call upon his congregations for their part to be "on-site missionaries" in their city after his departure? In his letters, Paul's assemblies are infrequently exhorted to share the gospel explicitly (see, e.g., the implicit encouragement in Phil 1:14: "most of the brothers and sisters . . . dare to *speak the word* with greater boldness and without fear;" cf. 1:7, 18).[69] More frequently, the congregations are presented as "recipients" of the message, who above all are encouraged to live faithfully according to the values of the gospel. However, it is clear that such a lifestyle "tells a story" (e.g., 1 Thess 1:6–9: "the word of the Lord has sounded forth from you not only in Macedonia and Achaia, but in every place your faith in God has become known, so that we have no need to speak about it"). Paul thus explicitly expects from his assemblies the *promotion* of the gospel, although he does not explicate that this implies (verbal) *proclamation*.[70] According to Dickson, this promotion of the gospel is achieved through the congregations being "partners in the gospel" (Phil 1:5), which for Paul involved the idea that "all of you share in God's grace with me, both in my imprisonment and in the defense and confirmation of the gospel" (Phil 1:7).[71] Paul considers it a success of such

---

67. Cf. Schnabel, *Mission*, 1244.

68. On Paul's highly individual "aftercare" for his assemblies in the different cities, see most recently Matthew Forrest Lowe, "In the Making and the Unmasking: Spiritual Formation as Paul's Missional 'Good News,' Then and Now," in *Is the Gospel Good News?*, ed. Stanley E. Porter and Hughson Ong, McMaster New Testament Studies (Eugene: Pickwick, 2018), forthcoming.

69. On this text, see Gorman, *Gospel*, 110–12. Gorman goes even further by arguing (partly from silence) that "like a dog, a community in Christ cannot help but bark" (45).

70. Cf. Dickson, *Mission-Commitment*, 311.

71. Dickson, *Mission-Commitment*, 131, 311.

participation in the gospel that many "through the testing of this ministry . . . glorify God by . . . obedience to the confession of the gospel of Christ and by the generosity of . . . sharing with them and with all others" (2 Cor 9:13). The believers' participation in the gospel is hence adequately coined as their "becoming the gospel."[72]

The attraction and radiance of such a life is emphasized by Paul also in other passages. For example, he encouraged the church in Rome to "take thought for what is noble in the sight of all" (Rom 12:17b). The fact that Paul can speak of "what is noble in the sight of all" shows the far-reaching compatibility of Pauline ethics with the basic ethical convictions of the ancient city dwellers (cf. Gal 5:23; 6:9; Phil 4:8; 1 Cor 9:19–22; 10:32–33). "The content of the paraenetic instructions which Paul gave demonstrates a definite inclusive ethical profile, directly in the middle of which stand such norms and values as are acknowledged by all people and enjoy general esteem, including among the non-Christian majority of society."[73] This inclusive ethical profile also implies the openness and comprehensibility of the worship service, so that outsiders may reach the positive conviction, "God is really among you" (1 Cor 14:24–25).

3. Conclusion

Paul's mission strategy among the cities demonstrates a close interconnection between basic missiological principles and the praxis based upon them. In the planning and execution of his missionary journeys Paul demonstrated flexibility, because conflicts and adversity forced him to take ways other than those he had planned. It is difficult to establish on the basis of his letters (and Acts) how far in advance and in how much detail Paul preplanned his travel routes. However, I have argued that Paul's Roman territoriality and the conditions of the urban landscape of the Roman Empire provided a framework for Paul's travel procedures among the cities. In retrospect, he interpreted his overarching geographical movement (shaped in an arc from Jerusalem to Illyricum) in the light of the prophecies in Isaiah 66. For him, the effective

---

72. Cf. n. 16 above.

73. Wolter, *Paulus*, 316. On the potentially missional function of an attractive ethos, see further Volker Rabens, "Philo's Attractive Ethics on the 'Religious Market' of Ancient Alexandria," in *Religions and Trade: Religious Formation, Transformation and Cross-Cultural Exchange between East and West*, ed. Peter Wick and Volker Rabens, DHR 5 (Leiden: Brill, 2014), 333–55.

motivation is the universal promise and demand of the gospel, which was to be proclaimed everywhere, especially wherever people had not yet heard, and especially among the gentiles.

Paul selected large cities such as Corinth and Ephesus for his mission. This choice brought with it abundant advantages for his work, ranging from a developed infrastructure to a breadth of job possibilities, to a great diversity of population. The latter point is significant in that it allowed Paul the possibility of attending the synagogue. These advantages served the purpose that people could hear the gospel, and eventually themselves become "partners in the gospel." This was a relational enterprise. For the apostle "mission" meant a reciprocal process in which he shared his life. This process manifested itself in the joint work with his coworkers with whom Paul traveled to the cities, in the work of urban industry as well as in the synagogues and houses in which Paul engaged with his fellow citizens. With the values that Paul communicated in this lifestyle, his congregations had a solid basis from which to lead a life attractive to further inhabitants of the cities and provinces.

"Outside the City Gate"

Center and Periphery in Paul's Preaching in Philippi

Cédric Brélaz

The colony of Philippi in the Roman province of Macedonia is considered an essential landmark for the geography of early Christianity. According to the Acts of the Apostles, this was the first city ever visited by Paul on European soil and the place where the first person converted to Christianity in mainland Greece. Because of the long passage devoted in Acts to the description of Paul's deeds there, the reputation of Philippi in the Christian tradition and culture extended far beyond the actual significance of the city within the Roman Empire. In addition, the narrative of Acts stresses two peculiarities with respect to the urban environment of Paul's preaching in Philippi: first, it is stated that Philippi was a Roman colony, which is the only instance where a colony is explicitly referred to as such in Acts; second, unlike in the other cities he visited, Paul had to get out of the city in order to find the place where the local Jewish (or Judaizing) community gathered.

This paper will explore the physical and symbolic topography of early Christianity in Philippi by recontextualizing Paul's action within the local urban environment of the colony. It will address four main issues regarding the interaction between Paul's presence in Philippi and the city of Philippi itself:

1. For what reason was Philippi deliberately characterized as a Roman colony in Acts 16:12 and why did Paul choose to stop in this city in eastern Macedonia?
2. What did the city center of Philippi look like at the time of Paul's visit and does the spatial framework of Paul's action in the colony as echoed in Acts find any counterpart on the ground?

3. What was the narrative function and the symbolic meaning of the shift between the venues of Paul's deeds in Philippi, first outside the city gate at the place of prayer and then in the middle of the public space?
4. Did the decision of Paul to focus on the town during his visit to Philippi have any implication as far as the social and ethnic composition of his audience was concerned?

This paper will argue that the apparent centrality of Philippi for early Christianity and the suggested centrality of Paul himself within the city as they emerge from the account of Acts have largely been constructed and magnified in order to comply with the programmatic intention of the narrative. Yet, it was not before the fourth century that the group originally established by Paul in Philippi became architecturally visible in the public space of the city and became as self-confident as the community depicted in Acts.

1. Philippi, (Not the First) City of Macedonia and Roman Colony

Philippi enjoys special treatment in the narrative of Acts. It was the first city where Paul and his followers preached after the apostle was convinced by the Holy Spirit to go over to Macedonia from Asia Minor. Moreover, a long passage of Acts is devoted to Paul's visit and deeds in the city (16:12–40)—longer than for most other cities he visited outside Judea—and one major event was believed to have happened there: the arrest and the subsequent jailing of the apostle by the local authorities. This is one of the only two instances in Acts where Paul was led to reveal his Roman citizenship.[1] The significance of Philippi for early Christianity was even more magnified later when in the fourth century the local church claimed to have been founded by the apostle and, to this day, the Eastern Orthodox Church celebrates Lydia as the first person to have converted to Christianity on European soil thanks to Paul's preaching in the city and has a baptistery to mark the site where the conversion is reputed to have taken place.

Despite the central position Philippi seems to have had in Acts for the narrative about the spread of Christianity in Europe and more broadly in the West, one should not overestimate the actual importance of the city in first-century Macedonia. Philippi was not "the leading city of that part of Macedonia," as it is sometimes understood from the text of Acts 16:12. Neighboring Amphipolis (where Paul just passed through) was still in the

---

1. The other instance is Acts 22:25–29.

first century CE the most thriving city in Eastern Macedonia.[2] It enjoyed the status of a free city—this means that it was formally not part of the Roman province of Macedonia and that it stood beyond the governor's jurisdiction[3]—and had direct access to the sea, which was not the case for Philippi, whose city center lay ca. 15 km from its harbor, Neapolis. The textual transmission of the passage about Philippi's status is uncertain and Peter Pilhofer convincingly argued that the lectio difficilior (ἥτις ἐστὶν πρώτης μερίδος τῆς Μακεδονίας πόλις rather than ἥτις ἐστὶν πρώτη τῆς μερίδος Μακεδονίας πόλις) should be preferred since it referred to Philippi as "a city of the first district of Macedonia," which was in fact true.[4] When the Antigonid kingdom was abolished in 168 BCE, the Romans divided Macedonia into four autonomous districts (μερίδες) in order to avoid a united state being rebuilt there.[5] Lying on the eastern fringes of the kingdom, Philippi was included in the first district of which Amphipolis was declared the capital city. Amphipolis had been for centuries the most important stronghold on the eastern border of the Macedonian kingdom.[6] In the meantime, Philippi had become in Late Hellenistic times a "small settlement" (κατοικία μικρά) according to Strabo.[7] The reference to these former districts might well have originated in the literary education of the author of Acts since they were mentioned for instance by Polybius.[8] It is worth noting, however, that μερίδες were still in use in the Roman imperial period. After the Roman province was created in 148 BCE, μερίδες became administrative units within the Macedonian

2. C. Koukouli-Chrysanthaki, "Amphipolis," in *Brill's Companion to Ancient Macedon: Studies in the Archaeology and History of Macedon, 650 BC–300 AD*, ed. Robin J. Lane Fox (Leiden: Brill, 2011), 409–36.

3. Éric Guerber, *Les cités grecques dans l'Empire romain. Les privilèges et les titres des cités de l'Orient hellénophone d'Octave Auguste à Dioclétien,* 2nd ed. (Rennes: Presses Universitaires de Rennes, 2010), 33–77.

4. Peter Pilhofer, *Philippi, I. Die erste christliche Gemeinde Europas*, WUNT 87 (Tübingen: Mohr Siebeck, 1995), 159–65. For a contrasting view, see Richard S. Ascough, "Civic Pride at Philippi: The Text-Critical Problem of Acts 16.12," *NTS* 44 (1998): 93–103.

5. Arthur M. Eckstein, "Macedonia and Rome, 221–146 BC," in *A Companion to Ancient Macedonia*, ed. Joseph Roisman and Ian Worthington (Chichester: Wiley-Blackwell, 2010), 225–50.

6. Louisa D. Loukopoulou, "*Provinciae Macedoniae finis orientalis*: The Establishment of the Eastern Frontier," in *Two Studies in Ancient Macedonian Topography*, ed. Miltiades B. Hatzopoulos and Louisa D. Loukopoulou, Meletēmata 3 (Athens: National Hellenic Research Foundation, 1987), 89–100.

7. Strabo, VII, frag. 17a (ed. S. Radt, Göttingen, 2002).

8. Livy, *Urb. cond.* 45.29.5–9, relying on a lost passage of Polybius. The expression μέρη is found in Diodorus, *Bibl. hist.*, 31.8.8, and Strabo, VII, frag. 47.

koinon, the federal, ethnic, and religious community linking Macedonians with one another.[9]

The accuracy of Acts 16:12 with respect to Philippi's status can also be seen through the use of the word κολωνία to describe the city. This is the only instance where a Roman colony is qualified as such in Acts. Yet, Paul visited many other Roman colonies in the Eastern Mediterranean, like Pisidian Antioch, Lystra, Iconium, Alexandria Troas and Corinth. If this precision had not been used at the beginning, the reader (ancient and modern) of Acts 16:12–40 would not have had any hint that Philippi was a Roman colony. In the whole passage, Philippi is depicted as a local community looking very much like any other Greek city throughout the Eastern provinces of the Roman Empire. Philippi is called a πόλις several times—which is the usual way in Greek to describe a local political entity, even if it was a colony dependent on the Roman state[10]—and generic words like ἀγορά or ἄρχοντες, though referring in this case to the forum and to the local magistrates of the Roman colony, can also be valid for a Greek city. Even titles such as στρατηγοί and ῥαβδοῦχοι, which serve here as the correct Greek equivalents for the Latin functions *duumviri* and *lictores*, could refer to Greek institutions as well.[11]

One might wonder what the purpose of using the technical term κολωνία, transliterated into Greek from Latin,[12] and of putting such an emphasis on the legal status of Philippi was. It is still possible that the word κολωνία was interpolated, since it stands in Acts 16:12 in apposition to πόλις. Κολωνία seems to have been used here as a comment on Philippi's status in order to make clear that, unlike most other local communities in the Greek-speaking provinces, that very political entity (πόλις) actually was part of the Roman state. The special concern of the author of Acts for institutions and for legal issues, however, was not limited to Philippi. In Thessalonica the title of the local magistrates is correctly phrased as πολιτάρχαι (Acts 17:6) and what is said about the proconsul's jurisdiction in Corinth (Acts 18:12–17) perfectly fits with the general framework of how Roman justice

9. Miltiades B. Hatzopoulos, *Macedonian Institutions under the Kings*, Meletēmata 22 (Athens: National Hellenic Research Foundation, 1996), 1:231–60, 352–59.

10. This term occurs in several Greek inscriptions in Philippi itself: see Peter Pilhofer, *Philippi, II, Katalog der Inschriften von Philippi*, 2nd ed., WUNT 119 (Tübingen: Mohr Siebeck, 2009) (cited below as Pilhofer II), nos. 22, 119, 127, 133, 137, 265, 267, 280, 301, 734.

11. Cédric Brélaz, *La sécurité publique en Asie Mineure sous le Principat (Ier–IIIème s. ap. J.-C.). Institutions municipales et institutions impériales dans l'Orient romain* (Basel: Schwabe, 2005), 74–85, 177–79.

12. Other instances regarding Philippi are Pilhofer II, nos. 273 and 711 line 3.

was administered in the provinces.[13] The focus on the status of Philippi as a Roman colony might be related to what proves to have been the most crucial moment during Paul's visit according to the account of Acts, namely the arrest, flogging, and subsequent jailing of Paul and Silas by the *duumviri*.

Indeed, the confession by Paul that he possessed Roman citizenship is the culmination of the whole episode of his visit in Philippi and prefigures his future appeal to the court of the emperor (Acts 25:10–13) and then his transfer to Rome where the tradition alleges he was sentenced to death. In any other Greek city, local authorities would of course neither have been allowed to flog or put in jail Roman citizens like Paul and Silas without trial.[14] But the fact that this occurred in a Roman colony, where local magistrates themselves were Roman citizens too and were supposed to observe Roman law carefully, made the event even more outrageous and the whole story more striking. In this respect, the precision of the beginning of the passage that Philippi was a κολωνία was perhaps intended to prime the reader for the growing dramatic intensity of the narrative.

Apart from these narratological aspects, more circumstantial reasons can certainly explain why Paul decided to visit Philippi, and this had to do with the location of the city on the Via Egnatia. It was usual for travelers coming from Western Asia Minor and going to Europe to pass over to Macedonia by boat starting from the Troad, as Paul did when he embarked in Alexandria Troas. The short sailing allowed travelers to save time by cutting through the northern Aegean and avoiding a long overland journey through Aegean Thrace. By doing so, travelers would reach the Via Egnatia when disembarking at the harbor of Neapolis. Then, if Paul visited Philippi, that was not because there was a substantial Jewish community in the city (it even seems that quite the opposite was the case), but because the colony was a major stop on the Via Egnatia.[15] The first important city travelers would come across in Macedonia was Philippi, since Neapolis—though it had been an autonomous city until late Hellenistic times—had now been turned into a dependent settlement integrated into the territory of the Roman colony.[16]

13. Julien Fournier, *Entre tutelle romaine et autonomie civique. L'administration judiciaire dans les provinces hellénophones de l'empire romain (129 av. J.-C.–235 apr. J.-C.)* (Athens: École française d'Athènes, 2010), 547, 579.

14. Fournier, *Entre*, 364–65.

15. Paul Collart, *Philippes, ville de Macédoine, depuis ses origines jusqu'à la fin de l'époque romaine* (Paris: de Boccard, 1937), 487–523.

16. Cédric Brélaz, *Corpus des inscriptions grecques et latines de Philippes. Tome II. La*

2. Mid-First-Century Philippi: Monumentalizing the Roman Colony

When Paul visited Philippi in the late 40s, the city had been undergoing considerable remodeling for the past few decades with regard to town planning and public building projects. Philippi was refounded as a Roman colony in 42 BCE by Marc Antony after the final battle of the civil war between the republicans and the heirs of Caesar. The settlement of hundreds (or even thousands) of Italian veterans in Philippi and in the surrounding area, and the creation of a new political entity—the *colonia* was now part of the state of the *populus Romanus*—made the previous Greek *polis* that was founded three centuries earlier by the king of Macedon Philip II disappear and caused dramatic changes with respect to demography, social structure, ethnic and cultural interactions, land ownership, and political institutions. The replacement of the Greek city by the Roman colony did not, however, instantaneously affect the physical organization of the town. Some of the most fundamental features of the town planning (dating back to the foundation of the city by the Macedonians in the fourth century BCE) were kept by the Roman colonists, such as the delimitation of the town by walls, the grid pattern of streets and blocks, and one of the major public buildings in the Classical and Hellenistic city, the theater that stood on the slopes of the acropolis.[17] Despite the reinforcement (and the formal refoundation) of the colony thanks to Octavian, who in 30 BCE settled in Philippi civilians he had expelled from Italy in order to seize their lands because of their support of Marc Antony, no substantial public works seem to have been carried out in the colony during the first four or five decades of its existence. This was in no way specific to Philippi. Roman colonies typically initiated public building projects at the earliest half a century after they were established, by which point the local elite had become wealthy enough to fund such works.[18]

The archaeological analysis of the forum has shown that the earliest monumental stage of the public space should be dated to the second quarter

---

colonie romaine. Partie 1. La vie publique de la colonie (Athens: École française d'Athènes, 2014), 41–42 (cited below as CIPh II.1).

17. Cédric Brélaz and Julien Demaille, "Traces du passé macédonien et influences de l'hellénisme dans les colonies de Dion et de Philippes," in L'héritage grec des colonies romaines d'Orient: interactions culturelles dans les provinces hellénophones de l'empire romain, ed. Cédric Brélaz (Paris: de Boccard, 2017), 119–56.

18. Rebecca J. Sweetman, "100 Years of Solitude: Colonies in the First Century of Their Foundation," in Roman Colonies in the First Century of Their Foundation, ed. Rebecca J. Sweetman (Oxford: Oxbow, 2011), 1–6.

of the first century CE, maybe under the reign of Claudius. Various archaeo-logical and epigraphic evidence suggests, however, that a public space such as a square, which might have been used for official activities and celebra-tions (including dedications to the emperors), did already exist under the Julian emperors, probably as early as the Augustan period.[19] At the time when Paul arrived at Philippi, the forum must have already had the general shape it would keep during the next centuries (with the exception of the later restructuring works that were carried out at different times, in particular in the mid–second century). This was a monumental quadrangular square surrounded by various public buildings sheltering the civic life of the colony, including a council hall, a judicial basilica, an archives building, a public library, a temple for the imperial cult, a speaker's podium and porticoes. In the Hellenistic period, above this flat area, on the slopes of the acropolis, there was a terrace with temples where epigraphic copies of the most im-portant public documents of the Greek city were displayed. This terrace now served as the *capitolium*, that is the sanctuary devoted to the main tutelary gods of the Roman state—as on the Capitoline Hill in Rome—which were found ubiquitously in every Roman colony all over the empire. This whole monumental and architectural layout looked very Roman indeed, even if the building material and the construction techniques were mostly Greek, which implies that Greek architects and craftsmen were hired for the works. Unlike in Corinth, where much more from the architectural heritage of the Greek city was kept (even if transformed and reinterpreted by the Roman colonists),[20] the city center of Philippi was drastically modified to ensure compliance with the Roman pattern.

This monumentalizing display of Romanness was the urban environ-ment in which Paul's deeds in Philippi took place, if we rely on the narrative of Acts, at least the episode of the apostle's arrest and jailing. A third-century CE Greek inscription from Philippi refers to the forum as the ἀγορά, as in Acts 16:19.[21] Several significant monuments were erected in the forum or in its immediate surroundings shortly before Paul's visit. A huge dedication to the imperial family, probably in honor of Claudius and his adopted son Nero whose name was deliberately erased because he had suffered *damnatio*

---

19. Michel Sève and Patrick Weber, *Guide du forum de Philippes* (Athens: École française d'Athènes, 2012), 11–17.

20. Benjamin W. Millis, "The Local Magistrates and Elite of Roman Corinth," in *Corinth in Contrast: Studies in Inequality*, ed. Steven J. Friesen, Sarah A. James and Daniel N. Scho-walter, NovTSup 155 (Leiden: Brill, 2014), 38–53.

21. Pilhofer II, no. 133 line 15.

memoriae, was carved on the front wall of a bathhouse close to the forum, commemorating the benefactions of the man who refurbished the baths and on this occasion gave donations to the whole population of the colony (including those who were not members of the civic elite and the people living in the countryside).[22] In the forum itself, an honorary monument supporting statues was erected to the emperor Claudius and to his relatives.[23] A very long inscription (nearly 20 meters), made of huge bronze letters of 62 cm (the biggest inscription ever in all Latin epigraphy after the dedication of the Pantheon in Rome!), was engraved on the floor of the square to commemorate the paving of the forum by a man who had been priest of the deified Augustus.[24] Only the fixing holes of the bronze letters have survived to the present, but this inscription visible from the *capitolium* and filling the whole central portion of the forum—long, big, and shining as it was—must have looked very impressive to anyone visiting the city center of Philippi at that time. On the contrary, several other monuments, though dating to the first century CE as well, did not yet stand in the forum at the time when Paul visited Philippi (as is sometimes stated in recent scholarship).[25] In particular, the statue base for the priestesses of the deified Livia standing before the temple of the imperial cult,[26] as well as the inscriptions referring to the soldier L. Tatinius Cnosus on the other side of the square,[27] were erected only in the Flavian period, and the blocks mentioning two prominent families of the colony, the Mucii and the Decimii, even if they were found in the fountains of the public place, actually belonged to funerary monuments that originally stood outside the city and were demolished in order to be reused as building material during reconstruction works in the forum in Late Antiquity.[28]

Strabo was indisputably right when he said that from a "small settlement" in late Hellenistic times Philippi significantly "grew" (ηὐξήθη) after it was refounded as a Roman colony in 42 BCE. As lavish as the monumentalized city center should have appeared to visitors in the mid–first century CE, Philippi remained a middle-range colony in the Imperial period in compari-

---

22. *CIPh* II.1, no. 6.
23. *CIPh* II.1, no. 5.
24. *CIPh* II.1, no. 66.
25. Pilhofer, *Philippi I*, 118–21.
26. *CIPh* II.1, no. 126.
27. *CIPh* II.1, nos. 84–85.
28. *CIPh* II.1, nos. 59, 119. The huge funerary altar standing next to the Via Egnatia and still visible today at Dikili Tash, in the Eastern necropolis of the city, was erected at the earliest under the reign of Nero: *CIPh* II.1, no. 63.

son with other Roman colonies visited by Paul in the Eastern Mediterranean. Philippi was not a world-class city like Corinth which, only a hundred years after it was rebuilt by Caesar, had regained its historical position as a major commercial hub and a leading city in mainland Greece. Corinth hosted the proconsul of Achaia's headquarters and resumed organizing the Isthmian games as the Greek city of Corinth had done until its destruction in 146 BCE. Neither was Philippi as thriving and powerful as the Roman colony of Pisidian Antioch, which had a close relationship with the emperors and where we know of seven families of senatorial rank and many equestrians who reached key positions in the imperial administration—while the only known senator from Philippi was not the descendant of the Italian colonists, but originated from the Thracian royal dynasty.[29] Philippi was undoubtedly an important city, but its influence was limited to a regional scale in eastern Macedonia and the colony could compete neither with Thessalonica, which served as the proconsul of Macedonia's headquarters, nor with Berea, which was the capital city of the Macedonian *koinon*.[30]

3. Outsiders in the Public Space: Asserting Christian Engagement in Roman Philippi

Paradoxically enough, the first thing Paul did after he entered Philippi, according to the account of Acts, was to get out of the city immediately to reach the place where local Jews used to gather. That place was said to have been located "outside the city gate" (ἔξω τῆς πύλης), by a river (16:13). Many attempts have been made to identify that place on the ground, especially the river, but the dramatic changes that the agrarian landscape and the hydrography in the surroundings of the archaeological site of Philippi encountered in the 1930s because of the draining of the plain of Drama make any identification very speculative.[31] Paul Collart asserted that πύλη should be assimilated

---

29. *CIPh* II.1, nos. 37–38.

30. Cédric Brélaz, "Le faciès institutionnel, social et religieux d'une colonie romaine dans la province de Macédoine," in *Philippes, de la Préhistoire à Byzance. Études d'archéologie et d'histoire*, ed. Julien Fournier (Athens: École française d'Athènes, 2016), 199–214.

31. Laurent Lespez, "L'évolution des paysages du Néolithique à la période ottomane dans la plaine de Philippes-Drama," in *Dikili Tash, village préhistorique de Macédoine orientale: recherches franco-helléniques dirigées par la Société archéologique d'Athènes et l'École française d'Athènes (1986–2001)*, ed. C. Koukouli-Chrysanthaki et al. (Athens: École française d'Athènes, 2008), 21–416.

to the monumental arch (the so-called "arch of Kiemer") that crossed the Via Egnatia 2 km westwards from the city wall.[32] But Collart's assumption was influenced by his own theory that pretends that the arch was delimiting the *pomoerium* or sacred boundary of the Roman colony and that foreign cults not formally allowed by the Roman state—such as the Jewish religion in his view—could only be practiced outside this limit. The numerous synagogues that were located within the city walls mentioned in Acts demonstrate, however, that worshipping outside the city was not a requirement for the Jews according to Roman law. Moreover, the "arch of Kiemer" certainly did not aim at showing the limit of the *pomoerium*, but more probably served as a monumentalized gate marking the entrance into the suburbs of the town of Philippi.[33] Still, the place where Paul met Lydia is said to have been located "outside the gate" (ἔξω τῆς πύλης)—or "outside the city" (ἔξω τῆς πόλεως) if we accept the most widespread reading in the textual transmission. Thus, that πύλη must have been one of the city gates.[34]

If the Jews gathered outside the city walls, this was certainly because there was no permanent building devoted to the Jewish cult within the city of Philippi. It is admitted that the word προσευχή used in 16:13 to describe the "place of prayer" Paul reached after he got out of the city can refer to permanent buildings like synagogues as well.[35] In this case however, the fact that the term synagogue was avoided—while it was used in Acts to refer to the meeting places of the local Jewish communities in most other cities— might have been deliberate. According to the account of Acts, it does not seem that there were a lot of Jews in Philippi at that time. Unlike in many cities where Paul was immediately able to find the local synagogue and to meet the Jewish community, the information the apostle could get about the existence of a meeting place for the Jews in Philippi was rather scant: actually, Paul headed to the river "where we were expecting there to be a place of prayer" (οὗ ἐνομίζομεν προσευχὴν εἶναι). Moreover, the first person to have faith in Paul's preaching, Lydia, was not really a Jew herself, but a "Godfearer" (16:14), a Judaizing pagan, and no other reference is made in Acts to the Jewish community in Philippi. The προσευχή outside the city walls, by the river, must then have been the place where the Judaizing people living in Philippi typically met and prayed.

32. Collart, *Philippes*, 320–25, 456–60.
33. *CIPh* II.1, 37–38.
34. Pilhofer, *Philippi I*, 165–74.
35. Philip A. Harland, *Greco-Roman Associations: Texts, Translations, and Commentary. II. North Coast of the Black Sea, Asia Minor* (Berlin: de Gruyter, 2014), 27–28.

This marginal presence of the Jewish (or Judaizing) community in Philippi and the peripheral range of Paul's action—preaching outside the city walls—sharply contrast with the implications the deeds of the apostle would have afterwards within the Roman colony. According to the narrative of Acts, Paul was immediately invited by Lydia to stay at her house after she converted to Christianity (16:15). Unlike the place of prayer, her house certainly stood within the city walls.[36] In the following days, Paul returned to the place of prayer, that is, outside the city. On his way to the προσευχή, Paul was yelled at several times by a female soothsayer until the apostle decided to exorcize her. From that very moment, all the following episodes of Paul's stay in Philippi were located in the town and even in the center of the Roman colony. The soothsayer's owners, accusing Paul of causing unrest in the city because of his preaching, dragged Paul and Silas into the public place (ἀγορά) before the local authorities (Acts 16:19). The case was then brought to the highest judicial and political authority in the colony, the *duumviri*, who had Paul and Silas flogged and jailed because they were allegedly rioting and spreading Jewish customs that would be contrary to the Roman way of life. The appearance of Paul and Silas before the most important magistrates in Philippi must have happened in the very heart of the Roman colony, in the forum itself as we are told in Acts, or in one of the public buildings around the square, like the basilica that was devoted to courts and trials—even if in this case the *duumviri* did not conduct a formal trial against Paul and instead took policing measures against him because of the emergency situation and the risk of riot in the city.

This account of Paul's adventures in the forum provided a symbolic transfer of early Christianity in Philippi from the periphery (where Paul met Lydia for the first time) to the center of the city. From an outsider being forced to get out of the city to meet with his fellow believers and to preach, Paul suddenly became a subject of public concern. Christianity gained through the appearance of Paul in a public venue (cf. δημοσίᾳ, "publicly" at 16:37), and by his confrontation with local authorities, a kind of official recognition. This is all the more true given that on this occasion Paul revealed that he was a Roman citizen and that he required that the *duumviri* personally come to the prison to release him from jail officially and confess that they should not have him flogged and jailed "without any trial" (ἀκατάκριτος) because of his status. By refusing to allow the *duumviri* to operate "covertly"

---

36. See also Acts 16:40: Paul and Silas entered one more time Lydia's house as soon as they were freed from jail.

(λάθρᾳ) one more time, Paul claimed that he and his followers were doing nothing wrong and that they deserved respect from local authorities. Disputing the procedure used by public authorities to arrest him because it was irregular was part of the argument of Paul (and of the later martyrological literature) and was meant to show that believing in the Lord did not lead to any breach of Roman law and that, ironically, the lawbreakers were those who were supposed to enforce it.[37]

This spatial, social, and even legal reintegration of Paul into the city and into the collective body of the city dwellers in Philippi, as well as into the wider community of Roman citizens, was meant to stress the importance of the message delivered by the apostle in the colony and to claim that Christianity should be a universal issue. The confrontation of Paul with public authorities is a recurring pattern in the narrative of Acts. In Pisidian Antioch, for instance, "the leaders of the city" (13:50) were informed by the Jews of Paul's preaching; in Athens the apostle was summoned before the Areopagus to expose what his beliefs were (17:19) and in Corinth he was brought to the court of the proconsul of Achaia (18:12–16); in Ephesus the situation was so serious because of the people rioting against Paul that the highest local official had to address the crowd gathered in the theater and to urge calm (19:35–40). In each case, the involvement of public authorities, either local or Roman, emphasizes the endurance of the apostle despite the hostility of the major part of the local population; and the staging of Paul's deeds in the most visible and official venues of the city suggests that Paul got a reputation going far beyond the groups he had founded around him and that his preaching was a matter of common interest regardless of any ethnic, social, or political identity, as well as of any former religious belonging.

4. Paul's Preaching in Philippi: Town vs. Countryside

Despite the focus in the account of Acts on the importance that Paul's preaching would allegedly have had for the public life in the colony, the visit of the apostle in the late 40s must have been a minor event on the ground for Philippi. As chaotic as it may appear, the arrest of Paul and Silas by the soothsayer's owners and their appearance in the forum before the *duumviri*, their being surrounded by the shouting crowd, then their flogging and jailing

---

37. Ari Z. Bryen, "Martyrdom, Rhetoric, and the Politics of Procedure," *ClAnt* 33 (2014): 243–80.

are nothing if not very realistic and are consistent with what we know of the daily duties of local magistrates in the Roman Empire with regard to law enforcement and policing. There is plenty of evidence for similar unrest in the Imperial period—whatever it arose from, whether for social, economic, political, or religious reasons—and this sort of summary justice that was administered by the *duumviri* against Paul and Silas certainly was a widespread practice in local communities.[38] The group itself that gathered around Paul was a very small community and, generally speaking, early Christianity remained a limited phenomenon in Philippi until the beginning of the fourth century.

From the very short prosopography of the first followers of Paul emerging from Acts and from the Epistle to the Philippians, we can infer that the apostle's audience in the colony was primarily made of Greek-speaking foreign residents who had moved from various parts of the eastern Mediterranean to settle in Philippi, certainly for business.[39] This was the case, for instance, with Lydia, the seller of purple who came from Thyatira. Non-biblical sources also point out the same close connection between the colony of Philippi and northwestern and western Asia Minor due to trade and to the migration of individuals from one region to the other in both directions.[40] The fact that Paul—apparently because of the absence of a substantial and properly structured Jewish community in Philippi—first sought to get in touch with the Greek-speaking (Judaizing) people among the local population, especially those who were active in the textile industry as he himself was, is in no way surprising. By doing so, however, Paul interacted with only a specific part of the inhabitants of the colony and deliberately set himself apart from the two major groups of the population in Philippi: the Roman colonists and the native Thracians.

Having a mixed population of Greeks and Thracians among its foreign residents was one of the peculiarities of the Roman colony of Philippi.[41] Thracians, who had been living in the area for centuries when Greeks first

38. Brélaz, *Sécurité publique*, 56–64, 271–75.

39. Richard S. Ascough, *Paul's Macedonian Associations: The Social Context of Philippians and 1 Thessalonians*, WUNT/2 161 (Tübingen: Mohr Siebeck, 2003), 122–28.

40. Cédric Brélaz, "Philippi: A Roman Colony within Its Regional Context," in *L'hégémonie romaine sur les communautés du Nord Égéen (IIe s. av. J.-C.–IIe s. ap. J.-C.): entre ruptures et continuités*, ed. Julien Fournier and Maria-Gabriella G. Parissaki (Athens: National Hellenic Research Foundation, 2017).

41. Peter Oakes, *Philippians: From People to Letter*, SNTSMS 110 (Cambridge: Cambridge University Press, 2000), 73.

arrived from the island of Thasos in the Archaic period to found settlements on the continent, still formed the majority of the population of eastern Macedonia in the Imperial period. The presence of Thracians in Philippi is mainly visible through their characteristic onomastics in the epigraphic record[42] and through the traditional cult deities that continued to be worshipped in the colony, also by the colonists of Italian origin, like the cult of the Hero Aulonites (*Heros Aulonites*; Ἥρως Αὐλωνείτης), a local variant of the so-called Thracian Horseman who was worshipped from the Hellenistic period in a sanctuary lying at the foot of Mount Pangaion.[43] The Thracian language, although it was not written, was probably still spoken in eastern Macedonia at that time. In the countryside surrounding the city of Philippi the Thracian population was predominant by far. Though they did not have civic rights in the colony, Thracians gathered into rural administrative units called *vici*. These villages and districts spread all over the territory of Philippi and enjoyed local autonomy, even if they formally belonged to the colony.[44] Apparently, Paul did not travel across the wide territory of the colony. We are told in Acts that the apostle only spent a few days in Philippi during his first visit (16:12). Once he disembarked at Neapolis, Paul headed straight toward Philippi. It does not seem that Paul went further into the countryside than the place of prayer that stood in the suburbs of the town. When he left Philippi, Paul must have gone through the territory of the colony using the Via Egnatia, but he certainly did not stop for longer stays in the countryside until he reached Amphipolis (17:1). Even there, he and his fellows only "went across" (διοδεύσαντες) the city, important as it was, as he did in Apollonia, in order to arrive at Thessalonica and to join the synagogue there, the first one he seems to have found during his journey through Macedonia.

Paul's focus on the town of Philippi would not have prevented him from meeting with Thracians. It is true that the city center was mainly inhabited by Roman colonists as well as Greek foreign residents dealing with production and trade. But native Thracians were not completely absent from the town: several votive reliefs carved on the rocks of the acropolis were dedicated to

---

42. Dan Dana, *Onomasticon Thracicum. Répertoire des noms indigènes de Thrace, Macédoine orientale, Mésies, Dacie et Bithynie*, Meletēmata 70 (Athens: National Hellenic Research Foundation, 2014).

43. *CIPh* II.1, 52–55.

44. Cédric Brélaz, "La langue des *incolae* sur le territoire de Philippes et les contacts linguistiques dans les colonies romaines d'Orient," in *Interpretatio. Traduire l'altérité dans les civilisations de l'Antiquité*, ed. Frédéric Colin, Olivier Huck, and Sylvie Vanséveren (Paris: de Boccard, 2015), 371–407.

deities of Thracian origin,[45] and cultic associations worshipping Thracian gods had their headquarters set up next to the forum, in the core of the Roman colony.[46] This evidence is later than the first century, but this suggests that Thracians would visit the city center too, at least from time to time, and this must have been the case since the colony was founded. Among the pagan population, Thracians might in theory have shared some common interests with Paul's followers. The most popular cult in eastern Macedonia, the cult of the Thracian Horseman or Hero God to whom we referred above, had strong chthonic and eschatological aspects, as is made clear by the heroizing depiction of the dead who was assimilated to the god on numerous funerary reliefs in the colony. On the other hand, the concern for the afterlife was crucial in the theology of Dionysus, who was worshipped in a specific sanctuary in Drama, north of Philippi, and whose cult included mystery initiation rites comparable to the devotion to another Thracian hero, Orpheus.[47]

Yet, as far as we can infer from the account of Acts and from the names of the members of the Christian community in Philippi from the time of Paul until the early Byzantine period, Christianity did not primarily affect the native population. It is worth noting that things happened in quite a different way in another Roman colony, in Lystra in Central Anatolia. There, the crowd spontaneously cheered Paul after the apostle had healed a man who could not walk. The crowd celebrated Paul and his friends as if they were themselves pagan gods. An interesting detail mentioned in Acts refers to the language shouted by the crowd: this was "in Lycaonian" (Λυκαονιστί [14:11]), an Anatolian language. Thus, we must conclude that, unlike in Philippi, Paul did interact with the native population of the colony in Lystra, even if in this case the apostle failed to make them abandon their traditional pagan beliefs and practice (14:14–18). Nor did Paul's preaching primarily address the Roman colonists of Italian origin who were still predominant in the town, especially in the monumentalized city center used by the civic elite for self-promotion and display through buildings, statues, and inscriptions. The only contact Paul had with members of the Italian elite of the colony was conflictual and occurred when the *duumviri* ordered him to be flogged and jailed by their escorts. But we cannot exclude the possibility that Roman citizens of lower social strata got acquainted with Paul's followers and their message.

45. Paul Collart and Pierre Ducrey, *Philippes I. Les reliefs rupestres* (Athens: École française d'Athènes, 1975).
46. Pilhofer II, no. 133 lines 14–16 mentions association headquarters located πρὸς τὴν ἀγορὰν παρὰ τὸ ὡρο[λ]όγιν.
47. *CIPh* II.1, 42–44.

Not all of the descendants of the first Italian colonists sent to Philippi by Marc Antony and Augustus belonged to the upper classes, and the social composition of some cultic associations in Philippi—including people of very different status (Roman citizens, freedmen, free foreigners, slaves) all representing the middle to middle-lower levels of the society[48]—seems to have been similar to what might have been the social background of the communities founded by Paul in Greece and Asia Minor.

5. Conclusion: From the City of Philip to the City of Paul

Early Christianity in Philippi was unquestionably an urban phenomenon. This does not mean however that all the city dwellers were affected by Paul's preaching. The deliberate choice of the apostle to focus on the Greek trading community living in the city center of Philippi in order to spread his message led to the exclusion from his mission of the two major ethnic and cultural groups of the colony: the Roman colonists (at least those who were part of the local elite) and the native population. Despite the apparent centrality— according to the narrative of Acts—of the figure and deeds of Paul in the public life of Philippi (after the apostle was brought into the forum to be sentenced by local authorities and after the miracle occurred in the prison), the Christian community evidently remained a very small group within the colony. Unlike many other cultic associations and the Jewish community itself, which by the third century had obtained a more institutionalized form as shown by an epitaph referring to the "synagogue,"[49] no archaeological or epigraphic record mentions the Christian group until the beginning of the fourth century. Yet, the epistle of Polycarp of Smyrna to the Philippians attests that in the second century the local church had grown and did possess an internal administrative organization.[50]

Surprisingly, when the first cathedral church was built during the first decades of the fourth century, Christianity in Philippi seems to have suddenly gained a central position in the city. The church, known already at that time as the "basilica of Paul" as it was phrased in the mosaic dedication on the floor,[51] was erected next to the forum in connection with an underground

48. Pilhofer II, nos. 163 (Silvanus's club), 509b (Apollo's club).

49. Pilhofer II, no. 387a.

50. Paul Lemerle, *Philippes et la Macédoine orientale à l'époque chrétienne et byzantine. Recherches d'histoire et d'archéologie* (Paris: de Boccard, 1945), 1:60–68.

51. Pilhofer II, no. 329.

tomb and *heroon* dating to Hellenistic times. During the early Byzantine period, greater basilicas were then built on the site of the marketplace and of the *capitolium*, replacing some of the most important public monuments in the center of the colony.[52] Local Christians had already been deeply aware and proud of the apostolic origin of their church since the second century, as stated by Polycarp and Tertullian.[53] But the construction of a church in honor of Paul at the core of the city in the fourth century was the culmination of the integration of the apostle's memory within the colony and from this point on was the expression of the focusing of the whole civic community (and not only of the Christian group, as had been the case so far) on the celebration of Christianity.

Some scholars have even argued that the Hellenistic tomb lying under the first cathedral church could have served as a martyrium or at least as a crypt devoted to St Paul.[54] In any case, the juxtaposition of the two buildings was not coincidental. The family of the man who had been originally buried in the tomb came from Thasos[55] and it is possible that in the Hellenistic period the hero cult that was worshipped there had something to do with the commemoration of the foundation of Krenides (which was the name of the city of Philippi before the king of Macedon conquered it in 356 BCE) by the Thasians in the mid–fourth century BCE.[56] Although it is very doubtful that the original hero cult to this Hellenistic benefactor had continued within the Roman colony, the memory and the acknowledgement of the sacred function of the place might have been kept until this space was reused by the church in the later Imperial period.[57]

52. Lemerle, *Philippes*, 281–513; Samuel Provost and Michael Boyd, "Philippi's Town Planning and the Size and Spatial Distribution of the Christian Settlement in the 4th–6th c. AD," in *Philippi, from Colonia Augusta to Communitas Christiana: Religion and Society in Transition*, ed. Steven J. Friesen et al. (Leiden: Brill, forthcoming).

53. Pilhofer, *Philippi I*, 206–28, 257–58.

54. Stylianos Pelekanidis, "Kultprobleme in Apostel-Paulus-Oktogon von Philippi im Zusammenhang mit einem aelteren Heroenkult," in *Atti del IX Congresso Internazionale di Archeologia Cristiana* (Vatican City: Pontificio Istituto di archeologia cristiana, 1978), 2:393–97; Charalambos Bakirtzis, "Paul and Philippi: The Archaeological Evidence," in *Philippi at the Time of Paul and after His Death*, ed. Charalambos Bakirtzis and Helmut Koester (Harrisburg: Trinity Press International, 1998), 37–48.

55. Pilhofer II, no. 327.

56. Angelos G. Zannis, *Le pays entre le Strymon et le Nestos: géographie et histoire (VIIe-IVe siècle avant J.-C.)*, Meletēmata 71 (Athens: National Hellenic Research Foundation, 2014), 523–39.

57. Cédric Brélaz, "The Authority of Paul's Memory and Early Christian Identity at

CÉDRIC BRÉLAZ

The replacement of this *heroon,* which—in the Hellenistic period at least—recalled the origins of the city, by a church devoted to the memory of Paul, was symptomatic of the importance gained by the figure of the apostle for local Christian identity in the fourth century. Even if the memory of the successive founders of Philippi (the Thasians with some Athenians, Philip II, Marc Antony, Octavian/Augustus) had not completely vanished at that time, especially the memory of Philip II since the city was named after him,[58] the real founder of Philippi was not considered in the early Byzantine period to have been Augustus, although the city continued to be named *colonia Iulia Augusta Philippiensium,* nor Constantine, who was celebrated as the new founder (*conditor*) of the colony because of some benefaction (not related to Christianity),[59] but the apostle Paul. Three centuries after Paul's visit in the city, the centrality of Christianity within the urban landscape of Philippi that the author of Acts claimed through the figure of the apostle was eventually achieved.

Philippi," in *Authority and Identity in Emerging Christianities in Asia Minor and Greece,* ed. Cilliers Breytenbach and Julien Ogereau (Leiden: Brill, forthcoming).

58. Cédric Brélaz, "Entre Philippe II, Auguste et Paul: la commémoration des origines dans la colonie romaine de Philippes," in *Une mémoire en actes: espaces, figures, discours,* ed. Stéphane Benoist, Anne Daguet-Gagey and Christine Hoët-van Cauwenberghe (Lille: Presses Universitaires du Septentrion, 2016), 119–38.

59. *CIPh* II.1, no. 29.

140

The City as Foil (Not Friend nor Foe)
Conformity and Subversion in 1 Corinthians 12:12–31

Helen Morris

1. Introduction

It is clear that Paul was familiar with urban environments and civic institutions, but how he viewed such structures is disputed.[1] The aim of this paper is to explore Paul's view of the city as revealed through his use of the body metaphor in 1 Corinthians 12:12–31 in comparison with contemporaneous examples. Is Paul against the city—does he see it as a foe? Does he embrace the city—does he see it as a friend? Or, is his stance toward the city more complex than either of these extremes? If so, how is it best depicted? To this end, aspects of both conformity and subversion in Paul's adoption and adaptation of this common motif will be explored. In addition, 1 Corinthians 12:12–31 will be read alongside 1 Corinthians 15:20–28 to see what light this sheds on the differences between Paul's body motif and its use in wider Greco-Roman culture.

---

1. See, for example, Bird's evaluation of the recent claims that Paul was anti-imperial in Michael F. Bird, "'One Who Will Arise to Rule over the Nations': Paul's Letter to the Romans and the Roman Empire," in *Jesus Is Lord, Caesar Is Not: Evaluating Empire in New Testament Studies*, ed. Scot McKnight and Joseph B. Modica (Downers Grove, IL: InterVarsity Press, 2013), 146–65.

2. The Body in Political Rhetoric

> A commonwealth resembles in some measure a human body. For each of
> them is composite and consists of many parts; and no one of their parts
> either has the same function or performs the same services to others. If
> . . . the feet should say that the whole body rests on them . . . the mouth,
> that it speaks; the head, that it sees . . . and then all these should say to
> the belly, "And you . . . what use are you to us? . . . [Y]ou are actually a
> hindrance and a trouble to us and . . . compel us to serve you. . . . " And if
> they therefore stopped serving the stomach . . . could the body possibly
> exist for any considerable time, and not rather be destroyed within a few
> days by the worst of all deaths, starvation?[2]

In these extracts, Dionysius retells Agrippa's[3] well-known fable about body
parts revolting against the stomach to warn the plebeians not to rise up
against the Senate.[4] References to the commonwealth as a body date back
to the fourth and fifth centuries BCE,[5] with Plato arguing that societies best
flourish when the individual members see themselves as one body so that,
for example, "when one of our fingers is hurt, the whole fellowship . . . is
sensible of the hurt . . . [and so too] . . . the pleasure felt when it is easy."[6]
The use of the body analogy to encourage social harmony is found in the first
century CE with Seneca's depiction of the emperor as the soul or head and
the state as his body.[7] In addition, Dio Chrysostom asserts that comrades
provide extra eyes with which to see and ears with which to hear.[8] Plutarch
also utilizes the body metaphor, maintaining that those who fail to live in
concord are like feet that trip each other up or a body that cuts off one of its
limbs.[9] Epictetus contends that citizens must not desire anything without
reference to the whole community, just as a hand or foot behaves in relation

---

2. Dionysius of Halicarnassus, *Ant. Rom.* 6.86.2–3.

3. Livy, *Urb. cond.* 2.32.7–11; cf. Anthony C. Thiselton, *The First Epistle to the Corinthians*, NIGTC (Grand Rapids: Eerdmans / Carlisle: Paternoster, 2000), 993.

4. Dionysius of Halicarnassus, *Ant. Rom.* 6.86.3–4.

5. Margaret M. Mitchell, *Paul and the Rhetoric of Reconciliation*, HUT 28 (Tübingen: Mohr Siebeck, 1991), 158.

6. Plato, *Resp.* 5.462c-d.

7. Seneca, *Clem.* 1.4.3–5.1; cf. Robert J. Banks, *Paul's Idea of Community: The Early House Churches in Their Cultural Setting* (Grand Rapids: Baker Academic, 1995), 66.

8. Dio Chrysostom, *1 Regn.* 32; *3 Regn.* 104; cf. Thiselton, *First*, 992; Mitchell, *Reconciliation*, 158–60.

9. Plutarch, *Mor.* 478–79; cf. Thiselton, *First*, 992.

to the body.[10] The body motif is also present in second-century texts such as Polyaenus's *Stratagems in War*, which records Iphicrates's warning to his army that while the cavalry, as the feet, are necessary, without the general, who is the head, the army has lost everything.[11] 1 Corinthians precedes the late-first-century and second-century texts, but Paul's first hearers would have recognized the body analogy as a means of encouraging unity within hierarchical political structures.[12] It was, as Banks notes, a metaphor that was *in the air*.[13]

3. Conformity and Subversion in Paul's Body of Christ Motif

Compare this political use of the body with Paul's use of the metaphor in 1 Corinthians 12:12–31:

> (12) For just as the body is one and yet has many parts, and as all the parts of the body are many but the body is one, so it is with Christ. (13) For by one Spirit we have all been baptized into one body—whether Jew or Greek, slave or free—we have all been saturated with one Spirit. (14) For the body is not one part but many. (15) If the foot said, "Since I'm not a hand, I'm not part of the body," would it, for this reason, not be part of the body? (16) And if the ear said, "Since I am not an eye, I'm not part of the body," would it, for this reason, not be part of the body? (17) If the whole body were an eye, where would the sense of hearing be? If it were all hearing, where would the sense of smell be? (18) Indeed, God has placed each of the parts in the body, as he has seen fit. (19) If it were all one part, where would the body be? (20) There are many parts, but one body. (21) Therefore the eye cannot say to the hand, "I have no need of you!" Nor, moreover, can the head say to the foot, "I have no need of you!" (22) In fact, more to the point, the parts of the body considered weak are indispensable. (23) Those parts of the body that we consider less honorable, we clothe in greater honor and the unpresentable parts we treat with greater modesty, (24) which our more respectable parts do not need. God has knit (συγκεράννυμι) the body together, giving greater

10. Epictetus, *Diatr.* 2.10.4–5; cf. Thiselton, *First*, 992.
11. Polyaenus, *Strateg.* 3.9.22; cf. Thiselton, *First*, 993; Dale B. Martin, *The Corinthian Body* (New Haven: Yale University Press, 1995), 93–94.
12. Thiselton, *First*, 992.
13. Banks, *Community*, 66.

honor to the parts that lacked it. (25) So there is no division in the body. Rather the parts are concerned about each other. (26) And if one part suffers, all the parts suffer together; if one part is praised, all the parts rejoice together. (27) Now you are Christ's body and individually parts of it. (28) God has placed in the church first apostles, second prophets, third teachers, then acts of power, then gifts of healing, helping gifts, gifts of administration, and different kinds of tongues. (29) Are all apostles? Are all prophets? Are all teachers? Do all work acts of power? (30) Do all have gifts of healing? Do all speak in tongues? Do all interpret? (31) But eagerly desire the greater gifts, and I will show you a far superior way.[14]

There is affinity between Paul's utilization of the body metaphor and contemporaneous examples. Mitchell notes that the motif in this pericope matches its wider political use even in the details.[15] Similarly, Martin, drawing on Mitchell's treatise, argues that this passage accords with the common rhetorical strategies and "topoi" of homonoia (concord/unity) speeches.[16] The presence of similarities between Paul's employment of the body metaphor and its use within wider Greco-Roman rhetoric does not negate the existence of marked differences. The extent and significance of these differences are disputed, however.

Some see Paul's application of the body motif as essentially conservative. Mitchell, for example, concedes that Paul "Christianizes" the motif by equating the church with the body of Christ but maintains that his use of the metaphor conforms to its use in the wider Greco-Roman world.[17] This supports her contention that Paul's primary aim in 1 Corinthians is to unify the divided Corinthian church.[18] Theissen also prioritizes conformity over subversion. In his view, Paul asks those of higher status to adapt their behavior for the benefit of the lower classes but does not challenge the hierarchical structure in which the believers' relationships were ordered.[19] Theissen depicts Paul's approach to social differences as "love-patriarchalism," wherein equality was extended to everyone, including women, foreigners, and slaves, but this equality was "internalized; it was true 'in Christ.'" In the political and

---

14. My translation.
15. Mitchell, *Reconciliation*, 159.
16. Martin, *Body*, 38–39.
17. Mitchell, *Reconciliation*, 157–64, esp. 160.
18. Mitchell, *Reconciliation*, 296.
19. Gerd Theissen, *The Social Setting of Pauline Christianity: Essays on Corinth*, trans. J. H. Schütz (Philadelphia: Fortress, 1975), 138–39.

social realm class-specific differences were essentially accepted, affirmed, and even religiously legitimated.[20]

Kim, in contrast, doubts that Paul would advocate a hierarchical unity.[21] He agrees that the Corinthian church stretched across a range of social strata within the urban population, from slaves to the upper classes, but disagrees that Paul would endorse love patriarchalism and so support the hierarchical boundaries that, for example, separated rich from poor.[22] Kim asserts:

> How could we believe that Paul would disregard the experiences of the most vulnerable, the slaves and victims of the Empire, when he talks about Christ crucified? How could we believe that the same Paul who made the cross central to his message would side with the hegemonic body politic based on the Stoic ideal of unity? It appears, to the contrary, that the image of Christ crucified deconstructs society's wisdom, power, and glory.[23]

What should one make of these divergent views on the degree to which Paul's body motif conforms with or subverts the metaphor's use in the wider Greco-Roman world? I argue below that the presence of both conformity and subversion is best explained eschatologically. Such a proposition is not intended as a headlong dive into the arms of the "apocalyptic Paul," were there indeed just one such Paul.[24] The assertion is, however, that Paul's body motif both conforms with and subverts contemporaneous uses because Paul believes in a kingdom that is both "now" and "not yet," as explored below. In particular, although Paul contends that this kingdom will only be fully realized by a supra-natural act of God in the future, he sees the church as an imperfect anticipation, or foretaste, of this future reality in the present. The church is to work out this reality *as a countercultural community*, within which believers' statuses are radically redefined, regardless of whether their location in Greco-Roman social strata is changed.

---

20. Theissen, *Social*, 109.

21. Yung-Suk Kim, *Christ's Body in Corinth* (Minneapolis: Fortress, 2008), 1.

22. Kim, *Body*, 17.

23. Kim, *Body*, 53.

24. Matlock notes, for example, that one of the weaknesses within the apocalyptic Paul movement is that it is not clear exactly who the apocalyptic Paul is. Different authors paint different pictures without adequately defining what they mean by "apocalyptic" (R. Barry Matlock, *Unveiling the Apocalyptic Paul: Paul's Interpreters and the Rhetoric of Criticism*, JSNTSup 127 [Sheffield: Sheffield Academic, 1996], e.g., 12–13, 327–28).

4. The Eschatological Tenor of Paul's Motif

The eschatological import of 1 Corinthians 12:12–31 is apparent early on through the sacramental overtones of βαπτίζειν and ποτίζειν (12:13), which mark the Corinthian community as the new covenant community.[25] The eschatological orientation of Paul's body motif is best seen, however, within three points of departure from wider uses of body to depict the city-state: the use of the metaphor to challenge the hierarchy that at least some within the Corinthian church had built up in their minds; the identification of the church as not just *a* body but *Christ's* body; and the application of the body metaphor to the church rather than the city-state. These three points of departure stand in stark contrast to the context in which Paul's body motif was penned, particularly as regards Corinth's socioeconomic climate and corresponding cultural values.

a. Corinth in Context

After its refounding in 44 BCE,[26] Corinth was populated by large numbers of freed-people,[27] keen to acquire status and wealth, alongside social elites,

25. Michelle V. Lee, *Paul, the Stoics, and the Body of Christ*, SNTSMS 137 (Cambridge: Cambridge University Press, 2006), 133.

26. Although there were some residents in the interim years, Corinth differed from many other Roman colonies in that there were no civic institutions in place when Roman citizens were resettled there (Christine M. Thomas, "Greek Heritage in Roman Corinth and Ephesos: Hybrid Identities and Strategies of Display in the Material Record of Traditional Mediterranean Religion," in *Corinth in Context: Comparative Studies on Religion and Society*, ed. Steven J. Friesen, Daniel N. Schowalter and James C. Walters, NovTSup 134 [Leiden: Brill, 2010], 117–47, here 118).

27. Benjamin W. Millis, "The Social and Ethnic Origins of the Colonists in Early Roman Corinth," in *Corinth in Context: Comparative Studies on Religion and Society*, ed. Steven J. Friesen, Daniel N. Schowalter and James C. Walters, NovTSup 134 (Leiden: Brill, 2010), 13–36, here 31. As Freisen notes, there has been much controversy over the repopulation of Corinth (Steven J. Friesen, "Introduction: Context, Comparison," in *Corinth in Context: Comparative Studies on Religion and Society*, ed. Steven J. Friesen, Daniel N. Schowalter and James C. Walters, NovTSup 134 [Leiden: Brill, 2010], 1–12, here 2). Witherington asserts that Corinth was "colonized by Romans—chiefly some of Caesar's veterans along with urban plebeians and freedmen and women from Rome itself and some Romanized Greeks" (Ben Witherington III, *Conflict and Community in Corinth: A Socio-Rhetorical Commentary on 1 and 2 Corinthians* [Grand Rapids: Eerdmans, 1994], 6). Thiselton also maintains that Corinth was refounded with those of the *Roman populace* and Gill maintains that Corinth's

who were drawn from the provinces to the provincial capital.[28] It was not long before Corinth thrived;[29] its natural resources supported production,[30] its strategic location, narrow isthmus, and two harbors facilitated trade,[31] the Isthmian Games drew in commerce,[32] and Corinth's religion brought financial and political benefits.[33] Not everyone benefitted equally from Corinth's wealth, however. Meggit points out that only around 1% of the Roman population were "wealthy," the remainder being at subsistence level.[34] This socioeconomic climate, including its inherent inequality, influenced Corinth's cultural norms, contributing to the prevalence of patronage and the pursuit of self-sufficiency, self-advancement, and even "consumerism" (which Thiselton defines as a "consumer-related, audience-orientated, approach to questions of meaning and truth," so as not to be anachronistic).[35]

These features of Corinth had infiltrated the Corinthian church. The Corinthian believers were enamored of elaborate rhetoric and pursued individual autonomy, personal success, and their own "local" theology.[36] In addition, the community was experiencing "conflict" (ἔρις; 1 Cor 1:11) and, although the nature of this rivalry is disputed, Theissen sees differentiation of wealth and status as the primary cause.[37] Theissen overstates his case;[38] any

---

Romanness should not be underestimated (Thiselton, *First*, 2; David W. J. Gill, "In Search of the Social Elite in the Corinthian Church," *TynBul* 44 [1993]:323–37, here 327). Freisen argues, however, that Millis—using "a wealth of new resources"—has more precisely identified the majority of migrants as *Greek* freed-people. He also supports Millis's conclusion that army veterans "were not a significant presence in the colony because it was founded for its strategic commercial position in a relatively stable area" (Friesen, "Introduction," 2).

28. Anthony C. Thiselton, "The Significance of Recent Research on 1 Corinthians for Hermeneutical Appropriation of This Epistle Today," *Neot* 40 (2006): 320–52, here 325. Regarding social elites moving to the capital, the Euryclids from Sparta are an example (Gill, "Elite," 329).

29. Gordon D. Fee, *The First Epistle to the Corinthians*, NICNT (Grand Rapids: Eerdmans, 1987), 2.

30. Witherington, *Conflict*, 10–11.

31. Thiselton, "Significance," 324.

32. Thiselton, "Significance," 325.

33. Robert S. Nash, *1 Corinthians*, SHBC (Macon, GA: Smyth & Helwys, 2009), 10 who notes that other cities had to give Corinth money for the emperor's birthday celebrations.

34. Justin J. Meggitt, *Paul, Poverty and Survival*, SNTW (Edinburgh: T&T Clark, 1998), 99, 153; cf. Nash, *1 Corinthians*, 19.

35. Thiselton, "Significance," 321, 325.

36. Thiselton, "Significance." 320.

37. Especially regarding meat sacrificed to idols and the celebration of the Lord's Supper (Theissen, *Social*, e.g., 98, 124–132, 160).

38. Differences in socioeconomic status are a particularly compelling explanation for

attempt to squeeze the whole of 1 Corinthians under one causative umbrella risks prohibiting each section from speaking for itself.[39] Nash, *pace* Theissen, questions how precisely the socioeconomic status of the believers can be ascertained and suggests that the believers may have been compensating for *a lack of status* in wider society by striving for prominence within the church.[40] Although Nash's view is plausible, the church in Corinth clearly represented a variety of social statuses (1:26), and it is likely that those in the higher strata were the most influential within the Corinthian church.[41] Differences in socioeconomic status at least contributed to the divisions and, even if socioeconomic inequality was not the only culprit, the Corinthian believers were clearly chasing status and prominence.[42] Paul saw this competitiveness, and the conflict it produced, as antithetical to the nature of the church as *Christ's* body.[43]

Paul's main three points of departure from wider uses of the body motif (his subversion of the Corinthian Christians' hierarchy, the identification of the church as specifically *Christ's body*, and the application of the metaphor to the church not the state) are particularly pertinent in light of this competitiveness, arrogance, division, and self-promotion.

5. Points of Departure

a. *The Subversion of the Corinthians' Hierarchy*

Rather than reinforce a fixed hierarchy, Paul's body motif subverts the hierarchy that at least some Corinthian believers had established in their minds.[44]

---

the problems with the Lord's Supper, for example. The existence of the different "parties" (cf. 1 Cor 1:12) is arguably better explained by the Corinthians' acquaintance with the sophist movement, within which "[a]ttachment to an eminent sophist could enhance one's own status" (Nash, *1 Corinthians*, 27).

39. Cf. Charles B. Cousar, "The Theological Task of 1 Corinthians: A Conversation with Gordon D. Fee and Victor Paul Furnish," in *1 and 2 Corinthians*, vol. 2 of *Pauline Theology*, ed. David Hay, SymS 22 (Minneapolis: Fortress, 1993), 90–102, here 93.

40. Nash, *1 Corinthians*, 22.

41. For compelling arguments that the Corinthian church consisted of at least some believers from the higher social strata see Gill, "Elite," esp. 328–37; Theissen, *Social*, 95–96.

42. On the disputes within which social status was clearly a factor see Gill, "Elite," 328–37; Theissen, *Social*, 98, 124–32, 160.

43. Nash, *1 Corinthians*, 22.

44. E.g., Thiselton, *First Epistle*, 1009.

Ἀναγκαῖος, for example, usually described parts such as the head and belly, which represented the social nobility.[45] In contrast, here it is the "weak," not the elite, who are indispensable (1 Cor 12:22). Moreover, the "less-honorable" are clothed in greater honor and the "unpresentable" are adorned (1 Cor 12:23–24).[46] The referents of these descriptors are hard to ascertain.[47] The designations "weak," "less-honorable," and "unpresentable" could, as Witherington proposes, refer to the weaker and seemingly less-gifted believers,[48] or, as Best argues, those whose work is in the background and thus over-looked.[49] Both suggestions are supported by the likelihood that there was a strong penchant for the more "showy" gifts of tongues and prophecy.[50] Regardless of the exact nature of these "weaker" members, rather than urging subordinates to stay in their place, which was the usual import of the body motif in wider Greco-Roman culture,[51] Paul adapts the body metaphor to urge the seemingly more gifted and privileged to value the contributions of their apparent inferiors (whether in terms of social status, spiritual gifts, or both).[52] Martin maintains that this is not a mere "compensatory move on Paul's part, by means of which those of lower status are to be compensated for their low position. . . . Rather, his rhetoric pushes for an actual reversal. . . . The lower is made higher, and the higher lower."[53]

Paul is not elevating those of previously low status to a position of authority above those of previously high status, however.[54] Equally, he is not depicting an imaginary or internal status change that simply reaffirms the existing hierarchy.[55] Instead, Paul is describing two contrasting ways of seeing status. In the world's eyes, the less honorable are still less honorable, but

---

45. Mark T. Finney, *Honour and Conflict in the Ancient World: 1 Corinthians in Its Greco-Roman Setting*, LNTS 460 (London: T&T Clark, 2012), 185.

46. Thiselton's rendering (Thiselton, *First Epistle*, 1008).

47. Ernest Best, *One Body in Christ: A Study in the Relationship of the Church to Christ in the Epistles of the Apostle Paul* (London: SPCK, 1955), 103.

48. Witherington, *Conflict*, 259.

49. Best, *Body*, 103.

50. Best, *Body*, 103.

51. E.g., David G. Horrell, "Σῶμα as a Basis for Ethics in Paul," in *Ethische Normen des frühen Christentums: Kontexte und Normen neutestamentlicher Ethik*, ed. Friedrich W. Horn, Ulrich Volp, and Ruben Zimmermann, WUNT 313 (Tübingen: Mohr Siebeck, 2013), 351–64, here 357.

52. Finney, *Conflict*, 183.

53. Martin, *Body*, 96.

54. Lee, *Stoics*, 145.

55. Lee, *Stoics*, 145.

HELEN MORRIS

the Corinthian believers should now see status, indeed the whole of reality, according to the "new age." In this "new age," those currently of low status will, as Lee notes, "enjoy high status as those who participate in the eschatological reality and thus shame the wise and the strong (1:27–28)."[56] Paul is not, however, simply affirming future equality to ease discontent in the present. Rather, as outlined below, the new way of viewing reality that he promotes should determine the Corinthian believers' *current* relationships with each other.[57]

b. Not "a" Body but Christ's Body

This new way of seeing is apparent in Paul's second point of departure from wider uses of the body metaphor: the church is not simply *a* body but *Christ's* body,[58] composed by the Spirit (12:13).[59] Thiselton warns that, though some have *overstated* the christological metaphysics of this designation (namely Robinson and those in his wake),[60] those who rightly emphasize the political background, and thus political implications, of the body metaphor must not *understate* the christological significance.[61] Paul makes the closest possible identification between the church and Christ without merging the two.[62] The church is a community whose life is determined by its incorporation into Christ as his body; it is not simply a community in which unity and good order must prevail. A believer's role within the church is not determined by inherited status, status climbing, social maneuvering, or hard work—the determinative factors within Greco-Roman

56. Lee, *Stoics*, 146.
57. Lee, *Stoics*, 148.
58. James W. Thompson, *The Church according to Paul: Rediscovering the Community Conformed to Christ* (Grand Rapids: Baker Academic, 2014), 71.
59. Schnabel notes that "der Geist die entscheidende Größe ist" (Eckhard J. Schnabel, *Der erste Brief des Paulus an die Korinther*, HTA [Wuppertal: Brockhaus/Giessen: Brunnen, 2006], 728). As Zizioulas asserts, the Spirit "is not something that 'animates' a Church which already somehow exists. The Spirit makes the Church *be*" (John Zizioulas, *Being as Communion: Studies on Personhood and the Church* [Crestwood, NY: St. Vladimir's Seminary, 1985], 132 [emphasis original]).
60. Thiselton, *First Epistle*, 996, referring to John A. T. Robinson, *The Body: A Study in Pauline Theology*, SBT (London: SCM, 1953).
61. Thiselton, *First Epistle*, 996, referring to Mitchell, *Reconciliation*, and Martin, *Body*.
62. Richard B. Hays, *First Corinthians*, IBC (Louisville: John Knox, 1997), 213.

urban societies.[63] Rather, "God has placed each of the parts in the body, as he has seen fit" (1 Cor 12:18).[64]

Christ is thus the foundation for the subversion of the Corinthians' hierarchy within Paul's body motif. The Corinthian believers' connection to Christ and, in Christ, their relationship with God through the Spirit is the fundamental reality to which they should ascribe. Christ's revelation of God is "cruciform"; he reveals God through "power-in-weakness."[65] Therefore, by identifying the church as specifically *Christ's* body, rather than promoting unity through the reinforcement of existing hierarchies,[66] and in stark contrast to the Corinthian Christians' striving for prominence and elevated status, Paul emphasizes the need for humility, interdependence, mutuality, and self-giving (esp. 12:14–21).[67]

The introduction of "first . . . second . . . third . . ." (12:28) could suggest that Paul challenges one hierarchy just to implement another, but his agenda is more complex than this. Hays suggests that the import of the sequence is temporal, indicating the order in which the gifts are required in the founding of churches.[68] The use of πρῶτος in Greco-Roman inscriptions to refer to those held in high esteem indicates, however, that notions of preeminence are hard to avoid.[69] Paul's aim is thus not to eradicate the concepts of honor and hierarchy; he does not envisage a charismatic community that is amorphously unstructured or anarchic.[70] Rather, he rede-

---

63. Although it was possible for freed slaves, for example, to rise quite high in society through the accumulation of wealth and influence (David E. Garland, *1 Corinthians*, BECNT [Grand Rapids: Baker Academic, 2003], 4), there were also fairly fixed hierarchies/social pyramids, consisting of networks of dependent relationships, most commonly "patron-client" (Nash, *1 Corinthians*, 11).

64. My translation. Thiselton argues that the rendering "God arranged" or "appointed" "weakens the sense in which . . . the call to Christian existence is inextricably bound up with his [God's] purposes for an individual within . . . the church" (Thiselton, *First Epistle*, 1004).

65. Michael J. Gorman, *Inhabiting the Cruciform God: Kenosis, Justification and Theosis in Paul's Narrative Soteriology* (Grand Rapids/Cambridge: Eerdmans, 2009), 32.

66. Martin, *Body*, 40, 92.

67. Lee, *Stoics*, 148; cf. Hays, *First Epistle*, 213.

68. Hays, *First*, 217.

69. Allen B. West, ed., *Corinth*. Vol. VIII, Part II: *Latin Inscriptions* (Cambridge, MA: Harvard University, 1931), no. 68 line 9 in reference to a Latin inscription dating to some time before 55 CE (the actual word on this inscription is *primus* but West notes that this is a translation of πρῶτος. For examples of Greek inscriptions he cites *OGIS* 544, 545, 652; cf. 528, 549.

70. "Charisma bedeutet darum keine amorphe Unstrukturiertheit oder ekklesiologische Anarchie" (Wolfgang Schrage, *Der erste Brief an die Korinther* EKK 7/1–4 [Neukirchen-Vluyn: Neukirchener, 1991–2001], 3:234).

fines authority and status on the basis of believers' relationship with Christ and Christ's example. Therefore, although the ranking "first . . . second . . . third" probably regards authority, responsibility, and even honor within the church,[71] Paul's view of these concepts is radically different from those of the wider Corinthian society. Earlier in 1 Corinthians, for example, Paul defines his status as an apostle in terms of being a "spectacle" (4:9), a "fool" (4:10), "hungry," "thirsty," "in rags," "brutally treated," "homeless" (4:11), "scum of the earth, refuse of the world" (4:13), and "a slave to everyone, to win as many as possible" (9:19).[72] *As an apostle* Paul faces indignity, hardships, and a low status in the world's eyes (e.g., 4:9–13) *but* (or, as Gorman contends, *because*) his status is high in the body of Christ.[73] "But" and "because" are not contradictory here. Rather,

> for Paul, the possession of a right to act in a certain way [i.e. his high status within the body of Christ] has an inherent, built-in mandate to exercise truly the status that provides the right by sometimes refraining from the exercise of that right out of love for others. This is not to *deny* one's apostolic or general Christian identity (and associated rights), or to void it . . . but to *exercise* it as an act of Christlike love. For Paul, love does not seek its own interest or edification but rather that of others . . . which is the core meaning of conformity to Christ.[74]

Similarly, the "greater" gifts (12:31a) are therefore greater because of their effectiveness in strengthening the body (14:3–5),[75] not because they afford status in the world's eyes.[76] Paul's instruction that his readers "be zealous" for these greater gifts is subversive compared to the usual import of the body motif. Any sense of predetermined or fixed order implied by 1 Corinthians 12:18 and 28–29 is held in dialectical tension with the fact that even these "greater" gifts are those that all can and should pursue (12:31).[77] Therefore,

---

71. Contra Witherington, who argues that the ranking is either depicting authority *or* responsibility (Witherington, *Conflict*, 261). However, authority and responsibility are so closely interconnected in Paul's mind that it is highly unlikely he would ever conceive of one without the other (e.g., 1 Cor 3:5–15; 4:1–2, 14–21).

72. Quotations here from NIV 2011.

73. Lee, *Stoics*, 146; Gorman, *Inhabiting*, 23–24.

74. Gorman, *Inhabiting*, 24 (emphasis original).

75. Witherington, *Conflict*, 261.

76. Lee, *Stoics*, 152.

77. Schrage argues that Paul promotes a flexible and changeable order in which all

although Martin maintains that Paul is *not* urging the Corinthian believers to pursue the greater gifts, but berating them for their preexisting zealousness in this regard,[78] this contention is derived by trumping the clear sense of Paul's exhortation with the cry that this contradicts his previous call for contentment (12:11).[79] The believers are zealous for spiritual gifts (14:12), but Paul's use of ζηλοῦν in reference to prophecy demonstrates that he is not criticising this zeal (14:1). Rather, he redirects his readers' zeal toward those gifts that are most suited "to the building up of the church" (πρὸς τὴν οἰκοδομὴν τῆς ἐκκλησίας [14:12]).[80] The gift of tongues, for example, primarily benefits the individual (14:2) and therefore, although the Corinthians probably put it first, it comes last in Paul's list, even though it does have value (14:5).[81]

Subversion is also evident in Paul's relativizing of both the greater and lesser gifts by noting that they will pass away (1 Cor 13:8). This eschatological relativizing is inconceivable within utilizations of the body motif elsewhere in Greco-Roman culture. One cannot imagine Senator Menenius, for example, who used the body metaphor to urge workers who had gone on strike to go back to work, relativizing his rhetoric on the importance of the belly being fed by then arguing that the role of the governing classes (= belly) would eventually cease.[82]

---

the gifts, except apostleship, are in principle open to all (Schrage, *Erste Brief*, 3:234). Thiselton also restricts the meaning of apostleship here to the uniquely authoritative and eschatological role of the original apostles, including Paul (Thiselton, *First Epistle*, 1015). If, however, the gift of apostleship is being used in its "root sense" to indicate a pioneering ministry role, then there is no reason why Paul's call to pursue the greater gifts could not also include this gift (Craig L. Blomberg, *1 Corinthians*, NIVAC [Grand Rapids: Zondervan, 1994], 247). See Clinton E. Arnold, *Ephesians*, ZECNT (Grand Rapids: Zondervan, 2010), 256, 259 for a compelling argument in favor of a two-tiered view of apostleship gifting.

78. Ralph P. Martin, *The Spirit and the Congregation: Studies in 1 Corinthians 12–15* (Grand Rapids: Eerdmans, 1984; repr., Eugene, OR: Wipf & Stock, 1997), 34.

79. Martin, *Congregation*, 34.

80. Thomas R. Schreiner, *Paul: Apostle of God's Glory in Christ* (Leicester: Apollos / Downers Grove, IL: InterVarsity Press, 2001), 357.

81. Chrysostom, *Hom. 1 Cor.* 32.2, as cited by Gerald Bray, ed., *1 and 2 Corinthians*, ACCSNT 7 (Downers Grove, IL: InterVarsity Press, 1999), 129; cf. Thiselton, *First Epistle*, 1015; Schrage, *Erste Brief*, 3:206.

82. Thiselton notes that Menenius's utilization of the body metaphor is recorded by Livy (*Urb. cond.* 2.32.7–11, as cited by Thiselton, *First Epistle*, 993).

c. The Application of the Body Metaphor to the Church, Not the State

Paul's challenge to the prevailing hierarchy and his redefinition of status and authority in light of the church's eschatological existence through its union with Christ acquire further significance in view of Paul's third main point of departure: whereas "body" generally referred to society as a whole, Paul applies this metaphor to the church.[83] As Dunn notes, this suggests that Paul sees the church as in some way a substitute for the state; belonging to the church relativizes any other citizenship.[84] Paul is not suggesting that the church usurp or overthrow the state. On the contrary, Paul's conformity with and subversion of contemporaneous uses of the body motif accord with the ambivalence within Paul's presentation of the church's relationship with the city-state elsewhere in 1 Corinthians. Elements of subversion are present in: 1:26–28 (the foolish shame the wise, and the weak shame the strong); 2:6 (the rulers of this age are brought to naught); 4:3–5 (to be judged by other humans is a tiny thing compared to God's judgment when the Lord comes); 6:1–8 (taking matters to a human court is shameful for those who will judge angels); and, most explicitly, 7:31 (this world is passing away). Social conformity, however, is indicated in 7:17–24, where Paul instructs his readers to stay in the position they are in, even slaves, unless they have the opportunity to gain freedom.[85]

This ambivalence, and that present within Paul's body motif, can be resolved by reading 1 Corinthians 12:12–31 in light of 15:20–28. In addition, consideration of Runesson's proposals regarding the nature of the church as an institution and attention to the "now/not yet" nature of Paul's eschatological framework adds greater clarity to the picture that emerges.

83. Martin, *Body*, 29, cf. 92.

84. James D. G. Dunn, "'The Body of Christ' in Paul," in *Worship, Theology and Ministry in the Early Church*, ed. Michael J. Wilkins and Terence Paige, JSNTSup 87 (Sheffield: Sheffield Academic, 1992), 146–62, here 161; cf. Lee, *Stoics*, 22.

85. Paul's view on slavery cannot be detached from the radical nature of Philemon, wherein Paul urges Philemon to welcome his slave Onesimus back as a *beloved brother* (Philemon 16). This example serves to show how distinct Paul envisaged the church community being from the wider world in which it was based.

6. Reading 1 Corinthians 12:12–31 alongside 15:20–28

a. 1 Corinthians 15:20–28

(20) But in fact Christ has been raised from the dead, the first fruit of those who have fallen asleep. (21) For since death came through a human being, through a human being resurrection from the dead has also come. (22) For just as in Adam all die, so too in Christ all will be made alive. (23) But each in its own order: the first fruit, Christ, then, with his coming, all who belong to Christ, (24) then the end, when he hands over the kingdom to God the Father, when he has nullified every ruler and every authority and power. (25) For he must reign until he has put all his enemies under his feet. (26) And the last enemy to be nullified is death. (27) For he has subjected all things under his feet—but when it says that all things have been subjected, it is clear that this excludes the one who subjected all things to him. (28) Indeed, when everything has been subjected to him, then the Son himself will be subject to the one who has subjected all things to him so that God will be all in all.[86]

Given that the main topic in view in this pericope, indeed the whole chapter, is the resurrection of the dead,[87] what connection can there be between Paul's polemic here and his body motif (12:12–31)? As Thiselton notes, these verses raise the question: in what sense does Christ, who is already the exalted Lord, not yet fully reign (1 Cor 15:25)?[88] One might also ask: in what sense is the earth the Lord's, the whole fullness of it (1 Cor 10:26; cf. Ps 24:1; 50:12), when only on Christ's return will God be all in all (1 Cor 15:28)? These questions are answered in part by the presence of one particular sphere in which Christ's rule and God's presence, through the Spirit, are most pronounced: amongst those whose harmonious, mutually edifying, unified, self-giving communal lives are predicated on their relationship with "the same Spirit, the same Lord" and "the same God" (τὸ αὐτὸ πνεῦμα, ὁ αὐτὸς κύριος, and ὁ αὐτὸς θεός [12:4–6]); those who proclaim, through that same Spirit, that "Jesus is Lord" (Κύριος Ἰησοῦς [12:3]); those who are "the body of Christ and each part a member of it" (σῶμα Χριστοῦ καὶ μέλη ἐκ μέρους

---

86. My translation.

87. E.g., Andrew T. Lincoln, *Paradise Now and Not Yet: Studies in the Role of the Heavenly Dimension in Paul's Thought with Special Reference to His Eschatology*, SNTSMS 43 (Cambridge: Cambridge University Press, 1981), 37, 50.

88. Thiselton, *First Epistle*, 1233.

[12:27]). In other words, the church, as the community in which Christ is most visibly "Lord" now, is to anticipate, and so provide a foretaste of, the future consummation of God's kingdom under Christ when Christ returns.

b. The Church as an "Association"

How is the church to outwork its identity as an anticipation of this kingdom? Runesson's exploration into the early church's institutional structures provides elucidation. He notes that non-state-run institutions ("associations"), such as the early church, were an alternative space to the domestic sphere, on the one hand, and the public, on the other; they were the only arena in which the rules of both could be reworked.[89] In associations, people could assume roles outside of the usual social, ethnic, and gender constraints.[90] Associations thus created the opportunity for *alternative worlds*, within which a slave, for example, could assume authority and status regardless of one's lack of power outside this realm.[91]

Runesson's assertions shed light on how Paul envisaged the church outworking its identity as Christ's body, but some notes of caution must be sounded. The early church was not as separate from the domestic sphere as this schema suggests, although Horrell warns against the assumption that the leaders of the earliest congregations were always heads of households.[92] Moreover, Runesson overstates his case in arguing that it was the association, as an established social entity, that *formed* Paul's thinking on ethnic, social, and gender equality.[93] Rather than relegating theology under sociology and anthropology, as Runesson proposes, one might simply note their inherent interaction.[94] Certainly, however, Paul seizes on this preexisting social structure as a means of working out his vision. In contrast to the marked societal integration that the Corinthian believers seem to enjoy,[95] Paul urges the

---

89. Anders Runesson, "Placing Paul: Institutional Structures and Theological Strategy in the World of the Early Christ-Believers," *SEÅ* 80 (2015): 43–57, here 52.

90. Runesson, "Placing Paul," 62.

91. Runesson, "Placing Paul," 45–46.

92. David G. Horrell, "Leadership Patterns and the Development of Ideology in Early Christianity," *Sociol. Relig.* 58 (1997): 323–41, here 327.

93. Runesson, "Placing Paul," 60–64.

94. Ward, *Participation*, 126–30.

95. John M. G. Barclay, "Thessalonica and Corinth: Social Contrasts in Pauline Christianity," *JSNT* 47 (1992): 49–74, esp. 50, 58, and 60.

church to live as a countercultural community, demonstrating to the wider world what communal relations can look like.[96]

Therefore, reading 1 Corinthians 12:12–31 alongside 15:20–28 indicates that the church is the community in which God's presence and Christ's lordship are manifest through the Spirit to a unique extent and the church is to work out its unique identity as a countercultural community. Outside of this community, a slave will probably remain a slave (Paul does not encourage slaves to violently pursue their freedom, and the church, as a minority group, was in no position to bring full-scale social change from the top-down).[97] However, *within* the community social differences are subverted and relativized such that the *apparently* weak, less-honorable, and unpresentable are actually indispensable, honored, and adorned. In addition, authority and status are redefined in relation to self-giving and building others up. Through living as a community that embodies these values, the church provides a foretaste and anticipation of the fullness of the kingdom that is to come.

c. "Now" and "Not Yet"

The church's anticipatory role can be read into, if not out of, Luther's analogy that currently the visibility of God's kingdom is "like beholding the sun through a cloud . . . one sees the light but not the sun itself. But after the clouds have passed, both light and sun are viewed simultaneously in one and the same object."[98] "Into, if not out of . . . " is an important qualification since Luther sees the current manifestation of the kingdom as restricted to the proclamation of the word and the sacraments, which seems unnecessarily reductionist. In contrast, placing 1 Corinthians 12:12–31 and 15:20–28 side by side, and reflecting on the institutional nature of the church as an alternative world, suggest that the church's life in its entirety, as Christ's body, is to exude this light and so provide a foretaste of the sun that will be revealed when the clouds part (to continue Luther's metaphor).

Ascribing an anticipatory role to the church's relationship with the

96. Dunn, "Body," 162.

97. Although as Meeks notes, through their construction of a "new world" they brought more cultural transformation than they could possibly have foreseen (Wayne A. Meeks, *The First Urban Christians: The Social World of the Apostle Paul*, 2nd ed. [New Haven: Yale University Press, 2003], 192).

98. Martin Luther, "Commentary on 1 Corinthians 15," in *Luther's Works*, ed. Hilton C. Oswald (St. Louis: Concordia, 1973), 18:57–213, here 124.

wider world, in this case Corinth, is not to assert that the church is God's kingdom in miniature in a fully realized or perfected sense. On the contrary, as Thiselton argues, a significant degree of coherence is found within 1 Corinthians if the disparate problems and issues that Paul addresses are seen to indicate both an over-realized eschatology and an overly ecstatic theology of the Spirit.[99] It may be that, as Barclay contends, rather than maintaining an over-realized eschatology, the Corinthian believers were simply non-eschatological. Either way, Paul seeks to correct a lack of future orientation in relation to the Corinthian church's behavior and worldview.[100] Despite his future emphasis, Paul does not deny the "now" aspect of the "now/not yet" tension that lies at the heart of his eschatological understanding.[101] This "now/not yet" tension indicates that the anticipation of the future consummation of all things that is manifest in the church, as the *current* locus of Christ's lordship, is imperfect and incomplete since the fullness of the kingdom has *not yet* arrived.

7. Conclusion

Paul's adoption and adaptation of the body motif demonstrates aspects of both subversion and conformity when compared to contemporaneous examples. Similarly, 1 Corinthians as a whole indicates some ambivalence as regards the church's relationship with the city-state. Coherence is afforded to Paul's view of the church's relationship with the city, however, when 1 Corinthians 12:12–31 is read alongside 1 Corinthians 15:20–28. Such a reading indicates that, on the one hand, the future subjection of all things under Christ's lordship is a supra-natural event that comes with God's initiative at the moment of Christ's return. It is not the church's job to usher in this event through political maneuvering or violent revolution. *The city is not a foe to be railed against, fought with, or displaced.* Thus, believers of low status (the "weak," "less-honorable," and "unpresentable") cannot, indeed should not, expect to be suddenly elevated, in social terms, above those who are higher up in society's pecking order.

On the other hand, the church, as the community in which Christ is

99. "Ecstatic" is preferable to Thiselton's "enthusiastic" as the problem is how the Spirit and the Spirit's work are perceived rather than over-enthusiasm toward the Spirit per se (Anthony Thiselton, "Realized Eschatology at Corinth," *NTS* 24 [1978]: 510–26, here 523).
100. Barclay, "Corinth," 64.
101. Lincoln, *Paradise*, 54.

most visibly "Lord" now, is to anticipate, and so provide a foretaste of, the future consummation of the kingdom when Christ returns. As a voluntary association, the church is to work out its eschatological identity as a counter-cultural community. The church is an alternative city of sorts. Thus, contra the Corinthian believers' excessive ease with their wider context, *the city is not a friend to be unthinkingly embraced*. Rather, the church, as a counter-community, is to be markedly different from the Greco-Roman state as usually promoted through the body motif. In contrast to reinforcing a hierarchical status quo, Paul asserts that through humility, unity-in-diversity, interdependence, mutuality, and, most importantly, *self-giving*, the Christian community is to anticipate a kingdom within which what is sown in dishonor is raised in glory, and what is sown in weakness is raised in power (15:43). For Paul, weakness really is strength, low status really is high status, and building up others should be every believer's goal.

The self-giving that Paul promotes markedly contrasts with the striving for personal elevation, progression, and status within wider Corinth, and the competitiveness and arrogance that this induced. Moreover, when Paul's utilization of the body motif is compared to contemporaneous examples, the radical nature of the mutuality, interdependence, and equality that he promotes is most clearly seen. Thus, rather than a friend to be unthinkingly embraced or a foe to be violently opposed, in view of Paul's body motif, *the city is best seen as a foil* against which the light that seeps through the clouds of a future kingdom still to come is most brightly seen.

Engaging—or Not Engaging—the City
Reading 1 and 2 Timothy and the Johannine Letters in the City of Ephesus

PAUL R. TREBILCO

1. The Salutaris Inscription

In 104 CE, C. Vibius Salutaris made a bequest to the city of Ephesus. A long inscription, giving details of this foundation, was set up in the theater of the city. From the inscription we learn that on procession days, thirty-one gold and silver type-statues and images, which included statues of Augustus, Trajan, and his wife Plotina and nine statues of Artemis,[1] were carried from the temple of Artemis outside the city wall to the Magnesian Gate, through the city to the theater, to the Koressos Gate and then back to the Artemisium.[2]

The procession occurred on the days the city assembly met, on important festivals such as the nativity of Artemis and on a number of other occasions. Rogers estimated that the procession would have occurred at least once every two weeks throughout the year,[3] and that the whole procession would have lasted at least ninety minutes on each occasion.[4] Since at least two hundred and sixty individuals were involved in the procession through the streets, it would have hindered, if not totally halted travel in the city on each occasion.[5] Salutaris clearly intended the procession to be a significant event in the city each time it occurred.

---

1. See the list of type-statues and images in Guy MacLean Rogers, *The Sacred Identity of Ephesos: Foundation Myths of a Roman City* (London: Routledge, 1991), 84–85.
2. For the route see Rogers, *Sacred Identity*, 85–107.
3. See Rogers, *Sacred Identity*, 83.
4. See Rogers, *Sacred Identity*, 110.
5. Rogers, *Sacred Identity*, 86.

The inscription shows the vitality of the cult of Artemis in Ephesus in 104 CE. Rogers has shown how Salutaris's foundation caused the people involved "to look (metaphorically) to the institutional structure of their city, to its Ionian foundation, and to the birth of the goddess Artemis, for their sense of social and historical identity in the complex and changing Roman world."[6] In particular, Salutaris's foundation, through focusing on the birth of the goddess, taught the people to look "to the birth of the goddess Artemis at Ephesos, for a theological sense of how Ephesian social and historical identity was grounded in a 'sacred reality,' which was impervious to all humanly wrought challenges."[7] This foundation shows us how central the goddess was to the identity of the city, and the intimate connection that existed between the city and its goddess.

Since the imperial family featured strongly among the statues, the foundation shows how the worship of Artemis and the imperial cult were integrated at the end of the first century CE. We should not think at all of competition between cults, but rather of the ability of the cult of Artemis to develop over time and in this way to include the worship of the emperors. There was a dynamism that meant the Artemis cult could adapt to a new day. But it is not as if Salutaris's foundation was "out of the blue." We know of the strength of the Artemis cult over previous centuries and of the imperial cult in the previous decades.[8]

In my view, in 104 CE there were two main strands of Christian tradition in Ephesus—the Pauline and the Johannine communities.[9] The Pauline community was founded by Paul around 52–55 CE and then received 1 and 2 Timothy perhaps around 80 CE. The Johannine community received 1–3 John perhaps around 90–100 CE.[10] The location and dates are of course

6. Rogers, *Sacred Identity*, 41.

7. Rogers, *Sacred Identity*, 69; see also 112–15, 145–47. The arrangements made by Salutaris were approved by the demos, so the foundation represented the attitude of the demos of Ephesus.

8. See further Guy MacLean Rogers, *The Mysteries of Artemis of Ephesos: Cult, Polis, and Change in the Graeco-Roman World* (New Haven: Yale University Press, 2012); Steven J. Friesen, *Imperial Cults and the Apocalypse of John: Reading Revelation in the Ruins* (Oxford: Oxford University Press, 2001).

9. For arguments in support of this paragraph, see Paul R. Trebilco, *The Early Christians in Ephesus from Paul to Ignatius*, WUNT 166 (Tübingen: Mohr Siebeck, 2004).

10. 2–3 John may have been written to house churches at some distance from the Elder and from the addressees of 1 John, since some travel is presupposed (see 2 John 12; 3 John 13–14). But it seems likely that Ephesus is the center of the movement or group attested to by 1–3 John; see Trebilco, *Early Christians*, 269–70.

debated. But since Ephesus was not unique as a city in the first two centuries CE, I hope that bringing 1–2 Timothy, 1–3 John, and the city of Ephesus together in a conversation is of interest even to those who would argue for different dates and locations for these letters.

That 1 and 2 Timothy were written to readers in Ephesus seems clear from 1 Tim 1:3 and 2 Tim 1:18 and 4:12. A strong case can be made that the Johannine letters were also written in Ephesus. The external evidence from the early Christian centuries favors Ephesus as the place where John's Gospel was written,[11] and given the very strong connections between the Gospel and the Johannine letters, it seems most likely that 1–3 John were also written in Ephesus, to Christians in the area. This is supported by the point that the oldest clear allusion to 1–2 John is by Polycarp of Smyrna in his Epistle to the Philippians, probably written around 115–120.[12] So before this date, these letters are known near Ephesus, which supports an Ephesian provenance.

How would the authors and readers of 1–2 Timothy and 1–3 John have responded to Salutaris's foundation and to the procession every two weeks? What theological response would they have given to life in the city of Artemis? And more generally, how can we characterize their overall attitude to the city in which they lived? Much of what I say here will be of the nature of an *implicit* theological response by the authors of these documents, since none of our documents give an explicit response to city life. Here I want to argue that 1–2 Timothy demonstrate a strong degree of engagement in city life, while 1–3 John demonstrate a high degree of disengagement.

2. Reading 1–2 Timothy in the City of Ephesus

a. First Timothy 2:1–7—Universalizing Prayer and Salvation

First Timothy 2:1–7 provides us with an entry point for this discussion. Here the Pastor expresses some principles that I think can be seen to govern how he thinks about the city, which means we see something of his theological approach to his urban environment:

11. See Trebilco, *Early Christians*, 241–63; the evidence comes from Papias, Irenaeus, Polycrates, *The Acts of John*, and Montanism.
12. In *Phil* 7:1–2 Polycarp shows his knowledge of 1 John 4:2–3 and 2 John 7, as well as other parts of 1 John; see Trebilco, *Early Christians*, 268. See further evidence and discussion in Trebilco, *Early Christians*, 263–71.

[1] First of all, then, I urge that supplications, prayers, intercessions, and thanksgivings be made for everyone (ὑπὲρ πάντων ἀνθρώπων), [2] for kings and all who are in high positions, so that we may lead a quiet and peaceable life in all godliness and dignity. [3] This is right and is acceptable in the sight of God our Savior, [4] who desires everyone to be saved and to come to the knowledge of the truth. [5] For there is one God; there is also one mediator between God and humankind, Christ Jesus, himself human, [6] who gave himself a ransom for all—this was attested at the right time. [7] For this I was appointed a herald and an apostle (I am telling the truth, I am not lying), a teacher of the Gentiles in faith and truth. (1 Tim 2:1–7)[13]

We see three important points with regard to how the Pastor views his city. First, this text has a strongly outward-looking perspective. The Pastor urges a range of different forms of prayer be made "on behalf of" or "concerning" all people (ὑπὲρ πάντων ἀνθρώπων).[14] The Pastor goes on to emphasize that prayer for those in authority is vital, but he *begins* by emphasizing prayer *for all*. This does not mean "everyone in our community," for that would be expressed as something like "prayer for all the household of God." Rather, the Pastor clearly means prayer is to be made for all, insiders *and* outsiders.

Such a universal scope of prayer is very unusual. Marshall notes: "What is said goes beyond Judaism in which prayer is said to have been offered only for neighbours and not for all people."[15] In addition, in the undisputed Paulines, we never find an explicit injunction calling for universal prayer.[16] Thus Quinn and Wacker call 1 Tim 2:1 "an innovation."[17] Robust theological justification

13. The NRSV translation is used in this chapter, unless otherwise indicated.

14. On ὑπέρ here, see I. Howard Marshall, *A Critical and Exegetical Commentary on the Pastoral Epistles*, ICC (Edinburgh: T & T Clark, 1999), 420.

15. Marshall, *Pastoral Epistles*, 420; see also Jürgen Roloff, *Der Erste Brief an Timotheus*, EKKNT 15 (Zürich: Benziger, 1988), 115. In Jer 36:7 (LXX) prayer is for the city in which they live, rather than being universal.

16. Jerome D. Quinn and William C. Wacker, *The First and Second Letters to Timothy*, ECC (Grand Rapids: Eerdmans, 2000), 175, suggest the injunction to pray for all in 1 Tim 2 has "a Pauline resonance about it" (175) and recalls 1 Thess 5:15–17, but this passage is somewhat different in focus, since it refers to doing good "to one another and to all," not to prayer.

17. Quinn and Wacker, *Timothy*, 175. Luke Timothy Johnson, *The First and Second Letters to Timothy*, AB 35A (New York: Doubleday, 2001), 196, notes: "In this composition, which is sometimes thought to signal a retrenchment within Pauline Christianity, we actually discover a more expansive vision: the community is to pray for all people, not simply for its own welfare—the motivation for the prayers for kings—because God 'wants all people to be saved and to come to recognition of truth' (2:4)."

for this new injunction is offered in 1 Tim 2:4, 6, for there the prayer of Christians is envisioned as "an extension and manifestation of God's saving will for humankind as that will has been revealed in the redemptive death of Christ Jesus 'for all, *hyper panton.*'"[18] This is strong justification for this innovation.

Secondly, the Pastor goes on to single out two groups in particular—prayer is to be "for kings and all who are in high positions." This would include city leaders. While, as noted above, the call for a universal scope in prayer is very unusual, prayer for those in authority is found elsewhere.[19] It is implicit here that rulers have a particular potential to cause difficulty for Christians, or to be forces bringing peace and stability. Prayers are to be offered to God for these rulers, that they may have an impact for peace, not for unrest or worse.

Thirdly, if 1 Tim 2:2 was taken alone, it might be thought that the goal of prayer was simply that the church might "lead a quiet and peaceable life in all godliness and dignity" (v. 2). However, in the context of 2:1–7, the thought is clearly that prayer has the church's mission in view, and a quiet life is *not* a *goal* in its own right. This is indicated by the description of God as "our Savior" (v. 3), by the clear statement of the universal scope of God's saving activity (v. 4), the tradition about Christ's mediatorial role (vv. 5–6) and the reference to Paul's activity as apostle and teacher of the gentiles (v. 7). The initial goal of prayer is that the church might have peace, *so that* believers can engage in mission, with salvation for individuals being the overall aim. Mission then is the overall reason that prayer is to be made concerning πάντες ἄνθρωποι ("all people"). In connection with this, the fourfold use of πᾶς ("all") in 2:1–7 gives the passage a strong "universal" emphasis. As Marshall notes: "The use of πᾶς here [with ἄνθρωποι in v. 1] and its repetition in vv. 2, 4 and 6 is thematic, establishing a universal emphasis. . . . The instruction is a pointer to the church's world consciousness."[20] Further, a number of studies have pointed to the importance of mission in the Pastorals.[21] In 1 Tim 2 then, there is a strong sense that the author is facing outward, in prayer but also in mission, and the letter's horizons can be thought of as very broad. But we see this "engagement outward" in other places too.

18. Quinn and Wacker, *Timothy*, 175.
19. E.g., Ezra 6:9–10; Bar 1:11; Let. Aris. 44–45.
20. Marshall, *Pastoral Epistles*, 420. See also Johnson, *Timothy*, 189.
21. A number of studies have emphasized the importance of salvation in the Pastorals and have highlighted what we might call the missional thrust of these letters. See, e.g., 1 Tim 4:16; see also Trebilco, *Early Christians*, 376–79; George M. Wieland, *The Significance of Salvation: A Study of Salvation Language in the Pastoral Epistles*, PBM (Milton Keynes: Paternoster, 2006).

b. *The Opinion of Outsiders Is of Concern*

The Pastor is sufficiently "engaged" in the life of the city to be concerned about what "outsiders" think and to endeavour to avoid offending the wider society. Clearly, an introverted group that was completely disengaged from its wider society would not be at all worried about the group's reputation among outsiders. This is far from the case in the Pastorals.

Note 1 Tim 3:7, which relates to an overseer: "Moreover, he must be *well thought of by outsiders*, so that he may not fall into disgrace and the snare of the devil." What we might call the "external reputation" of a leader is vitally important.[22] Note also 1 Tim 6:1: "Let all who are under the yoke of slavery regard their masters as worthy of all honor, so that the name of God and the teaching *may not be blasphemed*." Slaves should be respectful toward their masters because if they are not both God and Christian teaching will be "blasphemed" by outsiders and thus the church's reputation will be damaged.[23] Accordingly, the Pastor instructs readers who are slaves to behave in an appropriate way for the sake of the church's reputation and to avoid unnecessary slander being directed at the church.

First Timothy 5:7 is also revealing. In the context of giving instructions about the community's care of "real widows" who are genuinely alone (1 Tim 5:3, 5, 16), the Pastor writes: "Give these commands as well, so that they [the widows] may be *above reproach*." The reproach of an outsider is in view, as is shown by the comment that *even* "an unbeliever" would look after one's own family members (v. 8); it is the unbeliever who would reproach a believer who does not care for a "real widow" who is a family member. An outsider is seen as a real or potential objector to inappropriate behavior. There is clearly a strong concern that the community be seen to be respectable, and an anxiety about the impact that behavior that is negative in the view of outsiders could have on the reputation of the group.[24]

Thus, the Pastorals "are permeated with a strong concern for the opinion

---

22. John K. Goodrich, "Overseers as Stewards and the Qualifications for Leadership in the Pastoral Epistles," *ZNW* 104 (2013): 77–97, argues that the qualities required of overseers closely resemble "the popular idealization of the household steward" (85). By using a well-known contemporary model, the Pastor ensures that leaders chosen will "be well thought of by outsiders."

23. See also Titus 2:9–10.

24. See also 1 Tim 5:13. Another side of this desire not to cause offence is the concern to make a positive impression on others; see 1 Tim 6:14 and Titus 2:14 and 3:1–2, 8, 14 (relating to Crete).

of contemporary society."[25] Because it seems to matter a great deal that the behavior adopted by the members of the community should be acceptable in the eyes of outsiders, the Pastor advocates society-sanctioned behavior that will lead to acceptability.

This concern for the opinion of outsiders at least shows that social life was not confined to the Christian community; rather the community has a range of interactions with the wider society, to the extent that the Christian group knows what the wider community thinks of it. Further, that the wider society views the Christian group positively is regarded as vitally important. This is all evidence for significant contact and a strong degree of engagement with the wider community.

c. Doing "Good Works" for All

A prominent theme of 1–2 Timothy is that the readers should be involved in "good works."[26] The Pastor nowhere *explicitly* says that readers are "to do good" to outsiders.[27] However, given the focus on outsiders and the concern that the church has a good reputation with outsiders, it seems very likely that "good works" both within and *outside* the community are in view. It would be surprising if good works were thought of as "for members only," particularly given what is said in the case of the widows and the rich, as we will now see. A number of points are relevant here.

First, in 1 Tim 5:10 the widows who are to be enrolled are those who have "washed the feet of the saints," which clearly refers to acts of service to other Christians.[28] But this is just one of a list of "good works" that a widow should have demonstrated; the other activities are having "brought up children, shown hospitality . . . helped the afflicted, and devoted herself to *all kinds of good works* (παντὶ ἔργῳ ἀγαθῷ ἐπηκολούθησεν)." The final clause is clearly very broad, and hence refers to a wide range of potential "good works";[29]

25. Jouette M. Bassler, "The Widows' Tale: A Fresh Look at 1 Tim 5:3–16," *JBL* 103 (1984): 23–41, here 31.

26. See 1 Tim 2:10; 5:10, 25; 6:18; 2 Tim 2:21; 3:17; see also Titus 1:16; 2:7, 14; 3:1, 8, 14; see Marshall, *Pastoral Epistles*, 227–29.

27. Cf. 1 Thess 5:15; Rom 12:21; Gal 6:10.

28. See Paul R. Trebilco, *Self-designations and Group Identity in the New Testament* (Cambridge: Cambridge University Press, 2012), 149.

29. Marshall, *Pastoral Epistles*, 597 notes, "The reference is very broad, to whatever kind of good works the widow could find to do."

ἐπακολουθέω here means "to apply oneself to someth[ing] with eager dedication, [to] *follow after.*"[30] As Marshall notes, "The word implies that the widow has been zealous in finding opportunities for doing good and following them through."[31] It would seem most likely that this last injunction, with its very broad-ranging language, includes service to outsiders, which suggests that other elements in the list should not be interpreted narrowly to refer only to insiders. Hence, for example, "helping the afflicted" would refer to helping insiders *and* outsiders. These are deeds that the widow has done in the past, and so probably include things that have been done *before* she became a widow. Accordingly, they are certainly not "deeds only for widows," but are to be thought of as demonstrated by other Christians.[32]

Secondly, in 2 Tim 2:21 it is said that those who cleanse themselves and are "dedicated and useful to the owner of the house," who is clearly God, are to be "ready *for every good work* (εἰς πᾶν ἔργον ἀγαθὸν ἡτοιμασμένον)." Second Timothy 3:16–17 asserts that Scripture is inspired and useful for a range of purposes, "so that everyone who belongs to God may be proficient, equipped *for every good work* (πρὸς πᾶν ἔργον ἀγαθὸν ἐξηρτισμένος)." As in 1 Tim 5:10, both passages have a very broad-ranging reference to "every good work." We can suggest that in all three passages good works both within *and* beyond the community are in view.

Thirdly, the rich are "to do good, to be rich in good works, generous, and ready to share" (1 Tim 6:18). Benefaction both within and without the Christian community is likely to be in view.[33]

Finally, that good works in 1–2 Timothy have outsiders in view is strongly suggested by two passages in Titus, where it is evident that the prescribed "good works" include deeds done for outsiders. In Titus 3:1–2 we read: "Remind them to be subject to *rulers and authorities*, to be obedient, to be ready for every good work (πρὸς πᾶν ἔργον ἀγαθὸν ἑτοίμους εἶναι), to speak evil of no one, to avoid quarreling, to be gentle, and to show every courtesy to everyone." "To be ready for every good work" is situated between injunctions to obey and to be subject to rulers on the one hand, and to "speak evil of no one" on other, with the latter clearly including rulers and

30. BDAG, 358 s.v. §3 (emphasis original), with reference to 1 Tim 5:10.

31. Marshall, *Pastoral Epistles*, 597–98.

32. In the context of the Pastorals, "bringing up children" relates to Christian women, but there is nothing in the other elements that is restricted to women, and it is noteworthy that "washing the feet of the saints" seems to echo John 13, where all the men are instructed to undertake this task.

33. See also 1 Tim 2:10; 5:25. 2 Tim 2:24 may also have outsiders in view.

other outsiders. This structure shows that the beneficiaries of "every good work" are to include outsiders.

In Titus 3:8 the Pastor writes, "I desire that you insist on these things, so that those who have come to believe in God may be careful to *devote themselves to good works* (ἵνα φροντίζωσιν καλῶν ἔργων προΐστασθαι); these things are excellent and *profitable to everyone* (ὠφέλιμα τοῖς ἀνθρώποις)." That these "good works" are beneficial to "people" (the term translated "everyone" by the NRSV), who are contrasted in context with "those who believe in God," shows that these good works are to be done to outsiders. As Towner notes, "The reference is to outsiders to the faith among whom believers are meant to make a positive demonstration of what is truly 'good' in the acts they do for others."[34] This emphasis on "good works" for outsiders in Titus suggests that "good works" in 1–2 Timothy also have outsiders in view.

Accordingly, in 1–2 Timothy the author is exhorting readers in Ephesus to "do good to all," or to use Jeremiah's language, to "seek the welfare of the city."[35] This is an important theme in the letters; readers are to be involved in "good works" and in this way to engage positively in the life of the city, to the benefit of their fellow city-dwellers, even if they are not community members. Engagement is in part by "doing good." We have noted the outward-facing dimensions of the letter already; one dimension of "facing outward" is to do good to outsiders.

d. Adopting the Language of the City

Another dimension of "engagement" was the adoption of language that the believers heard around them and that was at home in the city, in order to express their Christian faith. This is a key way in which the urban environment affected the development and growth of the Christian movement in the early period. They "theologized" *using* local concepts and language. This was a two-way dialectic: there was engagement with the city by using the city's language, but also the city had an impact on the expression of Christian faith itself. Let me pick up two areas in which this engagement occurred— christology and the language of εὐσέβεια.

---

34. Philip H. Towner, *The Letters to Timothy and Titus*, NICNT (Grand Rapids: Eerdmans, 2006), 793–94. "Good works" are also referred to in Titus 1:16; 2:7, 14; 3:14.

35. Jer 29:7.

d.i. Christology: The Appearing of Our Lord Jesus Christ

As has often been recognized, the Pastorals present an "epiphany christology." The historical life of Jesus is spoken of as an "epiphany" or "appearance," and what is elsewhere spoken of as Christ's future parousia is here also called his "epiphany," "manifestation," or "appearance."[36] This effectively links the two "epiphanies" together.[37]

What is of interest here is that Artemis was also spoken of as "appearing." One expression relating to Artemis used in the Salutaris inscription was "the most *manifest* goddess." The use of epiphany language was also widespread in Greco-Roman religion, including in the imperial cult.[38]

Although the point is not explicitly polemical, the readers of 1–2 Timothy are being told by the author that the true "manifestation" of a god in this world is Jesus Christ, not Artemis. So the language does have a polemical edge to it, for those with ears to hear. But in addition, the language used in the city of Artemis is here being applied to Jesus. This is a contextualization of the message—the adoption of the epiphany schema and its associated language as a vehicle for the expression of the author's christology.

d.ii. The Language of εὐσέβεια[39]

Εὐσέβεια and its cognates are used eleven times in 1–2 Timothy.[40] These terms are not found in the undisputed Paulines, but are used, though fairly rarely, elsewhere in the NT.[41]

Εὐσέβεια was a popular term in the Hellenistic world, where it came to mean the worship paid to the gods in cultic activities rather than simply a rev-

---

36. For the first "appearance" of Jesus see 2 Tim 1:10, and Titus 2:11; for the second "appearance" of Jesus see 1 Tim 6:14; 2 Tim 4:1; 4:8; Titus 2:13. For παρουσία see for example 1 Cor 15:23; 1 Thess 2:19.

37. See I. Howard Marshall, "The Christology of the Pastoral Epistles," SNTSU 13 (1988): 157–77, here 169; Andrew Y. Lau, *Manifest in Flesh: The Epiphany Christology of the Pastoral Epistles*, WUNT/2 86 (Tübingen: Mohr Siebeck, 1996); Marshall, *Pastoral Epistles*, 287–96.

38. See Trebilco, *Early Christians*, 355–57.

39. On the term see Foerster in *TDNT* 7:168–96; Marshall, *Pastoral Epistles*, 135–44; Angela Standhartinger, "Eusebeia in den Pastoralbriefen. Ein Beitrag zum Einfluss römischen Denkens auf das entstehende Christentum," *NovT* 48 (2006): 51–82.

40. εὐσέβεια in 1 Tim 2:2; 3:16; 4:7–8; 6:3, 5, 6, 11; 2 Tim 3:5; εὐσεβεῖν in 1 Tim 5:4; εὐσεβῶς in 2 Tim 3:12; see also Titus 1:1 (εὐσέβεια) and Titus 2:12 (εὐσεβῶς).

41. εὐσέβεια is found in Acts 3:12; 2 Pet 1:3, 6; 3:11; εὐσεβεῖν in Acts 17:23; εὐσεβής in Acts 10:2; 2 Pet 2:9.

erent attitude, although outward worship was seen as the expression of inner attitudes.[42] Εὐσέβεια came to be seen as both a duty and a highly important virtue, and it was often referred to in inscriptions, including those from Ephesus.[43] Although εὐσέβεια is found comparatively rarely in the LXX, the εὐσέβ- word group is used a good deal by Philo and Josephus.[44] For these authors, εὐσέβεια "appears to gather together into one comprehensive idea the knowledge of God and the appropriate response."[45] It was a sufficiently broad concept for Hellenistic Judaism to use it to refer to knowledge of and loyalty to God, as well as to conduct that flowed from the "fear of the Lord." It comes closest to the idea of "religion," a term that is lacking in both Hebrew and Greek.

For the Pastor, εὐσέβεια encapsulates reverent knowledge of God and the appropriate conduct that flows from that knowledge. The term is rooted in the Christ-event (1 Tim 3:16; 2 Tim 3:12) and is closely related to the knowledge of God or of the gospel (1 Tim 6:3, 5, 11; Titus 1:1). It is thus used by the Pastor as a comprehensive term to describe the Christian life. Εὐσέβεια is also seen as something in which a person must train oneself, or something one should pursue (1 Tim 4:7-8; 6:11; Titus 2:12). It can be seen in specific activities, such as honoring parents (1 Tim 5:4).

Although the usage of εὐσέβεια in Hellenistic Judaism could, of itself, have led the Pastor to adopt the term, it seems more likely that its wide currency in the Greco-Roman world has led the Pastor to use it.[46] As Hellenistic Jews had adopted the term, so too does the Pastor.

Other examples of the adoption of the language of the city could be discussed in detail, including the language used for God, the use of "Savior" for God and Jesus, virtues given in various lists, the qualities required of leaders, the role of women and the understanding of the ideal household.[47]

In sum, there are three features at work here. First, it is likely that this

42. See Marshall, *Pastoral Epistles*, 136–39.

43. For example, the εὐσέβ- word group occurs six times in the Salutaris inscription (*IvEph* 27, lines 84, 118 (reconstructed), 367, 384, 418, 429); see also *IvEph* Indexes.

44. εὐσέβεια is found four times in the canonical books (Prov 1:7; 13:11; Isa 11:2; 33:6), four times in the Apocrypha (1 Esdr 1:23; Wis 10:12; Sir 49:3; 2 Macc 3:1), three times in 3 Macc, 47 times in 4 Macc. For εὐσεβής the figures are canonical books ten times; other books, 2 Macc 1:19; 12:45; Sir fifteen times, 4 Macc eleven times. εὐσεβεῖν and εὐσεβῶς occur six times and once respectively in the LXX. The εὐσέβ- word group is used 198 times by Philo and 148 times by Josephus; see Standhartinger, "*Eusebeia*," 70.

45. Marshall, *Pastoral Epistles*, 141; see also Jerome D. Quinn, *The Letter to Titus*, AB 35 (New York: Doubleday, 1990), 282–91.

46. See Quinn, *Titus*, 288.

47. See Trebilco, *Early Christians*, 357–69.

language resonates with the readers, which is why it is used by the Pastor. Readers know what it means and understand it. Accordingly, we can suggest that the readers are part of city life, engaged in the city and sharing in its vocabulary. Secondly, I have already noted the importance of mission. Salvation is a major theme in the letters and the author is concerned that the gospel be shared with others. In this context, the adoption of language familiar in the city probably had a missional edge. Language that communicated beyond the Christian assembly and into the wider city was used so that outsiders might understand the message. Thirdly, the city and its language and concepts had an impact on the expression of Christian faith itself.

e. Critique of the City

We have seen aspects of engagement with the city; but there are also dimensions of these letters that are countercultural. It is not as if the Christian community is, chameleon-like, a mere reflection of its wider culture. Rather, there are other areas where the language or attitudes of the Christian community critique the wider city in which they live.

e.i. One God—the King of Kings and Lord of Lords

As I have noted, the Salutaris inscription loudly proclaims the significance of Artemis to the city—there were nine statues of her in the fortnightly procession.[48] But there were also statues symbolizing the imperial cult. The religious life of the city was alive and well in 104 CE. How would readers of 1–2 Timothy respond? Two passages in particular suggest an answer:

> To the King of the ages, immortal, invisible, the only God, be honor and glory forever and ever. Amen. (1 Tim 1:17)
>   . . . [God] who is the blessed and only Sovereign, the King of kings and Lord of lords. It is he alone who has immortality and dwells in unapproachable light, whom no one has ever seen or can see; to him be honor and eternal dominion. Amen. (1 Tim 6:15–16)

There are no indications that these passages are polemical and so they do not *explicitly* address the wider culture. Although scholars have recently dis-

---

48. See the list of type-statues and images in Rogers, *Sacred Identity*, 84–85, 110.

cussed pagan monotheism (that is, the worship of one god in contexts that were neither Jewish nor Christian),[49] it is clear that most Ephesians in the late first century can be regarded as polytheists. Hence, with regard to 1 Tim 1:17 and 6:15–16, we can note how different such worship of the one God alone was from most Greco-Roman religious practice. A converted "gentile (Christian)" would surely have become aware of the difference between the religious life of the city and the beliefs of the community of which they were now a part. In the context of the worship of Artemis and the emperor, *we* proclaim the one King of kings and Lord of lords. He is "the only God," and this is the one God whom *we* worship in the city. In our "engagement," this is a non-negotiable element of difference between us and our neighbours.

e.ii. Being Rich

In 1 Tim 6:17–19 the Pastor shows that he knows a good deal about the position of the wealthy in contemporary culture and reflects some values that the wealthy would have found congenial. These include that one should not set one's hope on wealth since it provides a precarious foundation (v. 17c),[50] that wealth should be used for the benefit of others and that the wealthy person should be liberal and generous (v. 18c).[51] In vv. 17–19 then, the wealthy are being asked to play the same role in the Christian assembly and beyond it that they would have been expected to play in other social or political groupings. Wealthy Christians are to express their faith in a way that is familiar to the readers.

However, there are other features of the Pastor's instructions to the wealthy that go against contemporary expectations and exhibit a countercultural edge. First, the Pastor charges the rich "not to be haughty" (v. 17b). This

stands against a social world that lends social power to wealth by conferring on its possessors a presumption of moral superiority. Whatever

49. See Polymnia Athanassiadi and Michael Frede, eds., *Pagan Monotheism in Late Antiquity* (Oxford: Clarendon, 1999); Stephen Mitchell and Peter van Nuffelen, eds., *One God: Pagan Monotheism in the Roman Empire* (Cambridge: Cambridge University Press, 2010).

50. Note similarly Menander, *Dysk.* 284–86 (Arnott, LCL): "My message, then, is this: You may be very rich, but don't you bank on it (μήτ' αὐτός, εἰ σφόδρ' εὐπορεῖς, πίστευε τούτῳ), Don't trample, either, on us down-and-outs!"

51. For example, Aristotle held that wealth's power consisted in it being used to benefit others (*Rhet.* 1361a28); see also Reggie M. Kidd, *Wealth and Beneficence in the Pastoral Epistles. A "Bourgeois" Form of Early Christianity?* SBLDS 122 (Atlanta: Scholars, 1990), 126–30, 198–99.

else our author will concede to them, he will not have wealthy Christians thinking of themselves, to cite Dio Chrysostom . . . , as οἱ βελτίους "the better people" (*Oration* 48.9).[52]

Secondly, as I have noted, in the Greco-Roman city, the wealthy were expected to become benefactors and thus to lavish money and time on their cities. Those who were not wealthy reciprocated by giving public honor to benefactors, whose reward consisted largely of the honor and glory that they received. This system of reciprocity was fundamental to the life of the city.[53] Thus, εὐεργέτης "benefactor" is found several times in the Salutaris inscription[54] and in other Ephesian inscriptions,[55] and related terms are common.[56]

By contrast, what the Pastor says in 1 Tim 6:17–19 makes it clear that there is to be no earthly glory for Christian benefactors.[57] Wealthy people are expected to give generously, but they are not to expect any of the normally conferred honors or any reciprocity from those who benefited from their gifts. They are *only* "storing up for themselves the treasure of a good foundation for the future, so that they may take hold of the life that really is life" (1 Tim 6:19). The cultural norms of benefaction are in part adopted, in part repudiated.[58] As Countryman notes, the rich are "denied the honors, powers and rewards which Greco-Roman culture led them to expect in return for their beneficence."[59] Any reward for the rich or for anyone else is not immediate but belongs to another age and is from God (1 Tim 6:17–19). This is decidedly countercultural.

Thirdly, honor *is* to be given to three groups of people in the commu-

---

52. Kidd, *Wealth*, 131.

53. See for example Stephan Joubert, *Paul as Benefactor: Reciprocity, Strategy and Theological Reflection in Paul's Collection*, WUNT/2 124 (Tübingen: Mohr Siebeck, 2000), 37–58.

54. See *IvEph* 27, lines 76 and 327.

55. See for example, *IvEph* 22, line 70; 277; 286a, 297–98, 509, 614, 616, 619, 620, 621; see also *IvEph* vol. 8.1:31.

56. For εὐεργεσία (public service) see *IvEph* 212.10; 258; 1442.10, 1493.14; 3041, 3431, 3466. For εὐεργετεῖν (to do good service or to be proclaimed as a benefactor) see *IvEph* 695.4, 1087.6, 1419.2, 1440.12, 1442.9. 1449.9, 1455.11, 1458.7, 3048.15, 3110.8, 3251.11.

57. Note that the Pastor does not use εὐεργέτης in 1 Tim 6:17–19. So while he does adopt some language from the city (e.g., εὐσέβεια) he does not always do this. Perhaps in this case, the lack of use of εὐεργέτης is to emphasize that wealthy Christians are *not* to be treated like benefactors of the city.

58. See Kidd, *Wealth*, 200.

59. L. William Countryman, *The Rich Christian in the Church of the Early Empire: Contradictions and Accommodations* (Toronto: Mellen, 1980), 210.

nity: real widows (1 Tim 5:3), elders who preach and teach (1 Tim 5:17), and non-Christian masters of Christian slaves (1 Tim 6:1), who could defame the teaching. It is these groups, rather than the rich, who are to be honored.

Thus, the Pastor is aware of the position of the rich in society and shares in some features of contemporary city ideology in regard to the wealthy, but his thought also has a countercultural dimension to it, which means he can be seen to engage *critically* with a vital dimension of the ethos of the city—the system of reciprocity. As Kidd points out, "The Pastorals repudiate the presuppositions even as they appropriate the language of the cultural ideal of the wealthy *Bürger*."[60]

e.iii. *"The Present Age" and "the Age to Come"*

In two passages the author speaks of "the present age":

> . . . for Demas, in love with *this present age* (ἀγαπήσας τὸν νῦν αἰῶνα), has deserted me and gone to Thessalonica; Crescens has gone to Galatia, Titus to Dalmatia. (2 Tim 4:10)
>
> As for those who in *the present age* (ἐν τῷ νῦν αἰῶνι) are rich, command them not to be haughty, or to set their hopes on the uncertainty of riches, but rather on God who richly provides us with everything for our enjoyment. (1 Tim 6:17)

While it is not said in so many words that the "present age" is negative, there is a contrast made here between the "present" and an implied future age. Demas being "in love with this present age" is clearly a criticism. People may be rich "in the present age," but what matters is that they do good in order to accumulate treasure for the future age, where *"the life that really is life"* is to be found (1 Tim 6:19). *True* life in the future is clearly contrasted with "the present age."[61]

This is confirmed by 1 Tim 1:17: "To the King *of the ages* (Τῷ δὲ βασιλεῖ τῶν αἰώνων), immortal, invisible, the only God, be honor and glory forever and ever. Amen." God is King over all the ages, which are subject to God's rule.[62] Thus, city life is "the present age." It is implicitly—but only implicitly—critiqued from the perspective of the new age. This leads to at least a potential sense that much that is fundamental to the life of the city is relativized.

60. Kidd, *Wealth*, 158; see also 200.
61. This is connected to what is said about "eternal life"; see 1 Tim 1:16; 6:12.
62. See also 2 Tim 1:9.

f. Conclusions

We see significant engagement in the life of the city in 1–2 Timothy.[63] The Pastor has a strong outward-focus in prayer and in mission and is concerned about what outsiders thought of the community. Readers are encouraged to "do good" to outsiders as well as insiders, and we see the translation of important dimensions of Christian thought into language that was familiar in the city. However, the Pastor is also involved in at least an implicit critique of the city with regard to what is said about the one God, about wealth, and about "the present age." These are significant theologically determined differentiating factors for the community. We see then that the elements of engagement in city life that we have discerned led *both* to interaction and contextualization *and* to critique and critical engagement.

3. Reading the Johannine Letters in the City of Ephesus

The Johannine letters focus on the life of the group addressed and include a response to the distress caused by the recent departure of "the secession-ists" (1 John 2:18–25; 2 John 7). The author, whom I will call John, is not concerned to speak about relationships beyond the group, about "city life," or anything closely resembling it.[64] The topic of interactions with non-Christians is never addressed, there is no concern for what outsiders might think, no call to "do good" to all (although there is an emphasis on "loving the brother and sister"),[65] and no clear attempt to translate the gospel into the language of the wider culture.[66] Are these letters addressed to a group in Qumran-like isolation in a desert? We will return to this question below.

Here I will argue that the author does participate in wider society more

---

63. But note that in 2 Timothy the readers are instructed to expect persecution (2 Tim 1:8; 2:3, 9–12; 3:11–12; 4:5), which suggests that they are not so integrated socially as to avoid persecution.

64. Apart, that is, from the enigmatic reference to idols in 1 John 5:21, which I discuss below.

65. See e.g., 1 John 3:10–11, 13–18; 4:20; see also 1 John 2:9–10; 4:7–12. However, it is clear that ἀδελφός is a term for community members and not for outsiders; see Trebilco, *Early Christians*, 571–72.

66. Judith Lieu, *The Theology of the Johannine Epistles* (Cambridge: Cambridge University Press, 1991), 57, notes that 1 John is "focussed only on intra-communal relations." On "in-group" language in the letters, see Trebilco, *Early Christians*, 385–86.

than one might think. But the city is not seen as a place with which one would engage, but rather it seems to be somewhere to be avoided, somewhere that is fundamentally opposed to the life of the group. In fact, as far as possible, one is to be *neither* "in" nor "of" the city. But first, I will present evidence that suggests some involvement in wider city culture.

a. Indications of Some Involvement in Wider City Culture

a.i. The Letter Form of 2 and 3 John

2 and 3 John provide interesting evidence with regard to the author's involvement in wider culture. Both letters contain features that are found in the Hellenistic private letter. In 2 John 4 and 3 John 3 we have the expression "I was overjoyed" (ἐχάρην λίαν), a common way of writing of joy upon receiving a letter.[67] In addition, in 3 John 2 we find a conventional health wish, including the verb "to be healthy" (ὑγιαίνειν), a wish that is found in Hellenistic private letters.[68] In 3 John 6 we find the typical letter formula "you will do well" (καλῶς ποιήσεις) that "occurs exceptionally frequently in the papyrus letters."[69] All three expressions are not found elsewhere in the NT. Thus Funk concludes:

> It may then be said that the letter bodies of both II and III John are opened with forms and structures entirely characteristic of the common letter tradition. . . . There are thus certain formal and structural respects in which II and III John follow the common letter tradition, more closely, perhaps, than other letters in the NT, including those of Paul.[70]

In my view, the same author wrote all three Johannine letters.[71] While there are few signs of participation in wider culture shown by the author in 1 John, the acculturated letter form of 2 and 3 John suggests that the author had more

67. Robert W. Funk, "The Form and Structure of II and III John," *JBL* 86 (1967): 424–30, here 425; cf. Phil 4:10; Pol. *Phil.* 1:1.

68. Funk, "Form," 430.

69. Hans-Josef Klauck, *Ancient Letters and the New Testament: A Guide to Context and Exegesis* (Waco: Baylor University Press, 2006), 34.

70. Funk, "Form," 428; see also Judith Lieu, *The Second and Third Epistles of John: History and Background*, SNTW (Edinburgh: T&T Clark, 1986), 37–51.

71. See Trebilco, *Early Christians*, 264–67.

interaction with the wider cultural world than 1 John suggests.[72] Perhaps then it is the contents, genre, or audience of 1 John that has led the author, in writing that "letter," to show few signs of contact with the wider culture.

So 2–3 John and their author are more significantly a part of the wider culture than appears at first. We can suggest that the author and readers are not in fact isolated in some desert sect, but are indeed to be found in Ephesus and participate in the wider society to at least some extent. But how is city life portrayed and thought about in these letters?

On any reading, 1 John ends very strangely: "Little children, keep yourselves from idols" (1 John 5:21). There is much debate about what this injunction means.[73] It remains possible that it could relate to actual idols; in the context of the city of Ephesus, the real "idol" Artemis comes to mind. If this is the case, then the readers are sufficiently part of the city for the author to be concerned they might be involved in idol worship.

b. Dualism

One characteristic of the Johannine Letters is their very strong dualism. This is most obvious in the language about light and darkness.[74] There is also a very strong dualism between God and "the evil one" (see 1 John 5:19), which leads to an equally strong dualism between Christ and antichrist (1 John 2:18–22, 4:3; 2 John 7) and the children of God and the children of the devil (1 John 3:8–10). Another dimension of dualism evident here is that between God and the world, to which I now turn.

c. The World—ὁ κόσμος

"The world" is one of the terms that is used most often in the Johannine Letters for "outsiders."[75] If we are interested in how "the city" was conceived

---

72. Even if the author of 2 and 3 John is a different person from 1 John, the two authors are clearly related (probably as members of a school) and so the evidence of 2 and 3 John can shed light back on 1 John.

73. See the full discussion of ten possible interpretations in Raymond E. Brown, *The Epistles of John,* AB 30 (New York: Doubleday, 1982), 627–29.

74. E.g., 1 John 1:5–7; 2:8–11.

75. On ὁ κόσμος and the Johannine Letters see N. H. Cassem, "A Grammatical and Contextual Inventory of the Use of κόσμος in the Johannine Corpus with Some Implications

of or thought about in these letters, then language about "the world" is an important guide. One cannot simply equate ὁ κόσμος and the city, or transfer all that is said about "the world" to "the city," since ὁ κόσμος is clearly an overarching concept. But in my view, "the city" in which John lived is strongly tarred with the brush of "the world."

ὁ κόσμος is found 23 times in 1 John and once in 2 John and is used in a variety of ways, from positive (relating to the reach of salvation) and neutral (of the natural world) to the decidedly negative (of those who are opposed to God).[76] John's thinking about the world is most fully expressed in 1 John 2:15–17:

> [15] Do not love the world or the things in the world. The love of the Father is not in those who love the world; [16] for all that is in the world—the desire of the flesh, the desire of the eyes, the pride in riches—comes not from the Father but from the world (ὅτι πᾶν τὸ ἐν τῷ κόσμῳ, ἡ ἐπιθυμία τῆς σαρκὸς καὶ ἡ ἐπιθυμία τῶν ὀφθαλμῶν καὶ ἡ ἀλαζονεία τοῦ βίου, οὐκ ἔστιν ἐκ τοῦ πατρὸς ἀλλ᾽ ἐκ τοῦ κόσμου ἐστίν). [17] And the world and its desire are passing away, but those who do the will of God live forever.

John begins by exhorting his readers not to love "the world or the things in the world," since loving the world is incompatible with love toward the Father, so no one who loves the world can claim to love the Father (2:15b). The believer's love for the Father stands in total opposition to love for the world.

But to what exactly does ὁ κόσμος refer in 2:15? The three phrases in 2:16 elaborate on what constitutes ὁ κόσμος and explain why there is a basic incompatibility between "*all* that is in the world" (2:16) and the Father.[77]

The term "desire" (ἐπιθυμία), used twice ("the desire of the flesh, the

---

for a Johannine Cosmic Theology," *NTS* 19 (1972–73): 81–91; Rudolf Schnackenburg, *The Johannine Epistles. Introduction and Commentary* (New York: Crossroad, 1992), 125–28; see also more generally, Richard Bauckham, "Dualism and Soteriology in Johannine Theology," in *Beyond Bultmann: Reckoning a New Testament Theology*, ed. Bruce W. Longenecker and Mikeal C. Parsons (Waco: Baylor University Press, 2014), 133–53. The use of κόσμος in 1–3 John is related to the similar dualism in John's Gospel. If the Gospel is earlier than the Letters, as seems likely, then the dualism we see in 1–3 John is not a response to recent phenomena (such as the departure of the secessionists) but has been part of the thought of the author or his school for a considerable period of time.

76. In a positive sense: 2:2; 4:14; in a more neutral sense: 3:17; 4:1, 3, 4, 9, 17; 2 John 7; in a negative sense: 2:15–17 [6×]; 3:1, 13; 4:5 [3×]; 5:4 [2×], 5, 19.

77. On the relationship of the three elements see Schnackenburg, *Johannine Epistles*, 120–23.

desire of the eyes" [ἡ ἐπιθυμία τῆς σαρκός and ἡ ἐπιθυμία τῶν ὀφθαλμῶν]), generally has morally negative connotations in the NT, as it clearly does here.[78] The term "flesh" (σάρξ) here is "entirely negative, representing the human capacity for self-indulgence and self-preoccupation that ignores the requirements and purposes of God."[79] In conjunction with "desire" (ἐπιθυμία), "the desire of the flesh" (ἡ ἐπιθυμία τῆς σαρκός) refers to sexual desire, but probably also includes other vices such as gluttony and drunkenness.[80]

"The desire of the eyes" (ἡ ἐπιθυμία τῶν ὀφθαλμῶν) is again negative and involves desire that is activated by what people see, and that leads people to desire what others have.[81] The term ἀλαζονεία, in the phrase "the pride in riches" (ἡ ἀλαζονεία τοῦ βίου), has a range of meanings, including "boastfulness, pride, arrogance, ostentation."[82] βίος here is a reference to possessions, a sense that is in keeping with its only other use in 1 John (3:17).[83] The two words together give the sense of "the boastful possessions of life,"[84] and so point to arrogant boasting and self-confidence in human ability. The three words together constitute ὁ κόσμος for John, which is clearly to be understood as the world and its attractions understood apart from God.

What is said here is all-encompassing: "for *all* that is in the world (ὅτι πᾶν τὸ ἐν τῷ κόσμῳ) . . . comes not from the Father but from the world." This is a stark and total dualism, and it portrays a fundamental opposition between the two spheres, which explains why, if the readers love these things, "the love of the Father is not in him or her."

An additional reason why the world should not be loved is that "the world and its desire are passing away (ὁ κόσμος παράγεται καὶ ἡ ἐπιθυμία αὐτοῦ)" (2:17).[85] The present tense of the verb παράγειν emphasizes that this is an ongoing process occurring in the present. This reminds us of 2:8:

---

78. It is found thirty-eight times in the NT and is only positive in Luke 22:15; Phil 1:23; 1 Thess 2:17; see further Judith Lieu, *I, II and III John: A Commentary*, NTL (Louisville: Westminster John Knox, 2008), 94.

79. Lieu, *I, II and III John*, 94.

80. See Schnackenburg, *Johannine Epistles*, 122.

81. Colin G. Kruse, *The Letters of John*, PNTC (Grand Rapids: Eerdmans, 2000), 95.

82. John Painter, *1, 2, and 3 John*, SP 18 (Collegeville: Liturgical, 2002), 191.

83. See BDAG, 176–77 s.v. §2.

84. Painter, *1, 2, and 3 John*, 192.

85. The singular "desire" indicates that John has in view a whole negative mind-set that is opposed to God.

"the darkness is passing away (ἡ σκοτία παράγεται) and the true light is already shining (καὶ τὸ φῶς τὸ ἀληθινὸν ἤδη φαίνει)." All that is antithetical to God is passing away, and accordingly should not be loved. To speak of the transitory nature of the world is a "way of expressing the utter incompatibility between the sphere that represents God's will and intention, and all that opposes it."[86] Verse 17 closes with a note of contrast, pointing out the advantage of following this exhortation and so of doing the will of God—it leads to living forever.

What is the overall import of this passage? Lieu notes:

> First John is not advocating an ascetic rejection of any physical pleasures. Rather the author is drawing on what were probably conventional formulations in order to infuse the rather abstract concept of "the world" with the immediacy of potential threat. . . . At stake is the utter incompatibility of anything that might be identified with "world" and anything to be identified with the "Father," and the consequent need for readers to be single-minded about their loyalties.[87]

d. What Sociological Reality Corresponds to This Theological Understanding?

d.i. Not Qumran-like Isolation

But how much can this be translated into a *social position or a sociological reality*? Are the readers being urged to disengage totally from *all* relations with others? A number of passages in 1 John argue against this. First, 1 John 3:13 with its expectation of hatred against the community, shows that they are not actually totally disengaged from wider society. There is some sort of active interface with "the world," and the community is at least sufficiently a part of its wider context that it can be known by others, even if the outcome is hatred.[88] Secondly, 1 John 3:17 presupposes that some readers have "the world's goods," a clear reference to possessions.[89] This implies that readers are engaged in the *world's* production and commerce, and have sufficient

86. Lieu, *I, II and III John*, 96.
87. Lieu, *I, II and III John*, 95; the comment relates to 2:16b; see also Schnackenburg, *Johannine Epistles*, 125.
88. See Lieu, *I, II and III John*, 92.
89. See BDAG, 177.

surplus from that production to assist other believers. Thirdly, 1 John 2:15 presupposes that it is *possible* to love the world and that readers are sufficiently involved in the world for this to be an option. Fourthly, the statement that "the world does not know us" in 1 John 3:1 seems to be a reflection on experience, an experience where people in the surrounding culture have not come to "know," that is understand or comprehend, the identity of the group.

Readers are not *actually* living in Qumran-like isolation then. They are participating *to some extent* in wider society. They have experienced hatred and incomprehension from others; it is *possible* for them to "love the world" and some of them have an amount of the world's goods.

d.ii. Neither "in" nor "out of the World" but "out of God"

What does 1 John 2:15–17 mean in this context? I have suggested that it concerns disengagement from the world, having no loyalty or commitment to the world, and in no way to compromise their total commitment to God. It is about regarding "the world" as passing away, and as totally alien. We see here "two mutually exclusive patterns of loyalty."[90] So the theologizing about the city that we see here is almost totally negative. But we can develop this further.

Note 1 John 4:1: "Beloved, do not believe every spirit, but test the spirits to see whether they are from God (ἐκ τοῦ θεοῦ); for many false prophets *have gone out into the world* (ἐξεληλύθασιν εἰς τὸν κόσμον)." This implies that, wherever "we" are to be located, we are not "*in* the world." Those who have left us, the false prophets, and those who in 2:19 are said to have gone out from us, have gone to where *we are not*—they have "gone out *into* the world."[91] The same idea comes through 1 John 2:16: "for all that is *in* the world (ὅτι πᾶν τὸ ἐν τῷ κόσμῳ) . . . comes not from the Father but from the world (ἐκ τοῦ κόσμου)." John is saying that readers should not think of themselves as living "in" the world, in that place which is antithetical to God, for that is where their opponents are.

First John 4:5–6, speaking of the opponents, is even more revealing:

They are *from the world* (αὐτοὶ ἐκ τοῦ κόσμου εἰσίν); therefore what they say is *from the world* (ἐκ τοῦ κόσμου), and the world listens to them. We

---

90. Lieu, *I, II and III John*, 93.
91. Similarly, this is where the antichrist is: see 1 John 4:2–3; 2 John 7.

are *from God* (ἡμεῖς ἐκ τοῦ θεοῦ ἐσμεν). Whoever knows God listens to us, and whoever is *not from God* (ὃς οὐκ ἔστιν ἐκ τοῦ θεοῦ) does not listen to us. From this we know the spirit of truth and the spirit of error.[92]

The opponents are ἐκ τοῦ κόσμου and what they say is ἐκ τοῦ κόσμου. This is in striking contrast to the addressees who are ἐκ τοῦ θεοῦ (1 John 4:4). Theologically speaking then, for John believers are not ἐκ τοῦ κόσμου but ἐκ τοῦ θεοῦ. Obviously, they do *physically* live on earth, but they are not ἐκ τοῦ κόσμου.[93] This is the same contrast we saw in 1 John 2:16—all that is in the world (ὅτι πᾶν τὸ ἐν τῷ κόσμῳ) is *not* ἐκ τοῦ πατρός but ἐκ τοῦ κόσμου.

Lieu comments on this use of ἐκ: "This is an unusual use of the preposition and it seems to have been a Johannine formulation.... The phrase could be translated as 'come from' God (or the world), or even more strongly, as 'have as [their/your] origin' in God or the world."[94] We see again the sense that what is in the world is totally alien to believers, and is utterly incompatible with their true life and their true origin.

The sense of total incompatibility between the believers and "the world" is also expressed in the sense of battle between the two parties, which is clearest in 1 John 5:19, where John gives his final word on "the world": "We know that we are *out of God* (οἴδαμεν ὅτι ἐκ τοῦ θεοῦ ἐσμεν), and that the whole world lies under the power of the evil one (καὶ ὁ κόσμος ὅλος ἐν τῷ πονηρῷ κεῖται)." "The world" is most obviously the place that rejects God and Jesus his Son; it is perceived to be "anti-God," and in league with the evil one. By contrast, we are "out of God" (ἐκ τοῦ θεοῦ). God and the evil one, and hence God's people and the world, are resolutely and diametrically opposed to one another.[95]

One result of this emphatic opposition between the two spheres is that "the world hates you," about which readers should not be surprised (1 John 3:13). But in this battle, the outcome is assured, as 1 John 4:4 makes clear: "Little children, you are *from God* (ὑμεῖς ἐκ τοῦ θεοῦ ἐστε), and have conquered them; for the one who is in you is greater than the one who is in the

---

92. In 1 John 3:8-10 the opposition is between God and the devil. By contrast in 4:4-6 the world replaces the devil as the opposition to God.

93. See also John 8:23; 15:19; 17:6, 14-16; 18:36.

94. Lieu, *I, II and III John*, 95. The square brackets are added by Lieu.

95. Lieu, *I, II and III John*, 95, notes that here we sense "the immediacy of potential threat" that required "continuous vigilance."

world."[96] There is a strong sense of opposition, but the community is to be confident about the future, despite persecution and suffering.

John does not quite say that they are *not* in the world, since they do live on earth! If he were to say this, such a statement would easily be refutable, given the broad semantic range of ὁ κόσμος in 1–2 John. So John is willing to say we are "in this world" in 1 John 4:17: "Love has been perfected among us in this: that we may have boldness on the day of judgment, because as he is, *so are we in this world* (ὅτι καθὼς ἐκεῖνός ἐστιν καὶ ἡμεῖς ἐσμεν ἐν τῷ κόσμῳ τούτῳ)."[97] But Strecker remarks on the use of οὗτος here: "The demonstrative has a devaluative intent and emphasizes . . . the distance between the community and the world."[98] Even when John admits they are "in the world" he does so in a way that *devalues* "the world" (ὁ κόσμος)—it is only "*this* world."

In John's theological worldview then, it is the opposition who are truly "in the world." And of most importance, believers are not "from the world" (ἐκ τοῦ κόσμου) but "from God" (ἐκ τοῦ θεοῦ). Believers do not *belong* to the world; rather they belong to God, are of God, and are out of or from God.

We can suggest that this thinking about "the world" should completely color readers' attitudes to "the city," where they do not belong either. The total lack of positive engagement or positive regard for the world, and we can add, for the city in the Johannine Letters, is theologically motivated and is rooted in the strong dualism of us and them, light and darkness, God and the evil one, and God and the world, which is found in these letters.

The sociological reality to which this points is not a community in Qumran-like isolation, as we have pointed out. But the readers are to live as if this was their situation! The mental picture the community is to have of itself is of "no positive engagement or positive regard" for the city. They are to live in such a way as to show they are not "in the world" or "from the world" (ἐκ τοῦ κόσμου) but "from God" (ἐκ τοῦ θεοῦ).

---

96. See also 1 John 5:5.

97. Lieu, *I, II and III John*, 194 notes this represents "their current situation."

98. Georg Strecker, *The Johannine Letters: A Commentary on 1, 2, and 3 John*, Hermeneia (Minneapolis: Fortress, 1996), 166. He notes that this is the only time that 1 John speaks of "this world," but such a use is found in John 12:31b and 16:11, which states that "this world" "is subject to the devil's rule" (Strecker, *Johannine Letters*, 166 n. 29). See also John 11:9; 13:1.

e. Some Positive Elements of the Portrayal of "the World"

Yet some points do soften this picture. John believes that salvation is *for the world*,[99] showing again that he—and also his readers—are not totally closed off from their city. First John 2:2 reads: "and he is the atoning sacrifice for our sins, and not for ours only but also for the sins of the whole world." Further, 1 John 4:14 reads: "And we have seen and do testify that the Father has sent his Son as the Savior of the world."[100] This belief in salvation has not led to the group ameliorating its sense of intense division between "us" and "them." It is possible to cross from one side to the other through the Son who is the Savior of the world. But such a transition is so radical that it is spoken of as "being born of God" (ἐκ τοῦ θεοῦ).[101]

f. Conclusions

Although some positive statements are made about the world, the predominant sense is that the world is seen in strongly oppositional terms and that the community stood aloof from its social context and did not participate to any significant extent in the activities of the dominant culture. Further, there is little to suggest that the community was actively involved in outgoing mission.[102] There is rather a strong sense of separateness from the world. "The world" is seen as the community's enemy, an enemy who is to be shunned and who hates the community. Of course, we should not simply equate the world and "the city," but it seems clear that for the author, the city is tarred with the same brush as "the world," and the culture and life of the city belongs to the sphere of "the world."

4. Overall Conclusions

We see strongly contrasting ways in which the authors of the Pastorals and the Johannine Letters responded to their surroundings in the city. The Pastorals give a sense of significant engagement in the life of the city. The Pastor

99. Similar positive statements about the world are made in John's Gospel; see for example John 1:9; 3:16, 19; 6:14; 8:12; 9:39; 11:27; 12:46; 16:28; 17:2.
100. See also 1 John 4:9.
101. See 1 John 3:9; 4:7; 5:1, 4, 18; see also 2:29.
102. See Lieu, *Second and Third Epistles*, 182–86; Lieu, *Theology*, 85.

had a strong outward focus, concern was expressed about the community's reputation, readers were encouraged to "do good" to outsiders and we see significant contextualization of language. While there was some critique of the city, which differentiated the community from its context, the strongest sense was of positive engagement.

By contrast the Johannine Letters point to a strong but inwardly focused community that held aloof from its social context and did not engage to any significant extent with the dominant culture of their city. They lived with a strong sense of opposition from "out there"; their total loyalties were to God.

It is striking that these two quite different attitudes were probably both found in the city of Ephesus, though of course the provenance of these sets of letters is debated. But I suggest that both communities were responding to life in the same city. This makes their diverse responses even more remarkable.[103]

Why do we see strongly contrasting attitudes? Perhaps time is a factor here, since 1–3 John are probably to be dated at least a decade after 1–2 Timothy. However, in my view, 1–2 Timothy and the Johannine Letters are addressed to different communities.

Perhaps there are socioeconomic reasons at work. The readers of the Pastorals seem to include at least some wealthy people—there are rich people who are exhorted to become benefactors (1 Tim 6:17–19) and some women could wear expensive clothes, gold and pearls, which are clearly luxury items (1 Tim 2:9). There are also people who aspire to be rich (1 Tim 6:9–10).[104] By contrast, the only indication of some wealth in the Johannine Letters is 1 John 3:17, but "having the world's goods" need not involve much wealth, and clearly the ἀδελφοί mentioned who are in need are poor. It seems then that there were more wealthy people among the readers of the Pastorals, and this may well have led to a greater level of engagement in city life. But our evidence for socioeconomic level is unfortunately fragmentary.

But theological reasons are perhaps much more significant. The Pastorals stand in the tradition of Pauline theology. In this tradition, we see significant engagement with society, at least in 1 Corinthians (where Paul opposes a good deal of the wrong kind of involvement) but also in some of

---

103. On possible relationships between the two communities, see Trebilco, *Early Christians*, 589–617.

104. 1 Tim 5:16 speaks of a "believing woman" who has the means to help real widows. There are also slaves (1 Tim 6:1–2) and the "real widows" of 1 Tim 5:3–16 seem to be nearly destitute.

Paul's exhortations to do good to all or to look after enemies.[105] In addition, the strong focus on mission in the undisputed Paulines, which is present also in the Pastorals, clearly leads in certain directions with regard to engagement with context. By contrast, John's Gospel exhibits a similar stark dualism to that in evidence in 1–3 John, although in the Gospel there is a stronger emphasis on mission than in the letters. So perhaps theological thinking and developments within a particular theological tradition are key factors.

But the strongly contrasting ways of responding to city life in the books we have considered are of greatest significance. For the early Christians, there was no one paradigm of relating to their urban context but rather we see a considerable spectrum of interactions.

---

105. See for example, Rom 12:14–21; 1 Thess 5:15; Gal 6:10.

Urbanization and Literate Status in Early Christian Rome

Hermas and Justin Martyr as Examples

Chris Keith

1. Introduction

A maxim in studies of ancient literacy is that literate education was more readily available in urban areas than in rural areas. This essay will affirm this opinion but supplement it by arguing that, at the level of individuals, social class was the more determinative factor in the acquisition of a literate education. It will do so by considering early Christian Rome, a clear urban environment in which early Christianity was embedded. This focus on Rome is justified by the fact that scholars have two early Christian authors identified from this city who *also* discuss the distribution and usage of literate skills in manners related to class, *and* do so in the same chronological period (second century CE)—Hermas and Justin Martyr.[1] After presenting these two early Christians' descriptions of literacy, this essay will conclude by noting their significance for some recent proposals from New Testament scholars.

---

1. Since Hermas and Justin both refer to the reading and writing of books (see below in the main text), this essay will not address more limited forms of grapho-literacy such as graffiti or ossuary inscriptions. On the more advanced levels of education required for reading intricate texts or compositional writing, see Chris Keith, *The* Pericope Adulterae, *the Gospel of John, and the Literacy of Jesus*, NTTSD 38 (Leiden: Brill, 2009), 53–79.

2. Literacy and Urbanization

At the beginning of his landmark study, *Ancient Literacy*, Harris discusses the strong correlation between urbanization and literacy in terms of its relevance for setting historians' expectations for literacy rates in the Greco-Roman world.[2] Appealing to comparative evidence, he observes, for example, that the rise of "mass literacy" in eighteenth-century New England "was due in large part to urbanization."[3] Urbanization is thus, for Harris, a key "precondition" for "mass literacy," alongside other factors such as the printing press and publicly funded elementary education systems.[4] Their absence in antiquity indicates, for Harris, that "mass literacy" was never achieved. Similarly, based upon modern comparative evidence, he states that "cities were a crucial factor" for the spread of literacy in antiquity, and "at all events it is plain that rural patterns of living are inimical to the spread of literacy."[5] In support of this connection between agrarianism and illiteracy, he cites the frequent association of rural people with ignorance and illiteracy, such as Quintilian's usage of *illitteratus* ("illiterate," "unlearned") as essentially a synonym for *rusticus* ("rural," "rustic").[6]

a. Literacy and Urbanization in Second Temple Judaism and Early Christianity

Although both Harris and the theory of a connection between urbanization and literacy have received criticism,[7] studies related to Second Tem-

---

2. William V. Harris, *Ancient Literacy* (Cambridge, MA: Harvard University Press, 1989), 11–21.

3. Harris, *Ancient Literacy*, 13.

4. Harris, *Ancient Literacy*, 15: "No historical culture is known to have achieved more than a rather low level of craftsman's literacy without the printing press." On the lack of subsidisation of schools in the ancient world, see pp. 17, 245.

5. Harris, *Ancient Literacy*, 17.

6. Harris, *Ancient Literacy*, 17. See Quintilian, *Inst.* 2.21.16: "For even a rustic and illiterate litigant . . ." (*Nam et litigator rusticus illitteratusque*). Among others, Harris also notes Plutarch, *Arist.* 7.5.

7. An initial critical reaction to Harris was Mary Beard et al., *Literacy in the Roman World*, JRASup 3 (Ann Arbor: Journal of Roman Archaeology, 1991), which qualified and criticized Harris on minor issues but largely accepted his general argument for widespread illiteracy in ancient Greece and Rome. For a recent and succinct presentation of reactions to Harris, see Michael Owen Wise, *Language and Literacy in Roman Judea: A Study of the Bar*

ple Judaism and early Christianity have generally upheld the relevance and correctness of both for these contexts.[8] The strong connection between urbanism and literacy or, alternatively, agrarianism and illiteracy, stems from a variety of factors. In a 1992 study, Bar-Ilan presents some of these factors and concludes that "it is no exaggeration to say that the total literacy rate in the Land of Israel" among Jews in the first centuries CE "was probably less than 3%," which was up from the Maccabean period when it "was 1.5% if not lower."[9] Bar-Ilan arrives at this conclusion on the basis of three specific

---

Kokhba Documents, AYBRL (New Haven: Yale University Press, 2015), 21–26. Paul Rhodes Eddy and Gregory A. Boyd, *The Jesus Legend: A Case for the Historical Reliability of the Synoptic Jesus Tradition* (Grand Rapids: Baker Academic, 2007), 241–45, present Harris's thesis as more determinist than it is when, for example, they ask rhetorically, "Does literacy depend on public schools?" (244). Harris's view, however, concerns "mass literacy" specifically rather than "literacy" in general and is more tempered: "Schools are not always necessary for the teaching of the alphabet, and in these early-modern societies a great deal of literacy was acquired not in schools but in the home. A system of schools is nevertheless crucial, for they vastly reinforce basic literacy as well as spreading it, and they are symptomatic of societies which give high importance to mass education" (Harris, *Ancient Literacy*, 16). Similarly overlooking Harris's nuance is Brian J. Wright, "Ancient Literacy in New Testament Research: Incorporating a Few More Lines of Enquiry," *TJ* 36 (2015): 161–89. With regard to the connection between illiteracy and rusticity, Nicholas Everett, *Literacy in Lombard Italy, c. 568–774* (Cambridge: Cambridge University Press, 2003), 12–13, argues against an "economic-determinist view of literacy": "Despite humanist assumptions concerning the connections between ancient *urbanitas* and *litterae*, the history of literacy is full of examples that deny the validity of using urbanism as a guide to levels of literate activity." Everett is, of course, correct that exceptions exist, but they are not enough to suggest that there is no connection between urbanization and literacy.

8. On Second Temple Judaism and biblical studies scholars who generally affirm Harris, see Chris Keith, *Jesus' Literacy: Scribal Culture and the Teacher from Galilee*, LHJS 8 / LNTS 413 (London: T&T Clark, 2011), 3–4, 73–75; cf. also Wise, *Language*, 351, 355. For those who explicitly affirm the connection between urbanization and literacy, see, inter alia, Meir Bar-Ilan, "Illiteracy in the Land of Israel in the First Centuries CE," in *Essays in the Social Scientific Study of Judaism and Jewish Society*, ed. Simcha Fishbane, Stuart Schoenfeld, and Alain Goldschlaeger (New York: Ktav, 1992), 2:48–50; Albert I. Baumgarten, *The Flourishing of Jewish Sects in the Maccabean Era: An Interpretation*, JSJSup 55 (Atlanta: SBL, 1997), 137–51; Catherine Hezser, *Jewish Literacy in Roman Palestine*, TSAJ 81 (Tübingen: Mohr Siebeck, 2001), 496; Keith, *Pericope*, 71; Keith, *Jesus' Literacy*, 81–85.

9. Bar-Ilan, "Illiteracy," 55. However stark these conclusions might seem, the most detailed studies on Jewish literacy have broadly affirmed them. Hezser, *Jewish Literacy*, 496, explicitly affirms Bar-Ilan's view, suggesting that his estimate may, in fact, be too generous. Wise, *Language*, approaches the topic from the Bar Kokhba documents and concludes that, between Pompey and Hadrian, between 2.5 and 5 percent of adult Jews in Judea were able to read books, while perhaps 16 percent of adult Jews in Judea were able to sign their names

arguments, which he forms in light of a mixture of ancient and modern evidence. First, he argues for a strong correlation between illiteracy and agricultural societies: "The more agricultural the society, the less literate and the higher the birth rate."[10] Second, and similar to Harris, he argues that population growth leads to urbanization, which leads to increased literacy rates.[11] Third, Bar-Ilan argues for a correlation between literacy and life expectancy, though he forwards this argument with more hesitancy.[12]

Even if Bar-Ilan's brief study left much further work to be done and must function at a general level, it is difficult to disagree with his overall argument that, "even if imprecise or partial," there is indeed a correlation between urbanization and literacy on the one hand and agrarianism and illiteracy on the other hand.[13] As Harris and numerous medievalists have also demonstrated, this correlation is not restricted to ancient Palestine or the ancient Near East in general.[14] Furthermore, the strength of Bar-Ilan's argument actually lies not in the statistics but in the manner in which it forces historians to ask utterly practical questions about a first-century Palestinian culture in which the need and value for literate skills did not match those of industrialized cultures. For example, Bar-Ilan rightly asks, "Why should a farmer send his son to learn how to read when it entails a waste of working time (= money)? Why should he himself learn how to read if his culture is based on oral tradition (though with a written Torah)?"[15] Since education in the ancient world was not compulsory, this question throws into sharp

---

(350). As Wise states: "A literate society filled with illiterates—especially women: that was Roman Judea in a nutshell" (351).

10. Bar-Ilan, "Illiteracy," 48–50, quotation from 49.

11. Bar-Ilan, "Illiteracy," 50–52.

12. Bar-Ilan, "Illiteracy," 53: "The higher the literacy rate, the lower the number of infant deaths and the higher life expectancy. . . . Nonetheless, the explanation of this relationship between life expectancy and illiteracy is still rather vague." Bar-Ilan speculates that privileging the written word, and thus written information related to hygiene and other matters, leads to lower infant mortality and higher life expectancy. As this part of his argument is based primarily on evidence from modern societies, a more likely explanation is that cultures with sufficient governmental infrastructures for widespread healthcare also have sufficient infrastructures for widespread education systems, with designated tax funds for each social enterprise. In this sense, Bar-Ilan's point remains that "infant mortality and life expectancy may not be related directly to literacy, but they both proclaim the state of that society's progress."

13. Bar-Ilan, "Illiteracy," 48. Based upon Bar-Ilan, Baumgarten, *Flourishing*, 137, states, "Literacy often goes hand in hand with urbanization."

14. Harris, *Ancient Literacy*, 3–24.

15. Bar-Ilan, "Illiteracy," 55.

relief the fact that those children who received any elementary education at all were likely from the sector of society where the family could afford such a luxury. As Hezser observes,

> In addition to the actual teaching fees they would lose the money which their sons could have earned during the hours they spent at school. For many if not most parents this loss will have been exceedingly high. If they gave their sons an education at all, they are likely to have let them learn the skills which they needed for economic advancement only.[16]

Supporting these observations is the wealth of papyri from Jewish and Greco-Roman contexts that indicate that literacy was not necessary for an individual to engage literate culture for the purposes of, for example, registering a land deed or marriage contract. He or she could employ a professional scribe.[17] The non-compulsory nature of education also points to another factor connecting urbanization with opportunity for literate education; namely that there typically needed to be a dense enough population to justify the presence of a teacher of reading and writing.[18]

One can buttress the assertion of a connection between urbanization and literate education, or agrarianism and limited or no literate education, with further evidence. That some children received only as much education as was required or could be afforded is clear from the Greco-Roman Egyptian school papyri as well as "slow writers" such as the Egyptian village scribe Petaus or the Bar Kokhba–era Eleazar ben Eleazar. Petaus was literate enough to copy his formula for document submission mechanically but not literate enough to catch a mistake when he makes it and then repeats it (*P.Petaus* 121 [P.Köln inv. 328]).[19] He was similar to the pupils of the school

16. Hezser, *Jewish Literacy*, 67. Cf. also Wise, *Language*, 347.

17. For the occurrence of the formulae stating that one person wrote on behalf of another in the Jewish context, see the Babatha cache, especially *P.Yadin* 15.35–36, *P.Yadin* 16.35, and *P.Yadin* 22.34. For a non-Jewish occurrence, see P.Oxy. 1636.45–46, which is one among a plethora. See further Rita Calderini, "Gli ἀγράμματοι nell'Egitto greco-romano," *Aegyptus* 30 (1950): 14–41; Thomas J. Kraus, "'Uneducated', 'Ignorant', or Even 'Illiterate'? Aspects and Background for an Understanding of ΑΓΡΑΜΜΑΤΟΙ (and ΙΔΙΩΤΑΙ) in Acts 4.13," in his Ad fontes: *Original Manuscripts and Their Significance for Studying Early Christianity—Selected Essays*, TENTS 3 (Leiden: Brill, 2007), 149–67, as well as the helpful discussion of *P.Yadin* 44 in Wise, *Language*, 2–7.

18. Keith, *Pericope*, 64.

19. On Petaus, see Herbert C. Youtie, "Βραδέως γράφων: Between Literacy and Illiteracy," in his *Scriptiunculae II* (Amsterdam: Adolf M. Hakkert, 1973), 629–51, as well as Keith,

papyri who learned to write their names almost immediately, and prior to developed reading ability, in order to be able to demonstrate at least this skill in the likelihood that their education progressed no further.[20] Eleazar ben Eleazar, who signed *P.Yadin* 44, is an example of someone with such restricted literacy. His limited ability in producing Hebrew script garnered from Wise the assessment that "he did not so much write as draw."[21] The (from a contemporary perspective) stunted educational accomplishments of these individuals reflects a typicality in the ancient world—students gained only as much education as was required by their station in life or their family could afford.

These students, however, came from the sector of society that received at least some education. Based on the research of Harris, Bar-Ilan, Hezser, Wise, and many others, this was a stark minority and most individuals received no education at all.[22] In this sense, one should note the connection between manual labor, agrarianism, and literacy in Sirach's lauding of the scribe in Sir 38:24–39:1 (second century BCE). According to Sirach, "The wisdom of the scribe depends on the opportunity of leisure; only the one who has little business can become wise" (38:24 NRSV). Sirach thus directly correlates freedom from work with study, or at least the grapho-literate training required of a scribe. It can be no surprise, therefore, that he speaks of "the one who handles the plow," "drives oxen," and "whose talk is about bulls" (38:25) as fundamentally not being a scribe: "They are not sought out for the council of the people, nor do they attain eminence in the public assembly. They do not sit in the judge's seat, nor do they understand the decisions of the courts" (38:33). Such individuals join the artisan (38:27), the smith (38:28), the potter (38:29), and all who "rely on their hands" (38:31).[23]

Jesus' Literacy, 89; Thomas J. Kraus, "(Il)Literacy in Non-Literary Papyri from Graeco-Roman Egypt: Further Aspects to the Educational Ideal in Ancient Literary Sources and Modern Times," in his Ad fontes: *Original Manuscripts and Their Significance for Studying Early Christianity—Selected Essays*, TENTS 3 (Leiden: Brill, 2007), 107–29.

20. Raffaella Cribiore, *Gymnastics of the Mind: Greek Education in Hellenistic and Roman Egypt* (Princeton: Princeton University Press, 2001), 167; *Writing, Teachers, and Students in Graeco-Roman Egypt*, ASP 36 (Atlanta: Scholars, 1996), 10. Also noting that few students made it all the way through the pedagogical process is David M. Carr, *Writing on the Tablet of the Heart: Origins of Scripture and Literature* (New York: Oxford University Press, 2005), 183, 187, 192.

21. Wise, *Language*, 3, 59–60.

22. For a thorough discussion, see Keith, *Jesus' Literacy*, 71–123. Wise, *Language*, 345–55.

23. Cf. also the juxtaposition of Torah study and manual labor in the later y. Hag. 2:1,

Sirach praises such individuals and even assigns them an important role in the urban environment, since "without them no city can be inhabited" (38:32).[24] But he ultimately makes the contrast between the educated scribe, dealing with matters of texts and interpretation (39:2–3), and farmers and workers explicit: "How different the one who devotes himself to the study of the law of the Most High!" (39:1).

Sirach's identification of an artisan (τέκτων; 38:27) as someone who cannot function as an educated authority of the law is significant, as it is precisely why the audience of the Nazareth synagogue rejects Jesus as a synagogue teacher in Mark 6:3 (cf. Matt 13:55).[25] Similarly, the second-century critic of Christianity, Celsus, found laughable the fact that Christians would affirm an artisan (τέκτων) as their teacher.[26] He asks mockingly, "Would not an old woman who sings a story to lull a little child to sleep have been ashamed to whisper tales such as these?"[27] Importantly, Origen concedes to Celsus that Jesus "had no general education" and "received no serious instruction from men," just as he acknowledged that Jesus's disciples were "fisherfolk and tax-collectors who had not had even a primary education."[28]

b. Jerusalem, Galilee, and Literate Status

This evidence demonstrates that for many ancients there was a strong assumption that being from the class where one works on the land or works with one's hands for a living precluded the notion that such an individual would be an educated authoritative teacher.[29] It therefore exhibits a con-

---

77b and b. Yoma 35b, the latter of which envisions the poor responding to the question "How come you did not engage in Torah-study?" with, "I was poor and preoccupied with earning my living" (Jacob Neusner, trans., *The Babylonian Talmud: A Translation and Commentary*, 36 vols. [Peabody: Hendrickson, 2005]). The tractate then invokes Hillel as an example of one whose poverty did not stop his desire for studying Torah. On Hillel, see further below, n. 73.

24. *Pace* Richard A. Horsley, *Scribes, Visionaries, and the Politics of Second Temple Judea* (Louisville: Westminster John Knox, 2007), 55, 57, who claims Sirach "looks down on" manual laborers.

25. Keith, *Jesus' Literacy*, 132–39.

26. Origen, *Cels.* 6.34 (PG 11:1348).

27. Origen, *Cels.* 6.34 (Henry Chadwick, trans., *Origen: Contra Celsum* [Cambridge: Cambridge University Press, 1953]).

28. Origen, *Cels.* 1.29, 62 (Chadwick), respectively.

29. The point at present is not that manual labor and literate education could not co-

nection between agrarianism and illiteracy. This evidence is also capable of shedding some light on cultural assumptions that appear in the New Testament, especially the assumptions of those in Jerusalem regarding Galileans. Although there is no need, historically speaking, to think of Galilee as a "backwater," both the Gospel of John and the Acts of the Apostles portray Jerusalem authorities as identifying Galilee and Galileans with a lack of knowledge of the law and a concomitant illiteracy. "The Jews" are perplexed by Jesus, a Galilean (John 1:46), in John 7:15: "How does this man know letters (γράμματα οἶδεν) when he has never been taught (μὴ μεμαθηκώς)?" Their perplexity derives from the combination of their assumption that Jesus would be uneducated and the fact that his oral teaching seems to be indicative of a literate education.[30]

The claims of "the Jews" of John 7:15 are embedded in a narrative context that reflects the connection between non-urban contexts and lack of advanced literate skills and thus lack of intricate knowledge of written texts. The chief priests and the Pharisees (John 7:45) mockingly ask Nicodemus if he is also from Galilee in John 7:52 after he claims that judging Jesus without a hearing is against the law (7:51). They point out the supposed difference between Nicodemus and Galileans when they instruct him to "search" the law, which assumes his ability to consult it himself (7:52).[31] Rhetorically,

---

exist but that the degree to which they co-existed depended upon one's class. The evidence cited above indicates that, for those in the manual-labor class, literate education was generally impossible. The same cannot be said in the other direction. Those of the educated class often paired manual labor with Torah study. See, for example, m. 'Abot 2:2 or Philo's description of the Essenes in *Prob.* 12.81–82; *Hypoth.* 11.6–9. Later rabbinic tradition often portrays Shammai as engaged in manual labor, as he has a penchant for throwing his builder's cubit at questioners (b. Šabb. 31a). (Interestingly, b. Šabb. 31a also portrays a gentile who approaches Shammai and Hillel and needs first to be taught the Hebrew alphabet.) Cf. also b. Ber. 35b, which portrays something of a "good ole days" mentality. It claims that the "former generations" of rabbis "treated their study of Torah as their principal obligation, and their everyday work as their occasional task, and both this and that worked out well for them," whereas "the latter generations treat their everyday work as their principal obligation, and their study of Torah as their occasional task, and neither this nor that worked out well for them" (Neusner).

30. *Pace* scholars who use this passage to argue that Jesus was literate (e.g., Craig A. Evans, *Jesus and His World: The Archaeological Evidence* [London: SPCK, 2012], 81). The *author's* or *narrator's* claim is not that Jesus was literate, but that he taught like literate teachers (in contrast to Mark 1:22 // Matt 7:29), which was a problem because his audience assumed he was illiterate. For further discussion, see Chris Keith, "The Claim of John 7.15 and the Memory of Jesus' Literacy," *NTS* 56 (2010): 44–63.

31. The scribal-literate skill of being able to "search" a manuscript is attributed to Jesus

their chastisement places Nicodemus and Galileans in the same position as "the crowd" of John 7:49, which they claim "does not know the law."

In a similar fashion, the Jerusalem-based Sanhedrin in Acts 4:13 identifies Jesus's disciples Peter and John, whom the text earlier identified as "men of Galilee" (Acts 1:11), as "illiterate and unlearned" (ἀγράμματοι . . . καὶ ἰδιῶται).[32] Like the Jesus of John 7:15, the apostles prompt a response of "amazement" from the scribal authorities because of their oral preaching, with both authors using θαυμάζειν. In John, the Father undergirds Jesus's rhetorical skills (John 7:16), whereas, in Acts, the Holy Spirit undergirds the apostles' skills (Acts 4:8). In both cases, however, the point is the same—divine aid enables them to speak in a manner that their lack of education would normally prohibit. Therefore, John's Gospel and the Acts of the Apostles join other ancient sources in reflecting a prevalent assumption of illiteracy for those who dwell outside major urban centers.

c. Summary

Therefore, Second Temple Judaism and early Christianity, like the rest of the ancient world, exhibited a connection between urbanization and literacy, as well as a connection between agrarianism and illiteracy. In the rest of this essay, however, I suggest that the issue is not quite as simple as these general perceptions might suggest. To state it otherwise, even this evidence demonstrates that any thoughts of a *deterministic* relationship between urbanization and literacy, or agrarianism and illiteracy, would be shortsighted. The issue is not *primarily* where someone lives and works (that is, the city versus the countryside), but the class from which that person derives or, in the case of slaves trained as readers and copyists, the class of one's owners. When asking questions about an individual's literate status, then, the more important criterion is whether one is from a social class that affords one the

---

in Luke 4:17 after the text claims he stood up "in order to read" (ἀναγνῶναι) in Luke 4:16. I have argued elsewhere that this account of Jesus in Nazareth purposefully contradicts the Markan version, wherein Jesus is rejected as a synagogue teacher as a τέκτων (Mark 6:3), and that Mark's account is more historically likely (Keith, *Jesus' Literacy*, 124–88).

32. The Sanhedrin's further identification of Peter and John as companions of Jesus on the basis of their illiterate and unlearned status in Acts 4:13b presents an interesting discontinuity with Luke's portrayal of Jesus elsewhere in his Gospel as a scribal-literate teacher of the law (see n. 31 above). For further discussion, see Chris Keith, "The Oddity of the Reference to Jesus in Acts 4:13b," *JBL* 134 (2015): 791–811.

opportunity of literate education. This thesis is reinforced with evidence from two Christian authors from one of the most urban environments in early Christianity, ancient Rome.

3. Early Christian Rome

Two early Christian authors from the early- to mid-second century CE, Hermas and Justin Martyr, demonstrate that even in urban environments, accessibility of literate education was still primarily a function of social class.[33]

a. Hermas, Freedman, and "Slow Writer"

The *Shepherd of Hermas* was one of the most popular pieces of Christian literature in the early Church. If surviving manuscript witnesses are any indication of popularity, *Hermas* was even more popular than many texts that became canonical. Eleven second- and third-century manuscripts of *Hermas* survive and, as Hurtado notes, "This total exceeds the number of witnesses for any other text in Christian manuscripts of the period, except for the Psalms and the Gospels of Matthew and John."[34]

Important for present purposes are the provenance of *Hermas*, its authorship, and its depiction of literate abilities. According to lines 73–76 of the Muratorian fragment (ca. 200 CE), "Hermas wrote the *Shepherd* very recently, in our times, in the city of Rome, while bishop Pius, his brother, was occupying the chair of the church of the city of Rome."[35] The text itself

---

33. For the wider non-Christian book culture of Rome, see Ulrike Egelhaaf-Gaiser, "*Quaestiones Romanae*: Antiquarische Spaziergänge zwischen Kapitol und Venustempel," in *Von Rom nach Bagdad,* ed. Peter Gemeinhardt and Sebastian Günther (Tübingen: Mohr Siebeck, 2013), 163–87; William A. Johnson, *Readers and Reading Culture in the High Roman Empire*, CCS (New York: Oxford University Press, 2010), both of whom emphasize the significance of books and literate skills for the construction and reflection of elite identity. Thus, Egelhaaf-Gaiser, "*Quaestiones*," 169, refers to books as "die Vertreter der Bildungselite" ("the representatives of elite education"). Although focused upon a very specific sector of Roman society, such approaches nevertheless are important for considering the manners in which early Christians, an equally distinct (in some ways) sector of Roman society, used books to construct and reflect their identities (as notes Johnson, *Readers*, 15 n. 22).

34. Larry W. Hurtado, *The Earliest Christian Artifacts: Manuscripts and Christian Origins* (Grand Rapids: Eerdmans, 2006), 32–33.

35. Translation from Bruce M. Metzger, *The Canon of the New Testament: Its Origin,*

indicates a provenance of Rome also. The author opens by claiming he was formerly a slave who had been sold to a woman in Rome.[36] Hermas later claims that he, at one point, had some wealth (now gone), and was formerly dishonest in his business.[37] Although the author has crafted this text rhetorically, in the words of Verheyden, "There is no reason to suspect that the information he provides about himself, his troublesome family . . . and his ill-fated professional career . . . is wholly untrustworthy."[38] Similarly, Osiek affirms that Hermas was a freedman in Rome.[39]

With regard to Hermas's literate abilities, Hermas is educated but "his education level is limited."[40] When copying a book, Hermas claims, "I copied it all, letter by letter, for I could not make out the syllables."[41] In other words, Hermas was a "slow writer" like Petaus or Eleazar ben Eleazar who, though technically able to write, had to do so deliberately and without the more advanced ability to read what he was copying. (One should bear in mind that reading and writing were separately acquired skills in ancient pedagogy.[42]) Cicero describes a similar situation with regard to his scribes (*librarii*) Spintharo and Tiro. The former, like Hermas, can take dictation only syllable-by-syllable while the latter can follow whole sentences.[43]

Later, Hermas is instructed to write two "little books" (βιβλαρίδια; cf. Rev 10:2, 9, 10), which he is to send to Clement and Grapte, who will disseminate the works. Hermas is instructed to read what he has written in his city,

Development, and Significance (Oxford: Clarendon, 1987), 307. For a recent affirmation of a date of ca. 200 CE for the Muratorian fragment, see Joseph Verheyden, "The New Testament Canon," in *The New Cambridge History of the Bible: From the Beginnings to 600*, ed. James Carleton Paget and Joachim Schaper (Cambridge: Cambridge University Press, 2013), 399 n. 17. Lee Martin McDonald, *The Biblical Canon: Its Origin, Transmission, and Authority*, updated and rev. 3rd ed. (Peabody, MA: Hendrickson, 2008 [1995]), 369–78, favors a fourth-century dating.

36. Herm. Vis. 1.1.1 (1.1).

37. Herm. Vis. 3.6.7 (14.7); Mand. 3.5 (28.5), respectively.

38. Joseph Verheyden, "The *Shepherd of Hermas*," in *The Writings of the Apostolic Fathers*, ed. Paul Foster (London: T&T Clark, 2007), 64–65.

39. Carolyn Osiek, "The Oral World of Early Christianity in Rome: The Case of Hermas," in *Judaism and Christianity in First-Century Rome*, ed. Karl P. Donfried and Peter Richardson (Grand Rapids: Eerdmans, 1998), 152–53.

40. Osiek, "Oral," 154.

41. Herm. Vis. 2.1.4 (5.4) (Michael W. Holmes, ed. and trans., *The Apostolic Fathers: Greek Texts and English Translations*, 3rd ed. [Grand Rapids: Baker Academic, 2007]).

42. Keith, *Jesus' Literacy*, 93–95.

43. Cicero, *Att.* 13.25.

though he must do so "along with the elders who preside over the church."[44] The text does not clearly indicate that Hermas needs the aid of the elders due to his own limited reading abilities, though it is open to that interpretation, which would cohere with his aforementioned inability to identify syllables. After stating that he must read with the elders' assistance (whatever the nature of that assistance), the "elderly woman" who serves in the narrative as the Church personified refers to Hermas as "poorly instructed" (ἐνδεής).[45] Later in *Hermas*, like John in the Apocalypse, Hermas is instructed by an angel to write commandments, parables, and other things, which Hermas then claims he has done.[46] After further references to Hermas's lack of intelligence,[47] Hermas brings the text near a close by noting that he wrote it by taking dictation.[48]

Undoubtedly, these portrayals of Hermas's literate skills are products of a rhetorical flourish. His seeming lack of intelligence is a narrative device that requires mysteries to be revealed and explained to Hermas, and thus also the reader. Similarly, taking dictation from a celestial being has precedents in biblical tradition before Hermas, as far back as Moses taking dictation of the second set of stone tablets (Exod 34:27; cf. Deut 27:1–8) and as recent as John taking dictation in the Apocalypse (Rev 1:11, 19; 2:1, 8, 12, 18; 3:1, 7, 14; 14:13). Nevertheless, there is little reason to doubt that Hermas, as a freedman, could have had precisely the limited-yet-functional literate skills that he claims for himself. Elite individuals in the ancient world commonly employed slaves to read and write on their behalf,[49] and thus paid to educate them to varying levels of competence.[50] The reason for this is that, although reading and writing abilities were prized possessions among the educated elite and often praised as such,[51] they were also considered laborious tasks and easily dispensed to a trained slave.[52] Thus, "one might almost say that

44. Herm. Vis. 2.4.3 (8.3) (Holmes).
45. Herm. Vis. 3.1.2 (9.2) (Holmes).
46. Herm. Vis. 5.5–7 (25.5–7); Sim. 9.1.1 (78.1).
47. Herm. Sim. 9.2.6–7 (79.6–7); 9.14.4 (91.4).
48. Herm. Sim. 9.33.1–10.1.1 (110.1–111.1).
49. Cicero, *Att.* 13.25; Pliny the Younger, *Ep.* 3.5.
50. See P.Oxy. 724, a contract for a slave to learn shorthand.
51. For example, see Cicero, *Att.* 2.23; 7.3; Dio Chrysostom, *Dic. exercit.* 6; Quintilian, *Inst.* 1.1.28–29; 11.2.32; Philo, *Spec.* 4.160, 162.
52. Cicero, *Att.* 2.23; 4.16; 8.13; 7.2; *Rhet. Her.* 4.4.6. See further Larry W. Hurtado and Chris Keith, "Writing and Book Production in the Hellenistic and Roman Periods," in *The New Cambridge History of the Bible: From the Beginnings to 600*, ed. James Carleton Paget and Joachim Schaper (Cambridge: Cambridge University Press, 2013), 72.

there was a direct correlation between the social standing that guaranteed literacy and the means to avoid writing."[53] One should further remember that, although such limited abilities could be mocked as indicative of igno-rance by the truly educated,[54] in terms of the vast majority of the popula-tion even the ability to copy syllable-by-syllable was rare and a substantial accomplishment.

Hermas never explicitly states how he acquired his limited literate abil-ities. But it is quite significant that he was at one point a slave and at one point had some wealth. Although one is beyond the realm of the verifiable at this point, either of these realities is capable of explaining how Hermas came to acquire the ability to read and copy. One could even hazard an ed-ucated guess that they could be related, as manumitted slaves who had been trained in literate skills during their slavery were then equipped with a skill with which to earn a living, as is the case of Secundus the freedman who ran a bookshop in Rome.[55] Regardless of the merits of this guess, Hermas, as a manumitted semiliterate early Christian in an urban environment, exhibits a clear connection between literacy and social class.

b. Justin Martyr and the Roman Illiterate Christians

The theory that Hermas's acquisition of limited literate abilities was likely more directly reflective of his status as a slave in a wealthy home or as some-one who attained a moderate amount of wealth himself, rather than simply being geographically located in Rome, is strengthened by Justin Martyr's description of Roman Christians and their textual practices. Justin was born in Syria but became the "leader of a 'school-church' in Rome" by the mid–second century when he composed his *First Apology*.[56] In this work, he for-

---

53. Roger Bagnall, *Reading Papyri, Writing Ancient History*, AAW (New York: Rout-ledge, 1995), 25. Similarly, R. A. Derrenbacker, Jr., *Ancient Compositional Practices and the Synoptic Problem*, BETL 186 (Leuven: Peeters, 2005), 24.

54. Libanius, *Or.* 18.158 (mocking shorthand writers); Josephus, *J.W.* 1.24.3 §479 (village scribes).

55. Martial, *Epigr.* 4.72. Lionel Casson, *Libraries in the Ancient World* (New Haven: Yale University Press, 2001), 105: "The authors got nothing out of the sales [in bookshops]; . . . there was no such thing in the ancient world as copyrights or royalties. It was booksellers like Tryphon and Secundus who pocketed the profits."

56. Paul Parvis, "Justin Martyr," in *Early Christian Thinkers: The Lives and Legacies of Twelve Key Figures*, ed. Paul Foster (Downers Grove: IVP Academic, 2010), 1. On Justin, see further Sara Parvis and Paul Foster, eds., *Justin Martyr and His Worlds* (Minneapolis: For-

wards the argument that Plato was, in reality, dependent upon Moses, and thus claims, "It is not we, then, who have the same opinions as others, but everyone speaks in imitation of what we say."[57] In order to underscore the elementary nature of this observation, he states, "Among us, therefore, it is possible to hear and to learn these things from those who do not even know the formation of letters, being simple and uncouth in speech, but wise and trustworthy in mind, and some disabled and bereft of sight."[58]

This text contains a number of interesting aspects. First, Justin reveals that, as noted earlier, many Christians in Rome would have considered someone such as Hermas to be educated; for here Justin acknowledges that some of the Christians in Rome do not even know the alphabet. Second, this text alone demonstrates that an urban environment did not automatically lead to the acquisition of literacy on the individual level, even if it meant that such an education was geographically available. Similarly acknowledging Christian illiteracy is Origen in the third century. He concedes Celsus's charge that Christianity attracted a high number of illiterate individuals as simple common sense, thereby acknowledging its truth: "It was inevitable that in the great number of people overcome by the word, because there are many more vulgar and illiterate people than those who

---

tress, 2007); Hubertus R. Drobner, *The Fathers of the Church: A Comprehensive Introduction*, trans. Siegfried S. Schatzmann (Peabody, MA: Hendrickson, 2007), 77–86.

57. Justin Martyr, *1 Apol.* 60.10 (Minns and Parvis).

58. Justin Martyr, *1 Apol.* 60.11 (Minns and Parvis). I have placed the phrase that Minns and Parvis translate as "and some disabled and bereft of sight" (ὄντων καὶ πηρῶν καὶ χήρων τινῶν τὰς ὄψεις) back into the main text. Despite its presence in *Parisinus graecus* 450, the best manuscript of Justin's *First Apology*, Minns and Parvis remove the phrase from their critical text as a conjecture, stating, "We exclude the phrase as not being pertinent to the argument. It would be no more remarkable in Justin's world than in ours that a disabled or blind person should be able to impart wisdom" (Justin, Philosopher and Martyr, *Apologies*, ed. and trans. Denis Minns and Paul Parvis, OECT [Oxford: Oxford University Press, 2009], 237 n. 3). In addition to finding it odd that editors of a critical text would remove the reading of their best manuscript witness due only to their judgment of the unnecessary nature of the point made, I suggest that they have possibly missed the very point of Justin's employment of the blind in relation to the learning of literacy, as well as underestimated the socially stratified nature of ancient education. It is, of course, true that the blind could gain wisdom in a general sense. But they would not typically have been able to gain literacy in a time long before the invention of the Braille alphabet. Justin is pointing out that even those who have not had the opportunity to gain a literate education, whether as part of the majority poor or due to physical deformity, have acquired knowledge of simple matters such as Plato's dependence upon Moses.

have been trained in rational thinking, the former class should far outnumber the more intelligent."[59]

To return to Justin and the Roman illiterates, and third, Justin's claim indicates implicitly the connection between social class and literacy. The detailed level of textual knowledge that Justin's fuller argument, concerning Christ-types in the Old Testament, presumes is clearly the product of Justin's own education, which enabled him to learn the text in an intricate manner and write his own works expounding it. Beyond this, however, it is significant that he parallels the illiterate members of the church in Rome with the crippled and blind, both of whom would have carried social stigmas and the latter of whom would not physically have been able to read. In other words, Justin's elaborate hermeneutical argument demonstrates the connection between his social class and the acquisition of literate skills that enabled it[60] while his emphasis on the simplicity of the argument in reference to illiterates and social outcasts demonstrates the connection between their social class and the lack of sophistication that a literate education would have provided. The illiterate and blind cannot, after all, serve to shame Plato if they are not the illiterate and blind.

This brief sketch of the varying social classes in Justin's church in Rome provides a wider context for understanding Justin's references to the public reading of the gospels, and thus a "reading culture" of early Christian Rome.[61] In a famous passage a little later in his *First Apology*, Justin describes the activities of Sunday church services, which include the city folk and the country folk: "And on the day called Sunday there is an assembly of those who dwell in cities or the countryside, and the memoirs of the apostles or the writings of the prophets are read, for as long as there is time. Then, when the reader (ὁ ἀναγινώσκων) has stopped, the president, in an address, makes admonition and invitation of the imitation of their good things."[62] One of the primary functions of such a practice was to make available the contents of the manuscripts to the majority of illiterate individuals who could not access those texts for themselves. Notably, there is a single reader who reads on behalf of the church precisely because "among us . . . [are] those who do not even know the formation of letters."[63]

---

59. Origen, *Cels.* 1.27 (Chadwick). See also Clement of Alexandria, *Paed.* 3.11.78.

60. On Justin's identity as a Roman provincial able to write in Greek and his intellectual journey through philosophical schools, see Parvis, "Justin," 1–4.

61. The term "reading culture" is borrowed from Johnson, *Readers*, 9.

62. Justin Martyr, *1 Apol.* 67.3–4 (Minns and Parvis).

63. Justin Martyr, *1 Apol.* 60.11 (Minns and Parvis).

Justin's descriptions of the constituency of his church reveal that dwelling in Rome, or even within walking distance of it, does not lead to the ability to read for many in his church. The role of the lector in early Christian churches liturgically mirrors the role of appointed readers of the text in synagogues.[64] Behind this liturgical parallel, however, lies the similar social function of providing access to the written tradition for a majority illiterate audience. In this sense, Justin Martyr's description of his church in Rome confirms what Hermas's limited literate skills also indicate—even in a heavily urbanized town such as Rome, the acquisition and utilization of literate skills largely reflected the individual's (or his or her owner's) social class, not strictly the geographical location.

4. Conclusion

To conclude, therefore, although there is a connection between urbanization and literacy in the ancient world, one should be careful not to understand this connection in a deterministic manner. This general connection most likely reflects the fact that a more dense population will inevitably include more members of the educated classes, thus raising the overall literacy rate of an area. At the level of individuals, therefore, the question is not necessarily whether they were located within an urban environment, or whether urban characteristics had begun to appear in their locale, but whether they were from the educated class or, in the case of slaves, employed in them.

For New Testament scholars, this fact changes how several standard issues should be addressed. As an example, one may consider Bird's recent revival of the argument that the disciples recorded teachings of Jesus in notebooks that eventually could have served as sources for the gospel authors.[65] Bird states that "it was quite common among literary elites of the Greco-Roman world to take notes" of their teachers.[66] He is correct that this is a known practice; Quintilian even claims that two books have been published

---

64. See further Chris Keith, *Jesus against the Scribal Elite: The Origins of the Conflict* (Grand Rapids: Baker Academic, 2014), 33–36.

65. Michael F. Bird, *The Gospel of the Lord: How the Early Church Wrote the Story of Jesus* (Grand Rapids: Eerdmans, 2014), 45–48. The following two paragraphs are modified from Chris Keith, review of *The Gospel of the Lord: How the Early Church Wrote the Story of Jesus* by Michael F. Bird, *SCJ* 18 (2015): 144–47.

66. Bird, *Gospel*, 46.

in his name by this means.[67] Bird also correctly notes that there are likely early Christian *testimonia* collections of Old Testament passages by the time of Justin and Irenaeus in the second century and certainly by P.Ryl. 460 in the fourth century CE.[68] Bird therefore states that Q "may have started out as such a notebook" and that some of Justin Martyr's citations of sayings of Jesus "may" have been based on a notebook.[69]

Bird, however, nowhere demonstrates that Jesus's disciples came from the same socioeconomic class as the "literary elites of the Greco-Roman world" or educated early Christians such as Justin, Irenaeus, and Papias. The same issues arise with Bird's claim that early Jesus-followers could have preserved Jesus's teachings by way of their trained memories because "learning by memory was simply a part of ancient education."[70] In light of the discussion above, this question is pressing. New Testament traditions such as John 7:15 and Acts 4:13, as well as evidence from the patristic period (Origen) attest the common (though not ubiquitous) conviction that Jesus and his disciples were not from the educated class.

Bird is not alone in needing to give more thorough consideration to the issue of social class when it comes to the possible acquisition of literate skills, however. One may also note Evans's tentative argument that the historical Jesus was literate, which strangely takes John 7:15 and Acts 4:13 as indicating that Jesus and his disciples *were* literate, and nowhere addresses the serious class implications of the identification of Jesus as a τέκτων in Mark 6:3 or the identification of Peter and John as ἀγράμματοι and ἰδιῶται in Acts 4:13.[71] Alternatively, one may consider scholars who point to the Greek language's penetration of first-century Galilee as a supporting argument for James's authorship of the New Testament epistle attributed to him without considering whether James was from a class that would have received such an education, regardless of whether it was geographically available in Galilee.[72]

67. Quintilian, *Inst.* preface. See also the discussion of H. Gregory Snyder, *Teachers and Texts in the Ancient World: Philosophers, Jews, and Christians*, Religion in the First Christian Centuries (New York: Routledge, 2000), 43, 50, with regard to Stoics and Epicureans, respectively.

68. Bird, *Gospel*, 46–47.

69. Bird, *Gospel*, 47.

70. Bird, *Gospel*, 90.

71. Evans, *Jesus and His World*, 63–88 (see 81 on John 7:15 and Acts 4:13). Evans claims that "most commentators" take these passages in this way. He cites none, however, and most commentators actually take the opposite view. For further discussion, see Keith, "Claim"; Keith, "Oddity."

72. See the discussion in Dale C. Allison, Jr., *James*, ICC (London: Bloomsbury T&T Clark, 2013), 25–26.

Furthermore, this is not to suggest that there were no exceptions to the general rule about class restricting educational opportunities. In the rabbinic tradition, Hillel and Akiba have origins outside the scribal-literate class.[73] In early Christianity, Didymus the Blind went blind in childhood, never learned the alphabet, but became an important teacher in the Alexandrian school where he taught the likes of Rufinus and Jerome.[74] But, equally important, these scholars are presented precisely as exceptional. This point only further reinforces the argument of this essay. Outside of exceptional circumstances, the possibility of acquiring literate skills in the ancient world was partially dependent upon one's geographical proximity to an urban environment, but even more dependent upon one's own class or the class of one's owner.

---

73. According to b. Yoma 35b, Hillel overcame poverty to study Torah and thus serves as a counter-example to those who cite the need to earn a living as a reason for not studying Torah in a school setting. Obviously, the exaltation of Hillel as an example would not be necessary if poverty was not widely recognized as a reason that some do not pursue Torah study. According to b. Pesaḥ. 49b, Akiba was born an *am ha'arets* (literally "person of the land," though Neusner translates the term more specifically in educational terms as "un-lettered"). Akiba's origins and surprising access to Torah study are explained in rabbinic traditions that claim he married the daughter of Kalba Sabua, whom he had served as a shepherd, and that she put him through twenty-four years of Torah study (b. Ned. 50a; b. Ketub. 62b–63a). Akiba is therefore at the front of a long line of Scripture scholars who married above their station in life and whose spouse funded their studies, a line that continued with the present author.

74. Jerome, *Vir. ill.* 109.1. See further Keith, *Pericope,* 253–54.

Alexandria ad Aegyptum
The City That Inspired a Polyphony of Early Christian Theologies

Piotr Ashwin-Siejkowski

1. Centers of Scholarship in Alexandria

Sometime in the second century of the Common Era, Achilles Tatius wrote down these impressions on his arrival at Alexandria:

> I entered [Alexandria] by the Sun Gate, as it is called, and was instantly struck by the splendid beauty of the city, which filled my eyes with delight. From the Sun Gate to the Moon Gate—these are the guardian divinities of the entrances—led a straight double row of columns, about the middle of which lies the open part of the town, and in it so many streets that walking in them you would fancy yourself abroad while still at home. . . . I tried to cast my eyes down every street, but my gaze was still unsatisfied, and I could not grasp all the beauty of the spot at once; some parts I saw, some I was on the point of seeing, some I earnestly desired to see, some I could not pass by; that which I actually saw kept my gaze fixed, while that which I expected to see would drag it to the next. I explored therefore every street, and at last, my vision unsatisfied, exclaimed in weariness, "Ah, my eyes, we are beaten."[1]

Even after allowance is made for the highly rhetorical style of this description, this account still inspires our imagination. One element, however, is missing in this picture. The Alexandria visited by Tatius was not an empty,

1. *Leuc. Clit.* 5.1.1–5 (Gaselee, LCL).

silent metropolis. On the contrary, these streets were full of people, sailors, traders, and bankers who arrived at Alexandria's two most famous harbors guided by the splendid lighthouse on the rocky Pharos Island. Even if we do not believe Diodorus Siculus's claim that the total of the free population in Alexandria reached three hundred thousand people in 40 BCE,[2] still the extension of the built-up area of the *polis* suggests a population of approximately two hundred thousand by the beginning of the Christian era. The vibrant, cosmopolitan city attracted not only sellers and buyers: Alexandria, with its cultural tradition, appealed also to those who sought wisdom, wished to acquire philosophical and theological knowledge, or enjoyed theater, poetry, and literature. Why was Alexandria, not Rome, Athens, or Pergamum the intellectual oasis for so many academics, sophists, and students?

We have to mention the city's three largest and best-known intellectual centers: the *Mouseion*, the Royal Library, and the Serapeum Library. The Hellenistic *Mouseion* was an intellectual center in which scholars could research and discuss their ideas. At the same time, the institution also appears to be a center for teaching. If Fraser's assumption is correct,[3] which in my view is plausible, the Alexandrian *Mouseion* was modelled on the Hellenistic philosophical schools in Athens. As in the case of Plato's Academy,[4] the *Mouseion* attracted intellectuals who were devoted to the cult of Muses. Its members gave public lectures, probably from lectures halls within the building. In the Roman period, government support for the *Mouseion* continued. Under the emperors, membership of the *Mouseion* came to be seen as a reward to be given to both prominent Greek-speaking intellectuals and to important men of affairs.[5] As an academic institution, the *Mouseion* aimed to facilitate the highest level of culture in the city and in doing so it reassured its patrons and sponsors that Alexandria was seen as the leading place of Hellenistic intellectual life.

While the *Mouseion* had a more public, open role, the Royal Library held a private collection of literature available only to select groups of scholars. The original Library was built in proximity to the *Mouseion*, if not on its grounds. The collection of Greek manuscripts preserved in the Royal Library was said to be made up of more than four hundred and ninety thousand pa-

2. Diodorus, *Bibl. hist.*, 17.52 (Welles, LCL).
3. Peter M. Fraser, *Ptolemaic Alexandria* (Oxford: Clarendon, 1972), 314.
4. Pierre Boyancé, *Le culte des Muses chez les philosophes grecs. Études d'histoire et de psychologie religieuses* (Paris: Edition de Boccard, 1937), 261.
5. For the Ptolemaic background of this institution, see A. Erskine, "Culture and Power in Ptolemaic Egypt: The Museum and Library of Alexandria," *GR* 42 (1995): 38–48.

pyrus scrolls.[6] Although the Royal Library suffered its first decline in the late second century BCE and then again during the visit of Julius Caesar in 48/47 BCE when fire destroyed some of its collections, the building survived the cataclysm, while the damage to its collection was repaired by Antony's gift to Cleopatra of the contents of the other great Hellenistic library in Pergamum.[7]

The third institution, sometimes called "a daughter library" or "the outer library"—the Serapeum Library—was an annex to the Royal Library and contained duplicate books that were surplus to the requirement of the Royal Library. During the late Ptolemaic period its collection was estimated at nearly forty-three thousand papyrus rolls.[8] It is plausible that during the first century CE that collection became even bigger. All three institutions were active when the first Christian missionaries arrived in Alexandria; they were available to Christian teachers and exegetes who established their schools in this city. These institutions provided Christians not only with models of scholarship, such as various commentary techniques, but also with either public or private discussion. That discussion incorporated an apologetic defence of selected passages and inquisitive questioning of their meaning and significance. That Alexandrian spirit of debate was a very important feature of the city, which was made up of different ethnic and religious groups that from time to time turned to violence, such as that against the Jews in 38 CE.[9] In brief, Alexandria was a *polis* of contradictions; its academic institutions did not exist in a world of harmony and silent devotion to learning, but on the contrary, during the first century as well as later, it witnessed brutality and the violent power of the mob.[10]

2. The First Christians in the *Polis* and Their Literature

The origin of Christianity in Alexandria is shrouded in mist. The well-known legend of the role of John Mark in establishing the first Christian community

6. Ioannis Tzetzes, *Prolegomena de comoedia Aristophanis*, 2.10; see Robert Barnes, "Cloistered Bookworms in the Chicken-Coop of the Muses: The Ancient Library of Alexandria," in *The Library of Alexandria: Centre of Learning in the Ancient World*, ed. Roy Macleod (London: I. B. Tauris, 2005), 64–65; Edward J. Watts, *City and School in Late Antique Athens and Alexandria* (Berkeley: University of California, 2006), 149.

7. Fraser, *Ptolemaic Alexandria*, 335.

8. Ioannis Tzetzes, *Prolegomena de comoedia Aristophanis*, 2.10.

9. See, for instance, Philo, *Legat.* 121–22.

10. See Eusebius's note on the persecution of Christians in the city, in *Hist. eccl.* 6.41.

is part of Eusebius of Caesarea's larger theological outlook, which aimed to align what he proposed as "orthodoxy" with an apostolic origin.[11] Equally, the famous thesis of Walter Bauer about the "gnostic" origin of Christianity in Alexandria must be received critically.[12] Our first historical source, the Acts of the Apostles, mentions a certain "eloquent man" (ἀνὴρ λόγιος), Apollos of Alexandria (18:24–28),[13] who received "the baptism of John" (18:25). A more careful reading of this episode shows that Apollos was introduced to a recent religious tradition that had originated in Palestine. As an Alexandrian Jew, he was "mighty in Scriptures," which suggests his good—if not excellent—acquaintance with the LXX. That note hints not only at his intellectual ability to read (if not memorize) and comment on them, but also suggests his rhetorical, attractive, and convincing way of applying them to a Christian context. Apollos's technique impressed some Christians in Corinth.[14] As we read about Apollos's original views, we learn that his early knowledge about Jesus needed "correction" from other Christian teachers (i.e., Priscilla and Aquila).

I am inclined to propose that Christianity in Alexandria did not originate from one definite origin (either "orthodox"/"apostolic" or "heretical"/"gnostic") but from many sources and possibly simultaneously. Even with, in my view, the correct assumption that Jewish-Christian missionaries arrived in Alexandria,[15] they did not represent a "unanimous" group in a similar way to the first-century Jews,[16] or even Jewish-Christians, who were not "mono-

---

11. For discussion of relevant sources see Birger A. Pearson, "Earliest Christianity in Egypt: Some Observation," in *The Roots of Egyptian Christianity*, ed. Birger A. Pearson and James E. Goehring (Philadelphia: Fortress, 1986), 132–56, esp. 137–45.

12. Walter Bauer, *Orthodoxy and Heresy in Earliest Christianity*, ed. Robert A. Kraft and Gerhard Krodel, trans. Paul J. Achtemeier et al. (London: SCM, 1972); Birger A. Pearson, "Christianity in Egypt," *ABD* 1:954–60; Lewis Ayres, "Introduction," *JECS* 14 (2006): 395–98.

13. See also 1 Cor 1:12; 3:4–22; 4:6; 16:12; Acts 19:1; Bradley B. Blue, "Apollos" in *Dictionary of Paul and His Letters*, ed. Gerald F. Hawthorne, Ralph P. Martin and Daniel G. Reid (Downers Grove, IL: InterVarsity Press, 1993), 37–39.

14. Cf. 1 Cor 3:4–22.

15. See Albertus F. J. Klijn, "Jewish Christianity in Egypt," in *The Roots of Egyptian Christianity,* ed. Birger A. Pearson and James E. Goehring (Philadelphia: Fortress, 1986), 161–75 and other sources in Birger A. Pearson, "Earliest Christianity in Egypt," in *The World of Early Egyptian Christianity: Language, Literature, and Social Context. Essays in Honor of David W. Johnston,* ed. James E. Goehring and Janet A. Timbie, CUA Studies in Early Christianity (Washington: Catholic University of America, 2007), 99 n. 9.

16. Among many studies, I endorse Lee I. Levine, *Judaism and Hellenism in Antiquity: Conflict or Confluence?* (Seattle: University of Washington Press, 1988).

lithic" but rather had diverse theological viewpoints. Those missionaries did not arrive with only an oral tradition about Jesus the Messiah, but also with some notes and memoirs about Jesus the Savior.[17]

In early-second-century Alexandria, the activity of a number of Christian teachers with diverse theologies, such as Basilides,[18] Valentinus, Heracleon,[19] and Pantaenus, suggests that they found in this urban megapolis fertile soil for the dissemination of their doctrines. Those creative thinkers combined in their works various aspects of emerging Christian literature such as the gospels (the Gospel of John, in particular[20]) and Pauline motifs[21] with a philosophical (Stoic, Aristotelian, and Platonic) framework and an allegorical interpretation. Basilides, for instance, assimilated Aristotelian ideas into his theological views,[22] while Valentinus used poetry and mythology in his Christian theology.[23] Allegorical interpretation, so important to

---

17. According to Clement of Alexandria's letter to Theodore, Mark, the author of the Gospel, wrote his initial version in Rome during Peter's lifetime as a type of memoir. After Peter's martyrdom, Mark traveled to Alexandria and he brought "both his own notes and those of Peter, from which he transferred to his former book the things suitable to whatever makes for progress towards knowledge. Thus he composed a more spiritual gospel for the use of those who were perfected" (1.19–22). See Paul Foster, "Secret Mark," in *The Non-Canonical Gospels*, ed. Paul Foster (London: T&T Clark, 2008), 171–82, here 173. Although Clement's letter and the so-called *Secret Gospel of Mark* are still a subject of debate, there is no reason to doubt that early Christian missionaries and teachers carried some written testimonies about Jesus.

18. See more in Birger A. Pearson, "Basilides the Gnostic," in *A Companion to Second-Century Christian "Heretics,"* ed. Antti Marjanen and Petri Luomanen, VCSup 76 (Leiden: Brill, 2005), 1–31.

19. On both theologians and the Valentinian school, see Ismo Dunderberg, "The School of Valentinus," in *A Companion to Second-Century Christian "Heretics,"* ed. Antti Marjanen and Petri Luomanen, VCSup 76 (Leiden: Brill, 2005), 64–99, esp. 76–84, with a useful bibliography, 97–99.

20. Charles E. Hill challenges, as he puts it, "the Orthodox Johannophobia theory." In Hill's view, since Walter Bauer's famous study, recent scholarship has been dominated by a view that "Gnostic use of and affinity for John precipitated or perpetuated a long-standing attitude of suspicion or antagonism towards that Gospel, a phenomenon we may, for convenience, call 'orthodox Johannophobia.'" See his *The Johannine Corpus in the Early Church* (Oxford: Oxford University Press, 2004), 11.

21. See, for example, a very insightful paper by Judith L. Kovacs, "Participation of the Cross: Pauline Motifs in the *Excerpts from Theodotus*" in *Valentinianism: Proceedings of the Conference in Rome October 2013,* ed. Einar Thomassen (Leiden: Brill, forthcoming). I wish to thank Prof. Kovacs for allowing me to read her paper.

22. Ps.-Hippolytus, *Haer.* 7.20–27.

23. Ps.-Hippolytus, *Haer.* 6.37.7.

Valentinus and Heracleon,[24] was earlier endorsed and cherished in the Alexandrian milieu by a Jewish exegete and philosopher: Philo (c. 20 BCE–45 CE). Again, the preserved excerpts from their works show a great deal of acquaintance with the Alexandrian tradition of commentaries, philosophical inquisitiveness, and rhetorical skills.

In a similar way to those exegetes, some anonymous but valuable documents present a great variety of early Alexandrian theologies. The *Epistle of Barnabas*, the *Teachings of Silvanus,* and the *Kerygma Petri* illustrate that richness of outlooks, even that diversity of readership, if not audience. Each one of these narratives offers dissimilar points of contact with the Alexandrian exegetical traditions, each one reveals its own original theological agenda; however, they reflect various aspects of Alexandrian culture that encountered the Christian message. The *Epistle of Barnabas* shows its good acquaintance with allegory and the influence of Philo of Alexandria's thought.[25] This document was highly regarded by the Alexandrian mainstream theologians, who, like Clement, quoted it on a number of occasions.[26] The *Epistle* clearly shows that its author(s) was fully aware of competition with other Christian groups in Alexandria, as we may see in its polemical tone aimed at some ascetic, heretical, and Jewish Christians. The *Teachings of Silvanus* stands for yet another tradition in early Alexandrian Christianity.[27] This time the narrative is influenced by the Jewish sapiential tradition, which flourished earlier in Alexandria, and by a strong Middle Platonic stance.[28] The *Kerygma Petri,* although preserved only in

24. See Elaine H. Pagels, *The Johannine Gospel in Gnostic Exegesis: Heracleon's Commentary on John* (Atlanta: Scholars, 1989); David Dawson, *Allegorical Readers and Cultural Revision in Ancient Alexandria* (Berkeley: University of California, 1992).

25. For further details and discussion, see Pierre Prigent and Robert A. Kraft, eds., *L'Épître de Barnabé*, SC 172 (Paris: Cerf, 1971), 22.

26. Clement of Alexandria quoted this document at least twenty-five times in his works; see more in Annewies van den Hoek, "How Alexandrian Was Clement of Alexandria? Reflections on Clement and His Alexandrian Background," *HeyJ* 31 (1990): 179–94.

27. This document was discovered near Nag Hammadi and offers a much later (fourth century CE) Coptic translation of the treatise. Malcolm Peel highlights the affinity of the document with the Alexandrian intellectual ethos: "Broadly sketched, the affinities lie in the facts that both the Alexandrians and *Teach. Silv.* show the incorporation of Platonic and Stoic ideas into the Christian Faith through the philosophical catalyst of Middle Platonism." See his "Introduction" to *The Teachings of Silvanus* in *The Coptic Gnostic Library. Nag Hammadi Codex VII*, ed. Birger A. Pearson, NHMS 30 (Leiden: Brill, 1996), 265. This volume contains the edition and the English translation of the document.

28. See more in Jan Zandee, "'The Teachings of Silvanus' (NHC VII, 4) and Jewish Christianity," in *Studies in Gnosticism and Hellenistic Religions Presented to Gilles Quispel*

a few fragments, exemplifies some characteristics of Alexandrian theology with an emphasis on, for instance, the apophatic nature of God (frg. 2a) and Logos-Christology (frg.1a).[29] As noted by Pearson, the extracts offer a glimpse into this tradition of Christianity that would soon be embraced as its mainstream representation.[30]

Even more revealing is a careful study of the quoted Christian literature found in the author representing one of the main traditions of Christianity of this *polis* during the second century: Clement of Alexandria (c.150/160–215 CE). Clement, the polymath, theologian, and philosopher, preserved in his writings a vast number of references to Christian and non-Christian literature otherwise lost or even unknown. Stählin's index to Clement's work lists three hundred different literary sources, with more than a thousand references.[31] Clement's access to those sources could not happen without the Alexandrian libraries, which preserved Greco-Roman documents, but also without his placement in the city, which attracted different Christian teachers with their own dossiers. Alexandria, with its distinguished intellectual ethos, certainly helped to preserve, even if it did not actually produce, a diversity of emerging Christian commentaries, excerpts and letters. Clement's works reflect that diversity with great clarity. It should be noted that, while he refers to these Christian texts in multiple sources, he does not place them on the same level of authority as the gospels, which he believes have an apostolic origin (Mark, Luke, Matthew, and John). However, those "non-canonical" documents were quoted in order to support his mainstream theology. Among those "non-canonical" documents, for instance, Clement quotes the *Gospel of the Hebrews* on four occasions, and once he provides us with the correct identification of the document.[32] The *Gospel of the Egyptians*

---

on the Occasion of his 65th Birthday, ed. Roelof van den Broek and Maarten J. Vermaseren (Leiden: Brill, 1981), 498–584, here 547–48.

29. My references follow Wilhelm Schneemelcher's edition, *New Testament Apocrypha*, trans. Robert McL. Wilson (Louisville: Westminster John Knox, 2003), 2:37–38.

30. See Pearson, "Earliest Christianity in Egypt," 104.

31. According to Otto Stählin and Ursula Treu, vol. 4, pt. 1 of *Clemens Alexandrinus, Register*, 2nd ed., GCS 17 (Berlin: Akademie-Verlag, 1980), the largest source from among Christian Scriptures is the Pauline letters with 1273 references in comparison with the number of references to Plato (618), allusions to Homer (243) and to Philo of Alexandria (279). Annewies van den Hoek, "Techniques of Quotation in Clement of Alexandria: A View of Ancient Literary Working Methods," *VC* 50 (1996): 223–43, here 230.

32. *Strom.* 2.45.5 (with the full title); see also *Strom.* 5.96.3 (no title); *Paed.* 1.25.2 (no title) and *Strom.* 6.48.2.

is preserved in six quotations.[33] Other examples include his references to the *Kerygma Petri*—eight times,[34] and the *Apocalypse of Peter*—four times.[35] Even these few selected examples show that the urban context of Clement's work, with accessible resources either newly arrived or newly produced in the city, offered Clement a unique opportunity to include those colorful threads into the tapestry of his theology. The first generations of Alexandrian Christians brought to the *polis* or composed in the city a large quantity of literature that reflected their imaginative theologies, inquisitive minds, and more or less sophisticated taste for stories. The intellectual atmosphere of this cosmopolitan, lively, but also competitive megapolis encouraged a quest for literary novelty combined with Christian motifs about salvation.

3. The Catechetical School and Its Significance

In relation to Clement's (and earlier Pantaenus's) own use of literary sources, including Christian gospels and other documents, one important issue is still a subject of controversy. Again, we have to turn to Eusebius of Caesarea, but this time to introduce the dilemma. The ancient historian mentions "the school of sacred learning"[36] in Alexandria, suggesting its official ecclesiastical status. That sort of "school" would use Christian and other literature; the teaching, either in its early stage for the converts or in a later phase, would be focused on a written and maybe still oral Christian legacy. However, Eusebius's note does not provide us with any details of the education or literature used by the school. Eusebius's puzzling note leaves room for discussion. The enigma of the so-called catechetical "school" (*didaskaleion*) in Alexandria polarised modern scholars.[37] The majority of historians support one of two views. One group, with Gustave Bardy as its exponent, believe that *didaska-*

33. *Strom.* 3.45.3; 3.63.1–2; 3.64.1; 3.66.1–2; 3.92.2; *Exc.* 67.

34. *Strom.* 1.182.3; 6.39.1–41.5; 6.43.3; 6.48.1–2; 6.48.6; 6.58.1; 6.128.1–3, *Ecl.* 58.

35. *Ecl.* 41.1–2; 48.1–49.1.

36. *Hist. eccl.* 5.10.1.

37. Alain Le Boulluec, "L''école' d'Alexandrie. De quelques aventures d'un concept historiographique," in *Alexandria: Hellénisme, judaïsme et christianisme à Alexandrie. Mélanges offerts à Claude Mondésert*, SJ (Paris: Cerf , 1987), 403–17; Alain Le Boulluec, "Aux origines, encore, de l''école' d'Alexandrie," *Adamantius* 5 (1999): 7–36; Eric Osborn, *Clement of Alexandria* (Oxford: Oxford University Press, 2005), 19–24; Birger A. Pearson, "'The Catechetical School' in Alexandria," in *Origins to Constantine*, vol. 1 of *The Cambridge History of Christianity*, ed. Margaret M. Mitchell and Frances M. Young (Cambridge: Cambridge University Press, 2006), 340–42.

leion denoted a method of biblical interpretation, which was taught in a small inner Christian cell and was independent of the ecclesiastical authorities. In that view *didaskaleion* was not recognized by Christian leaders in Alexandria until the time of Demetrius, the bishop of Alexandria (189–231 CE). In Bardy's view, Pantaenus and Clement were two independent teachers offering an initial and then more advanced teaching to their disciples interested in theology and Christian philosophy.[38]

The second group of scholars, represented in this review by André Méhat, reexamined Eusebius's report. They acknowledge that the Christian school played a didactic role within the wider Alexandrian Church, including Pantaenus's contribution and then Clement of Alexandria's.[39] It was not a "private" school, but rather an established "chain" (or "channel") of education, which started with catechumens and led to advanced knowledge about the Christian faith.

Among other scholars there is an opinion that Clement, and possibly Pantaenus earlier, adapted in his teaching a model known to him and used in an Alexandrian Jewish milieu.[40] Within the Jewish community the central place belonged to the institution of the synagogue, where among other activities, such as worship or distributing charity, the same building served as a library and the place for study of the Torah.[41] In light of Clement's teaching about the connection, if not the similarity, between the "school of the divine Logos" and the "church," I endorse this hypothesis: Clement's school was also a community of worship. In the middle of the second century various schools of thought, including those that combined the quest for wisdom and the search for the salvation of the soul, flourished in Alexandria. In Alexandria the Hermetists produced an astonishing amalgam of Greek and Egyptian wisdom,[42] and the Valentinian branch of Christianity

38. Gustave Bardy, *La vie spirituelle d'après les Pères des trois premières siècles* (Paris: Bloud & Guy, 1935), 80; Gustave Bardy, "Aux Origines de l'École d'Alexandrie," *RSR* 27 (1937): 69–90.

39. André Méhat, *Études sur les "Stromates" de Clément d'Alexandrie*, Patristica Sorbonensia 7 (Paris: Le Seuil: 1966), 63; André Tuilier, "Les évangélistes et les docteurs de la primitive église et les origines de l'Ecole (didaskaleion) d'Alexandrie," StPatr 17 (1982): 738–49.

40. Roelof van den Broek, "Juden and Christen in Alexandrien im 2 und 3 Jahrhundert," in *Juden und Christen in der Antike*, ed. Johannes van Oort (Kampen: Kok, 1990), 181–96.

41. Lee I. Levine, *The Ancient Synagogue: The First Thousand Years* (New Haven: Yale University Press, 2000), 374–80.

42. Garth Fowden, *The Egyptian Hermes: A Historical Approach to the Later Pagan Mind* (Princeton: Princeton University Press, 1993), 161–65.

PIOTR ASHWIN-SIEJKOWSKI

was represented by Theodotus, a prominent exegete and theologian.[43] The shared teaching methods among those milieus focused on commentary on an authoritative text, followed by questions, answers, and discussion. The *didaskaleion*, mentioned by the church historian Eusebius of Caesarea, was one of many Christian schools in Alexandria and would share that didactic pattern with the crucial relationship between the teacher/catechists, the disciple/catechumen, and the holy text. Annewies van den Hoek highlights the role of Philo's legacy in Clement's exegetical activity.[44] Many elements of Philonic heritage now served in a Christian context, such as allegorical interpretation of the Holy Scriptures and openness to selective elements of Greco-Roman philosophy. Van den Hoek observes that in Clement's view, as reconstructed from his oeuvre, the opposition between school and church is "non-existent."[45] For Clement there was no separation between the liturgical public (worship) and private (prayer) life and the quest for true knowledge (*gnosis*). On the contrary, he would argue that Christians from the very beginning of their journey in faith should also endorse the study of the Scriptures and helpful traditions of philosophy. In brief, the church performed the role of the school, while the achievement of wisdom in a Christian school was only possible if that school and intellectual activity led to the life of prayer.[46] In that intellectual and spiritual atmosphere some second-century Christians, like Clement of Alexandria, not only preserved the richness of the gospels and other documents, but also contributed to the formation and development of the Christian canon of the Scriptures.[47]

43. Einar Thomassen, *The Spiritual Seed: The Church of the "Valentinians"* (Leiden: Brill, 2006), 28–38.

44. See Annewies van den Hoek, "The 'Catechetical' School of Early Christian Alexandria and Its Philonic Heritage," *HTR* 90 (1997): 59–87.

45. Van den Hoek, "Catechetical School," 71.

46. I have discussed Clement's view in my article "The Notion of 'Heresy' in Stromateis VII and Its Use in Clement of Alexandria's Polemic" in *The Seventh Book of the Stromateis: Proceedings of the Colloquium on Clement of Alexandria* (Olomouc, October 21–23, 2010), ed. Matyas Havrda, Vit Hušek, and Jana Plátová, VCSup 117 (Leiden: Brill, 2012), 277–90, here 286–88.

47. James A. Brooks highlights Clement's use of the notion of κανών: "Clement uses the word κανών twenty-one times [Stählin, *Clemens*, 4:494]. Invariably the word means *a standard or rule by which something is measured or judged*. He speaks of the 'canon of the church' [*Str.* 7.16.105] and an 'ecclesiastical canon' [*Strom.* 7.17.41], by which he means the inner principle of authority which the church possesses in the area of doctrine and conduct. Likewise he speaks of a 'canon of truth' [*Strom.* 7.16.94] and a 'canon of faith' [*Strom.* 4.15.98]. None of these, however, has anything to do with books. That use of the word did not emerge for another century. Although Clement did not use the word, the evidence col-

4. Conclusions

Alexandria, with its intellectual legacy, its urban institutions and privileged geographical location, was the ideal soil for the dissemination of the oral and soon-to-be written traditions about Jesus the Messiah, the Savior of the Greco-Roman *oikoumenē*. The specific Alexandrian location and intellectual tradition attracted a real diversity of Christian teachers, exegetes, and missionaries who passed on or produced a great number of commentaries with imaginative messages. Christians of various theological orientations found in this magnificent city a great opportunity. In Alexandria they promoted their ideas based on specific exegesis of the Scriptures, innovative imagination, and the power of rhetoric. Achilles Tatius's eyes were "beaten" by the splendour of Alexandrian architecture, and the minds of many scholars are still inspired by the polyphony of Alexandrian early Christian theologies.

---

lected in this study shows that he did have a concept of what is now called canonicity and an indefinite and fluid group of books which nevertheless constituted a provisional canon" (James A. Brooks, "Clement of Alexandria as a Witness to the Development of the New Testament Canon," *SC* 9 [1992]: 41–55, here 53–54).

PART II

Early Christian Thinking about Cities

City of God or Home of Traitors and Killers? Jerusalem according to Matthew

ANDERS RUNESSON

1. Introduction: The Standard Story and Its (Ancient) Contenders

Who were the first urban Christians?[1] Well, that depends on how we define "first," "urban," and "Christians"—and each of these terms would require at least monograph-length discussion. Much has, with or without such detailed terminological discussion, been written about this topic, most of it focused on Paul since his letters are a) early, b) written to city dwellers, and c) assumed to connect with later forms of Christ-belief in the Diaspora, beliefs with which modern (non-Jewish) Christians can identify.

But since Paul was neither a Christian[2] nor the first to bring the message

---

1. The title of Wayne A. Meeks's classic study, *The First Urban Christians: The Social World of the Apostle Paul*, 2nd ed. (New Haven: Yale University Press, 2003 [1986]). Much has happened in the study of Mediterranean societies, the role and function of synagogues and associations, and, of course, Paul, since Meeks's book was published. Some studies of interest include Todd D. Still and David G. Horrell, eds., *After the First Urban Christians: The Social-Scientific Study of Pauline Christianity Twenty-Five Years Later* (London: Bloomsbury, 2009); Reinhard von Bendemann and Markus Tiwald, eds., *Das frühe Christentum und die Stadt* (Stuttgart: Kohlhammer, 2012); Philip A. Harland, *Dynamics of Identity in the World of the Early Christians: Associations, Judeans, and Cultural Minorities* (London: T&T Clark, 2009); Anders Runesson, "Placing Paul: Institutional Structures and Theological Strategy in the World of the Early Christ-believers," *SEÅ* 80 (2015): 43–67. For the nature of first-century diaspora synagogues, see Anders Runesson, *The Origins of the Synagogue: A Socio-Historical Study* (Stockholm: Almqvist & Wiksell International, 2001), 401–76.

2. So also Pamela Eisenbaum, *Paul Was Not a Christian: The Original Message of a Misunderstood Apostle* (San Francisco: HarperOne, 2009); Anders Runesson, "The Question

about the Christ to an urban setting, perhaps we need to look elsewhere if we are aiming at understanding how the formation of the nascent movement and its theology was affected by urbanization. The standard story, after all, well-known to those who attended Sunday School, points to Jerusalem as the urban center where it all began immediately following Jesus's death and resurrection. From Jerusalem the message must be proclaimed to all the nations, as Luke's Gospel (24:47) and Acts (1:8) would have it. This focus on Jerusalem as the first urban center for the post-Easter formation of the Jesus movement seems to be supported by other early sources as well.

Paul acknowledges that not only "false believers" (Gal 2:4; ψευδάδελφοι) are found in Jerusalem, but also the "acknowledged leaders" (Gal 2:2), indeed "the acknowledged pillars" of the movement (Gal 2:9; οἱ δοκοῦντες στῦλοι εἶναι). Thus, in this urban hub we find "the apostles" (Gal 1:17), and names mentioned include Cephas,[3] James the brother of Jesus,[4] and John.[5] Indeed, just like the author of Luke-Acts, Paul understands his mission to take as its point of departure Jerusalem and, from there, he claims to have spread the gospel far and wide.[6] Wherever he goes, Paul is aware that "holy ones" are located in Jerusalem, and he takes special care to send money for the poor among this group.[7] For Paul, non-Jews are indebted to "the holy ones" in Jerusalem, since they have received a share in their spiritual

---

of Terminology: The Architecture of Contemporary Discussions on Paul," in *Paul within Judaism: Restoring the First-Century Context to the Apostle*, ed. Mark D. Nanos and Magnus Zetterholm (Minneapolis: Fortress, 2015), 53–77.

3. Gal 1:18, 2:9 (also called Peter at 2:7–8).

4. Gal 1:19, 2:9. For the identification of the James of 2:9 as the brother of Jesus, see Donald Guthrie, *Galatians*, NCB (Grand Rapids: Eerdmans, 1973), 82.

5. Gal 2:9. On the concord between Paul and the "acknowledged leaders," see, e.g., William M. Ramsay, *Historical Commentary on Galatians*, ed. Mark Wilson (1899; repr. Grand Rapids: Kregel, 1997), 53–54. Cf. Guthrie, *Galatians*, 82–83; Mark D. Nanos, *The Irony of Galatians: Paul's Letter in First-Century Context* (Minneapolis: Fortress, 2002), 147–52.

6. Rom 15:19: "From Jerusalem and as far around as Illyricum I have fully proclaimed the good news of Christ." One may note that Paul explains his traveling to faraway places as him aiming at proclaiming the Christ where no one else has (15:20–21). This may, indirectly, indicate why Galilee is ignored. The north, however, does not share Jerusalem's status as construed by "the apostle to the gentiles," despite the fact that Jesus was a Galilean working primarily among Galileans. The aim of the movement, it seems, is to "control" Jerusalem, i.e., the capital and center of the world; to replace the leadership there and transform Judaism (and, from Jerusalem, the rest of the world). See further Volker Rabens's essay in this volume, "Paul's Mission Strategy in the Urban Landscape of the First-Century Roman Empire."

7. Rom 15:25–26, 31; cf. 1 Cor 16:1, 3.

blessings.[8] As in Acts, then, it seems that Paul identifies the spiritual center of the movement to be in Jerusalem. Paul also speaks of ἐκκλησίαι that are "in Christ" in Judea, beyond Jerusalem, indicating the spread of the movement there, but we are not told whether these assemblies existed in villages, towns, or cities.[9] As for Galilee we hear nothing from Paul, and the same is true for all of the other texts included in the New Testament, except the Gospels of Mark, Matthew, and John.[10] From Josephus, we also know that James the brother of Jesus was executed in Jerusalem, implying that at least some of the leaders remained in the city.[11] As Rainer Riesner recently argued, "die Jerusalemer Gemeinde ist offensichtlich in unmittelbarem Zusammenhang mit den Osterereignissen im April des Jahres 30 n. Chr. entstanden."[12]

It cannot get much earlier than that, if we are looking for the first urban followers of Jesus. And we are still located in Jerusalem, far from any ideas about a "mission to the gentiles," or Pauline community formation in Antioch or Asia Minor. Urbanization happens, it seems, well before diasporization, and it originates in an internationally well-known city where Jewish believers in Jesus were surrounded by and operated among a population—including pilgrims from abroad visiting on a regular basis—quite familiar with the "big world" out there through countless influences in most areas of life, from everyday practices and beliefs to art and architecture.[13]

But is such a narrative, most recently also supported by James Charlesworth,[14] representative of the whole story? There are some disturbing details in Luke-Acts that may indicate that the author of these books is consciously hiding alternative stories, which may point to other, coterminous historical developments. To be more specific, there seems to be in

8. Rom 15:27.

9. Gal 1:22; 1 Thess 2:14.

10. Note also the isolated tradition in Acts 9:31, which indicates the assumed existence of Christ-believers in Galilee after the resurrection. Jerusalem, on the other hand, is referred to in Hebrews (12:22) and, significantly, in Revelation (3:12; 21:2, 10), as the center of the future realization of the victory of the God of Israel.

11. Josephus, *Ant.* 20.199–203.

12. "The Jerusalem community evidently arose in the immediate context of the Easter events in April in the year 30"; Rainer Riesner, "Zwischen Tempel und Obergemach: Jerusalem als erster messianische Stadtgemeinde," in *Das frühe Christentum und die Stadt,* ed. Reinhard von Bendemann and Markus Tiwald (Stuttgart: Kohlhammer, 2012), 69–91, here 74.

13. Cf. Acts 2:5, 9–11.

14. James H. Charlesworth, "The Temple and Jesus Followers," in *Jesus and the Temple: Textual and Archaeological Explorations,* ed. James H. Charlesworth (Minneapolis: Fortress, 2014), 183–212.

these two texts a programmatic marginalisation of Galilee in favor of Jerusalem as the center of the post-Easter movement. For example, while Mark,
Matthew, and John speak explicitly about the movement as returning to
Galilee directly after Jesus's death and resurrection, Luke re-writes Mark's
(and Matthew's, if you favor Markan priority without Q) twice (in Matthew
three times) repeated statement that Jesus will meet the disciples in Galilee
after he has been risen from the dead. Mark's "Go, tell his disciples and Peter
that he is going ahead of you to Galilee; there you will see him, just as he
told you" (16:7) is transformed in Luke, into: "Remember how he told you,
while he was still in Galilee . . ." (24:6).[15]

In fact, in Luke-Acts, contrary to Mark, Matthew, and John, the disciples are explicitly ordered to stay in Jerusalem,[16] and from there proclaim the
message of forgiveness through repentance to the entire world.[17] As the narrative in Acts reveals, this divine order to stay in the city is not time-limited,
and the leaders are presented as continuously praising God in the temple.
Indeed, throughout the story we find the key figures in the movement to be
located in Jerusalem: the eleven apostles (plus the replacement for Judas,
thus, contrary to the other gospels, restoring the symbolic significance of the
number twelve), Jesus's mother Mary and some other women, and Jesus's
brothers (Acts 1:13–14).

When all others leave Jerusalem due to persecution, the apostles stay
(Acts 8:1), and we find them there when Paul arrives in Acts 9:26–28. They
never leave, in fact; they again surface as leaders governing the movement
from the same city in Acts 15 and 21. It is also in Jerusalem that we find the
first organizational structuring of the movement, with different tasks as-
signed to different groups of people.[18] Even if disciples like Peter and John

15. Compare the wording of Luke 24:5–7 with that of the same scene in Mark 16:7
and Matt 28:7, 10 (cf. Mark 14:28; Matt 26:32). Note also John 20:17, where the geographical problem is avoided as Jesus tells Mary from Magdala to tell his brothers that
"I am ascending to my Father and your Father, to my God and your God." Still, John's
second ending (21:1–25) unfolds, geographically, in Galilee, assuming that the disciples
did indeed leave Jerusalem after the resurrection. As with Mark and Matthew, there is
no sign in John that they ever returned to Jerusalem, the implications of which shall be
discussed below. Cf. James D. G. Dunn on Luke 24:5–7 (*Beginning from Jerusalem*, vol. 2
of *Christianity in the Making* [Grand Rapids: Eerdmans, 2009], 138–39). Dunn, however,
never really pursues the full consequences of this rather radical difference between Luke
and the other gospels.

16. Luke 24:49; cf. Acts 1:4.

17. Luke 24:47.

18. Acts 6:1–6.

travel elsewhere, they always return to the center.[19] Indeed, when they travel, they do so representing the Jerusalem assembly as the leading group through which the Spirit works (e.g., Acts 8:14–17). The Jerusalem assembly is thus portrayed as both *establishing and controlling* a network of assemblies in Judea, Samaria, and the diaspora.[20] It is not surprising, then, that it is in Jerusalem that key decisions considered binding for all the ἐκκλησίαι are taken.[21] Interestingly for our purposes here, since God's Spirit is said to work through the leaders of the movement, and the movement itself is established in Jerusalem, we find in Luke-Acts a not-so-implicit claim that the Spirit of God is present in Jerusalem; indeed that God is residing in the temple itself and can be worshipped there.[22]

19. Even Paul does this, except in the context of his last journey to Rome where the story ends somewhat abruptly. There is nothing in that ending, though, suggesting that Jerusalem loses its carefully crafted status simply because Paul is preaching in Rome. There is certainly no pattern in Acts along the lines of "from Jerusalem to Rome," as is so often thought, if we by this expression understand a shift of the movement's headquarters to the empire's capital.

20. But not Galilee; see further below.

21. Acts 15:1–35; cf. 21:17–26. One may note that the Spirit works in special ways with the apostles, and is, in some aspects, dependent on the apostles' decisions and presence (Acts 8:17, 9:17, 15:28, 19:6). This reinforces, implicitly, Jerusalem as the center from where the Spirit proceeds: The Spirit acts through the apostles, and the apostles are located in Jerusalem. The "dependence" of the Spirit on the apostles should not be pressed too far, though, since the Spirit is also presented as controlling the apostles' movements (Acts 16:6–7) and initiating unexpected developments (Acts 10:44–48; note, however, that this giving of the Spirit happens during Peter's speech). For recent discussion of the Spirit in the gospels and Acts, see Anthony C. Thiselton, *The Holy Spirit in Biblical Teaching, through the Centuries, and Today* (Grand Rapids: Eerdmans, 2013), 33–69. See also James D. G. Dunn, *Baptism in the Holy Spirit: A Re-Examination of the New Testament Teaching on the Gift of the Spirit in Relation to Pentecostalism Today*, 2nd ed. (London: SCM, 2010), 38–102. None of these authors explore in any detail, however, the implications of the presentation of the Spirit in Acts for the status of Jerusalem in the world of this text.

22. On the temple in Luke-Acts, cf. Steve Walton, "A Tale of Two Perspectives? The Place of the Temple in Acts," in *Heaven on Earth: The Temple in Biblical Theology*, ed. T. Desmond Alexander and Simon Gathercole (Carlisle: Paternoster, 2004), 135–49; Peter Head, "The Temple in Luke's Gospel," in *Heaven on Earth: The Temple in Biblical Theology*, ed. T. Desmond Alexander and Simon Gathercole (Carlisle: Paternoster, 2004), 101–19. See also David R. McCabe, *How to Kill Things with Words: Ananias and Sapphira under the Prophetic Speech-Acts of Divine Judgment (Acts 4.32–5:11)*, LNTS 454 (London: T&T Clark, 2011), 223–24, n. 2 and literature referred to there. One may note that, through this rhetorical strategy, Luke-Acts manages to narratively imply, it seems, that Jesus's royal triumphal entry into Jerusalem was, after all–through his resurrection–successful. Jerusalem had been

In this study, I shall argue that these and similar claims by the author of Luke-Acts, despite finding support in some other early sources, are incompatible with Matthew's Gospel, especially if Matthew is read as a first-century Jewish text. Indeed, Luke's ideological focus on Jerusalem and its temple may even reveal hermeneutical inconsistencies within Luke's Gospel itself. In order to show this, we shall first look at Matthew's portrayal of the Jerusalem temple, being sensitive to the narrative progression of this text. Having thus identified what is arguably the key problem in Matthew's Gospel, indeed perhaps even the reason why Matthew was written at all in the first place, I will suggest that the author proposes two theo-ritual[23] solutions to the crisis with which the movement is faced in the story. We shall end by noting some implications of what has been said about Jerusalem's role in Matthew and Luke, respectively, as this relates to how we understand a) the eschatology of these texts, and b) the historical whereabouts of the earliest Jesus movement.

2. Matthew's Jerusalem

a. The City of the Great King

Jerusalem is described as a holy city in Matt 4:5 and 27:53, and there is no indication that the city loses this status as the narrative progresses. The reason for this sacred status of the city is implied in Matt 5:35, where Jesus states that Jerusalem is "the city of the great king"; thus, in this city the God of Israel dwells. If Jerusalem is understood as holy, it necessarily follows that the temple's status should be even more elevated.[24] It is thus not surprising to see how Matthew assumes and claims the temple's holiness throughout

---

"conquered" in the sense that the Spirit was now ruling from there the movement that was "invading" the empire, aiming, ultimately, at its heart: Rome.

23. By "theo-ritual" I mean to refer to a pattern of practice and thought in which what we term theology and ritual cannot be seen as separate issues, with the implication that they need to be understood and analyzed in conjunction with one another.

24. On the temple in Matthew's Gospel, see Daniel M. Gurtner, "Matthew's Theology of the Temple and the 'Parting of the Ways': Christian Origins and the First Gospel," in *Built upon the Rock: Studies in the Gospel of Matthew*, ed. Daniel M. Gurtner and John Nolland (Grand Rapids: Eerdmans, 2008), 128–53. Gurtner concludes: "the first evangelist has a remarkably consistent and positive portrayal of the temple. No negative word is uttered by either the evangelist or his Jesus about the temple *itself*" (130; emphasis original).

his narrative. The "holy place" in 24:15, whose desecration will indicate the beginning of apocalyptic disaster, surely refers to the temple.[25]

As with the city, the temple's holiness is based on the conviction, found also in the Torah, that it is the dwelling place of God (Matt 23:16–22). For Matthew, the holiness of the space needs to be taken more, not less, seriously than the author accuses the "scribes and Pharisees" of doing. What we see in Matt 23:16–22 is a critique of attitudes and rulings deemed too lenient in relationship to the holy. One may note in this regard the explicit comment in Matt 23:19 that, for Matthew, it is the sanctity of the altar that is said to make the sacrificial gift sacred. The gift belongs, in and of itself and regardless of the intentions of the giver, to the profane sphere (although it has to be pure, of course). It is when the pure sacrificial gift comes in (objective) contact with the holy that its status is transformed and becomes acceptable to the God of Israel, as is also indicated in the Hebrew Bible.[26] As elsewhere in Matthew, the problem is not that "scribes and Pharisees" keep the law, or keep it too strictly; they simply do not keep it rigorously enough. Lawlessness (ἀνομία) is the real problem in this narrative,[27] and this affects the fate of the temple too, as we shall see below.

Since the holy cannot be approached in a state of impurity, and (moral and ritual) purity rules are an important part of the law, it would be natural to expect in the text some signal about correct behavior in relation to the temple—and this is also what we find in Matt 5:23–26. Here the moral purity of a person is emphasized, so that if someone has sinned against another, they need to be reconciled before that person can approach the altar with a gift.[28] As in other forms of Judaism, the holy cannot coexist with the impure in Matthew's world.[29] This theo-ritual conviction, so central to the Jewish

25. Cf. Dan 9:26–27; 11:30–31; 12:10–12; 1 Macc 1:51–57; 2 Macc 6:1–9.

26. Cf. Exod 29:37 (NRSV): "The altar shall be most holy; whatever touches the altar shall become holy." For discussion, see John Nolland, *The Gospel of Matthew: A Commentary on the Greek Text*, NIGTC (Grand Rapids: Eerdmans, 2007), 935–36, who also refers to m. Zeb. 9:1, "the altar makes holy whatsoever is prescribed as its due" (trans. Danby).

27. Matt 5:20; 7:23; 13:41; 23:28; 24:12.

28. On the importance of reconciliation in relation to atonement, cf. m. Yoma 8:8–9.

29. The logic behind the ruling is that all relationships between human beings affect the relationship between humans and God (cf. Matt 6:12, 14–15; 18:21–35). Reconciliation is all the more important since Jesus has just equated anger with murder (Matt 5:21–22); bloodshed, together with sexual sins, idolatry, and deceit, is one of the severe sins that morally defile a person resulting in an impure status unacceptable within the temple precincts. For discussion, see Eyal Regev, "Moral Impurity and the Temple in Early Christianity in Light of Ancient Greek Practice and Qumranic Ideology," *HTR* 97 (2004): 383–411; cf. Paula

ritual system, is the single most important factor, I would argue, for understanding the aims of Jesus in Matthew.

In sum, then, there can be no doubt that, for Matthew, Jerusalem is *the*
city of God, and that no other urban center, either in Israel or in the Diaspora, can match or assume this status. Why, then, is the reader left with the
impression that Matthew's Jesus critiques and abandons both Jerusalem and
the temple, handing them over to destruction?

b. Defiled and Abandoned

It is precisely the holiness attributed to Jerusalem and the temple that triggers the downward spiral in Matthew's Gospel, which ends in complete disaster as the temple is pronounced defiled and, as a consequence, its destruction is predicted.[30] The temple cult is treated as valid in Matthew until the
infamous twenty-third chapter, where Jesus unleashes unprecedented accusations against the Pharisees and the scribes associated with them. Here, we
find a crescendo of charges, which begin somewhat quietly with claims that
Pharisees "make their phylacteries broad and their fringes long" (23:5) and
then deepens radically into accusations that they are guilty of all shedding of
innocent blood in history, including murder committed within the temple itself (23:35). Such shedding of blood in sacred space would inescapably result
in defilement. Consequently, due to the severity of the crimes committed,[31]

Fredriksen, "Did Jesus Oppose the Purity Laws?" *BRev* 11 (1995): 18–25, 42–47. See also
the important study by Jonathan Klawans, *Purity, Sacrifice, and the Temple: Symbolism and
Supersessionism in the Study of Ancient Judaism* (Oxford: Oxford University Press, 2006).

30. The idea of God abandoning Jerusalem and its temple builds on, indeed requires,
that this space is considered holy in the first place; profane space cannot be defiled in the
sense that sacred space can, and defiled sacred space cannot be equated with ordinary,
profane space. Jerusalem, even when defiled, retains special status, as it is called holy both
in the beginning and at the end of the Gospel. (Note also that the city is called holy even
when the devil himself is present in Matt 4:5.) Cf. discussion of the temple as sacred space
in the Dead Sea Scrolls by Alex P. Jassen, "The Dead Sea Scrolls and Violence: Sectarian
Formation and Eschatological Imagination," in *Violence, Scripture, and Textual Practice in
Early Judaism and Christianity*, ed. Raanan S. Boustan, Alex P. Jassen, and Calvin J. Roetzel
(Leiden: Brill, 2010), 27.

31. Some forms of less severe defilement may lead only to the necessity of purifying the
temple, as for example when in 164 BCE Judas Maccabeus purified the temple after the ritual
atrocities committed there under Seleucid rule. Not all defilement, thus, will necessarily
result in the destruction of the temple. On the issue of innocent blood in relation to the
destruction of the temple, see David M. Moffitt, "Righteous Bloodshed, Matthew's Passion

these accusations lead to the pronouncement that the temple has now been abandoned (23:38),[32] and that it must later be destroyed (24:1–2).

It is important to note that in Matthew the predicted fall of the temple is, contrary to later Christian interpretations, not related to the execution of Jesus, but to the Pharisees and their breaking of the Jewish law, as claimed by Matthew 23. The execution of Jesus is thus not the sin to which God responds with the destruction of Jerusalem, but the solution to the problem caused by the Pharisees. This, in my opinion, is the hermeneutical hub around which the entire narrative revolves. The logic goes something like this: the Mosaic law, which is, as we noted above, strongly emphasized in Matthew,[33] contains within it the means of atonement (the temple cult), and all of it is embraced by a covenant between God and Israel. If the temple, the space where heaven meets earth, and thus the place where atonement can be achieved, is destroyed, the covenant breaks down, since the law cannot make its doers righteous/acceptable to God without the means of atonement; "perfection"[34] in law requires atonement, since to be righteous means to follow the law *and* atone for trespasses.

So, here we stand at chapter 23 and the beginning of chapter 24, with a

---

Narrative, and the Temple's Destruction: Lamentations as a Matthean Intertext," *JBL* 125 (2006): 299–320; Catherine Sider Hamilton, "'His Blood Be upon Us': Innocent Blood and the Death of Jesus in Matthew," *CBQ* 70 (2008): 82–100.

32. In prophetic and rabbinic literature too, this type of serious sin (resulting in [moral] impurity) will result in God abandoning the temple; the same theo-ritual logic is applied to the fall of both the first and the second temple in these corpora of texts. Cf. Josephus, who shares the same view: the temple cannot be destroyed as long as God resides in it *J.W.* 6.124–28, 300 (cf. 300–309). See also *Ant.* 20.165–67; *J.W.* 2.254–57; cf. discussion in Doron Mendels, *The Rise and Fall of Jewish Nationalism* (Grand Rapids: Eerdmans, 1997), 301–2. Guilt for the destruction of the temple is always sought—in the Hebrew Bible, Josephus, as well as in rabbinic literature and the New Testament gospels—within the Jewish people, since if someone else, such as the Romans, would be accused, their god(s), by implication, would have to be judged to be stronger than the God of Israel. By blaming the Jewish leadership (the gospels), or Jewish "bandits" (Josephus), the Romans are transformed into a tool in the hands of the God of Israel as he punishes his people. This perspective on the temple strengthens the view that the gospels were written by Jews from an inner-Jewish perspective, even if they were meant to be read also by a non-Jewish audience (cf. Matt 28:18–20).

33. See, e.g., the paradigmatic statement in Matt 5:17–19, but note also how ἀνομία is consistently pointed to as the problem in the story generally (7:23, 13:41, 23:28, 24:12). For discussion, see Anders Runesson, *Divine Wrath and Salvation in Matthew: The Narrative World of the First Gospel* (Minneapolis: Fortress, 2016).

34. Cf. Matt 5:48, which is most likely meant to interpret Lev 19:2, so that "perfection" in Matthew implies holiness.

defiled temple abandoned by God, about to be destroyed together with the city.[35] What to do? How to save the people? Can the divine still be accessed without sacred space? Hardly. Can atonement be achieved without sacrifice? Unthinkable. Can God's people endure the final judgment without its covenant with God? Unfeasible. In other words: can the Jewish people survive without Jerusalem? Matthew's Gospel aims to answer this question in the affirmative, supplying the necessary theo-ritual tools to make it possible.

3. Restoring Judaism beyond the Temple

a. Covenant, Law, and Atonement

The aims of Matthew's Messiah are established already in the first chapter: to save his people from their sins (1:21). For Matthew, since the (Mosaic) law is still valid no matter what, this requires the restoration of the Mosaic covenant within which the law can be upheld the way it was meant to be; divine judgment is—and will be—based on obedience.[36] This, in turn, requires that people have access to valid means of atonement.

In Matthew's world Jesus takes care of all of this, beginning with the correct teaching of the law.[37] Then, when all is said and done (cf. 22:46), he transforms his soon-to-happen execution into a covenant-restoring sacrifice.[38] Intriguingly, this sacrifice simultaneously achieves atonement ("for the forgiveness of sins") and restores the covenant (Jesus's blood is the "blood of the covenant").[39] While this ritual is designed and devised in a room in Jerusalem, the actual sacrifice, i.e., Jesus's death, takes place outside the city gates.[40] This is, of course, narratively (and historically) necessary, but the

---

35. As implied in Matt 22:7.

36. This is stated and restated over and over again in Matthew, in various ways. See, e.g., 5:17–20, 7:21–27, 13:40–43, 22:11–14, 23:23–36, 25:14–30. (Matt 25:31–46 is a special case, aimed at non-Jews and non-Christ-believers; still, however, the criteria of judgment are based on doing what the God of Israel requires.) For discussion, see most recently Nathan Eubank, *Wages of Cross-Bearing and Debt of Sin: The Economy of Heaven in Matthew's Gospel*, BZNW 196 (Berlin: de Gruyter, 2013).

37. See especially Matthew 5–7, but halakhic decisions regarding specific questions are given in several other places in the Gospel (e.g., 12:1–8; 19:1–9; 23:16–23).

38. Matt 26:26–28. For discussion of how this is done, and how this ritual relates to the establishment of the Mosaic covenant in Sinai, see Runesson, *Divine Wrath*.

39. Matt 26:28.

40. Matt 27:32–33; cf. Matt 21:39. Note also how Heb 13:12–14 makes a theological point

procedure nevertheless aligns with a larger theme in Matthew, namely, that the temple has been abandoned by God and thus no longer provides a space where humans can access God. Strictly speaking, then, while Jerusalem still occupies a special place in Matthew's worldview,[41] it is no longer the city where God dwells.[42] Therefore, as in the case with the sectarian writings from Qumran,[43] *but contrary to the narrative of Luke-Acts*, the faithful should leave the city. When Matthew has the disciples leaving Jerusalem after Jesus's death this procedure is thus based on more than the simple idea that they should meet "at home"; it is a consequence of a theo-ritual motif that is deeply embedded in the structure of the Gospel.

Now, once sacred space has been disrupted Matthew needs to find a new way of establishing a connection point between heaven and earth, a way to restore God's presence among his people. For Matthew, the resurrection of the sacrificed Messiah provides the needed solution.

b. Rendering Sacred Space Portable

As the above has made clear, believers in Jesus cannot, for ritual and theological reasons, remain in Jerusalem, since God has abandoned the city and destruction looms. To this, we may add that the apocalyptic section in Matthew explicitly tells the disciples to leave Judea when the final suffering begins.[44] Further, just before Jesus is arrested, he tells his followers that after he has risen from the dead, he will meet them in Galilee (26:32). Then, after the resurrection, an angel tells Mary from Magdala and "the other Mary" outside the empty tomb that Jesus has been raised from the dead and is now going ahead of them to Galilee, and that they will see him there (28:7). As if this was not clear enough (Mark certainly thought it would be[45]), Matthew has

---

of the fact that Jesus dies outside the city gates and connects this to the current life of the communities for which the text is meant.

41. Like in the case of Revelation, Jerusalem, in its restored form, is envisioned as the center of the kingdom; it is, after all, "the city of the great king" (Matt 5:35; cf. 24:15). No other city can take this place in Matthean eschatological thought.

42. Cf. how God leaves the temple and Jerusalem before the destruction of the first temple in Ezekiel 10–11. See also Raymond E. Brown, *The Death of the Messiah: From Gethsemane to the Grave. A Commentary on the Passion Narratives in the Four Gospels*, ABRL (New York: Doubleday, 1994), 2:1101–2.

43. 1QS, 4QMMT, and the Pesharim.

44. Matt 24:15–18.

45. Mark 16:7.

Jesus himself repeat the command that the disciples leave Jerusalem and go to Galilee in order to meet him there (28:10). Consistent with this command Matthew recounts—adding to Mark and, again, contrary to Luke—that the eleven did indeed leave for Galilee and met Jesus on a previously agreed-upon mountain[46] where they prostrated (προσκυνέω) before him as one would before an image of the divine or a ruler.

From there, from Galilee—*not* from Jerusalem, as Luke would have it—these disciples are then sent out among the (non-Jewish) nations to make disciples of them all, inviting them into Jesus-centered Judaism and teaching them the (Mosaic) law.[47] For Matthew, then, the Jesus-group's postresurrection headquarters is by theological necessity located in Galilee, not in Jerusalem.[48] It would be theo-ritually impossible for Matthew to suggest or claim that followers of Jesus would return to Jerusalem and worship God in a temple that had been defiled and abandoned by God, waiting for its imminent destruction. It is simply not possible to harmonize Matthew's position with Luke's claims in this regard.[49]

The question is now: in the absence of the temple, how did Matthew construe access to the divine? How does this text conceptualize the sacred space needed to encounter the God of Israel in the period between the resurrection and the final judgment? In Matthew's world the problem of an access point to the divine is solved through reference to the community of Jesus followers. Matthew alone not only recounts the establishment of an ἐκκλησία but also outlines, albeit very briefly, the fundamental parts of its

---

46. R. T. France, *The Gospel of Matthew*, NICNT (Grand Rapids: Eerdmans, 2007), 1106, argues that εἰς τὸ ὄρος rather should be translated "into the hills."

47. Matt 28:16–20. On Matthew's mission as law-observant, see, e.g., David C. Sim, *The Gospel of Matthew and Christian Judaism*, SNTW (Edinburgh: T&T Clark, 1998); John Painter, "Matthew and John," in *Matthew and His Christian Contemporaries,* ed. David C. Sim and Boris Repschinski, LNTS 333 (London: T&T Clark, 2008), 66–86.

48. The movement away from Jerusalem is further supported by the fact that the Matthean Jesus speaks of sending, in the future, "prophets, sages, and scribes" to Jerusalem and Judea, where they will be killed, crucified, flogged, and pursued from town to town by (Jerusalem-based) Pharisees and the scribes associated with them. Indeed, as R. T. France has argued, Matthew, for whom the distinction between Galilee and Jerusalem is a matter of importance, displays a decisively anti-Jerusalem/Judean agenda. This agenda surfaces in the claim in Matt 28:11–15 that the false rumor about the disciples stealing Jesus's body is still, in the author's own day, widespread among *Judeans*; France, *Matthew*, 1106. As France also notes, Ἰουδαῖοι should not be translated "Jews" here since it refers specifically to people living in Judea.

49. Cf. Luke 24:53; Acts 2:42.

penal code.[50] Interestingly, the key exclusion mechanism operating in this group is based on the absolute requirement that members ask for and extend forgiveness to one another (18:15–35). What do such rules imply when understood in relation to notions of the sacred?

This type of forgiveness-oriented behavior creates, as previously noted in relation to the temple in 5:23–24, the necessary (moral) purity,[51] which will allow an individual to approach the divine. The divine presence in this case is represented by the risen Messiah himself, who appears among members in a way analogous to the Shekinah, the presence of the divine glory (Matt 18:20).[52] The reason for this absolute insistence on moral purity is, then, that it enables the presence of the divine in the midst of the assembly of the people. The ἐκκλησία is conceptualized as sacred "space," and becomes detached from geographical locations in a manner resembling the situation during the desert wandering before the First Temple period. God is, so to speak, "tenting" among his people.[53]

Such a theo-ritual conceptualization of divine presence on earth in (sacred community) spaces that are portable prepares well, as it happens, for the expansion of the movement beyond the land of Israel and into the dias-

50. Matt 16:18–19, 18:15–18.

51. On moral purity and impurity, cf. Matt 15:18–19.

52. One may note in relation to this motif that Jesus never leaves the world in Matthew, contrary to Luke-Acts and John, and there is no paraclete, as in John (but note Matt 10:20). I am grateful to Rebecca Runesson for discussion of this point and its implications. Note that Jesus's name, Immanuel (Matt 1:23), suggests that Jesus will take on the role of the Shekinah after his resurrection. Such a function of the risen Messiah (cf. Matt 28:20) also connects with the wilderness accounts in Exodus in the pre-temple era.

53. Cf. the tabernacle traditions of Exodus 25–35 (note Exod 40:34–38). Consider also that John 1:14 understands Jesus's earthly life in terms of God's "tenting" (σκηνοῦν) among his people. See, too, Rev 7:15 and 21:3, where, on the other hand, the "tent" of God is rather related to the eschatological new Jerusalem. Matthew's world of thought is closer to later rabbinic ideas about the Shekinah as present, after the destruction of the temple, among the people when they assemble for prayer or study of Torah. Cf. how the expression *miqdash me'at* ('little sanctuary') in Ezek 11:16 is interpreted in rabbinic literature, esp. the reference to synagogues in b. Meg. 29a: "Yet have I been to them as a little sanctuary. R. Isaac said: This refers to the synagogue and houses of learning in Babylon. R. Eleazar says: This refers to the house of our teacher in Babylon. Raba gave the following exposition: What is the meaning of the verse, Lord, thou hast been our dwelling [*ma'on*] place? This refers to synagogues and houses of learning. Abaye said: Formerly I used to study at home and pray in the synagogue, but when I noticed the words of David, O Lord, I love the habitation [*me'on*] of thy house, I began to study also in the synagogue" (*The Babylonian Talmud*, ed. I. Epstein, 17 vols. [London: Soncino, 1938]).

pora.[54] It is thus not surprising to see the same motif of community as sacred space elaborated on in similar ways in other early Jewish documents, including Paul's letters.[55] Indeed, as we know from inscriptions and papyri, many Jews in the diaspora regarded their synagogues as sacred space, although they continued to revere the Jerusalem temple as the abode of the God of Israel;[56] Philo, too, refers to the Essene συναγωγή as holy.[57] Matthew's solution to the loss of the Jerusalem temple and the establishment of the Messiah's ἐκκλησία as its (temporary) substitute,[58] may thus have made more sense to ancient Jews than is often assumed today. It is, in any case, certainly not a "Christian" idea, even if Christians later took Matthew to mean that the ἐκκλησία—often erroneously translated into English as "church"—was a non-Jewish institution that replaced the Jews as the people of God.

In sum, Matthew's position on the defiled status of the temple leads him to a theology of sacred space which is, contrary to the narrative in Luke-Acts, detached from Jerusalem. Matthew cannot, therefore, portray the leaders of the movement as located in Jerusalem or as worshipping in the temple, and he would certainly protest against the idea that the Spirit was

54. One should note, though, that such territorial expansion is not a necessary outcome of this type of notion of sacred space as indicated by the ideology of the Qumran sectarians, who also regarded their community as sacred. See discussion in Jassen, "The Dead Sea Scrolls and Violence," 30–31.

55. Cf. how Paul speaks of the communities he writes to as temple/sacred space, and how this requires them to live pure lives. For discussion, see Cecilia Wassen, "Do You Have to Be Pure in a Metaphorical Temple? Sanctuary Metaphors and Construction of Sacred Space in the Dead Sea Scrolls and Paul's Letters," in *Purity, Holiness, and Identity in Judaism and Christianity*, ed. Carl S. Ehrlich, Anders Runesson, and Eileen Schuller, WUNT 305 (Tübingen: Mohr Siebeck, 2013), 55–86. Cf. Annette Weissenrieder, "Do You Not Know That You Are God's Temple? Towards a New Perspective on Paul's Temple Image in 1 Corinthians 3:16," in *Contested Spaces: Houses and Temples in Roman Antiquity and the New Testament*, ed. David L. Balch and Annette Weissenrieder, WUNT 285 (Tübingen: Mohr Siebeck, 2012), 377–411. See also Runesson, "Placing Paul."

56. On this aspect of diaspora synagogues, see Anders Runesson, *Origins*, ch. 5; Anders Runesson, "Water and Worship: Ostia and the Ritual Bath in the Diaspora Synagogue," in *The Synagogue of Ancient Ostia and the Jews of Rome: Interdisciplinary Studies*, ed. Birger Olsson, Dieter Mitternacht, and Olof Brandt, Acta Instituti Romani Regni Sueciae 57 (Stockholm: Paul Åström, 2001), 115–29; Donald D. Binder, *Into the Temple Courts: The Place of the Synagogues in the Second-Temple Period*, SBLDS 169 (Atlanta, GA: SBL, 1999). For primary sources, consult the index in Anders Runesson, Donald D. Binder, and Birger Olsson, *The Ancient Synagogue from Its Origins to 200 CE: A Source Book*, AJEC 72 (Leiden: Brill, 2008).

57. Philo, *Prob.* 81.

58. Until the full realization of the kingdom of heaven.

channeled through Jerusalem leaders only, so that their decisions would have to be universally followed. What are we to make of such a clear case of irreconcilable differences in the deep structures of the theo-ritual worldviews of two groups within the same movement?[59]

4. Conclusion: From Galilee to the Ends of the Earth?

Four preliminary conclusions seem to follow from the above observations on Matthew in light of Luke-Acts with regard to the place of Jerusalem in these narrative worlds. First, while history seems to support Luke-Acts with regard to the post-Easter presence of believers in Jesus in Jerusalem, this creates a theo-ritual inconsistency in Luke itself, since Luke, too, mentions the abandonment of Jerusalem (Luke 13:34–35) as well as the apocalyptic request by Jesus that his disciples should leave the city when suffering begins (Luke 21:20–21). If we, on the other hand, take the story of Luke-Acts at face value, we have to conclude, based on the actual presence of the disciples—including the leaders—in Jerusalem, that Luke does not believe the narrative's current moment to be related to the beginning of the end.

Second, Matthew's story would hardly be possible to accept for Jesus-followers who were still living in Jerusalem and who believed that the Spirit was leading the movement from the temple city. The deep structure of the narrative carries within it halakhic and socio-ritual implications, and, as such, most likely indicates the existence of communities outside Jerusalem and beyond the authority range of the Jerusalem leaders. Such considerations should destabilize our confidence in Lukan claims to the contrary, and allow for the possibility of a different faction of the movement based in Galilee and engaged in a parallel mission.[60] After all, the earliest archaeolog-

59. While space will not allow consideration of Mark and John, it is of some interest to briefly note here that both of these Gospels support the Matthean version of the earliest history of the movement and its location, against Luke. For John, cf. 4:21–23, 21:1–25.

60. On Jesus believers in Galilee, see, e.g, Ekkehard W. Stegemann and Wolfgang Stegemann, *The Jesus Movement: A Social History of Its First Century* (Minneapolis: Fortress, 1999), 187–247. There has been much debate on this issue, however, and several scholars have dismissed the idea of Christ-groups in the Galilee as pure fantasy. See, e.g., Leonard Goppelt, *Apostolic and Post-Apostolic Times* (London: Black, 1970), 22; Martin Hengel and Anna Maria Schwemer, *Paul between Damascus and Antioch* (London: SCM, 1997), 30–31; both cited by Dunn, *Beginning from Jerusalem*, 136 n. 8. While some scholars have suggested that Q was the product of a community in the Galilee, I would suggest that Matthew's Gospel

ical evidence of Christ-groups in the land Matthew calls Israel comes from Galilee, not Jerusalem.[61]

Third, contrary to Luke, Matthew's story seems to merge the death and resurrection of Jesus with the beginning of the apocalyptic end time. This is hinted at by the fact that the disciples indeed leave Jerusalem after the resurrection, just as they were told to do in Matthew 24.

Fourth, while some scholars, such as Charlesworth, seem to believe that a perspective on Jerusalem and the temple such as that presented here for Matthew would be somewhat un-Jewish, and therefore something "negative," in my view Matthew's ritual and theological hermeneutics are consistently in line with what we see in other variants of Judaism, both predating and postdating the Gospel. Critiquing the temple and Jerusalem based on issues of defilement seems to me, indeed, to be a Jewish thing to do,[62] while ignoring the consequences of defilement, as Luke suggests, certainly does not. It may be, then, that Luke is simply reporting a different understanding of the ritual status of the temple, perhaps one that goes back to the earliest period since we know that, historically, at least some of the prominent Jewish followers of Jesus in fact stayed on in Jerusalem after Jesus's death. If this is the case, then we have in the first century two main interpretive trajectories within the Jesus movement, one of which understands the temple as defiled and Jerusalem as off limits until the kingdom has been established, and the other rejecting such views, considering the temple to be the continuously undefiled meeting place for heaven and earth where worship could still take place. Such disagreements, which are intertwined with different judgments with regard to halakhic issues, are not minor, but reveal signif-

---

in itself speaks in favor of such a location for those who produced the text; Q is, in my view, an unnecessary hypothesis in this regard.

61. The earliest archaeological remains of Christ-believers are found in Galilee, not in Jerusalem. The earliest phases of insula 1 in Capernaum indicate a late-first- or second-century place of gathering for what, according to the excavators, were likely Christ-believing Jews. See discussion in Anders Runesson, "Architecture, Conflict, and Identity Formation: Jews and Christians in Capernaum from the 1st to the 6th Century," in *Religion, Ethnicity, and Identity in Ancient Galilee: A Region in Transition,* ed. Jürgen Zangenberg, Harold W. Attridge, and Dale Martin, WUNT 210 (Tübingen: Mohr Siebeck, 2007), 231–57. On the early-third-century Christian prayer hall at Megiddo, built and used by non-Jews, see Yotam Tepper and Leah Di Segni, *A Christian Prayer Hall of the Third Century CE at Kefar `Othnay (Legio): Excavations at the Megiddo Prison 2005* (Jerusalem: Israel Antiquities Authority, 2006). Apart from these early remains, we have to look to Dura Europos and its "house church" for other pre-Constantinian archaeological remains related to Christ-believers.

62. Cf., e.g., Jer 7:1–34, and nn. 30–33 above.

icant disruption within the Jesus movement, developments that deserve careful further study.[63]

In the end, Matthew shows that apocalyptic expectations for some groups within the Jesus movement could lead to de-urbanization with regard to one specific city, the holy city of God, as this city, contrary to other urban centers, could be defiled by traitors and killers with disastrous consequences for the people as a whole. This process in turn resulted in a re-urbanization elsewhere in cities that could never attain, from a Jewish point of view, Jerusalem's status. It is in such cities we find, much later, "the first urban Christians."[64]

63. It seems, e.g., that the division between these approaches to Jerusalem and the temple coincides with differences in approach to non-Jews and their keeping or not of the Mosaic law, with Matthew and the Pharisaic "enemies" of Acts 15:5 on the one side, and the author of Luke-Acts and Paul on the other.

64. I am grateful to the conference participants as well as Rebecca Runesson for clarifying discussion of several issues dealt with in this study. Thanks are also due to Anna Runesson for discussion of Mark's relationship to Matthew on the topic of Galilee and Jerusalem and for bibliographic assistance.

Heavenly Citizenship and Earthly Authorities

Philippians 1:27 and 3:20 in Dialogue with Acts 16:11–40

STEVE WALTON

1. Christians and "City" Language

The variety of terms used by the early Christians to describe themselves as a community is intriguing. Paul Trebilco has provided a fine study of such language in his book *Self-Designations and Group Identity in the New Testament*[1] and, partly inspired by Trebilco's work, I myself have studied such language within the book of Acts in a recent article.[2] Trebilco and I agree that a primary source for the terms used is the Jewish Scriptures, especially in Greek, and that drawing from that well signals that the earliest Christians understood themselves as a restored and renewed Israel, and an "Israel *re-interpreted and re-understood* through the lens of Jesus as Messiah."[3]

Careful readers will notice that I write that the Jewish Scriptures are *a* primary source, not *the only* primary source for this language. George van Kooten provides an interesting response to Trebilco's work, arguing that ἐκκλησία τοῦ θεοῦ "assembly *of God*" as a self-designation for believing communities is derived from Greco-Roman political use in cities, rather than from Judaism.[4] Specifically, he claims that Paul used this collocation

---

1. Paul R. Trebilco, *Self-Designations and Group Identity in the New Testament* (Cambridge: Cambridge University Press, 2012); see also Paul R. Trebilco, "The Significance of the Distribution of Self-designations in Acts," *NovT* 54 (2012): 30–49.

2. Steve Walton, "Calling the Church Names: Learning about Christian Identity from Acts," *PRSt* 41 (2014): 223–41.

3. Walton, "Calling," 240–41 (emphasis original); Trebilco, *Self-Designations*, 307–11.

4. George H. van Kooten, "Ἐκκλησία τοῦ θεοῦ: The 'Church of God' and the Civic

to denote a believing community by contrast with the civic assembly of a Greek city.[5] Van Kooten's argument is cumulative, identifying five common features of the life of both forms of ἐκκλησία:[6] (i) both were places of instruction; (ii) both were places of factions and divisions; (iii) both valued rational discussion, and Paul opposes the presence of "mania" in the Corinthian assemblies (note 1 Cor 14:23); (iv) both had meetings that were in principle open to the public (principally citizens); and (v) both sought to prevent women present from speaking (indeed, the typical citizenry was male). I have argued elsewhere that this is not a strong list of parallels.[7] Nevertheless, it is highly likely that the use of ἐκκλησία by the believers would bring the citizen assembly to mind among Greek city dwellers—Luke himself uses that term for the riotous assembly in Ephesus (Acts 19:39), and it is likely that the regular citizen assembly met in the theater where the riot took place.[8] Thus whatever the origin of the use of ἐκκλησία for the Jesus communities, this echo would be heard and the parallel would be noticed.

Van Kooten's thinking is one root of this paper. He further suggested to me that ἐκκλησία in the NT is used in those writings that are addressed to, or deal with urban contexts that have a civic ἐκκλησία: (i) Paul's letters; (ii) the Revelation of John, addressed to the seven ἐκκλησίαι (1:11) in cities in Western Asia Minor; (iii) Matthew, probably written in Antioch; (iv) James (5:14), again written to (cities in) the Diaspora (1:1); (v) in Hebrews, although only in the LXX quotation in 2:12.[9] This is interesting corroborative evidence for his view. The suggestion van Kooten makes, in other words, is that the earliest Christians used terms from city life in city contexts, and thus self-identified (as we might say) as a "city within a city."[10]

A second root of this paper is Bruce Winter's exploration of Philippians 1:27–2:18,[11] in which he observes that the verb πολιτεύεσθαι (1:27) is now rarely translated "live as a citizen," although that might be expected to be its

---

Assemblies (ἐκκλησίαι) of the Greek Cities in the Roman Empire: A Response to Paul Trebilco and Richard A. Horsley," *NTS* 58 (2012): 522–48.

5. Van Kooten, "Church," 527.

6. Van Kooten, "Church," 539–47; for this summary, see Walton, "Calling," 231.

7. Walton, "Calling," 231.

8. Cf. Wayne A. Meeks, *The First Urban Christians: The Social World of the Apostle Paul* (New Haven/London: Yale University Press, 1983), 108.

9. George van Kooten, email message to author, February 24, 2014.

10. A phrase not used by van Kooten himself.

11. Bruce W. Winter, *Seek the Welfare of the City: Christians as Benefactors and Citizens* (Carlisle: Paternoster / Grand Rapids: Eerdmans, 1994), 81–104.

meaning.[12] Winter goes on to argue that the choice of this verb places the life of the believers "in the context of *politeia*," which we might call the "public square."[13] He observes that Paul's wider discussion in Philippians 1:27–2:18 locates Christian living in the public sphere, and in particular calls on the believing community to act for concord rather than discord—a recognized concern among ancient writers.[14] Paul's use of the terms "strife" (φθόνος), "envy" (ἔρις) in Phil 1:15, and "faction" (ἐριθεία) in Phil 1:17 bespeaks this concern, for if the Christian group(s) of Philippi were characterized in these ways, it would harm the gospel message in the public sphere, that is, among outsiders.[15] Thus, Winter argues, Paul calls the Philippian believers to live in the public sphere in ways that commend the gospel: the dispute between Euodia and Syntyche (Phil 4:2–3) is an example of the damage that discord can do. Such disputes were not uncommon in Roman colonies and could escalate into court cases.[16] Paul wishes to avoid this happening because of the damage it would do to the gospel's reputation; rather, he wants the Philippian believers to live in the public sphere in a non-factional lifestyle marked by concord rather than discord.

In Winter's very helpful essay, he argues that the use of the cognate noun πολίτευμα "citizenship" (3:20) should not affect the translation of πολιτεύεσθαι in 1:27, and this invites further reflection. The point of 3:20, he suggests, is a contrast of attitude and values that Paul wants to see between the false teachers and the believers.[17] That may be so (and we shall consider that below); nevertheless, if the verb connotes lifestyle in the public domain, what might the noun both denote and connote when qualified by "in the heavens" (ἐν οὐρανοῖς [3:20])?

In what follows, then, we shall address three issues concerning Paul's apparent use of "city" terminology in relation to the believing community: (i) What does Paul mean by heavenly citizenship (Phil 3:20)? Why does he use this metaphor and what does it signify about the believing community?; (ii) How should we understand Paul's use of his Roman citizenship in the account of his visit to Philippi in Acts 16:37?; (iii) How do the two citizenships—heavenly and Roman—relate to one another in Paul's thinking and in early Christian self-understanding (Phil 3:20 with 1:27, and with Acts 16:37)?

12. For those holding this view, see Winter, *Seek*, 82 n. 1.
13. Winter, *Seek*, 83–84.
14. E.g., Plutarch and Dio Chrysostom, discussed in Winter, *Seek*, 86–93.
15. Winter, *Seek*, 94–96, cites examples of these terms in Greek writers.
16. Winter, *Seek*, 100–101.
17. Winter, *Seek*, 103 n. 45.

2. "Our Citizenship Is in Heaven"

In order to understand Paul's use of "citizens of heaven" in Philippians 3:20, it will help us to consider both the social context of first-century Philippi, and specifically of Roman citizenship at that time and in that place.

a. First-Century Philippi [18]

It has been commonplace in studies of Philippians to note that the city was "refounded" as a Roman colony for military veterans in the wake of the decisive Battle of Philippi in 42 BCE. Antony and Octavian's forces overcame those of Cassius and Brutus.[19] A further influx of veterans came after the Battle of Actium in 31 BCE, when Octavian defeated Antony, this time veterans from Antony's defeated forces—an astute move by Octavian to win friends and influence veterans.[20] The location of Philippi, close to the territory of hostile Thrace in the first century BCE, meant that having a good number of veterans to hand was a good deterrent and safeguard for that corner of the empire, protecting the province of Macedonia.[21] The conclusion many go on to draw is that the Philippian church was composed primarily of Roman veterans, by assuming that the city's population was primarily Roman citizens and that the membership of the church reflected the population of the city. Those taking this approach then read the letter looking for evidence of veterans among the believers, and make that group the controlling factor in their exegesis.[22]

As Peter Oakes observes, almost every point of this reconstruction should be challenged.[23] Oakes offers a model of the development of Philippi as a Roman colony based on evidence from inscriptions, archaeology, and

---

18. For a valuable overview, see David W. J. Gill, "Macedonia," in *The Book of Acts in Its Graeco-Roman Setting*, ed. David W. J. Gill and Conrad H. Gempf, BAFCS 2 (Carlisle: Paternoster / Grand Rapids: Eerdmans, 1994), 397–417, here 411–13.

19. Gordon D. Fee, *Paul's Letter to the Philippians*, NICNT (Grand Rapids: Eerdmans, 1995), 25.

20. Peter Oakes, *Philippians: From People to Letter*, SNTSMS 110 (Cambridge: Cambridge University Press, 2000), 25 with n. 73.

21. Oakes, *Philippians*, 12.

22. Oakes, *Philippians*, 56.

23. Oakes, *Philippians*, 1–76; cf. the nuanced portrait of Philippi in Cédric Brélaz's essay in this volume.

literary sources. While such material is slim for the period of Paul's visit and the writing of Philippians, there is sufficient earlier material to build a plausible model of the development of the colony. Philippi was a city with fifteen satellite villages in the surrounding countryside,[24] and the area was strongly agricultural.[25] Although veterans settled there would have been given an allocation of land,[26] it is likely that many fell on hard times and had to sell their land.[27] There would also have been Greeks whose land was handed over to Roman veterans (for much land was seized when the Romans defeated Macedonia), and who then needed to rent land or work for a landowner.[28] We lack evidence of a Greek elite in the city; rather, power seems to have been concentrated in the hands of Romans.[29]

Oakes estimates the population in Paul's day to be ten to fifteen thousand.[30] The model Oakes develops gives a composition of the city's population of about forty percent Roman citizens and sixty percent Greeks (and others), so that the city was predominantly Greek with a significant Roman influence.[31] The whole is divided into: three percent elite; twenty percent peasant colonists who "commuted" daily from the city to their farmland outside the city (for there were relatively few rural settlements in the first century CE); thirty-seven percent service groups, who were craftworkers; twenty percent slaves, belonging to various of the above groups; and twenty percent poor, who had income below subsistence level.[32]

24. Oakes, *Philippians*, 32.

25. Oakes, *Philippians*, 20. David Gill reminds me that there were also gold mines in the vicinity (personal correspondence).

26. Peter Garnsey, *Social Status and Legal Privilege in the Roman Empire* (Oxford: Clarendon, 1970), 249 with references in n. 4.

27. For the allocation of land, see Appian, *Bell. civ.* 5.12, quoted in Oakes, *Philippians*, 26–27.

28. Oakes, *Philippians*, 28.

29. Oakes, *Philippians*, 33–34, 39.

30. Oakes, *Philippians*, 44–46. He bases his estimate on the size of the city as about 45 hectares with a population density similar to Pompeii.

31. Interestingly, Gill, "Macedonia," 413 reports that only sixty out of 421 inscriptions from Philippi are in Greek. However, the inscriptions that have been found are clearly a result of the places where digs have been undertaken, and these are predominantly in clearly Roman locations in Philippi (see discussion in Oakes, *Philippians*, 35–40).

32. On the identification of people as "poor" in this way, Oakes rightly critiques Meggitt's view that ninety-nine percent of the population were "poor," including all who lived at or near subsistence level, as unhelpful (Justin Meggitt, *Paul, Poverty and Survival*, SNTW [Edinburgh: T&T Clark, 1998], 50; Oakes, *Philippians*, 48). Oakes further notes that Paul speaks of "remembering the poor" (Gal 2:10), which can hardly mean almost everyone.

Oakes goes on to discuss whether the composition of the group of believers would reflect that of the city, and proposes that the likelihood is of a lower proportion of Romans in the believing community. His argument is that Paul, as the founder of the church, would have been more *spatially* accessible to city dwellers rather than those from outlying villages; that Paul would be more *socially* accessible to non-elite people, and that he normally socialized among craftworkers; and that Romans, especially members of the Roman elite, would find Paul less *"religiously"* accessible because of their loyalty to civic religions.[33] Oakes thus identifies the proportions of different social groups in the church (by contrast with the city at large) as follows: the proportion of elite in the church would be smaller than in the city at large, about one percent; the proportion of commuting colonist farmers would be lower, about fifteen percent; the proportion of service groups would be lower, about twenty-three percent; the proportion of slaves would be lower, about sixteen percent, and the proportion of poor would be higher, about thirty-five percent.[34] His proposal implies that Roman citizens were only thirty-six percent of the church, by contrast with forty percent in the wider city population.[35]

Oakes recognizes that this kind of modeling is not an exact science; nevertheless, his figures have a strong air of plausibility. Their implication is that the standard view, that the large majority of the church, and thus the audience of Philippians, were predominantly Roman citizens is seriously flawed. He goes on to note that the presence of Roman institutions in the letter, such as the praetorium (1:13), the household of Caesar (4:22), our key terms πολιτεύεσθαι (1:27) and πολίτευμα (3:20), and echoes of imperial terms[36] are sufficiently explained as reflecting the Romanness of the city's setting as a colony.[37] Thus Greek believers, and perhaps many non-elite Roman believers, would experience life as dominated by a small Roman elite with the massive machinery of the empire standing behind it. Terms—and, indeed, the official language of the colony, Latin—which echoed or reflected Roman institutions, power, or lifestyle would not be embraced as welcome by such people, but would seem to be an implied threat: thus, to claim that Christ was superior to the empire was startling (as we shall see).

33. Oakes, *Philippians*, 57–59.
34. Oakes, *Philippians*, 60–61.
35. Oakes, *Philippians*, 62.
36. Oakes, *Philippians*, 129–74; cf. n. 61 below.
37. Oakes, *Philippians*, 65–68.

b. Roman Citizenship

Our knowledge of Roman citizenship is considerable, although not without lacunae.[38] We have sufficient data to sketch the main lines of citizenship in the first century CE, and thus to paint in the setting in which the Philippian believers heard the term πολίτευμα. From the fifth century BCE onward, Roman citizenship, inherited by birth, was gradually extended, first to other parts of the Italian peninsula, and then further afield. In the Roman West, whole communities were given citizenship, notably in Gaul and Spain.[39] By contrast, in the Greek East, where Philippi is located, citizenship was generally given to particular individuals, often members of local elites, whom it was valuable to have as Roman allies.[40]

Roman citizenship gave a person identity, responsibility and privileges.[41] Citizens could vote in elections, stand for office (although in practice, normally only elite citizens could afford the financial commitments involved), enjoy legal protection (against, for example, being bound or condemned without trial) including a right of appeal to the emperor (*provocatio*),[42] could contract marriage under Roman law, and were protected by Roman commercial law in buying and selling.[43] Citizens were required to pay taxes and (in earlier periods) give military service,[44] and were subject to Roman law. Roman citizens "owed allegiance to Rome and Rome would protect" them.[45]

38. See, especially, A. N. Sherwin-White, *The Roman Citizenship*, 2nd ed. (Oxford: Clarendon, 1973); A. N. Sherwin-White, "The Roman Citizenship. A Survey of Its Development into a World Franchise," *ANRW* 1.2:23–58.

39. Sherwin-White, *Roman Citizenship*, 309.

40. Sherwin-White, *Roman Citizenship*, 245, 273; Garnsey, *Status*, 266.

41. On what follows, see Sherwin-White, *Roman Citizenship*, 264–65.

42. Although practice seems to have varied in the extent to which local Roman governors allowed this—it is debated whether local governors were compelled to accept such an appeal; see A. H. M. Jones, *Studies in Roman Government and Law* (Oxford: Blackwell, 1960), 56; Garnsey, *Status*, 263–64, 268; Eckhard J. Schnabel, *Acts*, ZECNT 5 (Grand Rapids: Zondervan, 2012), 992 n. 30; *contra* A. N. Sherwin-White, *Roman Society and Roman Law in the New Testament*, Sarum Lectures 1960–1961 (1963; Repr. Grand Rapids: Baker, 1981), 63–64; C. K. Barrett, *A Critical and Exegetical Commentary on the Acts of the Apostles*, 2 vols., ICC (Edinburgh: T&T Clark, 1994, 1998), 2:1131.

43. Francis Lyall, *Slaves, Citizens, Sons: Legal Metaphors in the Epistles* (Grand Rapids: Academie Books, 1984), 61–62.

44. Sherwin-White, *Roman Citizenship*, 234, 266–67.

45. Lyall, *Slaves*, 62. See fuller discussion of the nature and different types of Roman citizenship, and their rights and privileges in William W. Buckland and Peter G. Stein, *A Text-Book of Roman Law from Augustus to Justinian*, 3rd ed. (Cambridge: Cambridge Uni-

As an example of citizens being treated better than non-citizens, "in A.D. 17, when the Senate rounded on astrologers, the citizens among them were exiled, but the foreigners were put to death."[46]

What evidence could a citizen provide of his (and it was generally *his*) status as a Roman citizen?[47] A proconsul called Pompeius Strabo granted citizenship to a unit of Spanish cavalrymen in 89 BCE, and a bronze tablet records the grant and a list of their names. Sherwin-White suggests that each man would receive his own copy.[48] Octavian's veterans in 40 BCE received a copy of the document making them citizens with a list of the privileges thereby given to them. Under Claudius, a small bronze diptych, the *diploma civitas*, named a veteran who had been made a citizen and confirmed his status.[49] Civilians received a copy of the emperor's decree making them citizens. Those born as children of citizens had their birth registered within thirty days, and the father received a wooden diptych recording the registration. Falsification of Roman citizenship carried severe penalties, including execution.[50]

There is some debate over whether dual citizenship, that is holding both Roman citizenship and another citizenship, such as of a city, was allowed.[51] Cicero presents the situation in very clear-cut terms: a person either is or is not a Roman citizen,[52] and that understanding was accepted in earlier scholarship. However by the Principate, there seems to be at least a tacit acceptance of

---

versity Press, 1963), 86–100; Paul J. du Plessis, *Borkowski's Textbook on Roman Law*, 5th ed. (Oxford: Oxford University Press, 2015), 102–11.

46. Garnsey, *Status*, 261; see also 74, 268, describing both Pliny's execution of non-citizen Christians, and his response to Christian citizens: "being citizens of Rome, I directed them to be carried thither" (Pliny the Younger, *Ep.* 10.96 [Radice, LCL]).

47. For what follows, see Jane F. Gardner, "Proofs of Status in the Roman World," *BICS* 33 (1986): 1–14; Sherwin-White, *Roman Citizenship*, 314–16; Brian M. Rapske, *The Book of Acts and Paul in Roman Custody*, BAFCS 3 (Carlisle: Paternoster/Grand Rapids: Eerdmans, 1994), 130–32; Harry W. Tajra, *The Trial of St Paul: A Juridical Exegesis of the Second Half of the Acts of the Apostles*, WUNT/2 35 (Tübingen: Mohr Siebeck, 1989), 83–85; cf. Martin Hengel and Roland Deines, *The Pre-Christian Paul* (London: SCM, 1991), 102–4 (n. 61).

48. *ILS* 8888; Sherwin-White, *Roman Citizenship*, 315; text of the tablet: 294 n. 3.

49. A corpus of nearly two hundred *diplomata militaria* is presented in *CIL* 16 and its *Supplementum*, together with commentary, analyses of the components of this text type, and select photographs; see also Sherwin-White, *Roman Citizenship*, 315.

50. Epictetus, *Diatr.* 2.24.41 ("those who falsely claim Roman citizenship are severely punished"); Suetonius, *Claud.* 25 ("Those who usurped the privileges of Roman citizenship he executed in the Esquiline field").

51. See discussion in Sherwin-White, *Roman Citizenship*, 295–306.

52. Cicero, *Balb.* 28; cf. Cicero, *Leg.* 2.2.5; for discussion see Sherwin-White, *Roman Citizenship*, 154–55.

dual citizenship, although—of course—the Roman citizenship took priority if there was any dispute or tension between the two.[53] Paul is a good example of this: Luke presents him as a citizen of Tarsus as well as of Rome (Acts 21:39).

c. Philippians 3:20–21

Philippians 3:20–21 contrast with vv. 18–19: the table below sets out key phrases in order to see the links. Both vv. 18–19 and vv. 20–21 are unpacking the exhortation in v. 17 to imitate Paul and those like him: vv. 18–19 do this negatively, and vv. 20–21 positively. (English translations below are my own.)

vv. 18–19	vv. 20–21
πολλοὶ γὰρ περιπατοῦσιν . . . τοὺς ἐχθροὺς τοῦ σταυροῦ τοῦ Χριστοῦ "for many walk . . . as enemies of the cross of Christ"	(v 17b) σκοπεῖτε τοὺς οὕτως περιπατοῦντας καθὼς ἔχετε τύπον ἡμᾶς "pay attention to those who walk just as the model you have in us"
ὧν τὸ τέλος ἀπώλεια "whose end is destruction"	ὃς μετασχηματίσει τὸ σῶμα τῆς ταπεινώσεως ἡμῶν "who will transform our humble body"
ὧν ὁ θεὸς ἡ κοιλία "whose God is the belly"	ἐξ οὗ καὶ σωτῆρα ἀπεκδεχόμεθα κύριον Ἰησοῦν Χριστόν "from which we also await a savior, the Lord Jesus Christ"
ὧν . . . καὶ ἡ δόξα ἐν τῇ αἰσχύνῃ αὐτῶν "and whose glory is in their shame"	σύμμορφον τῷ σώματι τῆς δόξης αὐτοῦ "to be like his glorious body"

---

53. Sherwin-White, *Roman Citizenship*, 271–72.

οἱ τὰ ἐπίγεια φρονοῦντες	ἡμῶν γὰρ τὸ πολίτευμα ἐν οὐρανοῖς ὑπάρχει
"who set their minds on earthly things"	"for our citizenship is in heaven"

The point, therefore, of Paul's use of heavenly citizenship language is to re-inforce the contrast with these "enemies" who are earthly-minded. So why does Paul use citizenship language to convey this point?[54]

Πολίτευμα was used in various ways in Hellenistic Greek.[55] Josephus uses it for the Jews of Alexandria, who are a "foreign colony" within the city (*Ant.* 12.2.13 §108).[56] If this is at least part of the sense here, the portrait is of the believing community as exiles and sojourners, a thought familiar from other parts of the New Testament.[57] This is the "city within a city" idea that we noted earlier.

Πολίτευμα can also denote "citizenship," as we have been translating it until now.[58] Given the Roman colonial context in Philippi, and given that Paul does not use either the verbal form (πολιτεύεσθαι) or noun (πολίτευμα) in any other undisputed letter,[59] the use here looks deliber-ate[60] and, as Markus Bockmuehl observes, bespeaks "a depth of pastoral insight that is the fruit of Paul's long-standing familiarity with the Philip-

54. See the full and helpful discussion in Andrew T. Lincoln, *Paradise Now and Not Yet: Studies in the Role of the Heavenly Dimension in Paul's Thought with Special Reference to His Eschatology*, SNTSMS 43 (Cambridge: Cambridge University Press, 1981), 97–101, which draws on the key study of Walter Ruppel, "Politeuma: Bedeutungsgeschichte eines staatsrechtlichen Termus," *Phil* 82 (1927): 273–317, 440–61.

55. See the very helpful survey of usage in Gert Lüderitz, "What Is the Politeuma?," in *Studies in Early Jewish Epigraphy*, ed. Jan Willem van Henten and Pieter Willem van der Horst, AGJU 21 (Leiden: Brill, 1994), 183–225.

56. Cf. Let. Aris. 310; *TDNT* 6:519–20; contrast Lüderitz, *Studies*, here 204–8, who considers that the πολίτευμα in Let. Aris. is the community of Alexandria itself (so also John Reumann, *Philippians*, AYB 33B [New Haven: Yale University Press, 2008], 575–76). Lüderitz (*Studies*, 193–202) discusses other uses which clearly refer to a foreign colony; cf. Emil Schürer et al., *The History of the Jewish People in the Age of Jesus Christ (175 BC–AD 135)*, rev. ed. (Edinburgh: T&T Clark, 1973), 3:88–89, noting key sources for Jewish groups described as πολίτευμα. Each scholar cites other examples of πολίτευμα used for an ethnic group within a host community.

57. Cf. Heb 11, esp. vv 13–14; 1 Pet 1:17, 2:11. For the believers as a "colony of heaven" in Phil 3:20, see Peter-Ben Smit, *Paradigms of Being in Christ: A Study of the Epistle to the Philippians*, LNTS 476 (London: Bloomsbury T&T Clark, 2013), 134.

58. E.g., *SIG* 2.543, lines 6 and 32; see discussion in MM, 525 s.v.

59. πολιτεία is used in the disputed Eph 2:12 for "citizenship" in Israel.

60. With Lincoln, *Paradise*, 100.

pian context."[61] Although we may be tempted to take the parallel use in Philo (*Conf.* 78), which speaks of wise people who come from and return to "the heavenly country in which they live as citizens" (ὁ οὐράνιος χῶρος ἐν ᾧ πολιτεύονται), the rather Platonic view of Philo contrasts with the strongly earthy—and earthly—view of Paul. Paul expects the Lord Jesus Christ to come *from* heaven, by implication *to earth*. When Jesus comes he will transform Paul's body to be like his own, re-expressing the theology of resurrection in 1 Corinthians 15 (especially v. 49 "just as we have borne the likeness of the earthly man, so we shall bear the likeness of the heavenly man") into this setting. Such language is consistent with Pauline eschatology elsewhere, in which the redeemed do not go to heaven, but are present on a transformed earth.[62]

Given that the titles of "savior" and "Lord" were imperial titles, specifically used by Augustus in the Greek East, the comparison with Caesar coming from Rome to visit an outpost of his empire in Philippi is irresistible, and treats Caesar's claims to universal rule as parodies of the reality of the universal rule of Jesus as Lord.[63] Nevertheless, Paul does not turn the knife and say explicitly, "Jesus is Lord, Caesar is not." His dispute with Caesar is not the kind that involves attempting political or military overthrow of the emperor, for Paul is confident that every knee will bow to Jesus at the Last Day (Phil 2:10–11); it is simply that Caesar's rule is relativized by the rule of Jesus.[64]

Greeks in the Philippian church who were not part of the social elite would receive this as truly good news: their present, oppressive situation of being under the empire would not last forever—indeed, they were being assured that Christ already reigned and was already savior, making them citizens of heaven—a far greater honor than Roman citizenship. This meant that they need not fear what people, even Romans, might do to them.

Non-elite Romans, particularly those whose social situation was depressed because they had had to sell land given to them or their parents or grandparents as military veterans, would also receive this as good news, for their situation would not last interminably. Their present heavenly citizen-

61. Markus Bockmuehl, *The Epistle to the Philippians*, BNTC (London: Black, 1997), 233.

62. With N. T. Wright, *Paul and the Faithfulness of God*, COQG 4 (London: SPCK, 2013), 2:1292–93; cf. Lincoln, *Paradise*, 102.

63. For primary sources, see Oakes, *Philippians*, 138–40 (for σωτήρ), 149 (for κύριος), 160–62 (for universal rule).

64. Cf. Wright, *Faithfulness*, 2:1297.

ship was a foretaste of the world to come when injustice would be a past state of affairs (cf. 2 Pet 3:13 "in accordance with his promise we expectantly await new heavens and a new earth in which righteousness makes its home" [my translation]).

If there were elite Romans among the believers in Philippi, they would be encouraged not to fear Caesar and his associates, but to live as Christian people with the future in mind, as heavenly citizens, rather than spending their lives seeking the favor of the great and the good of the empire. They would be more ready to be publicly known as believers, and thus more ready to suffer for their faith.

3. Paul as Roman Citizen

So what of Paul himself as a Roman citizen? Luke presents Paul as "playing the card" of his Roman citizenship in Philippi, of all places (Acts 16:37). Is this picture plausible, both of Paul himself and within Roman law? If it is, how would it fit with the *heavenly* citizenship of which Paul writes in Philippians?

a. Was Paul a Roman Citizen?

Three passages in Acts mention Paul's Roman citizenship (16:37–39, 22:25–29, 25:7–12; cf. 26:32). In each case, Paul exercises his right as a Roman citizen to avoid unjust treatment or (in Philippi) to call the authorities to account following unjust treatment. A small number of scholars have cast doubt on this portrait as historically implausible.[65] Wolfgang Stegemann's weightiest objection is to assert that it would not be possible for Paul (and his father) to have been practicing Jews and Roman citizens.[66] On this claim

---

65. Notably John C. Lentz Jr., *Luke's Portrait of Paul*, SNTSMS 77 (Cambridge: Cambridge University Press, 1993), esp. 43–56 [see my review in *Anvil* 11 (1994): 62–64]; Wolfgang Stegemann, "War der Apostel Paulus ein römischer Bürger?," *ZNW* 78 (1987): 200–29; cf. Klaus Wengst, *Pax Romana and the Peace of Jesus Christ* (Philadelphia: Fortress, 1987), 74–75 (who is ambivalent about whether Paul was a Roman citizen: he concludes, "if he was, he attached no importance to it").

66. Stegemann, "Apostel," esp. 221–29; he also claims that Paul's low social status and Jewish background would prevent him or his family becoming Roman citizens, the lack of mention in Paul's letters of his Roman citizenship excludes it, and the Acts reports are Lu-

Martin Hengel acerbically observes, "Stegemann is completely overlooking what the sources say; clearly he does know them well enough."[67] Hengel is certainly right to point to the primary sources, for there is clear evidence of Jews in Rome itself who were devout in the practice of Judaism and Roman citizens: Philo indicates that Augustus knew that Jews lived in Rome, had synagogues, sent money to the Jerusalem temple for sacrifices, and were not deprived of their rights as Roman citizens.[68] Horace, Dio Cassius, and Juvenal object to the effectiveness of the Jewish engagement with pagans in Rome.[69] Jewish freedmen relocated to Judea and lived there as Roman citizens[70]—quite possibly the Jerusalem "synagogue of the freedmen" with whose members Stephen debated (Acts 6:9) was home to a number of such.

In sum, there is no plausible reason to reject Luke's testimony to Paul's Jewish ancestry being combined with Roman citizenship. But how do we understand his exercise of that citizenship in Philippi, according to Acts 16:37?

b. Is Paul's Exercise of His Roman Citizenship in Acts 16:37 Plausible in Roman Law?

Paul and Silas are imprisoned after being accused of advocating Jewish customs that Romans could not accept (Acts 16:20–21). This accusation results from the economic damage done by Paul's rather irritated deliverance of the young woman with the python spirit (vv. 16–19). The magistrates order lictors to beat Paul and Silas with rods (vv. 22–23), a standard means of extracting information from an accused non-Roman,[71] and acceptable as

---

kan creations with apologetic intent. For critique, see Rainer Riesner, *Paul's Early Period: Chronology, Mission Strategy, Theology* (Grand Rapids: Eerdmans, 1998), 151–54; Hengel and Deines, *Pre-Christian*, 6–8; Tajra, *Trial*, 87–89.

67. Hengel and Deines, *Pre-Christian*, 12.

68. *Legat.* 155–57 (discussion in Hengel and Deines, *Pre-Christian*, 11–132); cf. Tacitus, *Ann.* 2.85.4; text, translation, and discussion in Menahem Stern, *Greek and Latin Authors on Jews and Judaism* (Jerusalem: Israel Academy of Sciences and Humanities, 1974–84), 2:68–73, notably observing, "it seems that at the end of Tiberius's reign many Jewish lived at Rome and that at the beginning of the rule of Claudius (41 CE) the Jews in Rome were again numerous" (72).

69. Horace, *Sat.* 1.4.139–43 (discussion in Stern, *Authors*, 1:323); Dio Cassius 57.18.5a; 37.16.5–17.1 (discussion in Stern, *Authors*, 2:365, 353); Juvenal, *Sat.* 14.96–106 (discussion in Stern, *Authors*, 103–7); cf. Hengel and Deines, *Pre-Christian*, 13.

70. Hengel and Deines, *Pre-Christian*, 13 with n. 97.

71. Cf. Garnsey, *Status*, 136–41.

a way of punishing someone of low status who was accused by someone of high status (who would be presumed to be telling the truth).[72] They are then thrown into the innermost cell of the city prison (v, 23). Following the remarkable earthquake and the jailer's conversion during the night (vv. 25–34), the magistrates are ready to send Paul and Silas away. It is at this point—not earlier—that Luke presents Paul as speaking of their Roman citizenship and demanding that the magistrates come and let them go, rather than being dismissed merely by the jailer. If Paul was a Roman citizen, why wait until this point, and how would this situation be compatible with Roman law?

Peter Garnsey offers the possibility that the application of Roman law and justice could be variable in consistency from place to place.[73] He notes that some governors acted improperly, such as Galba crucifying a Roman citizen who had poisoned someone, in spite of the man citing "the laws" and claiming his Roman citizenship.[74] Garnsey goes on to note that the reports of such irregular actions found in Cicero, Suetonius, and Dio are disapproving, and thus may suggest that such abuses were unusual. In tune with Garnsey, Ramsay and Cadbury both considered that Paul and Silas may have spoken of their citizenship earlier, but been ignored.[75] However, this seems unlikely, for the authorities—both the magistrates and the lictors—would be rightly fearful of their positions if they acted illegally against a Roman citizen. For example, Paul's preemptive invocation of his Roman citizenship in Jerusalem led to the centurion, tribune, and other soldiers backing off rapidly from beating Paul (Acts 22:23–29). The Philippian officials were not high up the Roman chain, and would have those higher up to whom they answered.

Brian Rapske suggests three reasons why Paul and Silas might not have stated their Roman citizenship earlier.[76] First, to claim citizenship would necessarily delay events, and would probably mean that Paul and Silas would not be free to continue their mission travels and endeavours. It might well put financial pressure on Paul and Silas, far from friends and home, too.

Secondly, Paul and Silas's Jewishness is emphasized negatively in the accusation against them. The accusers present a stark either/or: either a

---

72. Rapske, *Paul*, 125; cf. 120–21; cf. Sherwin-White, *Society*, 82–83.

73. Garnsey, *Status*, 268.

74. Cicero, *Verr.* 2.5.65 §§167–68; Dio Cassius 63.2.3; Suetonius, *Galba* 9.

75. William M. Ramsay, *St. Paul the Traveller and Roman Citizen* (London: Hodder & Stoughton, 1895), 219.

76. Rapske, *Paul*, 133–34.

person is "Roman" ('Ρωμαῖος in v. 21) or he is "Jewish" ('Ιουδαῖος in v. 20). If Paul and Silas stated their Roman citizenship early in the going, it would have had negative implications for their Jewishness—and "Christianity" was not separate from Judaism at this time—and it would probably have been a bridge too far to explain that there was no necessary incompatibility in this Roman colony.

Thirdly, there would be a missiological cost to an early appeal to Roman citizenship, for it would have avoided facing the truth, which was that Paul and Silas were there to evangelize Romans and other inhabitants of the city, seeking to persuade them to believe in Jesus. Given that nascent Christianity was a "sect" within Judaism, at least in the eyes of these Romans, to hide behind Roman citizenship would be to leave non-Roman Philippian believers exposed. New believers might suspect that only Romans could be true believers—or, at least, that only Romans could *safely* be believers—and would see Paul and Silas's call to suffer for the gospel as hypocritical, since they had used their Roman citizenship to avoid such suffering.[77]

4. Roman Citizenship and Heavenly Citizenship

Rapske's three reasons are plausible and coherent, and also add up to a connection with Philippians 3:20-21. It was, we might say, Paul and Silas's heavenly citizenship that drove the way they used, or did not use, their earthly Roman citizenship.[78] Where appeal to their Roman citizenship might threaten the credibility of their heavenly citizenship, sheltering behind the Roman citizenship was not an option. Readiness to suffer for the gospel is such a point, as Rapske notes—and this is a significant theme in Philippians, both in Paul's suffering in prison and in the believers' present or future suffering. Paul's imprisonment had caused raised eyebrows among the believers, as 1:12-14 shows, notably that Paul writes, "the things that have happened to me have really (μᾶλλον) led to the progress of the gospel." The threat the Philippian believers face is suggested in 1:28, "not being frightened by anything from those who oppose you," by the example of Jesus, who readily went to suffering and death (2:5-8), by the warnings

---

77. Cf. Mark Reasoner, "Citizenship," *DPL*, 139-41, here 140 (§1.1).

78. Thus, Wengst overstates when he says of Phil 3:20, "Anyone who talks like this cannot attach any special value to Roman citizenship" (Wengst, *Pax Romana and the Peace of Jesus Christ*, 79). For my view, cf. Riesner, *Period*, 156.

against "the dogs" (3:2), whoever they are, and in the call to imitate Paul, who now suffers for the gospel (3:17) and says his highest ambition is to suffer like Christ in order that he may experience the heavenly power of resurrection (3:10–11).[79]

This line of thinking also connects Philippians 1:27 to 3:20–21, for 3:20–21 is prioritizing the believers' heavenly citizenship over their earthly citizenship, while at the same time Paul insists in 1:27 that their behavior in the public sphere should demonstrate appropriate citizenly deportment. The echo of the cognate verb and noun in these two places may be designed to lead Paul's letter-hearers in Philippi to see their earthly lifestyle as significant because it demonstrates their heavenly citizenship.

In my teens I learned a Christian song that was then very popular. It goes:

> Turn your eyes upon Jesus,
> Look full in his wonderful face,
> And the things of earth will grow strangely dim
> In the light of his glory and grace.[80]

In the light of this study, I am inclined to think the songwriter would have done better to write:

> . . . And the things of earth will grow strangely *important*
> In the light of his heavenly grace.

That is to say, earthly citizenly living is vitally important for Paul, for it is through such living that the glories of heavenly citizenship can be communicated to and experienced by those who are not yet citizens of heaven.

---

79. For a cogent, and widely accepted, case that the Philippian believers were suffering for their faith, with a helpful picture of what such suffering would look like for various groups in the church, see Oakes, *Philippians*, 77–84, 89–96. Joseph H. Hellerman, *Reconstructing Honor in Roman Philippi: Carmen Christi as Cursus Pudorum*, SNTSMS 132 (Cambridge: Cambridge University Press, 2005), esp. 129–56, argues that Paul is reconstructing "honor" as a category in contradistinction to the cultural mores of Roman society and in line with the example of Christ, seen particularly in Phil 2:6–11.

80. It is in fact the chorus of the hymn "O Soul, Are You Weary and Troubled?" by Helen H. Lemmel, written in 1922. See "O soul, are you weary and troubled," *The Canterbury Dictionary of Hymnology,* ed. J. R. Watson and Emma Hornby (Canterbury Press, 2013), http://www.hymnology.co.uk/o/o-soul,-are-you-weary-and-troubled.

5. Conclusion

We have seen that the direction in which Trebilco and Winter initially pointed us leads to a reading of both Philippians and Acts 16 that prioritizes heavenly citizenship over any earthly citizenship. In acting thus, Paul is strikingly using "city" language well known to the Roman and non-Roman inhabitants of Philippi and its surrounding districts, but applying it to the believing community—they are the "city within a city" called to shine as a light on a hill (cf. Matt 5:14) in order to present and embody the claim Jesus makes for the city.

Spiritual Geographies of the City
Exploring Spiritual Landscapes in Colossae

PAUL CLOKE

1. Introduction

This chapter seeks to identify and illustrate a series of alternative philo-sophical and analytical tools for understanding the city that can be derived from the invocation of non-representational ideas in human geography. In particular, it draws on the recognition in this work of so-called "affective landscapes" to develop an understanding of how "spiritual" presences and absences may be recognized as influential in the unfolding cultural imagina-tion and political-economic practices that characterize the city.[1] The chap-ter briefly demonstrates how a discernment of these spiritual landscapes is being practiced in the contemporary urban world. Then, somewhat more speculatively, it suggests how such understandings might be used to enhance the representational texts relating to the historic cities of the Bible. Using the example of Colossae,[2] the chapter suggests that the affective spiritual land-scapes therein would have influenced the hegemonic cultural imaginaries of the city, the forces and powers that had a hold over the lives of the people in the city, and the kinds of faithful improvisation recommended by Paul in his letter to the church in the city.

---

1. Here, I wish to acknowledge the expertise and influence of my friend and erstwhile colleague Dr. John-David Dewsbury of the School of Geographical Sciences, University of Bristol, not least for his formative thinking on the idea of "spiritual landscapes."

2. Brian J. Walsh and Sylvia C. Keesmaat, *Colossians Remixed: Subverting the Empire* (Downers Grove, IL: InterVarsity Press, 2004).

PAUL CLOKE

2. Landscapes of Affect

Social science has long been interested in how meaning can be ascribed to socioeconomic and cultural phenomena. Basic ideas suggesting that "things" exist in the material and cultural world and that they have perfectly clear meanings have largely been rejected as an oversimplification of the complexity of meaningfulness. Rather, theories of *representation*[3] have been used both to suggest that such meanings are produced rather than just found, and that this process of constructing meaning enters the very constitution of things, shaping rather than just reflecting their character. The idea of representation attempts to deal with complexity by organizing, understanding, and mediating the world through the construction of basic cognitive units that guide us to sets of assumed relations between appearance and reality. Representations can take the form of both concrete images and abstract concepts; they present a symbolic and iconic description of the physical material world. For example, nature is often represented as wilderness, and rural life as idyllic. In both cases, meanings become constructed that neglect other characteristics (for example elements of "tamed" nature or of dysfunctional rural life) that do not "fit" the representation concerned.

One of the most interesting and significant philosophical directions taken by social science in recent years has involved the development of nonrepresentational theories pioneered by Nigel Thrift.[4] The concern of these ideas is to provide a focus that takes seriously the ordinary practices by which life unfolds, and in particular to take fully into account the ways in which the preconscious, subconscious, and nonconscious playing out of life defies easy description and representation. Many researchers whose identity depends on measuring, explaining, and interpreting representational texts, signs, and significations will balk at the idea of accessing embodied life practices that somehow evade these processes and their attendant methodologies. However, nonrepresentational approaches to human geography have begun to open up ways of attending to embodied emotions, performances, and affects that are an integral part of being human and dwelling in particular places.

3. See, e.g., Stuart Hall, ed., *Representation: Cultural Representations and Signifying Practices* (London: Sage, 1997).
4. Nigel Thrift, *Non-representational Theory: Space, Politics, Affects* (London: Routledge, 2007). See also Ben Anderson and Paul Harrison, eds., *Taking Place: Non-representational Theories and Geography* (Aldershot: Ashgate, 2010).

Consider, for example, how powerful memories of places and/or events are so often fueled by haunting senses of presence and absence. I remember, when visiting Robben Island, the prison across the water from Cape Town where Nelson Mandela and other leaders of the African National Congress were incarcerated during the apartheid era, experiencing what I can only describe as a sense of ghostly and uncanny copresence of histories in the unfolding present.[5] There was something in the very pores of the prison's material fabric that conjured up a haunting ghostliness, transporting the historic birthing of truth and reconciliation in South Africa into direct relation with the embodied experience of the present day. A similar affect has been noted in other historic sites, ranging from industrial ruins to ecclesiastically sacred sites.[6] Equally, consider how engagement in contemporary pilgrimage is often associated with a spiritual power at work.[7] Even visits to small-scale UK Christian festivals such as New Wine and Greenbelt can be punctuated by spiritually affective power at work in the unfolding of events. The human staging of these festivals is periodically transcended by the emotional and relational performances that accrue: at New Wine a sense of the presence of the *Spirit* of God at work; at Greenbelt a sense of the powerful and hopeful *possibility* for the intersection of faith and justice to affect hopeful and ethical encounters and relations.[8] For these specific examples readers can substitute their own meaningful sites of pilgrimage, but whatever the specifics, participation often reflects some kind of spiritual force that exerts a powerful *affect* on embodied performance and emotional sensitivity.[9]

Each of these examples prompts, at least in part, a nonrepresentative grasp of what is *occurring*, inviting us to go beyond the previous comfort zones in which an obsession with representation and meaning emphasizes

5. For more information on his imprisonment, see Nelson Mandela, *Long Walk to Freedom* (London: Abacus, 1995).

6. See, for example, Tim Edensor, *Industrial Ruins: Space, Aesthetics and Materiality* (Oxford: Berg, 2005).

7. For an interesting account of pilgrimage, see Richard Scriven, "Geographies of Pilgrimage: Meaningful Movements and Embodied Mobilities," *Geogr. Compass* 8 (2014): 249–61.

8. Paul Cloke and Justin Beaumont, "Geographies of Postsecular Rapprochement in the City," *Prog. Hum. Geogr.* 37 (2013): 27–51.

9. See, for example, Matina Terzidou, "Religiousness as Tourist Practice" (PhD diss., University of Surrey, 2012); Dallen Timothy and Daniel Olsen, eds., *Tourism, Religion and Spiritual Journeys*, Contemporary Geographies of Leisure, Tourism and Mobility (New York: Routledge, 2006).

fixed, bounded, and often lifeless understanding, reaching out instead to that which is in an alive state of becoming. The problem here is not necessarily with representations and meanings themselves—clearly it should be possible to conceive of ways to bring together the representative and the nonrepresentative.[10] Rather, the problem is rooted in any overwhelming desire to engage in a process of representationalism by continually imposing fixed structures of meaning onto the world. By refocusing attention both to the performance of places and events, and to the manifestations of everyday life within these places and events,[11] we can begin to witness the vitality of these worlds as they unfold. Nonrepresentational theory, then, seeks to grasp the significance of "mundane everyday practices that shape the conduct of human beings towards others and themselves in particular sites."[12]

Any such approach has to be accompanied by a series of obvious prerequisites: that we take the body seriously, that we recognize the significance of precognitive aspects of embodied life, that we take the nonhuman world seriously and examine both how the social relates to the material and how the body evolves alongside and in relation to things, and that we give due attention to the technologies of being, especially the role of hybrid assemblages of connection or network. Hybridity here alerts us to the essential relations between the human and the nonhuman (including, for example, flora, fauna, technology, ideas, and discourses), and leads us to think less about humans in isolation and more about how humans need to be understood in terms of relational networks (such as food systems) or assembled spaces of relational achievements (such as restaurants or food banks). Perhaps most important of all, we need to take seriously the idea of "affect,"[13] which gives conceptual expression to a wide range of life experiences—background moods, shared atmospheres, fleeting feelings, emotional grasp, immediate visceral and neu-

10. For example, Hayden Lorimer has termed this bringing together as "more than representational." See his "Cultural Geography: The Busyness of Being 'More-Than-Representational'," *Prog. Hum. Geogr.* 32 (2005): 551–55.

11. See Nigel Thrift, "Afterwords," *Env. Plan. D* 18 (2000): 213–55; Nigel Thrift and John-David Dewsbury, "Dead Geographies and How to Make Them Live," *Env. Plan. D* 18 (2000): 411–32; Amanda Rogers, "Performances," in *Introducing Human Geographies*, ed. Paul Cloke, Philip Crang and Mark Goodwin (London: Routledge, 2014), 773–86.

12. Nigel Thrift, "The Still Point: Resistance, Expressive Embodiment and Dance" in *Geographies of Resistance*, ed. Steve Pile and Michael Keith (London: Routledge, 1997), 124–51, here 124.

13. See Ben Anderson, "Affects" in *Introducing Human Geographies*, ed. Paul Cloke, Philip Crang and Mark Goodwin, 3rd ed. (London: Routledge, 2014), 760–72.

rological responses—that speak to the process of becoming human at any given moment. As Ben Anderson has indicated,[14] affects are partly about a nonconscious background sense that flies under the radar of thought, deliberation, and reflection. Accordingly, affects can be individual, but they can also take a more collective shape in terms of shared atmospheres or vibes that are experienced by many in a particular place, and human geographers have taken a strong interest in the idea of "affective topologies" in which different affects are intensified or suppressed at different times in different places.[15] Thus, it is argued that affects are formed and emerge through particular geographies: through spaces of encounter between people and places; through wider geographies of connection or disconnection by which encounters get tangled up with economic, political, social, or cultural forces; and through the deliberate design of environments that condition affect.[16] Such topologies sometimes suggest particular kinds of affective landscapes in particular places.

3. Spiritual Landscapes

It is also possible to recognize some of the encounters that underlie these affective topologies as spiritual in nature, evoking the immanent sensation of something more going on than meets the eye.[17] Suggesting the need for an interpretative technology that exceeds that which is simply tangible and known about, human geographers have developed the idea of *spiritual landscapes* in order that understandings of local places can take the unseen spiritual world just as seriously as existing foci on the material landscapes of society, economy, politics, and culture. The argument here is that faith, belief, and religion can illuminate the notion of being and becoming in the world, reflecting an inhabitation or dwelling in different spiritual registers that goes alongside more representational registers of understanding what it is to inhabit or dwell in a place.

14. Anderson, "Affects," 764–65
15. See David Bissell, "Placing Affective Relations: Uncertain Geographies of Pain" in *Taking Place: Non-representational Theories and Geography*, ed. Ben Anderson and Paul Harrison (Aldershot: Ashgate, 2010), 79–98.
16. See Nigel Thrift, "Intensities of Feeling: Towards a Spatial Politics of Affect," *Geogr. Ann. B* 86 (2004): 57–78.
17. John-David Dewsbury and Paul Cloke, "Spiritual Landscapes: Existence, Performance and Immanence," *Soc. Cult. Geogr.* 10 (2009): 695–711.

As such, both "landscape" and "spiritual" are constructs of dwelling that require further explanation:

> By "landscapes" we refer to embodied practices of being in the world, including ways of seeing but extending beyond sight to both a sense of being that includes all senses, and an openness to being affected. By "spiritual" we refer to that part of the virtual in which faith forms a part of the move beyond rationality and of the possibility of other-worldly dispositions. Even for the most sceptical, the spiritual can suggest a form of performative presencing of some sense of spirit.[18]

In this way, the spiritual is not necessarily just about religion, and can be made manifest in at least three ways. First, people engage in particular practices because they believe in some form of the spiritual—this could involve engagements in prayer or contemplation, visits to places that are affective of some sense of spiritual evocation, or pondering on the aesthetic and affective connections in, for example, artwork or music. In such ways, places can become sacralised in one form or another.[19] Secondly, a belief in the spiritual means that certain things happen that would not have done so otherwise; that is, certain affects are produced that lead to profound experiences that are attributed to the spiritual realm. In this way, the spiritual can be a constitutive force that supplements other understandings of places that focus on, for example, the socioeconomic or the political. Thirdly, it can be postulated that the spiritual simply exists in and amongst the multiple contexts and practices of embodied life. Taking these three ideas of the spiritual together, it follows that the spiritual can be regarded as: "something constitutive of everyday life; cutting at that space between absence and presence, and manifesting itself at the immediate, and therefore non-metaphysical, level of the body."[20]

This is, then, the performance of believing that works both at and upon the relationship between the experience of space and of embodiment.[21] Spiritual landscapes thus become a tension between presences and absences and

---

18. Dewsbury and Cloke, "Spiritual Landscapes," 696.

19. See Lily Kong, "Mapping New Geographies of Religion: Politics and Poetics in Modernity," *Prog. Hum. Geogr.* 25 (2001): 211–33.

20. Dewsbury and Cloke, "Spiritual Landscapes," 697.

21. See Mitch Rose, "Gathering Dreams of 'Presence': A Project for the Cultural Landscape," *Env. Plan. D* 24 (2006): 537–54; Mitch Rose and John Wylie, "Animating Landscape," *Env. Plan. D* 24 (2006): 475–79.

between the performance and creation of the present. The rational/material is most obviously present, and the spiritual is often seemingly absent, but the ghostly presence of that unseen spiritual is nevertheless influential in how we make sense of our dwelling places and how we continue to develop them through our actions.

As an example, the renowned theologian Walter Wink[22] has written about the power of evil in terms of an outer visible structure (an "exteriority") and an inner spiritual reality (an "interiority"). He argues that the interior and exterior aspects of evil operate simultaneously, but that the invisible spiritual dimension of the powers of evil is often neglected.[23] While material structures of domination are often very visible in local contexts, the interior spiritual realities of such domination are discernible only as a kind of haunting enslavement that operates in the spiritual landscape to incarcerate humanity. Geographers are currently fascinated by this idea that being "human" in particular places involves both the visible/tangible and the virtual/intangible, with the latter including accounts of affective powers that are literally ineffable since they cannot be named. Theology, of course, has names for these seemingly ghostly presences and absences, and it seems vital that these kinds of spiritual landscapes should form an integral focus in the understanding of places in which and about which theology is invoked.

The idea that we need to take the performances and affects of spiritual landscapes seriously in the interpretation of "cities of God" depends for its relevance and utility on finding new ways of studying such phenomena.[24] Methodologies of scholarship have typically been geared toward the explanation, understanding, and *representation* of places as found in texts, attitudes, and activities. Sensitizing scholarship to the preconscious and nonconscious, to the ineffable and the affective, is no easy task, but progress has been made in a number of different ways. For example, it has been possible to develop ethnographic techniques to include how we sense things as well as how we talk about and do them. New forms of *sensory ethnography*[25] that give reflexive attention to the sensorial palette of human experience offer

---

22. Walter Wink, *Naming the Powers: The Language of Power in the New Testament,* vol. 1 of *The Powers* (Minneapolis: Fortress, 1984), 135.

23. Paul Cloke, "Emerging Geographies of Evil? Theo-ethics and Postsecular Possibilities," *Cultural Geographies* 18 (2011): 475–93.

24. I draw this phrase from Rodney Stark, *Cities of God: The Real Story of How Christianity Became an Urban Movement and Conquered Rome* (New York: HarperOne, 2007).

25. Sarah Pink, *Doing Sensory Ethnography* (London: Sage, 2009); Sarah Pink, *Situating Everyday Life* (London: Sage, 2012).

the possibility to relate knowledge without necessarily subjecting it to contemplative translation into frameworks of representation. Even so, ethnographies sometimes struggle to convey such imperceptibles as emotions, passions, desires, beliefs and faiths, which are easily elided by representation.

Accordingly, John-David Dewsbury[26] has advocated *witnessing* as a means of attending to differences that script the folded mix of emotions, desires, and intuitions in the aura and spirit of places and events. Seeking always to negotiate the connections between what we see and what we know, he challenges us to practice the belief that the intelligible comes from the sensible; in other words to start to form understandings from the orientation point of the body, to look at things in unusual ways, to have the courage to present rather than represent, to respond to the power that places have to move us. Witnessing, therefore, requires descriptive experimentation with "just" presenting manifestations, moments, performances, and so on in ways that will communicate their own meaning about the affective relationships of the world as displayed in unseen and unintended aspects of everyday life. It is about becoming accustomed to the immaterial and the spiritual in our thinking, citing the invisible energies that affect our being and becoming, witnessing what is felt, engaging in a wilder form of empiricism that feels before it contemplates.

For some, the witnessing of nonrepresentational worlds finds expression in certain forms of *psychogeography* and associated methodologies of walking. Merlin Coverley[27] explains that a focus on the connections between psychology and geography has taken myriad historical forms, some fueled by political radicalism and others more interested in playful provocation. However, in general psychogeography has involved a search for new ways of apprehending urban places by championing the mysteries that lie beneath and within what are often seen as the banal experiences of urban life. These mysterious and unknowable characteristics of urban life are most often encountered by practices of walking and wandering in the city, purposefully drifting in order that the vibe or sense of the place will reveal itself. In this way, walking also seems to offer a fruitful passageway into the practice of witnessing.[28] An excellent example of how these psychogeographies can be sensitized to spiritual landscapes is John Davies's narrative of walking

26. John-David Dewsbury, "Witnessing Space: Knowledge without Contemplation," *Env. Plan. A* 35 (2003): 1907–32.

27. Merlin Coverley, *Psychogeography* (Harpenden: Pocket Essentials, 2006).

28. John Wylie, "A Single Day's Walking: Narrating Self and Landscape on the South West Coast Path," *Trans. Inst. Br. Geog.* 30 (2005): 234–47.

coast-to-coast across the north of England, following the route of the M62 motorway.[29] As part of his journeying, Davies notes, for example, ghostly presences and absences presenting themselves in different guises, "be they the ghosts of communities no longer physically present in particular places but still active, 'dead roads' which had been cut off by the building of the M62 across them, or the 'spirits of place' which I tried at times to describe in my diary entries."[30]

It is clear here that there is a deliberate spiritual element to his journey, with the author leaning heavily on his faith in "a God who came to earth, who *incarnated* himself in the ordinary life of the common people."[31] Psychogeography for Davies, then, is a reading of everyday place and displacement in terms of a sacramental understanding of engaging with God in and through everyday experiences, conversations and events, both in terms of loss and suffering, and in terms of the presence of a powerful spirit of grace. As he puts it: "My fantasy is that once you have learned to 'read the everyday' then you are well equipped to start seeing the signs of 'heaven in the ordinary' in the previously unpromising places where people interact . . . and in the events which engage them there."[32]

In this example from John Davies, we can begin to see how psychogeographical surveying can address the spiritual interiorities of places and landscapes, noting the contours of presence and absence, but also being alerted to the tiny hints of incarnational grace that blossom amongst other geographies of power, exclusion, and marginalization.

4. Spiritual Landscapes in Colossae

I have for many years been fascinated by the New Testament account of the city of Colossae; it seems to be impregnated by the kinds of spiritual landscapes indicated above. Yet any move from sensory ethnography, witnessing, and psychogeographic engagement in the *here and now* to attempts at such engagements *through historic text* requires very careful consideration of multiple hermeneutical issues. First and foremost, we need to acknowledge the hermeneutical pitfalls in pondering what exactly we are doing when we

29. John Davies, "Walking the M62," http://www.johndavies.org.
30. Davies, "Walking," 13.
31. Davies, "Walking," 9.
32. Davies, "Walking," 10.

read, understand, or apply texts such as these.[33] Convoluted questions about what is happening behind the text, within the text, and in front of the text are variously overlain by ideological commitments to a plethora of interpretative strategies ranging from a search for truth and authentic meaning to a joyful quest for liberation from authorial and textual captivity. Any exploration for affective vibes, edges, and nuances is likely to fall foul of any and all of these hermeneutical prejudices. Secondly, any historic text will itself be a representational device, meaning that analysis of potentially affective powers and landscapes may well involve the worthwhile-but-challenging task of reading between the lines, searching the cracks, crevices, and between-spaces for glimpses of emotions, desires, and intuitions in the aura and spirit of the place. Inevitably here we have to rely on the *witnessing* provided by the author to glean hints about sensorial geographies or psychogeographies at work, realizing that these factors were certainly not Paul's primary focus in writing his letter.

As a further complication, although a deliberate and most enjoyable one, my interest in Colossae has been deepened and enhanced by Brian Walsh and Sylvia Keesmaat's creative and seminal interpretation in *Colossians Remixed*.[34] Bringing together serious historical study and detailed biblical exegesis with imaginative and discerning narrative of the emotional topography of living in and under empire, Walsh and Keesmaat use a witnessing of cultural and political landscapes in today's world to impregnate their descriptions of historic Colossae with an embodied sense of being in the world, and a distinct sense of the moods, atmosphere, emotional grasp, and visceral responses that pertained in that world. Their account, their re-witnessing of the city of Colossae, has played a very significant role in my capacity to think about the spiritual landscapes that are evident in that context. In effect, they are my hermeneutical guides in this speculative venture. They refer to Colossians as "a subversive tract for subversive living"[35] that insists on an alternative imagination and distinct cultural discernment. My hope is that the discernment of affective spiritual landscapes in Colossae can add a little to the subversion of fixed, bounded, and lifeless representations that eschew the emotional performance of place and the mundane everyday practices that help shape that city.

33. In this context, I have benefitted significantly from reading Stanley E. Porter and Beth M. Stowell, eds., *Biblical Hermeneutics: Five Views* (Downers Grove, IL: InterVarsity Press, 2012).

34. See n. 2.

35. Walsh and Keesmaat, *Colossians*, 9.

In the context of this chapter, I offer three sets of observations about the spiritual landscape pertaining in Colossae.

a. Affective Imaginaries of Colossae

It has been well documented that Colossae was an important city in first-century Asia Minor, situated as it was some 160 km from the port of Ephesus.[36] As part of the Roman Empire, the city lived under occupation, and its character and atmosphere must have been strongly conditioned by the subjugation and restricted self-determination that goes along with the physical and cultural trappings of a subaltern positioning under colonial rule. Reference in Colossians to "thrones, powers, rulers, authorities" (1:16) witnesses to the military and civic force of life in the empire, characterized by violent oppression, heavy taxation, and the imposition of all manner of cultural assimilation. The practices of everyday life in Colossae were carried out in an atmosphere of fear, uncertainty, and increasing social and cultural division. Impoverished peasants were particularly hard hit by the stringency of Roman taxation, with the result that wealthy Colossians were able to buy up cheaply the land previously owned by peasant farmers and enslave them as part of an emerging double jeopardy of colonial rule and bourgeois greed.

What is evident here is a series of contexts in which the Roman Empire maintained its sovereignty over the city. Most obviously, it established a *material* monopoly on the city based on its dominant military power, such that the major processes and practices of city life—political decisions, economic decisions and markets, social order and symbolic signification—were all brought into order by force or persuasion. Laws, rules, regulations, and orthodox practices were imposed by the colonial power and reinforced by those people in the city who were in a position to benefit from the opportunities available from postures of collaboration or acquiescence. However, along with this material monopoly came a less evident but equally powerful monopolizing by the Romans of the *imagination* of their Colossian subjects. In chapters three to five of their book, Walsh and Keesmaat capture something of this monopolized imagination in their re-witnessing of how embod-

36. For contextual information on Colossae, see, for example, Chistopher A. Beetham, *Echoes of Scripture in the Letter of Paul to the Colossians*, BibInt 96 (Atlanta: SBL Press, 2010); Douglas Moo, *The Letters to Colossians and Philemon,* PNTC (Grand Rapids: Zondervan, 2008); David W. Pao, *Colossians and Philemon*, ZECNT (Grand Rapids: Zondervan, 2012); N. T. Wright, *Colossians and Philemon*, TNTC (Leicester: Inter-Varsity Press, 2008).

ied lived practices in the city were engulfed by the enormity and inevitability of occupation and subjugation, reflected in particular by the unerring and overruling presence of the figure of Caesar in the places, events, and materials of the city.[37] Their imaginative account of daily life gives substance to the atmosphere and emotional context of a colonial imagination figure-headed by the cultural representation of its leader:

> I gazed around as I went about my business. Everywhere I turned there were images of Caesar. When I walked to the market, I saw his image in the square. I saw his image in the theatre, in the gymnasium, in the temples. And the coins with which I transacted my business all bore his likeness. Even my household was full of his image, from the idols of the emperor in the atrium to images on my jewellery and utensils and paintings on the walls. I noticed that my clay lamps were decorated with symbols of Roman victory, and my father's seal ring . . . was decorated with a kneeling Parthian, a symbol of Rome's dominance over its enemies.[38]

This monopolizing of the civic, public, and personal imaginations of the city will have provoked acknowledged and unspoken emotions and affects amongst the people of Colossae. Walter Brueggemann asserts that colonial control over the imagination produces a feeling amongst the subjugated population of being numbed, satiated, and thoroughly co-opted;[39] in other words, a monopoly over the imagination has an *affect* emotionally that goes well beyond the materiality of life. Numbed and satiated co-option affects both people who practice it, and those who are formed by its events, impinging on the embodied practice of everyday life through the performative presence of a spirit of weary inevitability and a sense of being immersed in subaltern power relations. These affective characteristics permeate the spiritual landscape of Colossae. The fact that Paul's letter to the Colossians is attempting to reshape the imaginaries of the city with an alternative to the Roman model suggests the power of ways of seeing, ways of sensing and ways of being open to an alternative spiritual landscape based on God-given wisdom and understanding, and fruitfulness within a model of God's kingdom:

37. Walsh and Keesmaat, *Colossians*, 49–95.
38. Walsh and Keesmaat, *Colossians*, 54.
39. Walter Brueggemann, *Interpretation and Obedience* (Minneapolis: Fortress, 1991), 185.

For this reason, since the day we heard about you, we have not stopped praying for you. We continually ask God to fill you with the knowledge of his will through all the wisdom and understanding that the Spirit gives, so that you may live a life worthy of the Lord and please him in every way: bearing fruit in every good work, growing in the knowledge of God, being strengthened with all power according to his glorious might so that you may have great endurance and patience, and giving joyful thanks to the Father, who has qualified you to share in the inheritance of his holy people in the kingdom of light. For he has rescued us from the dominion of darkness and brought us into the kingdom of the Son he loves, in whom we have redemption, the forgiveness of sins. (Col 1:9–14 NIV 1984)

Here an alternative imagination marked by strong and joyful endurance and patience, a prospect of rescue and redemption, and a spiritual sense of inheritance offers hope for other kinds of spiritual landscape in the colonial city; different senses of rhythm, disposition, and ethical impulse that may indicate the performative presencing of another sense of spirit based upon Christian faith.

b. Affective Powers in Colossae

In Colossians 1:9, Paul specifically prays that the people of the Colossian church will receive "all the wisdom and understanding that the Spirit gives." This invocation of alternative wisdom and understanding appears to be closely connected to the idea of everything "visible and invisible":

The Son is the image of the invisible God, the firstborn over all creation. For in him all things were created: things in heaven and on earth, visible and invisible, whether thrones or powers or rulers or authorities; all things have been created through him and for him. (Col 1:15–16 NIV 1984)

Here, the letter addresses the forces and practices that have a hold over the lives of the people of the city. Such forces include the "visible" manifestations of colonial rule and subordination, but also the "invisible" spiritual forces of empire—the powers behind, and sanctioning imperial power that were overwhelmingly responsible for structuring the lives of city dwellers. In other words, Paul's invocation of "visible and invisible" and "all things . . . in heaven

265

and earth" points us toward something that goes beyond the socioeconomic structures of political and military power. As Walsh and Keesmaat insist:

> The "powers" that legitimate and sanction the way power is exercised in the empire are not just military regiments or threats of capital punishment but the very structure of life including relationships of client and patron, slaves and masters . . . it has to do with "spiritual forces"—the spiritual forces of the empire.[40]

There are strong echoes here of Walter Wink's ideas about the simultaneous forces of exteriority and interiority of the power of evil. The outer, visible structure of the evil of empire is most readily recognized and understood, and the inner spiritual reality is often neglected because it is generally only perceived indirectly, by means of some form of projection.[41]

Accordingly, to understand the spiritual landscapes of Colossae, we need to recognize the real spiritual forces that emanate from real institutions and real systems of domination. As Paul suggests in his letter, the "dominion of darkness" (1:13) returns as a haunting enslavement, overpowering and incarcerating the humanity of Colossae. The thrones, powers, rulers, and authorities that form the exteriority of this darkness are at root spiritual in character, and this idolatrous spirit of empire *affects* the embodied practices and performances of living in the city. Once again, we can argue that the projections of these affective powers are perceived and made visible by Paul's reimagination of the city:

> So then, just as you received Christ Jesus as Lord, continue to live your lives in him, rooted and built up in him, strengthened in the faith as you were taught, and overflowing with thankfulness. See to it that no one takes you captive through hollow and deceptive philosophy, which depends on human tradition and the elemental spiritual forces of this world rather than on Christ. (Col 2:6–8 NIV 1984)

This re-imagination insists that the hollow and deceptive philosophy, human tradition, and elemental spiritual forces that are embedded in empire should be refused, and instead, Paul re-projects an alternative spiritual

---

40. Walsh and Keesmaat, *Colossians*, 92.
41. Wink, *Naming*, 185. See also Paul Cloke, "Emerging Geographies of Evil: Theoethics and Postsecular Possibilities," *Cult. Geogr.* 18 (2011): 475–93.

landscape in the image of invisible God. This idea of an alternative spiritual landscape needs to be understood both in terms of the undergirding power of God through the Holy Spirit to enable Colossian disciples to reimagine and reenact their city, and in terms of the capacity of these followers to bring their attitudes, actions, and everyday embodied performances into line with the flow and direction of the affective power of that godly Spirit. The perfect social imagination of God's kingdom, and the power of God's Spirit in and through people and places, becomes landscaped by the people of the Colossian church whose task it is—consciously and non-consciously—to reflect the fragrance of Christ by being salt and light in the city.

At least three aspects of this landscaping are evident in Paul's letter. First, there are clear alternative imaginaries at work in his discourses of rescue and bearing fruit. Paul talks of "rescue" from the dominion of darkness, and being brought into the kingdom of the Son (1:13), and he urges followers to bear fruit "in every good work" as they grow in the knowledge of God (1:10). Here he reflects a dramatic change of landscape, from the dominion of empire to a new kind of spiritual and practical kingdom based on following Christ, and fueled by the "energy" (1:29) that Christ works in and through his people. Secondly, these "big picture" changes to the spiritual landscape of the city are supported by clear alternative strategies for living out this alternative kingdom. Paul emphasizes the need to combat evil by setting aside self-indulgent and idolatrous characteristics of people's earthly nature (3:5)—characteristics that chimed with the spiritual interiorities of empire. Notably, these instructions are framed in the non-violent tactics of setting aside anger and malice (3:8). In these ways, Paul points to an alternative performance of life in the city capable of resisting the seemingly inevitable co-option into Roman cultures of living. Thirdly, Paul articulates the virtues necessary to effect a different way of living: "Clothe yourselves in compassion, kindness, humility, gentleness and patience. Bear with each other and forgive one another. . . . And over all these virtues put on love, which binds them all together in perfect unity" (3:12–14 NIV 1984).

Through the knowing and unknowing performance of these aspects of human relationship and interaction, Colossian disciples would not only live different kinds of lives for their own benefit, but they would produce affective waves of difference and alteriority through the city; others would be affected by their attitudes, behavior, and fragrance. However, this acknowledgement of the availability of alternative landscapes should not be taken as a simple process of performing social and spiritual blueprints. Rather, spiritual landscapes were contested as much through improvisation as through strict adherence to new rules and conventions.

c. Affective Landscapes of Improvisation

Paul's concern that the people of Colossae should not be fooled by hollow and deceptive philosophy represents a warning that such arguments may sound wise but that in reality they emanate from the powers of the world and they are constitutive of very worldly spiritual landscapes. This warning connects with the recommendation a little later in the letter that the Colossian church should "set your hearts on things above" (3:2). Here, it is important to understand Paul's insistence that the Christian message comes from somewhere, and is going somewhere, but in between requires a kind of *faithful improvisation*: an unfolding of individual and community life that is constantly becoming as the following of existing representations and rituals is mixed with a more immanent grasp of spiritual direction. As Walsh and Keesmaat explain:

> If we are to faithfully live out the biblical drama, then we will need to develop the imaginative skills necessary to improvise on this cosmic stage of creational redemption. Indeed it would be the height of infidelity and interpretative cowardice to simply repeat verbatim, over and over again, the earlier passages of the play. The task is not so much a matter of being able to quote the earlier script as it is to be able to continue it, to imaginatively discern what shape this story must take in our changing cultural context.[42]

Accordingly, we can readily imagine that the spiritual landscape of Colossae reflected just such processes and performances of improvisation—of being and becoming in different contexts and in response to different events—that were open to be affected by the spirit of God as discerned by Christians attempting to live out a life of faith.

Miroslav Volf writes about the constantly iterating practices of ascending to God to receive and discern prophetic messages, and returning to the world to *practice* the received message in mundane daily life.[43] Although the result of these iterations will be a complex and messy phenomenon of

---

42. Walsh and Keesmaat, *Colossians*, 134.
43. Miroslav Volf, *A Public Faith* (Grand Rapids: Brazos, 2011), 1–15.

praxis and performance, it can be understood as part of this wider development of faithful improvisation. It requires the development of a discerning attentiveness both to "what is in heaven" and to how the Christian narrative continues to be acted out. For example, Paul indicates the improvisation of hope in his reference to "Christ in you, the hope of glory" (Col 1:27). Hope can in many senses be understood as a performative force,[44] negotiated via the iterative ascending and descending alluded to in Volf's concept. It is unseen yet powerful and it affects both those who practice it and those who are formed through its events. Spiritual hope produces an ethical sensibility—a disposition that affects and is affected by the hope of something better—and as such illustrates one aspect of the kinds of landscapes of affective improvisation that helped to shape the lived topography and topology of Colossae. Paul's letter outlines a range of other ethical imaginaries, such as kindness (3:12), gentleness (3:12), love (1:4), gratitude (1:12), humility (3:12), and patience (1:11, 3:12), which would also inform and engender alternative praxis in the city, and thereby help to form a wider affective landscape of improvised agape, caritas, shalom, and cruciformity. Such affective improvisations would all contribute to the alternative spiritual landscape of the city.

5. Conclusion

The use of nonrepresentational ideas within human geography has opened up interesting lines of inquiry relating to how the processes of being and becoming human are affected both by non-conscious background senses that evade deliberation and reflection, and by the dawning of emotionally received feelings, shared atmospheres and background moods. These ideas are particularly valuable when dealing with the spiritual dimensions of how places and embodied lives interconnect, suggesting the spiritual as one affective co-constituent of everyday life that manifests at the edge between presences and absences in the form of immediate and immanent performance. As such, there is a clear application of concepts of affect and spiritual landscapes when seeking to witness to the unfolding role of faith and belief in contemporary place-lives through sensory ethnography and psychogeographic discernment. Application to historic text is more speculative be-

---

44. Julian Holloway, "The Space That Faith Makes: Towards a (Hopeful) Ethos of Engagement," in *Religion and Place: Landscape, Politics and Piety*, ed. Peter Hopkins, Lily Kong and Elizabeth Olson (New York: Springer, 2013), 203–18.

cause of the hermeneutical barriers involved. Nevertheless, any attempt to understand biblical texts in a way that combines faithful scholarship with a desire to be alert to the cultural issues of contemporary Christian faith will be enhanced by an acknowledgement of the nonrepresentational, however speculative. Such an understanding is in my view brilliantly undertaken in Walsh and Keesmaat's *Colossians Remixed*, and their re-witnessing of the contexts, events, and spiritual sensibilities in Colossae provokes a practice of imaginative discernment that can attempt to describe aspects of the spiritual landscapes at work in the city. The monopolistic nature of colonial imaginaries—underpinned by elemental spiritual forces—will have induced an affect of numb co-option and haunting enslavement and incarceration. The power and nature of this affective landscape only becomes fully evident when it is challenged and ultimately transgressed by Paul's reimagination of the spiritual landscape in the image of the invisible God. The force of this reimagination is in the alternative affective power of improvised practices of being and becoming that seesaw between imperfect spiritual discernment and tentative performance of faithful living. These subconscious and nonconscious dimensions of faith appear to be every bit as important to the character of the spiritual landscape in Colossae as their representational counterparts.

Re-Placing 1 Peter

From Place of Origin to Constructions of Space

DAVID G. HORRELL

Among the questions commentators regularly address when introducing a New Testament text are those concerning where it was written and where it was sent. In some cases the extant information makes this relatively clear and uncontroversial: 1 Corinthians was written from Ephesus and sent to Corinth; Romans was written in or near Corinth and sent to Rome. Such information often provides the basis for engaging with detailed studies of the history, culture, and archaeology of the specific city in view—as the countless monographs on some aspect of Paul's Corinthian letters illustrate. In other cases, notably the gospels, and some epistles such as James, 2 Peter, and Jude, there is no explicit information about the place of origin or the intended destination, though this has not prevented scholars from making learned but often somewhat speculative proposals.

In this essay, I begin by examining the range of scholarly proposals concerning 1 Peter's place of origin. The conclusions from this survey indicate that the kind of information the letter provides tells us not so much about physical location as about how the author constructs and presents the space where he depicts himself as writing the letter. This provides an impetus to turn to recent theoretical discussions of the notion of space, which have rejected any idea that space is merely a container within which human action takes place, and argued instead for a consideration of the ways in which space is constructed, represented, and imagined. Indeed, from this perspective, we may wonder whether decisions as to the actual location of the author are as illuminating for interpretation as is often assumed. Returning to the letter, this theoretical framework enables us to consider what may turn out to be a more illuminating issue: how the letter constructs space. This in turn provides a new perspective on 1 Peter's political stance.

1. Locating 1 Peter

The first letter of Peter informs us—at least ostensibly—both where it was written and where it was sent. The opening of the letter indicates the location of its addressees; they are scattered across a huge area covering much of Asia Minor, in Pontus, Galatia, Cappadocia, Asia, and Bithynia (1:1). These labels most likely indicate, as the large majority of commentators have agreed, the Roman provincial organization of Asia Minor, though it may be that the selected list suggests that the author has specific province-districts in view.[1] Whether or not the order of the list indicates a real or imaginary travel route for the letter carrier, most commentators have taken this to be a genuine indication as to the location of the letter's first recipients. Of course, the vast area and diverse terrain in view mean that 1 Peter cannot be interpreted against the backdrop of a specific city, as is so standardly done with 1 Corinthians, even though cities and towns are perhaps the most likely points for its distribution.[2] It is, rather, best seen as something of a circular letter, an early example of a kind of Christian encyclical (cf. Acts 15:23, Jas 1:1) standing, as Lutz Doering has shown, in the tradition of Jewish diaspora letters.[3]

1. See the important qualifications to the standard view that provinces are in view presented by Gudrun Guttenberger, *Passio Christiana: Die alltagsmartyrologische Position des Ersten Petrusbriefes*, SBS 223 (Stuttgart: Katholisches Bibelwerk, 2010), 72–77; and Lutz Doering, "Gottes Volk: Die Adressaten als 'Israel' im Ersten Petrusbrief," in *Bedrängnis und Identität: Studien zu Situation, Kommunikation und Theologie des 1. Petrusbriefes*, ed. David du Toit, BZNW 200 (Berlin: de Gruyter, 2013), 81–113, here 85–87.

2. For the argument that the addressees are most likely to be located in urban spaces, see David G. Horrell, "Aliens and Strangers? The Socioeconomic Location of the Addressees of 1 Peter," in *Engaging Economics: New Testament Scenarios and Early Christian Reception*, ed. Bruce Longenecker and Kelly Liebengood (Grand Rapids: Eerdmans, 2009), 176–202, revised and expanded in David G. Horrell, *Becoming Christian: Essays on 1 Peter and the Making of Christian Identity*, LNTS / EaChrCon 394 (London: Bloomsbury T&T Clark, 2013), 100–32, esp. 118–20; Travis B. Williams, *Persecution in 1 Peter: Differentiating and Contextualizing Early Christian Suffering*, NovTSup 145 (Leiden: Brill, 2012), 67–74.

3. Lutz Doering, "First Peter as Early Christian Diaspora Letter," in *The Catholic Epistles and Apostolic Tradition: A New Perspective on James to Jude*, ed. Karl-Wilhelm Niebuhr and Robert W. Wall (Waco, TX: Baylor University Press, 2009), 215–36, 441–57; Lutz Doering, *Ancient Jewish Letters and the Beginnings of Christian Epistolography*, WUNT 298 (Tübingen: Mohr Siebeck, 2012), 429–97.

The letter also tells us where it was written: in Babylon (5:13). There are two places called Babylon that might be in view here.[4] One, near Memphis and Heliopolis at the southern end of the Nile delta, was a small military stronghold founded, according to Josephus (*Ant.* 2.315), by Cambyses II, the Persian king who expanded the empire of Cyrus the Great into Egypt in the sixth century BCE.[5] Eusebius reports the tradition that Mark, also mentioned in 1 Pet 5:13, was the first to be sent to Egypt to preach the gospel, and the first to found churches in Alexandria (*Hist. eccl.* 2.16.1), but apart from this tenuous link there is nothing to support this Egyptian hypothesis, which has only very rarely received scholarly support.[6]

The Babylon in view is much more likely to be the Mesopotamian city on the Euphrates River, center of the ancient Babylonian empire. With the Babylonian conquest of Judah and the surrounding regions at the beginning of the sixth century BCE, there were several deportations of Jews to Babylon. Jerusalem itself was sacked and its temple destroyed in 587 BCE (cf., e.g., 2 Kgs 24:10–25:12; Jer 52:3–16; Josephus, *Ant.* 10.144–50).[7] A Jewish presence seems to have remained in Babylon even after the possibility of

---

4. W. Seufert, "Der Abfassungsort des ersten Petrusbriefes," *ZWT* 28 (1885): 146–56, here 148, also notes a third possible "Babylon": new-Babylon/Seleucia on the Tigris. On Seleucia, see below; the decisive objections against Mesopotamian Babylon as 1 Peter's place of origin largely apply to Seleucia too.

5. Josephus is describing the route of the Hebrews' exodus, and reports that "they took the road for Letopolis, at that time desert, afterwards the site of Babylon, founded by Cambyses when he subjugated Egypt" (*Ant.* 2.315 [Thackeray, LCL]). Diodorus Siculus (1.56.3) reports its origins by Babylonian captive laborers who rebelled against the ruler of Egypt, were granted an amnesty and established this colony. Strabo (*Geogr.* 17.1.30) provides a compatible, but much briefer, report of its origin, and adds that in his time it was the base for three legions guarding Egypt. Cf. John H. Elliott, *1 Peter: A New Translation with Introduction and Commentary*, AB 37B (New York: Doubleday, 2000), 883.

6. G. T. Manley, "Babylon on the Nile," *EvQ* 16 (1944): 138–46. Manley notes the evidence for the existence of such a Babylon (138–39), and argues that a Jewish colony was present there (139–40). His case for the "possibility" of 1 Peter's being written there, however, is based partly on assuming both the historicity of the flight of Jesus's family to Egypt (Matt 2:13–14) and the authenticity of 1 Peter, and partly on arguments against either Rome or Babylon on the Euphrates as likely settings (141–43). The tradition linking Mark with Alexandria (143) then becomes the crucial piece of positive evidence, along with the dogmatic preference that this solution is in no way "inconsistent with Scripture" (144).

7. For a recent historical overview, see Mario Liverani, *Israel's History and the History of Israel*, trans. Chiara Peri and Philip R. Davies, Bible World (London: Equinox, 2005), 183–99; also J. Alberto Soggin, *An Introduction to the History of Israel and Judah*, 3rd ed. (London: SCM, 1999), 259–87.

return from exile under the Persian ruler Cyrus the Great (cf. Philo, *Leg.* 216, 282; Josephus, *Ant.* 15.14).[8] By the first century CE, though, many may have departed (cf. Josephus, *Ant.* 18.310–79).[9] The city was reputedly virtually desolate in the early second century CE when Trajan visited it (Dio Cassius, *Hist. Rom.* 68.30.1), though the reports may be exaggerated and somewhat open to question. Strabo (*Geogr.* 16.1.5, 16) reports that Seleucia had become the major royal and urban center, while Babylon itself was largely deserted (cf. also Pliny, *Nat.* 6.30.121–123).[10]

The later importance of Babylonia as a center for Jewish life and literary production indicates that it once again became—and perhaps had always remained—a significant location for the Jewish community.[11] Yet we have no direct evidence, aside from this verse, to link Peter or this letter with Babylon (Acts 12:17 invites consideration, but is unspecific).[12] Moreover, the characteristics of the letter itself, together with other evidence we shall consider below, point to its origins in the regions north and west of Judea, in part contiguous with the scope of the Pauline mission, where Greek was the lingua franca and Rome the imperial power. Aside from its composition in Greek, the letter shows close similarities at various points with Paul's letters, as well as other early Christian traditions and writings in Greek,[13] and reflects the tensions inherent in negotiating Christian existence under the imperial structures of Roman governance, not least the name "Christian" (Χριστιανός), clearly a Latinism (2:13–17; cf. Rom 13:1–7).[14] The idea of

8. For discussion of both "returnees" and "remainees," see Liverani, *Israel's History*, 250–91.

9. Josephus here reports their departure for Seleucia, on the Tigris (*Ant.* 18.372), and thence, after a massacre of many, to Nearda and Nisibis (*Ant.* 18.379). Cf. also Manley, "Babylon," 143.

10. Cf. Elliott, *1 Peter*, 882.

11. See further Jacob Neusner, *A History of the Jews in Babylonia. I. The Parthian Period*, StPB 9 (Leiden: Brill, 1969).

12. Elliott, *1 Peter*, 882, puts it bluntly: "There is no evidence of any connection of Peter, Silvanus, or Mark with this Mesopotamian region." According to Seufert, "Abfassungsort," 149, Peter is not linked with Babylon in early Christian literature until the sixth century.

13. On these literary connections, see further David G. Horrell, "The Product of a Petrine Circle? A Reassessment of the Origin and Character of 1 Peter," *JSNT* 86 (2002): 29–60; Horrell, *Becoming Christian*, 7–44, esp. 12–28.

14. See further David G. Horrell, "The Label Χριστιανός: 1 Pet 4.16 and the Formation of Christian Identity," *JBL* 126 (2007): 361–81, revised and expanded in *Becoming Christian*, 164–210; David G. Horrell, "'Honour Everyone . . . ' (1 Pet. 2.17): The Social Strategy of 1 Peter and Its Significance for the Development of Christianity," in *To Set at Liberty: Essays on Early Christianity and Its Social World in Honor of John H. Elliott*, ed. Stephen K. Black (Sheffield: Sheffield Phoenix, 2014), 192–210.

the letter's origins in Babylon itself was supported by early Reformers such as Calvin, though this was clearly motivated by their opposition to Rome, whose ecclesial authority rested on the tradition of Peter's role as first bishop there.[15] Some older commentators have also taken this view,[16] but it is, as far as I know, very widely rejected in more recent commentaries.

The main alternative, favored by the majority of recent commentators, is to understand Babylon as a reference to Rome, an interpretation that dates back to the second century (and is later reflected in some minuscule manuscripts, which read "Rome" instead of "Babylon" [1611, 1890, 2138]).[17] Eusebius records Papias's report that Peter composed his first epistle "in Rome itself, which they say that he himself indicates, referring to the city metaphorically as Babylon (ἡ πόλις τροπικώτερον Βαβυλών)" (*Hist. eccl.* 2.15.2 [Lake, LCL]). There are various reasons to associate the letter with Rome.

1. Early Christian tradition locates Peter in Rome at the time of his death (and possibly once before, in the time of Claudius, though this earlier visit is much less securely attested).[18] The veracity of these traditions has certainly

15. E.g., John Calvin, *The Epistle of Paul the Apostle to the Hebrews and the First and Second Epistles of St. Peter*, Calvin's Commentaries (Edinburgh & London: Oliver & Boyd, 1963 [1551]), 228: "As they have rashly believed what they have said of the Roman episcopate of Peter without any likelihood in the conjecture, this allegorical figment ['that Rome is here allegorically called Babylon'] ought to be disregarded." Calvin also notes that Peter is likely to have traveled to where most Jews resided and that many were in Babylon and the surrounding areas.

16. Among German commentators, see Johannes E. Huther and Ernst Kühl, *Kritisch-exegetisches Handbuch über den 1. Brief des Petrus, den Brief des Judas, und den 2. Brief des Petrus*, 5th ed., KEK 12 (Göttingen: Vandenhoeck & Ruprecht, 1887), 64; Ernst Kühl, *Die Briefe Petri und Judae*, 6th ed., KEK 12 (Göttingen: Vandenhoeck & Ruprecht, 1897), 60; Bernhard Weiss, *A Commentary on the New Testament* (New York: Funk & Wagnalls, 1906), 4:297; Adolf Schlatter, *Die Briefe an die Thessalonicher und Philipper. Die Briefe des Petrus und Judas ausgelegt für Bibelleser*, ENT 12 (Calw & Stuttgart: Vereinsbuchhandlung, 1910), 140, 227. Among English-language commentaries, see, e.g., Henry Alford, *Epistle to the Hebrews: The Catholic Epistles of St. James and St. Peter: The Epistles of St. John and St. Jude: and the Revelation*, vol. 4 of *The Greek Testament* (Boston: Lee & Shepard, 1878), 128–31; Michael Ferrebee Sadler, *The General Epistles of SS. James, Peter, John, and Jude* (London: George Bell & Sons, 1891), xx, 148.

17. Representative examples include Elliott, *1 Peter*, 131–34; Reinhard Feldmeier, *The First Letter of Peter: A Commentary on the Greek Text* (Waco, TX: Baylor University Press, 2008), 40–42; Jacques Schlosser, *La première épître de Pierre*, CBNT 21 (Paris: Cerf, 2011), 38.

18. For Peter's death in Rome, see *1 Clem* 5.4; *Hist. eccl.* 2.25.5–6; 3.1.2 (citing Origen). See further Elliott, *1 Peter*, 885–86; Richard J. Bauckham, "The Martyrdom of Peter in Early Christian Literature," *ANRW* 2.26.1:539–95. For the tradition of Peter's visit in the time of

been contested, and it is difficult to separate legend from history, but there is no dissonance within the early sources themselves concerning the place of Peter's demise.[19]

2. Early Christian tradition also links Mark, mentioned in 1 Pet 5:13, with Rome. Papias famously describes Mark as Peter's "interpreter," who recorded Peter's memories in his Gospel (*Hist. eccl.* 3.39.15), and locates them both in Rome. He notes the reference to Mark in 1 Peter and, as we have seen, interprets Babylon as a reference to Rome (*Hist. eccl.* 2.15.2).

3. There are close affinities between 1 Peter and other documents linked with Rome, notably Paul's letter to the Romans and *1 Clement*, sent from Rome to Corinth around the end of the first century. Moreover, 1 Peter may represent the first instance of Rome, as a center of ecclesial authority, sending letters to other Christian communities, a practice to which both Hermas and Ignatius allude (Herm. Vis. 2.4.3 [8.3]; Ign. *Rom.* 3.1).

4. Finally, the use of the term Babylon to refer to Rome is well established in Jewish and Christian literature after 70 CE.[20] The use of the designation to signal Rome would, then, be entirely unsurprising in a Christian document from this period. It is unlikely that such a designation is intended as a cryptic code, deliberately concealing the reference to Rome, since it seems improbable that a document such as 1 Peter would need to veil its location in this way.[21]

All this gives good reason to place 1 Peter in Rome, but there are also reasons to be cautious. Traditions about Peter's travels and death link him with Rome, but these traditions are difficult to confirm. Moreover, they may at times contain the legendary accretion of supposed connections to Rome, reflecting the growing importance of that urban center for early Christianity

---

Claudius, possibly hinted at in Acts 12:17, see Eusebius, *Hist. eccl.* 2.14.6, 2.17.1; Jerome, *Vir. ill.* 1.1. Eckhard J. Schnabel, *Early Christian Mission* (Downers Grove, IL: InterVarsity Press / Leicester: Apollos, 2004), 2:721-27, after an extensive discussion, finds the evidence insufficient for any confident conclusions about Peter's supposed earlier visit to Rome.

19. See further Markus Bockmuehl, "Peter's Death in Rome? Back to Front and Upside Down," *SJT* 60 (2007): 1-23.

20. E.g., 4 Ezra 3.1, 28; 6 Ezra 15.43-63; Rev 17:5; 18:2, 10, 21; Sib. Or. 5.143, 5.159; 2 Bar. 8.5, 80.4 (in 2 Baruch the narrative of Babylon's destruction of the temple is used to lament Israel's fate post 70 CE). See discussion and further references in Claus-Hunno Hunzinger, "Babylon als Deckname für Rom und die Datierung des 1. Petrusbriefes," in *Gottes Wort und Gottes Land*, ed. Henning Graf Reventlow (Hertzberg: Vandenhoeck & Ruprecht, 1965), 67-77; Elliott, *1 Peter*, 137.

21. Cf. Leonhard Goppelt, *A Commentary on I Peter* (Grand Rapids: Eerdmans, 1993), 375; Elliott, *1 Peter*, 132.

and the importance too of the claims about the deaths of Peter and Paul in the city.[22] First Peter 5:13, with its linking of Peter with Mark (and Silvanus) and with Rome (assuming this understanding of "Babylon"), may even have been a stimulus to the growth of these traditions.[23] Furthermore, if 1 Peter was not actually written by Peter himself, its depiction as a letter written from Rome—encapsulated in the symbolic use of Babylon—may, as Norbert Brox points out, be part of the literary fiction of the letter rather than an indication as to its actual, historical place of origin.[24] Some scholars have therefore suggested that the letter may have originated somewhere in Asia Minor, in the areas to which it is addressed, rather than in Rome.[25] On this hypothesis, it would be a letter that *presents itself* as written by the apostle Peter from the ecclesial center of Rome, but would actually have emerged as a pseudonymous writing in Asia Minor.

Where then does all this leave us? One thing we must acknowledge is that, as in the case of many other New Testament writings, we can hardly be sure where 1 Peter was actually written. Even if plenty of evidence points to Rome, it is difficult to separate evidence that indicates a genuine historical origin in Rome from that which represents an association of the letter (and its author) with Rome. Also notable is that the explicit naming of place in 1 Peter (i.e., Babylon) is, as has long been recognized, a designation that conveys a sense of the character and significance of the implied place of the letter's origin, which is not literally Babylon. Indeed, while it is hard to be certain where the letter actually originated, we can more confidently say that it is a letter that depicts itself as written from Rome and identifies

22. Likewise, some of the letters attributed to Paul—Philemon, Colossians, 2 Timothy—are linked with Rome (as shown by the *subscriptiones* in NA27) due to convictions about the location of Paul's imprisonment and execution but may or may not have actually been written there.

23. Philipp Vielhauer, *Geschichte der urchristlichen Literatur: Einleitung in das Neue Testament, die Apokryphen und die Apostolischen Väter* (Berlin: de Gruyter, 1975), 260–61, for example, thinks that Papias's connection between Peter and Mark is derived from 1 Pet 5:13.

24. Norbert Brox, "Zur pseudepigraphischen Rahmung des ersten Petrusbriefes," *BZ* 19 (1975): 78–96, here 95; Norbert Brox, *Der erste Petrusbrief*, 3rd ed., EKKNT 21 (Zürich: Benziger / Neukirchener Verlag: Neukirchen-Vluyn, 1979), 42–43: "Vorsichtig kann man dann nur sagen, daß der 1Petr in Rom geschrieben sein will." Brox remains cautious about whether the place of origin is Asia Minor or Rome.

25. E.g., Hunzinger, "Babylon," 77; Jens Herzer, *Petrus oder Paulus? Studien über das Verhältnis des Ersten Petrusbriefes zur paulinischen Tradition*, WUNT 103 (Tübingen: Mohr Siebeck, 1998), 264–66; Paul A. Holloway, *Coping with Prejudice: 1 Peter in Social-Psychological Perspective*, WUNT 244 (Tübingen: Mohr Siebeck, 2009), 16–17.

Rome as Babylon. In this depiction we see something of how this author perceives Rome. This suggests, furthermore, that we may gain more insight into the significance of "place" in the letter if we focus our attention not on the question about whether the author was actually here or there, but rather on the significance of this kind of symbolic construction of space. In order to pursue such questions further, I turn next to some influential theorizing of the concept of space—theorizing that has recently begun to be taken up in the field of early Christian studies.[26]

2. Theorizing Space

An influential stimulus for rethinking notions of space is the complex and difficult work of the French philosopher Henri Lefebvre, in *The Production of Space,* which has been taken up in different ways in the work of the human geographers David Harvey and Edward Soja.[27] Their work is rich and detailed, and engages, from a critical and radical postmodern perspective, with diverse facets of contemporary capitalism and urbanism. Indeed, one thing that unites these three thinkers is their location broadly on the radical left. Due both to constraints of time and space (!) and also to the very different focus of this paper, I want to take from their work just two key points that offer a fresh orientation to the study of space.

The starting point is the concern to challenge the commonsense perception, based in Newtonian science and Cartesian philosophy, that space, like time, is simply there, a given, an empty container with fixed parameters within which human action takes place. The opening sentence of Lefebvre's *Production of Space,* for example, begins: "Not so many years ago, the word 'space' had a strictly geometrical meaning: the idea it evoked was simply that of an empty area."[28] By contrast, these theorists insist, space is produced

26. For a recent overview, see Eric C. Stewart, "New Testament Space/Spatiality," *BTB* 42 (2012): 139–50, esp. 145–47 on works in New Testament studies.

27. Henri Lefebvre, *The Production of Space,* trans. Donald Nicholson (Oxford: Blackwell, 1991); David Harvey, *The Condition of Postmodernity: An Inquiry into the Origins of Cultural Change* (Oxford: Blackwell, 1989); Edward W. Soja, *Thirdspace: Journeys to Los Angeles and Other Real-and-Imagined Places* (Oxford: Blackwell, 1996).

28. Lefebvre, *Production of Space,* 1. Cf. also Harvey, *Condition of Postmodernity,* 201–203; David Harvey, *Spaces of Hope* (Edinburgh: Edinburgh University Press, 2000), 182; Liam Kennedy, *Race and Urban Space in Contemporary American Culture,* ed. Peter Brooker, Tendencies: Identities, Texts, Cultures (Edinburgh: Edinburgh University Press,

and reproduced, constructed, shaped, represented. The same goes for time, hence the turn in social theory, such as Anthony Giddens's structuration theory, to make both time and space central to the theorizing of social reproduction and transformation: far from being merely the unalterable parameters within which human sociality takes place, time and space are bound up in the processes of social interaction.[29] As Harvey puts it,

> objective conceptions of time and space are necessarily created by the material practices of social reproduction, and to the degree that these latter vary geographically and historically, so we find that social time and social space are differently constructed. Each distinctive mode of production or social formation will, in short, embody a distinctive bundle of time and space practices and concepts.[30]

This insistence on the constructedness of space underpins a spatial turn, in which much greater attention is paid to what Soja calls "the *spatiality* of human life."[31]

A second key point, which follows from the first, is that the study of space needs to engage with various forms in which space is produced, experienced, and conceived. It will not do to think of space only as an objective, measurable, physical category. Lefebvre, Harvey, and Soja all present somewhat different threefold categorizations of spatial perspectives and practices.[32] Lefebvre's schema is adapted by Harvey in the following three categories: "material spatial practices" (the realm of "experience"), "representations of space" (the realm of "perception"), and "spaces of representation" (the realm of "imagination").[33] Soja's scheme, though also inspired by Lefebvre, is somewhat different: he speaks of "firstspace" as "focused on the 'real' material world," and "secondspace" as a "perspective that interprets

2000), 8–9; Matthew Sleeman, *Geography and the Ascension Narrative in Acts*, SNTSMS 146 (Cambridge: Cambridge University Press, 2009), 24.

29. See, e.g., Anthony Giddens, *Central Problems in Social Theory* (London: Macmillan, 1979), 198–233; Anthony Giddens, *The Constitution of Society: Outline of the Theory of Structuration* (Cambridge: Polity, 1984), 110–61. See also the discussion in Edward W. Soja, *Postmodern Geographies: The Reassertion of Space in Critical Social Theory* (London & New York: Verso, 1989), 138–56.

30. Harvey, *Condition of Postmodernity*, 204.

31. Soja, *Thirdspace*, 2 (emphasis original).

32. A concise tabular overview is provided by Sleeman, *Geography*, 43.

33. See Lefebvre, *Production of Space*, 38–39; Harvey, *Condition of Postmodernity*, 218–23, esp. table 3.1 on 220–21.

this reality through 'imagined' representations of reality."[34] "Thirdspace" is deliberately and explicitly a loosely defined category, but is intended to break down the binary dichotomy between the two first categories, between material space and imagined space, and to create new space and new possibilities for resistance—hence Soja's emblematic designation of "real-and-imagined places" (in the subtitle of the book).[35] Drawing on Lefebvre, Soja speaks of "spaces of representation"—Lefebvre's third category—as "the terrain for the generation of 'counterspaces,' spaces of resistance to the dominant order arising precisely from their subordinate, peripheral or marginalized positioning."[36] Indeed, drawing on radical thinkers such as Jacques Derrida, bell hooks, and Homi Bhabha, as well as Lefebvre, Soja stresses the ways in which thirdspace can, from the margins, challenge "all conventional modes of spatial thinking," disorientate and disrupt, and, fundamentally, offer "an alternative envisioning of spatiality."[37]

3. Re-Placing 1 Peter

What would this new theoretical orientation suggest by way of a reconsideration of the spatial location of 1 Peter? The obvious place to begin is with the issues considered above, concerning the indications in the letter regarding the place where it was written and the places to which it was sent. As we have already seen, the designation of the place of writing as Babylon is unlikely to represent direct information about the physical space of composition, "the place where I happen to be at the moment." In other words, even the traditional quest for historical information about the location of the letter's origins—with its conclusion that Babylon refers to Rome—already begins to indicate that there is more than merely physical information being conveyed.

It is highly significant that the crucial information about the origin and destination of the letter comes at the opening and closing of the letter (1:1;

34. Soja, *Thirdspace*, 6; cf. 10–11, 66–68, 74–82.

35. Cf. Soja, *Thirdspace*, 81: "*Thirdspace epistemologies* can now be briefly described as arising from the sympathetic deconstruction and heuristic reconstitution of the Firstspace-Secondspace duality, another example of what I have called thirding-as-Othering. Such thirding is designed not just to critique Firstspace and Secondspace modes of thought, but also to reinvigorate their approaches to spatial knowledge with new possibilities heretofore unthought of inside the traditional spatial disciplines" (emphasis original).

36. Soja, *Thirdspace*, 68.

37. Soja, *Thirdspace*, 163.

5:13), framing the whole composition and thus establishing a context for its interpretation.[38] We have already noted that the opening of the letter identifies its recipients as located in the Roman provinces (or province-districts) of Pontus, Galatia, Cappadocia, Asia, and Bithynia. But more crucial than this is the bracketing of all of these provinces under the more general designation "diaspora." The letter addresses itself to the elect strangers of the diaspora (1:1)—and specifically (reading the genitives that follow as effectively epexegetical) the parts of the diaspora denoted by the provincial names that follow.

One thing this indicates is that an essentially Jewish geography is taken as primary, more definitive, as it were, than the Roman organization of space—though this latter is not denied either. The recipients *are* in the diaspora, just as they are also (specifically) in Pontus, or wherever. To see these two designations of their spatial location side-by-side should also serve to underscore the importance of Soja's call to challenge any dichotomy between real and imagined space. It is not as if the place of the readers' location is *really* Pontus, Galatia, or wherever, but is *imagined* by the author as diaspora. Rather, *diaspora* represents a construction and organization of space, reflecting its own ideological orientation, just as does the Roman provincial system, albeit that the latter is undergirded and enforced by military, economic, and political power. Indeed, one reason to deconstruct the notion of space as simply a "given," the unalterable lie of the land, as it were, is to expose the hegemonic embodiment of political and social power in such assumptions: a crucial task of political critique is to expose what is presented and assumed as "the way things are" as a particular, contingent, and contestable construal enmeshed in particular configurations of production and power.

The specific designation of the readers' location as in diaspora does this in several ways (though these are, significantly, obscured in English translations that render diaspora "scattered," as, e.g., KJV, NIV). First, it assumes and articulates an alternative geographical configuration of the world, a different spatialized narrative about center and periphery from that which places Rome at the heart of the pacified *oikoumenē*.[39] Second, this particular

---

38. David G. Horrell, "Between Conformity and Resistance: Beyond the Balch-Elliott Debate towards a Postcolonial Reading of 1 Peter," in *Reading 1 Peter with New Eyes: Methodological Reassessments of the Letter of First Peter*, ed. Robert L. Webb and Betsy Bauman-Martin, LNTS 364 (London: T&T Clark, 2007), 124; Doering, *Jewish Letters*, 444.

39. On this latter subject, see esp. Claude Nicolet, *Space, Geography, and Politics in the Early Roman Empire*, Jerome Lectures 19 (Ann Arbor, MI: University of Michigan Press, 1991 [1988]).

designation makes sense of the readers' geographical location in terms of a Jewish history of imperial subjugation and consequent exile, a point to which we shall return. Third, the location in diaspora, combined with the description of the addressees as "strangers"—or, as elsewhere in the letter, "strangers and aliens" (2:11; cf. 1:17)—dislocates them from their wider society, giving them an identity marked by estrangement and marginality. They are no longer at home in the *oikoumenē*. Their labeling as "strangers and aliens" (πάροικοι καὶ παρεπίδημοι) is unlikely, *pace* John Elliott, to indicate their sociopolitical status prior to their conversion,[40] but this does not mean that it is a merely spiritual declaration that loses any political or social edge.[41] On the contrary, the readers' designation as "the elect strangers of the diaspora" configures their current spatial location and social existence in a distinctive way.

The declaration that the letter is being sent from Babylon (5:13) further reinforces its particular spatial configuration of the world. To address readers in the diaspora from a place called Babylon, wherever the author is really located, is to evoke the story of Judah's conquest by Babylon, the destruction of the temple and deportation of (some of) the people into exile, the origins of what came to be called the diaspora. Moreover, if, as seems most likely, the author intends to point to Rome as this new Babylon, then this identification configures the current imperial geography in terms of the historic experience of Judah, indicating that Rome now serves as the imperial power that oppresses and conquers God's people, effectively exiling them from their true home. As I have elsewhere noted, the author of 1 Peter

> does not depict—nor perhaps even long for—the downfall of "Babylon" in the vivid and detailed manner of the writer of Revelation, but he says enough to show that he and John share a common story about the character and achievements of this empire, a story which reflects the experience of the colonized and enslaved, not the powerful and dominant.[42]

To call Rome Babylon gives a certain kind of meaning and significance to the space that is the city of Rome; in Harvey's terms it *represents* that space

---

40. See esp. John H. Elliott, *A Home for the Homeless: A Social-Scientific Criticism of 1 Peter, Its Situation and Strategy*, 2nd ed. (Minneapolis: Fortress, 1990), 21–58; Elliott, *1 Peter*, 94.

41. See the discussion in Horrell, *Becoming Christian*, 114–20.

42. Horrell, "Between Conformity and Resistance," 126; Horrell, *Becoming Christian*, 225.

in a particular way, a way that construes its role and impact in a certain way—and a way that contrasts with the Romans' own celebration of their achievements, iconically in the *Res Gestae* of Augustus, as the establishment of peace.[43]

This kind of perspective on what Wei Hsien Wan calls the "spatial imagination"[44] of the author of 1 Peter also highlights how the questions we began with about the actual, physical location of the author—and the physical character of that space—might not be the most illuminating questions to pose, even assuming they can be answered. To illustrate, if a contemporary poet, say, of Caribbean origin, were writing about the experience of diasporic existence in London, how much would it illuminate the poetry to examine maps of the street layout in London during the period of the poem's composition? Much more important are the *perception* and experience of London, the way it feels as lived space and the way one gives meaning to that space. Moreover, in that sense it would not matter if one had written the poem in London, or in the Lake District, or even in Kingston, Jamaica; it is the experience and representation of space that is crucial to understanding the poem, more than its physical place of origin. Similarly, we arguably gain more insight into the character and meaning of 1 Peter when we explore the significance of the author's representational geography—the labeling of his location as Babylon and his addressees as in the diaspora—than when we debate whether he was actually in Rome or in Asia Minor, significant though such debates remain.

In an earlier outline of a postcolonial reading of 1 Peter, published in 2007, I suggested, again via an analysis of the framing of the letter, that the author of 1 Peter "invites its readers" into a "narrative of identity . . . which constructs a form of postcolonial awareness, which challenges positive acceptance or acquiescence and replaces it with a sense of dislocation and distance."[45] What I did not see then was what Wan's work in particular brings to light, namely that this narrative of identity also has spatial dimensions, or, put differently, entails a particular spatial configuration of the world and of the readers' place within it. In that earlier essay I also suggested that the positive counterpart to the dislocation expressed in the identification of the addressees as aliens and strangers in the diaspora

43. See further Nicolet, *Space*, 15–27.
44. See the next chapter in this volume, part of a wider doctoral research project on constructions of space and time in the Roman imperial cults in Asia Minor and 1 Peter.
45. Horrell, "Between Conformity and Resistance," 128; *Becoming Christian*, 227.

came in the author's bestowal of a new identity as God's chosen, elect people, a central theme in the opening half of the letter, and especially in 2:4–10.[46] Does this positive construction of identity also have spatial dimensions?

As Wan shows in the following chapter, the letter can indeed be seen to offer a positive spatial construction, juxtaposed with the spatial construction of Rome/Babylon and diaspora. One of the central images in the opening of that crucial passage (2:4–5) is of the letter's addressees as "living stones," being built into a "spiritual house" with Christ as "cornerstone." Since this spiritual house is one where sacrifices are offered by a priesthood, it is best, again *pace* Elliott,[47] to view this house as essentially a temple.[48] It is, I think, important not to treat this as merely a spiritual metaphor—or at least, to ensure that any use of such terms does not dissolve the social and political implications of this construction. Roman imperial temples dominated the urban spaces in which they were constructed, reconfiguring that space to reflect the ideology and reality of Rome's dominance.[49] Yet, according to the author of 1 Peter, the communities of believers in Christ, spread out across the land, are connected together as constituent parts of a different temple, one in which the virtues of their God are proclaimed to the world (2:9). In Soja's terms they constitute a kind of thirdspace, a construction of the imagination which forms a space of resistance to the dominant socio-political order, a positive counterpart to their "worldly" existence as dislocated strangers. Moreover, as Wan stresses, this community does have an irreducibly material existence, in the bodies of the believers who comprise the living stones.

---

46. Horrell, "Between Conformity and Resistance," 129–33; *Becoming Christian*, 227–29.

47. John H. Elliott, *The Elect and the Holy: An Exegetical Examination of 1 Peter 2:4–10 and the Phrase* basileion hierateuma, NovTSup 12 (Leiden: Brill, 1966), 156–59.

48. As Ramsay Michaels sagely remarks, "it is difficult to imagine a house intended for priesthood as being anything other than a temple of some sort" (J. Ramsey Michaels, *1 Peter*, WBC 49 [Waco, TX: Word, 1988], 100). See the more detailed arguments on this point in Wan's chapter below.

49. See Wei Hsien Wan's chapter below, and his doctoral thesis, "Reconfiguring the Universe: The Contest for Time and Space in the Roman Imperial Cults and 1 Peter" (PhD diss., University of Exeter, 2016); further Simon R. F. Price, *Rituals and Power: The Roman Imperial Cult in Asia Minor* (Cambridge: Cambridge University Press, 1984), esp. 133–46; Stephen Mitchell, *The Celts and the Impact of Roman Rule,* vol. 1 of *Anatolia: Land, Men, and Gods in Asia Minor* (Oxford: Clarendon, 1993), 100–17.

4. Constructions of Space and Forms of Resistance

Finally, we may ask how this approach to the spatial constructions of 1 Peter might inform our reflections on the letter's stance toward the Roman Empire. In recent years, there has been an energetic discussion about New Testament texts and their relationship to the Empire, with many readings, not least of Paul's letters, proposing that there is a much more anti-imperial stance than has generally been perceived.[50] First Peter has not received much attention in this regard, and in modern scholarship the established view is that it does not show any sign of conflict with, or opposition to, Rome. For example, Steven Bechtler comments on 2:13–17 that "[h]ere the letter enjoins fear of God and honor of the emperor in a single breath and commands subjection to the emperor as ὑπερέχων. Nor does 1 Peter elsewhere exhibit the kind of hostility to, or at least wariness of, Rome to be expected in a document dealing with imperial persecution."[51] Similarly, Elliott insists that "1 Peter engages in no negative critique of Rome and nowhere associates Roman officials with harassment of the believers."[52] In a stimulating attempt to consider 1 Peter's stance toward the Roman imperial cults, Warren Carter argues that the author of 1 Peter urges his readers to "go all the way" in accommodating to the demands of the cult, keeping their allegiance to Christ a matter of private, inward conviction (cf. 3:15).[53] I have previously sought to challenge this consensus by arguing that 1 Peter does indeed display signs of a clear but measured resistance—what I called a "polite resistance"—to the demands of Rome, and that the wording of passages such as 2:17 only makes sense in the setting of a nuanced negotiation of such a stance.[54]

50. Emblematic of this interest and perspective are Richard A. Horsley, ed., *Paul and Empire: Religion and Power in Roman Imperial Society* (Harrisburg, PA: Trinity Press International, 1997); Richard A. Horsley, ed., *Paul and Politics: Ekklesia, Israel, Imperium, Interpretation* (Harrisburg, PA: Trinity Press International, 2000); Richard A. Horsley, ed., *Paul and the Roman Imperial Order* (Harrisburg, PA: Trinity Press International, 2004); Warren Carter, *Matthew and Empire: Initial Explorations* (Harrisburg, PA: Trinity Press International, 2001); Warren Carter, *The Roman Empire and the New Testament: An Essential Guide* (Nashville: Abingdon, 2006).

51. Steven R. Bechtler, *Following in His Steps: Suffering, Community, and Christology in 1 Peter*, SBLDS 162 (Atlanta: Scholars, 1998), 50.

52. Elliott, *1 Peter*, 132.

53. Warren Carter, "Going All the Way? Honoring the Emperor and Sacrificing Wives and Slaves in 1 Peter 2.13–3.6," in *A Feminist Companion to the Catholic Epistles*, ed. Amy-Jill Levine and Maria Mayo Robbins (London: T&T Clark, 2004), 14–33.

54. Horrell, "Between Conformity and Resistance"; Horrell, *Becoming Christian,*

Considering the spatial construction of the letter offers another perspective on this issue. First Peter does not oppose or resist the Empire in the sense of rejecting its validity or refusing the structures of its governing rule (2:13–17). There is no open hostility or colorful denunciation of the Empire's rule nor graphic vision of its fiery demise (contrast Rev 13:1–18, 18:1–24). But what there is is an alternative geography, a spatial construction of the world that—without rejecting the imperial geography of provincial space—organizes it around the poles of Babylon and diaspora, thereby invoking a Jewish narrative of existence under empire, and constructs the trans-provincial community of believers in Christ as a kind of thirdspace, a real-and-imagined place that forms the positive location of life and hope. This alternative configuration of space, this form of representation and imagination, is, as Soja stresses, politically significant as a site of resistance, resistance to the dominant productions and constructions of space that structure human lives in particular ways. Outlining a different geography, a different representation of the world, may not sound revolutionary, but insofar as it stands against the ruling geographical configuration of the world it is resistance nonetheless, an insistence that this group of people will map their living otherwise, structure their existence in differently configured space, with a different central focus and goal for their lives.[55]

211–38; Horrell, "Honour Everyone." A broadly comparable perspective (on "differentiated resistance" in 1 Peter) is developed in Wai Lan Joyce Sun, "This Is True Grace of God: The Shaping of Social Behavioural Instructions by Theology in 1 Peter" (PhD diss., University of Edinburgh, 2012).

55. I would like to thank Wei Hsien Wan for comments on a draft of this essay and many discussions of its topic, and to acknowledge the stimulus of his own research on the ideas in this paper. We have coordinated our two contributions here, hoping that they complement one another and build a coherent overall perspective.

Repairing Social Vertigo

Spatial Production and Belonging in 1 Peter

Wei Hsien Wan

In his most recent collection of poems, *The Cartographer Tries to Map a Way to Zion*, Kei Miller stages an intriguing conflict between two voices who represent two different systems of knowledge, two ways of understanding space, place, and territory. The figure known as "the cartographer" takes an empirical approach to space, seeking to capture it in lines and measurements in order to comprehend it. His work lies at the service of dispassionate, objective knowledge:

> What I do is science. I show
> the earth as it is, without bias.
> I never fall in love. I never get involved
> with the muddy affairs of land.
>
> Too much passion unsteadies the hand.
> I aim to show the full
> of a place in just a glance.[1]

He is challenged, however, by "the rastaman," who resides in the very land the cartographer attempts to map. The rastaman rejects the cartographer's technical methods as reductionistic, and advocates instead the path of intimate experience and memory:

---

1. Kei Miller, *The Cartographer Tries to Map a Way to Zion* (Manchester: Carcanet, 2014), 18.

His [The cartographer's] work is to make thin and crushable
all that is big and as real as ourselves; is to make flat
all that is high and rolling; is to make invisible and wutliss
plenty things that poor people cyaa do without—like board
houses, and the corner shop from which Miss Katie sell
her famous peanut porridge.[2]

Throughout Miller's book, the cartographer and the rastaman engage in a
back-and-forth, each contesting the other's approach to space and knowledge of places.

Since what has been termed "the spatial turn" in the social sciences and
humanities, it is no longer possible to speak of space simply as an objective
grid of reality that we can measure and thus pin down, or a bounded area in
which things happen. The rastaman's critique of the cartographer's approach
finds theoretical expression in the work of scholars such as Henri Lefebvre,
Edward Soja, Doreen Massey, and David Harvey, among others.[3] These
thinkers have challenged what had been, for so long, taken for granted—
namely, the objective facticity and "given-ness" of space as something that
"simply is." They have instead underscored its constructed and symbolic
nature, drawing our attention to the diverse ways in which space is experienced, conceived, and imagined in human practice. It can no longer be
thought of as the passive stage on which our activities take place; rather,
it is transformed into a dynamic element of social life itself—caught up in,
forming, and being formed by our interactions with one another.

The cumulative force of this new phase of investigation, of analyzing
space, has not only compelled various disciplines to leave behind the notion
of space as a fixed or stable "container" in favor of far more fluid, dynamic
views, but has also given rise to multiple interrogations of the "hidden ter-

2. Miller, *Cartographer*, 17.

3. See especially Henri Lefebvre, *The Production of Space*, trans. Donald Nicholson-
Smith (Oxford: Blackwell, 1991); Doreen B. Massey, *For Space* (London: Sage, 2005);
Edward W. Soja, *Thirdspace: Journeys to Los Angeles and Other Real-and-Imagined Places*
(Oxford: Blackwell, 1996); David Harvey, *The Condition of Postmodernity: An Enquiry
into the Origins of Cultural Change* (Oxford: Blackwell, 1989). Useful summaries of the
contributions of these and other thinkers to the renewed study of spatiality are given in
Rob Kitchin and Phil Hubbard, eds., *Key Thinkers on Space and Place*, 2nd ed. (London:
Sage, 2010). For a brief but very helpful survey of the historical neglect of geography, the
spatial turn, and its relevance for Biblical Studies, see Matthew Sleeman, *Geography and
the Ascension Narrative in Acts*, SNTSMS 146 (Cambridge: Cambridge University Press,
2009), 22–56.

rains of ambiguity, contradiction, and struggle"[4] that in fact operate beneath what were once thought to be commonsensical or "plain" understandings of space. Space emerges as an arena of contest for different ways of thinking and living, shaped and reshaped both by power and responses to power within the complex web of human relations.

These contests of spatial imagination are of pivotal importance because symbolic orderings of space form an essential part of how we interpret the world and move in that world. The French anthropologist Pierre Bourdieu argues that the ways in which a particular group of people thinks of space "structures not only the group's representation of the world but the group itself, which orders itself in accordance with this representation."[5] Constructions of space (as well as time) are thus not merely inert ways of thinking about the world, but are in fact embedded in specific patterns of behavior and practices and, as such, constitutive of a community's social and political life.

The implications of these developments for the study of Christian origins are not difficult to see, concerned as the discipline is with the beliefs and practices of the earliest Christian communities. Indeed, several recent studies have begun to approach New Testament texts with keen attention to spatial questions.[6] In conjunction with its predecessors in this regard, the present essay brings the renewed perspectives on space to 1 Peter. In what follows, I will consider one aspect of the letter's spatial imagination, placing it alongside a contemporaneous but far more dominant form of spatial representation—that of first-century Roman imperialism. To allow for a comparative study, I take 1 Peter as an example of an early Christian approach to space (though it was likely one among several), and the practices of the imperial cults as representative of the spatial agenda of Rome. In particular, I argue that the author of 1 Peter scrambled the Roman construction of space to create room for a new way of social—and spatial—belonging that lay at the heart of emerging Christianity.

---

4. Harvey, *Condition*, 205.

5. Pierre Bourdieu, *Outline of a Theory of Practice*, trans. Richard Nice, Cambridge Studies in Social Anthropology 16 (Cambridge: Cambridge University Press, 1977), 163. Bourdieu is actually speaking here of time as well as space.

6. For a representative list, see Harry O. Maier, "From Material Place to Imagined Space: Emergent Christian Community as Thirdspace in the Shepherd of Hermas," in *Early Christian Communities between Ideal and Reality*, ed. Mark Grundeken and Joseph Verheyden, WUNT 342 (Tübingen: Mohr Siebeck, 2015), 144 n. 1.

1. The Imperial Cults and Imperial Reconfigurations of Space

a. Transformations in the Augustan Era and After

By the time of the spread of Christianity in the first century CE, the cultic veneration of rulers was already a well-established practice among the Hellenized communities of Asia Minor. Ruler cults in the region date to as early as the fifth century BCE.[7] Alexander the Great already received cultic veneration in his lifetime, as did his Seleucid successor Antiochus III and his queen Laodice.[8] As Roman presence in the Greek world increased throughout the second century BCE, there emerged corresponding cults to Roman power. At Chios, for example, we find a cult to the goddess Roma, marked by a procession, sacrifice and games. Elsewhere in the Hellenistic world there emerged cults collectively dedicated to "the Hearth of the Romans," "the People of the Romans," "the universal Roman benefactors," and even individual Roman officials.[9]

The rule of Augustus marked a watershed moment not only for the Roman Empire but also the evolution of Anatolian ruler cults. By 29 BCE, he had already granted sanctuaries to Roma and Julius Caesar at Nicaea and Ephesus, and was himself the recipient of divine honors at Pergamum and Nicomedia.[10] In 27 BCE, upon his taking the name *Sebastos* (the Greek equivalent of "Augustus"), the number of temples and sacrifices in his honor escalated, accompanied by a proliferation of cults to his successors and other members of the imperial family in subsequent years. Within only one year after Augustus took the title *Sebastos* in 27 BCE, as the epigraphic evidence shows, there was erected in Ephesus a statue of the *Sebastos* along with a sacred precinct (*temenos*), and the city of Philadelphia in Lydia had already consecrated a priest dedicated to the cult of Roma and Augustus.[11] A contemporary of Augustus, Nicolaus of Damascus, reporting from the eastern part of the empire, could thus say:

---

7. S. R. F. Price, *Rituals and Power: The Roman Imperial Cult in Asia Minor* (Cambridge: Cambridge University Press, 1984), 26.

8. Price, *Rituals and Power*, 37.

9. Price, *Rituals and Power*, 41–42.

10. Dio Cassius 51.20.6–9. For a discussion of the developments in Pergamum, see Steven J. Friesen, *Imperial Cults and the Apocalypse of John: Reading Revelation in the Ruins* (New York: Oxford University Press, 2001), 25–32.

11. Stephen Mitchell, *The Celts and the Impact of Roman Rule*, vol. 1 of *Anatolia: Land, Men, and Gods in Asia Minor* (Oxford: Clarendon, 1993), 100.

Because men call him by this name as a mark of esteem for his honor, they revere him with temples and sacrifices, organized by islands and continents, and as cities and provinces they match the greatness of his virtue and the scale of his benefactions toward them.[12]

Priests of the cult to Augustus are attested to in thirty-four cities in Asia Minor—"doubtless," Stephen Mitchell writes, "only a fraction of the original total."[13]

This spread of cultic veneration of the Roman emperor and his family inaugurated a series of crucial transformations of the urban landscape of various Anatolian cities. These transformations reflected a new imperial geography in which the known world was centered around Rome, as can be evidenced in several architectural practices in urban Anatolia.

Consistently, imperial temples and sanctuaries were built in the most prominent and prestigious locations in a city, thus emphasizing the looming and pervasive presence of Rome over the lives of the city's inhabitants and those of its dependents. At Eresos, a benefactor built an imperial temple and sanctuary (*naos*) in the most prominent part of the city's main square and another in the commercial harbor "so that no place should lack mark of his [the benefactor's] goodwill and piety toward the god [Augustus]."[14] Likewise, a temple to the *Theoi Soteres Sebastoi* at Sidyma, dating to the Claudian era, was built in the center, and in Cestrus two imperial temples faced each other across the main square.[15] The *Caesareum* at Laertes faced the city's main gates,[16] and in Stratonicea, the temple to the *Sebastoi Autokratores* was given prominence on a terrace above the local theater.[17]

In some instances, centrality of location could not be accomplished due to existing structures. The solution was to achieve visibility by other means. This was the case with Iotape, where the city center was already crammed into one arm of the bay. The Trajanic temple was, consequently, built on the opposite arm of the bay, so that it remained clearly visible from the city center.[18] Visibility also appeared to be a key criterion in Pergamum, where a massive substructure had to be engineered so that a temple jointly

12. FGrh 90 F. 125.1, quoted and translated in Mitchell, *Anatolia*, 1:100.
13. Mitchell, *Anatolia*, 1:100.
14. Price, *Rituals and Power*, 137, 249.
15. Price, *Rituals and Power*, 137, 263, 273.
16. Price, *Rituals and Power*, 137, 273.
17. Price, *Rituals and Power*, 137, 262.
18. Price, *Rituals and Power*, 137, 273.

consecrated to Trajan and Zeus Philios could occupy the highest point of the acropolis. (Although the location of the Pergamene provincial temple to Roma and Augustus, the first of its kind in the province of Asia, has not been determined, it may well have been located in the city center.[19]) The imperial temple of Ankara achieved visual prominence via its location on a hill on the west bank of the river that divided the Roman city. It thus towered over buildings such as the bath-gymnasium complex and the theater, communicating imperial protection over the city's civic life.[20] The Ephesian temple to the Sebastoi was likewise built to visually impress. Built on an artificially terraced slope of Mount Koressos, it had for its facade a looming three–story stoa that overlooked the open plaza, which in turn allowed the viewer to experience the full impact of the facade. In clear view of anyone approaching it from the city below, this imposing structure vividly communicated to the people of Ephesus the elevated, all-embracing presence and patronage of the emperor.[21] In Pisidian Antioch, the *Augusteum* departed from the custom of east-facing sanctuaries, built to face west on the city's eastern acropolis so that its awe-inspiring facade and propylon were plainly visible to the inhabitants below.[22]

b. An Empire State of Mind: Domination and Imperial Geography

The central locations and high visibility of these imperial buildings were by no means innocent criteria. Rather, they were key elements in the visual grammar of domination conveyed by Rome to its Anatolian subjects. Mitchell rightly observes that

> imperial buildings literally took over and dominated the urban landscape, thus symbolizing unequivocally the central position that emperor worship

19. Price, *Rituals and Power*, 137, 252.
20. Mitchell, *Anatolia,* 1:105.
21. Friesen, *Imperial Cults*, 50–52.
22. Benjamin B. Rubin, "(Re)presenting Empire: The Roman Imperial Cult in Asia Minor, 31 BC–AD 68" (PhD diss., University of Michigan, 2008), 59. Rubin does note that the tradition of east-facing temples is not rigidly observed in Anatolia. He cites the examples of the imperial temples in Ankara and Aphrodisias, both of which are built to face west. The point remains that in the case of Antioch, the orientation of the temple was conditioned by the need for the magnificent facade to face the city's inhabitants rather than away from them.

occupied in city life, and the overwhelming manner in which the emperor dominated the world view of his subjects.[23]

Architecture was thus placed at the service of empire. The strategic prominence of the imperial temples revealed the centrality of the body of the emperor to Rome's construction of Anatolian space. Power radiated, as if in concentric circles, from the body of the emperor to the bodies of his kin (fictive or real) and outward, beyond the city of Rome to the empire's furthest-flung territories. Distance from the center did not dilute this imperial presence, for everywhere Caesar's subjects were tangibly reminded of his authority, celebrated in ritual and made present to them in stone—in awe-inspiring columns, facades and plazas, whether in the heart of urban spaces or from some commanding hill. "Rome" was no longer confined to the imperial city, but every territory where the emperor's presence and power could be felt.[24]

The power to regulate space is also the power to regulate the movement of bodies in that space. The construction of these infrastructures required, in the first place, mobilization of economic machinery, including but not limited to material collaboration of a local ruling elite, the commandeering of skilled workers and slave labor, the supply of materials, and provisions for workers. The actual celebration of imperial festivals in cultic sites entailed a broader program of processions, sacrifices, and athletic contests that drew people into the city from the surrounding countryside and concentrated them at the specific location of the event.[25] Plazas and porticoes dotted with imperial statues allowed people to gather in engineered spaces that communicated Roman benefaction and wove the imperial family firmly into the fabric of social life. Towering temples drew eyes to look upward and hearts to marvel at their grandeur, and the reliefs on their facades depicted Rome's unstoppable victory over her enemies. Friesen hardly exaggerates when he describes the impact of the imperial cults in terms of cosmological reconfiguration: the institutions of cult "defined how space and time were to be experienced."[26]

23. Mitchell, *Anatolia*, 1:107.
24. On the remarkable shift of cultic focus from the city of Rome to the (mobile) personage of the emperor in the Augustan era, see Eric M. Orlin, "Augustan Religion: From Locative to Utopian," in *Rome and Religion: A Cross-Disciplinary Dialogue on the Imperial Cult*, ed. Jeffrey Brodd and Jonathan L. Reed (Atlanta: SBL, 2011), 49–59.
25. For a case study of how imperial festivals impacted civic life in Asia Minor, with Oenoanda as a model, see Stephen Mitchell, "Festivals, Games, and Civic Life in Roman Asia Minor," *JRS* 80 (2012): 183–93.
26. Friesen, *Imperial Cults*, 124.

As David Harvey points out, the organization (or reorganization) of space by means of specific practices—such as we find in the imperial cults—concretely shaped relationships between people, activities, things, and concepts.[27] The spatial practices of the imperial cults materialized an ideology at the heart of imperialism that was by no means particular to Rome—an ideology in which space became a commodity at the service of empire. The spatial reconfigurations brought about by the imperial cults linked the Roman Empire's acquired territories to the imperial city in a new geography of domination. By controlling the appropriation of spaces—that is, by infusing social and political life in the provinces with symbols of imperial presence, they envisioned the known world as a satellite of peripheries centered on Rome. The Roman-occupied regions of Anatolia such as Asia were thus construed as "'provincial,' subsidiary, dependent."[28] In at least this sense Rome became, in the words of Pliny the Elder, "the parent of all lands" and "the homeland of every people in the entire world."[29] This geography not only represented space in a particular way; by determining the terms of spatial representation, the imperial geography also *produced* space—that is, it stipulated the terms in which people were to think of, move, and live in that space. In doing so, it also constructed the identities of the inhabitants of Anatolia in a particular way—as dependent subjects of an expansive and expanding empire.[30]

2. The Locus of Belonging: The "Spiritual House" (1 Peter 2:5) as Spatial Production

Amid these innovations in the spatial imagination of Roman imperialism, we have yet another way of constructing space—that of the early Christians as represented to us in 1 Peter. As David Horrell points out in the preceding essay in this volume, the deployment of the diaspora-Babylon trope in the epistle challenges Rome's imperial geography with an alternative con-

27. Harvey, *The Condition of Postmodernity*, 216.
28. Friesen, *Imperial Cults*, 125.
29. *Nat.* 3.39.
30. Since my primary focus here is on the design of spaces rather than their cultic use properly speaking, I have not addressed the significance of imperial-cultic ritual in shaping the identity of Rome's subjects. On this, see Philip A. Harland, "Imperial Cults within Local Cultural Life: Associations in Roman Asia," *Ancient History Bulletin/Zeitschrift für Alte Geschichte* 17 (2003): 85–107 esp. 105–6.

strual of spatiality—one that decenters the empire both in time and space by evoking a powerful Jewish narrative of violence, subjugation, and exile.[31] By means of a temporal as well as spatial typology, the *oikoumenē* is reimagined as "diaspora" and Rome as Babylon, the archetypal aggressor of God's elect. The social existence of Christians in Anatolia is, correspondingly, a time of exile ("the time of your exile" [ὁ τῆς παροικίας ὑμῶν χρόνος, 1:17])—one of displacement, of nonbelonging—the trauma and experience of which looms so large in the Scriptures of Israel. And so, for the Petrine author, it is as it once was: in Babylon and Rome, history finds a rhyme. Had Qoheleth read our text, he might have chimed laconically, "What has been is what will be, and what has been done is what will be done; there is nothing new under the sun" (Eccl 1:9 NRSV).

If, then, 1 Peter dislocates its readers by casting Anatolia and imperial territories as a whole as exilic or alienating space, does the letter tell its readers where they might, in fact, belong? To put this in social terms: if true Christian existence were marked by nonbelonging within society at large, could Christians find belonging anywhere at all?

a. The οἶκος πνευματικός (1 Peter 2:5) and the Petrine Spatial Imagination

The author's response to this question is, I believe, in the affirmative, and lies in another trope deployed in his text. In the catena of "stone" passages of 2:4–8, he states that Christians are "being built into a spiritual house to be a holy priesthood, to offer spiritual sacrifices acceptable to God through Jesus Christ" (2:5). Various exegetes have dedicated their energies to the range of meanings possible for the "spiritual house" (οἶκος πνευματικός) here.[32] The

31. See also his earlier essay, "Between Conformity and Resistance: Beyond the Balch-Elliott Debate towards a Postcolonial Reading of 1 Peter," in *Becoming Christian: Essays on 1 Peter and the Making of Christian Identity*, LNTS 394 (London: Bloomsbury T&T Clark, 2013), 211–38, here 224–27.

32. E.g., Francis Wright Beare, *The First Epistle of Peter: The Greek Text with Introduction and Notes*, 3rd ed. (Oxford: Blackwell, 1970), 122; J. N. D. Kelly, *A Commentary on the Epistles of Peter and of Jude*, BNTC (London: Black, 1969), 89–90; Leonhard Goppelt, *A Commentary on I Peter*, ed. Ferdinand Hahn, trans. John E. Alsup (Grand Rapids: Eerdmans, 1993), 139–141; J. Ramsey Michaels, *1 Peter*, WBC 49 (Dallas, TX: Word, 1988), 99–101; John H. Elliott, *1 Peter: A New Translation with Introduction and Commentary*, AB 37B (New York: Doubleday, 2000), 414–18; Paul J. Achtemeier, *1 Peter*, Hermeneia (Minneapolis: Fortress, 1996), 154–59; Karen H. Jobes, *1 Peter*, BECNT (Grand Rapids: Baker, 2005), 150.

apparent ambiguity arises in large part because of the interpretive options in οἶκος, a word that can refer to both a group of people (household) or a physical edifice or building. Similarly, the adjectival πνευματικός can be understood in various ways, designating that which is "spiritual" as distinguished from the physical or fleshly (ψυχικός; e.g., 1 Cor 15:44, 46), as well as that which pertains to the realm of the human spirit (e.g., 1 Cor 14:14–16) or the spirit of God (e.g., 1 Cor 2:14; 12:1; 14:1).[33] While the expression οἶκος πνευματικός is complicated by the semantic range of its components, several contextual cues serve to allow us to elucidate more precisely its meaning—or, at the very least, its range of meaning.

It is helpful to begin with the observation that this passage occurs within a series of statements regarding the readers' Christian identity: as newborn infants (2:2), a spiritual priesthood (2:5), and, famously, "a chosen race, a royal priesthood, a holy nation, God's own people" (2:9 NRSV). The words οἶκος πνευματικός thus occur within a discussion about people—specifically, believers. It is also clear that the "stones" mentioned in this passage are persons. Christ is described as "a living stone, though rejected by mortals yet chosen and precious in God's sight" (2:4)—specifically, a cornerstone (ἀκρογωνιαῖος, 2:6)—and the readers are themselves "living stones" (λίθοι ζῶντες, 2:5). If the "stones" that make up the οἶκος are people, it would seem that the *primary* sense of οἶκος πνευματικός is, correspondingly, a community of people. But is it therefore necessary to conclude that this community is, specifically, a household?

To draw such a conclusion would be hasty and would impoverish the rich dynamics of the "stone" metaphor. The repeated references to stones—five times in 2:4–8, and seven if one includes the cornerstone (ἀκρογωνιαῖος, 2:6; κεφαλὴ γωνίας, 2:7)—yield an architectural density to the passage and foreground the structural aspect of this οἶκος. This is further augmented by the verb οἰκοδομεῖσθαι, which denotes the process of construction.[34] What we have here is precisely a play on the semantic flexibility of οἶκος as mean-

---

33. For a detailed discussion of πνευματικός in 1 Peter as well as the NT in general, see Edward Gordon Selwyn, *The First Epistle of St. Peter: The Greek Text with Introduction, Notes and Essays* (London: Macmillan, 1946), 281–85.

34. Cf. Selwyn, *First Epistle*, 160; Achtemeier, *1 Peter*, 155–56, 158–59; Jobes, *1 Peter*, 150. Though it does not directly affect my argument here, οἰκοδομεῖσθε can be taken as an indicative or imperative, and in the passive or middle voice; cf. F. J. A. Hort, *The First Epistle of Peter, I.1–II.17: The Greek Text with Introductory Lecture, Commentary, and Additional Notes* (1898; repr., Eugene, OR: Wipf & Stock, 2005), 109; Mark Dubis, *1 Peter: A Handbook on the Greek Text*, BHGNT (Waco, TX: Baylor University Press, 2010), 47–48.

ing both household and building. The two senses are not mutually exclusive but rather dependent on each other.[35] As a collective, the readers' integrity as a community in Christ depends on their being fitted together like the stones that make up a single edifice: they are a building of people dependent on Christ as the cornerstone. The corporate (and corporeal) sense of οἶκος is therefore derived from its spatial sense. Any attempt to reduce it to only one of these defuses the power of its imagery and impoverishes the dimensions of the text. Furthermore, as I shall argue below, the structure signified by οἶκος in 2:5 is not just any building, but specifically a temple.

On this point, John Elliott has been famously insistent that οἶκος in 2:5 carries only the sense of "household."[36] This position stems largely from the fact that he views οἶκος here as anticipating (and thus parallel in meaning to) βασίλειον in 2:9, which he takes as a substantive, meaning "royal residence" or "house of the king."[37] Moreover, he argues, as an appositive to ἱεράτευμα ἅγιον, which follows it, οἶκος makes better sense if understood as referring to a group of people, i.e., a household of (priestly) people.[38] For him, the οἶκος πνευματικός in 2:5 is identical to the οἶκος τοῦ θεοῦ in 4:17, where it clearly refers to the Christian community as God's household, and not to any structural edifice as such.[39] Elliott therefore maintains that οἶκος in 2:5 can only refer to a group of people (Christians), and cannot carry the spatial sense of "temple."[40]

I deem this position indefensible for several reasons. To begin with, given its semantic range, there is no definitive reason to suppose that οἶκος in 2:5 merely anticipates and is parallel to βασίλειον in 2:9,[41] or even that it

---

35. For a similar position, see Jobes (*1 Peter*, 150), who extends this versatility in meaning to the use of οἶκος in 4:17.

36. John H. Elliott, *The Elect and the Holy: An Exegetical Examination of I Peter 2, 4–10 and the Phrase* Basileion Hierateuma, NovTSup 12 (Leiden: Brill, 1966), 148–198; *A Home for the Homeless: A Social-Scientific Criticism of 1 Peter, Its Situation and Strategy* (Minneapolis: Fortress, 1981), 168–170; Elliott, *1 Peter*, 414–18.

37. Elliott, *Home*, 169; Elliott, *1 Peter*, 417. On βασίλειον as "royal residence," see Elliott, *1 Peter*, 435–37.

38. Elliott, *1 Peter*, 417.

39. Elliott, *Home*, 243.

40. Elliott's dismissal of the οἶκος-as-temple view is really quite sweeping: "temple, priesthood and cult play no central role in 1 Peter" (*Home*, 242). Earlier in the same work, he insists that even ἱεράτευμα in 2:5 "has not been employed to describe the community in cultic terms" (168) despite the explicitly liturgical words that follow it, "to offer spiritual sacrifices acceptable to God" (ἀνενέγκαι πνευματικὰς θυσίας εὐπροσδέκτους [τῷ] θεῷ [NRSV]).

41. As Michaels (*1 Peter*, 100–101) and Achtemeier (*1 Peter*, 159) both point out, the relationship between 2:5 and 2:9 is not as straightforward as Elliott contends.

is used in the exact same sense as in 4:17. The immediate context of its use ought to be accorded more weight than Elliott allows. Second, while it is true that οἶκος *can* function in apposition to ἱεράτευμα which follows,[42] it is first and foremost syntactically linked to the preceding images of "living stones" and construction: "you also, like living stones, let yourselves be built into a spiritual house" (καὶ αὐτοὶ ὡς λίθοι ζῶντες οἰκοδομεῖσθε οἶκος πνευματικός [2:5 author's translation]). This safeguards the sense of οἶκος as being, at the very least, a building. Third, Elliott's reading does not sufficiently take into consideration the collective impact of the "stone" texts in 2:4-8. The scriptural texts quoted in this section—Isa 28:16, Ps 118:22, and Isa 8:14-15—are, in their original context, references not to just any building, but to a very specific material edifice: the temple in Jerusalem. Finally, the occurrence of οἶκος within a verbal constellation that includes "priesthood" and "sacrifices" (ἱεράτευμα and θυσίαι, 2:5) is laden with cultic overtones, leading the majority of interpreters to conclude, not only that the Petrine author has a physical structure in mind, but that it is a temple.[43]

That the οἶκος of 2:5 refers to a temple is reinforced by its pairing with πνευματικός. The broader context suggests that this οἶκος is πνευματικός or "spiritual" not in the sense that it is invisible or nonmaterial (no cues in the context warrant this contrast), but rather that it is "of the spirit (of God)"— that is, "caused by or filled with the (divine) spirit."[44] This sense is brought out both by the fact that (1) οἶκος πνευματικός occurs in a section dedicated to the believers' identity (cf. 2:1-10 as a whole, but especially vv. 9-10); and (2) immediately following the explication of this identity, the author urges them "to abstain from carnal desires" (ἀπέχεσθαι τῶν σαρκικῶν ἐπιθυμιῶν)

42. Although this is not necessary, since εἰς in 2:5 can also be read as purposive to yield the reading: "a spiritual house *for* (the ministry of) a holy priesthood." On this, see Hort, *First Epistle*, 109; Michaels, *1 Peter*, 100.

43. Representative are Ernest Best, *1 Peter*, NCB (London: Oliphants, 1971), 101-102; Selwyn, *First Epistle*, 159-160; Kelly, *Commentary*, 89; Goppelt, *I Peter*, 140; Achtemeier, *1 Peter*, 156. Cf. Elliott, *Home*, 241-43. Even Michaels (*1 Peter*, 100), who leans in favor of Elliott's "house" or "household" reading, concedes that "it is difficult to imagine a house intended for priesthood as being anything other than a temple of some sort." So also David G. Horrell, *The Epistles of Peter and Jude*, EC (Peterborough: Epworth, 1998), 40.

44. BDAG, 678, s.v. πνευματικός §2; Achtemeier (*1 Peter*, 155-56): "The adjective πνευματικός ('spiritual') is not so much symbolic or metaphoric as it is intended to indicate its nature [i.e., that of the 'house']: it is the place where the Spirit is to be found." Cf. Selwyn, *First Epistle*, 160, 291. Elliott agrees with taking the adjective πνευματικός in this way ("controlled and animated by God's sanctifying spirit"; *1 Peter*, 418), although, as shown above, he does not allow for the house to be a temple (cf. *Home*, 168). Elliott, *1 Peter*, 418.

that wage war against their soul (2:11), reflecting the spiritual-carnal antithesis we find elsewhere in the New Testament (e.g., John 3:5–6; 1 Cor 3:1). This assertion regarding the readers' spiritual identity develops the author's initial description of them as those who have been made holy by God's Spirit (1:2) and are called to be holy as God is holy (1:16). Not surprisingly, the author later refers to them as people on whom "the divine Spirit of glory" rests (τὸ τῆς δόξης καὶ τὸ τοῦ θεοῦ πνεῦμα, 4:14), a description again redolent of a temple (cf. Eph 2:21–22).

We may thus conclude that οἶκος πνευματικός in 2:5 means "a spiritual house" in the sense of an edifice that stands in a particular relationship to God's Spirit. It is, as Horrell posits, "a building which belongs to God and where the Spirit is to be found."[45] More specifically, as the liturgically saturated vocabulary of the verse indicates, it is a temple whose constitutive building blocks ("living stones") are "quickened and governed by the Spirit of God,"[46] with Jesus as the living cornerstone (2:7). This temple is the locus of the offering of spiritual sacrifices, since the community not only constitutes the temple itself but also the holy priesthood that serves within it (2:5, 9). In the words of Selwyn, "the house is spiritual, because it consists of spiritual persons and exists for spiritual purposes."[47]

b. Contesting Spatial Imaginations

Although exegesis of 1 Peter has been dedicated to the range of meanings possible for this οἶκος πνευματικός—with the consensus leaning in favor of understanding it as a reference to God's temple—scholars have yet to tease out the spatial implications of this image. How does οἶκος πνευματικός fit into the author's spatial strategy, his construction of space, in the letter as a whole? The answer lies in taking more seriously the spatiality inherent in the very meaning of οἶκος πνευματικός itself.

45. Horrell, *Epistles*, 40. Similarly, Achtemeier, *1 Peter*, 155–56.
46. Selwyn, *First Epistle*, 283.
47. *First Epistle*, 284–85. Tempting though it may be to speculate as to where this temple stands in relation to the Jerusalem temple, any proposals must remain tenuous. Is the spiritual house he envisions simply an alternative temple, a more authentic temple, or, indeed, a *replacement* for the temple destroyed in the Jewish-Roman war? The author's silence on this matter is palpable, and is part of a broader exegetical mystery—that of Christians' relationship to Israel in the letter (cf. the concise discussion in Achtemeier, *1 Peter*, 69–72 and notes there).

The author sets before us the image of a temple made up of "living stones"—that is, Christians and Christ himself (*the* paradigmatic living stone and cornerstone). What we are confronted with is a way of envisioning Christian solidarity: a temple made up of material bodies, both those of believers and of the vindicated Jesus, who has now become its cornerstone (2:7). To read οἶκος πνευματικός in this way is not to take the expression in a wooden or hyperliteral sense, but rather to think of it as robustly material, spatial, and imaginative. It tells us that Christian bodies, spread throughout the Anatolian terrain in their respective communities, are simultaneously asked to conceive of themselves as a single, transspatial temple joined in Christ and animated by God's Spirit. While the corporate nature of this temple image is often appreciated by interpreters, its *corporeal* character has been less so. Yet the οἶκος πνευματικός is made up of actual, material, living bodies joined in solidarity with the once-broken, now-glorified body of Jesus. The architect of solidarity is none other than God, who is also the builder of this temple (the implied performer of οἰκοδομεῖσθε, 2:5). The bonds forged by this divine construction project are, I argue, as real in the author's mind as the mystical kinship invoked elsewhere in the letter: God is the Father (1:2, 3) over the household of believers (4:17) made up of siblings scattered throughout not only Asia Minor but also "the world" (2:17, 5:9; cf. 5:12: Silvanus as "brother").

The readers of 1 Peter, therefore, are not *only* to be thought of as aliens and sojourners. Their existence in the world is marked by estrangement, yes—but there is also a place where they belong: in the imagined but no less real οἶκος πνευματικός made up of their bodies and constituted as a divine collective. Scattered throughout Anatolia as dispersed communities, they are nonetheless united by one Father, one Lord, and one sanctifying Spirit (1:2). Already in the letter's opening we are presented with a paradox: the spatial dispersion of the recipients across the vastness of Roman Anatolia ("diaspora"), counterbalanced by their solidarity effected by divine election. The author underscores this paradox again toward the end of the letter, speaking of a family (ἀδελφότης, lit. "brotherhood") scattered throughout the world that is yet united in their share of Christ's sufferings (5:9; cf. 4:13). To paraphrase Paul, the temple is one and made up of many living stones, and all the living stones, though many, are one temple in Christ (cf. 1 Cor 3:16, 12:12).

This temple of living stones is by no means "other-worldly," but in fact very "this-worldly"—present in the here and now because of the believers who comprise it. That they live as aliens and sojourners in society need not necessarily imply that their only true home is in heaven—an inference Elliott has been so careful to guard against—but they belong to this world *in a different way*. In fact, it is precisely the temple's "this-worldliness" that causes the Christian experience of disjuncture from non-Christian bodies that inhabit shared spaces. The Christian experience of nonbelonging is tied to the liminal nature of their existence: they are a community unto themselves moving amid communities regulated according to a different logic. Despite this difference, their corporate identity as God's spiritual house does not change the fact that they continue to live in spheres governed by the dictates of the status quo. As the author's paraenetic concerns in the letter (esp. 2:11–3:7) indicate, Christians remain subject to regulations set by civic authorities, Christian slaves continue to be subject to the authority of their non-Christian masters, and Christian wives to that of their non-Christian husbands. What they must negotiate is how to live Christianly while remaining bound in daily practice and duty to non-Christian bodies—and this is precisely what the author sets out to help them do: to live out their exilic life in the fear of God (cf. 1:17; 2:12, 17).

3. Spatial Production, Resistance, Belonging

> I will draw a map of what you never see
> and guess me whose map will be bigger than whose?
> Guess me whose map will tell the larger truth?[48]

The reconfigurations of space reflected in the imperial cults sought to draw everybody—by which I mean *all bodies*—into a relationship with the rule of the Caesars. The structures and practices of the cults, from temples to festivals and everything in between, must be seen in terms of their very material, even *visceral*, effects: namely, the regulation of the movement of imperial subjects according to dictates of Roman power. In Harvey's terms, Rome's power to control the *appropriation* of space—i.e., the manner in which space is occupied by objects (buildings, squares, streets, etc.), activities (uses), and people (particular individuals, classes or groups)—amounts de facto to the Empire's *domination* of that space.[49]

Once the full force of this spatial imagination is appreciated, the Chris-

---

48. The rastaman, in Miller, *Cartographer*, 19.
49. Cf. Harvey, *Condition*, 122.

tian discourse of space in 1 Peter easily emerges as its competitor. If the imperial cults filled spaces with symbols and structures of Roman power radiating
from a center, 1 Peter disputed these attempts by asserting an alternative
view. Just as Caesar's power was not limited to the boundaries of the city
of Rome but was to be venerated in satellites of cult, the collective body of
believers transcended discrete boundaries by virtue of their divine election
in and through Christ. On the one hand, 1 Peter normalized the Christian
experience of nonbelonging in Roman spaces and redefined this alienation
as the hallmark of Christian existence. Believers were construed as aliens
and sojourners in diaspora. At the same time—and just as crucially—they
are living stones fitted together into a single, transspatial temple of cosmic
"brotherhood"—a universal Christian society bound together precisely by
estrangement and persecution. It was thus in their nonbelonging in Roman
space that they in fact belonged together. Their solidarity as one spiritual
house, one temple indwelt by God's spirit, is corollary to and counterbal-
ances the social vertigo they experience as aliens and sojourners, as inhabitants of the social margins. They are thus at once truly "at home" and truly
"homeless" (cf. Diogn. 5).

We must bear in mind that both the Roman and Petrine ways of imagin-
ing space were operative concurrently, on the same bodies, and in the same
space—Roman Anatolia. Each in their own right is an attempt to shape spatial, embodied practice—to modify how space is both conceived and lived
in and through the body. The Roman "units" of spatial imagination—that is,
the provinces that make up the imperial body politic—are acknowledged in
1 Peter (1:1)—along with their mechanics of governance (e.g., governors as
representatives of the emperor, 2:13–17), demonstrating the author's awareness of their existence. Yet it is precisely this awareness of them that brings
into sharper focus the distinctive features of his alternative spatial imagination—one that cuts across the boundaries imposed by the empire's geography of power and redefines space in terms of life and solidarity in Christ.
As such, the configuration of space in 1 Peter must be regarded as an act of
resistance, a genuine challenge to Roman hegemony because it imagined
that shared space—and indeed the world—very differently.

The space produced in 1 Peter, therefore, simultaneously dislocates and
relocates.[50] It dislocates the readers by rendering them aliens and sojourners,

50. Horrell, "Beyond Conformity," 229: "What [1 Peter] does . . . is to insert its readers
into a particular narrative of identity which 'places'—or rather, displaces—them in a specific
position vis-à-vis empire."

inhabitants of a diaspora. It relocates them—or rather, reveals their true location—within a spiritual house, situated not in another plane of existence or some distant heaven, but in the very same spaces of their dislocation. Where is this "spiritual house" in which they serve as priests, offering spiritual sacrifices? It is everywhere they are—in the very spaces of the daily grind occupied by their bodies and transformed by their activities. This material—even metaphysical—renovation of spatial practice is as real as their new birth in Christ (cf. 1:3, 23), and is in fact bound up with that new existence. Not surprisingly, the author's exhortation that they, like newborn infants, "grow into salvation" (2:2) is immediately followed by his injunction that they approach the living stone that is also the cornerstone of the spiritual house (2:4). The temple comes into being not simply because the readers are asked to think of space in a novel way, but because God is already at work in them, building them into a dwelling place for his Spirit of glory (cf. 4:14). This is the truth—the spatial reality—they must confess, and by which they must live.

Cities of Revelation
A Tale of Two (Kinds of) Cities

Ian Paul

It is now well established that the transition of early Christian faith from its origins in a Palestinian rural context to its growth in urban centers throughout the eastern Roman Empire marks a significant change in the cultural context for the development of Christian belief.[1] Of all the early Christian literature, it is arguable that none is dominated by the reality of the life of the city more than the book of Revelation.

It would be tempting to talk of the book as a "tale of two cities," in that the rhetorical strategy of the book is to polarize humanity according to their loyalty to the earthly city of Rome (in the form of its empire) or to the heavenly city, the new Jerusalem. This polarizing challenge for the reader is expressed in a series of binary oppositions that permeate the text of the book.[2]

---

1. The landmark exploration of this was Wayne A. Meeks, *The First Urban Christians: The Social World of the Apostle Paul*, 2nd ed. (New Haven: Yale University Press, 2003). The lasting contribution of this social-scientific approach was assessed in Todd D. Still and David G. Horrell, eds., *After the First Urban Christians: The Social-Scientific Study of Pauline Christianity Twenty-Five Years Later* (London: T&T Clark, 2010).

2. In that regard, the binary tensions within the narrative are actually captured quite well by the introduction to Dickens's novel of the same name: "It was the best of times, it was the worst of times, it was the age of wisdom, it was the age of foolishness, it was the epoch of belief, it was the epoch of incredulity, it was the season of Light, it was the season of Darkness, it was the spring of hope, it was the winter of despair, we had everything before us, we had nothing before us, we were all going direct to Heaven, we were all going direct the other way—in short, the period was so far like the present period, that some of its noisiest authorities insisted on its being received, for good or for evil, in the superlative degree of comparison only." Charles Dickens, *A Tale of Two Cities* (Ware: Wordsworth, 1999), 1.

These binary oppositions have been widely critiqued by feminist commentators,[3] but they appear to be central to the rhetorical strategy of the book in "raising the stakes" in relation to the allegiance of its first readers.[4] The book is less responding to a crisis than creating one—a crisis of loyalty.

But that is only part of the story of the role of cities in Revelation, since (in contrast to other kinds of Jewish apocalyptic), Revelation is given a specific urban setting, both by its form as a letter and by its being addressed to specific *ekklēsiai* in seven urban contexts in the Roman province of Asia.[5] Social scientific exploration of the text, based on an examination of material culture of these cities and their environs, has quite a different bearing on our reading of these contexts compared with its impact on our understanding of the role of Rome and Jerusalem because of the way the respective cities are handled in the text.

1. The Seven Cities

First, we turn to the function of the seven urban centers whose inhabitants are the addressees of the book as a whole. In what sense do they function as literal, actual contexts into which the text speaks, and to what extent are they metaphorical or rhetorical foils against which "John" presents his case? It might be hard for us to imagine, but a good part of the history of interpretation of Revelation did not treat the seven cities as historical contexts for reading this text in the way we might (for example) treat first-century Corinth as a context for reading Paul's letters.[6] This detachment from history originated

3. Perhaps the clearest exposition of this critique is that of Tina Pippin, *Death and Desire: Rhetoric of Gender in the Apocalypse of John* (Louisville: Westminster John Knox, 1992).

4. A major proponent of the idea that Revelation is not primarily comforting the challenged but challenging the comfortable—raising the stakes of loyalty to empire—is Leonard L. Thompson, *The Book of Revelation: Apocalypse and Empire* (New York: Oxford University Press, 1996).

5. There are intractable issues in translating the term *ekklēsia* by the English "church," since it has a background both in the Septuagint and in the life of the Greek city. Craig R. Koester, *Revelation: A New Translation with Introduction and Commentary*, AYB 38A (New Haven: Yale University Press, 2014) opts to use the word "assembly."

6. For two fascinating accounts of such de-historicized readings of Revelation, see Christopher Rowland, "British Interpretation of the Apocalypse: A Historical Perspective" and Jonathan Downing, "The Woman Clothed in the Sun: The Reception of Revelation 12 in British Millenarian Movements 1780–1820," both in *The Book of Revelation: Currents in British Research on the Apocalypse*, ed. Garrick Allen, Ian Paul, and Simon Woodman,

in two countermovements. The first was early chiliasm, with its (supposedly) literal reading of millennial expectation, whose end point in the modern era was dispensational premillennialism.[7] This was the tradition in which I first encountered the text of Revelation in a Baptist Church Bible study group; the question in reading Revelation 2–3 was not *where* were the cities located, but, in the context of a "church-historical" interpretive scheme, *when* are the cities located within the span of church history.[8] Although there is a process of dehistorizising within this hermeneutical strategy at the textual end, there is a curious (and paradoxical) rehistoricizing involved at the reader's end, in the process of application—though one detached from the context of Revelation. For example, Montanus believed the mountain on which the New Jerusalem would descend was in Phrygia,[9] while dispensational premillennialists regularly identify the events of Revelation with specific historical features of contemporary modern life.[10]

But the countermovement to this, Augustinian amillennialism, also dehistoricized the text, leading to "spiritual" interpretations that focused on the issues in the messages to the seven churches, rather than their relation to their historical context.[11]

Against both these reading traditions came the rise of interest in the

---

WUNT/2 411 (Tübingen: Mohr Siebeck, 2015), 225–44, 265–80. Some of the best recent exploration of the material culture of Corinth can be found in Steven J. Friesen, Daniel N. Schowalter, and James C. Walters, eds., *Corinth in Context: Comparative Studies on Religion and Society*, NovTSup 134 (Leiden: Brill, 2010).

7. For a useful overview of the history of interpretation, see Koester, *Revelation*, 29–65. For early patristic interpretation, see William C. Weinrich, ed., *Revelation*, ACCSNT 12 (Downers Grove, IL: InterVarsity Press, 2006). For selective examples from the history of interpretation, see Judith Kovacs and Christopher Rowland, *Revelation: The Apocalypse to Jesus Christ*, BBC (Malden, MA: Wiley, 2004).

8. See Koester, *Revelation*, 46–48. We were, of course, in the *last* age of the seven, as Christians have always thought themselves to be, and so were in danger of being lukewarm Laodiceans. We could easily see the danger of lukewarmness (as we understood it) by looking across to the Church of England—in which I was later ordained.

9. William Tabbernee, *Prophets and Gravestones: An Imaginative History of Montanists and Other Early Christians* (Grand Rapids: Baker Academic, 2009), 67.

10. Koester, *Revelation*, 59–61. Hal Lindsey, *The Late Great Planet Earth* (Grand Rapids: Zondervan, 1970) goes as far as predicting on which beaches in Israel amphibious Russian forces will land as forecast in the book of Revelation. See my exploration of this in Ian Paul, *The Ethics of the Book of Revelation*, Grove Ethics 136 (Cambridge: Grove, 2005).

11. Augustine's thoroughly antichiliastic reading is set out in *Civ.* 20, and is largely influenced by Tyconius and his opposition to the chiliasm of Victorinus. See Weinrich, *Revelation*, xx–xiv.

seven cities as actual historical contexts that could be explored in a way that would shed light on our reading of the text. The two names most commonly associated with the renewal of interest in the archaeology of Asia and its cities are William Ramsay from the turn of the twentieth century[12] and Colin Hemer working in the 1970s and 1980s.[13] It is still the case that nobody working on the historical context of Revelation can ignore these two scholars.[14] And there is no doubt that the contextual information here sheds some important light on the meaning, impact, and interpretation of the messages to the seven churches. Perhaps the most notable are:

(i) Smyrna addressed by Jesus as the one "who was dead and came to life" (ὃς ἐγένετο νεκρὸς καὶ ἔζησεν [Rev 2:8])[15] in relation to its own destruction and phoenix-like refounding;[16] the reward of the "crown of life" to those who remain faithful (Rev 2:10), in relation to the beauty of the city, its hosting of games and the symbol used on its coins.[17]

(ii) The description of Pergamum as "where Satan's throne is" (ὅπου ὁ θρόνος τοῦ σατανᾶ [Rev 2:13]) as a reference either to the temple of Zeus or the city as a center of the imperial cult;[18] the promise of a "white stone with a new name written on it" suggesting either acquittal from a charge, ownership, or relationship—though interestingly Hemer is agnostic on the various possible explanations, and simply notes from personal experience the contrast between imported white limestone and the local dark basalt.[19]

(iii) The call to Sardis to "wake up" (Rev 3:2), alluding to the fact that the city was captured not once but twice while the guards were asleep.[20]

12. William M. Ramsay, *The Letters to the Seven Churches*, ed. Mark W. Wilson, rev. ed. (Peabody, MA: Hendrickson, 1994).

13. Colin J. Hemer, *The Letters to the Seven Churches of Asia in Their Local Setting*, JSNTSup 11 (Sheffield: Sheffield Academic, 1989).

14. For a fascinating account (and ruthless critique) of Ramsay's work, see Steven J. Friesen, "Revelation, Realia, and Religion: Archaeology in the Interpretation of the Apocalypse," *HTR* 88 (1995): 291–314. On the influence of Ramsay, Friesen notes: "If Ramsay's archaeological arguments are implausible, his historical reconstructions unacceptable, and his thinking afflicted with imperialist values, why should he be discussed at all? An obvious reason is that a large number of his conclusions still circulate in commentaries and in secondary literature on Revelation. His conclusions are often accepted without critique and without an understanding of the assumptions that undergird his work" (300).

15. Biblical translations are the author's own throughout this essay.

16. Hemer, *Letters*, 61–64.

17. Hemer, *Letters*, 59–60, 70–76.

18. Hemer, *Letters*, 82–87.

19. Hemer, *Letters*, 96–104.

20. Hemer, *Letters*, 132–33.

(iv) The description of Laodicea as "poor, blind, and naked" (Rev 3:17) alluding to its wealth, its ophthalmic products, and its clothing manufacture;[21] and the Laodiceans' lukewarmness (Rev 3:16) relating to its water supply, first noted by Rudwick and Green in 1957.[22]

However, despite these gains, there are two major failings in this approach as exemplified by Ramsay and Hemer. The first is a consistent over-interpretation of the archaeological evidence. There is a fairly thoroughgoing use of the language of "we might suppose that" and "it must have been" peppering the catalogue of otherwise useful evidence. The most striking example of this is Ramsay's explanation of the term χαλκολίβανον; Steve Moyise notes that Ramsay "wrote with great confidence that it is a 'very hard alloyed metal, used for weapons, and under proper treatment assuming a brilliant polished gleam approximating to gold'—a remarkable insight given that the word is otherwise unattested."[23] He then notes Hemer's rather more cautious assessment:

The product, I *suggest*, was known there as χαλκολίβανον, which I *conjecture* to be a "copulative compound," literally rendered "copper-zinc," λίβανος being an *unrecorded* word, *perhaps* peculiar to the trade, for a metal obtained by distillation, and so derived from the verb λείβω.[24]

Moyise then observes:

Two things can be said of this. First, note the number of tentative expressions in this quotation (*suggest, conjecture, unrecorded word, perhaps*). For those who want to see a close connection between the seven messages and the places addressed (as a parallel to Paul's letters?), it sounds quite plausible but as with Ramsay, it is pure conjecture.[25]

21. Hemer, *Letters,* 196–201.

22. M. J. S. Rudwick and E. M. B. Green, "The Laodicean Lukewarmness," *ExpTim* 69 (1958): 176–78; cf. Hemer, *Letters,* 186–91. See also the supporting information in Stanley E. Porter, "Why the Laodiceans Received Lukewarm Water (Revelation 3:15–18)," *TynBul* 38 (1987): 143–49.

23. Ramsay, *Letters,* 329, cited by Steve Moyise, "From Revelatory Experience to Written Messages or Vice Versa: The Question of Revelation 1:12–18 and the Seven Letters to the Churches in Asia Minor," in *Epiphanies of the Divine in the Septuagint and the New Testament: Wechselseitige Wahrnehmungen. V. Internationales Symposium zum Corpus Judaeo-Hellenisticum Novi Testamenti,* ed. Roland Deines, WUNT (Tübingen: Mohr Siebeck, forthcoming).

24. Hemer, *Letters,* 116 (emphasis added), cited by Moyise, "Revelatory Experience," forthcoming.

25. Moyise, "Revelatory Experience," forthcoming.

This leads to the second problem in Hemer and Ramsay: the assumption that the local references have a fundamental role in shaping large parts of the text, going back to the opening vision of Jesus in Revelation 1—so that the direction of movement in composition is the assemblies and their context, the messages in Revelation 2–3, and then the composite vision of Jesus in Revelation 1.[26] Moyise offers a much more persuasive explanation—that John is constructing a vision that both draws on but also systematically alters the vision of the interpretive angel in Daniel 10, and then maps this onto the situations of the *ekklēsiai* to which he is writing—which follows the opposite direction of travel. Friesen had earlier noted that Hemer "attempted a defense of his assumption that the letters are permeated by allusions to local conditions" but also found that "very few parts of Hemer's case are convincing. Briefly put, his arguments lack substance."[27]

This then highlights a key methodological issue in reading Revelation in the context of the material culture of first-century Asia. John appears to be blending three "worlds" in the text. First, as Ramsay and Hemer have demonstrated, there is clear evidence of elements of the text that can only be explained by the historical context in which the text was formed. Aune has offered a parallel insight into the contribution of first-century imperial cult and Greco-Roman magical rituals whose footprint we can also clearly.[28]

Secondly, as numerous studies have demonstrated, the text of Revelation is also permeated by thoroughgoing but creative use of OT texts and ideas. There is a significant debate about how we might recognize the presence of OT influences, not least because John rarely if ever "cites" texts explicitly, and another debate about the extent to which the deployment of such influences was "deliberate" or "unconscious" on John's part. But even on a rough count there are 676 allusions in Revelation's 404 verses (the most at 128 from Isaiah).[29] More challenging is the nature of these allusions,

---

26. Such a movement is often reinforced by the idea that chapters 1 and 22 were added as an introduction and conclusion after the composition of the main body of the text, itself composed of two or more original visions or compositions. For a comprehensive discussion of these theories, see David E. Aune, *Revelation 1–5*, WBC 52A (Dallas: Word, 1997), cxviii–cvii.

27. Friesen, "Revelation, Realia, and Religion," 302.

28. These are explored respectively in the chapters "The Influence of Roman Imperial Court Ceremonial on the Apocalypse of John" and "The Apocalypse of John and Graeco-Roman Revelatory Magic" in *Apocalypticism, Prophecy, and Magic in Early Christianity: Collected Essays*, ed. David E. Aune (Grand Rapids: Baker Academic, 2008), 99–119, 347–67.

29. On the questions of method here, see my chapter "The Use of the Old Testament in

where the textual ideas are not just alluded to but also consistently reworked. Moyise demonstrates this very clearly in the examination of the relationship between the inaugural vision of Jesus and its "source" text in Daniel 10:

	Daniel's Vision (10:5–6)	John's Vision (1:12–18)
Clothing	linen with a belt of gold	long robe with a golden sash
Face	like lightning	like the sun
Eyes	like flaming torches	like a flame of fire
Legs/feet	like burnished bronze	like burnished bronze
Voice	like the sound of a multitude	like the sound of many waters
Seer's reaction	fell into a trance, face to the ground	fell at his feet as though dead
Divine response	hand touched him and told him not to fear	hand touched him and told him not to fear

The most consistent feature of John's use of Daniel is that he amends most of the features—though both the individual phrases and their composition into a vision are powerfully suggestive of Daniel. It is hard to imagine any well-informed reader in the first century failing to recognize the allusions—or failing to recognize how the text of Daniel has been altered.

Thirdly, these two worlds (the cultural and historical reality of John's readers, and the world of the Hebrew Bible) are not simply blended or intertwined; they are both reworked in the light of a third reality: the "Christ event" as John understands it, and John's depiction of Jesus as the lamb who was slain sharing the worship of the one seated on the throne. One of the most striking examples of this is in Revelation's use of Ezekiel; the frequent allusions, mostly in a similar order to the text in Ezekiel, are radically disrupted in the final visions, where John decisively declares, "And a temple I did not see in it" (Καὶ ναὸν οὐκ εἶδον ἐν αὐτῇ [Rev 21:22]). This is a striking contradiction to the climactic vision in Ezekiel—precisely because "the Lord

---

Revelation 12" in Steve Moyise, ed., *Old Testament in the New Testament: Essays in Honour of J. L. North*, JSNTSup 189 (Sheffield: Sheffield Academic, 2000), 256–76.

almighty and the Lamb are its temple." In the Lamb, God himself has become the place of mediation between God and his people.[30]

We therefore have to recognize that the depiction of the *ekklēsiai* in chapters 2 and 3 is not simply descriptive, but like the rest of the book has rhetorical goals. The key aspects of their characterization might well be metaphorical or symbolic—not least in the choice of these seven. There is some tension here between historical explanations (these are the most important, on a circular route)[31] and rhetorical explanations (these include all the examples of the ways churches go wrong as a lesson to others).

This then leads us to wider questions of the way the realities of life are depicted here, beyond the details of material culture. In terms of ecclesial reality, several commentators note how the life of the communities looks markedly different from what we might deduce from the Pauline correspondence, and take that as an indication that the date of Revelation is late. But more striking is the difference with (for example) what we might deduce from the writings of Ignatius. In his letter to the Smyrnaeans, we see quite clearly a focus on monarchical episcopacy ("You must all follow the bishop as Jesus Christ followed the Father" [8.1]) and what we might term (borrowing much later theological language) the "real presence" in the Eucharist ("believe in the blood of Christ" [6.1] and "the Eucharist is the flesh of our saviour" [6.2])[32]—both of which seem a good deal further away from the text of Revelation. Rather than telling us anything about dating, this might tell us something about the correspondence between the text and reality.

All this should make us cautious about using the text in "mirror-reading," or rather, as a clear glass window onto the first-century world.[33] Was there

---

30. See the landmark study of Jean-Pierre Ruiz, *Ezekiel in the Apocalypse: The Transformation of Prophetic Language in Revelation 16, 17–19, 10*, EurHS 376 (New York: Peter Lang, 1989) and the reflection on this in Steve Moyise, *The Old Testament in the Book of Revelation*, JSNTSup 115 (Sheffield: Sheffield Academic, 1995), 64–84. For a very different approach to this question, see Gregory K. Beale, *John's Use of the Old Testament in Revelation*, LNTS 443 (London: Bloomsbury T&T Clark, 2015), which includes a detailed critique of Moyise (41–59) drawing on the approach to validity in interpretation of E. D. Hirsch.

31. Rodney Stark estimates the size of the largest twenty-two cities in the empire in the first century, and it is striking that four of the seven cities in Revelation feature in this list (Ephesus, Pergamum, Smyrna, and Sardis). Rodney Stark, *The Rise of Christianity* (San Francisco: HarperCollins, 1997), 131.

32. Translation from Michael W. Holmes, ed., *The Apostolic Fathers: Greek Texts and English Translations*, 3rd ed. (Grand Rapids: Baker, 2007), 255–56.

33. The classic exposition of the issue of mirror-reading is John Barclay, "Mirror-Reading a Polemical Letter: Galatians as a Test Case," *JSNT* 31 (1987): 73–93.

really an individual that John is referring to using the biblical name Jezebel (2:20)? Or a Balaam (2:14)? Antipas (2:13) looks like a more straightforward reference—but what about the Nicolaitans (2:6, 15)? Given the etymology of the name (combining νικᾶν, "to conquer or triumph," and λαός, "people"), and the significance of the terms cognate with νικᾶν, and the fact that such cognates are key terms that link the material in chapters 2 to 3 with what follows in a very different genre, I would want to be very cautious about deducing anything of the social reality of the communities from this term. To say anything more definite about the meaning of the term might be speculative[34]—but in the complete absence of any historical evidence, and with the presence of biblical pseudonyms, these terms are best treated as part of John's rhetorical strategy.

This is not unrelated to the wider question of whether or not the Christians in Asia were subject to "persecution" (whatever we mean by that). Against Henry Barclay Swete's comprehensive catalogue demonstrating that Domitian was the second great persecutor[35] comes Leonard Thompson's counter-evidence,[36] along with observations about the text itself. The seven messages are not ones that, on face value, we might expect to read if all the communities were under pressure of persecution and needed encouragement—the powerful rebukes do not look like the strategy of an effective pastor if this were the case. But they *are* what we might expect to read if the Christ-followers were too assimilated with their culture and needed a challenge not to compromise.

A more helpful approach to the question about material culture of the seven cities is provided by Steven Friesen in his study of the imperial cult in Asia.[37] Friesen demonstrates the gradual encroachment of the cult into the physical center of cities in Asia, and corrects some common errors, such as the identity of the giant statue in Ephesus as Titus and not Domitian.[38] But the central part

34. As noted by Aune, *Revelation 1–5*, 149.

35. Henry Barclay Swete, ed., *The Apocalypse of St John: The Greek Text* (London: Macmillan, 1906), lxxvii–xciii.

36. Thompson, *Revelation*, 95–109.

37. Steven J. Friesen, *Imperial Cults and the Apocalypse of John: Reading Revelation in the Ruins* (New York: Oxford University Press, 2001). He has already signaled this fresh approach when he comments in the earlier article, "I argue that a different kind of engagement with archaeological evidence could bring significant benefits to the methods and findings of studies of Revelation in particular and New Testament studies in general" (Friesen, "Revelation, Realia, and Religion," 292).

38. Despite the labeling of the statue in the Museum of Ephesus. Friesen, *Cults*, 50.

of his thesis is the way that the material culture of the cities demonstrates how the imperial cult was the primary reference point in constructing reality for the first-century mind. This forms a bridge into our consideration of the two cities, Jerusalem and Rome, and how they are characterized in Revelation.

2. The Two Cities

The contrast between these two as centers of loyalty unfolds as the cycles of John's visions develop.[39] The anticipatory mention of the new Jerusalem as "the bride" in 19:7 leads into the climax of this contrast between Rome as whore and Jerusalem as bride.[40]

The first key thing to note is that these two cities are not mentioned by name, which alerts us to a fundamentally different dynamic in the way Revelation depicts them. The word "Rome" does not occur at all, though there is reference to the city Babylon six times, perhaps offering an additional connection with the numerology of 666 in Revelation 13:18.[41] "Jerusalem" is mentioned three times, twice as the "new" city (3:12 and 21:2)[42] and once as "coming down out of heaven from God" (21:10). Zion is mentioned once (14:1). The contrast here is that, while the references to the seven cities have some literal and some metaphorical or symbolic significance, the references to the two cities are entirely metaphorical, and of a particular type of metaphor: hypocatastasis.

The term hypocatastasis appears to have been coined in the modern era by the British theologian E. W. Bullinger, an Anglican clergyman who was a hyperdispensationalist; he believed that Jesus's teaching belonged to the dispensation of the Law, and is not relevant for the dispensation of the church, which only began after the end of the apostolic period following Acts 28:28.[43] But, like many of his fellow-travelers, he paid meticulous de-

39. For a helpful exposition of Revelation as a series of unfolding, cyclical visions, see Craig R. Koester, *Revelation and the End of All Things* (Grand Rapids: Eerdmans, 2001).

40. For an exploration of the female imagery, see Lynn R. Huber, *Like a Bride Adorned: Reading Metaphor in John's Apocalypse*, Emory Studies in Early Christianity 10 (London: T&T Clark, 2007).

41. On the significance of word frequencies, see particularly Richard Bauckham, *The Climax of Prophecy: Studies on the Book of Revelation* (Edinburgh: T&T Clark, 1993), 29–47.

42. Characteristically the phrase is repeated but with a difference—first as ἡ καινὴ Ἰερουσαλήμ and then as ἡ ἁγία Ἰερουσαλήμ. For other phrases repeated but always with variation see Bauckham, *Climax*, 22–29.

43. His teaching was regarded as "absolutely Satanic perversion of the truth" by the American fundamentalist Harry Ironside, in large part because it was schismatic and divided

tail to the use of language in the New Testament, and published commentaries, a lexicon, and in 1898 *Figures of Speech Used in the Bible Illustrated and Explained*.[44] On hypocatastasis, Bullinger comments:

> As a figure, it differs from Metaphor, because in a metaphor the two nouns are both named and given; while, in Hypocatastasis, only one is named and the other is implied, or as it were, is put down underneath out of sight. Hence Hypocatastasis is implied resemblance or representation: i.e., an implied Simile or Metaphor. If Metaphor is more forcible than Simile, then Hypocatastasis is more forcible than Metaphor, and expresses as it were the superlative degree of resemblance.
>
> For example, one may say to another, "You are like a beast." This would be Simile, tamely stating a fact. If, however, he said, "You are a beast" that would be Metaphor. But, if he said simply, "Beast!" that would be Hypocatastasis, for the other part of the Simile or Metaphor ("you"), would be implied and not stated.[45]

Bullinger claims that "So well known was it to the ancients, that it received this significant name," but it does not feature in standard works such as Aristotle's *Rhetoric*.[46]

The presence of this form of metaphor in Revelation has important consequences for the reading and interpretation of this text:

1. As we have noted, the description of Rome and Jerusalem is always and everywhere hypocatastatic—the referent of the metaphor (the subject) is suppressed or implied. Since this is a contrast to the way the seven cities in Revelation 1–3 are described, it suggests that we need to pay attention to the quite different function of the two cities in the narrative compared with the seven.

2. More widely, hypocatastatic metaphor is a form of language distinctively characteristic of Revelation. In his detailed comparative study of the

---

churches. Henry Allan Ironside, *Wrongly Dividing the Word of Truth: Ultra-Dispensationalism Examined in the Light of Holy Scripture*, 3rd ed. (New York: Loizeaux Bros., 1938), 9.

44. The original edition is available as a facsimile: E. W. Bullinger, *Figures of Speech Used in the Bible Explained and Illustrated* (Eastford, CT: Martino Fine Books, 2011). He was also interested in numerology, and his teaching is still influential in dispensationalist churches in Holland.

45. Bullinger, *Figures of Speech*, 744.

46. *LSJ* s.v. lists the term, but gives no citation from any ancient literature, although it does record the near cognate ὑποκαταστάτης. http://stephanus.tlg.uci.edu/lsj/#eid =111472&context=lsj&action=hw-list-click. This term continues to be used in modern Greek to mean "substitute" or "surrogate."

metaphors of Revelation 11 and those of Paul in 1 Cor 15, Andrew Harker highlights four aspects which set Revelation apart—its metaphors are original, open, substantive-based, and referent-suppressing.[47] The last two aspects arise from Revelation's metaphors being hypocatastatic:

Substantive-based: It seems that these allusive metaphors function particularly powerfully where (as often in Rev 11) they are noun-based, performing a form of naming (e.g., Sodom, Egypt, Beast).

Referent-suppressing: The emotive impact of this allusive naming is further heightened by the way in which the referent is swallowed up. The image from the Hebrew Scriptures is deployed straight into its new literary context becoming *the* organizing structure. To the extent that the hearer identifies the setting of the prophetic narrative of Rev 11 as one's own setting and hears what the Spirit says as the true diagnosis of the situation, the metaphors of the chapter cease to refer to "something else" but are an unveiling of reality, the true *Sitz im Leben* of the hearer.[48]

In his PhD thesis (as yet unpublished),[49] Harker goes on to demonstrate that this kind of language is characteristic of prophetic utterances, and so argues that Revelation constitutes the longest extended example of early Christian prophecy.

3. Although Revelation here contrasts with Paul, in this regard it resembles both the prophets of the Hebrew Bible and Jesus's own teaching. Bullinger notes examples from Jeremiah and the Psalms, as well as Matt 3:10, 5:29–30, 7:3–5, 7:6, 15:13, 15:26, 16:6, Mark 1:17, and John 2:19. In a sense, hypocatastatic metaphor is the essence of the parable, unexplained to the crowd, "Behold, a sower went out to sow . . ." (Mark 4:3).

4. Hypocatastatic metaphor creates the most powerful kind of language—it is primarily about exclamation rather than explanation. As Bullinger comments, "This figure, therefore, is calculated to arouse the mind and attract and excite the attention to the greatest extent."[50] This kind of

---

47. Andrew Harker, "Prophetically Called Sodom and Egypt: The Affective Power of Revelation 11:1–13," in *The Book of Revelation: Currents in British Research on the Apocalypse*, ed. Garrick Allen, Ian Paul, and Simon Woodman, WUNT/2 411 (Tübingen: Mohr Siebeck, 2015), 19–39.

48. Harker, "Prophetically Called," 39.

49. Andrew Harker, "Spiritually Called Sodom and Egypt: Getting to the Heart of Early Christian Prophecy through the Apocalypse of John" (PhD diss., London School of Theology / Middlesex University, 2011).

50. E. W. Bullinger, "Hypocatastasis; or Implication," *StudyLight.org*. http://www.studylight.org/lexicons/bullinger/hypocatastasis-or-implication.html.

speech offers challenge, provokes response, and invites decision. It is the kind of language used in strongly rhetorical or polemical contexts, often where conflicting claims are made about reality.

5. Hypocatastasis accounts for some of the major contended issues in the history of interpretation of the book of Revelation. Since the subject of the metaphor is suppressed or implied, it can leave open to dispute what that subject actually is.[51] Within historical-critical approaches, though there is a substantial consensus that "the Great City" is a hypocatastatic metaphor for Rome, principally because of its use in 17:18 and the four occurrences in chapter 18, there is a minority view that argues that its implied subject is in fact Jerusalem, principally because of its use in 11:8.[52] More radically, so-called "literal" futurist readings believe that the implied subject of the whole of the central narrative is not in the first century at all.

The "literalism" of such approaches is also due to hypocatastasis, since, unlike simile and "regular" metaphor, hypocatastatic metaphor shares exactly the same grammatical structure as literal statement. There is a powerful example of this in contemporary cinema in the 1990 film *Pretty Woman*.[53] Richard Gere has fallen in love with Julia Roberts, and everyone realizes it but him. Near the end of the film, he is returning a very expensive diamond necklace, and asks the hotel manager Mr. Thompson to take it back to the jewellers for him. Mr. Thompson asks to open the box and look at the necklace, and then comments, "It must be very difficult letting go of something so beautiful." Taken literally, this is simply a comment about the necklace; this is the (literal) implied subject of his comment. But taken as a hypocatastatic metaphor, the implied subject is Julia Roberts, and by making this statement the hotel manager is challenging Richard Gere to face up to the reality of his feelings. Grammatically the literal sense and the metaphorical sense are identical, so the sentence can function in both ways.[54]

51. I am here using the taxonomy of metaphor proposed by Paul Ricoeur of subject-vehicle-tenor. Paul Ricoeur, *The Rule of Metaphor: Multi-Disciplinary Studies of the Creation of Meaning in Language* (London: Routledge & Kegan Paul, 1978). For explication of Ricoeur's approach, see Ian Paul, "Paul Ricoeur's Hermeneutic of Metaphor and the Interpretation of Revelation 12 and 13" (PhD diss., Nottingham Trent University, 1998).

52. This interpretation is associated with the so-called "preterist" view of Revelation, which sees the destruction of Jerusalem identified with the coming of the kingdom of God, and believes that "the events of Revelation were entirely fulfilled in the first century"; Craig S. Keener, *Revelation*, NIVAC (Grand Rapids: Zondervan, 2000), 28.

53. J. F. Lawton, *Pretty Woman*, directed by Garry Marshall (Buena Vista, 1990).

54. A decade earlier, Peter Sellers starred in an entire film based on this ambiguity. In Jerzy Kosinski, *Being There*, directed by Hal Ashby (Warner Home Video, 1979), Sellers

6. Because the subject is implied rather than stated by hypocatastatic metaphor, it makes the text transferable from one context to another. Thus successive generations of readers of Revelation have seen events of their own day described in the text. If "the beast" is a referent-suppressing hypocatastatic metaphor for Roman imperial power, and characterizes the nature of imperial domination without actually naming the empire, might it not just as well describe later empires in history?

Given that the specific form of Revelation's metaphors explains so much about the history of its interpretation, it is perhaps surprising that this does not receive more attention from contemporary commentators.[55]

Within the text of Revelation, John offers some clear indicators that Rome and its empire are the subject of his metaphors, not least in the depiction of heavenly obeisance to the Almighty[56] and the numerology of 666 as a reference to Nero.[57] But, in a compound allusion that parallels his use of Dan 10 (noted above), John adapts the vision of the four empires in Dan 7:4–7 into a vision of a single empire in Revelation 13:1–2:

Daniel 7:4–7	Rev 13:1–2
The first was like a lion . . . a second beast, which looked like a bear . . . another beast looked like a leopard . . . and there before me was a fourth beast . . . it had ten horns.	And I saw a beast coming out of the sea. It had ten horns and seven heads, with ten crowns on its horns, and on each head a blasphemous name. The beast I saw resembled a leopard, but had feet like those of a bear and a mouth like that of a lion.

---

starred as a gardener who made simple (literal) statements about gardening and the weather, but these are interpreted as profound (hypocatastatic) metaphors about world affairs and the economy. In the end he gets elected President.

55. The only person who mentions the term "hypocatastasis" is G. K. Beale, *The Book of Revelation: A Commentary on the Greek Text*, NIGTC (Grand Rapids: Eerdmans, 2013), 57, though there is little evidence that this shapes Beale's interpretive strategy. Commentators often talk of Revelation's "symbolic" language, but the terminology of symbol should really refer to the extratextual world (a candle or flag might symbolize something); the linguistic phenomenon is metaphor.

56. David E. Aune, "The Influence of Roman Imperial Court Ceremonial on the Apocalypse of John," in *Apocalypticism, Prophecy, and Magic in Early Christianity: Collected Essays* (Grand Rapids: Baker Academic, 2008), 99–119.

57. Bauckham, *Climax*, 384–452.

Rome is not just one empire amongst many, but is the archetypal empire, and combines all the features of human imperial aspiration.

This implies that we must employ insights from social scientific study and the material culture of the first century in quite a different way when reading the two cities compared with the seven. For the seven cities, we use insights to locate the audience in their social, historical, and cultural context. But for the two cities, we use these insights to locate the audience in their ideological, spiritual, and theological context.

In reading of (the New) Jerusalem in Revelation 11 and 21, to ask the historical questions of whether the city is still standing or has now been conquered, or on which mountain the New Jerusalem will descend, is to misread the function and intention of the text. Much more important in chapter 11 is the ideological significance of Jerusalem as the sign of the presence of God amongst his people, and as the focal point of the people's gathering and worship throughout the Hebrew Bible. And in chapter 21, the walls and gates indicate the values of security and access, while the shape of the city indicates that it now functions theologically as the Holy of Holies, the space whose shape (as a cube) it replicates.

Likewise, the historical details of imperial worship present in Revelation 4–5 tell us something about the ideological claims of imperial power, and how the worship of the one on the throne and of the lamb function as a series of polemical counter-claims to cosmic power that therefore demands total loyalty. In a similar way, the list of cargoes in Revelation 18:11–13 can be correlated with actual goods traded between Rome and the provinces of the empire. But at least as important is its symbolic significance as a list of 28 (= 7 x 4) items, indicating Rome's total demand (seven as the number of completeness) over the whole earth (four as a natural number; compare Rev 7:1), usurping God's claim to be sovereign over the whole created order.[58]

Since Revelation offers this context-transcending characterization of imperial aspiration by means of its context-dependent hypocatastatic metaphors, it is no surprise that the text can be used to correlate Revelation's critique of empire with imperial aspirations in the contemporary world. Wes Howard-Brook and Anthony Gwyther characterize the binaries of imperial power as follows:[59]

58. See Bauckham, *Climax*, 338–83.
59. Wes Howard-Brook and Anthony Gwyther, *Unveiling Empire: Reading Revelation Then and Now* (Maryknoll, NY: Orbis, 199), 223–25.

Rome (Babylon)	(New) Jerusalem
Imperium	Empire (kingdom) of God (11:15, 12:10)
Pax Romana	Babylon the shedder of blood (16:6, 17:6)
Victoria	The victory of the lamb and his followers (17:14)
Fides	The faith(fulness) of Jesus (1:5)
Aeterna	"They will reign forever and ever" (22:5)

They then correlate the claims of contemporary neoliberal global capital with those of Rome, and then how the claims of Christian discipleship today, shaped by the text of Revelation, demand a decisive critique of capitalist consumerism.[60]

3. Conclusion

The Book of Revelation situates itself and its audience in the context of two sets of cities. The seven cities function as the *arena* of discipleship, the context in which the followers of the lamb must work out their loyalties and their commitments. Making use of social-scientific research and study of their material culture will give us vital insights into what those challenges were and how Revelation expresses them. But the two cities function as the *telos* of discipleship—the rival cities making incompatible claims on their citizens for total loyalty. Later readers of this text will be living and working in different contexts—they will have their own specific arenas in which they have to work out these questions of loyalty. But they will still be confronted with the rival claims of human empires and the kingdom of God—and will have the parallel decision to make about the *telos*, the goal of their discipleship.

60. Howard-Brook and Gwyther, *Unveiling Empire*, 236–60.

CONCLUSION

Research on Urban Christian Communities
Looking Ahead

DAVID W. J. GILL AND PAUL R. TREBILCO

The interdisciplinary approach to research on urban Christian communities has opened up new ways of thinking about common problems. New Testament scholars, classical archaeologists, and human geographers approach the evidence with different methodologies and insights. A roundtable discussion at the end of the conference provided an opportunity to review what had been achieved and to start exploring some of the ways forward.[1] We shall conclude by sketching some of the areas that require continuing and fresh exploration as a result of the analysis and discussion in this book.

There needs to be a better definition of the "city." In the Greek East, including Achaea, Macedonia, Asia, Syria, and Cyrenaica, the *polis* had been the main way to describe urban communities. This was a structure that had emerged by the eighth century BCE, and contained a range of social, political, and religious structures. The concept of the *polis* had spread with the expansion of the Hellenistic kingdoms under Alexander the Great and his successors, reaching as far as the Indus Valley. It is important to remember that there was no single structure for the *polis*, though the norm was to have one main urban center, the *astu*, with its surrounding countryside, the *chōra*. The *polis* itself is defined by the citizens who live within its territory, for example it would be usual to talk in terms of the *polis* of the Nemeans rather than the *polis* of Nemea.[2] It was the body of the citizens who defined the body

1. The roundtable consisted of David Gill, David Horrell, Joan Taylor, and Paul Trebilco.
2. Thus standard NT usage is to speak of (e.g.) ἐν Φιλίπποις "among the Philippians" (Phil 1:1), i.e. "in Philippi."

320

politic. This body would exclude women, children, slaves, and foreign residents, and yet each of those groups would contribute to the life and vitality of the community in which they resided. It would be worth contrasting how the Christian *ekklēsia* gave scope for members of these wider groups to take a full part in the Christian community, while at the same time they would be excluded from their civic *ekklēsia*.

The classic definition of the *polis* reminds us of the balance between the main urban center and its *chōra*. Within the territory there could be small towns as well as villages, and elite members of the urban communities could reside on their rural estates in more comfortable villas. These rural estates could have their own power structures relating to individual families. This structure of a city within its rural hinterland would be different for more rural provinces such as Galatia, which had developed its urban framework during the Hellenistic period and its annexation by Rome. The province of Judea would have been another anomaly because of the strength of Judaism as a unifying factor, in spite of its contacts with the Hellenistic kingdoms, as would the province of Egypt that retained so much of its pharaonic cultural identity.

This raises a parallel question about how far Christianity was able to reach rural communities. The estates of Sergius Paulus, governor of Cyprus, around Pisidian Antioch would be an obvious place to consider though there is unlikely to be much physical evidence.[3] By "rural" do we mean communities of perhaps a few thousand people? Are we talking in terms of dispersed dwelling in small family units, or in clusters of family groups? We perhaps need to remember that some *poleis* in the first century CE may have been no larger than the "small" rural communities found in other *poleis*.

As Christianity moved from the Greek East to Italy and the western provinces the urban structures would change. The "megacity" of Rome was unlike any urban community of the East, though perhaps Alexandria in Egypt would have been one of the most complex. At what levels and in which communities and networks would Christianity have engaged? As Christianity became established in the urban centers of Britannia, such as Calleva Atrebatum (Silchester) or Verulamium (St. Albans), where there is relatively early evidence for Christian communities both through archaeology and literary evidence, how would this urban experience have differed from cities in Gaul, Germania, or Hispania?

---

3. Acts 13:7; Stephen Mitchell, *The Rise of the Church,* vol. 2 of *Anatolia: Land, Men, and Gods in Asia Minor* (Oxford: Clarendon, 1995), 5-8.

Some of the urban settings in the eastern Mediterranean will have been heavily influenced by Rome. This would include the Romanized cities such as the great harbor city of Caesarea,[4] and colonies such as Philippi[5] and Corinth. However, other cities with established Hellenistic foundations would have had a less explicit Roman setting. Moreover, the structures of cities in the western provinces would have been different again.

There is scope to explore how communities interacted with each other. What was the interplay between the urban Christian communities of, say, Corinth and Alexandria? For the Greek *poleis* of Achaia, were the traditional links with their well-established colonies in southern Italy and Sicily exploited into the Roman period? To what extent did these established networks provide opportunities for the spread of Christianity through established structures of patronage? Is there a difference in the way that Christian communities became established in the Greek urban settlements such as Syracuse from the urban communities of northern Italy?

One of the cities overlooked in our essays was Syrian Antioch on the river Orontes. It was founded by Seleucus I Nicator in 300 BCE, and its inhabitants included large numbers from Macedonia and Athens. It received its autonomous status in 47 BCE from Julius Caesar. Yet this was the city in which the faith community was first called "Christians" (Acts 11:26). There is scope to collect further information to understand the place of this Seleucid foundation in the history of emerging Christian communities.

Some of our essays started to explore ethnic groups within cities. One of the strands was on the meaning of *Ioudaios*.[6] How far does Christianity engage with Roman citizens within the cities of the Greek East where citizenship was far from common outside the colonies? How does Christianity engage with different ethnic groups in the *poleis* of the Greek East that had themselves been founded with populations drawn from other urban communities? The emergence of major commercial centers supporting the movement of goods to Rome would have meant that there was some mobility of populations. Are there common patterns that emerge for Caesarea and Ephesus in contrast to, say, the colonial foundations of Corinth and Philippi?

New technologies will help us to understand the experience of living, and living out a Christian faith, in these urban communities. It could be at the level of how a church community could gather in domestic structures,

---

4. See Joan Taylor's essay above.
5. See Cédric Brélaz's essay above.
6. See Anthony Le Donne's essay above.

and what limits that places on a group in terms of size and interaction. This immediately raises the issue of what is a "typical" domestic space in the early first century CE, and even the question how far early-first-century domestic spaces have been excavated. There is also the wider issue of the visual landscape of cities. The arrival of any traveler to the port of Caesarea would have been faced with the imperial cult, but this visual impression would have been lost as the visitor left the harbor area. Yet for Christians there would be a constant reminder of the world of the Olympian and Capitoline deities, as well as more local cults, in the architecture of the city.

Any inhabitant of an ancient city would have been faced with numerous inscriptions and texts. Decisions by the political bodies, accounts, benefactions, as well as funerary texts would have provided the more formal texts, and alongside these would have been the informal texts and graffiti, as well as correspondence. How far would inhabitants of urban communities in the Greek East have used Latin on a regular basis? To what extent was Greek the more usual language? What was the place of local languages and dialects? Allied to this is the broader question of literacy within these urban communities. To what extent would uneducated (or unlettered) individuals have been able to engage with the teaching of the church? How reliant were these early Christian communities on educated leaders who could interact with the teaching in cities across their region?

The ancient world was in effect a series of urban and rural communities linked by a network of well-maintained roads allowing movement of goods and soldiers. How far do Paul's missionary travels concentrate on key urban locations? Did he target strategic hubs that would support Christian mission in surrounding communities and areas? This is particularly noticeable for Cyprus, southern Anatolia, and across Macedonia. At the same time there are coastal communities in mountainous regions that are more easily approached by the sea.

There is a need to develop a more nuanced approach to individual cities in the biblical texts. There are points when it seems that the available data for an individual city can be relatively limited. There is also a need to restrict information to particular periods of time. The resurgence of the use of Greek in Roman colonial settings in the second century CE is perhaps linked to the philhellenism of the emperor Hadrian (CE 117–138). Thus, trying to project the profile of a city from its later historical information back to the first century CE is more problematic. Scholars from different disciplines also need to develop a common language and intellectual framework that will assist with the understanding of urban identities in the ancient world.

The ancient world provides a backdrop of multiculturalism, religious diversity, pressures on space, poverty and wealth, and patronage. This was the setting of the early urban Christian communities. So how do we relate and translate those Roman imperial settings to our own urban worldwide environments that are connected by the internet and mobile communications? How do we understand the effect of cultural transposition as we engage with the ancient texts?

It is perhaps worth reflecting on the architectural setting of cities. The dominant buildings and structures would have been the temples of the Greek and Roman deities. Only by Late Antiquity would basilicas begin to make an impact on the cityscape. In a northern European setting so many medieval cities were dominated by cathedrals. Yet a visitor to the city of London today will observe that the medieval churches are dominated by the high-rise buildings of the financial sector. What were inhabitants of these urban communities observing and visualizing in the first century?

Our essays leave open the question of the emotional response to living in the ancient city. How did urban life intrude on everyday life? What sights, sounds, and smells influenced life choices? To what extent did urban dwellers experience the countryside on a regular basis, or was the *chōra* something that was traversed in order to reach another urban community? More broadly there is scope to work with human geographers on spiritual geography to understand the interaction between faith communities and the physical spaces that they occupy. This could be projected onto the ancient evidence.[7]

To what extent could the classical cities of the Roman Empire be considered "cities of God"?[8] To what extent did the Christian faith have a broad impact on life in the urban communities and how was this impact expressed in a visible way? At the same time, these same communities could be viewed as cities of *gods* as expressed through their patron deities, and with the religious structures, including the imperial cult, imposed on the social fabric in a number of subtle ways.

Much has been studied, and much has been learned already—and there is much still to study and learn. We invite our readers to become the people who will take these discussions forward, for they are vital to our understanding of earliest Christianity in its city settings, and will inform and inspire Christian engagement with city life today.

---

7. See Paul Cloke's essay above for an example of how this might work.

8. On this phrase, see Rodney Stark, *Cities of God: The Real Story of How Christianity Became an Urban Movement and Conquered Rome* (New York: HarperOne, 2007).

Works Cited

Primary Sources

Chrysostom, John. *Homilies on the Epistles of Paul to the Corinthians.* CCEL. http://www.ccel.org/ccel/schaff/npnf112.toc.html.

Clement of Alexandria. *Christ the Educator.* Translated by Simon P. Wood. Fathers of the Church 23. New York: Fathers of the Church, 1954.

Dio Chrysostom. *Discourses.* Translated by J. W. Cohoon. 5 vols. LCL. Cambridge, MA: Harvard University Press, 1932–51.

Diodorus Siculus. *Bibliotheca Historica.* Translated by C. Bradford Welles. LCL. Cambridge: Harvard University Press, 1963.

Dionysius of Halicarnassus. *Roman Antiquities.* 7 vols. LCL. Cambridge: MA: Harvard University Press, 1937–50.

Epictetus. *Dissertations.* The Internet Classics Archive. http://classics.mit.edu/Epictetus/discourses.html.

Eusebius of Caesarea. *History of the Church.* Translated and introduced by G. A. Williamson. London: Penguin, 1989.

(Pseudo-)Hippolytus. *Refutatio omnium haeresium.* Edited by Miroslav Marcovich. PTS 25. Berlin: de Gruyter, 1986.

Holmes, Michael W., ed. *The Apostolic Fathers: Greek Texts and English Translations.* 3rd ed. Grand Rapids: Baker Academic, 2007.

Josephus. Translated by H. St. J. Thackeray et al. 10 vols. LCL. London: Heinemann, 1926–65.

Justin Martyr. *Apologies.* Edited and translated by Denis Minns and Paul Parvis. OECT. Oxford: Oxford University Press, 2009.

Livy. *History of Rome (Ab Urbe Condita Libri).* Translated by B. O. Foster et al. 14 vols. LCL. Cambridge: Harvard University Press, 1919–59.

Philo of Alexandria. *Legatio ad Gaium.* Translated by F. H. Colson. LCL. Cambridge: Harvard University Press, 1962.

Plato. *Republic*. Translated by Paul Shorey. 2 vols. LCL. Cambridge: Harvard University Press, 1930–35.

Pliny. *Natural History*. Translated by H. Rackham. 10 vols. LCL. London. Heinemann, 1979.

Plutarch. *Lives*. Translated by Beradotte Perrinn. 11 vols. LCL. London: Heinemann, 1948.

Plutarch. *Moralia*. Translated by Frank Cole Babbitt et al. 16 vols. LCL. Cambridge, MA: Harvard University Press, 1927–2004.

Polyaenus. *Stratagems*. Attalus. http://www.attalus.org/info/polyaenus.html.

Prigent, Pierre, and Robert A. Kraft, eds. L'Épître *de Barnabé*. SC 172. Paris: Cerf, 1971.

Quintilian. *Institutio Oratio*. Translated by H. E. Butler. 4 vols. LCL. London: Heinemann, 1920–22.

Schneemelcher, Wilhelm, ed. *New Testament Apocrypha*. Translated by R. McL. Wilson. 2 vols. Louisville: Westminster John Knox, 2003.

Seneca. *Moral Essays*. Translated by J. W. Basore. 3 vols. LCL. Cambridge: Harvard University Press, 1928.

Tatius, Achilles. *The Adventures of Leucippe and Clitophon*. Translated by S. Gaselee. LCL. Cambridge: Harvard University Press, 1969.

Secondary Sources

Achtemeier, Paul J. *1 Peter*. Hermeneia. Minneapolis: Fortress, 1996.

Adinolfi, Federico, and Joan E. Taylor. "John the Baptist and Jesus the Baptist: A Narrative Critical Approach." *JSHJ* 10 (2012): 247–84.

Alcock, Susan E. *Graecia Capta: The Landscapes of Roman Greece*. Cambridge: Cambridge University Press, 1993.

Alford, Henry. *The Epistle to the Hebrews: The Catholic Epistles of St. James and St. Peter: The Epistles of St. John and St. Jude: and The Revelation*. Vol. 4 of *The Greek Testament*. Boston: Lee & Shepard, 1878.

Allen, Garrick, Ian Paul, and Simon Woodman, eds. *The Book of Revelation: Currents in British Research on the Apocalypse*. WUNT/2 411. Tübingen: Mohr Siebeck, 2015.

Allen, Roland. *Missionary Methods: St. Paul's or Ours?* 6th ed. Grand Rapids: Eerdmans, 1962.

Allison, Dale C, Jr. *James*. ICC. London: Bloomsbury T&T Clark, 2013.

Amselle, Jean-Loup. *Mestizo Logics: Anthropology of Identity in Africa and Elsewhere*. Translated by Claudia Royal. Stanford: Stanford University Press, 1998.

Anderson, Ben. "Affects." Pages 760–72 in *Introducing Human Geographies*. Edited by Paul Cloke, Philip Crang, and Mark Goodwin. 3rd ed. London: Routledge, 2014.

Anderson, Ben, and Paul Harrison, eds. *Taking Place: Non-representational Theories and Geography*. Aldershot: Ashgate, 2010.

Anderson, J. G. C. "Festivals of Mên Askaênos in the Roman Colony at Antioch of Pisidia." *JRS* 3 (1913): 267–300.

Arnold, Clinton E. *Ephesians*. ZECNT. Grand Rapids: Zondervan, 2010.

Ascough, Richard S. "Civic Pride at Philippi: The Text-Critical Problem of Acts 16.12." *NTS* 44 (1998): 93–103.

―――. *Paul's Macedonian Associations: The Social Context of Philippians and 1 Thessalonians.* WUNT/2 161. Tübingen: Mohr Siebeck, 2003.

Ashwin-Siejkowski, Piotr. "The Notion of 'Heresy' in *Stromateis* VII and Its Use in Clement of Alexandria's Polemic." Pages 277–90 in *The Seventh Book of the Stromateis: Proceedings of the Colloquium on Clement of Alexandria* (Olomouc, October 21–23, 2010). Edited by Matyáš Havrda, Vít Hušek, and Jana Plátová. VCSup 117. Leiden: Brill, 2012.

Attoh, Kafui A. "What *Kind* of Right Is the Right to the City?" *Prog. Hum. Geogr.* 35 (2011): 669–85.

Aune, David E. *Revelation 1–5.* WBC 52A. Dallas, TX: Word, 1997.

―――. *Apocalypticism, Prophecy and Magic in Early Christianity: Collected Essays.* Grand Rapids: Baker Academic, 2008.

Avi-Yonah, Michael. "Notes and News: Caesarea." *IEJ* 6 (1956): 260–61.

―――. "The Synagogue of Caesarea (Preliminary Report)." *Louis Rabinowitz Bulletin for the Study of Ancient Synagogues* 3 (1960): 44–48.

―――. "Historical Geography." Pages 78–116 in vol. 1 of *The Jewish People in the First Century: Historical Geography, Political History, Social, Cultural and Religious Life and Institutions.* Edited by Shemuel Safrai and Menahem Stern. CRINT. Assen: Van Gorcum, 1974.

Ayres, Lewis. "Introduction." *JECS* 14 (2006): 395–98.

Bagnall, Roger. *Reading Papyri, Writing Ancient History.* Approaching the Ancient World. New York: Routledge, 1995.

Bakirtzis, Charalambos. "Paul and Philippi: The Archaeological Evidence." Pages 37–48 in *Philippi at the Time of Paul and after His Death.* Edited by Charalambos Bakirtzis and Helmut Koester. Harrisburg: Trinity Press International, 1998.

Banks, Robert J. *Paul's Idea of Community: The Early House Churches in Their Cultural Setting.* Grand Rapids: Baker Academic, 1995.

Barclay, John M. G. "Mirror-Reading a Polemical Letter: Galatians as a Test Case." *JSNT* 31 (1987): 73–93.

―――. "Thessalonica and Corinth: Social Contrasts in Pauline Christianity." *JSNT* 47 (1992): 49–74.

―――. *Jews in the Mediterranean Diaspora: From Alexander to Trajan (323 BCE–117 CE).* Berkeley: University of California Press, 1996.

Bardy, Gustav. *La vie spirituelle d'après les Pères des trois premières siècles.* Paris: Bloud & Guy, 1935.

―――. "Aux Origines de l'École d'Alexandrie." *RSR* 27 (1937): 69–90.

Bar-Ilan, Meir. "Illiteracy in the Land of Israel in the First Centuries CE." Pages 46–61 in vol. 2 of *Essays in the Social Scientific Study of Judaism and Jewish Society.* Edited by Simcha Fishbane, Stuart Schoenfeld, and Alain Goldschlaeger. New York: Ktav, 1992.

Barnes, Robert. "Cloistered Bookworms in the Chicken-Coop of the Muses: The Ancient Library of Alexandria." Pages 64–65 in *The Library of Alexandria: Centre of Learning in the Ancient World.* Edited by Roy Macleod. London: I. B. Tauris, 2005.

Barram, Michael. *Mission and Moral Reflection in Paul.* SBL 75. New York: Lang, 2006.

Barreto, Eric. *Ethnic Negotiations: The Function of Race and Ethnicity in Acts 16.* WUNT/2 294. Tübingen: Mohr Siebeck, 2010.

Barrett, C. K. "Attitudes to the Temple in the Acts of the Apostles." Pages 345–67 in *Templum Amicitiae: Essays on the Second Temple Presented to Ernst Bammel.* Edited by William Horbury. JSNTSup 48. Sheffield: Sheffield Academic, 1991.

———. *The Acts of the Apostles.* ICC. 2 vols. Edinburgh: T&T Clark, 1994, 1998.

Barton, Stephen C. "Why Do Things Move People? The Jerusalem Temple as Emotional Repository." *JSNT* 37 (2015): 351–80.

Bassler, Jouette M. "The Widows' Tale: A Fresh Look at 1 Tim 5:3–16." *JBL* 103 (1984): 23–41.

Bauckham, Richard. "The Martyrdom of Peter in Early Christian Literature." *ANRW* 26.1:539–95. Part 2, *Principat*, 26.1. Edited by Wolfgang Haase. Berlin: de Gruyter, 1992.

———. *The Climax of Prophecy: Studies on the Book of Revelation.* Edinburgh: T&T Clark, 1993.

———. "Dualism and Soteriology in Johannine Theology." Pages 133–53 in *Beyond Bultmann: Reckoning a New Testament Theology.* Edited by Bruce W. Longenecker and Mikeal C. Parsons. Waco, TX: Baylor University Press, 2014.

Bauer, Walter. *Orthodoxy and Heresy in Earliest Christianity.* Translated by Paul J. Achtemeier et al. Edited by Robert A. Kraft and Gerhard Krodel. London: SCM, 1972.

Bauer, Walter, Frederick William Danker, William F. Arndt, and F. Wilbur Gingrich. *Greek English Lexicon of the New Testament and Other Early Christian Literature.* 3rd ed. Chicago, 2000.

Baumgarten, Albert I. *The Flourishing of Jewish Sects in the Maccabean Era: An Interpretation.* JSJSup 55. Atlanta: SBL, 1997.

Beale, Gregory K. *The Book of Revelation: A Commentary on the Greek Text.* NIGTC. Grand Rapids: Eerdmans, 2013.

———. *John's Use of the Old Testament in Revelation.* LNTS 443. London: Bloomsbury T&T Clark, 2015.

Beare, Francis Wright. *The First Epistle of Peter: The Greek Text with Introduction and Notes.* 3rd ed. Oxford: Blackwell, 1970.

Bechtler, Steven R. *Following in His Steps: Suffering, Community and Christology in 1 Peter.* SBLDS 162. Atlanta: Scholars, 1998.

Beetham, Christopher. *Echoes of Scripture in the Letter of Paul to the Colossians.* BibInt 96. Atlanta: SBL, 2010.

Bendemann, Reinhard von, and Markus Tiwald, eds. *Das frühe Christentum und die Stadt.* Stuttgart: Kohlhammer, 2012.

Bendemann, Reinhard von, and Markus Tiwald. "Das frühe Christentum und die Stadt—Einleitung und Grundlegung." Pages 9–42 in *Das frühe Christentum und die Stadt.* Edited by Reinhard von Bendemann and Markus Tiwald. BWANT 198. Stuttgart: Kohlhammer, 2012.

Best, Ernest. *One Body in Christ: A Study in the Relationship of the Church to Christ in the Epistles of the Apostle Paul.* London: SPCK, 1955.

———. *1 Peter.* NCB. London: Oliphants, 1971.

Betz, Hans Dieter. *Galatians: A Commentary on Paul's Letter to the Churches in Galatia.* Hermeneia. Philadelphia: Fortress, 1979.

Binder, Donald D. *Into the Temple Courts: The Place of the Synagogues in the Second-Temple Period.* SBLDS 169. Atlanta: SBL, 1999.

Bird, Michael F. "'One Who Will Arise to Rule over the Nations': Paul's Letter to the Romans and the Roman Empire." Pages 146–165 in *Jesus Is Lord, Caesar Is Not: Evaluating Empire in New Testament Studies.* Edited by Scot McKnight and Joseph B. Modica. Downers Grove, IL: InterVarsity Press. 2013.

———. *The Gospel of the Lord: How the Early Church Wrote the Story of Jesus.* Grand Rapids: Eerdmans, 2014.

Birley, Anthony R. *Officers of the Second Augustan Legion in Britain.* Cardiff: National Museum of Wales, 1990.

Bissell, David. "Placing Affective Relations: Uncertain Geographies of Pain." Pages 79–98 in *Taking Place: Non-representational Theories and Geography.* Edited by Ben Anderson and Paul Harrison. Aldershot: Ashgate, 2010.

Blomberg, Craig L. *1 Corinthians.* NIVAC. Grand Rapids: Zondervan, 1994.

Blue, Bradley B. "Apollos." Pages 37–39 in *Dictionary of Paul and His Letters.* Edited by Gerald F. Hawthorne, Ralph P. Martin, and Daniel G. Reid. Downers Grove, IL: InterVarsity Press, 1993.

Boas, Franz. "Changes in Bodily Form of Descendants of Immigrants." *Am. Anthropol.* 14 (1912): 530–63.

Bockmuehl, Markus. *The Epistle to the Philippians.* BNTC. London: Black, 1997.

———. "Peter's Death in Rome? Back to Front and Upside Down." *SJT* 60 (2007): 1–23.

Boer, Roland. *Criticism of Heaven: On Marxism and Theology.* Leiden: Brill, 2005.

Bonhoeffer, Dietrich. *The Cost of Discipleship.* Translated by R. H. Fuller. New York: Touchstone, 1995. Translation of *Nachfolge.* Munich: Chr. Kaiser, 1937.

Borse, Udo. "Paulus in Jerusalem." Pages 43–64 in *Kontinuität und Einheit: Festschrift für Franz Mußner.* Edited by Paul-Gerhard Müller and Werner Stenger. Freiburg, Basel, Vienna: Herder, 1981. Republished as pages 251–76 in *Studien zur Entstehung und Auslegung des Neuen Testaments.* Edited by Regina Börschel et al. SBAB 21. Stuttgart: Katholisches Bibelwerk, 1996.

Botha, Peter J. J. *Orality and Literacy in Early Christianity.* Biblical Performance Criticism 5. Eugene, OR: Cascade, 2012.

Bourdieu, Pierre. *Outline of a Theory of Practice.* Translated by Richard Nice. Cambridge Studies in Social Anthropology 16. Cambridge: Cambridge University Press, 1977.

Bowers, W. Paul. "Mission." Page 608–19 in *Dictionary of Paul and the Letters.* Edited by Gerald F. Hawthorne, Ralph P. Martin, and Daniel G. Reid. Downers Grove, IL: Inter Varsity Press, 1993.

Boyancé, Pierre. *Le culte des Muses chez les philosophes grecs. Études d'histoire et de psychologie religieuses.* Paris: Edition de Boccard, 1937.

Bray, Gerald, ed. *1 and 2 Corinthians.* ACCSNT 7. Downers Grove, IL: InterVarsity Press, 1999.

Brélaz, Cédric. *La sécurité publique en Asie Mineure sous le Principat (Ier–IIIème s. ap. J.-C.). Institutions municipales et institutions impériales dans l'Orient romain.* Basel: Schwabe, 2005.

———. *Corpus des inscriptions grecques et latines de Philippes. Tome II. La colonie romaine. Partie 1. La vie publique de la colonie.* Athens: École française d'Athènes, 2014.

———. "La langue des *incolae* sur le territoire de Philippes et les contacts linguistiques dans les colonies romaines d'Orient." Pages 371–407 in *Interpretatio. Traduire l'altérité dans les civilisations de l'Antiquité.* Edited by Frédéric Colin and Olivier Huck. Paris: de Boccard, 2015.

———. "Entre Philippe II, Auguste et Paul: la commémoration des origines dans la colonie romaine de Philippes." In *Une mémoire en actes: espaces, figures, discours.* Edited by Stéphane Benoist, Anne Daguet-Gagey and Christine Hoët-van Cauwenberghe. Lille: Presses Universitaires du Septentrion, 2016.

———. "Philippi: A Roman Colony within Its Regional Context." In *L'hégémonie romaine sur les communautés du Nord Égéen (IIᵉ s. av. J.-C.– IIᵉ s. ap. J.-C.): entre ruptures et continuités.* Edited by Julien Fournier and Maria-Gabriella G. Parissaki. Athens: National Hellenic Research Foundation, forthcoming.

Brélaz, Cédric, and Julien Demaille. "Traces du passé macédonien et influences de l'hellénisme dans les colonies de Dion et de Philippes." In *L'héritage grec des colonies romaines d'Orient: interactions culturelles dans les provinces hellénophones de l'empire romain.* Edited by Cédric Brélaz. Paris: de Boccard, forthcoming.

Bremmer, Jan N. *The Rise of Christianity through the Eyes of Gibbon, Harnack, and Rodney Stark.* 2nd ed. Groningen: Barkhuis, 2010.

Broek, Roelof van den. "Juden and Christen in Alexandrien im 2. und 3. Jahrhundert." Pages 181–96 in *Juden und Christen in der Antike.* Edited by Johannes van Oort. Kampen: Kok, 1990.

Brooks, James A. "Clement of Alexandria as a Witness to the Development of the New Testament Canon." *SC* 9 (1992): 41–55.

Brown, Raymond E. *The Epistles of John,* AB 30. New York: Doubleday, 1982.

———. *The Death of the Messiah: From Gethsemane to the Grave. A Commentary on the Passion Narratives in the Four Gospels.* 2 vols. ABRL. New York: Doubleday, 1994.

Brox, Norbert. "Zur pseudepigraphischen Rahmung des ersten Petrusbriefes." *BZ* 19 (1975): 78–96.

———. *Der erste Petrusbrief.* 3rd ed. EKKNT 21. Zürich/Neukirchen-Vluyn: Benziger, 1989.

Bruce, F. F. *The Epistle of Paul to the Galatians: A Commentary on the Greek Text.* NIGTC. Exeter: Paternoster, 1982.

Brueggemann, Walter. *Interpretation and Obedience.* Minneapolis: Fortress, 1991.

Brunt, P. A., and J. M. Moore, eds. *Res Gestae Divi Augusti: The Achievements of the Divine Augustus.* Oxford: Oxford University Press, 1967.

Bryen, Ari Z. "Martyrdom, Rhetoric and the Politics of Procedure." *ClAnt* 33 (2014): 243–80.

Buckland, William W., and Peter G. Stein. *A Text-book of Roman Law from Augustus to Justinian.* 3rd ed. Cambridge: Cambridge University Press, 1963.

Bullinger, E. W. *Figures of Speech Used in the Bible Explained and Illustrated.* Eastford, CT: Martino Fine Books, 2011.

———. "Hypocatastasis; or Implication—Bullinger's Figures of Speech Used in the Bible." *StudyLight.org.* http://www.studylight.org/lexicons/bullinger/hypocatastasis-or-implication.html.

Burrell, Barbara. "Palace to Praetorium: The Romanization of Caesarea." Pages 228–47 in *Caesarea Maritima, A Retrospective after Two Millennia*. Edited by Avner Raban and Kenneth Holum. DMOA 21. Leiden: Brill, 1996.

———. "Herod's Caesarea on Sebastos: Urban Structures and Influences," Pages 117–233 in *Herod and Augustus: Papers Presented at the IJS Conference, 21st–23rd June 2005*. Edited by David M. Jacobson and Nikos Kokkinos. Leiden: Brill, 2009.

Burrell, Barbara, Kathryn Gleason, and Ehud Netser. "Uncovering Herod's Seaside Palace." *BAR* 19 (1993): 50–57.

Butler, Chris. *Henri Lefebvre: Spatial Politics, Everyday Life and the Right to the City*. Abingdon: Routledge, 2012.

Byrne, Maurice A. "The Date of the City Gate of Antioch." Pages 193–200 in *First International Conference on Antioch in Pisidia*. Edited by Thomas Drew-Bear, Mehmet Taşlıalan, and Christine M. Thomas. Ismit: Kocaeli, 2000.

Byrne, Maurice A., and Guy Labarre, eds. *Nouvelles inscriptions d'Antioche de Pisidie d'après les note-books de W. M. Ramsay*. IGSK 67. Bonn: Habelt, 2006.

Calderini, Rita. "Gli ἀγράμματοι nell'Egitto greco-romano." *Aeg* 30 (1950): 14–41.

Calvin, John. *The Epistle of Paul the Apostle to the Hebrews and the First and Second Epistles of St. Peter*. Translated by William B. Johnston. Calvin's Commentaries. Edinburgh & London: Oliver & Boyd, 1963.

Campbell, William S. *The "We" Passages in the Acts of the Apostles: The Narrator as Narrative Character*. SBLStBL 14. Atlanta: SBL, 2007.

Carr, David M. *Writing on the Tablet of the Heart: Origins of Scripture and Literature*. New York: Oxford University Press, 2005.

Carter, Warren. *Matthew and Empire: Initial Explorations*. Harrisburg, PA: Trinity Press International, 2001.

———. "Going All the Way? Honoring the Emperor and Sacrificing Wives and Slaves in 1 Peter 2.13–3.6." Pages 14–33 in *A Feminist Companion to the Catholic Epistles*. Edited by Amy-Jill Levine and Maria Mayo Robbins. London: T&T Clark, 2004.

———. *The Roman Empire and the New Testament: An Essential Guide*. Nashville: Abingdon, 2006.

Cartledge, Paul, and Antony Spawforth. *Hellenistic and Roman Sparta: A Tale of Two Cities*. States and Cities of Ancient Greece. London: Routledge, 1989.

Cassem, N. H. "A Grammatical and Contextual Inventory of the Use of κόσμος in the Johannine Corpus with Some Implications for a Johannine Cosmic Theology." *NTS* 19 (1972–73): 81–91.

Casson, Lionel. *Libraries in the Ancient World*. New Haven: Yale University Press, 2001.

Cavanagh, William G., Joost Crouwel, R. W. V. Catling, and Graham Shipley. *The Lakonia Survey: Archaeological Data*. Vol. 2 of *Continuity and Change in a Greek Rural Landscape*. BSASup 27. London: British School at Athens, 1996.

———. *The Lakonia Survey: Methodology and Interpretation*. Vol. 1 of *Continuity and Change in a Greek Rural Landscape*. BSASup 26. London: British School at Athens, 2003.

Charlesworth, James H. "The Temple and Jesus Followers." Pages 183–212 in *Jesus and the Temple: Textual and Archaeological Explorations*. Edited by James H. Charlesworth. Minneapolis: Fortress, 2014.

Ciampa, Roy E. "Paul's Theology of the Gospel." Pages 180–91 in *Paul as Missionary: Identity, Activity, Theology, and Practice*. Edited by Trevor J. Burke and Brian S. Rosner. LNTS 420. London: T&T Clark, 2011.

Clark, Andrew C. *Parallel Lives: The Relation of Paul to the Apostles in the Lucan Perspective*. PBM. Carlisle: Paternoster, 2001.

Clarke, Andrew D. "Another Corinthian Erastus Inscription." *TynBul* 42 (1991): 146–51.

———. *Secular and Christian Leadership in Corinth: A Socio-historical and Exegetical Study of 1 Corinthians 1–6*. AGJU 18. Leiden: Brill, 1993.

Cloke, Paul. "Emerging Geographies of Evil? Theo-ethics and Postsecular Possibilities." *Cult. Geogr.* 18 (2011): 475–93.

Cloke, Paul, and Justin Beaumont. "Geographies of Postsecular Rapprochement in the City." *Prog. Hum. Geogr.* 37 (2013): 27–51.

Cohen, Edward E. *The Athenian Nation*. Princeton: Princeton University Press, 2000.

Cohen, Shaye J. D. *The Beginnings of Jewishness: Boundaries, Varieties, Uncertainties*. Berkeley: University of California Press, 1999.

Collart, Paul. "Inscriptions de Philippes." *BCH* 56 (1932): 192–231.

———. *Philippes, ville de Macédoine, depuis ses origines jusqu'à la fin de l'époque romaine*. Paris: de Boccard, 1937.

———. "Inscriptions de Philippes." *BCH* 62 (1938): 409–32.

Collart, Paul, and Pierre Ducrey. *Philippes I. Les reliefs rupestres*. Athens: École française d'Athènes, 1975.

Cotton, Hannah M., and William Eck. "Governors and Their Personnel on Latin Inscriptions from Caesarea Maritima." *PIASH* 7/7 (2001): 215–40.

Countryman, L. William. *The Rich Christian in the Church of the Early Empire: Contradictions and Accommodations*. Toronto: Edwin Mellen, 1980.

Cousar, Charles B. "The Theological Task of 1 Corinthians: A Conversation with Gordon D. Fee and Victor Paul Furnish." Pages 90–102 in *1 and 2 Corinthians*. Edited by David Hay. Vol. 2 of *Pauline Theology*. SymS 22. Minneapolis: Fortress, 1993.

Cousland, J. R. C. Review of Bruce W. Winter, *Philo and Paul among the Sophists. Bryn Mawr Classical Review* (1999). http://bmcr.brynmawr.edu/1999/1999-02-13.html.

Coverley, Merlin. *Psychogeography*. Harpenden: Pocket Essentials, 2006.

Cranfield, C.E.B. *A Critical and Exegetical Commentary on the Epistle to the Romans*. 2 vols. ICC. Edinburgh: T&T Clark, 1975–1979.

Cribiore, Raffaella. *Writing, Teachers and Students in Graeco-Roman Egypt*. ASP 36. Atlanta: Scholars, 1996.

———. *Gymnastics of the Mind: Greek Education in Hellenistic and Roman Egypt*. Princeton: Princeton University Press, 2001.

Dalongeville, R., Maria Lakakis, and Athanassios D. Rizakis, eds. *Paysages d'Achaie: le bassin du Peiros et la plaine occidentale*. Meletēmata 15. Athens: De Boccard, 1992.

Dana, Dan. *Onomasticon Thracicum. Répertoire des noms indigènes de Thrace, Macédoine orientale, Mésies, Dacie et Bithynie*. Meletēmata 70. Athens: National Hellenic Research Foundation, 2014.

Davies, John. "Walking the M62." http://www.johndavies.org.

Dawson, David. *Allegorical Readers and Cultural Revision in Ancient Alexandria*. Berkeley: University of California, 1992.

Delaney, David. *The Spatial, the Legal and the Pragmatics of World-Making: Nomospheric Investigations.* Abingdon: Routledge, 2010.

Derrenbacker, R. A., Jr. *Ancient Compositional Practices and the Synoptic Problem.* BETL 186. Leuven: Peeters, 2005.

Dewsbury, John-David. "Witnessing Space: Knowledge without Contemplation." *Env. Plan. A* 35 (2003): 1907–32.

Dewsbury, John-David, and Paul Cloke. "Spiritual Landscapes: Existence, Performance and Immanence." *Soc. Cult. Geogr.* 10 (2009): 695–711.

Dickens, Charles. *A Tale of Two Cities.* Ware: Wordsworth, 1999.

Dickson, John P. *Mission-Commitment in Ancient Judaism and in the Pauline Communities: The Shape, Extent and Background of Early Christian Mission.* WUNT/2 159. Tübingen: Mohr Siebeck, 2003.

Dinkler, Michal Beth. "'The Thoughts of Many Hearts Shall Be Revealed': Listening in on Lukan Interior Monologues." *JBL* 133 (2015): 373–99.

Doering, Lutz. "First Peter as Early Christian Diaspora Letter." Pages 215–36, 441–47 in *The Catholic Epistles and Apostolic Tradition: A New Perspective on James to Jude.* Edited by Karl-Wilhelm Niebuhr and Robert W. Wall. Waco, TX: Baylor University Press, 2009.

———. *Ancient Jewish Letters and the Beginnings of Christian Epistolography.* WUNT 298. Tübingen: Mohr Siebeck, 2012.

———. "Gottes Volk: Die Adressaten als 'Israel' im Ersten Petrusbrief." Pages 81–113 in *Bedrängnis und Identität: Studies zu Situation, Kommunikation und Theologie des 1. Petrusbriefes.* Edited by David du Toit. BZNW 200. Berlin: De Gruyter, 2013.

Downey, Glanville. "Caesarea and the Christian Church." Pages 23–42 in *Studies in the History of Caesarea Maritima.* Vol. 1 of *The Joint Expedition to Caesarea Maritima.* BASORSup 19. Edited by Charles T. Fritsch. Missoula, MT: Scholars, 1975.

Drobner, Hubertus R. *The Fathers of the Church: A Comprehensive Introduction.* Translated by Siegfried S. Schatzmann. Peabody, MA: Hendrickson, 2007.

Dubis, Mark. *1 Peter: A Handbook on the Greek Text.* BHGNT. Waco, TX: Baylor University Press, 2010.

Dunderberg, Ismo. "The School of Valentinus." Pages 64–99 in *A Companion to Second-Century Christian "Heretics."* Edited by Antti Marjanen and Petri Luomanen. VCSup 76. Leiden: Brill, 2005.

Dunn, James D. G. *Romans 9–16.* WBC 38B. Texas: Word, 1988.

———. "'The Body of Christ' in Paul." Pages 146–62 in *Worship, Theology, and Ministry in the Early Church.* Edited by Michael J. Wilkins and Terence Paige. JSNTSup 87. Sheffield: Sheffield Academic, 1992.

———. *Beginning from Jerusalem.* Christianity in the Making 2. Grand Rapids: Eerdmans, 2009.

———. *Baptism in the Holy Spirit: A Re-examination of the New Testament Teaching on the Gift of the Spirit in Relation to Pentecostalism Today.* 2nd ed. London: SCM, 2010.

Du Plessis, Paul J. *Borkowski's Textbook on Roman Law.* 5th ed. Oxford: Oxford University Press, 2015.

Dyck, Jonathan. "Philo, Alexandria and Empire: The Politics of Allegorical Interpretation." Pages 149–74 in *Jews in the Hellenistic and Roman Cities*. Edited by John R. Bartlett. London: Routledge 2002.

Dyson, Stephen L. *Ancient Marbles to American Shores: Classical Archaeology in the United States*. Philadelphia: University of Pennsylvania Press, 1998.

Ebel, Eva. *Die Attraktivität früher christlicher Gemeinden: Die Gemeinde von Korinth im Spiegel griechisch-römischer Vereine*. WUNT/2 178. Tübingen: Mohr Siebeck, 2004.

———. "Paul's Missionary Activity." Pages 111–20 in *Paul: Life, Setting, Work, Letters*. Edited by Oda Wischmeyer. London: T&T Clark, 2012.

Ebner, Martin. *Die Stadt als Lebensraum der ersten Christen*. Vol. 1 of *Das Urchristentum in seiner Umwelt*. GNT 1/1. Göttingen: Vandenhoeck & Ruprecht, 2012.

Eckert, Jost. "Die Kollekte des Paulus für Jerusalem." Pages 65–80 in *Kontinuität und Einheit. Festschrift für Franz Mußner*. Edited by Paul-Gerhard Müller and Werner Stenger, Freiburg, Basel, Vienna: Herder, 1981.

Eckstein, Arthur. M. "Macedonia and Rome, 221–146 BC." Pages 225–50 in *A Companion to Ancient Macedonia*. Edited by Joseph Roisman and Ian Worthington. Chichester: Wiley-Blackwell, 2010.

Eddy, Paul Rhodes, and Gregory A. Boyd. *The Jesus Legend: A Case for the Historical Reliability of the Synoptic Tradition*. Grand Rapids: Baker Academic, 2007.

Edensor, Tim. *Industrial Ruins: Space, Aesthetics and Materiality*. Oxford: Berg, 2005.

Ehrensperger, Kathy. *Paul at the Crossroads of Cultures: Theologizing in the Space Between*. LNTS 456. London: Bloomsbury T&T Clark, 2013.

Eisenbaum, Pamela. *Paul Was Not a Christian: The Original Message of a Misunderstood Apostle*. San Francisco: HarperOne, 2009.

Elden, Stuart. "Politics, Philosophy, Geography: Henri Lefebvre in Recent Anglo-American Scholarship." *Antipode* 10 (2001): 809–25.

Elliott, John H. *The Elect and the Holy: An Exegetical Examination of 1 Peter 2:4–10 and the Phrase* basileion hierateuma. NovTSup 12. Leiden: Brill, 1966.

———. *A Home for the Homeless: A Social-Scientific Criticism of 1 Peter, Its Situation and Strategy*. 2nd ed. Minneapolis: Fortress, 1990 [1981].

———. *1 Peter: A New Translation with Introduction and Commentary*. AB 37B. New York: Doubleday, 2000.

Elliott, Susan M. "Choose Your Mother, Choose Your Master: Galatians 4:21–5:1 in the Shadow of the Anatolian Mother of the Gods." *JBL* 118 (1999): 661–83.

Engels, Donald. *Roman Corinth: An Alternative Model for the Classical City*. Chicago: University of Chicago Press, 1990.

Erskine, Andrew. "Culture and Power in Ptolemaic Egypt: The Museum and Library of Alexandria." *GR* 42 (1995): 38–48.

Eubank, Nathan. *Wages of Cross-Bearing and Debt of Sin: The Economy of Heaven in Matthew's Gospel*. BZNW 196. Berlin: de Gruyter, 2013.

Evans, Craig A. *Jesus and His World: The Archaeological Evidence*. London: SPCK, 2012.

Evans, Elizabeth. *Physiognomics in the Ancient World*. TAPS 59. Philadelphia: American Philosophical Society, 1969.

Everett, Nicholas. *Literacy in Lombard Italy, c. 568–774*. Cambridge: Cambridge University Press, 2003.

Faust, Avraham. *Judah in the Neo-Babylonian Period: The Archaeology of Desolation.* Atlanta: SBL, 2012.

Favro, Diane G. *The Urban Image of Augustan Rome.* Cambridge: Cambridge University Press, 1996.

Fee, Gordon D. *The First Epistle to the Corinthians.* NICNT. Grand Rapids: Eerdmans, 1987.

―――. *Paul's Letter to the Philippians.* NICNT. Grand Rapids: Eerdmans, 1995.

Feldmeier, Reinhard. *The First Letter of Peter: A Commentary on the Greek Text.* Translated by Peter H. Davids. Waco, TX: Baylor University Press, 2008.

Fergus, Donald. *"Lebensraum*—Just What Is This 'Habitat' or 'Living Space' That Dietrich Bonhoeffer Claimed for the Church?" *SJT* 67 (2014): 70–84.

Finger, Reta. *Of Widows and Meals: Communal Meals in the Book of Acts.* Grand Rapids: Eerdmans, 2007.

Finney, Mark T. *Honour and Conflict in the Ancient World: 1 Corinthians in Its Greco-Roman Setting.* LNTS 460. London: T&T Clark, 2012.

Flessen, Bonnie. *An Exemplary Man: Cornelius and Characterization in Acts 10.* Eugene, OR: Wipf & Stock, 2011.

Foster, Paul. "Secret Mark." Pages 171–82 in *The Non-Canonical Gospels.* Edited by Paul Foster. London: T&T Clark, 2008.

Fournier, J. *Entre tutelle romaine et autonomie civique. L'administration judiciaire dans les provinces hellénophones de l'empire romain (129 av. J.-C.–235 apr. J.-C.).* Athens: École française d'Athènes, 2010.

Fowden, Garth. *The Egyptian Hermes. A Historical Approach to the Later Pagan Mind.* Princeton: Princeton University Press, 1993.

Foxhall, Lin, David W. J. Gill, and Hamish A. Forbes. "The Inscriptions of Methana." Pages 269–77 in *A Rough and Rocky Place: The Landscape and Settlement History of the Methana Peninsula, Greece. Results of the Methana Survey Project Sponsored by the British School at Athens and the University of Liverpool.* Edited by Christopher B. Mee and Hamish A. Forbes. Liverpool: Liverpool University Press, 1997.

France, R. T. *The Gospel of Matthew.* NICNT. Grand Rapids: Eerdmans, 2007.

Fraser, M. Peter. *Ptolemaic Alexandria.* Oxford: Clarendon, 1972.

Fredriksen, Paula. "Did Jesus Oppose the Purity Laws?" *BRev* 11 (1995): 18–25, 42–47.

Freedman, David Noel, ed. *Anchor Bible Dictionary.* 6 vols. New York: Doubleday, 1992.

French, David H. "The Roman Road-system of Asia Minor." *ANRW* 7.2:698–729. Part 2, *Principat,* 7.2. Edited by Hildegard Temporini and Wolfgang Haase. Berlin: de Gruyter, 1980.

―――. *Roman Roads and Milestones of Asia Minor,* fasc. 2: *An Interim Catalogue of Milestones.* British Archaeological Reports International Series 392. Oxford: British Archaeological Reports, 1988.

Frey, Jörg. "Die Ausbreitung des frühen Christentums: Perspektiven für die gegenwärtige Praxis der Kirche." Pages 86–112 in *Kirche zwischen postmoderner Kultur und Evangelium.* Edited by Martin Reppenhagen. Neukirchen-Vluyn: Neukirchener Verlag, 2010.

Friesen, Steven J. "Revelation, Realia and Religion: Archaeology in the Interpretation of the Apocalypse." *HTR* 88 (1995): 291–314.

———. *Imperial Cults and the Apocalypse of John: Reading Revelation in the Ruins*. New York: Oxford University Press, 2001.

———. "Prospects for a Demography of the Pauline Mission: Corinth among the Churches." Pages 351–70 in *Urban Religion in Roman Corinth: Interdisciplinary Approaches*. Edited by Daniel N. Schowalter and Steven J. Friesen. HTS 53. Cambridge, MA: Harvard University Press, 2005.

———. "Introduction: Context, Comparison." Pages 1–12 in *Corinth in Context: Comparative Studies on Religion and Society*. Edited by Steven J. Friesen, Daniel N. Schowalter, and James C. Walters. NovTSup 134. Leiden: Brill, 2010.

Friesen, Steven J., Daniel N. Schowalter, and James C. Walters, eds. *Corinth in Context: Comparative Studies on Religion and Society*. NovTSup 134. Leiden: Brill, 2010.

Funk, Robert W. "The Form and Structure of II and III John." *JBL* 86 (1967): 424–30.

Gardner, Jane F. "Proofs of Status in the Roman World." *BICS* 33 (1986): 1–14.

Garland, David E. *1 Corinthians*. BECNT. Grand Rapids: Baker Academic, 2003.

Garnsey, Peter. *Social Status and Legal Privilege in the Roman Empire*. Oxford: Clarendon, 1970.

Garrett, Bradley L. *Explore Everything: Place-Hacking the City*. London: Verso, 2013.

Giddens, Anthony. *Central Problems in Social Theory*. London & Basingstoke: Macmillan, 1979.

———. *The Constitution of Society: Outline of the Theory of Structuration*. Cambridge: Polity, 1984.

Gill, David. W. J. "Erastus the Aedile." *TynBul* 40 (1989): 293–301.

———. "Behind the Classical Façade, Local Religions in the Roman Empire." Pages 85–100 in *One Lord, One God: Christianity in a World of Religious Pluralism*. Edited by Andrew D. Clarke and Bruce W. Winter. 2nd ed. Grand Rapids: Baker, 1992.

———. "Corinth: A Roman Colony in Achaea." *BZ* 37 (1993): 259–64.

———. "In Search of the Social Elite in the Corinthian Church." *TynBul* 44 (1993): 323–37.

———. "Macedonia." Pages 397–417 in *The Book of Acts in Its Graeco-Roman Setting*. Edited by David W. J. Gill and Conrad H. Gempf. BAFCS 2. Carlisle: Paternoster/ Grand Rapids: Eerdmans, 1994.

———. "Paul's Travels through Cyprus (Acts 13:4–12)." *TynBul* 46 (1995): 219–28.

———. "The Roman Empire as a Context for the New Testament." Pages 388–406 in *Handbook to Exegesis of the New Testament*. Edited by Stanley E. Porter. NTTS 25. Leiden: Brill, 1997.

———. "1 Corinthians." Pages 100–193 in vol. 3 of the *Zondervan Illustrated Bible Backgrounds Commentary: Romans to Philemon*. Edited by Clinton E. Arnold. 4 vols. Grand Rapids: Zondervan, 2002.

———. "The British School at Athens and Archaeological Research in the Late Ottoman Empire." Pages 223–55 in vol. 1 of *Archaeology, Anthropology and Heritage in the Balkans and Anatolia: The Life and Times of F. W. Hasluck, 1878–1920*. Edited by D. Shankland. 2 vols. Istanbul: Isis, 2004.

————. *Sifting the Soil of Greece: The Early Years of the British School at Athens (1886–1919)*. BICSSup 111. London: Institute of Classical Studies, 2011.

Gill, David W. J., and Conrad H. Gempf, eds. *The Book of Acts in Its Graeco-Roman Setting*. BAFCS 2. Carlisle: Paternoster/Grand Rapids: Eerdmans, 1994.

Gill, David W. J., and Moyer V. Hubbard. *1 and 2 Corinthians*. Zondervan Illustrated Bible Backgrounds Commentary. Grand Rapids: Zondervan, 2007.

Gleason, Kathryn. "Ruler and Spectacle: The Promontary Palace." Pages 208–27 in *Caesarea Maritima, A Retrospective after Two Millennia*. Edited by Avner Raban and Kenneth Holum. DMOA 21. Leiden: Brill, 1996.

Gleason, Kathryn, Barbara Burrell, Ehud Netzer, Laurel Taylor, and J. Howard Williams. "The Promontory Palace at Caesarea Maritima: Preliminary Evidence for Herod's Praetorium." *JRA* 11 (1998): 23–52.

Goodrich, John K. "Overseers as Stewards and the Qualifications for Leadership in the Pastoral Epistles." *ZNW* 104 (2013): 77–97.

Goppelt, Leonard. *Apostolic and Post-Apostolic Times*. London: Black, 1970.

————. *A Commentary on I Peter*. Edited by Ferdinand Hahn. Translated by John E. Alsup. Grand Rapids: Eerdmans, 1993.

Gorman, Michael J. *Inhabiting the Cruciform God: Kenosis, Justification and Theosis in Paul's Narrative Soteriology*. Grand Rapids: Eerdmans, 2009.

————. *Becoming the Gospel: Paul, Participation, and Mission*. Grand Rapids: Eerdmans, 2015.

Govaars, Marylinda, Marie Spiro, and L. Michael White. *The Joint Expedition to Caesarea Maritima Excavation Reports: Field O: The "Synagogue" Site*. Boston: American Schools of Oriental Research, 2009.

Gravlee, Clarence C., H. Russell Bernard, and William R. Leonard. "Heredity, Environment and Cranial Form: A Reanalysis of Boas's Immigrant Data." *Am Anthropol.* 105 (2003): 125–38.

Guerber, E. *Les cités grecques dans l'Empire romain. Les privilèges et les titres des cités de l'Orient hellénophone d'Octave Auguste à Dioclétien*. 2nd ed. Rennes: Presses Universitaires de Rennes, 2010.

Gunn, David M. "Narrative Criticism." Pages 201–29 in *To Each Its Own Meaning: An Introduction to Biblical Criticisms and Their Applications*. Edited by Stephen R. Hayes and Steven L. MacKenzie. Rev. ed. Louisville: Westminster John Knox, 1999.

Gurtner, Daniel M. "Matthew's Theology of the Temple and the 'Parting of the Ways': Christian Origins and the First Gospel." Pages 128–53 in *Built upon the Rock: Studies in the Gospel of Matthew*. Edited by Daniel M. Gurtner and John Nolland. Grand Rapids: Eerdmans, 2008.

Guthrie, Donald. *Galatians*. NCB. Grand Rapids: Eerdmans, 1973.

Guttenberger, Gudrun. Passio Christiana: *Die alltagsmartyrologische Position des Ersten Petrusbriefes*. SBS 223. Stuttgart: Katholisches Bibelwerk, 2010.

Hadas-Lebel, Mireille. *Philo of Alexandria: A Thinker in the Jewish Diaspora*. SPhA 7. Leiden: Brill, 2012.

Hall, Jonathan. *Ethnic Identity in Greek Antiquity*. New York: Cambridge University Press, 1997.

Hall, Stuart, ed. *Representation: Cultural Representations and Signifying Practices.* London: Sage, 1997.

Hamilton, Catherine S. "His Blood Be upon Us': Innocent Blood and the Death of Jesus in Matthew." *CBQ* 70 (2008): 82–100.

Hansen, Inge Lyse. *Hellenistic and Roman Butrint.* London: Butrint Foundation, 2009.

Hardie, Margaret M. "The Shrine of Mên Askaenos at Pisidian Antioch." *JHS* 32 (1912): 111–50.

Harker, Andrew. "Spiritually Called Sodom and Egypt: Getting to the Heart of Early Christian Prophecy through the Apocalypse of John." PhD diss., London School of Theology / Middlesex University, 2011.

———. "Prophetically Called Sodom and Egypt: The Affective Power of Revelation 11:1–13." Pages 19–39 in *The Book of Revelation: Currents in British Research on the Apocalypse.* Edited by Garrick Allen, Ian Paul, and Simon Woodman. WUNT/2 411. Tübingen: Mohr Siebeck, 2015.

Harland, Philip A. "Imperial Cults within Local Cultural Life: Associations in Roman Asia." *Ancient History Bulletin/Zeitschrift für Alte Geschichte* 17 (2003): 85–107.

———. *Dynamics of Identity in the World of the Early Christians: Associations, Judeans and Cultural Minorities.* New York: T&T Clark, 2009.

———. *Greco-Roman Associations: Texts, Translations and Commentary. II. North Coast of the Black Sea, Asia Minor.* Berlin: de Gruyter, 2014.

Harnack, Adolf von. *Die Mission in Wort und Tat.* Vol. 1 of *Die Mission und Ausbreitung des Christentums in den ersten drei Jahrhunderten.* 4th ed. Leipzig: Hinrichs, 1924.

Harris, Wiliam V. *Ancient Literacy.* Cambridge: Harvard University Press, 1989.

Harvey, David. *The Condition of Postmodernity: An Enquiry into the Origins of Cultural Change.* Oxford: Blackwell, 1989.

———. *Spaces of Hope.* Edinburgh: Edinburgh University Press, 2000.

Hatzopoulos, Miltiades B. *Macedonian Institutions under the Kings.* 2 vols. Meletēmata 22. Athens: National Hellenic Research Foundation, 1996.

Hawthorne, Gerald F. *Philippians.* WBC 43. Waco, TX: Word, 1983.

Hays, Richard B. *First Corinthians.* IBC. Louisville: John Knox, 1997.

Head, Peter. "The Temple in Luke's Gospel." Pages 101–19 in *Heaven on Earth: The Temple in Biblical Theology.* Edited by T. Desmond Alexander and Simon Gathercole. Carlisle: Paternoster, 2004.

Hellerman, Joseph H. *Reconstructing Honor in Roman Philippi: Carmen Christi as Cursus Pudorum.* SNTSMS 132. Cambridge: Cambridge University Press, 2005.

Hemer, Colin J. "First Person Narrative in Acts 27–28." *TynBul* 36 (1985): 79–109.

———. *The Book of Acts in the Setting of Hellenistic History.* Edited by Conrad H. Gempf. WUNT 49. Tübingen: Mohr Siebeck, 1989.

———. *The Letters to the Seven Churches of Asia in Their Local Setting.* JSNTSup 11. Sheffield: Sheffield Academic, 1989.

Hengel, Martin. *Between Jesus and Paul: Studies in the Earliest History of Christianity.* Translated by John Bowden. London: SCM, 1983.

Hengel, Martin, and Roland Deines. *The Pre-Christian Paul.* London: SCM, 1991.

Hengel, Martin, and Anna Maria Schwemer. *Paul between Damascus and Antioch.* London: SCM, 1997.

Herzer, Jens. *Petrus oder Paulus? Studien über das Verhältnis des Ersten Petrusbriefes zur paulinischen Tradition.* WUNT 103. Tübingen: Mohr Siebeck, 1998.

Hezser, Catherine. *Jewish Literacy in Roman Palestine.* TSAJ 81. Tübingen: Mohr Siebeck, 2001.

Hill, Charles E. *The Johannine Corpus in the Early Church.* Oxford: Oxford University Press, 2004.

Hock, Ronald F. *The Social Context of Paul's Ministry: Tentmaking and Apostleship.* Philadelphia: Fortress, 1980.

Hoek, Annewies van den. "How Alexandrian Was Clement of Alexandria? Reflections on Clement and His Alexandrian Background." *HeyJ* 31 (1990): 179–94.

Hofius, Otfried. "Paulus - Missionar und Theologe." Pages 1–16 in *Paulusstudien II.* By Otfried Hofius. WUNT 143. Tübingen: Mohr Siebeck, 2002.

Holloway, Julian. "The Space That Faith Makes: Towards a (Hopeful) Ethos of Engagement." Pages 203–18 in *Religion and Place: Landscape, Politics and Piety.* Edited by Peter Hopkins, Lily Kong, and Elizabeth Olson. New York: Springer, 2013.

Holloway, Paul A. *Coping with Prejudice: 1 Peter in Social-Psychological Perspective.* WUNT 244. Tübingen: Mohr Siebeck, 2009.

Holum, Kenneth G. "The Temple Platform: A Progress Report." Pages 12–34 in *Caesarea Papers 2: Herod's Temple, the Provincial Governor's Praetorium and Granaries, the Later Harbor, a Gold Coin Hoard, and Other Studies.* Edited by Kenneth G. Holum, Avner Raban, and Joseph Patrich. JRASup 35. Portsmouth, RI: Journal of Roman Archaeology, 1999.

Holum, Kenneth G., Robert L. Hohlfelder, Robert J. Bull, and Avner Raban. *King Herod's Dream: Caesarea on the Sea.* New York: Norton, 1988.

Honigman, Sylvie. "Philon, Flavius Josèphe, et la citoyenneté alexandrine: vers une utopie politique." *JJS* 48 (1997): 62–90.

Horrell, David G. "Leadership Patterns and the Development of Ideology in Early Christianity." *Sociol. Relig.* 58 (1997): 323–41.

———. *The Epistles of Peter and Jude.* EC. Peterborough: Epworth, 1998.

———. "The Product of a Petrine Circle? A Reassessment of the Origin and Character of 1 Peter." *JSNT* 86 (2002): 29–60.

———. "The Label Χριστιανός: 1 Pet 4.16 and the Formation of Christian Identity." *JBL* 126 (2007): 361–81.

———. "Aliens and Strangers? The Socioeconomic Location of the Addressees of 1 Peter." Pages 176–202 in *Engaging Economics: New Testament Scenarios and Early Christian Reception.* Edited by Bruce Longenecker and Kelly Liebengood. Grand Rapids: Eerdmans, 2009.

———. *Becoming Christian: Essays on 1 Peter and the Making of Christian Identity.* LNTS / EaChrCon 394. London: Bloomsbury T&T Clark, 2013.

———. "Between Conformity and Resistance: Beyond the Balch-Elliott Debate towards a Postcolonial Reading of 1 Peter." Pages 111–43 in *Reading 1 Peter with New Eyes: Methodological Reassessments of the Letter of First Peter.* Edited by Robert L. Webb and Betsy Bauman-Martin. LNTS 364. London: T&T Clark, 2007. Reprinted as pages 211–38 in *Becoming Christian: Essays on 1 Peter and the Making of Christian Identity.* Edited by David G. Horrell. LNTS 394. London: Bloomsbury T&T Clark, 2013.

————. "Σῶμα as a Basis for Ethics in Paul." Pages 351–64 in *Ethische Normen des frühen Christentums: Kontexte und Normen neutestamentlicher Ethik*. Edited by Friedrich W. Horn, Ulrich Volp, and Ruben Zimmermann. WUNT 313. Tübingen: Mohr Siebeck, 2013.

————. "'Honour Everyone . . .' (1 Pet. 2.17): The Social Strategy of 1 Peter and Its Significance for the Development of Christianity." Pages 192–210 in *To Set at Liberty: Essays on Early Christianity and Its Social World in Honor of John H. Elliott*. Edited by Stephen K. Black. Sheffield: Sheffield Phoenix, 2014.

Horsley, Richard A., ed. *Paul and Empire: Religion and Power in Roman Imperial Society*. Harrisburg, PA: Trinity Press International, 1997.

————, ed. *Paul and Politics: Ekklesia, Israel, Imperium, Interpretation*. Harrisburg, PA: Trinity Press International, 2000.

————, ed. *Paul and the Roman Imperial Order*. Harrisburg, PA: Trinity Press International, 2004.

————. *Scribes, Visionaries and the Politics of Second Temple Judea*. Louisville: Westminster John Knox, 2007.

Hort, F. J. A. *The First Epistle of St. Peter, I.1–II.17: The Greek Text with Introductory Lecture, Commentary and Additional Notes*. 1898. Reprinted: Eugene, OR: Wipf & Stock, 2005.

Howard-Brook, Wes, and Anthony Gwyther. *Unveiling Empire: Reading Revelation Then and Now*. Maryknoll, NY: Orbis, 1999.

Huber, Lynn R. *Like a Bride Adorned: Reading Metaphor in John's Apocalypse*. Emory Studies in Early Christianity 10. London: T&T Clark, 2007.

Hunzinger, Claus-Hunno. "Babylon als Deckname für Rom und die Datierung des 1. Petrusbriefes." Pages 67–77 in *Gottes Wort und Gottes Land*. Edited by Henning Graf Reventlow. Göttingen: Vandenhoeck & Ruprecht, 1965.

Hurtado, Larry W. *The Earliest Christian Artifacts: Manuscripts and Christian Origins*. Grand Rapids: Eerdmans, 2006.

Hurtado, Larry W., and Chris Keith. "Writing and Book Production in the Hellenistic and Roman Periods." Pages 63–80 in *The New Cambridge History of the Bible: From the Beginnings to 600*. Edited by Joachim Schaper and James Carleton Paget. Cambridge: Cambridge University Press, 2013.

Hurwit, Jeffrey M. *The Athenian Acropolis: History, Mythology and Archaeology from the Neolithic Era to the Present*. Cambridge: Cambridge University Press, 1999.

Hutchinson, John, and Anthony D. Smith. "Introduction." Pages 3–16 in *Ethnicity*. Edited by John Hutchinson and Anthony D. Smith. Oxford: Oxford University Press, 1996.

Huther, Johannes E., and Ernst Kühl. *Kritisch-exegetisches Handbuch über den 1. Brief des Petrus, den Brief des Judas, und den 2. Brief des Petrus*. 5th ed. KEK 12. Göttingen: Vandenhoeck & Ruprecht, 1887.

Hvalvik, Reidar. "Paul as a Jewish Believer—According to the Book of Acts." Pages 121–53 in *Jewish Believers in Jesus: The Early Centuries*. Edited by Oskar Skarsaune and Reidar Hvalvik. 2nd ed. Peabody, MA: Hendrickson, 2007.

Ironside, Henry Allan. *Wrongly Dividing the Word of Truth: Ultra-Dispensationalism Examined in the Light of Holy Scripture*. 3rd ed. New York: Loizeaux Bros, 1938.

Isaac, Benjamin. *The Invention of Racism in Classical Antiquity.* Princeton: Princeton University Press, 2004.

Isin, Engin F. *Being Political: Genealogies of Citizenship.* Minneapolis: University of Minnesota Press, 2002.

Jameson, Michael H., Curtis N. Runnels, and Tjeerd van Andel. *A Greek Countryside: The Southern Argolid from Prehistory to the Present Day.* Stanford: Stanford University Press, 1994.

Jassen, Alex P. "The Dead Sea Scrolls and Violence: Sectarian Formation and Eschatological Imagination." Pages 13–44 in *Violence, Scripture and Textual Practice in Early Judaism and Christianity.* Edited by Raanan S. Boustan, Alex P. Jassen and Calvin J. Roetzel. Leiden: Brill, 2010.

Jewett, Robert. *Romans: A Commentary.* Hermeneia. Philadelphia: Fortress, 2006.

Jobes, Karen H. *1 Peter.* BECNT. Grand Rapids: Baker, 2005.

Johnson, Luke Timothy. *The Acts of the Apostles.* SP 5. Collegeville, MN: Liturgical, 1992.

———. *The First and Second Letters to Timothy.* AB 35A. New York: Doubleday, 2001.

Johnson, William A. *Readers and Reading Culture in the High Roman Empire.* Classical Culture and Society. New York: Oxford University Press, 2010.

Jones, A. H. M. *The Greek City from Alexander to Justinian.* Oxford: Clarendon, 1940.

———. *Studies in Roman Government and Law.* Oxford: Blackwell, 1960.

Jones, Christopher M. "'The Wealth of Nations Shall Come to You': Light, Tribute and Implacement in Isaiah 60." *VT* 64 (2014): 611–22.

Jones, Christopher P. "ἔθνος and γένος in Herodotus." *CQ* 46 (1996): 315–20.

Joubert, Stephan. *Paul as Benefactor: Reciprocity, Strategy and Theological Reflection in Paul's Collection.* WUNT/2 124. Tübingen: Mohr Siebeck, 2000.

Kahn, Lisa C. "King Herod's Temple of Roma and Augustus at Caesarea Maritima." Pages 130–45 in *Caesarea Maritima: A Retrospective after Two Millennia.* Edited by Avner Raban and Kenneth G. Holum. Leiden: Brill, 1996.

Kartzow, Marianne Bjelland. *Gossip and Gender: Othering of Speech in the Pastoral Epistles.* BZNW 164. Berlin: de Gruyter, 2009.

Kasher, Aryeh. "The Isopoliteia Question in Caesarea Maritima." *JQR* 68 (1978): 16–27.

———. *The Jews in Hellenistic and Roman Egypt: The Struggle for Equal Rights.* TSAJ 7. Tübingen: Mohr Siebeck, 1985.

Kearsley, Rosalinde A. "Women in Public Life in the Roman East: Iunia Theodora, Claudia Metrodora and Phoebe, Benefactress of Paul." *TynBul* 50 (1999): 189–211.

Keener, Craig S. *Revelation.* NIVAC. Grand Rapids: Zondervan, 2000.

———. *Acts: An Exegetical Commentary.* 4 vols. Grand Rapids: Baker, 2012–15.

Keith, Chris. *The* Pericope Adulterae, *the Gospel of John and the Literacy of Jesus.* NTTSD 38. Leiden: Brill, 2009.

———. "The Claim of John 7.15 and the Memory of Jesus' Literacy." *NTS* 56 (2010): 44–63.

———. *Jesus' Literacy: Scribal Culture and the Teacher from Galilee.* LHJS 8 / LNTS 413. London: T&T Clark, 2011.

———. *Jesus against the Scribal Elite: The Origins of the Conflict.* Grand Rapids: Baker Academic, 2014.

———. "The Oddity of the Reference to Jesus in Acts 4:13b." *JBL* 134 (2015): 791–811.

————. Review of *The Gospel of the Lord: How the Early Church Wrote the Story of Jesus* by Michael F. Bird. *SCJ* 18 (2015): 144–47.

Kelly, J. N. D. *A Commentary on the Epistles of Peter and of Jude*. BNTC. London: Black, 1969.

Kennedy, Liam. *Race and Urban Space in Contemporary American Culture*. Edited by Peter Brooker. Tendencies: Identities, Texts, Cultures. Edinburgh: Edinburgh University Press, 2000.

Kent, John Harvey. *The Inscriptions, 1926–1950*. Corinth: Results. Vol. 8, Part 3. Princeton: American School of Classical Studies at Athens, 1966.

Kidd, Reggie M. *Wealth and Beneficence in the Pastoral Epistles. A "Bourgeois" Form of Early Christianity?* SBLDS 122. Atlanta: Scholars, 1990.

Kim, Yung-Suk. *Christ's Body in Corinth*. Minneapolis: Fortress, 2008.

Kitchin, Rob, and Phil Hubbard, eds. *Key Thinkers on Space and Place*. 2nd ed. London: Sage, 2010.

Klauck, Hans-Josef. *Ancient Letters and the New Testament: A Guide to Context and Exegesis*. Waco, TX: Baylor University Press, 2006.

Klawans, Jonathan. *Purity, Sacrifice, and the Temple: Symbolism and Supersessionism in the Study of Ancient Judaism*. Oxford: Oxford University Press, 2006.

Klijn, Albertus F. J. "Jewish Christianity in Egypt." Pages 161–75 in *The Roots of Egyptian Christianity*. Edited by Birger A. Pearson and James E. Goehring. Philadelphia: Fortress, 1986.

Koester, Craig R. *Revelation and the End of All Things*. Grand Rapids: Eerdmans, 2001.

————. *Revelation: A New Translation with Introduction and Commentary*. AYB 38A. New Haven: Yale University Press, 2014.

Kong, Lily. "Mapping New Geographies of Religion: Politics and Poetics in Modernity." *Prog. Hum. Geogr.* 25 (2001): 211–33.

Kooten, George H. van. "Ἐκκλησία τοῦ θεοῦ: The 'Church of God' and the Civic Assemblies (ἐκκλησίαι) of the Greek Cities in the Roman Empire: A Response to Paul Trebilco and Richard A. Horsley." *NTS* 58 (2012): 522–48.

Kos, M. Šašel. "A Latin Epitaph of a Roman Legionary from Corinth." *JRS* 68 (1978): 22–25.

Kosinski, Jerzy. *Being There*. Directed by Hal Ashby. Warner Home Video, 1979.

Koukouli-Chrysanthaki, Ch. "Amphipolis." Pages 409–36 in *Brill's Companion to Ancient Macedon. Studies in the Archaeology and History of Macedon, 650 BC–300 CE*. Edited by Robin J. Lane Fox. Leiden: Brill, 2011.

————. "Philippi." Pages 437–52 in *Brill's Companion to Ancient Macedonia: Studies in Archaeology and the History of Macedonia, 650 BC–300 CE*. Edited by Robin J. Lane Fox. Leiden: Brill, 2011.

Koukouli-Chrysanthaki, Ch., and Charalambos Bakirtzis. *Philippi*. Athens: Ministry of Culture, 2003.

Kovacs, Judith. "Participation of the Cross: Pauline Motifs in the *Excerpts from Theodotus*." In *Valentinianism: Proceedings of the Conference in Rome, October 2013*. Edited by Einar Thomassen. Leiden: Brill, forthcoming.

Kovacs, Judith, and Christopher Rowland. *Revelation: The Apocalypse to Jesus Christ*. Malden, MA: Wiley, 2004.

Kraus, Thomas J. "(Il)Literacy in Non-Literary Papyri from Graeco-Roman Egypt:

Further Aspects to the Educational Ideal in Ancient Literary Sources and Modern Times." Pages 107–29 in his Ad fontes: *Original Manuscripts and Their Significance for Studying Early Christianity—Selected Essays*. TENTS 3. Leiden: Brill, 2007.

————. "'Uneducated', 'Ignorant', or Even 'Illiterate'? Aspects and Background for an Understanding of ΑΓΡΑΜΜΑΤΟΙ (and ΙΔΙΩΤΑΙ) in Acts 4.13." Pages 149–67 in his Ad fontes: *Original Manuscripts and Their Significance for Studying Early Christianity—Selected Essays*. TENTS 3. Leiden: Brill, 2007.

Krentz, Edgar. "Caesarea and Early Christianity." Pages 261–71 in *Caesarea Papers: Straton's Tower, Herod's Harbour, and Roman and Byzantine Caesarea*. Edited by Robert Lindley Vann. JRASup 5. Ann Arbor, MI: Journal of Roman Archaeology, 1992.

Kruse, Colin G. *The Letters of John*. PNTC. Grand Rapids: Eerdmans, 2000.

Kühl, Ernst. *Die Briefe Petri und Judae*. 6th ed. KEK 12. Göttingen: Vandenhoeck & Ruprecht, 1897.

Kurz, William S. *Reading Luke-Acts: Dynamics of Biblical Narrative*. Louisville: Westminster John Knox, 1993.

Lane, Eugene N. *Corpus monumentorum religionis dei Menis*. 4 vols. EPRO 19. Leiden: Brill, 1971–1978.

Lau, Andrew Y. *Manifest in Flesh: The Epiphany Christology of the Pastoral Epistles*. WUNT/2 86. Tübingen: Mohr Siebeck, 1996.

Lawton, J. F. *Pretty Woman*. Directed by Garry Marshall. Buena Vista, 1990.

Le Boulluec, Alain. "'L''école' d'Alexandrie. De quelques aventures d'un concept historiographique." Pages 403–17 in *Alexandrina: Hellénisme, judaïsme et christianisme à Alexandrie. Mélanges offerts à Claude Mondésert, SJ*. Paris: Cerf, 1987.

————. "Aux origines, encore, de l''école' d'Alexandrie." *Adamantius* 5 (1999): 7–36.

Le Donne, Anthony. *The Wife of Jesus: Ancient Texts and Modern Scandals*. London: Oneworld, 2014.

Lee, Michelle V. *Paul, the Stoics and the Body of Christ*. SNTSMS 137. Cambridge: Cambridge University Press, 2006.

Lefebvre, Henri. *The Production of Space*. Translated by Donald Nicholson. Oxford: Blackwell, 1991.

————. *Writings on Cities*. Translated by Eleonore Kofman and Elizabeth Lebas. Oxford: Blackwell, 1996.

————. *Critique of Everyday Life: The One-Volume Edition*. Translated by John Moore. London: Verso, 2014.

Lehmann, Clayton M., and Kenneth G. Holum. *The Greek and Latin Inscriptions of Caesarea Maritima*. Boston: American Schools of Oriental Research, 2000.

Lemerle, Paul. *Philippes et la Macédoine orientale à l'époque chrétienne et byzantine. Recherches d'histoire et d'archéologie*. 2 vols. Paris: de Boccard, 1945.

Lentz, John C., Jr. *Luke's Portrait of Paul*. SNTSMS 77. Cambridge: Cambridge University Press, 1993.

Leonhardt, Jutta. *Jewish Worship in Philo of Alexandria*. TSAJ 84. Tübingen: Mohr Siebeck, 2001.

Leonhardt-Balzer, Jutta. "Priests and Priesthood in Philo." Pages 121–47 in *Was 70 CE a Watershed in Jewish History? On Jews and Judaism before and after the Destruction of the Second Temple.* Edited by Daniel R. Schwartz, Zeev Weiss, in collaboration with Ruth A. Clements. AJEC 78. Leiden: Brill, 2011.

Lespez, Laurent. "L'évolution des paysages du Néolithique à la période ottomane dans la plaine de Philippes-Drama." Pages 21–416 in *Dikili Tash, village préhistorique de Macédoine orientale: recherches franco-helléniques dirigées par la Société archéologique d'Athènes et l'École française d'Athènes (1986–2001).* Edited by Haïdo Koukouli-Chryssanthaki, René Treuil, Laurent Lespez, and Dimitra Malamidou. Athens: École française d'Athènes, 2008.

Levick, Barbara. "Two Pisidian Colonial Families." *JRS* 48 (1958): 74–78.

———. "Two Inscriptions from Pisidian Antioch." *AnSt* 15 (1965): 53–62.

———. *Roman Colonies in Southern Asia Minor.* Oxford: Oxford University Press, 1967.

———. "Unpublished Inscriptions from Pisidian Antioch." *AnSt* 17 (1967): 101–21.

———. "Dedications to Mên Askaenos." *AnSt* 20 (1970): 37–50.

Levine, Lee I. "The Jewish-Greek Conflict in First-Century Caesarea." *JJS* 25 (1974): 381–97.

———. *Caesarea under Roman Rule.* SJLA 7. Leiden: Brill, 1975.

———. *Judaism and Hellenism in Antiquity: Conflict or Confluence?* Seattle: University of Washington Press, 1988.

———. "The Jewish Community at Caesarea in Late Antiquity." Pages 268–73 in *Caesarea Papers: Straton's Tower, Herod's Harbour, and Roman and Byzantine Caesarea.* Edited by Robert Lindley Vann. JRASup 5. Ann Arbor, MI: Journal of Roman Archaeology, 1992.

———. *The Ancient Synagogue. The First Thousand Years.* New Haven: Yale University Press, 2000.

Levinskaya, Irina. "The Italian Cohort in Acts 10:1." Pages 106–25 in *The New Testament in Its First Century Setting: Essays on Context and Background in Honour of B. W. Winter on His 65th Birthday.* Edited by Peter J. Williams, Andrew D. Clarke, Peter M. Head, and David Instone-Brewer. Grand Rapids: Eerdmans, 2004.

Lieber, Andrea. "Between Motherland and Fatherland: Diaspora, Pilgrimage and the Spiritualization of Sacrifice in Philo of Alexandria." Pages 193–210 in *Heavenly Tablets: Interpretation, Identity and Tradition in Ancient Judaism.* Edited by Lynn R. LiDonnici and Andrea Lieber. JSJSup 119. Leiden: Brill, 2007.

Lietaert Peerbolte, L. J. *Paul the Missionary.* CBET 34. Leuven: Peeters, 2003.

Lieu, Judith. *The Second and Third Epistles of John: History and Background.* SNTW. Edinburgh: T&T Clark, 1986.

———. *The Theology of the Johannine Epistles.* Cambridge: Cambridge University Press, 1991.

———. *I, II and III John: A Commentary.* NTL. Louisville: WJK, 2008.

Lincoln, Andrew T. *Paradise Now and Not Yet: Studies in the Role of the Heavenly Dimension in Paul's Thought with Special Reference to His Eschatology.* SNTSMS 43. Cambridge: Cambridge University Press, 1981.

Lindsey, Hal. *The Late Great Planet Earth.* Grand Rapids: Zondervan, 1970.

Liverani, Mario. *Israel's History and the History of Israel.* Translated by Chiara Peri and Philip R. Davies. Bible World. London: Equinox, 2005.

Longenecker, Bruce W. "Socio-Economic Profiling of the First Urban Christians." Pages 36–59 in *After the First Urban Christians: The Social-Scientific Study of Pau-*

line Christianity Twenty-Five Years Later. Edited by Todd D. Still and David G. Horrell. London: Continuum, 2009.

———. *Remember the Poor: Paul, Poverty, and the Greco-Roman World*. Grand Rapids: Eerdmans, 2010.

Lorimer, Hayden. "Telling Small Stories: Spaces of Knowledge and the Practice of Geography." *Trans. Inst. Brit. Geog.* 28 (2003): 197–217.

———. "Cultural Geography: The Busyness of Being 'More-Than-Representational.'" *Prog. Hum. Geogr.* 32 (2005): 551–55.

Loukopoulou, Louisa D. "*Provinciae Macedoniae finis orientalis*: The Establishment of the Eastern Frontier." Pages 89–100 in *Two Studies in Ancient Macedonian Topography*. Edited by Miltiades B. Hatzopoulos and Louisa D. Loukopoulou. Meletēmata 3. Athens: National Hellenic Research Foundation, 1987.

Lowe, Matthew Forrest. "In the Making and the Unmasking: Spiritual Formation as Paul's Missional 'Good News,' Then and Now." In *Is the Gospel Good News?* Edited by Stanley E. Porter and Hughson Ong. McMaster NT Studies Series. Eugene: Pickwick, forthcoming.

Lüderitz, Gert. "What Is the Politeuma?" Pages 183–225 in *Studies in Early Jewish Epigraphy*. Edited by Jan Willem van Henten and Pieter Willem van der Horst. AGJU 21. Leiden: Brill, 1994.

Luther, Martin. "Commentary on 1 Corinthians 15." Pages 57–213 in vol. 18 of *Luther's Works*. Edited by Hilton C. Oswald. 55 vols. St. Louis: Concordia, 1973.

Lyall, Francis. *Slaves, Citizens, Sons: Legal Metaphors in the Epistles*. Grand Rapids: Academie Books, 1984.

Magda, Ksenija. *Paul's Territoriality and Mission Strategy: Searching for the Geographical Awareness Paradigm behind Romans*. WUNT/2 266. Tübingen: Mohr Siebeck, 2009.

Maier, Harry O. "From Material Place to Imagined Space: Emergent Christian Community as Thirdspace in the Shepherd of Hermas." Pages 143–60 in *Early Christian Communities between Ideal and Reality*. Edited by Mark Grundeken and Joseph Verheyden. WUNT 342. Tübingen: Mohr Siebeck, 2015.

Malbon, Elizabeth Struthers. *Narrative Space and Mythic Meaning in Mark*. NVBS. San Francisco: Harper & Row, 1986.

Malherbe, Abraham J. *Social Aspects of Early Christianity*. Rockwell Lectures. 2nd ed. Philadelphia: Fortress, 1983.

Mandela, Nelson. *Long Walk to Freedom*. London: Abacus, 1995.

Manley, G. T. "Babylon on the Nile." *EvQ* 16 (1944): 138–46.

Marger, Martin N. *Race and Ethnic Relations: American and Global Perspectives*. Belmont, CA: Wadsworth, 2012.

Marguerat, Daniel. *Paul in Acts and Paul in His Letters*. WUNT 310. Tübingen: Mohr Siebeck, 2013.

Marshall, I. Howard. "The Christology of the Pastoral Epistles." *SNTSU* 13 (1988): 157–77.

———. *A Critical and Exegetical Commentary on the Pastoral Epistles*. ICC. Edinburgh: T&T Clark, 1999.

Martin, Dale B. *The Corinthian Body*. New Haven: Yale University Press, 1995.

Martin, Ralph P. *The Spirit and the Congregation: Studies in 1 Corinthians 12–15.* Grand Rapids: Eerdmans, 1984. Repr., Eugene, OR: Wipf & Stock, 1997.

Martyn, J. Louis. *Galatians: A New Translation with Introduction and Commentary.* AB 33A. New York: Doubleday, 1997.

Mason, Steve. "Josephus and Luke-Acts." Pages 185–229 in his *Josephus and the New Testament.* Peabody, MA: Hendrickson, 1992.

———. *Josephus, Judea and Christian Origins: Methods and Categories.* Peabody, MA: Hendrickson, 2009.

Massey, Doreen B. *For Space.* London: Sage, 2005.

Matlock, R. Barry. *Unveiling the Apocalyptic Paul: Paul's Interpreters and the Rhetoric of Criticism.* JSNTSup 127. Sheffield: Sheffield Academic, 1996.

McCabe, David R. *How to Kill Things with Words: Ananias and Sapphira under the Prophetic Speech-Acts of Divine Judgment (Acts 4.32–5.11).* LNTS 454. London: T&T Clark, 2011.

McDonald, Lee Martin. *The Biblical Canon: Its Origins, Transmission and Authority.* Updated and rev. 3rd ed. Peabody, MA: Hendrickson, 2008.

McDonald, William Andrew, and George Robert Rapp, Jr., eds. *The Minnesota Messenia Expedition: Reconstructing a Bronze Age Regional Environment.* Minneapolis: University of Minnesota Press, 1972.

McGinn, Thoma A. J. "Paul's Women." *CR* 55 (2005): 645–47.

Mee, Christopher B., and Hamish A. Forbes, eds. *A Rough and Rocky Place: The Landscape and Settlement History of the Methana Peninsula, Greece. Results of the Methana Survey Project Sponsored by the British School at Athens and the University of Liverpool.* Liverpool: Liverpool University Press, 1997.

Meeks, Wayne A. *The First Urban Christians: The Social World of the Apostle Paul.* New Haven: Yale University Press, 1983. 2nd ed. 2003.

Meggitt, Justin. *Paul, Poverty and Survival.* SNTW. Edinburgh: T&T Clark, 1998.

Méhat, André. *Études sur les "Stromates" de Clément d'Alexandrie.* Patristica Sorbonensia 7. Paris: Le Seuil, 1966.

Mélèze-Modrzejewski, Joseph. "Esperances et illusions du judaïsme alexandrin." Pages 221–35 in *Profesorowi Janowi Kodrebskiemu in Memoriam: Mélanges à la mémoire de Jan Kodrębski.* Edited by Anna Pikulska-Robaczkiewicz. Łodz: Łodz Publishing House, 2000.

Mendels, Doron. *The Rise and Fall of Jewish Nationalism.* Grand Rapids: Eerdmans, 1997.

Meshorer, Ya'akov. *Jewish Coins of the Second Temple Period.* Tel Aviv: Am Hassefer & Massada, 1967.

Metzger, Bruce M. *The Canon of the New Testament: Its Origin, Development and Significance.* Oxford: Clarendon, 1987.

Michaels, J. Ramsey. *1 Peter.* WBC 49. Waco, TX: Word, 1988.

Millar, Fergus. *The Roman Empire and Its Neighbours.* 2nd ed. London: Duckworth, 1981.

———. *The Roman Near East 31 BC–CE 337.* Cambridge, MA: Harvard University Press, 1993.

Miller, James C. "The Jewish Context of Paul's Gentile Mission." *TynBul* 58 (2007): 101–15.

Miller, Kei. *The Cartographer Tries to Map a Way to Zion*. Manchester: Carcanet, 2014.

Millis, Benjamin W. "'Miserable Huts' in Post-146 BC Corinth." *Hesperia* 75 (2006): 397–404.

———. "The Social and Ethnic Origins of the Colonists in Early Roman Corinth." Pages 13–36 in *Corinth in Context: Comparative Studies on Religion and Society*. Edited by Steven J. Friesen, Daniel N. Schowalter, and James C. Walters. NovTSup 134. Leiden: Brill, 2010.

———. "The Local Magistrates and Elite of Roman Corinth." Pages 38–53 in *Corinth in Contrast: Studies in Inequality*. Edited by Steven J. Friesen, Sarah A. James, and Daniel N. Schowalter. NovTSup 155. Leiden: Brill, 2014.

Mitchell, Margaret M. *Paul and the Rhetoric of Reconciliation*. HUT 28. Tübingen: Mohr Siebeck, 1991.

Mitchell, Stephen. *Anatolia: Land, Men, and Gods in Asia Minor*. 2 vols. Oxford: Clarendon, 1993–1995.

———. "Festivals, Games and Civic Life in Roman Asia Minor." *JRS* 80 (2012): 183–93.

Mitchell, Stephen, and Marc Waelkens. *Pisidian Antioch: The Site and Its Monument*. London: Duckworth / Classical Press of Wales, 1998.

Moffitt, David M. "Righteous Bloodshed, Matthew's Passion Narrative and the Temple's Destruction: Lamentations as a Matthean Intertext." *JBL* 125 (2006): 299–320.

Moo, Douglas. *The Letters to Colossians and Philemon*. PNTC. Grand Rapids: Zondervan, 2008.

Morgan, Catherine. "Ethnic Expression on the Early Iron Age and Early Archaic Greek Mainland: Where Should We Be Looking?" Pages 11–36 in *Ethnic Constructs in Antiquity: The Role of Power and Tradition*. Edited by Ton Derks and Nico Roymans. Amsterdam Archaeological Studies 13. Amsterdam: Amsterdam University Press, 2009.

Morley, Neville. "Cities in Context: Urban Systems in Roman Italy." Pages 42–58 in *Roman Urbanism: Beyond the Consumer City*. Edited by Helen M. Parkins. London: Routledge, 1997.

Moyise, Steve. *The Old Testament in the Book of Revelation*. JSNTSup 115. Sheffield: Sheffield Academic, 1995.

———, ed. *Old Testament in the New Testament: Essays in Honour of J. L. North*. JSNTSup 189. Sheffield: Sheffield Academic, 2000.

———. "From Revelatory Experience to Written Messages or Vice Versa: The Question of Revelation 1:12–18 and the Seven Letters to the Churches in Asia Minor." In *Epiphanies of the Divine in the Septuagint and the New Testament: Wechselseitige Wahrnehmungen. V. Internationales Symposium zum Corpus Judaeo-Hellenisticum Novi Testamenti*. Edited by Roland Deines. WUNT. Tübingen: Mohr Siebeck, forthcoming.

Mußner, Franz. *Der Galaterbrief*. HTKNT 9. 2nd ed. Freiburg: Herder, 2002.

Nanos, Mark D. *The Irony of Galatians: Paul's Letter in First-Century Context*. Minneapolis: Fortress, 2002.

Nash, Robert S. *1 Corinthians*. SHBC. Macon, GA: Smyth & Helwys, 2009.

Nenna, Marie-Dominique, ed. *L'École française d'Athènes. L'espace grec. 150 ans de fouilles de l'École française d'Athènes*. Paris: Fayard, 1996.

Netzer, Ehud. "The Promontory Palace." Pages 193–207 in *Caesarea Maritima: A Retro-*

spective after Two Millennia. Edited by Avner Raban and Kenneth Holum. DMOA 21. Leiden: Brill, 1996.

Neusner, Jacob. *A History of the Jews in Babylonia. I. The Parthian Period.* StPB 9. Leiden: Brill, 1969.

———, trans. *The Babylonian Talmud: A Translation and Commentary.* 36 vols. Peabody, MA: Hendrickson, 2005.

Nicolet, Claude. *Space, Geography and Politics in the Early Roman Empire.* Jerome Lectures 19. Ann Arbor, MI: University of Michigan Press, 1991.

Niehoff, Maren. *Philo on Jewish Identity and Culture.* TSAJ 86. Tübingen: Mohr Siebeck, 2001.

Noack, Christian. *Gottesbewußtsein: Exegetische Studien zur Soteriologie und Mystik bei Philo von Alexandria.* WUNT/2 116. Tübingen: Mohr Siebeck, 2000.

Nobbs, Alanna. "Cyprus." Pages 279–89 in *The Book of Acts in Its Graeco-Roman Setting.* Edited by David W. J. Gill and Conrad H. Gempf. BAFCS 2. Carlisle: Paternoster/ Grand Rapids: Eerdmans, 1994.

Nolland, John. *The Gospel of Matthew: A Commentary on the Greek Text.* NIGTC. Grand Rapids: Eerdmans, 2007.

Oakes, Peter. *Philippians: From People to Letter.* SNTSMS 110. Cambridge: Cambridge University Press, 2000.

———. "Contours of the Urban Environment." Pages 21–35 in *After the First Urban Christians: The Social-Scientific Study of Pauline Christianity Twenty-Five Years Later.* Edited by Todd D. Still and David G. Horrell. London: Continuum, 2009.

Oleson, John Peter, and Graham Branton. "The Technology of King Herod's Harbour." Pages 49–67 in *Caesarea Papers: Straton's Tower, Herod's Harbour, and Roman and Byzantine Caesarea.* Edited by Robert Lindley Vann. JRASup 5. Ann Arbor, MI: Journal of Roman Archaeology, 1992.

Ollrog, Wolf-Henning. *Paulus und seine Mitarbeiter: Untersuchungen zu Theorie und Praxis der paulinischen Mission.* WMANT 50. Neukirchen-Vluyn: Neukirchener Verlag, 1979.

Omi, Michael, and Howard Winant. *Racial Formation in the United States: From the 1960s to the 1980s.* New York: Routledge, 1986.

Orlin, Eric M. "Augustan Religion: From Locative to Utopian." Pages 49–59 in *Rome and Religion: A Cross-Disciplinary Dialogue on the Imperial Cult.* Edited by Jeffrey Brodd and Jonathan L. Reed. Atlanta: SBL, 2011.

Osborn, Eric. *Clement of Alexandria.* Oxford: Oxford University Press, 2005.

Osiek, Carolyn. "The Oral World of Early Christianity in Rome: The Case of Hermas." Pages 151–72 in *Judaism and Christianity in First-Century Rome.* Edited by Karl P. Donfried and Peter Richardson. Grand Rapids: Eerdmans, 1998.

Owens, E. J. *The City in the Greek and Roman World.* London: Routledge, 1991.

Pagels, Elaine H. *The Johannine Gospel in Gnostic Exegesis: Heracleon's Commentary on John.* Atlanta: Scholars, 1989.

Painter, John. *1, 2 and 3 John.* SP 18. Collegeville: Liturgical, 2002.

———. "Matthew and John." Pages 66–86 in *Matthew and His Christian Contemporaries.* Edited by David C. Sim and Boris Repschinski. LNTS 333. London: T&T Clark, 2008.

Pallas, Demetrios I., Séraphin Charitonidis, and Jacques Vénencie. "Inscriptions lyciennes trouvées à Solômos près de Corinthe." *BCH* 83 (1959): 496–508.

Pao, David W. *Colossians and Philemon.* ZECNT. Grand Rapids: Zondervan, 2012.

Parsons, Mikeal C. *Acts.* Paideia. Grand Rapids, Baker, 2008.

Parvis, Paul. "Justin Martyr." Pages 1–14 in *Early Christian Thinkers: The Lives and Legacies of Twelve Key Figures.* Edited by Paul Foster. Downers Grove, IL: IVP Academic, 2010.

Parvis, Sara, and Paul Foster, eds. *Justin Martyr and His Worlds.* Minneapolis: Fortress, 2007.

Patrich, Joseph. "Caesarea in the Time of Eusebius." Pages 1–24 in *Reconsidering Eusebius: Papers on Literary, Historical and Theological Issues.* Edited by Sabrina Inowlocki and Claudio Zamagni. VCSup 107. Leiden: Brill, 2011.

Paul, Ian. "Paul Ricoeur's Hermeneutic of Metaphor and the Interpretation of Revelation 12 and 13." PhD diss., Nottingham Trent University, 1998.

———. "The Use of the Old Testament in Revelation 12." Pages 256–76 in *Old Testament in the New Testament: Essays in Honour of J. L. North.* Edited by Steve Moyise. JSNTSup 189. Sheffield: Sheffield Academic, 2000.

———. *The Ethics of the Book of Revelation.* Grove Ethics 136. Cambridge: Grove, 2005.

Pearce, Sarah. "Jerusalem as 'Mother-City' in the Writings of Philo of Alexandra." Pages 19–36 in *Negotiating Diaspora: Jewish Strategies in the Roman Empire.* Edited by John M. G. Barclay. LSTS 45. London: T&T Clark, 2004.

Pearson, Birger A. "Earliest Christianity in Egypt: Some Observations." Pages 132–60 in *The Roots of Egyptian Christianity.* Edited by Birger A. Pearson and James E. Goehring, Philadelphia: Fortress, 1986.

———. "Basilides the Gnostic." Pages 1–31 in *A Companion to Second-Century Christian "Heretics."* Edited by Antti Marjanen and Petri Luomanen. VCSup 76. Leiden: Brill, 2005.

———. "'The Catechetical School' in Alexandria." Pages 340–42 in vol. 1 of *The Cambridge History of Christianity.* Edited by Margaret M. Mitchell and Frances M. Young. Cambridge: Cambridge University Press, 2006.

———. "Earliest Christianity in Egypt." Pages 97–112 in *The World of Early Egyptian Christianity: Language, Literature, and Social Context. Essays in Honor of David W. Johnston.* Edited by James E. Goehring and Janet A. Timbie. CUA Studies in Early Christianity. Washington: Catholic University of America, 2007.

Peel, Malcolm. "Introduction." Pages 249–76 in *The Teaching of Silvanus,* in *Nag Hammadi Codex VII. The Coptic Gnostic Library.* Edited by Birger A. Pearson. NHMS 30. Leiden: Brill, 1996.

Pelekanidis, Stylianos. "Kultprobleme in Apostel-Paulus-Oktogon von Philippi im Zusammenhang mit einem aelteren Heroenkult." Pages 393–97 in vol. 2 of *Atti del IX Congresso Internazionale di Archeologia Cristiana.* 2 vols. Vatican City: Pontificio Istituto di archeologia cristiana, 1978.

Peltonen, Matti. "Clues, Margins and Monads: The Micro-Macro Link in Historical Research." *Hist. Theory* 40 (2002): 347–59.

Pervo, Richard I. *Acts.* Hermeneia. Minneapolis: Fortress, 2008.

Peterson, David G. *The Acts of the Apostles.* PNTC. Grand Rapids: Eerdmans, 2009.

Pilhofer, Peter. *Philippi, I. Die erste christliche Gemeinde Europas.* WUNT 87. Tübingen: Mohr Siebeck, 1995.

———. *Philippi, II. Katalog der Inschriften von Philippi.* 2nd ed. WUNT/2 119. Tübingen: Mohr Siebeck, 2009.

Pinder, David. "Subverting Cartography: The Situationalists and Maps of the City." *Env. Plan. A* 28 (1996): 405–28.

———. "'Old Paris Is No More': Geographies of Spectacle and Anti-Spectacle." *Antipode* 32 (2000): 357–86.

———. "Reconstituting the Possible: Lefebvre, Utopia and the Urban Question." *Int. J. Urb. Reg. Res.* 39 (2015): 28–45.

Pink, Sarah. *Doing Sensory Ethnography.* London: Sage, 2009.

———. *Situating Everyday Life.* London: Sage, 2012.

Pippin, Tina. *Death and Desire: Rhetoric of Gender in the Apocalypse of John.* Louisville: Westminster John Knox, 1992.

Poncin, Marie-Dominique. "Les prêtrises publiques dans la colonie de Philippes." *Cahiers du Centre Gustave Glotz* 12 (2001): 229–52.

Porter, Stanley E. "Why the Laodiceans Received Lukewarm Water (Revelation 3:15–18)." *TynBul* 38 (1987): 143–49.

———. *The Paul of Acts: Essays in Literary Criticism, Rhetoric and Theology.* WUNT 115. Tübingen: Mohr Siebeck, 1999.

Porter, Stanley E., and Beth M. Stowell, eds. *Biblical Hermeneutics: Five Views.* Downers Grove, IL: InterVarsity Press, 2012.

Powell, Mark Allan. *What Is Narrative Criticism?* GBS. Minneapolis: Fortress, 1990.

Praeder, Susan M. "The Problem of First Person Narration in Acts." *NovT* 29 (1987): 193–218.

Price, Simon R. F. *Rituals and Power: The Roman Imperial Cult in Asia Minor.* Cambridge: Cambridge University Press, 1984.

Purcell, Mark. "Urban Democracy and the Local Trap." *Urban Stud.* 43 (2006): 1921–41.

Quinn, Jerome D. *The Letter to Titus.* AB 35. New York: Doubleday, 1990.

Quinn, Jerome D., and William C. Wacker. *The First and Second Letters to Timothy.* ECC. Grand Rapids: Eerdmans, 2000.

Raban, Avner, ed. *Harbour Archaeology: Proceedings of the First International Workshop on Ancient Mediterranean Harbours, Caesarea Maritima, 24–28.6.83.* BAR International Series 257. Oxford: Biblical Archaeology Review, 1985.

———. "Καισαρεια η προς Σεβαστω λιμενι: Two Harbours for Two Entities." Pages 68–74 in *Caesarea Papers: Straton's Tower, Herod's Harbour, and Roman and Byzantine Caesarea.* Edited by Robert Lindley. JRASup 5. Ann Arbor, MI: Journal of Roman Archaeology, 1992.

———. "Sebastos: The Royal Harbour at Caesarea Maritima—A Short-lived Giant." *The International Journal of Nautical Archaeology* 21 (1992): 111–24.

Raban, Avner, and Robert L. Hohlfelder. *The Site and the Excavations.* Vol. 1 of *The Harbours of Caesarea Maritima.* Edited by John Peter Oleson. BAR International Series 491. Oxford: Biblical Archaeology Review, 1989.

Raban, Avner, Robert L. Hohlfelder, Kenneth G. Holum, Robert Stieglitz, and R. Lindley Vann. "Caesarea and Its Harbours: A Preliminary Report on the 1988 Season." *IEJ* 40 (1990): 241–56.

Raban, Avner, Eduard G. Reinhardt, Matthew McGrath, and Nina Hodge. "The Underwater Excavations, 1993–94." Pages 152–68 in *Caesarea Papers 2: Herod's Temple, the Provincial Governor's Praetorium and Granaries, the Later Harbor, a Gold Coin Hoard, and Other Studies*. Edited by Kenneth G. Holum, Avner Raban, and Joseph Patrich. JRASup 35. Portsmouth, RI: Journal of Roman Archaeology, 1999.

Raban, Avner, and Robert Stieglitz. "Caesarea, Ancient Harbor, 1987." *IEJ* 38 (1988): 273–78.

———. "Caesarea and Its Harbor—1987–1988." *Excavations and Surveys in Israel* 7–8 (1988–89): 33–41.

Raban, Avner, Ronni Toueg, Shalom Yankelevitz, and Yael Arnon. "Land Excavations in the Inner Harbour (1993–94)." Pages 198–224 in *Caesarea Papers 2: Herod's Temple, the Provincial Governor's Praetorium and Granaries, the Later Harbor, a Gold Coin Hoard, and Other Studies*. Edited by Kenneth G. Holum, Avner Raban, and Joseph Patrich. JRASup 35. Portsmouth, RI: Journal of Roman Archaeology, 1999.

Rabens, Volker. "Power from In Between: The Relational Experience of the Holy Spirit and Spiritual Gifts in Paul's Churches." Pages 138–55 in *The Spirit and Christ in the New Testament and Christian Theology: Essays in Honor of Max Turner*. Edited by I. Howard Marshall, Volker Rabens, and Cornelis Bennema. Grand Rapids: Eerdmans, 2012.

———. "'Von Jerusalem aus und rings umher . . .' (Röm. 15,19): Die paulinische Missionsstrategie im Dickicht der Städte." Pages 219–37 in *Das frühe Christentum und die Stadt*. Edited by Reinhard von Bendemann and Markus Tiwald. BWANT 198. Stuttgart: Kohlhammer, 2012.

———. *The Holy Spirit and Ethics in Paul: Transformation and Empowering for Religious-Ethical Life*. WUNT/2 283. 2nd ed. Tübingen: Mohr Siebeck, 2013.

———. "Inclusion of and Demarcation from 'Outsiders': Mission and Ethics in Paul's Second Letter to the Corinthians." Pages 290–323 in *Sensitivity towards Outsiders: Exploring the Dynamic Relationship between Mission and Ethics in the New Testament and Early Christianity*. Edited by Jacobus Kok, Tobias Nicklas, Dieter T. Roth and Christopher M. Hays. WUNT/2 364. Tübingen: Mohr Siebeck, 2014.

———. "Philo's Attractive Ethics on the 'Religious Market' of Ancient Alexandria." Pages 333–55 in *Religions and Trade: Religious Formation, Transformation and Cross-Cultural Exchange between East and West*. Edited by Peter Wick and Volker Rabens. DHR 5. Leiden: Brill, 2014.

———. "*Pneuma* and the Beholding of God: Reading Paul in the Context of Philonic Mystical Traditions." Pages 293–329 in *The Holy Spirit, Inspiration, and the Cultures of Antiquity: Multidisciplinary Perspectives*. Edited by Jörg Frey and John R. Levison. Ekstasis 5. Berlin: de Gruyter, 2014.

———. "The Faithfulness of God and Its Effects on Faithful Living: A Critical Analysis of Tom Wright's Faithfulness to Paul's Ethics." Pages 555–80 in *God and the Faithfulness of Paul: A Critical Examination of the Pauline Theology of N. T. Wright*. Edited by Michael F. Bird, Christoph Heilig, and Jay Thomas Hewitt. WUNT/2 413. Tübingen: Mohr Siebeck, 2016.

Ramsay, William M. *St Paul the Traveler and Roman Citizen*. London: Hodder & Stoughton, 1895.

———. "Cornelius and the Italic Cohort." *The Expositor* 5/4 (1896): 194–201.

———. *Historical Commentary on Galatians*. 1899. Repr., Grand Rapids: Kregel, 1997.

———. *The Cities of St. Paul: Their Influence on His Life and Thought. The Cities of Eastern Asia Minor*. Dale Memorial Lectures 1907. London: Hodder and Stoughton, 1907.

———. "Colonia Caesarea (Pisidian Antioch) in the Augustan Age." *JRS* 6 (1916): 83–134.

———. "Studies in the Roman Province of Galatia VI. Some Inscriptions of Colonia Caesarea Antiochea." *JRS* 14 (1924): 172–205.

———. "Studies in the Roman Province of Galatia. X. The Romans in Galatia." *JRS* 16 (1926): 201–15.

———. *The Letters to the Seven Churches*. Edited by Mark W. Wilson. Revised ed. Peabody, MA: Hendrickson, 1994.

Rapske, Brian M. *The Book of Acts and Paul in Roman Custody*. BAFCS 3. Carlisle: Paternoster / Grand Rapids: Eerdmans, 1994.

Redaelli, Eleonora. "Becoming a Creative City: Perspectives from Augustus' Rome." *Urban Geogr.* 36 (2015): 608–23.

Regev, Eyal. "Moral Impurity and the Temple in Early Christianity in Light of Ancient Greek Practice and Qumranic Ideology." *HTR* 97 (2004): 383–411.

Reinbold, Wolfgang. *Propaganda und Mission im ältesten Christentum: Eine Untersuchung zu den Modalitäten der Ausbreitung der frühen Kirche*. FRLANT 188. Göttingen: Vandenhoeck & Ruprecht, 2000.

Reinhartz, Adele. "The Vanishing Jews of Antiquity." http://www.marginalia.lareviewofbooks.org/vanishing-jews-antiquity-adele-reinhartz/.

Reiser, Marius. "Hat Paulus Heiden bekehrt?" *BZ* 39 (1995): 76–91.

Resseguie, James L. *Narrative Criticism of the New Testament: An Introduction*. Grand Rapids: Baker Academic, 2005.

Reumann, John. *Philippians*. AYB 33B. New Haven: Yale University Press, 2008.

Ricoeur, Paul. *The Rule of Metaphor: Multi-Disciplinary Studies of the Creation of Meaning in Language*. London: Routledge & Kegan Paul, 1978.

Riesner, Rainer. *Die Frühzeit des Apostels Paulus: Studien zur Chronologie, Missionstrategie und Theologie*. WUNT 71. Tübingen: Mohr Siebeck, 1994.

———. *Paul's Early Period: Chronology, Mission Strategy, Theology*. Grand Rapids: Eerdmans, 1998.

———. "Zwischen Tempel und Obergemach: Jerusalem als erster messianische Stadtgemeinde." Pages 69–91 in *Das frühe Christentum und die Stadt*. Edited by Reinhard von Bendemann and Markus Tiwald. Stuttgart: Kohlhammer, 2012.

Rizakis, Athanassios D. *Achaie I. Sources textuelles et histoire regionale*. Meletēmata 20. Athens: De Boccard, 1995.

———. "La carrière équestre de C. Vibius Quartus." *MEFRA* 115 (2003): 535–48.

Robbins, Vernon K. "By Land and by Sea: The We-Passages and Ancient Sea Voyages." Pages 215–42 in *Perspectives on Luke-Acts*. Edited by Charles Talbert. Danville, VA: Association of Baptist Professors of Religion, 1978.

Robert, Louis. *Les gladiateurs dans l'Orient grec*. BEHEH 278. Paris: Champion, 1940.

Robinson, David M. "A Preliminary Report on the Excavations at Pisidian Antioch and at Sizma." *AJA* 28 (1924): 435–44.

———. "Notes on Inscriptions from Antioch in Pisidia." *JRS* 15 (1925): 253–62.

———. "Roman Sculptures from Colonia Caesarea (Pisidian Antioch)." *ArtB* 9 (1926): 5–69.

Robinson, John A. T. *The Body: A Study in Pauline Theology.* SBT. London: SCM, 1953.

Robinson, Thomas. *Who Were the First Christians? Dismantling the Urban Thesis.* Oxford: Oxford University Press, 2017.

Rogers, Amanda. "Performances." Pages 773–86 in *Introducing Human Geographies.* Edited by Paul Cloke, Philip Crang, and Mark Goodwin. 3rd ed. London: Routledge, 2014.

Rogers, Guy McLean. *The Sacred Identity of Ephesos: Foundation Myths of a Roman City.* London: Routledge, 1991.

———. *The Mysteries of Artemis of Ephesos: Cult, Polis and Change in the Graeco-Roman World.* New Haven: Yale University Press, 2012.

Rohrbaugh, Richard L. *The New Testament in Cross-Cultural Perspective.* Eugene, OR: Cascade, 2014.

Roll, Israel. "The Roman Road System in Judaea." *The Jerusalem Cathedra* 3 (1983): 136–62.

———. "Roman Roads to Caesarea Maritima." Pages 30–33 in *Caesarea—A Mercantile City by the Sea.* Edited by Ofra Rimon. Haifa: University of Haifa, 1993.

———. "Roman Roads to Caesarea Maritima." Pages 549–58 in *Caesarea Maritima: A Retrospective after Two Millennia.* Edited by Avner Raban and Kenneth G. Holum. Leiden: Brill, 1996.

Roller, Duane W. *The Building Program of Herod the Great.* Berkeley: University of California Press, 1998.

Roloff, Jürgen. *Der Erste Brief an Timotheus.* EKKNT 15. Zürich: Benziger, 1988.

Romano, David Gilman. *Athletics and Mathematics in Archaic Corinth.* MAPS 206. Philadelphia: American Philosophical Society, 1993.

———. "City Planning, Centuriation, and Land Division in Roman Corinth: *Colonia Laus Iulia Corinthiensis and Colonia Iulia Flavia Augusta Corinthiensis.*" Pages 279–301 in *Corinth, The Centenary: 1896–1996.* Edited by Charles K. Williams II and Nancy Bookidis. Princeton: American School of Classical Studies at Athens, 2003.

———. "Roman Surveyors in Corinth." *PAPS* 150 (2006): 62–85.

Rose, Mitch. "Gathering Dreams of 'Presence': A Project for the Cultural Landscape." *Env. Plan. D* 24 (2006): 537–54.

Rose, Mitch, and John Wylie. "Animating Landscape." *Env. Plan. D* 24 (2006): 475–79.

Rubin, Benjamin B. "(Re)presenting Empire: The Roman Imperial Cult in Asia Minor, 31 BC–CE 68." PhD diss., University of Michigan, 2008.

Rudolph, David J. *A Jew to the Jews: Jewish Contours of Pauline Flexibility in 1 Corinthians 9:19–23.* WUNT/2 304. Tübingen: Mohr Siebeck, 2011.

Rudwick, M. J. S., and E. M. B. Green. "The Laodicean Lukewarmness." *ExpTim* 69 (1958): 176–78.

Ruiz, Jean-Pierre. *Ezekiel in the Apocalypse: The Transformation of Prophetic Language in Revelation 16, 17–19, 10.* European University Studies. Series XXIII Theology 376. New York: Peter Lang, 1989.

Runesson, Anders. *The Origins of the Synagogue: A Socio-Historical Study*. Stockholm: Almqvist & Wiksell International, 2001.

———. "Water and Worship: Ostia and the Ritual Bath in the Diaspora Synagogue." Pages 115–29 in *The Synagogue of Ancient Ostia and the Jews of Rome: Interdisciplinary Studies*. Edited by Birger Olsson, Dieter Mitternacht, and Olof Brandt. Acta Instituti Romani Regni Sueciae 57. Stockholm: Paul Åström, 2001.

———. "Architecture, Conflict, and Identity Formation: Jews and Christians in Capernaum from the 1st to the 6th Century." Pages 231–57 in *Religion, Ethnicity and Identity in Ancient Galilee: A Region in Transition*. Edited by Jürgen Zangenberg, Harold W. Attridge, and Dale Martin. WUNT 210. Tübingen: Mohr Siebeck, 2007.

———. "Placing Paul: Institutional Structures and Theological Strategy in the World of the Early Christ-Believers." *SEÅ* 80 (2015): 43–67.

———. "The Question of Terminology: The Architecture of Contemporary Discussions on Paul." Pages 53–77 in *Paul within Judaism: Restoring the First-Century Context to the Apostle*. Edited by Mark D. Nanos and Magnus Zetterholm. Minneapolis: Fortress, 2015.

———. *Divine Wrath and Salvation in Matthew: A Historical Study of the Narrative World of the First Gospel*. Minneapolis: Fortress, 2016.

Runesson, Anders, Donald D. Binder, and Birger Olsson, eds. *The Ancient Synagogue from Its Origins to 200 CE: A Source Book*. AJEC 72. Leiden: Brill, 2008.

Runia, David T. "Philo, Alexandrian and Jew." Pages 1–18 in *Exegesis and Philosophy: Studies on Philo of Alexandria*. Edited by David T. Runia. VCS 332. Aldershot: Variorum, 1990.

———. "Polis and Megalopolis: Philo and the Founding of Alexandria." Pages 398–412 in *Exegesis and Philosophy: Studies on Philo of Alexandria*. Edited by David T. Runia. VCS 332. Aldershot: Variorum, 1990.

———. "The Idea and the Reality of the City in the Thought of Philo of Alexandria." *JHI* 61 (2000): 361–79.

Ruppel, Walter. "*Politeuma*: Bedeutungsgeschichte eines staatsrechtlichen Termus." *Phil* 82 (1927): 273–317, 440–61.

Sack, Robert David. *Human Territoriality: Its Theory and History*. Cambridge Studies in Historical Geography. Cambridge: Cambridge University Press, 1986.

———. *Homo Geographicus: A Framework for Action, Awareness, and Moral Concern*. Baltimore: Johns Hopkins University Press, 1997.

Sadler, Michael Ferrebee. *The General Epistles of SS. James, Peter, John and Jude*. London: George Bell & Sons, 1891.

Sanders, E. P. *Judaism: Practice and Belief 63 BCE–66 CE*. London: SCM, 1992.

Sandnes, Karl Olav. "A Missionary Strategy in 1 Corinthians 9.19–23?" Pages 128–41 in *Paul as Missionary: Identity, Activity, Theology, and Practice*. Edited by Trevor J. Burke and Brian S. Rosner. LNTS 420. London: T&T Clark, 2011.

Schell, Vítor Hugo. *Die Areopagrede des Paulus und Reden bei Josephus: Eine vergleichende Studie zu Apg 17 und dem historiographischen Werk des Josephus*. WUNT/2 419. Tübingen: Mohr Siebeck, 2016.

Schlatter, Adolf. *Die Briefe an die Thessalonicher und Philipper. Die Briefe des Petrus und Judas ausgelegt für Bibelleser*. ENT 12. Calw & Stuttgart: Vereinsbuchhandlung, 1910.

Schlosser, Jacques. *La première épître de Pierre.* CbNT 21. Paris: Cerf, 2011.

Schmeller, Thomas. *Paulus und die 'Diatribe': Eine vergleichende Stilinterpretation.* NTA 19. Münster: Aschendorff, 1987.

Schnabel, Eckhard J. *Urchristliche Mission.* Wuppertal: Brockhaus, 2002.

———. *Early Christian Mission.* 2 vols. Downers Grove, IL: InterVarsity Press, 2004.

———. *Der erste Brief des Paulus an die Korinther.* HTA. Wuppertal: Brockhaus, 2006.

———. *Paul, the Missionary: Realities, Strategies, and Methods.* Downers Grove, IL: IVP Academic / Nottingham: Apollos, 2008.

———. *Acts.* ZECNT 5. Grand Rapids: Zondervan, 2012.

———. "Evangelism and the Mission of the Church." Pages 683–707 in *God and the Faithfulness of Paul: A Critical Examination of the Pauline Theology of N. T. Wright.* Edited by Michael F. Bird, Christoph Heilig, and Jay Thomas Hewitt. WUNT/2 413. Tübingen: Mohr Siebeck, 2016.

Schnackenburg, Rudolf. *The Johannine Epistles. Introduction and Commentary.* New York: Crossroad, 1992.

Schrage, Wolfgang. *Der erste Brief an die Korinther.* 4 vols. EKK 7/1–4. Neukirchen-Vluyn: Neukirchener, 1991–2001.

Schreiber, Stefan. *Paulus als Wundertäter: Redaktionsgeschichtliche Untersuchungen zur Apostelgeschichte und den authentischen Paulusbriefen.* BZNW 79. Berlin: De Gruyter, 1996.

Schreiner, Thomas R. *Paul: Apostle of God's Glory in Christ.* Leicester: Apollos, 2001.

Schürer, Emil, Geza Vermes, Fergus Millar, and Martin Goodman. *The History of the Jewish People in the Age of Jesus Christ (175 BC–CE 135).* 4 vols. Rev. ed. Edinburgh: T&T Clark, 1973–86.

Schwabe, Moses. "The Synagogue of Caesarea and Its Inscriptions." Pages 433–50 in vol. 2 of *Alexander Marx: Jubilee Volume on the Occasion of His Seventieth Birthday.* Edited by Saul Lieberman. 2 vols. New York: Jewish Theological Seminary, 1950.

Schwartz, Daniel R. "Temple or City: What Did Hellenistic Jews See in Jerusalem?" Pages 114–27 in *The Centrality of Jerusalem: Historical Perspectives.* Edited by Marcel Poorthuis and Chana Safrai. Kampen: Kok Pharos, 1996.

———. "'Judean' or 'Jew'? How Should We Translate *Ioudaios* in Josephus?" Pages 3–37 in *Jewish Identity in the Greco-Roman World.* Edited by Jörg Frey, Daniel R. Schwartz, and Stephanie Gripentrog. AGJU 71. Leiden: Brill, 2007.

Schwartz, Seth. "How Many Judaisms Were There? A Critique of Neusner and Smith on Definition and Mason and Boyarin on Categorization." *JAJ* 2 (2011): 208–38.

Scott, James M. *Paul and the Nations: The Old Testament and Jewish Background of Paul's Mission to the Nations with Special Reference to the Destination of Galatians.* WUNT 84. Tübingen: Mohr Siebeck, 1995.

Scriven, Richard. "Geographies of Pilgrimage: Meaningful Movements and Embodied Mobilities." *Geogr. Compass* 8 (2014): 249–61.

Selwyn, Edward Gordon. *The First Epistle of St. Peter: The Greek Text with Introduction, Notes and Essays.* London: Macmillan, 1946.

Seufert, W. "Der Abfassungsort des ersten Petrusbriefes." *ZWT* 28 (1885): 146–56.

Sève, Michel, and Patrick Weber. *Guide du forum de Philippes.* Athens: École française d'Athènes, 2012.

Sheller, Mimi, and John Urry. "The New Mobilities Paradigm." *Env. Plan. A* 38 (2006): 207–26.

Shepherd, Robert. *Ancient Mining*. London: Institution of Mining and Metallurgy by Elsevier Applied Science, 1993.

Sherwin-White, A. N. *Roman Society and Roman Law in the New Testament*. Sarum Lectures 1960–1961. 1963. Repr., Grand Rapids: Baker, 1981.

———. "The Roman Citizenship. A Survey of Its Development into a World Franchise." *ANRW* 1.2:23–58. Part 1, *Von den Anfängen Roms bis zum Ausgang der Republik*, 2. Edited by Hildegard Temporini. New York: de Gruyter, 1972.

———. *The Roman Citizenship*. 2nd ed. Oxford: Clarendon, 1973.

Sim, David C. *The Gospel of Matthew and Christian Judaism*. SNTW. Edinburgh: T&T Clark, 1998.

Skinner, Matthew L. *Locating Paul: Places of Custody as Narrative Settings in Acts 21–28*. ABib 13. Atlanta: SBL, 2003.

Sleeman, Matthew. *Geography and the Ascension Narrative in Acts*. SNTSMS 146. Cambridge: Cambridge University Press, 2009.

———. "Critical Spatial Theory 2.0." Pages 49–66 in *Constructions of Space V: Place, Space and Identity in the Ancient Mediterranean World*. Edited by Gert T. M. Prinsloo and Christl M. Maier. LHBOTS 576. London: Bloomsbury T&T Clark, 2013.

Smit, Peter-Ben. *Paradigms of Being in Christ: A Study of the Epistle to the Philippians*. LNTS 476. London: Bloomsbury T&T Clark, 2013.

Smith, Roland R. R. *Hellenistic Royal Portraits*. Oxford Monographs on Classical Archaeology. Oxford: Clarendon, 1988.

Snyder, H. Gregory. *Teachers and Texts in the Ancient World: Philosophers, Jews, and Christians*. Religion in the First Christian Centuries. New York: Routledge, 2000.

Soggin, J. Alberto. *An Introduction to the History of Israel and Judah*. 3rd ed. London: SCM, 1999.

Soja, Edward W. *Postmodern Geographies: The Reassertion of Space in Critical Social Theory*. London: Verso, 1989.

———. *Thirdspace: Journeys to Los Angeles and Other Real-and-Imagined Places*. Oxford: Blackwell, 1996.

Souzis, A. E. "Momentary Ambiances: Psychogeography in Action." *Cult. Geogr.* 22 (2015): 193–201.

Spawforth, Antony J. S. "Balbilla, the Euryclids and Memorials for a Greek Magnate." *ABSA* 73 (1978): 249–60.

———. "Roman Corinth and the Ancient Urban Economy." *CR* 42 (1992): 119–20.

———. "Roman Corinth: The Formation of a Colonial Élite." Pages 167–82 in *Roman Onomastics in the Greek East: Social and Political Aspects*. Edited by Athanassios D. Rizakis. Meletēmata 21. Athens: De Boccard, 1996.

Spencer, F. Scott. *Journeying through Acts: A Literary-Cultural Reading*. Peabody, MA: Hendrickson, 2004.

Sperber, Daniel. *The City in Roman Palestine*. Oxford: Oxford University Press, 1998.

Stählin, Otto, and Ursula Treu. *Clemens Alexandrinus. Register*. Vol. 4, part 1. 2nd ed. GCS 17. Berlin: Akademie-Verlag, 1980.

Standhartinger, Angela. "*Eusebeia* in den Pastoralbriefen. Ein Beitrag zum Einfluss römischen Denkens auf das entstehende Christentum." *NovT* 48 (2006): 51–82.

Stanley, Farland H., Jr. "The South Flank of the Temple Platform (Area Z2, 1993–95 excavations)." Pages 35–40 in *Caesarea Papers 2: Herod's Temple, the Provincial Governor's Praetorium and Granaries, the Later Harbor, a Gold Coin Hoard, and Other Studies.* Edited by Kenneth G. Holum, Avner Raban, and Joseph Patrich. JRASup 35. Portsmouth, RI: Journal of Roman Archaeology, 1999.

Stark, Rodney. *The Rise of Christianity.* San Francisco: HarperCollins, 1997.

———. *Cities of God: The Real Story of How Christianity Became an Urban Movement and Conquered Rome.* New York: HarperOne, 2007.

Ste. Croix, E. M. *The Class Struggle in the Ancient Greek World.* London: Duckworth, 1981.

Stegemann, Ekkehard W., and Stegemann, Wolfgang. *Urchristliche Sozialgeschichte: Die Anfänge im Judentum und die Christusgemeinden in der mediterranen Welt.* Stuttgart: Kohlhammer, 1997.

———. *The Jesus Movement: A Social History of Its First Century.* Minneapolis: Fortress, 1999.

Stegemann, Wolfgang. "War der Apostel Paulus ein römischer Bürger?" *ZNW* 78 (1987): 200–29.

Stern, Menahem. *Greek and Latin Authors on Jews and Judaism.* 3 vols. Jerusalem: Israel Academy of Sciences and Humanities, 1974–84.

Stewart, Eric C. "New Testament Space/Spatiality." *BTB* 42 (2012): 139–50.

Still, Todd D., and David G. Horrell, eds. *After the First Urban Christians: The Social-Scientific Study of Pauline Christianity Twenty-Five Years Later.* London: Bloomsbury T&T Clark, 2009.

Stott, John R. W. *The Message of Acts.* BST. Leicester: Inter-Varsity Press, 1990.

Stowers, Stanley K. "Social Status, Public Speaking and Private Teaching: The Circumstances of Paul's Preaching Activity." *NovT* 26 (1984): 59–82.

———. "Does Pauline Christianity Resemble a Hellenistic Philosophy?" Pages 81–102 in *Paul beyond the Judaism/Hellenism Divide.* Edited by Troels Engberg-Pedersen. Louisville: Westminster John Knox, 2001.

Strecker, Georg. *The Johannine Letters: A Commentary on 1, 2 and 3 John.* Hermeneia. Minneapolis: Fortress, 1996.

Sun, Wai Lan Joyce. "This Is True Grace of God: The Shaping of Social Behavioural Instructions by Theology in 1 Peter." PhD diss., University of Edinburgh, 2012.

Sweetman, Rebecca J., ed. *Roman Colonies in the First Century of Their Foundation.* Oxford: Oxbow, 2001.

Swete, Henry Barclay, ed. *The Apocalypse of St John: The Greek Text.* London: Macmillan, 1906.

Tabbernee, William. *Prophets and Gravestones: An Imaginative History of Montanists and Other Early Christians.* Grand Rapids: Baker Academic, 2009.

Tajra, Harry W. *The Trial of St Paul: A Juridical Exegesis of the Second Half of the Acts of the Apostles.* WUNT/2 35. Tübingen: Mohr Siebeck, 1989.

Tannehill, Robert C. *The Narrative Unity of Luke-Acts: A Literary Interpretation.* 2 vols. Philadelphia: Fortress, 1986, 1990.

Taylor, Joan E., ed. *The Onomasticon by Eusebius of Caesarea: Palestine in the*

Fourth Century. Translated by Greville Freeman-Grenville. Jerusalem: Carta, 2003.

———. "Pontius Pilate and the Imperial Cult in Roman Judaea." *NTS* 52 (2006): 555–82.

———. "The *Nazoraeans* as a 'Sect' in 'Sectarian' Judaism? A Reconsideration of the Current View via the Narrative of Acts and the Meaning of *Hairesis*." Pages 87–118 in *Sects and Sectarianism in Jewish History*. Edited by Sacha Stern. Leiden: Brill, 2011.

———. "Two by Two: The Ark-etypal Language of Mark's Apostolic Pairings." Pages 58–82 in *The Body in Biblical, Christian and Jewish Texts*. Edited by Joan E. Taylor. London: Bloomsbury T&T Clark, 2014.

Tcherikover, Victor A., and Alexander Fuks. *Corpus Papyrorum Judaicarum*. 3 vols. Cambridge, MA: Harvard University Press, 1957–64.

Tepper, Yotam, and Leah Di Segni. *A Christian Prayer Hall of the Third Century CE at Kefar ˋOthnay (Legio): Excavations at the Megiddo Prison 2005*. Jerusalem: Israel Antiquities Authority, 2006.

Terzidou, Matina. "Religiousness as Tourist Practice." PhD diss., University of Surrey, 2012.

Theissen, Gerd. *The Social Setting of Pauline Christianity: Essays on Corinth*. Translated by John H. Schütz. Philadelphia: Fortress, 1975.

———. *Studien zur Soziologie des Urchristentums*. 3rd ed. Tübingen: Mohr Siebeck, 1989.

Thiselton, Anthony C. "Realized Eschatology at Corinth." *NTS* 24 (1978): 510–26.

———. *The First Epistle to the Corinthians: A Commentary on the Greek Text*. NIGTC. Grand Rapids: Eerdmans, 2000.

———. "The Significance of Recent Research on 1 Corinthians for Hermeneutical Apppropriation of This Epistle Today." *Neot* 40 (2006): 320–52.

———. *The Holy Spirit in Biblical Teaching, through the Centuries and Today*. Grand Rapids: Eerdmans, 2013.

Thomas, Christine M. "Greek Heritage in Roman Corinth and Ephos: Hybrid Identities and Strategies of Display in the Material Record of Traditional Mediterranean Religion." Pages 117–47 in *Corinth in Context: Comparative Studies on Religion and Society*. Edited by Steven J. Friesen, Daniel N. Schowalter, and James C. Walters. NovTSup 134. Leiden: Brill, 2010.

Thomassen, Einar. "The 'Catechetical' School of Early Christian Alexandria and Its Philonic Heritage." *HTR* 90 (1997): 59–87.

———. *The Spiritual Seed: The Church of the "Valentinians."* Leiden: Brill, 2006.

Thompson, James W. *The Church according to Paul: Rediscovering the Community Conformed to Christ*. Grand Rapids: Baker Academic, 2014.

Thompson, Leonard L. *The Book of Revelation: Apocalypse and Empire*. New ed. New York: Oxford University Press, 1996.

Thrall, Margaret E. *A Critical and Exegetical Commentary on the Second Epistle to the Corinthians*. 2 vols. ICC. Edinburgh: T&T Clark, 1994–2000.

Thrift, Nigel. "The Still Point: Resistance, Expressive Embodiment and Dance." Pages 124–51 in *Geographies of Resistance*. Edited by Steve Pile and Michael Keith. London: Routledge, 1997.

———. "Afterwords." *Env. Plan. D* 18 (2000): 213–55.

———. "Intensities of Feeling: Towards a Spatial Politics of Affect." *Geogr. Ann. B* 86 (2004): 57–78.

———. *Non-representational Theory: Space, Politics, Affects.* London: Routledge, 2007.

Thrift, Nigel, and John-David Dewsbury. "Dead Geographies and How to Make Them Live." *Env. Plan. D* 18 (2000): 411–32.

Timothy, Dallen, and Daniel Olsen, eds. *Tourism, Religion and Spiritual Journeys.* Contemporary Geographies of Leisure, Tourism and Mobility. New York: Routledge, 2006.

Towner, Philip H. *The Letters to Timothy and Titus.* NICNT. Grand Rapids: Eerdmans, 2006.

Trebilco, Paul R. *Jewish Communities in Asia Minor.* SNTSMS 69. Cambridge: Cambridge University Press, 1991.

———. *The Early Christians in Ephesus from Paul to Ignatius.* WUNT/2 166. Tübingen: Mohr Siebeck, 2004.

———. *Self-Designations and Group Identity in the New Testament.* Cambridge: Cambridge University Press, 2012.

———. "The Significance of the Distribution of Self-Designations in Acts." *NovT* 54 (2012): 30–49.

Tripp, Jeffrey M. "A Tale of Two Riots: The *Synkrisis* of the Temples of Ephesus and Jerusalem in Acts 19–23." *JSNT* 37 (2014): 86–111.

Tuilier, André. "Les évangélistes et les docteurs de la primitive église et les origines de l'Ecole (didaskaleion) d'Alexandrie." *StPat* 17 (1982): 738–49.

Tzetzes, Ioannis. *Prolegomena de comoedia Aristophanis.* Pages 22–38 in *Prolegomena de comoedia scholia in Acharnenses, Equites, Nubes.* Edited by Nigel G. Wilson. Vol. 1 of *Scholia in Aristophanem.* Edited by W. J. Koster. Scripta Academica Groningana. Groningen: Bouma, 1975.

Uitermark, Justus, Walter Nicholls, and Maarten Loopmans. "Cities and Social Movements: Theorizing beyond the Right to the City." *Env. Plan. A* 44 (2012): 2546–54.

———. "Techniques of Quotation in Clement of Alexandria: A View of Ancient Literary Working Methods." *VC* 50 (1996): 223–43.

Verheyden, Joseph. "The *Shepherd of Hermas.*" Pages 63–71 in *The Writings of the Apostolic Fathers.* Edited by Paul Foster. London: T&T Clark, 2007.

———. "The New Testament Canon." Pages 389–411 in *The New Cambridge History of the Bible: From the Beginnings to 600.* Edited by Joachim Schaper and James Carleton Paget. Cambridge: Cambridge University Press, 2013.

Vielhauer, Philipp. *Geschichte der urchristlichen Literatur: Einleitung in das Neue Testament, die Apokryphen und die Apostolischen Väter.* Berlin: de Gruyter, 1975.

Vlassopoulos, Kostas. *Unthinking the Greek Polis: Ancient Greek History beyond Eurocentrism.* Cambridge: Cambridge University Press, 2007.

Volf, Miroslav. *A Public Faith.* Grand Rapids: Brazos, 2011.

Vorholt, Robert. "Alle Wege führen nach Rom: Die Hauptstadt im Blickfeld des Paulus." Pages 208–18 in *Das frühe Christentum und die Stadt.* Edited by Reinhard von Bendemann and Markus Tiwald. BWANT 198. Stuttgart: Kohlhammer, 2012.

Walbank, Mary E. Hoskins. "Pausanias, Octavia and Temple E at Corinth." *ABSA* 84 (1989): 361–94.

———. "The Foundation and Planning of Early Roman Corinth." *JRA* 10 (1997): 95–130.

———. "What's in a Name? Corinth under the Flavians." *ZPE* 139 (2002): 251–64.

———. "Aspects of Corinthian Coins in the Late 1st and Early 2nd Centuries AC." Pages 337–49 in *Corinth, The Centenary: 1896–1996*. Edited by Charles K. Williams II and Nancy Bookidis. Corinth 20. Princeton: American School of Classical Studies at Athens, 2003.

Walsh, Brian J., and Sylvia C. Keesmaat. *Colossians Remixed: Subverting the Empire*. Downers Grove, IL: IVP Academic, 2004.

Walton, Steve. Review of *Luke's Portrait of Paul*, by John C. Lentz, Jr. *Anvil* 11 (1994): 62–64.

———. "A Tale of Two Perspectives? The Place of the Temple in Acts." Pages 135–49 in *Heaven on Earth: The Temple in Biblical Theology*. Edited by T. Desmond Alexander and Simon Gathercole. Carlisle: Paternoster, 2004.

———. "Paul, Patronage and Pay: What Do We Know about the Apostle's Financial Support?" Pages 220–33 in *Paul as Missionary: Identity, Activity, Theology, and Practice*. Edited by Trevor J. Burke and Brian S. Rosner. LNTS 420. London: T&T Clark, 2011.

———. "Calling the Church Names: Learning about Christian Identity from Acts." *PRSt* 41 (2014): 223–41.

Wankel, Hermann, et al. *Die Inschriften von Ephesos*. IGSK 11.1–17.4. Bonn: Rudolf Habelt, 1979–1984.

Warf, Barney, and Santa Arias, eds. *The Spatial Turn: Interdisciplinary Perspectives*. London: Routledge, 2009.

Wassen, Cecilia. "Do You Have to Be Pure in a Metaphorical Temple? Sanctuary Metaphors and Construction of Sacred Space in the Dead Sea Scrolls and Paul's Letters." Pages 55–86 in *Purity, Holiness and Identity in Judaism and Christianity*. Edited by Carl S. Ehrlich, Anders Runesson, and Eileen Schuller. WUNT 305. Tübingen: Mohr Siebeck, 2013.

Watts, Edward J. *City and School in Late Antique Athens and Alexandria*. Berkeley: University of California, 2006.

Webb, William J. *Returning Home: New Covenant and Second Exodus as the Context for 2 Corinthians 6.14–7.1*. JSNTSup 85. Sheffield: JSOT, 1993.

Weber, Patrick, and Michel Sève. "Le côté Nord du forum de Philippes." *BCH* 110 (1986): 531–81.

———. "Un monument honorifique au forum de Philippes." *BCH* 112 (1988): 467–79.

Weinrich, William C., ed. *Revelation*. ACCSNT 12. Downers Grove, IL: InterVarsity Press, 2006.

Weiss, Bernhard. *A Commentary on the New Testament*. 4 vols. New York & London: Funk & Wagnalls, 1906.

Weissenrieder, Annette. "Do You Not Know That You Are God's Temple? Towards a New Perspective on Paul's Temple Image in 1 Corinthians 3:16." Pages 377–411 in

Contested Spaces: Houses and Temples in Roman Antiquity and the New Testament. Edited by David L. Balch and Annette Weissenrieder. WUNT 285. Tübingen: Mohr Siebeck, 2012.

Welborn, L. L. *An End to Enmity: Paul and the "Wrongdoer" of Second Corinthians.* BZNW 185. Berlin: de Gruyter, 2011.

Wengst, Klaus. *Pax Romana and the Peace of Jesus Christ.* Philadelphia: Fortress, 1987.

West, Allen B., ed. *Corinth:* Vol. VIII, Part II, *Latin Inscriptions.* Cambridge, MA: Harvard University Press, 1931.

Wick, Peter, and Volker Rabens, eds. *Religions and Trade: Religious Formation, Transformation and Cross-Cultural Exchange between East and West.* Dynamics in the History of Religions 5. Leiden: Brill, 2014.

Wieland, George M. *The Significance of Salvation: A Study of Salvation Language in the Pastoral Epistles.* PBM. Milton Keynes: Paternoster, 2006.

Wilk, Florian. *Die Bedeutung des Jesajabuches für Paulus.* FRLANT 179. Göttingen: Vandenhoeck & Ruprecht, 1998.

Williams, Charles K., III. "The Refounding of Corinth: Some Roman Religious Attitudes." Pages 26–37 in *Roman Architecture in the Greek World.* Edited by Sarah Macready and F. H. Thompson. Occasional Papers NS 10. London: Society of Antiquaries of London, 1987.

Williams, Travis B. *Persecution in 1 Peter: Differentiating and Contextualizing Early Christian Suffering.* NovTSup 145. Leiden: Brill, 2012.

Wink, Walter. *Naming the Powers: The Language of Power in the New Testament.* Vol. 1 of *The Powers.* Minneapolis: Fortress, 1984.

Winter, Bruce W. *Seek the Welfare of the City: Christians as Benefactors and Citizens.* Grand Rapids: Eerdmans, 1994.

———. *Philo and Paul among the Sophists.* SNTSMS 96. Cambridge: Cambridge University Press, 1997.

———. "The Imperial Cult and the Early Christians in Pisidian Antioch (Acts 13 and Galatians 6)." Pages 60–68 in *First International Conference on Antioch in Pisidia.* Edited by Thomas Drew-Bear, Mehmet Taşlıalan, and Christine M. Thomas. Ismit: Kocaeli, 2000.

———. *After Paul Left Corinth: The Influence of Secular Ethics and Social Change.* Grand Rapids: Eerdmans, 2001.

———. *Roman Wives, Roman Widows: The Appearance of New Women and the Pauline Communities.* Grand Rapids: Eerdmans, 2003.

———. *Divine Honours for the Caesars: The First Christians' Responses.* Grand Rapids: Eerdmans, 2015.

Wise, Michael Owen. *Language and Literacy in Roman Judaea: A Study of the Bar Kokhba Documents.* AYBRL. New Haven: Yale University Press, 2015.

Witherington, Ben, III. *Conflict and Community in Corinth: A Socio-Rhetorical Commentary on 1 and 2 Corinthians.* Grand Rapids: Eerdmans, 1994.

———. *The Acts of the Apostles: A Socio-Rhetorical Commentary.* Grand Rapids: Eerdmans, 1998.

Wolfson, Harry A. "Philo on Jewish Citizenship in Alexandria." *JBL* 63 (1944): 165–68.

Wolter, Michael. *Paulus: Ein Grundriss seiner Theologie.* Neukirchen: Neukirchener Verlag, 2011.

Wright, Brian J. "Ancient Literacy in New Testament Research: Incorporating a Few More Lines of Enquiry." *TJ* 36 (2015): 161–89.

Wright, N. T. *Colossians and Philemon*. TNTC. Leicester: Inter-Varsity Press, 2008.

———. *Paul and the Faithfulness of God*. 2 vols. COQG 4. London: SPCK, 2013.

Wylie, John. "A Single Day's Walking: Narrating Self and Landscape on the South West Coast Path." *Trans. Inst. Br. Geog.* 30 (2005): 234–47.

Youtie, Herbert C. "Βραδέως γράφων: Between Literacy and Illiteracy." Pages 629–51 in his *Scriptiunculae II*. Amsterdam: Adolf M. Hakkert, 1973.

Zandee, Jan. "'The Teaching of Silvanus' (NHC VII, 4) and Jewish Christianity." Pages 498–584 in *Studies in Gnosticism and Hellenistic Religions Presented to Gilles Quispel on the Occasion of His 65th Birthday*. Edited by Roelof van den Broek and M. J. Vermaseren, Leiden: Brill, 1981.

Zanker, Paul. *The Power of Images in the Age of Augustus*. Translated by Alan Shapiro. Thomas Spencer Jerome Lectures. Ann Arbor: University of Michigan Press, 1990.

Zannis, Angelos G. *Le pays entre le Strymon et le Nestos: géographie et histoire (VIIe-IVe siècle avant J.-C.)*. Meletēmata 71. Athens: National Hellenic Research Foundation, 2014.

Zeller, Dieter. *Juden und Heiden in der Mission des Paulus: Studien zum Römerbrief*. Stuttgart: Verlag Katholisches Bibelwerk, 1973.

Zizioulas, John. *Being as Communion: Studies on Personhood and the Church*. Crestwood, NY: St. Vladimir's Seminary, 1985.

Index of Authors

INDEX OF AUTHORS

Thompson, Leonard L., 305, 312
Thrall, Margaret E., 118
Thrift, Nigel, 254, 256, 257
Timbie, Janet A., 208
Timothy, Dallen, 255
Tiwald, Markus, 86, 100, 113, 219, 221
Towner, Philip H., 168
Trebilco, Paul R., xiv, 76, 161, 162, 164, 166, 169, 170, 175, 176, 185, 236, 252, 320
Treu, Ursula, 211
Tripp, Jeffrey M., 33
Tuilier, André, 213
Tzetzes, Ioannis, 207

Uitermark, Justus, 23
Urry, John, 40

Vann, Robert Lindley, 43, 57, 59, 61
Vanséveren, Sylvie, 136
Vénencie, Jacques, 72
Verheyden, Joseph, 197, 289
Vermaseren, Maarten J., 211
Vielhauer, Philipp, 277
Vlassopoulos, Kostas, 10, 12
Volf, Miroslav, 268–69
Volp, Ulrich, 149
Vorholt, Robert, 86

Wacker, William C., 163–64
Waelkens, Marc, 75, 76, 77, 78, 80, 81, 82, 84
Walbank, Mary E. Hoskins, 70, 71, 72
Wall, Robert W., 272
Walsh, Brian J., 253, 262–64, 266, 268, 270
Walters, James C., 146, 306
Walton, Steve, xiv, 37, 116, 117, 223, 236–37
Wan, Wei Hsien, xiv, 283–84, 286
Warf, Barney, 21
Wassen, Cecilia, 232
Watson, J. R., 251
Watts, Edward J., 207
Webb, Robert L., 282
Webb, William J., 110
Weber, Patrick, 74, 129
Weinrich, William C., 306

Weiss, Bernhard, 275
Weiss, Zeev, 92
Weissenrieder, Annette, 232
Welborn, L. L., 72
Wengst, Klaus, 247, 250
West, Allen B., 151
White, L. Michael, 62
Wick, Peter, 111, 121
Wieland, George M., 164
Wilk, Florian, 110
Wilkins, Michael J., 154
Williams, Charles K., II, 71
Williams, Peter J., 48
Williams, Travis B., 272
Wilson, Mark W., 220, 307
Wilson, Robert M., 211
Winant, Howard, 4
Wink, Walter, 259, 266
Winter, Bruce W., 71, 73, 80, 82–83, 85, 237–38, 252
Wischmeyer, Oda, 102
Wise, Michael Owen, 188, 189–90, 191, 192
Witherington, Ben, III, 27, 34, 35, 146, 147, 149, 152
Wolfson, Harry A., 94
Wolter, Michael, 114, 121
Woodman, Simon, 305, 315
Worthington, Ian, 125
Wright, Brian J., 189
Wright, N. T., 107–8, 246, 263
Wylie, John, 258, 260

Young, Frances M., 212
Youtie, Herbert C., 191

Zamagni, Claudio, 66
Zandee, Jan, 210
Zangenberg, Jürgen, 234
Zanker, Paul, 8
Zannis, Angelos G., 139
Zeller, Dieter, 106
Zetterholm, Magnus, 220
Zimmermann, Ruben, 149
Zizioulas, John, 150

Index of Subjects

1 Peter, 271–86; locating the place of origin (Rome/Babylon), 272–78, 280–84; readers' location in the diaspora, 281–82, 284, 294–303; reconsidering place of origin and construction of space, 280–84; spatial imagination and construction of space, 283–84, 294–303; "spiritual house" (οἶκος πνευματικός) and spatial belonging, 284, 294–303; stance of resistance to the Roman Empire, 285–86, 301–3; viewing the "spiritual house" as a temple, 284, 297–301

"affective landscapes," 253, 254–57, 268–70. *See also* spiritual landscapes and non-representational theories in human geography

Alexandria, 205–15; centers of scholarship and intellectual life, 205–7; diverse first Christian theologies, teachers, and literature, 207–12, 215; early Jewish-Christian missionaries in, 207, 208–9; Eusebius on Mark and the first Christian community, 207–8, 273; growth of Christianity and early Christian theologies in, 205–15; the *Mouseion*, 206–7; Philo on Jewish community of, 94–95; Philo's attitudes toward, 93–95; Royal Library and Greek manuscript collection, 206–7; Serapeum Library, 206, 207; so-called catechetical "school" (*didaskaleion*) and its significance, 212–14

Ankara, imperial temple of, 292

Apocalypse of Peter, 212

Apollos of Alexandria, 208

Augustus: and Caesarea Maritima, 57–60; and founding of Philippi, 140; imperial cult of, 57–59, 82, 160, 290–92; and link between the diaspora and Jerusalem, 93, 96–97, 112, 248; *Res Gestae* of, 82, 283; on the Roman colonies, 69; statue at Ephesus, 160; Suetonius's physiognomic description of, 7–8; temple at Caesarea, 57–59

Basilides, 209–10

body motif and Paul's view of the Corinthian church (1 Cor 12:12–31), 141–59; application to the church, not the city-state, 154; and Corinth's socioeconomic context and cultural values, 146–48; eschatological anticipation of God's kingdom (reading 1 Cor 12:12–31 alongside 15:20–28), 155–58; as essentially conservative (prioritizing conformity), 144–45; future orientation and the church's relationship with the world ("now"/"not yet" tension), 157–58, 159; Paul's christology and the church as not just *a* body but *Christ's body*, 150–53; as subversion of the Corinthians' social hierarchy, 148–50, 151–52; vision of the church as an "association" and countercultural community, 156–57, 159; and wider uses of body metaphor in the Greco-Roman world, 142–46, 148–54, 158

seeking job opportunities and workplace
in each city, 113, 116–17; and social status
of Pauline congregations, 113–15; Stark's
three hypotheses, 100–101; travel procedures, 102–12; travel with coworkers/
companions, 27–28, 115; as "word and
work," 105
Pergamum: description in Revelation, 307;
Hellenistic library at, 207; imperial cult
and temple, 291–92, 307
Philippi, 69, 73–75, 123–40, 236–52; arrest
and imprisonment of Paul and Silas, 133,
134–35, 248–50; difference from Corinth
or Pisidian Antioch, 131; establishment
of the Roman colony, 74, 128, 130–31;
first cathedral church (in honor of Paul),
138–40; imperial cult and city center's
displays, 128–31; importance for early
Christianity, 124, 140; importance in
first-century Macedonia, 124–27; inscriptions and Latin epigraphy, 74; location on
the Via Egnatia, 73–74, 127, 136; Lydia's
house "outside the gate," 132–34; marginal
presence of the Jewish community
(gathering outside the city gate), 131–34;
origins and the settlement by Philip
II of Macedon, 73–74, 128, 140; Paul's
Roman citizenship, 124, 127, 133, 247–50;
physical organization and city center,
128–31; portrayed in the Acts narrative,
123, 124–27, 131–38; recontextualizing
Paul's mission and preaching in, 123–40;
Roman forum and architecture, 74; the
shift between town and countryside in
Paul's preaching in, 134–38; social context
and demographic composition, 134–38,
239–41, 246–47; spatial framework of
Paul's action in, 131–34; symbolic transfer
of Christianity from the periphery to
the city center, 133–34; use of the word
κολωνία to describe, 126–27; women's
roles, 75, 133
Philo of Alexandria: Alexandria as ultimate
model city and home, 93–95; on Alexandrian Jewish community, 94–95; concept
of colony and mother city, 15–16, 89–90;
and diaspora Jewish attitudes to *metropoleis*, 89–95; and Jerusalem (as *metropolis*),
15–16, 89–92, 96; *metropolis* as metaphor
for relationship between the Logos and
other divine powers, 89–92; and Rome
(Roman imperial culture), 95–97; on Zion
as *metropolis*, 90

Pisidian Antioch, 69, 75–84, 131; archaeological excavations, 75–76; in biblical
texts and classical scholarship, 76–84;
cult of Mên and classical sanctuary of
Mên Askaênos, 80–81; difference from
Philippi, 131; and "elementary principles
of the world" in Paul's letter to Galatians, 78–81; imperial cult, 82–83, 292;
inscription relating to wild-animal hunts
and gladiatorial shows, 83–84; inscriptions and epigraphy, 77–78, 83–84; Paul's
arrival in, 76–78; Paul's letter to Galatians,
78–81, 84; Paul's mission to gentiles of,
78–79, 82–83; reception of Paul and Barnabas by the chief men of the city, 77–78;
Sergius Paulus and his family, 76–77, 321;
social elite, 78, 84, 131
poliscentrism: and Hellenistic perceptions of
ethnos, 9–13, 19; Second Temple *Ioudaioi*
as poliscentric people, 13–19. *See also* ethnicity and Second Temple Jews/Judeans

race, 4–9. *See also* ethnicity and Second
Temple Jews/Judeans
Revelation's cities, 304–19; characterization
of imperial power in Rome (Babylon) and
(New) Jerusalem, 318–19; Daniel's vision/
John's vision, 310, 317–18; and depiction
of *ekklēsiai*, 305–13; depictions of material
culture and realities of life, 311–13; Ezekiel
and depiction of Jesus (as lamb who was
slain), 310–11; functions of, 309, 319;
Hebrew Bible texts and ideas in, 309–11;
hypocatastasis metaphor and descriptions
of Rome and Jerusalem, 313–19; John's
adaptation of Daniel's vision of the four
empires, 317–18; and "literal" futurist
readings of Revelation, 316–17; read
in light of Augustinian amillennialism,
306–7; read in light of chiliasm, 306; read
in light of the actual historical contexts,
307–9; the seven cities, 305–13
Roman citizenship in Philippi, 236–52; and
early Christians' use of "city" language,
236–38, 252; how Roman citizenship
and heavenly citizenship relate to one
another, 250–51; identity, responsibility, and privileges of, 242–44; Paul's
possession of Roman citizenship, 124,
127, 133, 247–50; Paul's use of heavenly
citizenship language, 244–47; Roman law
and the plausibility of Paul's exercise of

Index of Scripture and Ancient Sources

Off.
1.42   116

Verr.
2.5.65 §§167–68   249

Dio Cassius

Hist. Rom.
37.16.5–17.1   248
51.20.6–9   290
57.18.5a   248
63.2.3   249
68.30.1   274

Dio Chrysostom

1 Regn.
32   142

3 Regn.
104   142

Dic. exercit.
6   198

Oration
48.9   173

Diodorus Siculus

Bibl. hist.
1.56.3   273
17.52   206
31.8.8   125

Dionysius of Halicarnassus

Ant. rom.
6.86.2–3   142
6.86.3–4   142

Epictetus

Diatr.
2.10.4–5   143
2.24.41   243

Herodotus

Hist.
1.90–91   11

Homer

Od.
19.245   7

Horace

Sat.
1.4.139–43   248

John Malalas

Chron.
10:261, lines 13–16   62

Juvenal

Sat.
14.96–106   248

Libanius

Or.
18.158   199

Livy

Urb. cond.
2.32.7–11   142, 153
45.29.5–9   125

Martial

Epigr.
4.72   199

Menander

Dysk.
284–86   172

Plato

Laws
5.747d   8

Resp.
5.462c–d   142

Pliny the Elder

Nat.
3.39   294
5.70   45
6.30.121–123   274

Pliny the Younger

Ep.
3.5   198
10.96   243

Plutarch

Arist.
7.5   188

Mor.
478–79   142

Polyaenus

Strateg.
3.9.22   143

Polycarp

Phil
1:1   176
7:1–2   162

Pseudo–Aristotle

Physiognomics
808b 11–13   6

Pseudo–Hippolytus

Haer.
6.37.7   209
7.20–27   209

Quintilian

Inst.
1.1.28–29   198
2.21.16   188
11.2.32   198

Seneca

Clem.
1.4.3–5.1   142

Strabo

Geogr.
12.8.14   80
16.1.5   274
16.2.37–38   14
16.16   274
17.1.30   273

VII
frag. 17a   125
frag. 47   125